GEORGE FREEDLEY and JOHN A. REEVES

A History of the

THEATRE

With hundreds of Illustrations
from Photographs, Playbills,
Contemporary Prints, etc.

CROWN PUBLISHERS · NEW YORK

THIS BOOK IS DEDICATED TO FREDERICK H. KOCH OF THE CAROLINA PLAYMAKERS, WHOSE FINE SPIRIT AND KEEN ENTHUSIASM HAVE BEEN AN INSPIRATION TO US ALL

ACKNOWLEDGEMENTS

WE WISH to thank the various persons and institutions who have been so cooperative with us in our compilation of this history. Our first thanks go to Elizabeth Perkins Barrett and the staff of the Theatre Collection and to Eunice Wilson and Julia Gardner and the staff of the 58th Street Branch of the New York Public Library.

We acknowledge our indebtedness to Ludlow Bull of the Metropolitan Museum of Art and Yale University for reading the chapter on the Egyptian theatre and for his suggestions in regard to its writing. We particularly appreciate the generous cooperation of Louis E. Laflin, Jr. who gave us days of his time in the research and preparation of this same chapter.

Allardyce Nicoll, Franz Rapp and Elemer Nagy of Yale University have been most gracious in their cooperation in our search for illustrations as have Janos Sholz, Esther Johnston, Florence Overton, Rosamond Gilder, Herbert Bittner, Julia Gardner, Elizabeth Reynolds Hapgood, Louis V. Ledoux, Edith Hamilton, Robert Van Rosen, H. M. Lydenberg and the New York Public Library, A. J. Wall and Bella C. Landauer of the New York Historical Society, May Davenport Seymour of the Museum of the City of New York, Frederick H. Koch of the University of North Carolina, Gilmor Brown of the Pasadena Community Playhouse, Frederic McConnell of the Play House of Cleveland, the Folger Shakespeare Library, the Metropolitan Museum of Art, the Cincinnati Museum Association and the Museum of Modern Art. Thanks are also due Frederick J. Kiesler for his illuminating explanation of his "space-stage" and to Donald Oenslager specifically for his permission to reproduce a Galli-Bibiena drawing in his possession. The designers of New York have been most gracious in their response to our request for permission to reproduce their designs which appear, duly acknowledged, in this volume.

We are grateful to Edmund Fuller, Hildegard and George Hilton, Vernon Tanner and Stuart Sherman for their research and editorial assistance.

GEORGE FREEDLEY AND JOHN A. REEVES

CONTENTS

LIST OF ILLUSTRATIONS

PROLOGUE

This is an objective history of the theatre which is written with the express purpose of setting down within the confines of a single volume the main events which have occurred since the drama's inception in Egypt thirty-two hundred years before Christ. The travail of war and destruction, the ever-recurring religious and political turmoil, the moral and social stress through which the drama passed is indicated in the background of its development. Its various forms and appearances in all parts of the world are described in as much detail as space allows. Drama has been wedded to religion and consigned to the devil but it still endures five thousand years after its birth under the hot skies of Egypt.

No attempt has been made to re-evaluate drama nor the theatrical impulses which prompted its evocation. The main trends and principal events are chronicled in what we hope is a simple and concise fashion. The actors whose voices have declaimed the lines of the poets, or who as mimes or dancers have created their own theatre, are given full share in this chronological account of theatrical art. We have described the architectural qualities of the buildings, their changes and structural development, the gradual passing from the light of day into the artificial darkness of the playhouse as it has come down to us. The characteristics of stage costume, the introduction and use of the mask and make-up, the invention and elaboration of scenery are indicated in words or pictures. The illustrations are included to illuminate the text and in some instances to replace laborious descriptions of buildings, decoration or scenic investiture.

This account is, as far as is possible, strictly chronological because it is our feeling that many well written stage histories have confused the issue by too constant shifting both of scene and of emphasis. It is our hope that by this we may have eliminated some of the pitfalls for the unwary and the inquiring. We have placed the chapters on the Far-Eastern theatre immediately before those dealing with the eighteenth century in Europe at which point the infiltration of Oriental culture through as dissimilar writers as Voltaire and Goethe is most apparent.

This is a history of the whole theatre; plays, playwrights, artists, actors have been granted their dates when known and plots of plays have been included only when absolutely essential to the proper evaluation of the period in question because this is not intended to be merely a chronicle of the drama. Plays exist in their own niche which has been determined by examination of proper authorities so that our findings may set forth the best regarded and best documented viewpoint. Whenever in the interests of clarity or, to our minds, in strict justice to the person or his work, an opposing and personal judgment is offered, the popular criticism is also included.

We acknowledge our indebtedness to the scholars and artists who have trod the path we now tread. The voluminous six volumes of Mantzius and those five handsomely illustrated ones of Dubech together with the brilliant shorter accounts of Sheldon Cheney, Allardyce Nicoll, Glenn Hughes and Thomas Wood Stevens have been pleasant sources of inspiration. It is our hope that this present *History of the Theatre* combines the good qualities of these gentlemen with the simplicity and clarity which we sought to achieve.

The theatre as we know it is a sophisticated art with mass appeal; it blends all of painting and sculpture with architecture and poetry to create dramatic production. It wasn't always thus because the theatre began in the religious impulse in the hearts and souls of men in the mysterious and remote antiquity of the valley of the Nile.

EGYPT,

THE BEGINNING OF THE THEATRE

THE story of Egypt has been an incompletely understood record for centuries. Herodotus had much to tell but few if any historians of the theatre seemed to be cognizant of the fact that he recorded the religious festivals and the origin of the worship of Dionysos which was later to be transferred to the dramatic festivals in Greece. For hundreds of years much of this information has been unrecognized by the world of theatre scholarship because of the difficulty of the study of the Egyptian language, literature and art. We can but conjecture about the drama from the published records of such Egyptologists as Champollion, Maspero, Naville, Erman, Petrie, Sethe, Breasted, DeBuck and Drioton. Any exact interpretations of drama remain to be established by scholars and Egyptologists of the present and future.

Although this chapter enters a controversial field because the Egyptologists have not yet established all the actual theatrical facts, the history of world theatre can be extended back a thousand or more years further than was previously possible. Now over five thousand unbroken years look down on New York, London and Moscow which remain the great theatre capitals despite the destruction of a war-torn world. Paris surrendered its claim in a mess of boulevardism long ago and in 1933 Berlin chose a political regeneration and world aggrandizement rather than cultural development, consciously surrendering her claims to be considered a contender for the world capital of the theatre. Everything that is written from now on can be safely said to derive at least in part from those actor-priests who long, long ago believed that the best way to inculcate religion was through the development of a drama on the banks of the Nile.

Thanks are due to the generosity of Louis E. Laflin, Jr., who led us to the sources on which we base this chapter and who has received advice from Dr. Ludlow Bull of the Metropolitan Museum of Art and Yale University. All that theatre historians have discussed about ancient Egypt is the famous *Abydos Passion Play*, also known as the *Osiris Passion Play*, from the name of the god whose history was celebrated. (The text of this play does not exist, nor do we know that it was written down. All that remains are the accounts of participants or witnesses beginning with Ikhernofret about 1868 B.C.)

There were actually many types of drama in Egypt: the *Pyramid Texts*, of which at least fifty-five exist; the *Coronation Festival Plays*, several of which survive in some form; *Heb Seds* (*Coronation Jubilees*), physical evidences of which still exist in great number; *Passion Plays*, at least three; and at least one *Medicinal Play* recognized by Egyptology (possibly also a *Passion Play*).

The story of these dramas goes back at least to 3200 B.C., and the content of the *Pyramid Texts* seems to indicate that it may be extended as far back as 4000 B.C. Nine existing examples of texts came from royal pyramids through the VI Dynasty and forty-six from later nobles' tombs, some as late as the XXX Dynasty. These texts were written on the interior walls of the pyramids and tombs which were sealed against posterity. The earliest tombs in Pre-Dynastic times took the form of Mounds which were constructed over the graves scooped out of the sand. In the I and II Dynasties the royal tombs became *Mastabas* (Arabic word for bench) which were rectangular in shape and of considerable height and length. In the III Dynasty appeared the first Pyramid built in step-formation as though several *mastabas* had been placed one upon another. In the IV Dynasty came the familiar smooth-sided great pyramids which were followed by smaller pyramids in the V Dynasty and later.

The Pyramid Texts, the earliest of which survive from the reigns of the last king of the V Dynasty and five pharaohs and three queens of the VI Dynasty (around 2700 B.C.), contain internal evidence which date portions of them as having been composed from approximately 4000 B.C., at least before the First Union of the Kingdom of Upper and Lower Egypt.

It may be asked why we agree with Gaston Maspero who in 1882 called the *Pyramid Texts* drama. If the hieroglyphic texts themselves are examined, the directions for action and the indications of various characters speaking become apparent as stage directions and identification of actors to a mind trained to look for dramatic indications. On rare occasions the characters' names precede the speeches. Frequently characters identify themselves within the speech, as: "I am Horus," "I am Nut." In most cases the character of Osiris was identified with the dead king (whose part, of course, had to be played by a priest); that of Horus with the living king (who may have been played by himself). Animal masks were undoubtedly employed in the presentation of these *Pyramid Texts* and other Egyptian dramas.

These dramatic and religious texts were probably theatrically represented by the priests, who lived in buildings near the *mastaba* or pyramid. The actor-priests and their performances were endowed in memory of the deceased and were financed by taxes from towns, which revenues were set aside in perpetuity for that purpose. There are accounts of the violation of these endowments as in the case of a long dead queen whose fund was appropriated by the reigning Pharaoh to endow the tomb of a recently deceased noble.

The plot of the *Pyramid Texts* dealt with the ascent of the soul of the deceased to become one of the Imperishable Stars, or the resurrection of the body, or both. "Ho, King Unis! Thou didst not depart dead, thou didst depart living." Also, "This King Pepy dies not" and "He dies not; this King Pepy lives forever." The resurrection of the king calls for an apparent physical representation which could have been accomplished if a priest portrayed the role of the king. If the body of the King did not appear to come to life, much of the religious significance would have been lost. In the Mediaeval *Mystery Plays*, had the Three Marys found the stone still in place in front of the Holy Sepulchre, the audience would have had difficulty in picturing the physical resurrection. When the Egyptian priest said, "Throw off thy wrappings," or "Throw off the sand," or "Throw off the bricks," if the corpse had remained motionless and no physical action had taken place, the emotional and theatrical effect would have been lost. The wrappings refer to mummification, the bricks to the burial under the *mastaba*, and the sand to the earliest grave of all, under the mound.

In the *Pyramid Texts* all things which might duplicate in after-life the creature comforts which the king enjoyed on earth were presented: bread, beer, eye-paint, embalming fluid (that is *natron*), wine, grain, poultry, perfume, flowers, clothing, crowns and sceptres.

The next earliest extant drama in point of composition was the famed *Memphite Drama*, probably a *Coronation Festival Play* of about 3100 B.C. The royal city of Memphis, situated near the junction of Upper and Lower Egypt, became the capital at the beginning of the I Dynasty. The *Memphite Drama* celebrates the claims to supreme godhood of Ptah, of whom it is stated that "Ptah the Great is the heart and tongue of the gods." For "heart" read "intelligence" or "mind" as these words were lacking in the Egyptian vocabulary. For "tongue" read "spoken word" or "utterance." Ptah is said to have created Atum and the latter's divine Ennead, and to have established the development of religion and culture, and brought about the physical development of the country. This is an interesting parallel to the achievements of Prometheus.

This drama had an absorbing history of survival. In the eighth century B.C. the Ethiopian Pharaoh Shabaka found a manuscript which "the worms had eaten," indicating that it was on leather or papyrus. He called this a "work of the ancestors" which indicates that he had no idea of the enormous extent of its antiquity. He ordered it copied on stone for "the house of his father Ptah-South-of-His-Wall." Fortunately for us, this stone is still in existence in the British Museum, where it is to be found in mutilated form, due to the fact that it had been used for a long time by modern Egyptians as a nether millstone. A large portion of the inscription is obliterated and what remains has puzzled scholars for years. A number of incorrect translations were made until Breasted translated it correctly in 1901. Erman suspected it was drama in 1911 and Sethe confirmed this suspicion in 1928.

The next probable *Coronation Festival Play* dates from the reign of Senwosret I of the XII Dynasty (about 2000 B.C.) in the period known as the Middle Kingdom (M. K.). Such festival pieces celebrated the elevation of the pharaoh to the throne.

The *Heb Sed* celebrates the Coronation Jubilee. This doubtless symbolizes the renewal of the king's power through death and resurrection and usually took place after thirty years of his reign and occasionally at intervals thereafter. These festivals could and did sometimes occur earlier. This explains Naville's confusion concerning the *Heb Sed* of Osorkon II, fourth king of the XXIII Dynasty at Bubastis in the twenty-second year of his reign. This *Heb Sed* has been handsomely recorded, though its reconstruction is debatable, by Edouard Henri Naville (1844-1926). Mme. Naville drew copies of the inscriptions which suffered in accuracy from her prudery and elimination of anything phallic. Naville divides the *Heb Sed* as follows:

(1) First Ascent to the Pavilion (on the south side of the walls of the temple).
(2) The Rising of the God and the Assembling of Divinities.
(3) Second Ascent to the Pavilion (on the north side of the temple).
(4) The Offerings and the Shrine of the North.

When Napoleon invaded Egypt in 1798, his plan to attack Britain not being propitious at the time, he took with him draughtsmen and artists who were commissioned to turn out the handsome volumes sponsored by the French Emperor. However, these draughtsmen did not know the language, prettied things up and were very inaccurate in the pictures and the texts which they gratuitously restored. The principal discovery of the campaign was the famous Rosetta Stone found in 1798 (now in the British Museum) which was the direct reason for the beginnings of the Science of Egyptology. The hieroglyphic version of the inscription on this stone was the first text in that script to be translated in modern times. It was published by Champollion in 1822.

Egyptology has so far recognized but one example of *Medicinal Drama*. This is to be found on the Metternich Stela which is now located in the Chateau Metternich, Kynsvart, Bohemia. The purpose of the drama is magical or faith healing. It is the story of the goddess Isis whose child Horus has been bitten by a scorpion and involves artificial respiration and a magical cure.

Now we come to the only Egyptian play known to theatre historians, the *Abydos Passion Play* (sometimes called the *Osiris Passion Play*). Pages have been devoted to this single work though all that can be said about it is strictly from secondary sources. It seems to be mentioned in the *Pyramid Texts;* otherwise its earliest surviving record is in the reign of King Senwosret III, the fifth ruler of the XII Dynasty, who was on the throne from 1887-1849 B.C.; though the celebration itself possibly dates back at least to the V Dynasty (shortly before 2500 B.C.).

This play enacted the story of the treacherous death and dismemberment of Osiris, the reassembling of his limbs by his wife-sister, Isis, and their son, Horus.

According to Ikhernofret, who refurbished the play for Senwosret III, he participated in the drama, which he described as follows, according to the translation accorded him by Breasted in *The Development of Religion and Thought in Ancient Egypt* (1912). This outline of the play is all that has been written down and preserved:

(1) "I celebrated the 'Procession of the god Upwawet' when he proceeded to champion his father (Osiris)." (This was probably a mock fight in front of the House of Osiris at Abydos in which the audience participated.)

(2) "I repulsed those who were hostile to the Neshmet barque, and I overthrew the enemies of Osiris." (This indicates a mock naval encounter on the Nile in which the audience joined.)

(3) "I celebrated the 'Great Procession,' following the god in his

footsteps." (In this scene probably Osiris was slain by Seth, an episode too sacred for Ikhernofret to mention.)

(4) "I sailed the divine barque, while Thoth . . . the voyage." (Here the body of Osiris was recovered by his family led by Thoth, the god of Speech, after a voyage in a boat, followed by the audience in their barques.)

(5) "I equipped the barque (called) 'Shining in Truth,' of the Lord of Abydos, with a chapel; I put on his beautiful regalia when he went forth to the district of Pekar." (This suggests the embalmment or possibly a description of Ikhenofret's production duties.)

(6) "I led the way of the god to his tomb in Pekar." (This scene was the funeral procession to the tomb of Osiris, the audience following as mourners. The actual setting was the tomb of King Djer of the I Dynasty, at some distance away.)

(7) "I championed Wennofer (Osiris) on 'That Day of the Great Battle'; I overthrew all the enemies upon the shores of Nedyet." (In this scene Seth dug up the body of his brother, Osiris, and dismembered it. Half of the audience supported Seth while the other half joined Horus and the family of Osiris who reassembled his limbs after the battle.)

(8) "I caused him to proceed into the barque (called) 'The Great'; it bore his beauty; I gladdened the heart of the eastern highlands; I [put] jubilation in the western highlands, when they saw the beauty of the Neshmet barque. It landed at Abydos and they brought [Osiris, First of the Westerners, Lord] of Abydos to his palace." (This was the great Resurrection Scene, also too sacred to mention.)

This drama was performed at Abydos at least until the latter part of the XXVI Dynasty between 569 and 526 B.C.

In 449 B.C. Herodotus found two other *Passion Plays*, one at Busiris (Dedu) and one at Sais. The still later *Osirian Festival of Canopus* was probably also dramatic. This was the same as the *Festival of Osiris-Apis* (Serapis). The last *Festival of Canopus* was held before 391 A.D. during the reign of Theodosius the Great, when the *Serapeum* (place of performance) was burned and Christianity was made the official religion. Christianity continued as the official religion until 640 when the Arabs overran the country, making Egypt a province of the Caliph.

Egyptian plays were performed in regularly appointed places most of which had been constructed for that purpose. The *Coronation Festival Plays*, the *Heb Seds* and the *Pyramid Texts* were presented in what Egyptologists call "mortuary temples" because they were, except during the XVIII-XX Dynasties, attached to the tombs of kings. The *Abydos Passion Play* and the *Medicinal Drama* were presented at the "houses of the gods." For thirty-five hundred years the theatre endured, with dark ages before and after the Middle Kingdom, and a brief hiatus of suppression under Akh-en-Aton (also spelled Ikhnaton) in 1375 B. C., only to be restored by the famous Tut-ankh-Amun twenty-five years later.

THE GLORY THAT WAS GREECE

In the wild hills and deep ravines of mountainous Greece the greatest drama the world has ever known was created. In the cold, clear air of dawn, the priests and choric singers assembled with the populace of the cities to celebrate the Dionysiac rites. Out of the dithyramb, their song of intoxicated rejoicing at the rebirth of Dionysos, God of Wine and Fertility, tragedy was born. It drew its material from the epic, taking its form from the lyric, and its name from the sacrificial goat (*tragos*).

According to Herodotus, the Dionysiac festival had its inception in Egypt and was transferred to Attica. This festival is commonly considered the fountain head of the theatre in Greece. The date of the transfer to Greece is unknown but evidence of Greek drama in Syria exists from about 1250 B.C., eight hundred years before Herodotus visited the banks of the Nile. Two sacred dramas written on clay tablets in the cuneiform alphabet were found in the ruins of Ras Shamra. These possess the form of Attic drama, the first having to do with the need of rain to insure a good crop and the second seems to deal with the Phoenician story of Daniel. These findings by Theodor Gaster, coupled with the similarity of Tammuz (Adonis) and Dionysos worship, suggest a possible road the drama may have taken in its journey from Egypt to Greece.

There were four Dionysiac festivals each year. The rural *Dionysia* occurred in the month of *Poseidon*, which included December and the early part of January. The *phallus*, more or less realistically depicted, was an object of worship as a symbol of fertility and phallic songs of crudity and obscenity were sung. These rites were like those of all early peoples, the American Indian, the African, the South Sea Islander, and still persist today in the remote portions of New Guinea and in certain regions of Australia.

These gatherings were formal but one can imagine the peasants coming for long distances along mountain paths, meeting others on their way to the festival, stopping for conversation. The talk turns to the songs to be sung, someone begins singing, others take it up, the feet begin to move in the ancient figures of the dance and theatre is created unconsciously.

When they reached the appointed place, perhaps the wine had been passed freely around and constraints were abandoned and the chorus joined in lustily in the responses or colloquy with the one whose natural leadership made him begin the ceremonies. Out of this came the *Coryphaeus* (head-man), the choral leader. These words had been chanted as the villagers and neighboring country people had marched to the altar of Dionysos where a goat was sacrificed. Songs and dances followed and with the end of the religious ceremonies, country sporting contests took place.

The second festival of each year was the *Lenaea* which came in the month of *Gamelion*, the marriage month, January and the beginning of February in our calendar. It was in this celebration that comedy was emphasized, but of that, more later.

The third was the *Anthesteria* in the month of flowers, *Anthesterion* (February and the early days of March, though the weather was like our spring). This festival had little of theatric interest, being the opening of the wine casks (*Pithoigia*) and the setting out of pots of food for the souls of the dead (*Chythroi*), as well as *Choes*, a children's festival. None of these were suitable for dramatic performances.

The fourth and final was the all-important City *Dionysia* or Great *Dionysia*, which took place in the month of stags (*Elaphebolion*), being March to the beginning of April. This was celebrated by all city and state officials and even by officers of the Attic Federated States, during the period of its existence. Tragedy held first place here just as comedy did at the *Lenaea*.

This celebration in honor of Dionysos Eleuthereus, which developed from the sacred Eleusinian Mysteries, took place from the first within the walls of the city of Athens, hence its name (City) which distinguished it from the *Anthesteria* and the *Lenaea* which in the beginning were held outside the city. The first of the City *Dionysia* seems to have taken place in 534 B.C. at the instance of Pisistratus, tyrant of Athens. This new *Thereus* was made the occasion of a contest in tragedy, an important development. Before the contest took place, a colorful procession known as the *Proagon* was held in memory of the god. All of the state officials under the leadership of the *Archon*, together with the priests and the *choregus* bore the statue of Dionysos from its temple to a point south of the Acropolis near

the Academy on the road to Eleutherae, a town on the northern borders of Attica from whence Dionysos had first come to Athens. There
the procession turned and retraced its steps to the city. The rich robes
were the most beautiful part of the whole festival. The statue was
seated in a festival car, drawn by two men dressed as the attendant
sprites of Dionysos; sitting on either side of the statue were two men
playing on flutes. The knowledge of these details comes from paintings on vases which also show the sacrificial bull with a citizen on
either side and ahead of them two youths bearing branches, another
with a basket and a fourth with a censer from which incense perfumed the air. At the beginning of this whole procession was a youth,
doubtless a trumpeter.

No one knows whether these paintings are accurate representations
of the rites themselves but it is reasonable to suppose that they are
similar to what actually took place.

The whole of the first day was occupied with religious rites and
festivities at the furthest point the procession reached. Then the return over the same route originally travelled by Dionysos was made
in the dark, lighted by the flaming torches which illuminated the
faces of the celebrants. Thus the god was brought back to his theatre,
at a point near his temple, so that he might be present at all performances during the festivals.

At first there was no theatre building, merely a hollow below a hillside; later there was a wooden structure; and finally a great stone
theatre, the Theatre of Dionysos, which will be described later.

The day following the procession was given over to lyrical contests which lasted until late in the afternoon and sometimes even into
the third day. These were amateur contests at which dithyrambs were
performed by five choruses of boys and five choruses of men, each
chorus numbering fifty. The group, totaling five hundred in all, was
chosen evenly from the ten Attic tribes. The honor of participating
was considerable and each bore his own expenses. Thus the finest
talent in Attica was assembled for these contests and the honor of
winning was a tribal honor, though the tripod, the prize of victory,
was awarded to the *choregus*. This was erected in some public place
at the *choregus'* expense. In fact all of the other expenses of the festival were borne by a group of wealthy men, who in turn were so
honored, and who were known as the *choregi*. When actors were
introduced to the dramatic contests, their salaries were paid by the
state.

The dithyramb was a song of revelry to the god, Dionysos, and
was sung to the musical accompaniment of the flute. In the beginning

these dithyrambs related events in the life of the god and were comparable to the Egyptian *Abydos Passion Play*.

In time, other incidents in the lives of legendary heroes were added to the dithyramb proper. The humanity of these stories appealed to the audiences as the religious significance of the Dionysiac Festivals declined in interest. Then there occurred a partial secularization: upon occasion, the dithyrambs were sung entirely in honor of heroes, rather than of Dionysos. Herodotus mentions dithyrambs honoring Adrastus, a legendary Greek King, and undoubtedly other heroes were so honored. The secular dithyrambs evolved into what we know as tragedy—dramas about mortals. The Dionysiac dithyrambs evolved into what we know as satyric comedy—dramas about gods, half gods and satyrs. Thus, both tragedy and satyric comedy derived from the dithyramb.

The artistic quality of these forms was raised to approximate the form of a play by the celebrated Arion who first (according to Herodotus) placed spoken lines among the lyrical songs of his dithyramb and gave the whole composition a title. This composition was sung, spoken and performed with pantomimic action and was essentially a play.

This form of dithyramb play, both tragic and satyric, was widely adopted and became an important part of the Dionysiac Festivals.

Thus, on the third or fourth day, depending on the extent of the dithyrambic contests, the audience assembled in the half-darkness before dawn to attend a play contest. Dawn found most of them on the hillside because space was always at a premium, particularly so after the stone theatre was built, though the overflow was taken care of on the hill behind the theatre seats. At sunrise the contest began as the audience sat, chilled, reverent and expectant. The contestants were poets, each offering a tetralogy—four dramas or plays. Three plays were performed in the morning, one after the other until noon when the audience dispersed. Late in the afternoon they reassembled for the fourth play, a satyric drama, and the tetralogy was completed. For three days these tetralogies were shown and on the final day the judges selected the victor.

These judges were chosen by an elaborate process in order to prevent corruption or intimidation. Undoubtedly they were often afraid to go counter to the opinions of the wealthy and influential but in all probability the dramatist secured a reasonably fair hearing as these judges represented the general intelligence of the Athenian public. Much depended, just as it does today, on the standards of production.

Some days before the festival, the Council together with the *choregi* (whose purses and good taste determined the excellence of

the presentation) elected by lot a preliminary list of judges from the
ten Attic tribes. Their names were inscribed on clay tablets and
placed in urns, one for each tribe, and were sealed in the sight of the
choregi and *prytanes* (members of the Council), turned over to the
treasurers and placed in the Acropolis. The secret of this preliminary
list was carefully guarded. Those whose names were included were
probably summoned by the *Archon* to be present at the drawing. One
name was chosen by lot from each urn and after all had taken the
oath of impartiality, these ten voted on the plays. Their votes were
placed in a single urn and after the contest five lists were drawn, this
determining the victors. All might know how these judges had voted.
The remaining lists were destroyed without publication. The names
of the victorious poet and *choregus* were announced and the men
were crowned with ivy, after which they made a solemn sacrifice.
Then a great banquet was held for them, to which came all their
friends. All of the plays of the tetralogy performed in the contest
were based on a common subject. It is not known whether this was
an invention of Aeschylus or an inheritance from his predecessors.
The plays were short so that their presentation on a single day was
possible. It was Sophocles who abandoned this system and wrote his
plays on subjects independent of each other. This set a fashion and
was soon imitated by his contemporaries and successors. On the
death of Aeschylus the tetralogy was abandoned and was never even
attempted by Euripides. Thus by the end of the fifth century B.C.
this form became extinct. Even the number of plays produced by
each poet declined as the dramas increased in length. By the latter
half of the fourth century the poets ceased to contribute a satyric
drama each, one being considered enough for the festival. With the
decline of the vitality of Attic tragedy, the number of dramas decreased to two. Finally the Hellenic poets in Alexandria became more
celebrated than those in Athens, although the latter continued to contribute new plays and many revivals to the contests.

At each of the festivals three poets competed and each was required
to produce four plays; a tetralogy if on a subject which ran through
all the dramas, or a *didaskalia* (a teaching for a chorus) each of which
was an independent artistic piece. The three tragedies were known as
a trilogy, a term which has persisted until the present day. The leading American dramatist, Eugene O'Neill, utilized this form in *Mourning Becomes Electra*, which is a clear instance of a subject common to
all the plays. The story of Electra (seen in a setting of New England
during the American Civil War) carries its impact so clearly both to
the auditor and reader that it is as though it were one play.

ARION, whose renown was celebrated by Herodotus, was a native of Lesbos, though he lived most of his life in Corinth. There he was at the court of the tyrant, Periander. He was undoubtedly the greatest harpist of his time and he improved the dithyramb in regularity and order. He was said to have "invented" this form, though this was manifestly impossible. It is a characteristic Greek habit of ascribing invention to the person who was at most the systematizer. He is even said to have introduced the circular arrangement of the chorus, which evidently came from the practice of grouping itself around the altar. Living at the end of the seventh century and the beginning of the sixth, he probably set the number of dancers at fifty, which persisted until the end. His most important contribution was the insertion of "spoken verses" in the middle of the dithyrambs. These were brief colloquies between the *choryphaeus* and the members of the chorus concerning the exploits of Dionysos which would clarify the story told in the songs.

THESPIS was born about the beginning of the sixth century in Icaria where his youth and early manhood were spent. There he conceived the idea of improving the dithyramb in a simple but far-reaching manner, namely by introducing the first actor. (Of course if the Egyptian connection is accepted, then Thespis' invention had been anticipated by the priests of Osiris for at least two thousand years.) Thus a tragic drama was possible. The days of simple narrative were over. Formerly the chorus and the leader had related events that had happened and had discussed them in poetry and song. It was always, however, from the point of view of the outsider. The chorus was costumed as satyrs but no effort had been made to imitate the protagonists of the story. With the first actor, disguises were introduced, and the actor and the *choryphaeus* could impersonate scenes from the life of the god. Thespis is also credited with the introduction of the mask in Greece which permitted quick change of character without any alteration in dress. This mask of unpainted linen was considered an improvement over the earlier method of painting the face with white lead and covering it with cinnabar. Visible dramatic action was introduced to the spectators and the line between narrative and dramatic poetry was passed, so that it is understandable how in ancient times Thespis came to be considered the inventor of tragedy.

Beginning in Icaria, he transferred his activities to Athens where he may have begun to exhibit plays as early as 560 B.C., though they were yet private enterprises and were not recognized by the state. According to tradition Solon frowned upon his efforts, contending that he deceived the public by having an actor impersonate a god

or king and that these deceptions would be introduced into public
life. There may have been some truth in his statement because soon
afterwards Pisistratus persuaded the public, by self-inflicted wounds,
that he needed a bodyguard and so was able to establish himself as a
tyrant, a habit which has been imitated by would-be dictators ever
since.

In 534 B.C., the self-same Pisistratus established the first public contest for tragedy in Athens and Thespis was the first victor. This was
truly poetic justice since it was due to his energies that the contest
had come about. No play of his survives and he passed into obscurity;
doubtless he died soon after as he was an old man in his hour of
triumph.

CHOERILUS, the successor of Thespis, is credited with the introduction of women's masks which were probably light in color, as the
men's were dark in the vase-paintings where the habits of the stage
were probably recorded. He is believed to have flourished in the fifty
years between 523 and 482 B.C.; to have composed one hundred and
sixty plays; and to have won thirteen victories in the dramatic contests. He undoubtedly competed against Aeschylus and Pratinas. Success is attributed to him in satyric drama, an invention of the younger
Pratinas and the *Alope* is the only recorded title of which some fragments exist. His style was said to be determinedly precious.

PRATINAS was a native of Phlius and competed with Aeschylus and
Choerilus. He wrote fifty plays, thirty-two of which were satyric,
thereby lending credence to the theory that he composed satyric
dramas for the tetralogies of others, whilst they wrote their own
tragedies. Certainly he was the first to compose satyric plays of the
type known in the fifth century.

Satyric drama was closely related to tragedy. Though the former
was often gay, frolicking and obscene, as were the disguised satyrs
of the chorus, nonetheless the principal characters were gods or
heroes. In addition to the tragic characters however were the *silenus*,
autolycus and *polyphemus*, a choice disreputable assembly. The
stories of these dramas were the same as those of the tragedies but
were treated from a humorous point of view. Satyric drama is not to
be confused with Greek comedy which will be treated later.

PHRYNICHUS, the tragedian, was only slightly the senior of Aeschylus, whose invention of the second actor he adopted in the *Phoenissae*,
476 B.C. His plays doubtless had high literary merit. Aristophanes
praised his lyrics but ridiculed the crudity and extreme simplicity of
the handling of the actors in his plays. His first victory came in 512-
509 B.C. and he introduced women as characters, though played of

course by men. *The Capture of Miletus* was enormously successful in his time. It is deeply to be regretted that only scattered fragments of his plays exist because he was highly regarded by an age that knew and listened to the tragic writings of Aeschylus, Sophocles and Euripides.

AESCHYLUS (525-456 B.C.) was born in Eleusis. In 500 he began to compete in the tragic contests but did not win a prize until 485. He lived in perilous times for Greece as Xerxes and the Persians sought to conquer and despoil the country. He was a warrior at Marathon and it is probable that he was present at Salamis because of the vividness of the description of the victory in *The Persians*. Unlike the other dramatists of his day he spent long periods of time out of his country. His second and last visit to Sicily was permanent. According to popular legend, he was seated on the side of a hill near Gela when an eagle flew over in search of a rock on which to crush the tortoise it carried in its beak and mistook his bald head for a stone. So died the man who is called the first great tragic writer.

His principal innovation as a dramatist was the introduction of the second actor in his plays. (This statement is included because it is generally taken to be true. However if the Egyptians used at least two actors, the dead king and the living king, and at Abydos many speaking parts, then the Greeks may have used more actors than was supposed previously, before the connection between Egypt and Greece was understood.) Thus a more complicated plot could be portrayed and it was possible to decrease the importance of the chorus and offer more flexibility to the drama. To be able to bring the conflicting dramatic forces face to face in the persons of actors strengthened them and the sympathetic and pathetic scenes were immeasurably heightened. He wrote between seventy and ninety plays of which only seven are extant. Nonetheless these suffice to trace his development as a dramatist. *The Suppliants*, his earliest play to survive, uses the chorus of *Danaides* as the protagonist and only a single actor is utilized. *The Persians*, *Seven Against Thebes*, and *Prometheus Bound* employ two actors, but by the time he wrote the *Oresteia* (a tetralogy, the satyric play is missing) which contains the *Agamemnon*, *The Libation Bearers* and the *Eumenides*, he borrowed the third actor from Sophocles, his younger rival.

The Suppliants (*Hiketides*, sometimes called the *Supplices* or *Suppliant Women*) concerns itself with fifty maidens, the daughters of Danaus, who have fled from Egypt to avoid an enforced marriage. This is the first play to have a dramatic situation which arises in the conflict between king and herald, but there is slight attempt at characterization. *The Persians* (*Persae*), almost twenty years later in point of writing, is the next play to have survived. In this drama the importance of religion in the make-up of Aeschylus is stressed. The defeat of the Persians is accomplished as an act of God. Instead of the remoteness of time which is characteristic of the Greeks, he has chosen the remoteness of distance to achieve the nobility and grandeur which is always characteristic of his writing. This was part of a series of four plays which seems to have had no continuity of subject matter (the others no longer exist) and therefore could not properly be considered a tetralogy.

The *Seven Against Thebes* won first prize at its production in 467 B.C. as part of a true tetralogy. It concerns the quarrels of the sons of Oedipus and is graphic in its treatment of war for which it was praised by Aristophanes in *The Frogs. Prometheus Bound*, though undated, was probably produced about 465 because the importance of the choral odes is diminished and the dialogue overshadows all. It is concerned with the punishment of Prometheus by Zeus for the offense of teaching mankind the use of fire for which crime he is chained to a rock. This play is one of the noblest of Aeschylus; its very suggestiveness of outline emphasizes man's struggle against inhumanity regardless of source, a constant striving after liberty. It had a profound influence on such later lovers of liberty as Goethe, Byron and Shelley, who wrote *Prometheus Unbound*.

The *Orestiae* is composed of three great plays. The *Agamemnon* is a magnificent portrayal of guilt and retribution and as such has had a profound influence on dramatic literature. It is concerned with the murder of Agamemnon by his wife, Clytemnestra, and her lover, Aegisthus; their subsequent death at the hands of Orestes, her son, is treated in the *Libation Bearers*. In the *Eumenides* Orestes is haunted by the Furies until his arrival in Athens. There he is tried and acquitted. The theme is so great, the conception so magnificent, that this tetralogy ranks in the eyes of many as the greatest of the Greek tragedies. Its very severity makes it less attractive to modern auditors who are accustomed to more careful embroidering of theatrical subjects, but this is the quality that endeared it to the Greeks themselves.

In addition to his contributions to the refinement of dramatic structure, Aeschylus is responsible for some innovations in the staging of plays. He introduced definite costume for the actors, increased their height by the use of higher buskins, *kothurni*, and enlarged the size of the masks. These were all, of course, borrowed from the worship of Dionysos. He also decorated theatres, bringing in paintings and mechanical devices.

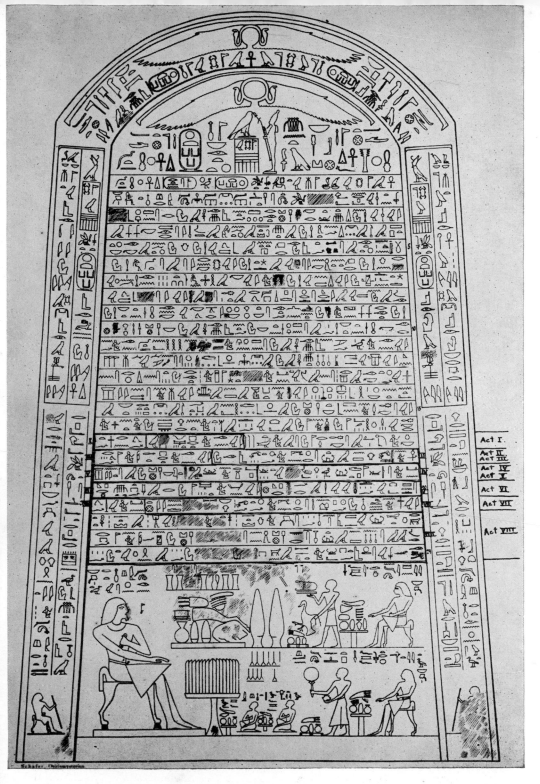

1. HIEROGLYPHICS ON IKHERNOFRET STONE (1868 B.C.) DEPICTING AN ACCOUNT OF THE ABYDOS
PASSION PLAY. Act divisions are superimposed by Louis E. Laflin, Jr.

Schaefer, *"Untersuchungen zur Geschichte und Alterumskunde Aegyptens."*

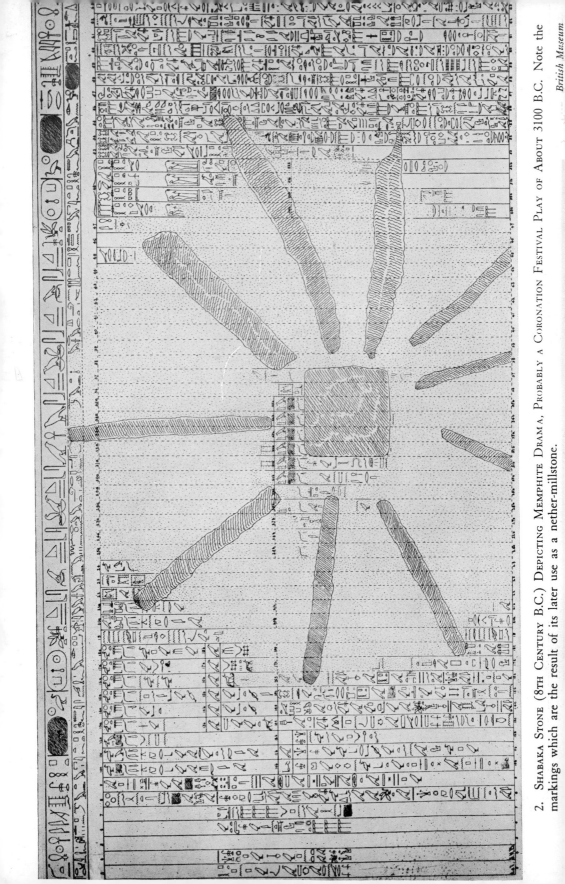

2. Shabaka Stone (8th Century B.C.) Depicting Memphite Drama, Probably a Coronation Festival Play of About 3100 B.C. Note the markings which are the result of its later use as a nether-millstone.

British Museum

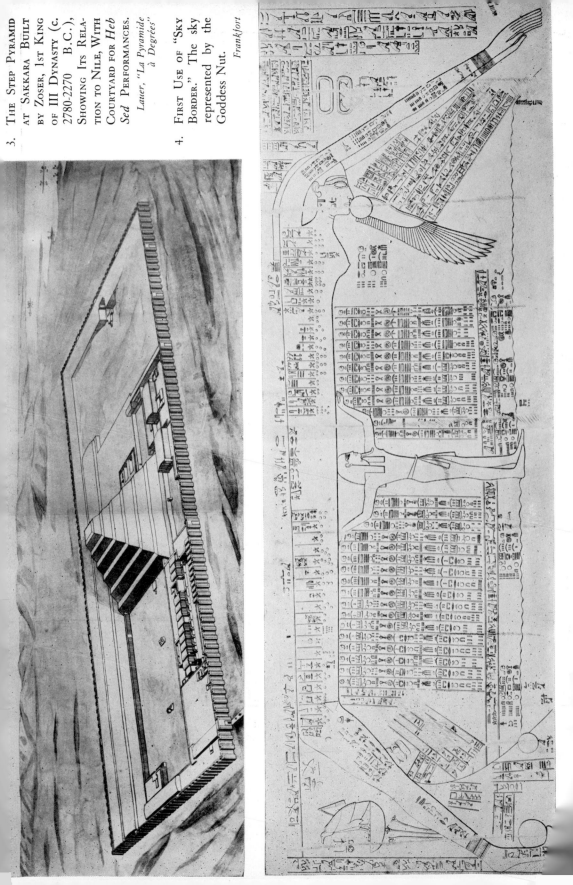

3. THE STEP PYRAMID AT SAKKARA BUILT BY ZOSER, 1ST KING OF III DYNASTY (c. 2780-2270 B.C.), SHOWING ITS RELATION TO NILE, WITH COURTYARD FOR *Heb Sed* PERFORMANCES.

Lauer, "La Pyramide à Degrées"

4. FIRST USE OF "SKY BORDER." The sky represented by the Goddess Nut.

Frankfort

5. **Reconstruction of the Temple at Deir El-Bahri Where Dramatic Performances Probably Took Place.** Shown from above looking down the causeways leading to the Nile. Photograph of model.

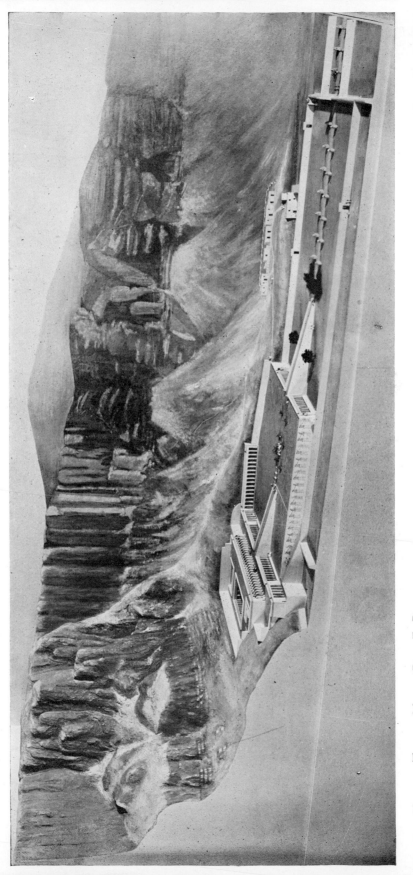

6. SIDE VIEW OF TEMPLE MODEL, DEIR EL-BAHRI.

7. IMITATION OF A ROLL CURTAIN IN TILE AT THE III DYNASTY STEP
PYRAMID OF ZOSER.

Lauer, "La Pyramide à Degrées"

8. MASK OF BES METTERNICH STONE. Compare with masks of Greek and Roman Mimes.

Golenisheff, "Das Metternichstele"

11. DETAIL SHOWING CONSTRUCTION OF PRIESTS' MASKS

Mariette-Bey, Dendérah

9. TEMPLE DETAIL. (*See No. 10*).

10. RECONSTRUCTION OF A MORTUARY TEMPLE. PROBABLY USED FOR DRAMATIC PURPOSES. Detail above, left.

Borchardt, "Das Grabdenkmal des Koenigs Sa-Hu-Re"

12. Greek Theatre at Epidaurus Showing Circular Orchestra.

13. GREEK THEATRE AT DELPHI. *Courtesy of Julia Gardner*

14. THEATRE OF DIONYSOS AT ATHENS. *Courtesy of Julia Gardner*

16. CONJECTURAL RECONSTRUC-
TION OF THE THEATRE OF
DIONYSOS ABOUT THE MIDDLE
OF THE FIFTH CENTURY, B.C.
Designed by Heinrich Bulle
under the direction of Franz
Rapp. A performance of
Aeschylus's *Agamemnon* is
depicted.

Courtesy of Franz Rapp

17. HELLENISTIC THEATRE AT TAORMINA, SICILY.

Courtesy of Julia Gardner

18. Greek Theatre at Segesta in Sicily.

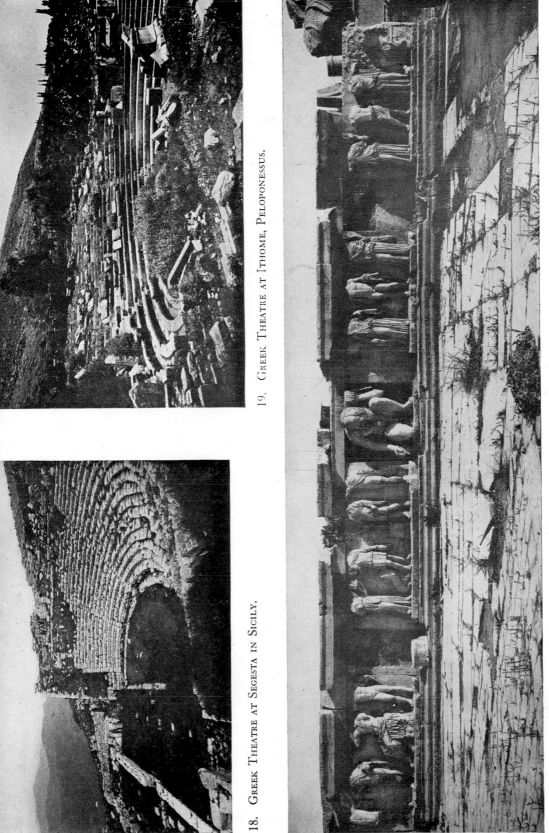

19. Greek Theatre at Ithome, Peloponessus.

20. Architectural and Sculptural Detail of the Theatre of Dionysos at Athens.

Courtesy of Julia Gardner

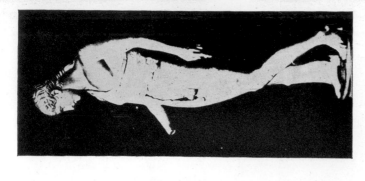

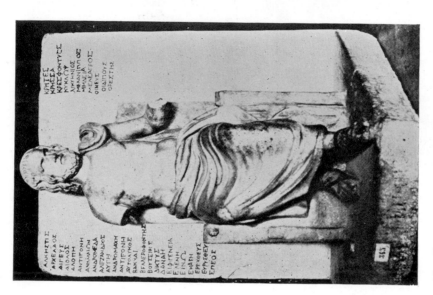

22. EURIPIDES. A list of his plays is carved
behind him.

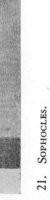

21. SOPHOCLES.

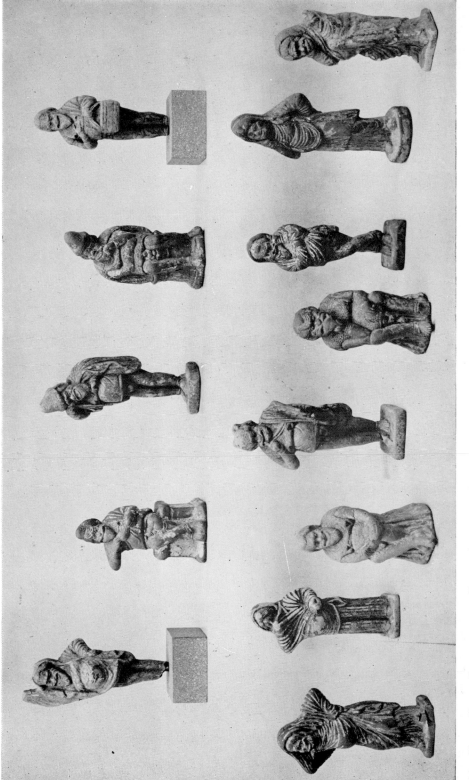

24. Terra Cotta Statuettes of Greek Actors of Old Comedy.

25, 26, 27, 28, 29, 30, 31. GREEK MASKS AND FIGURES.

Metropolitan Museum

32, 33, 34. SCENES FROM GREEK DRAMA. The upper is a satyric play and
the lower a *phlyakes* (also a favorite dramatic form of the Romans).

Metropolitan Museum

35, 36, 37, 38, 39. GREEK VASES SHOWING DRAMATIC SCENES.

SOPHOCLES (497-c.406 B.C.) was born (when Aeschylus was a young man of twenty-eight) in Colonys, a village one mile north of Athens and was the son of the wealthy but unaristocratic Sophillus. It was there that he passed his boyhood which so indelibly fixed his memory that its scenes are celebrated in *Oedipus Coloneus* which was written when he was nearly ninety. His education was complete and according to the Greek custom included music, dancing and the athletics of the gymnasium. At the age of sixteen, he was chosen because of the beauty of his face and body, as well as his conspicuous success in the arts of music and dance, to lead the singing and play the harp for the chorus of boys in celebration of the victory over the Persians.

In 468, when he was twenty-eight, and Aeschylus a man of late middle years, they competed for the tragic prize. The competition was keen and the feeling high and Sophocles was the victor. For the next sixty years he continued to write plays and stage-manage them, though rarely acting in them because of his deficiencies in voice. He was victorious eighteen times in the City *Dionysia* and several times in the *Lenaea,* and is said never to have been less than second in the list of winners.

He lived in an important period of Greek history—his life coincided with the life of the Athenian Empire. He was not a great figure in political life but like other writers did his share. He was twice elected general, the highest office in the state, first with Pericles in 440 and in his later years with Nicias, but his part was a subordinate one. He also carried out certain functions of the priest in connection with Asclepius to whom he composed a paean which continued to be sung until the third century A.D.

These duties are in keeping with his strong religious feelings. He was the great idealist of the Greek dramatists. According to Aristotle, it was he who, in comparing his own work with that of Euripides, said that "I drew men as they ought to be—Euripides drew them as they are." Plutarch records that he said of his own development as a dramatist, "My dramatic wild oats were imitations of Aeschylus' pomp, then I evolved my own harsh mannerism; finally I embraced that style which is best, as most adapted to the portrayal of human nature."

The principal innovation in dramatic form introduced by Sophocles was the third actor, according to authorities on the Greek drama. Thus was completed the cycle begun a century before by Thespis when he "introduced" the first actor and "began" the movement which resulted in the complete subordination of the chorus to dramatic action. Practically all scenes could be acted without their assistance and the choral odes became interludes in the drama. The chorus no longer had anything at stake in the action. It became more detached in its point of view; in fact it acts as a foil to the actors on the stage. Sophocles refined the drama enormously. This can easily be seen if his plays are compared with the earlier efforts of other playwrights. In sheer creativeness, however, he was probably the inferior of Aeschylus. Another difference between the two dramatists was Sophocles' abandonment of the tetralogy and his lengthening of dialogue, thereby making four plays too long. This also simplified the construction of the play, making each drama complete in itself and no longer dependent on an earlier piece for the audience's understanding nor on a later one for the conclusion of the dramatic action of the trilogy or tetralogy. The language was made more human though it was still idealistic in tone. The characters had taken on the shape of heroes rather than that of the Aeschylean titans. It is especially in the delineation of character that Sophocles excels. He never keeps his audience in doubt as to the final outcome of the play as the modern dramatist must do. How often our critics and those who attend the theatre disparage a play for this reason. The Greeks however were never troubled by this. They were as familiar with their plots as were the later Elizabethans. It is in the depiction of character development under stress and in the occasional revelation of tenderness at unexpected moments which won the Hellenes. Aeschylus was primarily a moralist, sometimes to his detriment as a dramatist. In contrast, Sophocles is reticent in his approach but he never loses sight of the mysteriousness and incredibility of destiny, and the power of religion in the world. This becomes apparent in the unconscious tragic irony which he so often utilizes when the words or actions of a character draw the attention of the audience to his appointed but (to him) unforeseen end.

He developed the use of painted scenery and is credited with increasing the number of the chorus from twelve to fifteen, although this change has never been understood because the chorus was early fixed at fifty and many authorities believe this number was never lowered. He was the first to introduce the use of Phrygian music in tragedy.

There are but seven plays extant of the more than one hundred and ten plays which we know he wrote. Some authorities place the figure as high as one hundred and thirty. Their chronology is very uncertain because there are no historical allusions which might help in dating them. We know that the *Philoctetes* was produced in 409

B.C. and that *Oedipus Coloneus* was played in 401 B.C. In point of structure, which is all we have to go on, the *Antigone* and the *Ajax* are probably the earliest. Authorities disagree and we can but follow modern preference in placing the *Ajax* first. This play (circa 440 B.C.) is frequently called Sophocles' earliest extant play because, though the play calls for three actors, his use of them is more tentative than in the *Antigone*.

This latter play was probably produced the following year and is often the most admired of his plays because of modern sympathy with the heroine. The *Electra* is next in point of writing and is more often revived than any of Sophocles' works and is related in subject matter to Euripides' play of the same name and to Aeschylus' *Libation Bearers*. *Oedipus Tyrannus* (also known as *Oedipus, the King* and *Oedipus Rex*) is probably a later play than *Electra* and from Aristotle's time it was considered a model of tragedy. The next is the *Women of Trachnis* (*The Trachiniae*) and is the least interesting of all to the modern mind. When the author was eighty-seven, the before mentioned *Philoctetes* was performed and represents the highest skill in play-construction Sophocles demonstrated. The last extant play is *Oedipus Coloneus* (402-401 B.C.) produced posthumously by his grandson who also bore his name, Sophocles having died in c.406.

EURIPIDES (485-406 B.C.) was born at Salamis. Tradition put his birth as the day of the battle in 480 but the Parian Marble is probably more reliable. He was the son of well-to-do parents which fact permitted him to devote himself entirely to the drama and to amass a library (a great rarity in his time) and thus to own the first recorded theatre collection. Unlike Sophocles he cared little for social life and saw only those few intimates for whom he cared. Anaxagoras, Protagoras and Socrates (as tradition would have it) were his close friends. Much of his time was spent in a cave at Salamis which he had had reconstructed as a study.

His dramatic powers were widely recognized in Athens but his rewards in the contests were few. In his nearly one hundred plays he won first prize only four times. A fifth victory came after his death when his tetralogy which included the *Bacchae* was produced.

His contributions to dramatic technique are not large but they are significant. He always made excellent and economical use of his material. Whenever he introduced a character, he used that character. Aristophanes in *The Frogs* makes him rebuke Aeschylus for bringing characters on to the stage without giving them lines to speak. He also clarified the prologues of Aeschylus and Sophocles and turned them into what we recognize by that term. He employed them to place the story of the play in its proper sequence in the legend.

When he was already an old man he accepted the invitation of the Macedonian King, Archelaus, to reside in his court where he received the highest honors and where his latest plays were performed. On his death he quickly won the position denied him generally in life and his plays were performed over the entire ancient world. Nine of his nineteen extant dramas were used as school texts and he, along with Homer, Virgil and Horace were studied in ancient times.

The *Alcestis* (438 B.C.) won second prize, Sophocles being victor with a play unknown to us. It is the fourth play of the tetralogy but it is not satyric, being tragic with some features of comedy. Many of the plays of Euripides are more properly tragi-comedies, in that they end in joy. It is in this that the dramatist can be said to imitate life more closely than his two great predecessors. The *Medea* (431 B.C.) was the first play of a tetralogy and obtained only third prize, Sophocles being second and Euphorion, son of Aeschylus, the winner. It concerns itself with the wrongs put upon Medea by her husband, Jason, and the terrible revenge she takes. It reveals knowingly the position of women in Greek life. It also shows a great tragic character divided against itself which is expressed in mental, rather than dramatic action, and as such, is the forerunner of the modern psychological drama.

The *Children of Heracles* (*Heracleidae*) was produced about 430 B.C. though the exact date is unknown. It is a short play and is one of the least admired of his works, though the style is marked with the easy and smooth flowing qualities that are characteristic of Euripides.

The *Hippolytus* (428 B.C.) won first place in the contest and recounts most beautifully the love Phaedra, wife of Theseus, bore for her step-son, Hippolytus, and her suicide and the son's later death. Racine used this legend in his greatest play, *Phèdre*. The *Hecuba* (circa 425 B.C.) was greatly successful throughout all antiquity as the comments of contemporary critics prove. It has little standing today, probably because it breaks up into two plays with forced and slight connection. The best thing in it is the chorus describing the last hours of Troy, but this is only remotely concerned with the drama's plot. The *Andromache* may have been produced about 430 B.C. but its première did not take place in Athens. Perhaps this explains the fact that while purportedly concerned with the heroic age, it is in part a tract against the holding of slaves in fifth century Attica and is couched in terse and idiomatic dialogue equal to the poet's best.

The Madness of Heracles (*Hercules Furens*) was written about 421 B.C. This date derives from the famous choral lyric concerning old age which would suggest that the dramatist had but recently passed into his sixties. *The Suppliant Women* (*Supplices* or *The Suppliants*) was produced about 420 B.C. and is one of his least interesting plays, having no characterization worthy of the name. The story is unlike Aeschylus' play despite the duplication of title.

The exact date of the next drama is unknown but is presumed to be about 412 B.C.; it is entitled *Ion* and is an attack on Olympian theology in which Apollo is shown to be a liar and a cheat and the Delphic Oracle to be human and not divine. The play is technically a melodrama, not a tragedy. Shortly before *Ion* had come the *Trojan Women* (*Troades*) which lost the prize to Xenocles in 415 B.C. This is considered one of the greatest indictments of war in the sweep of world literature and as such has known frequent revival in a present day world hungry for peace. *Iphigenia Among the Taurians* (*Iphigenia in Tauris*) was produced about 414 B.C. It is one of his finest plays technically and the spirit of adventure in this tragi-comedy is winning to modern ears.

The *Electra* was played about 413 B.C. and holds a special claim on the attention of students of Greek drama because the subject matter is the same as Aeschylus' religious *Libation Bearers* and Sophocles' emotional *Electra*. Euripides was interested in the ethics of matricide and shows that a crime left unmolested is less likely to cause anguish than the punishment of it at the expense of one's natural love of one's parents. *Helen* (*Helena*) was produced in 412 B.C. and is a burlesque of his own writings. It is incredibly light and pretty for a serious effort. Legend has it that it was written for a private performance for a group of women who were celebrating the festival, Thesmorphoria, on the island of Helene. Next comes the *Phoenician Women* (*Phoenissae*) in 410 B.C. which was enormously popular in the ancient world and was one of the three plays (*Hecuba* and *Orestes* were the others) chosen by the Byzantine scholars to represent Euripides. Because of this, the play has been lengthened by whole passages, interpolated by later poets, as well as individual lines by actors and copyists. The *Orestes* was first played in 408 B.C. and revived in 341. It is a brilliant study of the growing insanity of Orestes which is stimulated by the malice of Electra. It is anti-religious in feeling as the viperish Electra and the shallow Helen attribute their troubles to the gods. *The Bacchantes* (*Bacchae*) came in 405 B.C. after the death of Euripides. It is an example of the same primitive dramaturgy which suggests Aeschylus; at the same time it has great lyric loveliness and propounds a theology the import of which still confounds scholars.

Iphigenia in Aulis was produced by his son in 406 B.C. and is a masterpiece in character drawing. Left unfinished at his death, the younger Euripides completed it and later scribes added their own additions. Though his last play, it shows no weakening. In fact he seemed to be on the verge of discovering new forms which make the piece almost a transition into the New Comedy of Menander.

There are numerous fragments of plays left to us but there is only one left unconsidered. That is the *Cyclops*, which is the only whole satyric drama which survives to this day. Most authorities decline to date the production but the distinguished scholar, Roy C. Flickinger, sets it at about 440 B.C. It is seven hundred lines long, slight in content, with only rudimentary attempts at characterization. The *Rhesus* is sometimes ascribed to Euripides but many authorities argue against this. It has decided vigor of action but is almost totally lacking in psychology and the lyrics are of little value. It is probable that it is a very early work of the dramatist who was a great artist, a great teacher, and one who loved beauty and worshipped intelligence.

Tragedies were also performed at the *Lenaea* which was mentioned before but the principal contribution of this largely domestic festival was comedy. Coming as it did late in January when storms on the Aegean and Mediterranean would hold ships at home, there were few strangers present. It was a peculiarly Athenian celebration in honor of *Dionysos Lenaeus* and took place in an enclosure known as the *Lenaeum*, near the market place. There was a simple procession and the festival was much shorter though the form in general was the same. It continued to be celebrated at least as late as the second century A.D. It was probably its comic tradition which caused its long survival.

Aristotle says that comedy came from the Dionysiac ritual and that its development was parallel to that of tragedy. Despite the discrediting of most of his teachings, this one is still accepted—as the Doric mimes from Hegara in Doria took on comic form. Thus rude social satire became comedy. Old Comedy, as it is now defined, existed from approximately 500 B.C. until 400 B.C. Aristophanes was its greatest exponent and he ranks as the finest comic writer of Greece.

Old Comedy was marked by bawdiness and great license in speech. It was at this time that the tongue was freed and writers and actors might say what they thought without any restraint. This developed with the rise of Greek democracy and declined with the democratic spirit. The actors wore tights and padded themselves front and back and frequently wore giant phalli since this type of drama came out of the phallic ceremonies of Dionysos. By the beginning of Middle Comedy (circa 400-320 B.C.) these had become modified or had disappeared. Humor was primitive and Gargantuan. Fertility has always been a subject both of reverence and fun and world drama has developed along those lines.

ARISTOPHANES (c.450-c.380 B.C.) was the son of Philippos of Aegina and therefore a transplanted son of Athens, which like New York drew many adopted citizens. Almost all details of his life are conjectural. The dramatist's first play was produced in his early twenties, *The Banqueters* (427 B.C.) and was an attack on the new techniques in education. Aristophanes has been called an aristocrat, a reactionary, a conservative and various names of a so-called derogative nature. In all probability he was an aristocrat of the soul who deplored the vulgarity which of necessity comes with the uplifting of the masses. Believing in the necessity of a democracy of intellect and art, he resented the blatancy of many who were its protagonists. A great deal has been made of his criticisms of Euripides and his exaltation of Aeschylus and Sophocles but too little attention has been paid to his able defense of Euripides' position in *The Acharnians, Thesmophoriazusae* and *The Frogs.*

Like his first play, *The Babylonians* (426 B.C.) was brought out in the name of a contemporary actor. It is likely that the authorship was perfectly well known, however. It is known that the dramatist believed that he had a great deal to learn and so was willing to observe the work of other directors and actors during the production of his first three plays. This particular piece attacked the foreign as well as the domestic policies of Athens.

The earliest extant play is *The Acharnians* (425 B.C.) which was the third in point of production. This was concerned with the follies of the war party in Athens during the Peloponnesian War with Sparta which had brought overcrowding and plague to the city, the latter of which caused the death of Pericles. Cleon had persisted in carrying on this war and Aristophanes used the bawdy strokes of comic writing to muster the peace party against the government. He lived almost entirely in wartime and it is a tribute to Greek democracy that both he and his plays managed to survive the destructive spirit abroad at such times. This play is a prelude to his outright attack on Cleon in *The Knights* (424 B.C.) which was produced at the *Lenaea.* This play, entirely political in subject matter, has less of interest to modern readers than some.

His next play was so unsuccessful that it only obtained third place.

The Clouds (423 B.C.) and was entirely rewritten, in which version it survives. This attacks Socrates and Greek education and was so damaging to the scholar that he attributed his conviction and death to Aristophanes' travesty. *The Wasps* (422 B.C.) was devoted to a critical study of the perversion of judicial power and the desirability of jury duty in Athens since payment for such service had been instituted. Cleon sought to divert the citizens with a pretense of ruling whilst he was the real power in the city-state. In this play in a *parabasis* he compliments his own writing of *The Clouds* which was undoubtedly slighted because the bold and amusing indecencies dear to the hearts of the theatre public had been largely sublimated. Probably because of this, the ending of The *Wasps* was riotous and the leading character danced the indecent *cordax*.

Aristophanes' plays (he wrote forty in all, of which eleven survive and the titles of twenty-six additional are known) crowd fast upon each other. The *Peace* (421 B.C.) again pleads for a settlement of the difficulties with Sparta and an end of the war which was undermining Athenian civilization. This is one of the cleanest and dullest plays, a fact which may have had something to do with its only receiving second place. However, there are many lyric passages describing the beauties of peace in the Attic country. Subsequent plays perished and the much admired *Birds* (414 B.C.) is the next extant drama. Undoubtedly concerned with Alcibiades, it has much that reminds us of *A Midsummer Night's Dream* and in the beautiful costuming of the chorus as the birds of Attica we are reminded of Rostand's *Chantecler*.

Then came another anti-war play which as such takes rank with the great plays of all time devoted to peace. *Lysistrata* (411 B.C.) has much to commend it to modern audiences. Several brilliant translations and productions have been made in America and England since the First World War. The bold humor of a league of women to bring about the sexual starvation of men and so force an end to war is one that tickles the modern sense of humor. The very end of the play in a riotous festival has become popular in a day of great theatrical freedom. This play was performed in the fall of the year and the following spring (410 B.C.) saw the production of *The Women at the Festival of Demeter* (*Thesmophoriazusae*), which was another attack on Euripides. Some of Aristophanes' brightest lines are written at the expense of this great tragic writer whom he delighted to ridicule. In many of Euripides' plays women were painted in an unfavorable light. His *Phaedra* was considered typical by the satirist so Aristophanes pictures the plight of Euripides who must secure some dramatist to appear at the Women's Assembly to plead his cause in this play. Again in *The Frogs* (405 B.C.) he was pilloried and, coming as it did shortly after his death and that of Sophocles, Aristophanes chose this one in which to compare these two playwrights with Aeschylus. Passages of sublime beauty are contrasted with the cry of the chorus "Brekekekex, ko-ax, ko-ax" on the shores of the River Styx, which has found echo in modern university songs and cheers. It is this combination of wit, as well as humor, with lyric passages and high-minded songs that makes Aristophanes a great dramatist.

Women in Parliament (*The Ecclesiazusae*) circa 393 B.C. differs greatly from his earlier plays because open political satire was less possible due to the decline of Athens as a great power. This piece satirized women's rights and seems almost to travesty Plato's *Republic* which was yet to be published. *Plutus* (produced in an early version in 408 B.C. which has not survived) was revised and staged in 388 B.C. The freedom of speech enjoyed in the great days of Athens is strictly limited and the dramatist is circumscribed in his speech by the hostility to criticism and so took refuge in allegory. There is no *parabasis* and the chorus has declined. Old Comedy is over and the period of transition known as Middle Comedy is upon us.

There is no exact line of demarcation between the first and second forms of Greek comedy. Aristophanes belonged to both periods and two of his plays not mentioned before, *Aeolosicon* and *Cocalus* (which includes a "seduction" and a "recognition later" imitated by Menander) produced by one of his sons, definitely belong to Middle Comedy. The decline of the chorus under Aristophanes eventually continues to extinction in this period because the humbled state of Athens could no longer finance productions requiring the choruses of the great period. The Thirty Tyrants endeavored to suppress personal satire but that merely forced the poets to use the kind of subterfuge that modern American dramatists employ in such plays as *The Man Who Came to Dinner* or *The Royal Family*. This made it necessary to transform the comedy of character into the comedy of manners. There are approximately forty writers of this period whose names remain. Of these perhaps the most important were Antiphanes, who wrote three hundred plays of a critical and social nature, and the handsome and effeminate Anaxandrides, who is credited with the introduction of love affairs of low nature in his comedies.

New Comedy commenced about 330 B.C. and continued throughout the whole period of Macedonian supremacy in Greece. The unqualified right of free speech had disappeared and even the modified form known in Middle Comedy was very much limited by the parlous state of Athenian political affairs. Of necessity the dramatists concerned themselves with the personal problems of the average citizen, no longer singling out the great and near-great. Their handling of plots became more skilful if more stereotyped. They chose such characters and situations as were likely to arouse a mirthful response in their auditors. The types included the mercenary courtesan, the scheming and greedy slave, the captain of the mercenary troops with his purse overflowing with recently paid gold, the dissolute scion of a wealthy family and the frequently deceived *pater familias,* whether stern or kindly.

MENANDER (c.342-c.291 B.C.) was born in Athens, son of Diopeithes, an important Greek general. He was celebrated for his observation and knowledge of character which is reflected in his more than a hundred plays, eight of which won the comic prize. Some authorities say that he was a pleasure-loving and effeminate person, while others remind us of his rakish affair with the notorious prostitute, Glycera. His plays, which record his admiration of Euripides, survive only in the Roman adaptations of Plautus and Terence. Philemon (c.300-c.233 B.C.), Diphilas and Posidippus, who began to produce plays notorious for their indecency two years after Menander's death, were three other leading writers of New Comedy.

It is not our intention to describe all the theatres of Greece, Asia Minor and Sicily which were under Greek influence but to describe a typical theatre and to allow your eye to detect in ample illustrations the variations on the theme which later architects introduced at the behest of far-seeing dramatists and actors. Naturally the physical location of the theatre to some extent controlled its form but as places for playing were usually on a plain before a hillside, the later buildings, first wood and then stone, were shaped by their surroundings. As you would expect from a theatre which stems directly from religious worship, there is a *thymele* (altar) which was first located in the center of a circular dancing space for the chorus known as the *orchestra.* This circular arrangement permitted the performance of the dithyramb in honor of Dionysos and the audience arranged themselves around the ring on the hillside and plain. The statue of the god which had been carried in the procession was placed near the altar so that he might enjoy the dithyrambs and later the dramatic performances in his honor.

The Theatre of Dionysos in Athens is the most celebrated of all the Greek theatres as it was here that the City *Dionysia* was celebrated and the works of Thespis, Aeschylus, Sophocles and Euripides received their first performances. The orchestra circle was near the old temple and hard by the Sacred Grove which doubtless hid the booth or hut known as the *skene* (from which the modern *scene* was derived) which was a retiring room where the actor changed his mask or costume. This was possible while the chorus was performing. There was a natural terrace above the orchestra which could be utilized for appearances of the gods. The sloping approach gave rise to the expression of "ascending" the stage when the actor made his entrances and "descending" when he made his exit.

Before the first actor existed, the *choryphaeus* used to ascend the sacrificial table which was beside the altar, both being called *thymele*, for his interrogation of the chorus. This passed with the erection of a temporary *skene* on the edge, or more properly, within the orchestra circle as the actor increased and the chorus declined in importance. These scene buildings were first erected every year and were wooden but were later replaced by permanent handsome stone structure begun in the time of Pericles and completed under the Thirty Tyrants at the end of the fifth century B.C. There were usually three doors, though sometimes only one, which suggested houses in a street. Projecting on either side were wings known as *paraskenia* built probably between 420 and 400 B.C. at which time the orchestra was reduced in size and the retaining walls (*analemmata*) of the auditorium were moved northward to provide sufficient space. This was done at the time of the erection of the new temple in which was placed the ivory and gold statue of Dionysos which was created by Alkamenes, famous pupil of the celebrated Phidias.

This permitted a playing space framed on three sides by the walls of the scene building; the three doors were in the back wall and there were steps in front of this terrace-like playing space which led down into the orchestra where the chorus remained. It is now believed that there were also doors in the side walls as well. On the roof of this building there was occasionally an *episkenion* which was a little like a penthouse on a modern apartment house. The dressing rooms of the actors and chorus had been placed in the sides of the same building (the *paraskenia*) and interior staircases led to the *episkenion*.

A good deal of our knowledge of the structure of theatre buildings comes from internal evidence in the plays themselves. Aeschylus' *Eumenides* calls for two different temples, that of Apollo in Delphi and that of Pallas Athena in Athens; Euripides' *Iphigenia Among the Taurians* needs several buildings. Therefore the *paraskenia* becomes necessary for proper representations of the drama. The extent of the stage, perhaps sixty-five feet deep and equally wide, made natural the movement from one part to another to suggest travel to a different

place. In this they were like the simultaneous stages in use in France
and other countries during the Middle Ages.

The earliest permanent scene building in Athens was similar in shape
to the beautiful theatre at Epidauros. Like this theatre, which ancients
and moderns agree to be most harmonious of all, the auditorium was
semi-circular and designed to be easily filled and emptied at performance time. In the very front row were benches for the city officials
and the priests. These were later replaced by individual thrones, some
of which were handsomely decorated. The most important one stands
today, that for the Priest of Dionysos. It was in the period of Lykurgos
that the auditorium itself was improved and a covered foyer was
provided for the audience at intermission time and in case of storm.
It is important to remember that, though the theatre building was
gradually improved and enlarged in the Classical Period, there was no
raised stage. That came later in the Hellenistic Period.

There was scenery in the Greek theatre despite popular belief that
the scene buildings provided the only background. Sometimes it consisted of a scene painted on the building itself and often the scene was
painted on canvas backdrops or flats and placed against the building
to represent certain locales. Vitruvius, writing in the last century
before the Christian era and Pollux, two hundred years later, are our
principal authorities for this information. They both record the use of
periaktoi (triangular revolving prisms) on which were painted scenes;
architectural buildings for tragedy and comedy and a pastoral scene
for satyr-plays. One was placed on either side of the stage. The convention of turning the right one alone to indicate a different locality
in the same city, and both for a complete change of scene seems to
have become general. They may have existed in the Classical Period
but it was not until the Hellenistic that we found indisputable evidence. This principle of scene changing is reflected in the Renaissance
stage and may be found as late as the eighteenth century Drottningholm Court Theatre near Stockholm. Another mechanical device was
the *scaena ductilis* in which the flats or backdrops were arranged in
layers, so that when the front screens were removed, the next scene
emerged. This method in all probability was introduced during the
great period of literary composition because of usefulness in connection with the *eccyclema*. This was a movable platform to illustrate
the interiors required in many of the plays of Euripides, which like a
wagon-stage, was wheeled out from the center door and the *scaena
ductilis* employed to provide background. The flying machine for the
ascent into heaven, located in the *episkenion* and the *deus ex machina*
(operated by a winch) by which the gods were made to appear to

settle the fate of the protagonist and so to end the play, were two important mechanical aids to production.

The costumes of the tragic actor resembled those in use in daily life but their color and style were more handsome. The variegated tunic was occasionally ornamented with stripes or with flower designs or animal figures and was worn with a high girdle which made it assume graceful lines. This undergarment reached to the feet. The overgarments were the *himation*, a long mantle around the right shoulder covering most of the body, and the *chlamys*, a short cloak worn over the left shoulder. Mourning was signified by black, grey, yellow or dirty white. Hats were not worn except when a journey was being made which was reflected in drama. The actor's height was increased by the *kothurnos*, a stout boot with a thick sole. Masks were worn by the actor to make his countenance visible to the countless thousands and to give additional resonance to his voice and so add to its carrying power. Expressions could not change so that the actor had to rely on a wide range of voice and gesture. If the action of the play required that the effects of an accident or injury be shown, a new mask had to be used. The features were not characterized and boldness was their keynote. Pollux enumerated twenty-eight kinds of masks for ordinary tragedy. The *onkos* was a prolongation on the crown of the mask to add height and physical importance to the actor. Comic masks for fictitious personages were grotesque in character having wide open mouths and distorted features in Old Comedy. Those of real personages such as Euripides and Sophocles in the plays of Aristophanes had natural features. In New Comedy though the costumes remained true to nature, the masks were always exaggerated. This was due to the size of the theatres which made it necessary to enlarge the features in order to carry any impression to the audiences. A dark sun burnt complexion stood for vigorous health and was worn by soldiers, country boys and athletes. Whiteness of complexion denoted effeminacy and extreme pallor was the consequence of love or illness. Red cheeks and hair were given to rascals. Curly, thick hair denoted vigor while close-cropped hair was a sign of niggardliness.

In Old Comedy the actors regularly wore the grossly exaggerated phallus. They were also heavily padded, wearing flesh-colored tights resembling nakedness which completely covered the body. Whereas in New Comedy the phallus was no longer worn and the costume resembled that in ordinary life.

The actors who appeared in these plays were three in number. The first was called the *protagonist*, the second the *deuteragonist* and the third, who played the minor characters, was known as the *tritagonist*. They all held a very honorable position in their national life. It was not until the Roman era that their profession became so degraded in the eyes of the public that it took eighteen hundred years to rehabilitate the social standing of actors. When English society lionized Sir Henry Irving and Sir George Alexander, they were unconsciously restoring the actor to an approximation of his status in Greek life.

In the beginning it was the dramatist who shone as he played the leading part but when Aeschylus added the second actor, the poets ceased to perform in the principal part and the profession of the actor began to assume an important place in the theatre. This had taken place by the middle of the fifth century. Though paid by the state, they were first chosen by individuals but soon it was evident that their importance justified their selection by the state itself. Sophocles is believed to be the first playwright to have considered the talents and capacities of his actors when writing his dramas. Undoubtedly Euripides counted on the fine voices of actors to carry certain sections of his plays. In the end this was harmful to drama and by the time of Aristotle, the success of a play depended on the abilities of the actor rather than on the genius of the dramatist. This made the selection of actors a matter of supreme importance as they were assigned to an individual playwright by lot. As this soon demonstrated its unfairness, actors rotated in turn in parts written by the poets. Acting contests to determine the greatest tragic actor were established at the City *Dionysia* about 446 B.C. and at the *Lenaea* in 420 B.C. and for the prowess of the comic actor at least by 442 B.C. Among the famous actors of antiquity were Aristodemus, who twice served as an Athenian ambassador; Neoptolemos, who was frequently at the court of Philip of Macedon; Athenodoros, who was a friend of Alexander the Great and Thettalos who was a particular friend of Alexander and several times his emissary. Cleander was Aeschylus' favorite actor and Tlepolemos was constantly used by Sophocles. Phrynichos, said to be the first to portray feminine characters, Kallippides and Lysikrates were other famous actors. A list of the most successful would fill many pages, so high was the standard of acting in the Greek theatre.

There is perhaps no better way to sum up the importance of Greece to the theatre world than to discuss the contribution of Aristotle to dramatic criticism. Despite modern research which doubts his thoroughness in matters pertaining to the history and development of drama, the basic principles of the art still stand as outlined. In warning it should be stated that one should not be too *literal* in reading and interpreting his dramatic dicta.

ARISTOTLE (384-322 B.C.) was born in Stagirus and at eighteen went to Athens where for twenty years he became the pupil and favorite disciple of Plato at the Academy. After the death of his master, he spent three years with Hermias at Atarneos. In circa 343 B.C. he went to the court of Macedon to tutor the young Alexander and remained for eight years. On his return to Athens he founded the Peripatetic School and taught in the Lyceum. At the time of Alexander's death he was forced to flee the country and died in Chalcis in Euboea. He wrote a great many scientific and philosophical treatises but it is his *Poetics* which concerns us. In this he defended the proposition that poetry is superior to history because it is scientific and universal and exhibits the qualities of whole classes of mankind, while history merely records events and actions. He contends that the purpose of tragedy is to excite fear and pity and so the protagonist must be a person both of virtue and of evil like most of us in order that the spectators may be moved by the tragedy of his death and apply it to themselves. This dictum is frequently violated and is the one that is most attacked. Aristotle's criticisms of the great dramatists, while they are now considered unfair to Euripides, do give us a clear, if biased picture of dramaturgy as practiced in the Classic Period and as evaluated by a philosophic mind. Had he read and heeded Herodotus, it is probable that he would have made fewer errors in fact about the origin and development of drama and stage in Greece. Then his pronouncements would have been of more value to the modern student.

Many of the great impulses of the theatre, whether in drama or in problems of stagecraft, stem from the Greek. Shelley so idealized it that he said all elements of modern drama derived from it, an undoubted exaggeration. Nonetheless the theatre as we know it received wholesome stimulus from Greek thought which created the Renaissance, and so through that, the development of the modern drama.

III

ROMAN GRANDEUR

IN THE deep south of Italy as well as in the mountainous, verdant and wine-growing isle of Sicily, the theatre of Greece found a foothold. The settlers crossing the seas carried with them their drama and plays continued to be performed even while wars went on. Doubtless it was during the ill-fated Athenian expedition against Sicily that certain captured Greek soldiers won their freedom because of their ability to recite passages from the plays of Euripides. Some of the finest theatres of the Hellenistic period are to be found in Sicily, notably at Taormina and at Syracuse. The style of tragic writing and playing remained the same as in Greece but in comedy it departed sharply from the Grecian mold. There was a throwback to the ancient Doric mimes with which comedy was allied.

These comic pieces had no chorus and closely resembled the mimes of Epicharmus who was writing at Syracuse in the fifth century B.C., and of the later Heroda. At first they parodied mythology, later dropping this subject to burlesque tragedy itself. It is well to keep in mind the ability of the pagan writer to ridicule, or see ridiculed on the stage his most sacred religious mysteries without being in any way shaken in his beliefs. This led to the writing of *hilario tragodia* in which Rinthon of Tartenum, living about 300 B.C. excelled. His was no new form. He simply turned into literary form the mimes of the famous actors, Kleon and Nymphodoros.

The more general name for both plays and actors was *phlyakes*, coming from the word meaning gossips. Heracles as well as Odysseus was a favorite hero and he was permitted even to insult and ridicule Zeus. Rinthon's piece about Zeus and Alkmene, *Amphitruo*, doubtless had its influence on Plautus' *Amphitruo*. There is little literary evidence of the *phlyakes'* existence and it is primarily in the vase paintings that we find all that we know. They were undoubtedly phallephoric; most of the actors were grotesquely padded and usually wore a short chiton. Wide-mouthed, grotesque masks were used throughout and the scenes had to do with eating, drinking, theft of wine or food, browbeating of elderly husbands by shrewish wives, intrigues and other phases of ordinary lusty life. These subjects are those that belonged to the ancient Dorian mimes which arose in or near Megara and extended south into Egypt and west into Italy. The continuity of the Greek in the Roman theatre is one of the most distinguishable characteristics in the latter.

These *phlyakes* developed a characteristic stage of a rough platform of boards with unornamented posts and curtains or panels below the level of the stage. There were from four to seven movable steps which were used either at the front or on the sides of the stage. There seems to have been a simple background for actors, later called the *frons scaenae* by the Romans, which probably contained doors and was roofed over; altars and thrones were frequently used.

Shortly after the rise of the *phlyakes*, there developed the apparently indigenous *fabula Atellana* in the Oscan Atella, the present day Aversa. We can not be sure how much influence the Greek farces had on the native Oscans as they were perhaps played not in Greek but in the language of the Roman peninsula. Diomedes contended that Atellan farce was akin in comic style and language to the Attic satyric drama. Certainly they were short because they are often referred to as *exodium*, after pieces, which followed the tragedies in Roman festivals. They were in all probability played before the Oscans for a long time before their Latinization in Rome itself.

The basic principles of the farces remained the same after transplanting and they had a hardy life in the capital because, although they were said to be dying fifty years before Christ, they still survived five hundred years after His death. When the *fabula Atellana* became a literary form, it produced two writers of importance. The first was L. POMPONIUS BONONIENSIS who flourished in the first century B.C. and wrote over seventy plays of which the titles and a few fragments remain. These are enough to indicate that while some satirized foreigners and others burlesqued mythology, most of them were concerned with the ordinary events of daily life. Not so much is known of NOVIUS whose forty-four plays exist only in title, but he is credited with Pomponius with introducing to Rome the Atellan style of writing. This is not to be taken that the *fabula Atellana* was previously unknown but merely that Roman writers had not used the form.

The farces were licentious in speech and in the beginning ridiculed the bucolic customs of neighboring Campania which appeared foreign, therefore barbaric and foolish to Oscan eyes. Like the *phlyakes* they developed masks of abnormal ugliness of which there were five main types: *Bucco*, the fool; *Dossenus*, sometimes called *Mandacus*, usually hunchbacked, beaknosed with a prominent wart, probably witty, certainly sharp-tongued; *Maccus,* a stupid, gluttonous, awkward fool; *Pappus,* the good-humored, gullible old man; and *Cicirrus;* though not usually mentioned in antiquity, modern scholarship has deduced the existence of this animal or bird-like mime. The costumes were like those of the *phlyakes* and the actors undoubtedly wore the large leather phalli characteristic of ancient farce. These pieces became popular in Rome with amateur and professional alike as the masks and costumes satisfactorily concealed their identity. The gilded youth, either in search of a thrill or else yielding to a latent dramatic impulse, or both, performed these farces in private and in public.

Despite their survival into the sixth century A.D., they were being supplanted by the pure mime by the middle of the second century. The popular theatre had so much dynamic force that it survived the strictures of the Church and the suppressions of the Dark Ages to re-emerge in the *commedia dell'arte* and even in the religious plays of the Church itself.

Even before the introduction of farces from Atella, the Romans formed a drama of their own which was based in part on the famous *Fescennine Verses* commonly chanted at marriage ceremonies. These poems celebrating the marital rites had no theatrical importance but did to some extent influence play construction. This came about through the mingling of these verses with the *histriones* to form the *satura,* or the *fabulae saturae,* which are not to be confused with the satyric drama of the Greeks. As their name suggests, these were miniature scenes of daily life and were used as the concluding pieces at tragic contests, the before mentioned *exodium.* The *satura* was later supplanted by the *fabula Atellana.*

The occasion of the first performances of the *saturae* was in 364 B.C. at the *Ludi* (Games) which were held in Rome, when a troupe of Etruscans were brought to participate in the *Ludi Etrusci.* These actors, who performed in a tongue unknown to their audience, excited amusement by their pantomimic action and phallephoric comedy which was understandable to them. By 240 B.C. comedies and tragedies were being regularly acted at the *Ludi Romani,* as they were then called, in the month of September. These games became so popular that more and more occasions were found for their celebration.

By 220 B.C. the *Ludi Plebeii,* or popular games, were introduced and from 212 B.C., the *Ludi Apollinares* were performed to honor the god Apollo. In 214 B.C. theatrical performances lasting about four days were introduced at the *Ludi Romani* and from 194 B.C. the *Ludi Megalenses* were established as the Megalensian games to honor the *Magna Mater* (Great Mother). In addition there were the *Ludi Pub-*

lici, public religious celebrations and the *Ludi Votivi*, plays in honor of triumphs or dedications of temples supported by private munificence and, of course, the *Ludi Funebres* where scenic displays took place in connection with funerals of distinguished citizens, financed by their families or other private persons. By about 200 B.C. Rome devoted forty-eight days each year to official dramatic and scenic productions. Many new celebrations were added 50 B.C. including the *Ludi Victoriae Caesaris* to celebrate the victories of Julius Caesar, or as they were also known, the *Ludi Veneris Genetricis*. These were in honor of the dedication of the temple of Venus Genetrix in 46 B.C., which Caesar erected to honor his own military exploits in the name of Venus, the Fruitful Mother. So popular were all forms of theatrical art despite the effort on the part of the doughty and virtuous Roman senators to censor the theatre, that the number of these days eventually grew to one hundred and seventy-five during the fourth century A.D. According to the calendar of Furius Dionysius Philocalus, 354 A.D., these holidays were occupying almost six months of the year. One hundred and one were given over to plays and theatrical entertainment, sixty-four to chariot races and ten to gladiatorial combats.

The history of the Roman theatre building is curious and derives from many sources. One source, of course, was from the performance of the *phlyakes*, *fabula Atellana* and other farces on a raised wooden stage. This octangular acting space (*pulpitum*) with a scene-building (*scaena*) behind it, was high enough so that the standing audience could follow the action. This meant that theatres could be situated anywhere, not merely on hillsides as in Greece or in the Hellenistic theatres of Syria, Egypt and southern Italy from which the Roman playhouses were also descended. It was a long time before the Romans felt the need of an auditorium and for several centuries the theatres were always constructed of wood. The first stage known to be erected in the city of Rome was in 364 B.C. for the *histriones* (this Etruscan term for mimes and dancers was adopted by the Romans for all actors). It was in 179 B.C., nearly two hundred years later that a true theatre was built near the Temple of Apollo. This wooden structure was soon torn down and similar structures met the same fate. A stone building was begun but it so roused the ire of many honorable citizens that in 154 B.C., a year after its inception, P. Scipio Nasica induced the Senate to order its destruction on the somewhat dubious ground that it would be injurious to public morals. The Senate also decreed that no one should provide seats for an audience in the *cavea* (hollow, the place where the audience stood) nor should anyone sit down himself at any dramatic performance within the city proper or within a mile of the gates. Knowing the perfectly natural desire of people to be comfortable, this august legislative body reasoned that if they could make theatre-going uncomfortable, they would reduce it to a minimum. There are those today who say that there is a conspiracy between theatrical producers, box-office men, the real estate interests and labor unions to make modern playgoing as uncomfortable and expensive as is possible without breaking down the system completely. Their motive does not have the same hiigh morality as that of the Roman Senate.

Of these enormous wooden structures that were so wastefully destroyed, though frugality was also called a Roman virtue, the most famous was the one erected in the aedileship of M. Aemilius Scaurus in 58 B.C. According to the historian Pliny, the building was ornamented with three hundred and sixty columns, three thousand statues (possibly exaggerated); the scene house was three stories high; and the auditorium had a capacity of eighty thousand, which we doubt.

Three years later, due to the resourcefulness of Pompey, Rome achieved a permanent stone structure which, according to Plutarch, was copied from the Hellenistic theatre at Mytilene on the island of Lesbos. The great Roman placed a shrine to Venus Victrix at the highest point in the rear of the auditorium so that the seats would serve as steps to reach the temple and absolve them from the dangerous and illegal status of being theatre seats. Vitruvius said that the auditorium was capable of seating forty thousand auditors. This theatre was remodelled and rebuilt in 32 B.C. by Augustus Caesar and later by Tiberius, Caligula and others so that it eventually became typically Roman and seated approximately ten thousand.

Pliny says that the rivalry between Pompey and Caesar was so great that when the latter heard of this theatre, he feared its probable effect on his own popularity and so also desired to construct a playhouse. Being absent on a military campaign, he entrusted the task to his friend and confidant Curio who caused two wooden theatres to be built. On the occasion of their dedication, after the morning performances in each, one theatre was revolved on pivots so that it faced the other to form an amphitheatre for gladiatorial spectacles and racing in the afternoon. This was the first Roman amphitheatre, a characteristic architectural development of their civilization and one to have a profound effect on the construction of modern athletic stadia all over the world.

In addition there was built by L. Cornelius Balbus, friend of Pompey and sometime dramatist, another permanent theatre which was opened in 13 B.C. A second and more famous playhouse was planned by Julius Caesar, built by Augustus and dedicated in the same year, though Pliny dates it as 11 B.C. It was built as a memorial to Marcellus, nephew and adopted son of Augustus, on the south-west slope of the Capitoline Hill and remains today as one of the great monuments of modern Rome, this Theatre of Marcellus near the Tiber.

These were the only three permanent theatre buildings of the city unless we include the small *Odeum* erected by the Emperor Domitian (51-96 A.D.), or the gigantic Colosseum or the enormous Circus Maximus but the latter two were not true theatre buildings. The Colosseum, built by Vespasian and Titus was six hundred and twelve feet long and five hundred and fifteen feet at the widest point of the ellipse and seated eighty-seven thousand souls with standing room for fifteen thousand more. Here gladiatorial contests and, when the Arena was filled with water, naval battles were held until the sixth century.

The oldest of the places of amusement in Rome was the Circus Maximus which was built under the reign of Tarquin I (c.616-c.578 B.C.) at which time it had wooden seats. It was twice restored and in the reign of Julius Caesar the lower seats were replaced with stone, the upper tiers still being of wood; these latter burned in the reign of the Emperor Nero and again under Domitian who rebuilt them of stone and marble. The building was restored and enlarged by Constantine the Great at which time it was reputed to have seated a quarter of a million people. Although this was the most famous, there were other circuses such as the Circus Flaminius, Hadrian's Circus and the one built by Maxentius (311 A.D.) in honor of his deified son, Romulus, which is the best preserved circus today.

In the Colosseum and other circuses the contests were athletic and finally gory as the taste for that kind of entertainment increased. It was there that the games became gladiatorial combats, first by pairs and finally by small armies waging bloody warfare. Human beings were pitted against wild beasts and the stubborn Christian minority was notoriously persecuted. Arenas were flooded and naval battles were enacted in deadly earnest. These contests won fame under Pompey and Julius Caesar, and under the emperors became vilely debased. Nero, Caligula and Heliogabalus, to name but a few, won ill fame even in that time for their perversions, cruelty and bestiality. The sadistic details are sickening even to a so-called hard-boiled modern of today.

A typical Roman theatre of the period of highest development had a highly ornamented scene house (Greek *episkenion*) known as the *frons scaena*. In front of this was the stage proper (*pulpitum*), long and low, perhaps five feet above the level of the orchestra which had been made semi-circular in contrast to the circular orchestra of the Greeks. Steps led down from the richly decorated stage and the front

wall, *hyposcenium*, which contained doors and was handsomely ornamented. In contrast to the high stages of the Hellenistic theatres of
the late Greek period the acting platform was lowered to five feet
so as to provide better sight lines for the audience. This was due to
the fact that the orchestra was frequently used for seating the Roman
Senate and other distinguished guests. The *cavea* or auditorium had
become semi-circular to permit a better view of the stage. Some of
the stages were roofed—notably the Roman theatre at Orange in
France (the roof does not survive) and Aspendos in Asia Minor. A
gaily-painted canvas was suspended over the theatre to shield the spectators from the hot afternoon sun and a curtain was sometimes provided to hide scene changes. This curtain (*auleum*) came up from
below in contrast to the modern asbestos curtain (which comes down
from above) but we do not know its exact use. The walls of the theatre
were as high as the scene house, sometimes three or four stories. The
exteriors of these were treated in handsome architectural detail and the
joining of these walls to the *frons scaenae* made the stage and auditorium a single unit. This meant that the separate entrances, *paradoi*,
of the Greek theatre had been swallowed up and had become the
vomitoria, covered passages, exits and entrances of the Roman theatre.
The theatre building in early Roman days had a religious connection
which passed, leaving it entirely secular. Perhaps because of this, even
if handsomer and richer, it nevertheless lacked the austere grandeur
of the Greek theatre.

In the beginning the actor was engaged by the poet somewhat in
the same way as he was in Greece. Subsequently his status changed.
A large professional class sprang up. This was made up of troupes
largely recruited from the slaves who had been brought from Southern
Italy and Greece itself, many of whom had been actors before their
capture. These were contracted for the exhibitions under the direction of the aediles who were responsible for dramatic performances.

Some actors achieved real fame, notably the celebrated Q. Roscius
Gallus (died 62 B.C.), better known as Roscius, whose very name has
become a symbol of great acting so that to be termed a "Second
Roscius" or a "Young Roscius" is considered high praise indeed.
Roscius attained such wealth and distinction that he was freed and
knighted by Sulla. He was a man of many talents and of considerable
intellectual attainments as was his younger contemporary, Clodius
Aesopus, a native of Greece who died in 54 B.C.

The ordinary variety of actor received but poor financial return
for his work and all too often a flogging as well. A man was unfor-
gettably demeaned if he were forced to become an actor. Julius
Caesar, by promise of gifts and high honors, persuaded the Roman

knight and writer of mimes, Decimus Laberius, to enter the acting contest against Publilius Syrus, the prologue of which still exists. Laberius made so many veiled attacks on Caesar that victory was awarded to his rival. Though his knighthood was restored, the sixty year old man was disgraced in the eyes of his fellow citizens and he died a few years later.

The costume worn by the actor was similar to the Greek garb, the tragic *syrmata* and the short costumes for comedy which suggest both the *phlyakes* and the literary comedy. Both the *crepida* (the Greek *kothurnos*), high-heeled boot, for the tragedian and *saccus*, a soft slipper (the Greek *embas*), for the comedian were taken over to Italy. Roscius introduced the mask. Up to his time it was not in use because of the intimate arrangement of the dramatic performances. This innovation was disapproved but by persistence he finally proved the value of using this *persona* (from the Latin *personare*, to sound through). It was a mask which covered the whole head and added volume and projection to the voice, a useful contrivance in the huge later theatre. It was decorated with hair and painted to resemble the complexion of the character. This superseded the *galeri* (wigs) which were worn up to the introduction of the mask. White hair portrayed old age; black, youth and vigor; red denoted slaves and rogues. These masks were realistic, though somewhat exaggerated in tragedy and completely grotesque in the *mimes*.

The first Roman dramatist of real importance was LIVIUS ANDRONICUS, who was a child in 272 B.C. when his native Tarentum was taken by the Romans. He had been brought up in a city which so loved the theatre that the citizens were attending a dramatic performance instead of manning their defenses when the Roman fleet sailed into the harbor. From 240 to 207 B.C. he translated into Latin the Greek tragic writers, Sophocles and Euripides, as well as some of the comedies of Attica. He is the first known translator of the ancient world and has to his credit such tragedies as *Achilles*, *Ajax*, *The Trojan Horse*, *Aegisthus* and such comedies as *Gladiolus*, *Lusius* and *Virgus*. He is credited also with the first production both of comedy and tragedy at the *Ludi Romani* in 240 B.C.

NAEVIUS (flourished 235-204 B.C.) though born in Campania, was a Roman citizen. He borrowed liberally from Euripides and his nine tragedies, including the *Danae*, the *Trojan Horse* (a favorite title in the Greek and Roman theatre), *Hector*, *Hesione* and *Iphigenia* (another favorite), were known as *fabulae palliatae*. This name came from the Greek word, *pallium*, meaning mantle. He created the *fabulae praetextatae*, a characteristic Roman drama which took its name from the purple striped patrician toga. Two of these dramas were *Romulus* and *Clastidium*, which despite their supposed Roman subjects, were really blendings of two Greek plays of the New Comedy period. His political references won the vengeance of the Metelli, who choked off at the source these beginnings of realistic drama.

ENNIUS (239-169 B.C.) came from the countryside east of Tarentum. He wrote twenty tragedies mostly borrowed from the *Iliad* or from Euripides, as well as two plays on Italian subjects, *The Sabine Women* and *Ambracia*.

TITUS MACCIUS PLAUTUS (c.254-184 B.C.) was considered by the Romans to be their greatest comic dramatist; indeed his name with those of Terence and Seneca constitute the sole surviving names of any real importance. He was born in Sarsina in Umbria and is believed to have begun his association with the theatre as a stage carpenter or scene-shifter (now known as stagehand or grip). His writing seems to have been begun in 207 B.C. at the time of the imprisonment of Naevius but most of the twenty extant plays belong to the last ten years of his life and were only published after his death. The manuscripts were left to various actors who composed the prologues and who provided many of the known or supposed interpolations. Many plays were attributed to him, one hundred and thirty in all. However Varro, the most learned Roman critic and writer, credits Plautus with twenty-one dramas. He adds that there were possibly nineteen additional titles but he was doubtful as to their authenticity. Naevius' writings appealed to the tastes and spirit of the aristocracy while Plautus' were popular among the masses whom he understood and who understood him. He was most popular in his own time and in the generation that followed but he continued to be acted during the time of Cicero who greatly admired his comedies. His work was in the discard during the first century of the Roman Empire but the archaic revival of the second century restored his popularity and caused the preservation of his works. These were to reappear during the Renaissance and were to influence both Shakespeare and Molière, who in turn were to influence the whole field of modern drama.

Plautus was a man of great vitality with the spirit of the sea and adventure in his veins so that his writing partook of the lusty qualities of both. The New Comedy of Greece was his principal source of inspiration. He borrowed plots, scenes, characters and undoubtedly some of his dialogue which he adapted freely to Roman uses. Almost all of his play titles were in Latin, while those of Terence, a more conscious imitator, were in Greek. All of his characters were Attic and supposedly lived in Greek towns but in reality he made them, as well as their customs, Roman. He depicts graphically the life of his own time and his own country. He avoided politics because of the rigorousness of Roman censorship but reflections of recent events in his country's history do appear, particularly the growing estrangement between the wealthy ruling class and the poor working class, a potential danger in any country. If the wealthy lose understanding and sympathy for the problems of the poor, disaster is not far distant for all. That however was not a prime consideration for Plautus; he was no propagandist but simply reflected the life of the day as it appeared to him.

His writings are filled with metaphors taken from Roman business and military life and puns and plays on words which do not translate successfully. He makes use of lyric monologue along with regular dialogue. This is quite different from the Greek original, coming as it does from the old *saturae*, the earliest dramatic efforts of the Roman mind as opposed to the Attic sources. The plot of his *Amphitruo* was imitated by Molière and Dryden and by so many others that when Jean Giraudoux used the story in our time he entitled his play *Amphitryon 38*.

It was with comedy that this Roman writer was concerned; not until modern times was the serious purpose of his plays thought of. He is said to have written his own epitaph, "After Plautus died, comedy mourns, the stage is deserted; then laughter, mirth and jest all wept in company." His plays among others include *The Trinummus*, *The Braggart Soldier* (*Miles Gloriosus*, which was to give its name to a character in Renaissance comedy), *The Captives*, *The Merchant*, *Truculentus*, and *The Stratagem Defeated*.

Publius Terentius Afer, better known to us as TERENCE, (c.185-159 B.C.) born in Carthage, was the slave of a Roman Senator, Terentius Lucanus, who recognized his remarkable intelligence and wit and so gave him an excellent education and, what was even more important, his freedom, early in life. This came after a childhood in the Phoenician colonies of North Africa followed by a period of slavery in Rome where he was bathed in Greek culture. He lived on intimate terms with Scipio Africanus Minor, the poet Laelius, and Luclius, the satirist, all of whom found him an attractive and stimulating companion.

His plays had mixed success. His first piece, *Andria* (*The Andrian*), was offered to the aediles, superintendents of the theatres and dramatic productions. He was commanded to recite to Caecilius, the official critic, who found it excellent. *Eunuchus* (*The Eunuch*) met with so much *éclat* that it was acted twice in a single day and the author received 8,000 sesterces for it, the greatest price paid for a comedy up to that time. It is commonly believed that Laelius and Scipio assisted Terence in the writing of his plays. Certainly he did little to refute this assertion; in fact he may have considered himself honored by the imputation.

Where Plautus chose his characters and scenes from the whole comic field of Greece, Terence borrowed only from Menander, whose work he particularly admired and whom he considered the outstanding writer of New Comedy. Like Plautus, he combined several plays to form the complicated plot esteemed by the Romans, but he was more polished and skilful than his predecessor. To the modern mind his plots seem overladen with unnecessary intricacy and recent revivals have caused severe criticism on this score. He kept everything within the realm of possibility—or, rather, in that of probability. He was successful in handling psychological development. This is true in *The Eunuch* and particularly in his handling of the two old men in *Adelphi* (*The Brothers*). His six plays, all of which survive, also include *Heauton, Tunorumenos* (*The Self-Tormentor*), *Hecyra* (*The Mother-in-law*) and *Phormio*.

Contrary to one's expectation this refinement of handling, despite its praise from the small group of intellectuals, met only opposition and critical abuse from the public in general. Nevertheless, he has received high rank in ancient writing from critics a thousand and two thousand years later. His imitation of Greek comedy is remarkably faithful and was indubitably a labor of love. He bitterly resented the popular criticism of his day and defended his point of view in his prologues. Finally, when he was almost twenty-five, either to remove the charge of plagiarism or to study Greek customs at first hand, he left Rome never to return. It is presumed that he died at sea a year later.

Writing as he did contrary to the methods of Plautus, casting scorn upon the multitude and only concerning himself with the criticism of the few, he failed to live to see the plays of Plautus disappear (later to reappear) from favor and the point of view of the aristocrats prevail.

Other writers of this period include PACUVIUS (c.220-c.130 B.C.), who wrote about twelve tragedies derived from or modelled after Euripides and at least one *fabula praetextata*. STATIUS CAECILIUS, mentioned in connection with Terence, wrote some forty comedies deriving from Greek New Comedy, particularly Menander, which would naturally have attracted Terence; and ACCIUS (170-c.86 B.C.), an important early Roman tragic writer whose first play was *Atreus*, probably written under the influence of Aeschylus, though Euripides and Sophocles were also models whom he admired. In addition there were QUINTUS ENNIUS (239-169 B.C.) born in Rudiae in Calabria, who modelled his tragedies on Euripides; STRABO, the orator; QUINTUS

TULLIUS CICERO, brother of the great Cicero; LUCIUS CORNELIUS BAL-
BUS; and finally the great JULIUS CAESAR, none of whose plays survive.

LUCIUS ANNAEUS SENECA (c.4 B.C.-65 A.D.) was the second son of
the statesman and philosopher, Seneca the Elder. He was born in Spain
in Cordoba and studied in Rome under the stoic teacher, Attalus,
whom he greatly admired and whose philosophy of religion and life
he emulated. He won a fine reputation in law and was progressing
favorably when the Emperor Caligula, who disliked him, threatened
his life. Identified with Julia, daughter of Germanicus, his career received a further set-back when she fell from favor. At the instigation
of the notorious Messalina, the succeeding Emperor Claudius I banished him to Corsica in 41 A.D. There he spent eight long years in
study, writing, waiting and flattering Claudius in the hope that his exile
would be ended. This came about under the influence of Nero's mother, Agrippina, who had him recalled for an appointment as *praetor*
and to act as tutor to her son, then a boy of eleven. He was her confi-
dential adviser and on the succession of her son in 54 he shared the
administration of affairs with Burrus, the praetorian prefect and in 57
became consul. Both the large fortune which he had amassed and his
opposition to Nero's efforts to murder his mother naturally enough
won the Emperor's dislike. The death of Burrus in 62 quickened the
downfall of Seneca. He pleaded ill health and offered up his wealth but
escape was impossible and he continued in his official position, an unhappy figure-head. Finally, on the pretext of his involvement in Piso's
conspiracy, he was given the choice of suicide or a shameful death.
Seneca chose an honorable suicide and in part atoned for a weak and
ignoble life.

Seneca's recognized plays, eight of which survive, were not primarily intended to be acted but were meant to be read, or to have
individual scenes recited in theatres, at banquets or at parties in the
houses and palaces of Rome. It was his plan to utilize the plots of
Greek tragedies and to translate them into terms understandable to
Romans. His drama was sentimental but he outlined a dramatic form
which is popular to this day. His work is not of the first rank but his
influence on Classical French tragedy in Corneille and Racine, as well
as on the eighteenth century English dramatists such as Rowe, Cibber
and Murphy makes him an important figure. His plays include *The
Daughters of Troy* (*Troades*), *Hercules, Agamemnon, Thyestes,
Hercules Oetaeus, Phoenissae* or *Thebais, Medea, Oedipus* and possibly *Octavia* though modern scholarship doubts that this last play
was Seneca's.

For all practical purposes it can be said that the literary drama ends with Seneca. People undoubtedly continued to write for their own amusement and for private and public performances but only scenes from plays were given, no dramas in toto. It was in the mime, the circus and gladiatorial combat that Roman drama continued to exist.

The Romans always liked a show, and the bare austerities of the Greeks with three actors at most were soon discarded by them. It is recorded that Pompey was hailed with delight by the audience because in the *Clytemnestra* Agamemnon's return was preceded by a procession of six hundred pack-mules. It was this love of display, despite the persistence of protean acting in the mimes themselves, that enhanced the popularity of pantomimes. Mimes were performed with gaiety, broad humors and occasional handsome extravagance.

The characters remained the same as those described before but more and more mimes were being written and the mimograph became more popular than ever. There were many dramatists whose names alone are known. Attalus, Accius, Aesopus, Cneus, Matius, Nucula to whom Cicero ascribed the invention of the mimes, and Aemilius Severianus are among those mimic writers whose works have perished as surely as the mimic actors who played them. The most famous of those of whom some record survives are Catullus, Decimus, Laberius, Lentulus, Philistion and Publilius Syrus.

Three mimes of Q. Lutatius Catullus are known to us because of contemporary mention. The author lived at the time of the emperors Tiberius, Claudius and Nero; according to Juvenal, his *Phasma* (*The Ghost*) was the gluttonous Damasippus who had wasted his patrimony and hired out his very voice to the mimes. The same authority describes the second mime as *Fugitivus Scurra* (*The Fugitive Jester*), sometimes termed by modern scholars *The Fugitive Slave*. The third concerned itself with the crucifixion of the slave, Laureolus, and Juvenal tells us that the actor, Lentulus, played the part with such cunning and viciousness that he deserved a true crucifixion at the end of the piece. On some occasions the part of Laureolus was played by a real criminal who actually died in agony on the cross. This was for the benefit of the spectators whose gladiatorial contests had taught them to enjoy bloody and cruel amusements.

DECIMUS LABERIUS (c.106-43 B.C.), whose disgrace was recorded when he was induced by Julius Caesar to act as a mime in actors' contests against Publilius Syrus, was a Roman knight whose farces were celebrated for their flashing wit. Marcus Fronto rates him with Plautus for his satiric style. No play survives, but forty-three titles remain to suggest their nature. Among them are the *Aulularia* (also the name of a play by Plautus), *Augus* (*The Soothsayer*), *Hetaera* (*The Cour-*

tesan), *Piscator* (*The Fisherman*), *Lacus Avernus* (*Lake Avernus*) and *Saturnalia*. He was fond of puns and rustic and unusual words which he imported if it suited his purpose.

The mimic writer, LENTULUS, is not to be confused with the mime of the same name listed as having played in a farce of Catullus (in fact some persisted in ascribing that mime to him). Tertullian refers to him and in his defense of religion he takes care to point out the licentiousness of the portrayal of the gods by the mimographs. It is evident that he had Lentulus, among others, in mind when he wrote this. Only one title remains to us *Catinenses* (*The Citizens of Catina*), a town on the east coast of Sicily.

PHILISTION, the Graeco-Roman, was first noticed in 6 B.C. by St. Jerome (Hieronymus) who referred to him as an Asiatic mime. He seems in all probability to have written in Greek but was undoubtedly famous in Rome. Martial in his *Epigram* spoke of the mimes of the merry Philistion and he continues to be mentioned by critics and literary historians as late as Izetzes in the twelfth century. His mimes were of sufficient importance to merit comparison with the comedies of Menander. The writer Suidas ascribes a *Philogelos* to him and a manuscript giving short mimic scenes and which may have descended from this has been preserved.

PUBLILIUS, surnamed Syrus because of his probable birth at Antioch in Syria, was brought to Rome as a slave and was a student of the same Laberius whom he defeated in 46 B.C. His grace and wit won him the admiration of two such dissimilar men as Cicero and Petronius. None of his plays survive but the titles of two, *Putatores* and *Murmurcones*, do exist. His principal work was *Publilii Syri mimi sententiae* (*Maxims of the Mime, Publilius Syrus*), the sharp sayings of which have also been attributed to Seneca, though the cutting style is not characteristic of the latter.

Despite the fact that the mime undoubtedly descended directly from the Doric mime, it was not until the time of the Roman Empire that it won its highest esteem. All authorities unite in referring to it as being a play of low life. This appealed both to the masses, and the classes who found it typified the humors and rigors of their own exalted existence. The so-called Oxyrhynchus Mime was discovered to be primarily an adventure play and as such was not unlike some Elizabethan dramas. This Egyptian papyrus makes it possible for us to read the simple story of a Greek girl who finds herself in a barbarous country. After pretending to dedicate herself to religion in order to avoid the attentions of a savage king who is in love with her, she escapes. Then as now, adultery was a favorite theme judging from the fulminations of the contemporary Christian Fathers against it. There were also the mimes which ridiculed Christianity, particularly the ceremony of baptism. Apparently the practice of immersion was extremely amusing to the Latin mind because this is burlesqued over and over again. Our evidence of this frequently comes from the *Acta Santorum* (*Acts of the Saints*). In this there are recorded occasions when the mime who was burlesquing a Christian character was illumined by a new faith, and actual belief in Christ. He threw off his acting and proclaimed loudly to the assembled audience that he had become a true believer and so attained martyrdom. The Christian writers bitterly attacked obscenity and contended that frequently the mimic adulteries were actually performed on the stage. However, much of that must be taken with a grain of salt as the righteous have been known to see more evil than actually exists. That such orgies took place in mimes performed privately at the Emperor's Court or in the houses of the wealthy is undoubtedly true, but that such public displays were customary is certainly out of line with what we know in general of the Roman theatre.

One of the provinces of the mime was satire. This won great popularity and frequent censorship for it. There was no subject the actors hesitated to ridicule; even the Emperor and the gods were not exempt. Of the two the latter were a great deal less dangerous. Both the considerable vices of Commodus and the virtues of Augustus won prompt suppression when mentioned but the mimes never failed to utilize such subjects regardless of the severity of possible punishment by the state. Short or long, these plays had gaiety and employed numerous actors, grotesque masks and bright costumes. Most important of all was the fact that they were the people's mouthpiece when an injustice had been done, an impropriety of state had become flagrant or when an official of the Empire had betrayed his trust.

The last important form of Roman drama was the *pantomimus* or *pantomime*. This was serious in intent and was a form of the interpretative dance. It is believed from pictorial evidence that a single dancer portrayed all of the characters as indicated by changes of mask and costume. There is an ivory relief in Berlin depicting a pantomimic actor with his harp, sword and masks. Undoubtedly a chorus gave background to the ballet and certainly additional principal dancers were introduced to heighten the dramatic conflict.

These pantomimes took place against a musical accompaniment of wind, brass and string instruments. Like the modern tap dancer, the dancer wore a *scabellum* (clapper) under his foot in order to keep the rhythm. It is reported by Livy, the historian, to have had its inception in Livius Andronicus who found his voice grew hoarse when he was called on to encore portions of his plays, and so hit on the device of having a boy sing the words while he acted them out with vigorous gesture and rhythmic movement.

During the reign of Augustus there came into prominence two of the greatest pantomimic dancers, Pylades of Cilicia and Bathyllus of Alexandria. They introduced a more sophisticated type of dance because their art was deeper and more versatile. Juvenal called Bathyllus tender and said that in the scandalous ballet of *Leda and the Swan* he was the only one who could instruct the sophisticated Thymele, celebrated actress of mimes. Other famous dancers were Hylas and two actors named Paris, the younger of whom was mentioned by Juvenal. These pantomimes were serious and largely tragic and derived their themes either from the Greek and Roman tragedies or from some mythological sources that were used by the tragic dramatists. Many of them were highly lascivious and the sensual, not to say pornographic, was emphasized. Perhaps it was because of this that the comic rather than the serious mime won and held the hearts of the people. Comedy is remembered pleasantly but no one waxes sentimental over pornography.

There are several general conclusions to be drawn concerning the whole Roman theatre. One is that the orderliness natural to the Romans made them establish set forms of the drama to be adhered to, though the whole might be censored by the stringent morality peculiar to the stoic mind. The stage and auditorium of the Roman theatres were joined in one structural whole and in a perfection of architectural unity. The austerity and bareness of the Greek ideal soon passed from the Latin mind and the embellishments, sentimentality and strict sense of order brought about a type of drama that has adhered to this day. We owe more to the Romans than a brief outline of their relatively unimportant literary drama would illustrate.

IV

MIMETIC MIRACULOUS MEDIEVALISM

IT IS with a feeling of dismay that we plunge into the dark and turgid waters which lie between the fall of Rome (476) and the capture of Constantinople (1453) which precipitated the Renaissance. Vile, cruel, obscene as the Roman stage had become, it was at least sufficiently documented so that we may write of it with the authority based on known experience. However with the submerging of the Latin culture by German barbarism, even though this may have improved moral standards, wedded to the righteous censor of a militant church, the creative arts were temporarily lost. Or at least they can be said to have disappeared from view. There are a few isolated instances in the next five hundred years to suggest that the theatre continued to have a *sub rosa* existence.

The orthodox view has been that the theatre mysteriously ended its profane glory in the indecencies of the late Empire, to be reborn in the church drama of the middle ages, half a milliennium later. It is the contention of such scholars as Reich, Nicoll, Duchartre that the theatre continued to function. It is with these dissidents that we ally ourselves.

Earlier we have spoken of the condemnation of the stage by the Roman Church which saw its worshippers attending mimetic spectacles and games rather than the holy office of the Mass. Saint John Chrysostom (c.347-407) censured the effeminate manners and dress of the youth, the old man with the shaven head who was always ready to be the butt of jokes, the courtesan who invited attention, the fornication and adultery. Tertullian and Cyprian (died 258) joined in this vituperative chorus and it found echo in the Church Councils. Those several at Carthage, and at Arras decreed in 452 that actors, *histriones*, might not be admitted to Communion while they plied the trade of acting. However in his celebrated *Confessions*, St. Augustine (345-430) admits that dramatic spectacles enraptured him in his youth.

Proof that mimes continued exists in a fifth-sixth century comment on Gregory of Nazianzus that the phallus was still indicated by a leather appendage; this would indicate that the comic theatrical art persisted. Theodosius I encouraged the stage, though he relegated the professional actors to an even lower social position. Theodoric the Great, who said that the theatre was a good way of handling the conquered Romans and persuading them to accept German domination, reconstructed a theatre in Rome through his minister Cassiodorus. During the sixth century Choricus defended the whole mimic stage and argued its value point by point with Chrysostom, Tertullian and the others. Of course he was arguing for North Africa but there is no reason to suppose that the theatre had entirely disappeared both from the Western and Eastern Roman Empires.

It has been stated that Justinian I closed the theatres in Constantinople but evidently this condition did not obtain long because we know that performances took place there in the seventh century. The Emperor having married the famous Theodora, whom both scandal and history record as a shameless mimetic, decreed that a nobleman might marry an actress provided she abandoned her profession. This is important not only because it shows Theodora's influence on Justinian but that performances were still held. Both Nicoll and Delbrueck draw our attention to the Diptych of Anastatius (517) in the *Bibliothèque Nationale* which shows some kind of dramatic burlesque taking place. Several others exist in various European libraries and museums to record the occurrence of *spectacula*.

Sisebert, King of Spain from 612 to 621, refers to the popularity of *ludis theatriis* at marriages and feasts, saying that he believed that the clergy should leave the place when they were performed. At the same time in Constantinople performances continued to be so popular that the Trullan Council in 691 threatened the deposition of priests and excommunication of those of the laity who dared to attend them.

One of the most valuable sources of information of this period is the famous seventh century *Originum seu etymologiarum libri xx* of Isidore of Seville which speaks of theatre buildings in the past tense but refers indignantly to the shameless mimes and *histriones* in the present. This would certainly seem to corroborate our point. In the eighth century John of Damascus, who is credited with having written a religious drama, condemned secular performances as a rival of the Mass, thereby condemning his own play. Certainly these scenic displays offered competition to the Greek religious drama, *The Death of Christ*, written in 790 by Stephanos the Sabbaite. In the next century, 813, the Council of Tours decreed that the clergy should not witness the obscenity of actors and in 816 the Council at Aix-la-Chapelle again stated that priests must not be present at plays given on the stage or at marriages. Over and over the Church thunders against the theatre.

What is most important in the history of the Western Roman Empire is the edict of Charlemagne, who ruled from 800 to 814, stating that no actor could put on a robe of priestly rank except under penalty of corporal punishment or banishment. This would indicate either that anti-Christian mimes persisted or, which is more probable, the actors submitted to the church and were performing in religious plays. This would place the beginnings of the ecclesiastical drama in the early part of the ninth century, a view which is held by some authorities but has been impossible to document further.

The secular theatre certainly continued in the persons of the *ioculatores* (jongleurs) who carried over the duties of mime and combined them with those of the Teuton *scop*. So the minstrel-singer, poet-singer, actor-singer who chanted the exploits of the German, Anglo-Saxon and Norse warriors came to be one with the comic actor (imitator of humanity) for Greece and Rome. Like most general statements this is not strictly true but the passage of time and the amalgamation of duties and interests approximated its culmination. All these wandering minstrels, sword-dancers and acrobats joined with the true mime and came to belong to the class of *histriones*.

Juggling and acrobatic tricks were as much a part of the medieval fool as was his quick wit. His motley costume and long ass's ears such as are worn by Touchstone in *As You Like It* are familiar to every school child. These actors took their part in the *Feast of the Fools* and the *Feast of the Ass,* favorite diversions of a later period in France and England.

The ecclesiastical drama began with the elaboration of the Mass itself and seems to have come about first in France. There, liturgical dramas were called *mystères* (mysteries); in Italy they were the *sacre rappresentazioni;* in England, miracle plays (sometimes called mystery plays); in Germany, *Geistspiele*. These plays were written in Latin and not until later were they set down in the language of the people. In the case of England this was delayed further because they were played for a long time in Anglo-Norman, the speech of the nobility and gentry.

This extension of the church ritual was apparent in the dedication of a church. A member of the clergy was concealed behind the closed doors. The bishop and procession of priests approached and the bishop cried out, "Lift up your gates, oh ye rulers, and be ye lifted up, ye everlasting portals; and the King of Glory shall come in." A scornful voice (the spirit of evil) was heard calling harshly from within, "Who *is* this King of Glory?" The bishop and all the clergy replied triumphantly, "The Lord of Hosts, He *is* the King of Glory." The doors were swung open and the forces of righteousness marched in while the hidden priest slipped out to join the others.

Another instance came in the ceremonial held on Good Friday. After the adoration of the crucifix it was carried in the procession as though it were the body of Christ and was to be hidden in a sepulchre built for the occasion near the altar. The *Concordia Regularis* of St. Ethelwold, drawn up between 965 and 975 for Winchester records this *trope* or extension of the Mass. Quietly on Easter morn during the third lesson of the service, four of the priests approached the sepulchre. One seated himself and holding a palm took the part of the Angel. At the third response, the three approached tentatively as if searching for something. They represented the three Marys come to anoint the body of Jesus. When the Angel perceived them he began to sing in a sweet medium voice, *"Quem Quaeritis (in sepulchro, o'Christicolae) . . ."* When he had finished, the three chanted *"Jesum Nazarenum (crucifixum, o caelicolae)."* The angel replied:

"Non est hic, surrexit sicut praedixerat.
Ite nuntiate quia surrexit a mortuis."

Then the three turned to the choir and said:

"Alleluia! resurrexit Dominus."

And so on until the holy drama was acted out. These were the simple and beautiful beginnings of liturgical drama.

Christ's Passion, long attributed to the before-mentioned Gregory Nazianzine of the late fourth century, now believed to be a concoction of Aeschylus and Euripides made by Johannes Tzetzes six hundred years later, is one of the earliest known dramas of the medieval period but stemmed from the Greek tragic writers rather than from the Christian Church. A holy German nun, Hrosvitha (c.935-c.1000) in the tenth century composed six plays modelled on the comedies of Terence whom she had read and admired. In an effort to remove the license of the Roman original, she wrote to teach strict morality. If these plays were performed at the time, their audience was made up of her fellow nuns and benefactors of the convent.

Other than these literary efforts, the dramas of the period were based on the Holy Mysteries of the Bible, hence their name of mystery plays. The miracles were taken from events in the lives of the saints, though by the fourteenth century the two were used interchangeably in ordinary speech.

The first of the mysteries was the famous *Représentation d'Adam*, (*Ordo repraesentationis Adae*), a Norman-French mystery of the twelfth century. This play begins with an admonition to the actors to pick up their cues and "to be mindful not to add or subtract a syllable in the verses and to see that they pronounced all distinctly." This suggests a source for Hamlet's celebrated speech to the players. This earliest play in French drama was played in the square before the church and all the actors, even the one who represented God, reentered the church when they were not occupied in the action. In France it was customary to build a number of *mansions* in a straight line whenever possible, whether inside of the church or outside so that the actors progressed from one place to another. If Heaven was at one end, frequently to the right of the crucifix, Hell was at the other and between them, if the church structure permitted, there were Limbo, the Golden Gate, the Palace of the Bishops, Pilate's House, Jerusalem, the Temple, Bethlehem and other points depending on the story. This arrangement always held good when the performance was out of doors.

The mouth of Hell was of great importance to the medieval audience and far surpassed Heaven in interest. Mechanical devices were contrived that permitted the enormous jaws to open and close, emitting smoke and flame when the unfortunate wicked were prodded into it by shaggy, hairy, black devils with pitchforks. When the devils embarked on a foray into the world, the jaws opened and the howls of the damned were heard as their tormentors leaped out to carry on their nefarious designs upon the blessed. It was here that many of the humorous episodes and later obscenities were introduced.

In France these scenes were more frankly intended for entertainment than they were in England. It was in this scene that the theatrical machinist made best use of his skill and at Mons no less than seventeen persons were necessary for the scenic devices of Hell alone.

The simplicity of the medieval theatre lay in the faith that the auditors and performers had in the holiness of their purpose. The staging was far from simple. Tempests, earthquakes, buildings on fire, sudden lights, miraculous appearances from above, mysterious or sacred disappearances were common to all the cycles of plays. The stage manager's promptscript as recorded in Lee Simonson's brilliant *The Stage Is Set* (which is one of the best contemporary criticisms of theatrical production) lists certain expenditures which indicate the Belasco realism of medieval staging. Among the items are "To Jehan Foucquart, called Docque Docque, for feeding certain birds of every variety to be used for the Creation: 6s. To Ghendart, sergeant at Nimy, for live rabbits for the Creation of the Beasts and birds: 5s. For two live lambs, for the aforesaid Creation and also for the sacrifice of Abel and Abraham: 32s."

Whilst these magnificent performances were taking place, a great festival was decreed for the city and the gates in the outside walls were shut so that there might be no interruption from a marauding force at such a sacred time. The empty streets were patrolled by armed guards to protect the citizens and their property while they were participating, either as spectators or actors, in the great mysteries in the cathedral itself or in the public square set aside for these performances. This recalls the aforementioned capture of Tarentum while its citizens were so absorbed in a dramatic production. At this time the French had the forethought to guard against foreign attack and to dismiss internal disturbances at a time when their love of God and their love of the theatre coincided.

The arrangements varied from country to country as the Lucerne Easter play and *Donaueschingen* play illustrate. These performances sometimes were given in a structure resembling the old Roman arena, with tiers of seats raised in a complete circle for the spectators. Religious plays, *sacrae repraesentationes*, were given in the Colosseum in Rome, in *corrales* in Spain and in *rounds* in Cornwall in the south-west of England.

Sometimes the pageant wagon was used in place of the fixed mansion in France and in The Netherlands. This of course was only possible when the mysteries were given out of doors. The most general use of them, however, was made in England. The pageant wagon was constructed in two levels and roofed over. The uprights supported curtains which shut the lower half from view so that it might serve as a dressing-room. The play took place on the upper level. David Rogers in *Breauarye* (1609) records that in the "productions at Chester," the "pagiente" was "a highe place made like a howse with ij rowmes, being open on ye tope; the lower rowme they apparrelled & dressed themselves; and in the higher rowme they played; and they stood upon 6 wheeles" ("4 wheeles" in another version).

The following list gives some idea of the costumes worn as reprinted by Sir E. K. Chambers, renowned authority on the medieval stage:

"Inventory of ye p'ticulars appartaynyng to ye Company of ye Grocers, a.d. 1565.
A Pageant, yt is to saye, a Howse of Waynskott paynted and buylded on a Carte wt fowre whelys.
A square topp to sett over ye sayde Howse.
A Gryffon, gylte, wt a fane to sette on ye sayde toppe.

A bygger Iron fane to sett on ye ende of ye Pageante.
iiij^{xx} iij small Fanes belongyng to ye same Pageante.
A Rybbe colleryd Red.
A cote & hosen wt a bagg & capp for dolor, stayned.
2 cotes and a payre hosen for Eve, stayned.
A cote & hosen for Adam, steyned.
A cote wt hosen & tayle for ye serpente, steyned, wt a wt heare.
A cote of yellow buckram wt ye Grocers' arms for ye Pendon
bearer.
An Angell's Cote & over hoses of Apis Skynns.
3 paynted clothes to hang abowte ye Pageant.
A face & heare for ye Father.
2 hearys for Adam & Eve.
4 head stallis brode Inkle wth knopps & tassells.
6 Horsse Clothes, stayned, wt knopps & tassells.
Item, Weights, &c."

For a long time the actors were drawn from the priests within the
church, the monks and the lay brothers. The feminine parts were
played by young altar boys, though in time women and even girls
occasionally played them. This of course could only have happened
after the dramas had been withdrawn from the church edifice and
taken into the public square. At first the dramas were primarily concerned with the festivals of the church and so took place on those days
within the church itself. As the building constricted the action, the
plays were removed. They were no longer reserved for exact festival
days and came to be performed at Whitsuntide or on Corpus Christi
day. By the middle of the fourteenth century the relation of the
plays to church liturgy had weakened greatly. Writers had sprung up
who wrote consciously on religious topics and the people in the towns
took it upon themselves to stage the productions. The various workers' guilds made themselves responsible for certain plays within the
cycle. This was particularly true in England where existed the four
great series of miracle plays called York, Chester, Wakefield (or
Townley because of the ownership of the manuscript by that family)
and Coventry.

Other than the *trope* of the disappearance of Christ's body from
the tomb and the mystery of *Adam*, little has been said of the early
plays themselves. In France comes the earliest development. John
Bodel of Arras wrote *Le Jeu de Saint Nicholas* in the thirteenth century (which set the play in the Holy Land where the Crusaders were
fighting the infidels. All the Christians were killed save a certain
Prudhomme, who prayed to St. Nicholas to the amazement of the

Saracen king. He was told that this saint would safely guard his treasure. Some thieves stole the king's money but St. Nicholas appeared before them and ordered them to give it up. The king was convinced and he and all his hosts became Christians and Nicholas was vindicated). This subject was also popular in England in a somewhat different play of Hilarius and was frequently performed by the altar boys during the *Festival of the Boy Bishop.*

Another popular play was written by Ruteboeuf (c.1230-c.1280) a contemporary of the canonized Louis IX, and was entitled *Le Miracle de St. Theophile.* It concerned the ambitious Saint who sold himself to the devil, repented of his bargain and by the gracious intercession of the Virgin Mary, was freed. This unthinking kindness of Mary provoked a series of plays in France and are sometimes called Marys (*Maries*) or Mary-plays.

There were two other dramas in the France of this period which have survived and which deserve mention because of their genuine comic and satiric qualities. Not having read Aristophanes, but unbeknownst having caught some of his spirit, the *trouvère*, Adam de la Halle (1230-1288) wrote *Le Jeu de la Feuillée* (c.1262) which satirized the citizens of his native Arras. His *Le Jeu de Robin et de Marion* was idyllic and was the earliest example of comic opera.

There were also the famous Mary-plays, *Les Miracles de Notre-Dame* which recounted all kinds of miracles of the Virgin. The humanity of Mary and her interest in the poor and afflicted held the love and attention of the audience. One of the most famous of this series was that of *Robert le Diable*, which has found form in later drama and opera. Maeterlinck and other mystic modern dramatists have gone to these for their plays.

There were three cycles of mystery plays in France though the word itself was not used until 1402 when Charles VI (1368-1422) licensed the famous *Confrérie de la Passion*, an organization of citizens and craftsmen to present mysteries. The first of these was *Le Mystère du Viel Testament* consisting of 44,325 verses, and was printed by Pierre le Dru about 1500. It was played in its entirety by the *Confrères* at the *Hôtel de Flandres* in 1542 and twenty performances were necessary to complete the cycle. One of the most touching plays in this group was *Abraham et des Enfants*, the counterpart of the English *Abraham and Isaac*. The *Mystère de Nouveau Testament* exists in seven versions. The best known is that of Arnoul Greban, circa 1450 and comprises 34,574 verses. The third cycle was called *Les Actes des Apôtres*. The apostle plays were written by Arnoul and Simon Greban and comprise 61,968 lines. When played in 1536 at Bourges they took forty days. One of the most famous performances of these passion plays took place at Valenciennes in 1547.

Before these cycles developed however, there were a series of yearly festivals which were humorous and even bawdy in intent and in fact. The first of these was *The Feast of the Ass*. This grew partly out of the serious use of the donkey by Balaam, the procession of the Prophets, The Flight into Egypt and The Entry into Jerusalem. It grew partly out of the pagan rites of the Teutons, Celts, Romans. The Greeks themselves were progenitors because of their rites at the coming of spring or at the beginning of the year. As far back as the reign of Michael III (842-867), ruler of the Eastern Roman Empire, the court buffoon, Theophilus, dressed as the patriarch and, attended by false metropolitans, burlesqued the holy office of the Mass. A manuscript of the late twelfth and early thirteenth century still survives at the British Museum which records what is called the "Prose" of the Ass, a chant to be intoned in praise of that estimable animal with a braying refrain of hee-haws. The lower orders of the priesthood, the sub-deacons and secular clergy took part in the riotous tomfoolery. There was much drinking and the censing was done with sausages and pudding. With this ribald affair was mingled the prose of the *Feast of Fools*. A chief person seriously called the Bishop, Archbishop or Pope of Fools, celebrated a mock Mass in an atmosphere of buffoonery, noise and leaping about. The participants were dressed in motley costumes or in no clothes at all. This was true in France, Germany and Italy but they were slightly more decorous in England, or so English writers would have us believe. For a long time the church endeavored to stamp out these practices and by the end of the fourteenth century may be said to have done so, though curious survivals of the ritual appear in unlikely places even today.

Another festival was that of the *Boy Bishop*. The altar and choir boys elected one of their number "Bishop" on the fifth of December, the eve of St. Nicholas. The date of the beginning of the festival was originally the date of the election. Subsequently the celebration was transferred to December 27th, the eve of the Feast of the Holy Innocents. Though attended by night dances, masquerades and plays, this festival was reverent and of course took place in the church. The bishop was always the senior boy "so long as he was sufficiently good-looking," according to the York Minister Statutes. Tributes were levied on the gentry and clergy and in the two weeks of holiday (literally, as school vacations were not established until the eighteenth century) substantial sums were received.

The favorite plays for these occasions were the *Massacre of the Innocents* and the before mentioned St. Nicholas play of Hilarius which lent itself to presentation by boys. This recounted the little miracle of St. Nicholas whose image was left to guard the treasure whilst the faithful were away in the Holy Land, fighting the infidel. When they returned and found the treasure had been stolen, they beat the statue for being unfaithful to their trust. St. Nicholas himself learns of this and goes secretly to the thieves, reveals himself and forces them to return the treasure. The warriors are overjoyed and then honor the saint for his valiant and truthworthy efforts on their behalf.

But to return to the great cycles of English mystery plays, the earliest in point of composition is the Chester, though it is possible that it may have been preceded by the Cornish. This latter cycle consisted of four plays, *The Beginning of the World* (*Origo Mundi*), *The Passion of Our Lord* (*Passio Domini*) which included *The Death of Pilate* and *The Resurrection and Ascension* (*Resurrectio Domini*). These date from the fourteenth century. The Chester Cycle came into existence in the first third of the same century, though some of its partisans place it in the thirteenth century. The York Cycle came along between 1340 and 1350 according to their editor, but other authorities date them somewhat later. The Wakefield (Townley) Cycle comes slightly later and shows the influence of York. The last in point of time were the so-called Coventry Plays and were in all probability performed elsewhere than in Coventry as this town already possessed several miracle plays of its own which are still extant. The Coventry Plays are sometimes called the N—— Towns Cycle. The 1468 manuscript would indicate that they may have been used by a strolling company of players who substituted the name of the town in which they played at the *Festival of Corpus Christi*.

The plays were performed by the craftsmen's guilds and seem to have been divided somewhat according to the type of work done by each guild. For instance, in Beverley and Lincoln, the cooks presented *The Harrowing of Hell* (that favorite of the mediaeval audience) because they were accustomed to baking, boiling, taking things out and putting things into the fire. There too, as might be expected, the watermen performed the Noah play and had one of the sure-fire comedy scenes which had great possibility of comic enlargement. At York with appropriate assignments, the shipwrights conducted *The Construction of the Ark*, the fishmongers *The Flood*, the goldsmiths *The Three Kings* and the barbers *The Baptism of Jesus*. The priests at Beverley attended to *The Coronation of the Virgin*.

Each municipality controlled the production of these plays and the license for performance was granted to the individual guild. If for any reason the performance was not given on the *Feast Day of Corpus Christi,* or was omitted altogether, the Guild was fined. The expenses of these elaborate presentations were paid for by a tax which was levied on each member of the guild. Occasionally, as the sumptuousness of the productions grew and became lengthened, an outside craft or individual would contribute a share. A modern equivalent would be the magnificent Mardi Gras at New Orleans. However, the expense eventually became burdensome and this, coupled with the Protestant Reformation gradually caused the cessation of these performances toward the end of the sixteenth century. The Protestant objection to seeing portrayed the events in the lives of the saints and the miracles of the Virgin Mary were responsible. The need for this kind of religious solace not found in sermons or ritual was answered in the seventeenth century in another literary medium by Bunyan in *The Pilgrim's Progress.*

Perhaps it might be well to give a more exact picture of the extent and nature of these representations by listing the titles included in the Chester Cycle. Various manuscripts of this cycle exist in the British Museum, in the Bodleian Library at Oxford, in the library of the Duke of Devonshire. It is possible for one to see a script which seven centuries ago was carried about by an excited stage manager whose duties were comparable in modern times only in such productions as *The Miracle, The Eternal Road* or *Jumbo.*

The manuscript plays vary from one to twenty-five and according to Sir E. K. Chambers run in about this order: *The fallinge of Lucifer; the creation of ye worlde; Noah and his shipp; Abraham & Isacke; King Balack & Balaam with Moyses; Nativytie of our Lord; The Shepperdes offeringe: Kinge Harrald & ye mounte victoriall; Ye 3 Kinges of Collen; the destroyeinge of the childeren by Herod; Purification of our Ladye; The pinackle, with ye woman of Canan; The rising of Lazarus from death to liffe; The cominge of Christe to Jerusalem; Christs maundy with his desiples; The scourginge of Christe; The Crusifienge of Christ; The harrowinge of The Ressurection; The Castle of Emaus & the Apostles; The Ascension of Christe; Whitsonday ye makeinge of the Creede; Prophetes before ye day of Dome; Antecriste; Domes Daye.*

The very names of the plays make abundantly clear the interest and intentions of the authors and producers. *Antecriste* and *Domes Daye* are suggestive enough to make the blood run cold, the righteous shiver and the sinners repent. All of them however were not so frightening: the pathos of *Abraham and Isaac* really communicates with the modern mind, and the hilarity of the *Second Shepherd's Play* is still funny.

There is a tremendous modern fascination in reading the lists of expenses for actors and production costs for we find there such items as: a rope for Judas 2d., a girdle for God 3d., an earthquake 3s 4d., 4d. for attending to it and 2d. for covering it, whatever the pillar device for "ye erthequakes" might be. Pilate was the best paid of the actors, Herod and Caiaphas next, with Jesus and Judas next in financial return.

Alongside the mysteries and miracles there existed the moralities, which contrary to popular belief were contemporaries and not successors of the already described forms. Though the word "morality" was not in use at the time, this form was generally termed "moral," "goodly" or "pithy Interlude." The first of which we have knowledge is the *Play of the Lord's Prayer* which was performed in York before 1384 and until 1582. The seven vices of Pride, Lust, Sloth, Gluttony, Hatred, Avarice and Anger were portrayed for the instruction of the auditors. The characters in these plays were allegorical and in some instances derived from miracles though they existed along with the liturgical drama. Undoubtedly allegory was rendered more popular by the success of *Le Roman de la Rose*. Interludes were a popular means of performing moralities.

The Devil and Vice claimed exclusively for the morality, were also used in the interlude and some moralities have neither. The interlude could be both serious and merry; in fact at times it was a kind of mystery play itself in England, while in France it was sometimes a light "interlude" or a mystery play of deep religious significance.

By 1550 the term in England came to be used synonymously with comedy, certainly Udall used it in his imitations of Plautus and Terence.

The moralities varied greatly in length, the celebrated and beautiful *Perseverance* had 3,500 lines, *Bien-Avisé, Mal-Avisé* produced in 1439 had 8,000, and the giants, *L'Homme Pécheur* with 22,000 and *L'Homme Juste* (both written in the reign of Louis XII) with 30,000 lines.

The farce and *sottie* developed in France. The most famous farce was *Maître Pierre Pathelin* (1470), which was so popular that when it was printed it went through twenty-five editions prior to 1600, and is frequently revived at the present time. The *sotties* were the merry entertainments which France wove into the already described *Feast of the Ass* and *Feast of the Fools*. One of the most celebrated of these was the *Jeu du Prince des Sots*, written by Pierre Gringoire, 1475-80 to 1544, and produced at the *Halles de Paris,* 24 February, 1512, at the behest of Louis XII. He wished to inflame the popular mind against the papacy and to attack Pope Julius II who had turned against him.

It is not possible to turn from the Middle Ages without some consideration of Germany, Italy and Spain. In the first named country the mysteries and miracles were approximately like those of France and England. Several of these passion plays continued until the present day; those of Freiburg and Oberammergau being the most famous and best attended.

The most characteristic plays of the German stage were the Shrovetide plays which centered in Nuremberg, the center of learning and industry throughout the mediaeval period as well as during the Renaissance. These pieces were not unlike the French farces except that they were much shorter. They began with *der Einschreier* (the prologue) which was recited by one of the fools and announced the arrival of his companions. At the completion of the playlets there was a general invitation to join the dance.

The subject matter was similar to the French except for the representation of the peasants in a coarse and ugly light, their virtue and bravery always being subject to crude questioning. The fact that these plays were always written by townsfolk may explain the dislike, distrust and ridicule heaped upon country people. The most famous one (though not written at Nuremberg) was the Neithart Play, also the longest as it exceeds 2,000 verses. There were two groups of characters involved, the ducal or court party and the uncouth peasants. The plot consisted of a joke, which was perpetrated by the latter, their cruel punishment by the nobles and finally by the devil himself. The greatest writer of this type of play was Hans Sachs (1494-1576) who was prolific in all literary forms as well. Of his 198 plays, eighteen were tragedies, sixty-five comedies, sixty-four Shrovetide-plays, and ten others which he merely termed "plays." His Shrovetide-plays were his best and he undoubtedly cleansed the form of much of its obscenity. His other plays lie between the Middle Ages and the Renaissance so his definition of them as tragedies and comedies is not very exact. His most famous was a *Fastnachtspiel* (Shrovetide-play) entitled *Der fahrende Schueler mit dem Teufelbanner* (*The Wandering Scholar and Exorcist*) which achieved unity of place and action, and a certain differentiation of character, a distinct advance over his predecessors.

The theatre in Italy possessed a history not too dissimilar from that of France and England. The liturgical drama developed as early here as elsewhere but it is not definite at just what point the *trope* became *sacre rappresentazioni*. Uberto Benvoglienti reports a passion play in Sienna on Good Friday about the year 1200 and Apostolo Zeno speaks of a performance, whether spoken or in pantomime, in 1234 in Padua. Shortly after that a religious revival, inspired by the old hermit Raniere Fasani, took place and led to the rise of the *Disciplinati di Gesu Cristo*. In this excited people marched with bare breasts and feet through the cold of a severe Umbrian winter, lashing themselves and imploring God's mercy in a sacred chant called a laud. These took several forms but the dialogue form turned into a crude drama spoken in Italian. The most famous of these developed as the *Passion of Revello* and was produced in that city in 1490; it was influenced by the French mysteries and was written in cultured Italian, not in Latin nor in the dialect of the common people.

The performances of the *devozioni* of Italy were similar in technique to the French. There was a series of mansions, and Hell was located at one side and usually a little below the spectators. The dependence on factual display of the miraculous ascensions and descents, are all like the French too. The plays themselves were based on the New Testament and the lives of the saints and martyrs, rather than on the Old Testament upon which both France and England largely depended.

In all probability the theatre in Spain persisted as late as the seventh century but the Arab invasion in 711 and the domination of the whole country by the Saracens effectively checked any dramatic effort. The Arab mind resists the theatre and it is a fact that wherever they are in control the theatre diminishes as it has done in Turkey. The establishment of the Christian Kingdoms of Navarre, Castile and Aragon provided a place where the theatre could be revived. Just when this happened is not clear, but by the middle of the thirteenth century the religious drama had gained such a foothold that abuses had already been introduced. The experience of Spain paralleled that of France and England; the first plays were extensions of the Mass and were followed by nativity and passion plays performed by the clergy in the churches. However certain buffooneries came to be introduced by the priests themselves. This abuse gave rise to the edict of Alfonso X about 1260 which forbade these practices and denied villages the right of production. It also prohibited production for any monetary gain and stated definitely that all performances must be under the authority of the bishop or archbishop or under persons properly designated by them.

The really curious thing about the religious drama in Spain is that all physical evidence of its actual existence has entirely disappeared. Not a vestige of a play survives as it does in all of the other principal nations of Western Europe. In fact there is no exact account to which we may turn for confirmation of our conjectures concerning the early theatre except for the already quoted *Siete Partida* of Alfonso X. We do know that with the institution of the often mentioned *Feast of Corpus Christi* in 1264 by Pope Urban IV, many religious dramatic performances took place. These were called *autos sacramentales* and took place as late as the end of the sixteenth century. Beginning as they did in the church and on the piazza in front of the church, they were transferred to wagons known as "cars" and drawn throughout the city. The procession was called *La fiesta de los Carros*. Details concerning the expenses for these performances have been found in municipal archives of various Spanish cities from which much practical information has been learned concerning them.

To sum up, the experience in all countries seems to have been remarkably similar. Despite barbarian pressure from without, moralistic strictures, general and total ignorance, the people were disinclined to cast out entirely some form of secular theatrical art. The *scop, jongleur*, minstrel, sword-dancer, fool, as well as the actor survived if only in a hidden fashion. Realizing the tremendous hold the dramatic instinct had on all its peoples, the mediaeval Church translated its religious history and dogma into a theatre form which would appeal to its communicants and so strengthen its hold on their consciences as well as their emotions. For hundreds of years this form flourished inside and outside the church, at first under ecclesiastical and finally under secular control. The Holy Church performed a valuable service to the professional and amateur theatre of today as is evidenced in countless ways.

V

THE WRITTEN DRAMA OF THE ITALIAN

RENAISSANCE

As the mystery play emerged from the churches into the squares and the *sacra rappresentazione* took its place as a morality play devoted didactically to the instruction of a youth unwilling to be educated, a great political event occurred. Proud Byzantium, the Constantinople of recent centuries, the Istanbul of the present day, fell at the hands of the Islam Turks. The Saracens had no literature, no art worth naming, no real theatre and no appreciation of it. Intolerant of art, bigoted and cruel, they seized the Eastern European capital of culture in 1453. From the city fled the actors, scholars, artists and artisans who had made it beautiful and memorable. To Venice, seaport of the Adriatic, Mantua, Ferrara, Florence they went and Italy awoke to a great revival of the classic arts of Greece and Rome.

Its effect on the Theatre was distinctly disappointing. Great painters, sculptors and architects abound in the annals of the Italian Renaissance but the names of dramatists and actors are few and poor. The opening of minds and hearts to the spirit of the ancient world seems to have had an opposite effect in the field of the theatre. Stilted imitation of Greek tragedy, the faint and sentimental pastorals of Virgil's *Bucolics*, and bawdy, loosely constructed copies of Terence, and Plautus' imitations of Menander's comedies are all that we find. Perhaps this is so because Italy was not ready for a great national drama as were England, Spain and France when the Renaissance reached those countries. There was no focal point where the theatre might be attached and receive the enlightened encouragement a genuine center of culture could have given it. The quickening minds and spirits in the other countries had brought about their establishment as nations. Italy remained a conglomeration of small, quarreling principalities, divided between foreign conquerors and petty princes who had a passion for intrigue. In this direction the

63

Italians wasted enough energy to have sustained the combined dramatic genius of Sophocles, Shakespeare and Ibsen. The cruelty and immorality, wholesale disregard of decency and low moral standards of ancient Rome were repeated in Renaissance Italy. Perhaps this is characteristic of the Italian temperament and therefor we should not be surprised that Christianity brought no improvement in social decency.

The fifteenth century found the *names* of dramatists emerging from the communal and anonymous authorship of the medieval drama so that individual responsibility can be assigned for the successes and failures. The first two are of important poets who are represented with a drama each. Angelo Poliziano (1454-1494) produced *Orfeo* probably in 1471 or 1472 and *Il Timone* was produced before 1494, the year of the death of its author, Matteo Maria Boiardo (c.1434-1494). The first was a kind of *sacra rappresentazione* with Christian elements transposed into pagan mythology and the second was a crudely constructed comedy. Both of these were written in Italian, the vulgar tongue. Certain precious dramas in Latin preceded them if you are willing to admit such scholarly diversions into the ranks of Italian drama. Among these were the *Philogenia* of Ugolino Pisani, produced in Parma in 1430, Leon Battista Alberti's *Philodoxius*, Gregorio Corrado's *Progne* and Leonardo Bruni's *Polissena*.

Curiously enough with all the material for tragic drama about them the Italian writers ignored what the great Elizabethans, Shakespeare, Webster, Massinger found as the very meat of historical tragedy. Perhaps living in an age of violent deaths, parricides, incest, and other horrors was quite enough to make them write of it all in a comic style with no thought of satire. Their plays satirize themselves to the modern reader. At the same time their style was graceful, witty and polished. Their pastoral comedies were tender and sentimental in an age where poison and hired *bravi* flourished. They were performed for the *haut monde* of the court; there was no cultured middle class and the style of drama was above the heads of the proletariat. It is only in a place where you have a high general intelligence in your audience that you have great drama such as that in Athens, Elizabethan London, seventeenth century Paris, nineteenth century Bergen and Oslo, twentieth century New York. The whole of their literature took its tone from the cultivated *novella* in which form the witty if monotonous Giovanni Boccaccio (1313-1375) excelled.

For some now unknown reason *Sofonisba*, a tragedy by Giovanni Giorgio Trissino (1478-1550) was not acted until 1562 though it was

completed in 1515 and went through six editions before its representation. This is considered the first Italian tragedy and abounds
with the author's misconceptions of Aristotle's *Poetics*. Instead of
being a consecutively dramatic story it is a pale reflection of Attic
tragedy chiefly interesting because of Trissino's effort to reform
orthography and to refine Italian composition. It was a scholarly
attempt which was a success as far as contemporary theorists were
concerned but it has no modern significance.

Another learned man of the period, GIOVANNI RUCELLAI (1475-
1526), of the famous family of Florence, wrote *Rosmunda* at the
same time that Trissino was composing *Sofonisba*. The former piece
was played in the Rucellai gardens before Pope Leo X. The play is
mercifully brief despite its static quality and over-use of the device
of the Messenger. It is imitative of Seneca who in turn was imitative
of the Greeks. There is no life to it, but his *Oreste* has a beauty of
style that is suggestive of the original *Iphigenia in Tauris*.

An important drama of this time was *Canace* by Sperone Speroni
which had the same lack of dramatic incident in the scenes shown
to the audience. There is no attempt to display action nor is there
any interchange between the characters to build stature. *Orbecche*
by GIOVANNI BATTISTA GIRALDI (1504-1573) was a horrible play
about a child who innocently discloses to her father the adultery between his wife and their eldest son. His murder of the guilty pair
only fixes the fate of Orbecche because the mother wills evil upon
her from the grave. The girl secretly marries a lowborn man and
has two children by him. When her father learns of this he kills
the father and children and sends the head and hands of the husband
to his daughter. This is finally too much for her. She stabs her father
to death and commits suicide. This is the kind of "tragedy" that was
customary in sixteenth century Italy. The characters were stock
characters just as those of the Roman mime were. There was no
effort to differentiate between one heroine and another and the
villains and heroes were cut from an endlessly same pattern. Thus
the finely differentiated characterization which is the only excuse for
a play of this kind did not exist. We accept our Mr. Dulcimer in *The
Green Bay Tree* because the character rings true though the subject matter may be repulsive to most of us.

The writers of this period whose work seems best to us are those
who were willing to translate without distortion the Greek tragedies
into their own Italian terms. These are few and far between because
Seneca's alterations and embroideries are invariably followed rather
than the natural felicity of the Greeks. Luigi Alamanni (1495-1556)
was one of the few writers to make a beautiful translation of the

Antigone, Lodovico Dolce (1508?-1568) spoiled *The Phoenician Women* in his alteration of the play which he called *Giocasta*. The most extravagant remodelling of a play was Giovanni Andrea dell'Anguillera's reworking of *Oedipus Rex* as *Edippo*. He gave it a new final act and added odd bits as well as whole scenes from Seneca. All of this makes it quite evident why Italian tragedy was a failure. It was not the work of dramatists writing out of the heat of their own lives and imagination but the conscious construction of dead plays by scholars who wrote for an audience of fellow-scholars.

It was in the field of comedy that the dramatists had most success. Even there they were not content to develop the comic vernacular found in the *sacre rappresentazioni* but must needs rewrite Plautus and Terence. In the south of Italy and centering on Naples there was a native comic farce form which might have been the basis for a national comedy since it partook of both comedy and tragedy. But as always where the humanists were concerned, it was to the ancient world they turned. Those lands looked fresh and invigorating after the thralldom of the Dark Ages so that the eyes of the writers were blinded to forms about them which were readily available. Besides, this classic heritage was a common meeting ground for the Venetians, Florentines and Neapolitans who were otherwise separated among small states. It was the common denominator of the courts of Italy and their devoted followers.

The first step was in the enactment of Terence and Plautus in Latin according to the Renaissance ideas of what constituted the ancient methods of staging. This was caused by a misreading of the theatrical dicta of Vitruvius and Horace. We have only to examine the illustration depicting the Terentian stage and to compare it with a true Roman theatre to understand the profound misconception they had of the ancient playhouses. These revivals were most popular in Rome towards the end of the fifteenth century and particularly at the Vatican during the pontificates of Popes Sixtus IV and Innocent VIII. The *Menaechmi* was performed in 1502 at the marriage of Lucrezia Borgia to Alfonso d'Este, eldest son to the Duke of Ferrara. This play followed one of the famous banquets which included a *morisco* (a simplified *ballet d'action*) in which Cesare Borgia acted. As the music rose for the glorious finale the guests danced with the performers and the Pope looked on approvingly. This was a period when every entertainment was enriched by theatrical displays for which distinguished artists contributed scenery or novel scenic effects. The great Leonardo da Vinci designed a festival in Milan in 1489 which was called *Il Paradiso* because of the glorious paradise created by this versatile man of the Renaissance. There was a revolving heaven with seven planets represented by actors, and all of it bespoke the praises of the recently married Isabella of Aragon.

It was at the court of Ferrara and under the sponsorship of Duke Ercole d'Este that many pastoral comedies as well as translations of the comic Roman twins were played. In 1486 was played the Latin comedy *Menaechmi* and in 1487 Nicolà da Correggio's *Favolo di Cefalo*, at the wedding of Lucrezia d'Este to Annibale Bentivoglio. It was a mythological pastoral based on the seventh book of Ovid's *Metamorphoses*, and was somewhat the same as Poliziano's *Orfeo*. These plays were idyllic in style and largely pagan in content.

Coupled with the pastorals were the eclogues, which were arranged as dialogues and were frequently recited as *intermezzi* by costumed actors. These simple pieces gradually became more and more complicated as additional characters, many scenes and handsome settings were introduced. Shepherds and shepherdesses were favorite characters in these pieces and a certain quiet pleasantness pervaded them though there is a melancholy which is quite different from the bucolics of old. They gradually assembled these qualities and eventually were known as "masques", in France and England; in Italy they were called *maschere* and in Spain *máscaras*. It is well to remember that the theatre of all these countries was in a fluid state. This was due to the interchangeability of nationality among the rulers and frequent change of masters of the various cities. The Spanish and French rulers of Italy both took and gave artistically and the marriage of a Medici into the French house of Valois or Bourbon was the signal for the gaiety which took theatrical form in dance, music and drama. These masques and entries employed the greatest artists of the day, Giovanni Maria Cecchi, Filippo Brunelleschi, Baldassarre Peruzzi, and Alfonso Parigi the younger, to name a few. Performances in the Italy of this period were given only at court or in a public square under courtly auspices. There were no theatres as most of the surviving Roman and Greek theatres had fallen into such a state of disrepair as to be unusable. Later theatres were to be attached to the palaces themselves but during the early Italian Renaissance temporary structures were set up in the *cortiles* of the residences of the princes. The change from the scattered scene picture of the Middle Ages, with the buildings set in a line or a square, was superseded by the contemporary concept of what Roman staging was like. The upper stage for playing and the lower for dressing was more like the pageant wagon than the theatre of Marcellus. The small theatres in palaces for royal or noble entertainment came into being during the seventeenth and first half of the eighteenth century. The most notable however, was the famous *Teatro Olimpico* at Vicenza designed by Andrea Palladio in 1565, with the famous architectural perspective of streets converging. This, and the handsome *Teatro Farnese* at Parma built in 1618-19, represent the most outstanding Renaissance theatres.

It is time now to turn from the minor literary figures who laid the foundation for literary Italian drama to its five major exponents. The first of these was Bernardo Dovizio (1470-1520) called BIBBIENA from the little town of Bibbiena near Arezzo, where he was born. He was destined for the church in which career he had some success. He allied himself with Cardinal Giovanni de' Medici, a highly politic move and one which proved of much value to him. His churchly posts are not our concern however except for the fact that his elevation to the cardinalate in 1513 terminated his dramatic career.

Sometime between 1504 and 1513 his chief work *Calandria* was played at Urbino (in 1508 according to John Addington Symonds, whose account of the Italian Renaissance combines the rare qualities of scholarship with literary brilliance). Plautus' *Menaechmi* so influenced Dovizio that his piece reads not unlike a free adaptation from the Latin. The remarkable physical resemblance between brother and sister and their masquerading in male and female costume, recalling the devices of *Twelfth Night,* was important to the plot. The wittiness of the *novella* was apparent in the writing. By special command of Pope Pius X it was again performed in 1514 in the private theatre of the Vatican in honor of Isabella of Mantua. The Pope genuinely loved the theatre and attended all the performances he could even though it shocked some of the ambassadors to his court.

LUDOVICO ARIOSTO (1474-1533) was a native of Ferrara where his family was old and respected. The greater part of his life was spent in writing for the theatre, and he was an actor, director and manager as well. His ability in all fields made him a Renaissance counterpart of Boucicault, Belasco or George Abbott. He translated Latin comedies to be staged but unfortunately none of them survive. It was not until 1508 that his own play *Cassaria* was performed in Ferrara. There was no great variety in his plots; a sum of money was always urgently needed for the hero which in the end was always secured by the wiliness of his servant. There were invariably pairs of young men, pairs of girls, pairs of valets, a convention which was similar to that of the then developing *commedia dell'arte.* The renowned obscenity of his prologues was not matched by any like qualities in the texts. There, there was a genial and innocent satire in the well-constructed plots which still attracts readers. At the same time it details the point of view of the so-called "reform element" in Ferrara. The next year came *I Suppositi* which won so much acclaim that it was repeated in Rome in 1509 for the benefit of Leo X's court. At the personal behest of the Pope for a new play, Ariosto finished his *Negromante*, which he had been working on for ten years. *Léna* was produced in 1528. In 1532 he drew the plans for and advised in the building of a permanent theatre in his native Ferrara which burned down on New Year's Eve of the same year. His last play, *Scolastica*, which was unfinished at his death was subsequently finished by his brother Gabrielle. Thus he was working right up to the end.

NICCOLÓ MACHIAVELLI (1469-1527) was born in the brilliant Firenze of the Renaissance. His fame as a wily diplomat and treacherous statesman has been emphasized out of all relation both to his own importance and to his wickedness; in his evil he was no better and no worse than others of his time. We are concerned with his plays and his life only in so far as it is reflected in his writings. The work for which he is best remembered, of course, is *Il Principe* which outlined a plan for a new state and was published in 1532. From our point of view his most important work is his play *La Mandragola*, printed in Rome in 1524. Although offensive in its obscenity, it is a careful documentary play of the customs, morals and standards of thinking in Machiavelli's own time. It analyses stupidity, vileness, folly from the point of view of one who was not shocked by the natural tenor of his surroundings, but who complacently accepted them. The result was not an outcry against the existence of such corruption but was instead an amused and understanding chronicling of the lives of the people and their neighbors.

His other plays include the doubtful *Commedia in Versi* which could have been but a crude outpouring of his youth. Some have attacked his authorship of *Commedia in Prosa* but the mark of his thinking is upon it. It concerns itself with a plot which he later-used in *La Clizia* and *La Mandragola*. The servant Margherita and the friar Fra Alberigo, who are instruments of immorality, are matched by the calculations of the heroine Caterina, and the senile amours of her old husband Amerigo. It is a comedy of corruption and succeeds all too well. *La Clizia* is a brilliant study of Italian family life with well-thought out and expertly created characters. The whole structure is somewhat weakened by the arbitrary and conventional happy ending which provides a wealthy, long-lost father for the heroine; the hero, who has been entirely practical about the matter, as befitted a gallant of his day, is then able to marry her.

PIETRO ARETINO (1492-1556) was born in Arezzo. Perhaps he took advantage of the very defects in his education to declare war on the artificial conventions of Latin comedy that scholars had created out of the whole cloth. One such convention was that a character might not appear in a play more than five times. He desired, as did Machiavelli, that all his writing should reflect the characters of the people about him, but at the same time they should come and go naturally. He was neither a profound thinker nor a genius. Although his characters are shallow they are vivid and lively but are hampered by his loose play-structure. Having been a servant himself he was privy to the backstairs gossip of the Italian courts and his plays reveal this in salacious strokes. They are dramatic memoirs of the brothels and criminal hang-outs of Rome. His comedies include *La Cortigiana*, which indignantly reveals the reality of life at court; genially indecent *Il Marescalo; Talanta*, which deals with the tenuous devices in the life of a courtesan; and finally *L' Ipocrita* and *Il Filosofo* which are scarcely as successful in the writing—the strokes are too broad, the insight too shallow.

We cannot close any consideration of the literary drama of the fifteenth and sixteenth centuries in Italy without some mention of the celebrated and mad poet, Torquato Tasso (1544-1595) who was born in the South Italian town of Sorrento. It was necessary to place him under restraint in 1576 but by then the two works for which he is still known had been produced. The first of these was *Aminta* played in 1573 at a pleasure resort of the Este family on an island in the River Po at Ferrara. Its idyllic quality set the style for the pastoral comedy which flowered in Shakespeare's *As You Like It* and in the paintings of Boucher and Watteau two centuries later. The shepherd Aminta loves the chaste maiden, Sylvia, who is sternly attached to the worship of Diana. Not even when he rescued her from assault by a lecherous satyr did she relent. Finally in desperation he endeavors to kill himself. This awakens in the maiden the realization that she has come to care for him, and so love conquers all. The gracefulness of the theme and the artistry of its writing fascinated all who saw it or read any of its two hundred printings. This, with his great literary epic *Gerusalemme Liberata*, written between 1563 and 1575, will always recall the name of Tasso to the literary mind of the subsequent period in the history of the world. May his troubled soul rest in peace.

VI

ITALIAN IMPROVISED COMEDY

AT A time when the current outpouring of literary drama was of no lasting importance and the stuffy revivals of the Latin of Seneca and Terence were amusing no one but the pedants, there began to spring up a great popular comedy. There are those who say that this comedy had a direct unbroken descent from the Doric mimes of the ancient Greeks and there are many valid arguments for this viewpoint. Certainly the similarity of the masks, stock characters and plots is more than mere coincidence. The popular view in the eighteenth century was that the *commedia dell' arte* was a continuation of the *fabulae Atellanae* of the Oscans and the Romans. The distinguished student of the mime, Hermann Reich, contends that this theory is wrong and that the *commedia* descended from the Byzantine mimes of the Eastern Roman Empire who were driven out by the capture of Constantinople in 1453. Certain other authorities state that all of these comic actors had perished and that the *commedia* is but an imitation of the Greek and Roman mime and was inspired by the revival of culture and learning. Whichever side we espouse the continuity of the theatre, whether actual or spiritual, is plain.

The exact date when this unwritten comedy was first played is unknown. Its beginnings were early in the sixteenth century and by 1550-1575 it was flourishing. Troupes of players had been established and its popularity extended from the public squares of Florence, Bologna and Venice to the courts of princes of state and church in all of civilized Europe. Its name has varied and it is properly called *commedia improvvisa* (improved comedy), *commedia a soggetto* (subject comedy), *commedia non scritta* (unwritten comedy), *commedia a maschera* (masked comedy) or *commedia dell' arte all' improvviso*, which means professional improvised comedy. Whether *arte* is used to denote a craft, a guild, or the perfection of professional playing, the meaning is clear.

It might be well to define what we mean by "unwritten comedy". The actual speeches were not written down but the plot, locale, and names of the characters were. Naturally plays of this kind depended on the brilliance, the wit and knowledge of the actors. Their memories must have been prodigious because there were set speeches that might be drawn on to fit any occasion. Tags and good entrance and exit lines were as essential to win applause and esteem, as was a real sense of the stage. No matter how good an actor might be in a scene there was always the danger of a weak partner who was too slow on cues and unable to sustain the repartee. Or even worse, an over-eager actor might cut into the best speeches too soon. It promoted a naturalness in acting that is sometimes mistakenly claimed for the cinema but it placed a burden on the actor that but few could successfully sustain. That of course accounts for the unevenness of performances and the long delays in assembling a new troupe for a foreign tour if any of the better players were unwilling to venture to Paris, Barcelona, Munich or London. There are records of a long correspondence between Marie de' Medici in Paris and the Duke of Mantua concerning his effort in 1616-17 to arrange a return visit of the Accesi troupe. The famous Martinelli had declined to leave Italy and so it was a difficult task for the Duke to assemble a properly balanced company.

When a performance was to be given, a *scenario* (the before-mentioned plot) was read to the company by the manager, who was usually the author and leading actor. He was variously called *il guido maestro, il concertatore*, or more commonly *il corago*. He explained to them the progress of the plot, and location of the houses so that no actor might make any untoward mistakes in performance, the names of the characters so no lover might miscall his inamorata in the midst of an impassioned love scene. He arranged for the entrances and exits and timed the actors for their soliloquies or pantomimic action. He also assigned the *lazzi* (from the Lombard mispronunciation of the Tuscan *lacci*, meaning ribbon), which tie up the disconnected parts of the action and give sequence to the plot. These *lazzi* can take many forms: acrobatic, musical or humorous. It is not intended to infer that they relate to the main plot (they may have a plot of their own) but they do connect the disjointed sections of the play. Some of the actors were great gymnasts as was the famous *Scaramouche* (Tiberio Fiorilli) who when he was nearly eighty-three could box another actor's ear with his foot. Somersaults were popular. The famous comedian, Tommaso Antonio Visentini, in the eighteenth century could somersault without spilling a glass of wine in his hand. Such feats secured the enthusiastic approbation of the audience.

The *scenari* were occasionally serious, sometimes pastoral but mainly comic. A secret marriage between two lovers, their persecution and eventual escape is told in *L'Alvida*, which may be found in the theatre collection of La Scala in Milan. Even in these tragic pieces strange or comic characters were introduced. There were no complete tragedies in this form. The pastoral type recalls *The Tempest* and probably was not too far removed in subject matter if not in form.

The overwhelming majority were comic. Of these the dusty remains of a few *scenari* survive but the bare bones give us no idea of the plays because few if any speeches were written down in the early period. In the eighteenth century when the *comédies mixtes* were played, a large portion of the play included set speeches and so had more literary value, at least those that are left to us have. The two principal concerns were love and amusing intrigue. The lovers were always balanced by the cranky old father or fathers, the comic or covetous servants. The old men were frequently cuckolded and occasionally were farcical lovers themselves. Mistaken identity, girls masquerading as men or vice versa, were favorite themes.

Each actor, according to his type, had a *repertorio*, or stock of lines for all occasions; endearments for love scenes and curses for quarrels, clever lines to titillate the ears of the courtly spectators. There was a tremendous variety in the names of the characters but certain main types stood out, though their number varied.

Perhaps we might begin with the least important characters, the "straight parts." There were usually two *innamorati* with the complementary *innamorate*, though occasionally there were three and sometimes only one pair of lovers. The men had many names, some of which were Ottavio, Florindo, Flavio, Polidorio, Virginio. The lover was usually handicapped by parental interference or occasionally by the rivalry of his own father for the hand of the lady, or was sometimes the lover of an old man's wife. The actor who played these young parts had to be as well read as the gentleman of the period; he had to have a good manner and an elegant Tuscan pronunciation of Italian (which might be said to parallel the Oxford accent of English in theatrical esteem); he had to be handsomely dressed and have had with him a tiny copy of Petrarch in his hand, a necessity for all lovers of that period

Balancing the handsome, highly perfumed gallants were the lovely *innamorate* who bore frequently such names as Felice, Adriana, Eularia, Isabella, Silvia, Valeria, Laura among others. Richly dressed they had to have a modest demeanor and were not required to be as erudite as the *innamorati*. These lovely ladies were usually the daughters of the two old men, but occasionally an orphan girl or a dashing young widow was substituted for variety. They must have had to strive for different effects and connotations as do the singers of double entendre songs in the night clubs of today because similarity of subject matter is likely to bore the audience unless a constant search for novelty is maintained.

To follow the general outline of the distinguished Allardyce Nicoll in his authoritative *Masks, Mimes and Miracles* in describing the stock characters of Italian comedy seems best, as he is the clearest of all modern authorities on this subject. The serving-maid, or *fontesca*, was a semi-serious character who was the invariable companion of the beautiful maiden. Her most famous name was Colombina but she was also known as Pasquella, Ricciolina, Argentina, Corallina, Franchasquina as well as by others. In her earlier days she was occasionally coarse but she was always witty and full of brightness. Sometimes she was a *soubrette* and the feminine counterpart of Arlechino.

Undoubtedly descended from the Roman *Miles gloriosus* was the *Capitano* who was inevitably Spanish because Spain was the military boss of Italy. Boastful and cowardly with a grotesquely long nose and enormous black moustaches on his mask, the captain was a huge success. Despite this caricaturing of their soldiers, there is good evidence that the character amused the Spanish when the acting troupes invaded the Iberian peninsula. His speech was full of violent extravagance and his bragging was insufferable but it evidently had enough basis in reality to convulse his auditors with laughter. Politically and militarily subservient to the proud Castilians, the gay Italians could still laugh at the pomposities of their conquerors.

It might be well to make it clear once and for all that all of the actors except the lovers and the serving-maid wore masks. These were close fitting and permitted some facial expression by contortion, but they were never removed. The masks and stock costumes were the official designation of the character. They might vary slightly, but their general outlines had to be retained.

Next come the old men, the Venetian *Pantalone* and the Bolognese *Dottore*. The former is invariably the old father or the cuckolded husband, the greedy, talkative, avaricious old man of various plots. He wore a red vest, breeches and full hose with Turkish slippers (natural to his Venetian origin), a black coat with flowing sleeves, almost touching the ground which permitted the gestures a voluble actor loves. His soft cap, rising from the brown mask with the prominent hooked nose and long grey beard, suggests the fez of Asia Minor. His dialect was Venetian but was as full of aphorisms as Shakespeare's Danish Polonius. His appearance was that of a dignified and distinguished citizen (though phallephoric, an inheritance from the mime), who all too often cast aside his gravity when angry, as in scenes with his servants.

The character of *Dottore* was complementary to *Pantalone* but was sometimes dispensed with to provide a place for the popular character, *Coviello*. The characteristics of the doctor remained whether his specific part was retained or not. In the beginning his doctorate was of law, as was appropriate for a native of Bologna, medicine not being ascribed to him until late in the sixteen hundreds. He was never so wealthy as his friend and was usually the father of the lover, though he might be the deceived husband or the learned minister of a monarch. He was boastful of his learning, his speeches being interlarded with Latin phrases, a trait which the other characters frequently ridiculed. His hypocrisy and pedantry were definitely comic in quality as they rolled forth in dignified Bolognese accent. He frequently aspired to seem younger than his years entitled him, despite the soberness of his doctor's cap and gown, black relieved by white collar and cuffs. Often a large white handkerchief protruded from his pocket.

There were occasionally other old men, many of them of Neapolitan origin. Pasquariello, Cola, Cassandro, and Ciccombimbo were their names. Their features may be seen in many prints of the period, sometimes as rich citizens, sometimes even as servants with some of the qualities of the *zanne*.

These *zanne* were the servants who provided much of the comedy in these pieces where a command of "ad libbing" was paramount, a habit that famous actors running from Roscius to Barrymore have found profitable. These farcical servitors could be counted on to make use of incidents occurring in the audience to brighten their improvisations with a technique that variety, vaudeville and night club entertainment has borrowed for the past century. It is in these fields that the modern audience can find something that brings home the variety, timeliness and personality of Italian comedy.

There were a number of these servants who began perhaps as a *zanni* and expanded to include some of the names we best remember, Arlecchino, Scaramuccia, Mezzetino. Authorities differ aciduously on point of origin but a good case can be made out for the derivation of *zanni* from the Roman *sannio*, who was, one of the stock characters of Latin farce, the fool in the mimes. One of the earliest extant authorities on the *commedia dell' arte*, Andrea Perrucci, in 1699 divides the *zanne* as to type. He says that the first had to be quick in mind and body, sharp and clever, and have an off-color connotation which would make the audience laugh. The second, for contrast, was the dolt, stupid and dull, who was like William in *As You Like It* and other Elizabethan comic characters.

It would be simple if we could assign Arlecchino to the first and Brighella to the second as Lucien Duchartre does in his admirable treatments of the subject. While this is frequently true other combinations of characters and names appear, especially as the *commedia* expanded and developed throughout the seventeenth and early eighteenth centuries. Duchartre is quite right in granting Arlecchino (our Harlequin) first place in so far as popularity and use are concerned. Histories of his development and derivation have been written and the future may see them continued as new scholars advance new theories based either on as yet unmade discoveries or an unadvanced postulates. You have only to read a few to understand the fascination his character offers to the professional student of the theatre. It is not the place here for us to go into a long disquisition on the subject. Suffice it to say that this gaily dressed character who, decorating his costume with a small hat, shoes without heels, and a black mask from which his eyes peered through slits, is a perennial favorite.

He was particularly adept in his performance of *lazzi* and was always an acrobat of real ability so that his tumbling, falls, and dancing carried a spirit of brightness and gaiety. His wit was variable; with the extinction of it he could and did become the dull second servant. Restore it and he was back as usual in the clever role of valet, the sly one whose cynical advice to his master was likely to advance the material cause of the *innamorato*. Other relatives of Arlecchino such as Truffaldino, Tracagnino, Trivellino exist but their tendency is always to disappear so that it is the most distinguished representative of their family that we remember.

The *Brighella* type of *zanni* seems to date from the seventeenth century though an earlier place for him is claimed. He had many counterparts which varied considerably and should not be taken to be his equivalent. Licentious, witty, cruel, the born cynic, he was most popular in the eighteenth century, but his life extended into the harlequinades of the first half of the nineteenth century when the formerly unwritten comedy had become largely literary. *Scapino*, from whom some think *Brighella* descended, is of earlier origin, and while not so bold he has most of the characteristics of the more distinguished character. *Mezzetino* and *Mescolino* were one and the same and came into being in the seventeenth century through a mixture of the witty and stupid traits of the earlier two servants. *Scara-muccia*, or to employ his more familiar name (to us) *Scaramouche*, was one of the *zanne* though certain characteristics made the famous theatre historian, Riccoboni, ally him to the *capitano*. In France he became one of the most popular characters in the whole range of comedy.

Pulcinella was a wooden type of servant whose stupidity quickly endeared him to his audience and whose popularity in puppets and marionettes extends to the Punch of this very day. His large crooked nose and high peaked cap continue to characterize him. He is closely allied through a fairly sound genealogy to the Roman mime. *Pedrolino* who has become through a change of habits and background our *Pierrot*, is the last of the important *zanne* though it would be easily possible to list the merry names of the others almost indefinitely. Another variation is *Pagliacci* whom Leoncavallo's short opera and Caruso's magnificent singing has made a household word throughout the modern world. All of these servants, no matter what their names, brightened the hearts and loosened the laughter of audiences in the palaces, streets and theatres of Europe for three hundred years.

What interests us now is the formation of those troupes who brought so much gaiety with them and whose success made foreigners jealous of the Italian actors. The earliest known contract seems to have been dated in France in 1530, thus showing that the companies passed over the Alps to the further portions of the continent at an early period. Among the most famous of the players was Angelo Beolco, known as Il Ruzzante. The troupe whose personnel is first known to us is that of Maffeo's troupe which in 1545 included Maffeo dei Re of Padua, Thofano de Bastian, Zuane of Treviso, Bragato of St. Luca and others. By 1551 there was a rival company in Rome headed by one Marcantonio. In 1564 in the same city a contract for a new company names him Marco Antonio de Gabiati. In 1567 the appellation of Venetian was added—was he perhaps of a Venetian company?

We have to work so much with isolated court contracts and receipts of payment to actors, written by people ignorant or careless of names, that those names vary in such a way as to leave us in the dark concerning the activities of individual actors and of whole troupes. Soldino of Florence and Anton Maria of Venice may have headed separate companies or even have been part of the same troupe. Alberto Ganassa managed a famous company though his early years are unknown; his name first appears in Mantua in 1568. With him was the celebrated Vicenza Armani, who soon was stabbed to death in Cremona. To them in 1570 were added a *Flaminia* and a *Pantalone* of a rival troupe. This union brought about the famous Gelosi, the best known of all the comedians. From 1571 to 1573 they acted in Lyons and in Paris where they finally split up. The main section went to Ferrara and Venice while Ganassa went to London where he acted in 1574. In 1575 he joined up with the rest of the troupe in Madrid. He played mostly in Spain until he was imprisoned in 1582; all evidence of his career is lost after December 1583.

The main group of Gelosi played in Italy and attracted so much attention that Henri III of France and Poland expressed a desire to see a performance in Venice. They were acting in Milan but made haste to go to the celebrated seaport to play for the king. They made so great an impression on him that two years later he invited them to his place at Blois. This was indeed an honor as they were playing their regular circuit through the North Italian cities, always contriving to leave before their welcome was worn out. Thus the audience bade them farewell regretfully and welcomed them joyfully upon their return. This trip to France had to be carefully planned as travelling from country to country was hazardous in those days. They left early in December 1576 but fell into the hands of the politically hostile Huguenots, who demanded a ransom from the king for their release. This Henri was willing to pay and on the 25th of January, 1577, they arrived at Blois to the evident pleasure of the monarch and his court who loved any real excuse for gaiety. There they remained until late in the spring. After having made satisfactory arrangements with the *Confrérie de la Passion*, who had the monopoly rights on acting in Paris, they moved on to the capital where they opened May 19th at the *Hôtel de Bourbon*.

In the company was undoubtedly the celebrated Isabella Andreini (1562-1604) born in Padua, whose death in Lyons caused the mourning of audiences in all the countries in which she had ever played. Famous for her beauty and acting ability she was no less acclaimed for her virtue. Poets praised her in their verses. The great Tasso composed a sonnet in her honor, while Gherardo Borgogni and Isaac des Ryer were eulogistic in their rhapsodic praise. A painting of her hangs in the *Musée Carnavalet* in Paris. This learned lady was the wife of the fine musician and actor, Francesco Andreini. Their son Giovanni Battista was also an excellent actor, a writer of pornographic plays and author of a collection of sonnets celebrating actors who had become martyrs for their religious faith.

It would prove extremely interesting for us to give in full detail the history of this troupe and all of those wandering Italian actors who brought so much joy with their gay comedies at a time when the mind was beginning to recover from the stupefaction of the

Middle Ages. That is manifestly impossible so that the best we can do is to describe briefly some of the more celebrated troupes who played despite opposition of church and state authorities. It is quite true that the *commedia* was often obscene, usually in words or gestures. They were accused of displaying a naked man fleeing from a fire and a woman stripped, or nearly so, by robbers and left tied to a tree by the most diaphanous of bonds which left none of her charms invisible to the audience. Even the Gelosi themselves, in a piece called *Le Burle d'Isabella* had the lovers appear in most inadequate attire and enjoy a remarkably free kind of lovemaking.

The Church was frequently quite severe in punishments meted out to the poor actors despite the fact that many of the cardinals admired them and viewed their playing with equanimity, yes, even pleasure. When they were allowed to play a strict watch was kept upon them to make certain that they went to confession three times a year and were avid in the performance of their religious duties. St. Charles Borromeo, one of the great saints of the church, had a strong predilection for the *commedia*, and actors were always welcome in Milan during his archbishopric. However he practised censorship of the scripts but seems to have been a benevolent despot in the exercise of his churchly prerogative. In many cities no such latitude was allowed and the poor actors were liable to be thrown into prison, or even condemned to death if their productions offended the church authorities. At the very least, the nearness of hell-fire was preached to those of the theatrical profession. Despite all this, the *commedia* survived, doubtless because it answered a gay need in a constantly beset world.

Certainly these interferences by church and state kept the actors moving. This was perhaps a good thing for them because their audiences never tired of them. If outside interference didn't come, the actors themselves pushed on to the next city where a fair, a carnival, or perhaps a court wedding was to take place.

But to return to the make-up of these troupes which alternately delighted and scandalized, the one most closely allied to the Gelosi was the Uniti. Some deny that there ever was such a company and that the name came from the union of some of the Gelosi with actors from the Confidenti. Certainly with the dissolution of the Gelosi upon the death of Isabella Andreini in 1604, and the retirement of her husband Giovanni, the Uniti also disappeared from history. The Confidenti were frequently related to the Andreini troupe from their formation in the 1570's. After 1604 probably many from that company joined up with their friendly rivals. All was far from friendly in their own ranks because of a quarrel between their two leading ladies who were at the proverbial dagger's point. This is related to us in their letters which were written in the haste of anger and malice. It was settled by the departure of one of them a few years before the troupe's disbanding in 1621. Other important groups are the Accesi, the Desiosi and the Fedeli but space does not permit a study of the make-up of the entourage of these actors who lived as vividly off stage as they did on.

In Italy, the Duke of Mantua was the ruler most likely to patronize the players but as previous statements prove the *commedia dell' arte* was every whit as popular outside Italy as it was in its native land. The Court of France was particularly partial to their art, probably because of the royal alliances with the Medici family. Parliament was usually hostile but that was merely part of its plan to embarrass the royal family if possible. Certainly its anti-foreign strictures were primarily aimed at the Italians as the English, Greek and Spanish actors were permitted to play without interference; perhaps it was a facet of France's foreign policy. In addition to the sniping of the country's legislative body and the active interference of the Huguenots whenever possible, there was the opposition of the professional French actors who resented the favors heaped upon alien comedians by the court. The Italian companies were forced to charge a lower rate of admission than their heavy expenses for scenery, costume, and traveling would permit. Despite this they were even officially charged with gouging the public and so were driven out of the country. Even the efforts of the king could not prevent their banishment.

All of the previously mentioned principal companies played in France during the last thirty years of the sixteenth and first quarter of the seventeenth century. Charles IX and his sombre mother, Catherine de Medici, invited Ganassa to make his first appearance at a time when they were plotting the Massacre of St. Bartholomew. They felt that the antics of the actors would be an excellent blind for their machinations. Charles' brother, Henri III, was fond of private theatricals and masquerades so naturally he recalled the comic Italians. Henri IV, who was all things to all men, finding his people enjoyed the *commedia dell' arte*, encouraged performances in Paris. His son Louis XIII who married Marie of the Medicis, naturally consoled his wife with her favorite actors.

William Kemp, favorite comic actor of England, made several tours of the continent and is believed to have seen and admired the famous Italian Tristano Martinelli of the Accesi company in Rome in 1600. Foreign companies penetrated to Bavaria, Spain, Austria and London where they had considerable success. By the middle of the

40. SMALL ROMAN THEATRE AT TAORMINA.

Courtesy of Julia Gardner

41. DETAIL OF POMPEIAN WALL-PAINTING OF A ROMAN STAGE.

Yale-Rockefeller Theatre Colle...

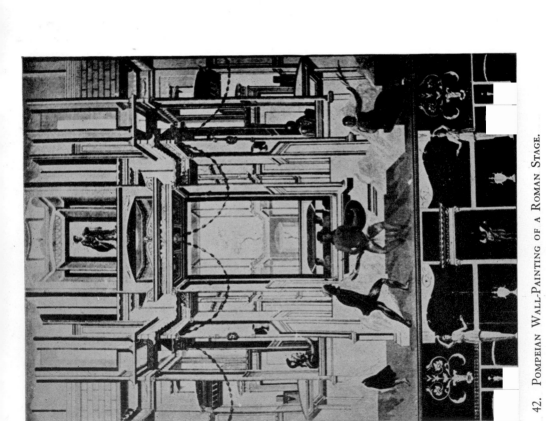

43. ACTORS IN ATELLAN FARCES.

In Camei

42. POMPEIAN WALL-PAINTING OF A ROMAN STAGE.

Yale-Rockefeller Theatre Collection

44. ROMAN COMEDY ON THE MEDIAEVAL STAGE.

Yale-Rockefeller Theatre Collection

45. ROMAN THEATRE AT POMPEII. *Streit, "Das Theater"*

46. "Christ's Descent Into Hell" By a Follower of Hieronymus Bosch. *Metropolitan Museum*
Note similarity to the hell-mouth of the mystery plays.

47, 48. Mediaeval Devil Costumes.
Hermann, "Forschungen Zur
Deutschen Theater Geschichte."

49. Hrosvitha, (c. 932–c. 1000).
Dubeche, "Histoire Illustré du Théatre"

51. MEDIAEVAL "MARY PLAY", POPULAR IN FRANCE.

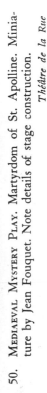

50. MEDIAEVAL MYSTERY PLAY. Martyrdom of St. Apolline. Miniature by Jean Fouquet. Note details of stage construction.

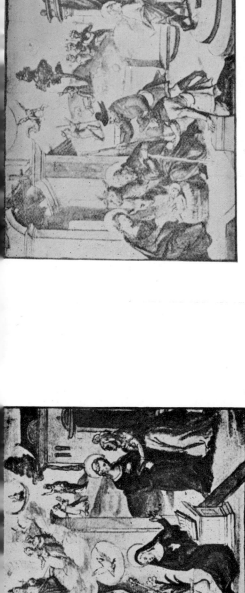

52. The Annunciation.

53. The Conception of the Virgin.

54. Circumcision, and the Adoration.

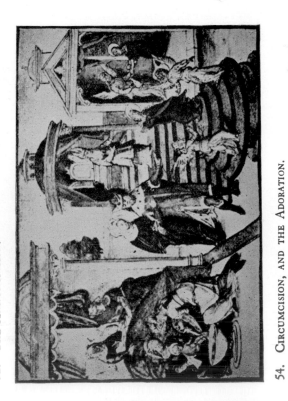

55. Massacre of the Innocents.

56, 57, 58. ART IMITATES LIFE IN THESE SCENES RESEMBLING MYSTERY PLAYS.

59. PAINTING BY JÉRÔME BOSCH OF A MEDIAEVAL JONGLEUR. Note the similarity to a modern carnival pitchman.

60. FRENCH OPEN-AIR STAGE, 1542.   *Théâtre de la Rue*

61, 62, 63, 64. RENAISSANCE PERFORMANCES OF TERENCE.

Streit, "Das Theater"

67. Torquato Tasso.

65. Swan With Knight Astride, Francesco Primaticcio.
(1504-1570). *Yale-Rockefeller Theatre Collection*

66. Allegorical Personage For Court Pageant, Francesco
Primaticcio. *National Museum, Stockholm*

68, 69. THE *Teatro Olimpico* AT VICENZA, 1584. Designed by Scamozzi.

70. SCENE IN *Teatro Olimpico*, 1584. SCAMOZZI.

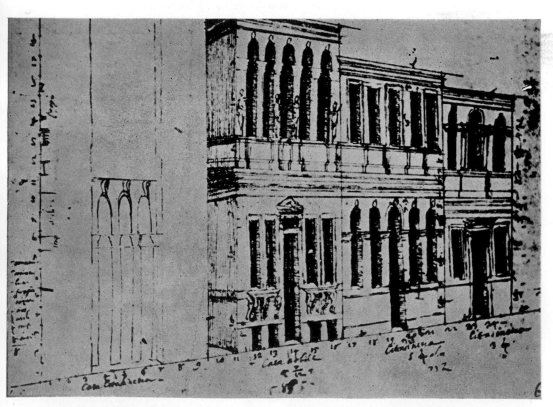

71. STREET SCENE, BY SCAMOZZI. 1584.

72, 73. BERNARDO BUONTALENTI, DESIGNS FOR MARRIAGE FESTIVITIES OF FERDINAND DE MEDICI,
1589.
Yale-Rockefeller Theatre Collection

74. BERNARDO BUONTALENTI. Music of the Spheres.

75. BERNARDO BUONTALENTI. Design for the City of Dis.

76. BARTOLOMEO NERONA. Design for *L'Ortensio*, 1560.

77. ATRIO DEL PALAZZO D'ALESSANDRO, 17TH CENTURY.

78. THE SETTING FOR TRAGEDY, BY SERLIO.

79. THE SETTING FOR COMEDY, BY SERLIO.

Sebastiano Serlio. "De Architectura"

eighteenth century improvised comedy had penetrated to all the courts of Europe.

Aside from freeing the theatre from the absurd artificiality of the beginning Italian literary drama, one of the most important achievements of the *commedia dell' arte* was the introduction of women onto the stage on equal (frequently even more favorable) terms with men. Occasionally they appeared as themselves in the Middle Ages but the widespread use of them in female parts sprang out of Italian comedy. In France men appeared in old women's parts as late as Molière; in England it was not until the Restoration in 1660 that women were established as playing themselves.

These wandering companies of actors who influenced the whole theatre world frequently only contained ten members, though twelve seems to have been the average. With carts of scenery, a portable stage for the countryside or small town, many changes of costume, the inevitable masks which were an essential of each character, the musical instruments with which they made merry, these indomitable players brought the wit and comic genius of Italy to the whole of Europe.

VII

PROUD, IGNORANT SPAIN AND DEPENDENT,

NEIGHBORING PORTUGAL

THE influences from the East that swept over Italy in the middle of the fifteenth century slowly penetrated into the cruel land that held her captive. The rapacious rulers of the Italian states stemmed largely from highborn Spanish families whose tastes in the theatre were cultivated in Milan, Parma, or Mantua. They carried ideas back to Spain which brought about a cultural awakening in their native land. It is not intended that the inference be created that the Spanish theatre was not a national one, because it was. In fact it can be said to be the first theatre to attain true nationality in the European Renaissance. Italy had not achieved political unity but Spain and her drama was a flowering of this natural national pride. We know that the theatre in Spain was smothered by the anti-literary Saracens and that the energies of the Castilians had been expended in the reconquest of their country. The medieval period brought into being an active theatre under the aegis of the Church. These religious *autos* continued to be performed until the middle of the eighteenth century. The extravagances and secular excesses in connection with the parades preceding them caused the civil authorities to ban them.

When we discussed the church theatre of the Middle Ages we said that there was almost no physical evidence of its existence in Spain because practically all of the plays that still exist date from the fifteenth and sixteenth centuries. This was due in part to a resumption of control over production by the Church and a natural return to pietism by the most secular dramatists who were exhausted by the depravity and loose thinking of the age in which they lived.

What held true for Spain was an axiom for Portugal as well. The beginnings of the Portuguese drama developed independently of the Spanish but along similar lines. The real domination of their theatre by the Castilians did not come until the smaller nation of the Iberian peninsula had produced a dramatist or two of sufficient influence and importance to be claimed in part by arrogant Spain. Methods of production were similar in the two countries so that only Portuguese *deviations* from this norm will be mentioned.

Theatre has a way of stemming from the dramatists, named or un-named, so that perhaps it is always best to begin with them. This was true in Spain where the author became the *autor* or leader of the traveling company and frequently the principal actor as well. This was a totally unconscious return to the Greek ideal which was very imperfectly understood at the time. The ecclesiastical drama has been mentioned in an earlier chapter but it will be necessary to return to it from time to time in our treatment of individual dramatists. Now we will turn our attention to the secular writers and the development of the professional theatre because the sixteenth century had an im-pressive array of actors who were paid for their services.

RODRIGO COTA, the elder, of Toledo is credited with having written a few simple *eclogues* such as *The Couplets of Mingo Revulgo* and *A Dialogue Between Love and an Old Man* between 1472 and 1480, but his principal claim to fame comes from his reputed (and probably actual) writing of the first of the famous and notorious *Celestina*, in 1480. This piece of dramatic writing acquired twenty more acts at the hand of Fernando de Rojas of Montalbán but was probably never staged. A portion of it was incorporated in Cepeda's *Comedia Selvage* in 1582, and Alfonso Vaz de Velasco produced his *Jealous Man* in 1602 which was founded on *Celestina* though the characters were re-named. It was so bold and frequently so obscene that it was used as a moral warning to the young. It went through at least thirty editions and was widely read by the small educated circle that existed in the years following its publication in 1499. Its translation into Latin made it available to scholars everywhere. It was also turned into English, German, Dutch, Italian and French. It is really a dramatized romance of strong theatrical feeling, with an easy and sometimes brilliant style which was the highwater point of the period; nor has it often been equalled.

The first dramatist who wrote directly for the secular theatre was the variously spelled JUAN DE LA ENZINA (1468-1534). He wrote under the patronage of the first Duke and Duchess of Alva to whom he dedicated the first edition of his work in 1496. King Ferdinand, Queen Isabella, Prince John and the Duke's son, Don Garcia de Toledo were also his sponsors. He called his plays, really eclogues, *representaciones*, some of which were in a sense merely adaptations of Virgil's *eclogues* turned into the history of the ruling family of

Spain and the ducal house of Alva. Six of his so-called plays were intended to be represented during the Church festivals of Easter and Christmas, or during Lent. Five of them record the life of his own times in Salamanca, particularly the one treating with the eternal quarrel between Town and Gown which he might have observed in this university seat. The plays were largely lacking in plot and had casts varying from two to six but they were written to be acted and were. These were concerned with Portugal as well as Spain. His style was imitated by Gil Vicente the Portuguese, whose writings the Spaniards also claim.

Before Gil Vicente wrote, however, there was FRANCISCO SÁ DE MIRANDA (1495-1558), who has been called the Portuguese Horace. Spanish drama was still struggling with form so that it was to the Italians, Bibbiena and Ariosto, to whom he turned for guidance. This automatically gives us Plautus and Terence at third hand; their importance only becomes apparent to us as we see how much influence, good and bad, they had on the fifteenth-seventeenth centuries in Europe. Just as Pope Leo X had encouraged performances in the Vatican, the Infante, Cardinal Henry promoted them in Lisbon. But we have no assurance that the productions had any more influence on the average citizen than the Italian plays which preceded them. His plays, *Os Estrangeiros* and *Os Vilhalpandos* were loosely constructed but were occasionally spirited and satirical. Among other things they condemned the immoral life of the Roman clergy. This is evidence that the Portuguese Church looked with disfavor on certain aspects of its mother church, particularly so as this author was a deeply religious man.

GIL VICENTE, about whom wildest conjectures abound and bitter scholarly wars have raged, was Portuguese by birth and bi-lingual in his writings which seem to lie between 1502 and 1536. He has been called a peasant and a gentleman. He is said to have been a humble goldsmith and the intimate of Kings Manuel the Great and John III. That he wrote plays for production at their court is undoubtedly true. His earliest play was written on the occasion of John's birth; great charm lay in the account of a herdsman's simple wonder as he entered the palace with other shepherds to bear gifts to the royal infant. This so pleased Manuel's Castilian queen that she asked Vicente to provide a nativity play for Christmas. In many of his plays he combined the qualities of the mysteries with secular accounts of Spanish and Portuguese history. Most of his pieces were *autos*, and they became famous because of their lyric poetry, not because of their plots or dramatic structure. *O Viudo* acted at court in 1514,

Ribena in 1521, *Don Duardos* and *Templo d'Apollo* played in 1526 at the marriage of a Portuguese princess and Charles V, Emperor of the Holy Roman Empire, are his most famous dramas.

BARTOLOMÉ DE TORRES NAHARRO (1480-1530) came from the Portuguese border of Spain near Badajoz but sometime after 1513 went to the court of Pope Leo X where he wrote a play satirizing the vices of the court and was forced to flee to Naples where he lived until his death. His eight plays were written in verse and their subject matter was the life of the nobility, the clergy and their servants. When he kept to this theme, his plays had the ring of truth, but his conception of history was indeed vague. The *comedias* (a form he and Lope de Rueda are said to have invented) *Trofea*, *Hymenea* and *Serafina* are his best known pieces; they are fluent and have many passages of easy dialogue, but their language was often gross. Their outspoken attacks on the Church caused their ban by the Inquisition.

It was not until the arrival on the scene of LOPE DE RUEDA, who flourished from 1554 until his death in 1565, that a popular theatre vein may be said to have been tapped. His *comedias* were written in prose and his long experience as manager of a wandering troupe of thespians stood him in good stead in perfecting his dramatic structure. His company seems to have played in the principal towns and cities, for in 1554 he appeared before Philip II in an *auto* at Benavente; four years later he performed a comedy on the occasion of the dedication of the new cathedral at Segovia. His successes and his failures (he had to pawn a part of his theatrical costumes in Madrid in 1561) are noted in the various municipal records. That same year he acted *autos* in Toledo and was well rewarded by the queen for two performances of his comedies in October and November. He invented the *paso*, a short interlude involving a single dramatic situation, but it was his gay and natural dialogue coupled with his establishment of a highly regarded acting company that add special lustre to his name. He was a practical man of the theatre who fashioned his comedies and interludes out of the tastes of his audience and the known acting abilities of his company.

Though quoted frequently it may be just as well to summarize Cervantes' account of the costumes, scenery and properties of a traveling company in Lope de Rueda's time. The properties were carried in a sack and consisted of four white pellices trimmed with gilded leather, together with wigs, beards and staffs for four. No scenic machinery existed as the stage was formed by making a hollow square of benches with boards laid across. A large woolen blanket was hung at the back behind which the costumes were changed and the ballad-singers and musicians performed. Pedro Nabarro, who succeeded

Lope de Rueda, brought the musicians out onto the open stage, discarded the beards and introduced thunder, lightning, battles and other scenic devices. Under him the sacks were cast aside and trunks and chests took their place, though the costumes of the secular companies were still simple. It was only in the religious productions subsidized by the Church or in the Italian *commedia dell' arte* troupes that rich dresses and robes were worn.

While Lope de Rueda was establishing a professional theatre in Spain two Portuguese dramatists were upholding their nation's honor if not adding greatly to its glory. These were LUIZ DE CAMOËNS (or CAMÕES) (1524-1580) and ANTONIO FERREIRA (1528-1569), who wrote *Castro*, the first tragedy in Portuguese and the second in modern European literature. Camoëns seems to have written plays out of a sense of patriotism for the novel form was his natural *métier*. On the whole he preferred native subjects for his plots. Our primary interest in him is that he used Plautus as the source of one of his best known plays, *Os Amphytryões*, yet another telling of the Amphitryon legend. It was Ferreira's intention to found a lasting national drama and so he scorned all foreign tongues. His plays were written only in Portuguese and his lyric tragedy was based on that subject dear to the poets of his country, the celebrated Inez de Castro. With these men died the first and last attempt to establish an indigenous theatre in Portugal and since their day her poets and dramatists have been content to imitate the Spanish.

MIGUEL DE CERVANTES (1547-1616) the famous author of the immortal *Don Quixote* and the apt describer of the theatrical equipment of Lope de Rueda's professional company, was also a playwright. The fame of his satiric story has obscured his eminence in the theatre world for which he wrote a number of unimportant comedies and some well-known *autos*. The true poetry of *Numancia* inspired Shelley, an admirer of the Spanish theatre. At the end of the second act of his *El Rufián dichoso* we find the celebrated dialogue between Curiosity and Comedy: Curiosity asks Comedy why she does not respect the rules; Comedy replies that only in that way lies progress.

Against the unrelieved black background of the recently promulgated Holy Office of the Inquisition, one of the gayest, most dashing theatre men of all time was born. LOPE FELIX DE VEGA CARPIO (1562-1635) was the contemporary of Shakespeare in more ways than one. If ever there were a lively spirit in the theatre it was Lope's, with his innumerable love affairs, wives, mistresses and children, and a writing output that staggers the imagination. From whence had come such enormous energy? Each portion of his manner of living was full enough for most men, but he combined the vigor of a titan with the sparkling eye of a lover, the felicitous phrase of a courtier, the ease of expression of the born theatre man. When one thinks of the cruel, dark and ignorant tradition of Spain, it is even harder to understand how so buoyant and rich a personality came out of the sharp austerity of his surroundings. Frequently in hot water with the church and civil authorities, shocking in his treatment of some of the gallant ladies who loved him, understanding in his handling of his noble patrons, and resolved to be saved from hell fire he became a priest, backslid but climbed triumphantly on to the portal of heaven in the end. And who will say that St. Peter could resist his blandishments?

Born in Madrid in 1562, he was a brilliant student under the tutelage of the Jesuits. He translated Claudius at ten and wrote his first play, *El verdadero amante*, at twelve. From then on he never stopped writing until his score numbered the amazing figures of 1500 to 1800 dramas of all kinds. Of these 458 survive in text or manuscript and his distinguished biographer, Hugo Rennert, who has checked 673 titles is convinced that two-thirds of his plays have perished.

He fell in love with Elena Osorio, daughter of Jerónimo Velázquez, the *autor* or manager of a theatrical troupe. She was married to an actor but that did not interfere with her dalliance with Lope as he continued to contribute comedies to her father's repertoire. Quarreling with Velázquez and tiring of the whole family, he chose to ridicule them in writing, even the fair Elena herself. Resenting this, Jerónimo brought suit for libel against him in December 1587 and Lope was arrested in the *Corral de las Comedias* also known as the *Teatro de la Cruz*. Convicted, he was sentenced to exile from Madrid for ten years. In 1588 after he had married Isabel de Urbina, poor woman, he joined the expedition of the so-called Invincible Armada to conquer England for the glory of the Church and Spain. With the failure of that high enterprise he returned to his native land and settled in Valencia.

This was all happening in a period of real progress in our dramatic world. The *Corradía de la Sagrada Pasión*, in order that it might raise funds for the maintenance of its hospital, was granted the right to own a theatre in Madrid. This playhouse could be rented out to visiting troupes. So, in 1579, just three years after the elder Burbage had opened The Theatre on the South Bank of the Thames, the *Teatro de la Cruz* was inaugurated in the *Calle de la Cruz*, Madrid. This type of theatre, popularly called *corral* was not unlike the Elizabethan theatres. These *corrals* were little more than courtyards with a fixed stage at one end. Seats were placed on balconies or in the railed windows of the houses adjoining. If a householder declined to sell or rent to the hospital, he had to pay to watch the plays from his windows.

In front of the stage was a row of benches and a row of raised seats ran around the *corral*. The rest of the open space was used for standees. Opposite the stage was the *cazuela*, a gallery reserved for women who were frequently "not so good as they should have been" and who attracted as much attention from the hot-blooded men as did the actors who had to compete with them for the interest of the audience. The stage and sides of the courtyard were covered with a roof but only an awning shielded the "pit" from the glare of the Iberian sun, a device which recalls the Roman theatre.

In 1582 the *Teatro del Príncipe* was opened on the site of the *Corral de la Pacheca* which dated from 1568. Five years later native born actresses were licensed to make their first professional appearance on the Madrid stage, though they had been unofficially playing since Ganassa's tour in 1574. Actors were numerous in Spain and more than 2,000 names have been recorded. A profitable study could be made of their lives and contributions to the histrionic art. Some of them are particularly famous, especially the actresses who were associated with Lope de Vega in a professional or personal capacity. For Jusepa Vaca he wrote *Las almenas de toro* and called Micaela de Luxan Lucinda in his sonnets. He was very much in love with the latter who bore him four children. There was also the earlier mentioned Elena whom he celebrated as Filis. Roque de Figueroa, *autor* and friend of Lope's, managed a company and acted before the King, court and commoners from 1623 until his death in 1651. Nicolás de los Ríos was a famous manager and actor from 1570 until his death in 1610. He was so important that the French Ambassador recognized his influence and demanded he be silenced when a play offended him in 1601. The King soon missed the troupe and so restored Ríos to favor in September of the same year. Baltasar Pinedo (flourished 1596-1621) was a favorite of Tirso de Molina. As *autor* he produced *El Colmenero divino* and *Como han de ser los Amigos* in 1621. The Prada family was especially famous. Its founder, Antonio de Prada (1584?-1651), was greatly admired for his managerial and acting abilities by Calderón de la Barca.

In May 1598 (Isabel having died in 1595) Lope married Juana de Guardo. This marriage seems to have been a happy one and produced his only legitimate son, Carlos. Lopito, his son by Micaela, was a great favorite who followed in his father's tread as a writer. In 1605 Lope became the favorite of the twenty-six year old Duke of Sessa. He not only acted as his secretary, but also wrote his sonnets and advised him in his love affairs. And all this was in addition to his own voluminous correspondence which is our greatest source of information concerning the various amatory and professional alliances he formed in his long lifetime.

The patronage Lope received from the Duke of Sessa was an absolute necessity in the Europe of his time. How else could a literary artist survive? Occasional performances of innumerable plays did not bring all the gold needed. Nor was copyright necessarily respected beyond the reach of one's sword or the incomparably longer arm of one's protector. Perhaps he received more financial return from his plays than did other writers but then his needs were always greater. By 1599 the royal court had become conscious of the playwright's genius and the festivities attending royal marriages were occasions for many of his plays. Several of his *autos* were used by the church at the beatification of Santa Teresa and the canonization of the patron of Madrid, San Isidro. On these occasions the simple stage properties (a single curtain and insignificant scenery) were replaced with rich scenery financed from kingly and ecclesiastical coffers. These sets were used to embroider the background for the gravity and stateliness of his formal dramas.

Encouraged by church and state, Lope returned to Madrid in 1610 and set up an establishment in the *Calle de Francos*. There he lived contentedly until his death twenty-five years later. That is not to say that he retired from active life. Far from it. The death of his beloved son Carlos and of his devoted wife Doña Juana so preyed on his mind that he contemplated taking Holy Orders. He was ordained for the priesthood in Toledo in March, 1614. Though intended to bring order into his life this change of status was not successful. 1616 found him pursuing a mysterious lady, one Lucía de Salcedo, who was probably an actress in Sánchez' troupe. This did not last long however, for he soon fell in love with a young married woman, Doña Marta de Nevares Santoyo, whose husband survived the disgrace for three long years. Lope honored this mistress by making her the leading character in his eclogue *Amarilis* in 1632, a year after her death.

He continued to write plays and lyric poems and such epics as *Dragontea* which maligned Sir Francis Drake; *Corona Trágica* which praised Mary, Queen of Scots; and *Dorotea* (1632) a narrative in dialogue modelled on *Celestina* and which celebrated his affair of long ago with Elena Osorio. In this preoccupation with the polishing of his poems for publication one is mindful of Shakespeare who was so proud of his *Rape of Lucrece* and *Venus and Adonis*. Their disregard for the literary importance of those plays that made them famous, their concern with popular taste and the commercial success of their pieces, disregarding the literary importance, are characteristic of both men.

A number of Lope's plays were printed prior to 1618 but it was not until that date that he began to consider publication of his work to be of sufficient importance to attend to it himself. For seven years he turned his attention to this preparation for immortality but it bored him. During the last ten years of his life no volumes were issued. After his death his daughter published one collection of his plays which he had arranged.

Broken by the death of his Amarilis, the elopement of their daughter Antonia Clara, and the death of his brilliant son Lopito, he died quietly in his home on August 27, 1635. His declining years had brought him the adulation of the great and the strange from all over the world. The Duke of Sessa was at his bedside when he died, and because of the magnitude of the nobleman's arrangements, his funeral lasted for nine days.

It is difficult even to discuss his dramatic output because of its enormous volume. Certain plays stand out, particularly *Fuente Ovejuna*, because the modern world has chosen to consider this an early stirring of the proletariat. *El perro del hortelano, El caballero de Olmedo, San Isidro labrador, La dama boba, El Maestro de danza.* In addition we must mention *El castigo sin venganza* which is celebrated for its lyricism; *El peregrino en su Patria; La Estrella de Sevilla*, his most important historical play; and his last piece, *Las bizarrías de Belisa*, written in 1634 almost sixty years after the first play of his childhood.

Lope de Vega is important to us because he was the first prominent dramatist in Spain and one of the golden dozen of truly great; he reformed the theatre in his own country; his popularity enormously widened the influence of dramatic art everywhere; he increased the number of theatres and actors in the Iberian peninsula; and finally because he had so much influence on such masters of the theatre as Corneille and Molière, to name two of the greatest.

Living at the same time as Lope de Vega were four other men who must be considered: GUILLEM DE CASTRO, TIRSO DE MOLINA, JUAN RUIZ DE ALARCÓN and CALDERÓN DE LA BARCA. The first of these was born in 1569 and died in 1631; his principal contribution to the theatre was his creation of the great character of El Cid in *Las Mocedades de Cid*, which served as literary inspiration for Corneille's *Le Cid*. TIRSO DE MOLINA (*nom de théâtre* for Gabriel Téllez, 1571-1648) had far greater importance than de Castro. He lived and died a devout ecclesiastic in the church in which Lope neither distinguished himself for his piety nor for his devotion to duty. His principal contribution to the theatre, in fact to the whole literary and cultural world, is the character of Don Juan in *El burlador de Sevilla* (*The Deceiver of Seville*).

In real life this character was killed by certain Franciscan friars for a supposedly serious offense and he was said to have been removed to Hades by supernatural means. Molière, Byron, Rostand and Mozart have been the most illustrious employers of the Don Juan legend.

From Molina's ordination as a priest in 1601 until his death, he combined his ecclesiastical duties, which he placed first, with the writing of some four hundred plays. About eighty of these survive. Besides the Don Juan piece, his best known plays are *El Condenado por desconfiao* (*The Double Damned*), which treated in great detail the doubts and mental temptations that an intelligent Christian encounters in his efforts to save his soul; *La prudencia en la mujer* (*Prudence in Woman*), his best-liked historical piece; and *Don Gil de las calzas verdes* (*Don Gil of the Green Trousers*), a much lighter play.

JUAN RUIZ DE ALARCÓN (1580(81)-1639) was born of a noble Spanish family in Mexico. He is claimed as the father of the Mexican theatre and remains its most illustrious name because the country has been so consistently under Spanish influence. Alarcón was greatly impressed by the style and personality of Lope de Vega but did not imitate his fecundity as he wrote scarcely more than twenty plays. His best known are: *Las paredes oyen* (*Walls Have Ears*); *La verdad Sospechosa* (*The Suspicious Truth*), on which Corneille based *Le Menteur; La prueba de las promesas* (*The Proof of the Promises*); and *El tejedor de Segovia* (*The Weaver of Segovia*), the plot of which might be compared with Schiller's *Die Raeuber*.

PEDRO CALDERÓN DE LA BARCA (Pedro Calderón de la Barca Hanao de lar Barreda y Riano, 1600-1681) was born in Madrid of a noble family from the northern town of Santander. Though at first a soldier, he began his theatrical career certainly by 1629. In 1635 he became manager and director of the court performances. He dominated his own age as thoroughly as Lope did the one preceding. It is difficult to estimate his importance because in the seventeenth century he was as overrated as he was minimized in the eighteenth century.

The failure of a love affair made him turn to the Church as a career. He was ordained a priest in 1651, became Honorary Royal Chaplain and finally Superior of the Congregation of St. Peter. His inclination had been to give up the theatre but kingly command forbade his doing this. He continued to write plays and was in fact composing a new *auto* when he died, thirty years after entering the priesthood. It is easy to see that Calderón emulated Tirso de Molina rather than Lope de Vega in his attitude toward religion.

The chief characteristic of his plays is his lyricism; in this form he assumed high rank in his own country. This sweetness was however coupled with the severe fault of gongorism which resembled the

Euphuism of English literature. This deliberate extravagance, exasperating bombast and studied obscurity marred much of his work, though it usually only appeared as purple patches in the well-wrought whole. Perhaps one hundred and twenty plays survive; eighty of these being *autos*. They fall into three groups whose characteristics are, devotion to Catholic Christianity, loyalty to the Spanish crown, and a high sense of honor. The best known of his *autos* are *Encantos de la culpa* (*Sorceries of Sin*) and *La devoción de la cruz* (*Devotion of the Cross*). In this form he is absolutely supreme. His "cape and sword" plays of adventure and swashbuckling are considered by some more brilliant than Lope's. Perhaps his best known in this group is *La dama duende*, which is variously translated as *The Female Ghost*, *The Fairy Lady*, etc. He was at his best however in his graver pieces rather than in his comedies. There are three that deserve mention: *El médico de su honra* (*The Doctor of His Own Honor*), which has been compared to *Othello*, but always to Shakespeare's advantage; *La vida es sueño* (*Life Is A Dream*), a philosophical drama of a youth whose beastly fate is foretold, his parents strive to thwart the oracle by imprisoning him and bring about the very end they feared (to be compared with Franz Werfel's *Goat Song*); and the social drama, *El alcalde de Zalamea* (*The Mayor of Zalamea*), which broadens the theme of honor to encompass peasant and noble alike.

Calderón was the last of the great Spanish theatre figures. He lived and wrote in the first generations of the decline of the Spanish Empire. This degeneration continued in a worldly and literary way though the end of the nineteenth and beginning of the present century have seen an awakening in their theatre. Calderón had a great influence on the European theatre. This was a mixed blessing for he inculcated the artificiality of his own country at the same time he was preaching thoughtfulness, gravity and a philosophical approach to life.

⊷§ VIII §⊶

ENGLAND'S AWAKENING

(1550-1642)

THE lechery and pompous desire of Henry VIII for self-aggrandizement brought about a severance of connection between England's state religion and the Church of Rome. Unwisely opposed by the Church, his vanity fanned by those who protested against the temporal power of the ecclesiastics, Henry broke once and for all with the conditions of thinking and living which dominated Europe. Similarly reformers in France, Germany and Italy were objecting to the medieval mind that had passed unknowingly with the coming of the Renaissance. England's physical location made the rapid development of a conservative protestantism relatively easy once its monarch decided that the desirable Anne Boleyn was more important than his Catholic soul. This was his pretext. The cause lay in his wish to make England a nation.

The national life of any country determines its art and literature. With Britain's recognizance of itself as an entity, the rapid growth of a great literature was possible because she was fortunate in possessing many men of first class writing ability. As Italy had expressed her reawakening in the graphic and graven arts, so England found her way through literature and the development of a professional means of translating writing into theatrical performance.

Henry VIII died in 1548 and for five years Edward VI, a pious and weak child, was ruled by his bigoted Protestants. He was followed by the even more stupid repressions of a restored Rome under Mary, a quiet, devout, unhappy, misunderstood woman called "bloody," for she tried to turn back the hands of a clock which was never meant to run backwards. Finally in 1558 began the reign of the vain, red-headed, alert, niggardly, capable, scheming, brilliant, suspicious nationalist, Elizabeth, who loved the theatre if it cost her no money and who patronized the arts with a financial temperance that only the stingy can comprehend. Her name stands for England's

93

glorious period in dramatic history which has never since been equaled.

The sixteenth and seventeenth centuries in English theatre, established the transition from the medieval mystery and morality through the glories of tragedy and full comedy down to the brilliant, mannered and obscene comedies of the restored Stuarts, relatives and wasteful successors to the acquisitive Tudors. From the squares of London, through the inn courtyards of Southwark, and the provincial towns of bustling middle-class England, to the formal, partially endowed and royally patronized professional theatres of Drury Lane and Lincoln's Inn Fields the journey was accomplished with the ease of assured affluence. Shakespeare's "squeaking Cleopatras," the boys who had minced through feminine roles since the theatre began in England, finally found replacement in 1660 when the moral releases of Stuart restoration offset the essential prudery and hypocrisy of the people who constituted the audiences of D'Avenant and Killigrew.

In early sixteenth century England interludes were being written which, in their merry qualities, were akin to *Maître Pierre Pathélin* in France and the pieces of Hans Sachs in Germany. The leading farce writer was JOHN HEYWOOD (c.1500-c.1580), instructor to the boys of St. Paul's Cathedral, who left behind six interludes. The most famous of these were the hilarious *The Four P's* (published 1543-47), the slightly obscene *Merry Play of John, Tyb, and Sir John,* and *The Play of the Weather.* A favorite of Queen Mary, he fled the country on Elizabeth's accession and died in exile at Malines.

England's first comedy *Ralph Roister Doister* (1550) was, naturally enough, an imitation of the Roman by NICHOLAS UDALL (c. 1505-1556). Despite its ancient and continental origin this play managed to catch the characteristics of its own native land in its middle-class English story. Udall was a teacher at Eton and later at Westminster so he would have been familiar with Plautus from whom he borrowed. The play is reputed to have been first performed at Eton during the Christmas holidays in the year of its publication. This merry, rowdy comedy is still occasionally revived. But *Gammer Gurton's Needle*, the second English comedy in point of time, is more often staged by present day producers. The latter piece finds quick favor in Anglo-Saxon circles everywhere. Some twenty years ago it was played by a perspicacious group of amateurs for the remote mountaineers of Virginia and Kentucky to their almost Elizabethan appreciation. Variously ascribed, the authorship seems to belong to William Stevenson who died in 1575, though John Bridges, Bishop of Oxford is sometimes named. For a long time its rhymed doggerel was believed to have been written by John Still, Bishop of Bath and Wells. Its gay humors are truly national and the gossip which embroils the village over the loss of Gammer Gurton's needle suggests similar devices which were to be used later by Lady Gregory in *Spreading the News*.

England's national drama was born at a time when her court was under the influence of Italian poetry and romance. Edmund Spenser, Sir Philip Sydney, Raleigh, and Princess Mary Tudor were devotees of Italia so that it is natural that Seneca's declamatory style should also win favor and admirers in England. Certainly Jasper Heywood, Alexander Neville, John Studley and others set to work to render his correct Latin into rhymed English. Not content with translation and imitation, certain other playwrights were composing national historical tragedies. The first of these was the chronicle play *King Johan* (1548) which described the king's disputes with the Pope and is really a morality play lauding an unworthy subject. Written by the vigorous Protestant bishop John Bale, it was intended for religious controversy rather than for theatrical entertainment. Thomas Sackville's *The Mirror for Magistrates* (1557) was an historical romance rather than a play. Several other authors wove the plot around the great and unfortunate names in English history from the time of the Norman Conquest down to 1400. This monumental work bore fruit in the first true English tragedy, *Gorboduc; or, Ferrex and Porrex* by Thomas Sackville and Thomas Norton, which was performed before Queen Elizabeth on January 17, 1561. The play was in blank verse and was heavily influenced by Seneca in that all significant events took place off-stage and were either reported by messengers or interpreted from the dumb-show before each act. This latter was an attempt to imitate the Euripidean prologue. Its only contemporary connotation was its interest in good and responsible government; perhaps an indirect compliment to Elizabeth was intended. Certainly most of the writers and all of the managers and actors were highly conscious of the need to flatter this capable, capricious woman. Demanding praise, withholding favor where it was denied, she rewarded adulation in cavalier fashion.

GEORGE GASCOIGNE (1535 or 1536-1577), made the first English translation from Greek tragedy, *Jocasta*. He was responsible for a prose translation of Ariosto's *I Suppositi*. This comedy, *The Supposes*, received an amateur production by the barristers of Gray's Inn Court in 1566. These literal adaptations from the Italian were as lukewarm, and to us uninteresting, as the correct effusions of the French of the same period.

The second tragedy *The Misfortunes of Arthur*, did not come until twenty years later and was from the pen of Thomas Hughes. Played by the Society of Gray's Inn before the Queen at Greenwich in 1587 it was less pretentious than *Gorboduc* and the "Ghost," favorite character of Elizabethan drama, played a prominent part.

Before we say anything of the dramatists who immediately preceded Marlowe, Shakespeare and Jonson, it is necessary for us to understand the whole workings of the theatre which ranked with that of the Greeks as the greatest of all time. By 1576 there was a professional playhouse in London so that it was no longer necessary to depend on the inn courtyards and public squares as places of performance. Outside the capital they served their purpose for another hundred years.

JAMES BURBAGE (d. 1597), who first appears as a member of the Earl of Leicester's Men on May 7, 1576, was determined to erect a playhouse. This he did and called it The Theatre. Construction was not the cumbersome and lengthy process it is in the modern world and the same year saw it opened. It was built at a cost of seven hundred pounds on a site between Shoreditch and Finsbury Fields in a neighborhood north of the Thames and beyond the jurisdiction of the civil authorities. It is said to have entertained fifteen hundred people at a performance but the receipts and admission rates which have been established for the Elizabethan theatres do not suggest so large a seating capacity. The location of the building was important because at the beginning of this great period the Puritans who had been encouraged by their success in revolting against Catholicism, hoped to stamp out the theatre. The Lord Mayor was hostile to the players and all kinds of penalties were imposed upon them; but the Queen and the Court liked them and protected them.

The building was of wood and a square stage extended out into the enclosure (pit). This was open to the sky and meant that performances could only take place during the day. Fair or not, the groundlings stood before the stage. In case of rain or drizzle they were unprotected from the weather as were the actors on the forestage. The rear of the stage was capped with a balcony (useful in such plays as *Romeo and Juliet*). Partial protection against the elements was provided by a strip of canvas called "the sky." The nobility and the middle class who paid more for their places were seated on chairs, stools and benches under a roof. They were not influenced by erratic weather so the performance could continue; the management could thus keep the shillings and pence which amounted to all too few pounds. The space beneath the balcony was concealed by a curtain, and was called the inner stage, the "within" of Shakespearean stage-directions. It must be understood that each of the theatres varied somewhat in size, interior and exterior, but it is our intention to give you a composite picture of all. The building was usually circular ("this wooden O" says Shakespeare in the opening chorus of *King Henry V*). It was a utilitarian stage which did not admit of scenic display as did the picture stage of the Italian theatre; but it was one which encouraged solo acting, star parts, rich poetic descriptions of background, handsome and even extravagant costumes. It was not possible to skimp on the expense of the actors' dress because the audience was too close. A portion of the stage was even occupied by richly attired young gallants who would have been critical of anything but the best.

Admission prices varied somewhat but the standard according to Ben Jonson seems to have been 6d. for the pit on up to half a crown for the best places. A seat upon the stage cost a shilling more and was collected backstage by the doorkeeper. Economic need introduced this pernicious practice of seating people on stage and it was only by royal proclamation by Charles II that it was ended; obedience to this ruling on the part of the nobility came reluctantly and grumblingly.

The playhouse was a very much more satisfactory place for the management than the inn yard where people had assembled in such crowds that the collector had a difficult time securing his admissions. Paying at the door made it possible for the producer to be sure of his box office receipts. That there was only one door was attested to by the famous fire which destroyed the Globe Theatre during the first performance of *King Henry VIII*, June 29, 1613. Sir Henry Wotton's contemporary account of the fire states specifically, "only one man had his breeches set on fire, that would have perhaps broyled him, if he had not by the benefit of a provident wit put it out with a bottle of ale."

Scarcely was The Theatre opened in 1576 than The Curtain was built not far away in Moorfields. The second playhouse shared its name with the Curtain Road in Shoreditch, a street which survives at the time of this writing. Perhaps it was the same year (1576) or in 1577. Certainly we know little that is factual about it. The owners seem to have formed an offensive and defensive alliance with The Theatre against the Puritan authorities' efforts to prevent performances; their prosperities and depressions were simultaneous. Certainly they were both mentioned when the order came in 1597 to pull down the playhouses. The command was not carried out as proven by the Privy Council's admonition to the Curtain in 1601 concerning satiric attacks in the manner of Aristophanes.

The alliances between the two theatres permitted the Burbage company also to play at the Curtain. In fact Jonson's *Everyman In His Humour* was acted there. We do not know when the building was pulled down; perhaps it was not until the Civil War of 1642-47.

We do not know when the theatre situated south of the Thames and called Newington Butts was built, nor do we know that it was more than a stage in an inn courtyard, but we do have evidence that it was owned by Philip Henslowe (d.1616) the pawnbroker, manager and father-in-law of the towering actor, Edward Alleyn.

In 1592 the Rose with its thatched roof was built on the same side of the river. It was there that the Lord Admiral's Men played and it was for this company that the shining Christopher Marlowe wrote. Nevertheless Burbage's and other companies performed there as is evidenced by entries in Henslowe's noted diary, a great source of information for scholars.

But this cooperation did not go on for long because the Lord Chamberlain's Men (the company of Burbage and Shakespeare) determined to move south of the Thames to establish the famous theatre which took the name of Globe (in 1598-9) from the sign which hung in front of it. To most of us this is the best known playhouse in the world. It was near the Rose and the bear-baiting pit, known as the Bear-garden, under the management of Alleyn. A poster for the theatre existed as late as this year in the remarkable theatre collection of the Dulwich College Library.

The Globe was circular in shape like The Theatre, and was opened with a performance of *King Henry V*. Shakespeare's greatest plays and many of Jonson's finest were produced there. During this same period the Lord Chamberlain's Men took the position of the first acting company of Elizabethan England. Due to Shakespeare's glowing pen, the fine acting of Richard Burbage (the first Hamlet) and the sound management of Shakespeare and the Burbages, the troupe was a huge success.

After the Bard returned to Stratford in 1611, Richard continued the enterprise alone. When the theatre, together with the costumes and the physical equipment, burned in an hour in 1613 the details were recorded in a street song called *A Sonnet About the Sad Fire in the Globe Theatre in London*. This ended with the sound advice that the New Globe should be supplied with a tiled roof instead of the thatch which had caught fire from the cannon shots that heralded the king's entrance in *Henry VIII*. It is pleasant to relate that dramatic criticism was for once taken seriously and 1614 saw a new and fairer Globe with a tiled roof. The theatre continued profitably for a long time. In 1635 the Burbage family still held the controlling interest, but their good actors had gone and the quality of their productions had declined. James Shirley, in the prologue to his *Rosania; or, The Doubtful Heir* (1640) apologized for the refinement of his pieces as he had intended them for the smaller purlieus of the private Blackfriars. He hoped the lewdly noisy pit at the Globe would take his efforts kindly. It seems to have been a gratuitous kind of insult. The end of a great period was near, however, because the delighted Puritans pulled down the house on April 15, 1644.

In answer to the competition of the Globe Henslowe and Alleyn determined to abandon the Rose to the fate of lesser companies and to build the handsomest scenic structure in London, scorning all expense in constructing its (comparative) magnificence. We have a very exact description of its dimensions in Henslowe's diary; the stage was to be 43 feet across, it was to have a tiled roof with gutters at the back to carry off rain and not to empty on the heads of the actors on the stage or the spectators in the edge of the yard. It took its name from the statue of the Goddess of Fortune which stood in front of it. Such magnificence naturally aroused the ire of the bigoted. Then city officials planned to restrict the number of playhouses in or near London (the claim for jurisdiction without the city was extra-legal) to two, nor were the Globe and Fortune to play more than twice a week nor must they play on Sunday. This ruling was, as usual, never enforced.

The Fortune burned down in 1621 and was rebuilt, probably in the next year. It survived the Civil War and Cromwell's regime only to be pulled down shortly after Charles II's return to England. An advertisement in *Mercurius Politicus* for February 14, 1661 announced that it was to be torn down to permit the construction of twenty-three houses with gardens. This gives a good idea of the space the theatre occupied.

The Burbage syndicate had also remodelled the Blackfriars, a private theatre within the City. This was the home of a famous company of boy actors who flourished in London; it was later the house of the King's company and probably existed until the end of the Civil War. 1647 has been put as the date of its destruction.

Much of our knowledge of the physical condition and importance of the theatres has been gained from the visit to London in 1596 of the distinguished Dutch scholar, Johan de Witt. He left a description and a drawing of the Swan Theatre, the magnificence of which impressed him. He claimed that it seated three thousand people, not far short of the capacity of the Center Theatre in Radio City. Many think de Witt's figure is grossly exaggerated. Because of its location near the Paris Garden Stairs to the Thames it has also been called the Paris Garden. Its company is unknown but its proprietor was Francis Langley. Of its repertory we are uninformed, though de Witt's drawing, which was first thought to represent a scene from *Twelfth Night*, may have been from an earlier comedy on the same subject. The date of the closing of this theatre is not known but in 1632 Shackerley Marmyon, in his drama *Holland's Leaguer*, referred to the playhouse when he said that it, "like a dying swanne, hangs her head and sings her own dirge."

With The Theatre and the Newington no longer in existence it was probably in 1599 that the courtyard of an inn was turned into a regular public theatre henceforth called the Red Bull. It was situated in St. John's Street, Clerkenwell, and the company was that of the Queen, but little is known of its history until William Prynne's vitriolic attack on actors and the stage, *Histriomastix*, appeared in 1633. (This violent book specifically attacked the performances of French actresses in London in 1629 and was believed also to have been aimed at Queen Henrietta Maria, who had acted in the court masques.) It is then mentioned as having been remodelled and enlarged and continued to survive through the Cromwellian period as a private theatre for secret performances. Samuel Pepys records a visit on March 23, 1661 when he saw a poor performance of *All's Lost by Lust* with scarce a hundred in the house. That it existed in 1663 but was not used, is determined by a reference to it as a lodging home for spiders in Sir William D'Avenant's *A Theatre To Let*. After that is silence.

The year that the Globe burned, Henslowe and Alleyn, who had admired the beauty of the Swan, determined to construct a playhouse as much like it as possible. Together with Jacob Meade, once keeper of the Royal Menagerie, they turned his bear pit into a handsome theatre. The specifications called for it to have a roof of tile, the stage to have a canopied heaven, the house to be three stories with the foundation of brick. The stage was placed on horses so that it might be removed for the baitings which later caused the fair name of Hope to be abandoned and to be replaced by the more descriptive one of Bear Garden. The company was Lady Elizabeth's Players and included the young and brilliant Nathaniel Field (1587-1633), formerly a child actor, as the leading man. With the reopening of the Globe, he doubtless joined with Ben Jonson, Fletcher, Massinger and others who identified themselves with the King's Men, the old Lord Chamberlain's company. It was not long after that the management pushed forward its animal attractions and the name was changed. This policy continued until 1642 when it became illegal to bait bears. The last mention of it was in 1691, as recorded by Ordish in his *Early London Theatres*, when it was mentioned as a very superior glass factory.

In 1617 various sources speak of a new private playhouse known as the Cockpit, from an earlier use of the house, though on Shrove Tuesday, the apprentices of London in their annual disorder pillaged and burned it while they were attacking the taverns and houses of ill fame that existed in Drury Lane. After this it seems also to have employed the name of Phoenix and was used by a troupe of boy actors. When the Theatre Royal was built in Drury Lane in 1663 it was abandoned. There remains but one more theatre of this period which was originally the refectory of the dissolved Whitefriars where the Queen's Children played in 1608-10. In 1629 the nearby Salisbury Court was opened and the children moved over and changed their name to The King's Children, Queen Anne, wife of James I, having died. This private theatre continued to be used until shortly after the Restoration.

The names of the companies of players in Elizabethan and Stuart England changed frequently and much misinformation has grown up because many authorities have become confused and unable to follow the various changes. The death of a royal or noble patron, that is one who lent the official sanction of his name, meant that the actors had to secure a new sponsor at once in order to continue playing.

The two most distinguished troupes were Burbage's company, known successively as Lord Leicester's Men, Lord Strange's Men (then the Earl of Derby's Men as Strange became Derby), Lord Hunsdon's Men, (Hunsdon became Lord Chamberlain) so, The Lord Chamberlain's Men and finally as the King's Men; and Henslowe's (later Alleyn's) players, called the Lord Admiral's Servants, subsequently known as the Prince's Men. In addition there were the Children of the Chapel, a troupe whose personnel changed as the boys grew up and passed on to other work, theatrical or otherwise, and whose name and management changed and they became successively the Queen's Children, the King's Children, etc., which represented a continuity of idea if not of troupe. It is not to be inferred that there were no other companies playing. Only the two most important adult companies are described for continuity's sake. Lord Sussex's Men, the Earl of Pembroke's Servants, the Earl of Worcester's Men are other acting troupes which existed in Elizabethan England.

Complete anonymity among English actors disappeared in the sixteenth century and we learn the names and careers of the most distinguished. Richard Tarleton (d. 1588), the jester and interlude player from the Middle Ages, was the gayest clown of all. Some people think that he inspired Hamlet's famous "Alas, poor Yorick" speech. According to Heywood, Tarleton's successor was one William Kemp who danced a morris dance from London to Norwich in nine days during the Lenten period of 1599. This he celebrated in his pamphlet describing the exploit, which smacks a trifle of the dance marathons of the nineteen-twenties in our own country. His fame and that of other English actors was displayed to the Continent in various tours. Both in 1579 and in 1586 a company had appeared in Elsinore where Denmark's king frequently held court. Among the actors were the well-known comedians, Kemp, Thomas Pope, George

Bryan and Kemp's "boy" Daniel Jones, with whom he travelled. Many of them played in Saxony but Kemp returned to England where he acted both for Burbage and Henslowe.

The most famous tragedians of the period were EDWARD ALLEYN (1565-1625) and Richard Burbage. The former seems to have had an exaggerated style of acting and it is believed by some that Shakespeare aimed his barbs at him in his pronouncement on acting in *Hamlet*. Nonetheless he was the leading actor of his company because he played Faustus in Marlowe's *Doctor Faustus* and Barabbas in his *The Jew of Malta*, Orlando in Greene's *Orlando Furioso* and Hieronimo in Kyd's *The Spanish Tragedy*. Although younger than Shakespeare, he may have adhered to an older school of acting if "out-heroding Herod" was intended for him, as Mantzius seems to think in his *History of Theatrical Art*. He was a good business man and a devoted husband who prospered and became a friend of the aristocracy. Upon his death he left his Dulwich estate together with endowment for its support, as a school for poor children under the name of God's Gift. This survives as Dulwich College, where his records and those of his father-in-law, Henslowe, are still preserved.

RICHARD BURBAGE (1567?-1619), son of the actor and manager James, was brought up in the theatre. His fame is enhanced because he created so many of Shakespeare's and Jonson's heroes. We know that he played Hamlet, Othello, King Lear, King Richard III and it is conjectured that he acted the principal parts in many others. He played in *Sejanus*, *Every Man In His Humour*, as well as in Marston's *The Malcontent*. He was a careful and successful theatre manager who steered a sure course, having profited as a youth by close attention to his father's methods.

Of Shakespeare's acting ability we have little exact knowledge nor do we know exactly what he played except the Ghost in *Hamlet*. Probably he acted old Knowell in *Every Man In His Humour* as well as a lesser part in *Sejanus*, and his brother in his dotage recalled that when young he had seen William play Adam in *As You Like It*. This is all we know about Shakespeare's parts beyond the fact that he was for a long time inclined to think of himself as an actor rather than an author. It was probably his *acting* that Robert Greene attacked in his posthumous *Groat's Worth of Wit, bought with a Million of Repentance* in 1592, though many authorities consider that it was his dramaturgy.

The actor's lot was not an easy one because Henslowe seems to have made as much money by loans to actors as he did by employing them in his theatres in their professional capacities. Their incomes came from a share, or more usually a small fraction of a share, of the company's receipts. When business was bad actor and manager starved together though the latter usually came out of it in better shape than even the highest paid actor, because he possessed several *whole* shares.

Scenery practically did not exist and properties were sparse. Background came out of the poet's descriptions and physical richness and beauty from the actors' costumes. When these were lost, as in the burning of the old Globe and the Fortune, it was an almost overwhelming blow, which only the generosity of a noble patron could rectify by gift of gold or kind. Much could be written about the staging and acting of the period but Sir E. K. Chambers' brilliant four-volume *Elizabethan Stage* covers these matters thoroughly.

JOHN LYLY (1554-1606) wrote a novel entitled *Euphues* which was so vague and alliterative in style that it gave its name to Euphuism (an affected or artificial style of writing). His plays were pretty, romantic and charming and were intended as compliments to the capricious Elizabeth whose favor he sought. *Campaspe, Sappho and Phaon, Midas, Endimion* and *The Woman In the Moon* won him contemporary fame and admiration of the court. They were often performed by the boy troupes of actors, the Children of the Chapel and Children of St. Paul's.

ROBERT GREENE (1560-1592) was an uneven writer but his best work ranks high in the Elizabethan period, particularly his comedies, *George-a-Greene the Pinner of Wakefield* and *Friar Bacon and Friar Bungay* which partook of both pastoral and romantic comedy. Having led a debauched life himself, he was a most ardent champion of pure women in his plays. Finally his viciousness provoked a reaction and he became a bitter castigator of his former fellow-dramatists. His previously-mentioned pamphlet in which he attacked Shakespeare, must have been a desperate effort to salve his conscience when he realized his vice-ridden body was wearing out and death was near.

THOMAS KYD (1558-1594) was, next to Marlowe, the greatest exponent of blood-and-thunder plays and bombastic tragedy of this period. His *The Spanish Tragedy* (1592) was greatly admired by the crowds, if scorned by the few, and was frequently played. It was cruel, mysterious and intended to shock the sensibilities of his audience. Kyd understood theatrical limitations and made good use of his stage. His lost play the *Ur-Hamlet* is believed to be the original of Shakespeare's tragedy. He is said to have had a hand in writing the latter's *Titus Andronicus;* certainly its vigorous bombast suggests Kyd. *Arden of Faversham* (1585 or 1592), a fine domestic tragedy, is sometimes ascribed to him. Involved in the charges of atheism against Marlowe, he was imprisoned and tortured. Upon his release he felt the disgrace so keenly that he died a year later.

GEORGE PEELE (1558?-1598) was among the famous University Wits who included Marlowe, Greene, Nashe and Kyd (who was not a university man). Though his exploits as recounted in *The Merrie Jests of George Peele* (1607) were largely fictitious, he was one of the bohemians of London. His *Edward I* (1593) seems to have survived better than his elegant comedy, *The Arraignment of Paris* in 1584 (which was probably influenced by Lyly and Greene); though at the time it was considered his best play. *The Old Wives' Tale* (1595) was a delicate kind of fantasy, a tender satire.

THOMAS NASHE (1567-1601) was another of those Elizabethan writers who burnt themselves out in thirty or forty years because they crowded so much fierce living and loving into them. His principal hatred was of Puritanism which he attacked with every literary means at his satiric command; pamphlets, novels, plays. In 1592 he wrote the satirical masque, *Summer's Last Will and Testament* and in 1596 after Marlowe's untimely death he prepared his friend's *Queen Dido* for the stage despite his own attacks on Kit's style when he was alive. He has also been considered part-author of the piece. His only other play was the political satire, *The Isle of Dogs*, never published and now lost, which was considered seditious and caused his imprisonment. Thus ended the career of "railing Nashe," and all the careers of the scholar poets as some have called them, that is all save Thomas Lodge who collaborated with Greene on *The Wounds of Civil War* (1594), and the greatest of them all, the rowdy, tempestuous, hot and glowing Kit.

CHRISTOPHER MARLOWE (1564-1593), son of a Canterbury shoemaker, nevertheless a Cambridge man, was the only one of these broiling Elizabethans who could challenge Shakespeare on his own ground. From *Tamburlaine the Great* in 1587, produced in London before he had received his Master's degree from Cambridge, until his death six years later he had written six tragedies (one unfinished) and an heroic poem, *Hero and Leander*. Marlowe's "mighty line" and glorious use of blank verse cover in part his imperfect characterization and love of the sound rather than the meaning of words. He began the development of heroic tragedy by rescuing it from the classic sameness of Seneca and restoring it to the grandeur of Aeschylus, Sophocles and Euripides. He was the first dramatist in more than fifteen hundred years to recognize their importance. He understood and valued the spirit which lay behind their writing and was not guilty of the slavish and superficial imitation of it which makes previous European tragedy of so little literary importance.

Tamburlaine depicts the rise of a young peasant lad to transcendent power by ruthless means which have been used before and since.

It typifies the Elizabethan desire for glory and advancement clothed in magnificent language. This youth tortures the Emperor and Empress until they kill themselves and he seizes the throne for himself. Though not the first tragedy in blank verse, it was the first written for a public theatre and was certainly a first in importance because Marlowe strained himself to prove that this form could be more effective than rhyme.

The Faust legend is a prolific one in literature; it first appears in 1587 in an anonymous unliterary German story version. This was followed by an English ballad probably based on the folk-book which had crossed the channel early in 1588. In 1589 Marlowe took the bare bones of a plot in which a sensualist sells his soul for twenty-four years of earthly bliss, and transformed it into a tragedy of intellectual desire reaching beyond the limits of the material mind (*The Tragical History of Dr. Faustus*). The version we possess is presumably incomplete and we are inclined to think it formless but it is suited to imaginative staging. The brilliant, showy revival of *Dr. Faustus* made by John Houseman and Orson Welles in 1937 for the Federal Theatre Project is a case in point. The play was extremely popular and continued to be performed up to the middle of the eighteenth century. Eventually it became a marionette show which was the form in which Goethe first became acquainted with it.

His next play *The Jew of Malta* (1589), was structurally and poetically an advance over his first pieces, though the version we know is that of Thomas Heywood and leaves much to be desired. In this he created the avaricious Barabbas, a Jewish monster, who served Shakespeare as a model for Shylock and gave Edward Alleyn a magnificent acting part when the play was produced by the Lord Admiral's Men. It was hugely popular in its day and had been acted thirty-six times by 1592.

Probably his highest peak of creation came in *Edward II* dated by some as having been written in 1590. This play is frequently compared with *King Richard II* and *King Richard III*, and has usually been ranked above them; an opinion which, despite attack in recent years, is probably still tenable. Certainly the infatuations of Edward for Gaveston and the young Spenser (comparable to Richard II's weaknesses) brought about an alienation of the nobles (and in Marlowe's play, Queen Isabella who is considerably more of a person than the Queen in Shakespeare's drama), and finally his death. There are passages of great beauty in this play though it is rarely revived. It was performed in 1592.

The Massacre of Paris was written about 1590 and is the poorest of his plays. It represents a historically inaccurate picture of the struggle between the Duc de Guise and the French Huguenots. *Dido, Queen of Carthage*, his final and unfinished play was completed by Nashe; though some authorities, including John Gassner in his able *Masters of the Drama*, assign this to an earlier period when he was still an undergraduate at Cambridge.

Marlowe's contribution to the English theatre was one of personality, passion and glorious poetry all too frequently marred by overstraining. His plots were weak, but his mastery of language makes one forgive all. Next to Shakespeare, he was the greatest tragic dramatist of England.

WILLIAM SHAKESPEARE (1564-1616) was born in Stratford-upon-Avon, which he loved so dearly that in 1597 he bought a house, New Place, to which he retired permanently in 1611. He was the son of John Shakespeare, a freeholder and glover, and Mary Arden, daughter of a well-known family. John Shakespeare became an alderman and city chamberlain in Stratford but by 1577, through improvidence, he had lost his money and most of his position in political affairs. This coincides with William's removal from school, which is conjectured to have been the well regarded Stratford Grammar School, and his employment by his father. In five short years he had become involved with Anne Hathaway who was some eight years his senior. He married her in November, 1532 and six months later their daughter Susanna was born. There were also twins, Hamnet and Judith, born in 1585. By the time he had reached man's estate he was burdened with a wife and three children and no proper means of caring for them. His early love of the theatre (the players used to come to Stratford) coupled with sheer necessity probably forced him forth to London where, by 1592, he had become successful enough to cause Greene to cast slurs at him in the before-mentioned pamphlet.

So many traditions and such an infinite amount of apocrypha have grown up about him that it is difficult to separate truth from adulation or local interest stories. He seems to have become first a hanger-on at the theatre, knowing the players, observing, learning his profession until the time when he could go back-stage to become a call boy, then stage manager, actor, dramatist. But probably by 1591 he had become aligned with the Burbages and wrote, or adapted, *King Henry VI, Parts II* and *III*. When Greene attacked him, Greene's publisher Henry Chettle defended him in these words, "Myself have seen his demeanor nor less civil than he excellent in the quality he professes. Besides, divers of worship have reported his uprightness of dealing, which argues his honesty, and his facetious grace in writing, that approves his art." Shakespeare had arrived. From this point on there is a steady progression in his dramatic development and theatrical success.

The importance of Shakespeare to us lies in his universality of thought, his comprehension of human motives and the frailties of the flesh, his masterly depiction of character through his majestic lines and economical use of words. His poetry is full and flowing with all the robust qualities of a man who has lived and loved in a time when the senses of the world were quickened by the fire of the new-born English Renaissance. The tempo of his plays is that of the new regard for action in a country which had flexed its muscles and demonstrated its national power. The swift moving action carried with it the imagination of the spectators who saw the mighty towers and deep forests of his poetic imagination. He loved the very words with which he depicted the stories of his plays and chose them lovingly out of the reservoir of English literature, giving them new meanings, coining them when necessity arose. Their sound and color were all important to him as well as to us.

His characters live in our minds and thoughts today. Who does not know the fat and jolly, braggart Falstaff? The melancholy Dane, the impetuous Percy known as Hotspur, the gay, boyish yet eternally feminine Rosalind? Do we not decorate our speech with unconscious Shakespearean allusions, even with his very words, "a rose by any other name," "all the world's a stage"? Could we write or speak as we do had Shakespeare never lived? Brought up in childhood with Lamb's *Tales from Shakespeare* we know the stories of his great plays before we know their lines. Our education in English-speaking countries presupposes a knowledge and an appreciation of our greatest poet, our noblest dramatist.

Though we should like to dwell in considerable detail upon the plots and sources of his plays, we have vigorously guarded against it. We have set down in as exact fashion as we can the puzzling and muchly debated chronology of their creation. We have indicated a few of the oft-disputed facts of his personal and professional life to guide those who had and should find far fuller explanations from the men whose lives have been devoted to analyzing the scattered and confusing skeins of known fact and vast conjecture. That is the province of the Shakespearean specialist.

In 1593 came the erotic poem, *Venus and Adonis*, and in 1594, *The Rape of Lucrece*, both dedicated to his patron the handsome Earl of Southampton, to whom many of his sonnets were written. It is mere conjecture that his relationship with him may have been similar to that of Lope de Vega with the Duke of Sessa. Certainly he received monetary aid from Southampton which he used to purchase shares in Burbage's company. This investment assured him of a market for his plays, and suitable performances. It was not necessary for him to stoop to the pandering which the Spanish dramatists were frequently driven to in order to secure a production of their dramas in the *corrales*.

In 1590-91 he wrote parts two and three of *King Henry VI*, which he based on *The First Part of the Contention* and *The True Tragedy of Richard Duke of York*, and from which he took more than 3,200 lines; the authorship of these older plays is unknown to us. He wrote part one of this trilogy in 1591-92. Next, probably because of the sequence of historical events, came *King Richard III*, in which he was influenced by Marlowe, and some say Marlowe had a hand in the actual composition. *The Comedy of Errors*, a reworking of *The Menaechmi*, was accomplished in 1592-93. *Titus Andronicus*, which is frequently doubted as being one of his plays because of its bloody *Grand Guignol* qualities and crudity of construction, was written in this period as was *The Taming of the Shrew*, probably in 1594. The sub-plot was taken from Gascoigne's *The Supposes*, an adaptation of Ariosto's *I Suppositi*. This piece represents a great advance in comedy as well as in construction of plot over *The Comedy of Errors*.

His plays pour forth in profusion, he can be said to have blossomed in royal and noble favor; in 1596 he was granted a coat of arms and Queen Elizabeth so esteemed him that she asked him to continue the adventures of Sir John Falstaff from *Henry IV*. Accordingly he wrote *The Merry Wives of Windsor*, which suffers from many of the faults of commissioned plays. It was probably first acted in 1600, though Leslie Hotson in *Shakespeare Versus Shallow* (1931) dates it as 1597.

In 1594-95 came *The Two Gentlemen of Verona*, a romantic comedy which profited from preliminary plays of Robert Greene though it did not derive from them; *Love's Labour's Lost*, a self-critical piece; and finally his first great tragedy, *Romeo and Juliet*. This piece made good use of the mood of erotic poetry which his narrative poems had developed. It also contains a good understanding of theatrical effectiveness and provides his first great role for a woman.

King Richard II (1595-96) treated a problem similar to that in Marlowe's *Edward II* but it had much broader implications in reference to government and the right of a responsible nobility to force an abdication. Being friendly with Essex and unconscious of his plotting, Shakespeare was persuaded to perform this piece on February 7, 1601, the eve of the rebellion against Elizabeth. The dramatist escaped retribution but he undoubtedly was saddened by the death of Essex because his "dark plays" followed.

The same year he wrote *A Midsummer Night's Dream*, probably to celebrate a court wedding. It had many of the qualities of the masque, a form introduced into England from Italy. During the latter part of 1596 or early in 1597 he returned to historical tragedy in *King John*, distinctly one of his lesser plays, though it did produce an excellent child portrait of Prince Arthur whose terror is described in the play's best scene. This, with Edward III in Marlowe's *Edward II*, are the best portrayals of children in the Elizabethan period. Also in 1597 one of his best comedies was produced, *The Merchant of Venice*. 1597-98 saw the chronicle plays, *King Henry IV*, *Parts I and II*, and *King Henry V*, which brought onto the stage some of his most likeable characters, Prince Hal, Hotspur and the never-to-be-forgotten Falstaff, whom everyone has loved since the time of Elizabeth. These are but a few instances of the humanity of the poet's characters which has endeared him to a world-wide audience. In 1599-1600 came *Julius Caesar*, too often memorized, too little played. *As You Like It*, *Much Ado About Nothing*, *Twelfth Night*, were the climax of the happy plays, the period of cloudless writing before Essex's fall.

In 1601 appeared the play regarded above all others as his masterpiece, *Hamlet*, registered in 1602 and printed in 1603. Some consider *King Lear* a finer play, but actors and audiences have always preferred the unhappy Danish prince, the supreme example of the play of revenge, the test of great acting, the aspiration of every thespian playing in English. Germans and Scandinavians have a similar regard for it; the love of the French is perhaps tempered by the difficulty of securing a satisfactory translation, though Mounet-Sully and the dynamic Sarah Bernhardt have been acclaimed in the role by Gallic audiences.

Essex's death and Elizabeth's growing tyranny are reflected in the bitter comedy of woman's fickleness in *Troilus and Cressida* (1603). The so-called dark comedy, *Measure For Measure*, was performed at court December 26, 1604; *Othello* (which may also reflect Essex) was shown there on November first; *All's Well That Ends Well* probably came in the same year.

Elizabeth was dead and her eccentric Scottish cousin, James I, had ascended the throne. These new plays, together with a selection of earlier pieces, were revived for the royal occasion. They were played at the express command of the King and Shakespeare's and Burbage's company accepted royal patronage and became the King's Men.

Pericles was performed before the Venetian Ambassador to the Court of St. James in January, 1606; on Boxing Day (December 26th) of the same year, the great *King Lear* (written 1604) was played. *Antony and Cleopatra* was registered May 20, 1608, and *Coriolanus* came the same year. Forman saw a performance of *Macbeth* on April 20, 1611, but though the play was written by 1605-06 it was not published until the Folio of 1623. Forman also witnessed a production of *Cymbeline* (1609) in April, 1611, and *The Winter's Tale* (1610) in May of the same year. The latter was performed at Court on November fifth, four days after the serene comedy *The Tempest* was acted. As has been stated previously, the première of *King Henry VIII* which was written in collaboration with John Fletcher, was the occasion of the burning of the Globe. Though doubted by some, it seems probable that Shakespeare also lent an aiding hand to Fletcher in the composition of *The Two Noble Kinsmen* in 1613. This sums up a list that covers the work of the greatest dramatist England and perhaps the world has produced. It is interesting to note how much more prolific were the great Greek dramatists but the difference in tempo of living and longevity probably accounts for it. It also must be remembered that the complexity of Shakespeare's style added to the necessity of his limiting the number of plays he wrote.

His various plays were published separately in quarto form and were four times gathered to form the famous folios in 1623 (edited by John Hemminge and Henry Condell), 1632, 1663 and the faulty folio of 1685. Texts varied so much that it necessitated the work of innumerable editors from Nicholas Rowe (1709), Edward Capell, Alexander Pope, Edmund Malone, James Orchard Halliwell-Phillipps and Alexander Dyce to Horace Howard Furness, Ashley Thorndyke and Leslie Hotson to disentangle the scholarly and bibliographical problems. Then there have been forgeries of entire plays as perpetrated by William Ireland and falsified records of production as committed by John Payne Collier as well as the baffling problem of authorship. Scholars have ascribed his plays to Francis Bacon and to the Earl of Oxford among others; they have puzzled over the identity of Mr. W. H. in his dedication of his *Sonnets* published in 1609; and have generally been so interested in the details as to have missed the substance which people of the theatre, including his great audience, have understood and appreciated.

Love of people, richness of characterization, advance in dramatic structure, magnificent poetry that sings on the lips of the actor and in the brain of the reader and auditor, keen observation of what lay about him, great understanding of the technique of staging and the actor's art, but above all that humanity which only a genius who knew and understood and loved human beings in their endless struggle for love, life and soul, are the characteristics which mark this man as England's greatest dramatist. He was more than that. He was and is eternal and of all times and of all peoples.

BEN JONSON (1573-1637) was born in and educated at Westminster. Through the generous interest of the scholar William Camden, who took him under his tutelage, he became one of the most learned men in England and eventually received honorary degrees from both Oxford and Cambridge. This evidently did not make him charitable towards others' deficiencies because he disparagingly refers to Shakespeare's "Small Latin and less Greek."

His father having died before his birth, his mother married a bricklayer. When the boy grew up his step-father pressed him into the business. Naturally enough the rare Ben didn't care for this work so he enlisted in the English army and fought with the Dutch Protestants against the Spanish. About 1592 he returned to London where he married and had a son, who lived only a few years. At this period Jonson led a generally bohemian and casually literary existence, acting in various plays for Henslowe's company and doing an occasional play-doctoring job for the Lord Admiral's Men. However when his first original play was performed it was done by Burbage's company.

Every Man In His Humour was a realistic comedy with no building up of heroic characters. It is in essence a middle-class drama which records the day by day happenings of a group of eccentrics in the Elizabethan world. The play holds up well, both in reading and in playing.

He seems to have been mentally and physically quarrelsome. The latter quality led to a duel with Gabriel Spencer, a fellow actor, in which Spencer was killed. Jonson was imprisoned for a year and while confined he embraced Catholicism. To celebrate his release his next play, *Every Man Out of His Humour* was produced in 1599. This was a grotesque caricature of all that he detested in London and two years later in 1601 he satirized the nobility in *Cynthia's Revels* and then involved himself in a war with his fellow theatre men. This would progress naturally out of his pre-eminence in the literary circle which centered on the Mermaid Tavern, which has later emulations in the coffee house assemblages of Joseph Addison, Sir Richard Steele and Colley Cibber in early eighteenth century Queen Anne London; America and New York found a latter-day renaissance in the celebrated Algonquin Round Table.

If you gather "wits" together, especially hard drinking, passionate, quarrelsome Elizabethans, an explosion is bound to follow. It did and in a thorough fashion when John Marston painted an uncomplimentary portrait of Jonson in *Histriomastix*. Ben countered with *Every Man Out of His Humour* only to have Marston thrust back at him in *Jack Drum's Entertainment* and Jonson answered with the before-mentioned *Cynthia's Revels*. Dekker was attacked as well in this piece; it might have been an ungrateful thrust at a former collaborator. Marston defended both Dekker and himself in *What You Will* and

Jonson responded with *The Poetaster* (1601), in which many think Shakespeare is praised under the name of Virgil, but the learned Chambers doubts this. However Shakespeare seems to have taken up the cudgels for his friends, Marston and Dekker, as Jonson has been identified as Ajax in *Troilus and Cressida*. Dekker counter-attacked with *Satiromastix*. However, it all may have been a put-up job, a well-published feud of two good friends like the Walter Winchell and Ben Bernie of our own times. At any rate in 1604 Jonson and Marston collaborated with Chapman on *Eastward Ho*, a first-rate comedy.

Sejanus (1603) was a tragedy on the Roman model but is chiefly notable today for its exposé of the methods of dictators who are hostile to the human spirit. In this there seems to have been a covert reference to the disintegration of Elizabeth's reign. His sardonic comedy *Volpone*, hailed in 1605, was another delving into Italy and was set in Venice. In this play he had an excellent opportunity to satirize his world, cloaking it as he did with Italian and animal masks in his biting attack on human greed. *Epicoene; or, The Silent Woman* (1609) is a comedy of humor about Morose, a miserly man who abhors noise and even plans to marry a dumb wife. A bold boy in disguise is saddled on him by a scheming nephew; the boy talks so endlessly that Morose is glad to pay the nephew to call off the talkative "bride." *The Alchemist* (1610) is a sharp and satirical comedy about greed, that human failing and actual obsession that constantly troubled the reformer in Jonson.

In an effort to establish his affinity with the classic writers, as became a learned man and scholar, he returned to the method of *Sejanus* in his next play *Catiline, His Conspiracy* (1611) but it was truly a failure. This perhaps prompted his return to satiric comedy in *Bartholomew Fair* in 1614 which is gayer and funnier than most of his plays. By 1616 all of his important work was done, though he continued to write until his death in 1637. He issued the first folio of his plays in 1616, the year in which both Shakespeare and Beaumont died. It is perhaps unfair to dismiss completely this later work because it was then that he composed many masques that were performed in the Banqueting Hall of Whitehall under James I and Charles I. But more will be said about these productions later.

Quite aside from the dramatic merit of these masques, Jonson's position in the theatre was eminent. He was really the founder of a school of satiric writing and had more immediate influence than Shakespeare. By his bad disposition and generally quarrelsome nature he negated much positive good he might have done. He created in England a comedy of humors and his plays had a purging effect on his own country. He had little, in fact, he had no sympathy with Puritanism.

80. Comedy Scene, Not Later Than 1622.
Corsen manuscript title page. Note Serlian
side wings and raised upper stage.

IL NATAL DE FIORI IRRIGATI DAL FONTE PEGASEO COL BALLO DELL AVRE

81. Setting by Alfonso Parigi, 1628.

82. STAGE OF THE FARNESE THEATRE, PARMA, 1618.

83. AUDITORIUM OF THE FARNESE THEATRE.

Yale-Rockefeller Theatre Collection

, 85. FIREWORKS AND MASQUE. Festival at Assum, Germany, 1616. *Spencer Collection, N.Y.P.L.*

86. The Duke De Guise As An American King.

87. Other Participants in A Ballet On An American Theme. France, 1662.

Spencer Collection. N. Y. Public Library

88. TRIUMPHAL CAR. Festival at Assum, Germany, 1616.

PAGEANT CAR. From festival above.

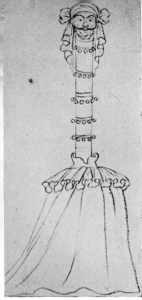

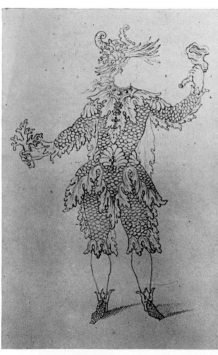

90—96. Costume Designs by Jean Berain (c. 1673-1700.) Note trick costume with telescoping neck. Note construction of camel.

Yale-Rockefeller Theatre Collection

Le monde n'est que tromperie
ou du moins charlatanerie.
Nous agitons nostre Cerveau
Comme TABARIN son chapeau.

chacun ioue son personnage,
tel se pense plus que luy sage
qui est plus que luy charlatan.
Messieurs Dieu vous donne bon.

97. TABARIN'S FAMOUS STREET SHOW. Paris, 1620.   *Théâtre De La Rue*

8. A TYPICAL SCENE OF HORSEPLAY IN COMMEDIA DELL'ARTE.

            Yale-Rockefeller Theatre Collection

99. COMEDY. Magny as "The Old Man."

100. COMEDY. DuMoulin as a Peasant.

Yale-Rockefeller Theatre Collection

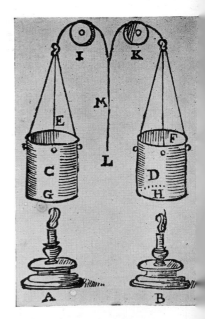

101. CANDLE DIMMERS, 1638. B
Sabbatini, in *Practica di Fa
bricar Scena.*

102. PAGEANT COSTUME, FRANCESCO PRIMATICCIO.

103. BONARELLI, *Il Solimano*, FLORENCE, 1620. Engraved by Jacques Callot.

104. LUIGI BURNACINI. INTERIOR OF THE IMPERIAL THEATRE, VIENNA, 1668.

105. Design For *Le Roman de Paris,* 1631.

106. Rock Scene, *Il Dono del Re,* Rivoli, 1645.

107. Design For *Il Dono del Re*, Rivoli, 1645.

108. Domenico Mauro, Design, *La Favore Degli Dei*, Parma, 1690.

109. Opera Setting, Turin, 1681.

110. Design For the Ballet *L'Unione Perla*, Turin, 1660.

111, 112. Designs For the Ballet *L'Unione Perla*, Turin, 1660. Note painted back drop above and side panels below.

113-116. Three Designs By Giacomo Torelli For *Andromède*, 1650. Upper right, Design For *Il Bellero Fonte*, 1642. *Yale-Rockefeller Theatre Collection*

117. Design For *Noces de Tétis*, Torelli, 1654.

118. Design For *Il Bellero Fonte*, Torelli, 1642.

Yale-Rockefeller Theatre Collection

119. Design For *Il Bellero Fonte*, Torelli, 1642.

120. PERFORMANCE AT SAINT-LAURENT FAIR, 1786. *Le Théâtre de la Rue*

121. *L'Amour au Théâtre Italien*, BY WATTEAU.

Nor did he have any patience with the kind of corruption he found rampant. This was the kind of corruption that rarely excites puritans' revolt because their own movement is often tarred with it, that is with avarice and provinciality. His wit and ever-wagging tongue dominated the Mermaid group and frequently his great dramatic merit is overlooked in his bitter speech, though by his own admission he sought to gauge public taste, being unsuccessful at first, but ending up sufficiently well.

Beaumont and Fletcher, sons of bishops and English gentlemen, are an inseparable pair, a kind of Elizabethan Siamese twins accustomed to communal living until 1613 when FRANCIS BEAUMONT (1584-1616) married an heiress, Ursula Isley. JOHN FLETCHER (1579-1625) survived his partner for nine years and worked with other collaborators, but with none of them did he combine talents as satisfactorily as he did with Beaumont. They both produced plays separately, Fletcher wrote *The Faithful Shepherdess* (1609 or 1610), based on Guarini's *Pastor Fido; Wit Without Money* (1614?); *Bonduca and Valentinian* acted before 1619; *The Loyal Subject* (1618); *The Mad Lover* played before 1619; *The Humorous Lieutenant* (1619-20); *Women Pleased* (1620); and among a long list of others, the famous and much played *Rule a Wife and Have a Wife* acted in 1624.

Beaumont is credited with the delicacy, restraint and depth lacking in Fletcher (who is to be credited with buoyancy, facility and shallowness) but was not so prolific as his collaborator when working alone. He evidently had the type of mind which blossoms in fellowship. In 1602 he wrote the poem (doubted by some) *Salmacis and Hermaphroditus* and about the time of his marriage in 1613, the pleasant and graceful *A Masque For the Inner Temple.*

It should be mentioned that Fletcher wrote *King Henry VIII* and *The Two Noble Kinsmen* with Shakespeare; collaborated with Rowley and Massinger on *The Fair Maid of the Inn* (1626), as well as with Middleton and Massinger. However, his most important work was done with Beaumont. Their *The Knight of the Burning Pestle* was a delightful burlesque on the theatre. They also wrote *The Woman Hater* (1607), *Philaster; or, Love Lies-A-Bleeding* (1610-11) the supposed source of *Cymbeline*, and the much praised and highly regarded drama, *The Maid's Tragedy* (played not later than 1611, printed 1619).

Of the remaining Elizabethans, Massinger is certainly the most important, so we will disregard strict chronology and consider him last. GEORGE CHAPMAN (1559?-1634) was not primarily a dramatist. If he hadn't lived in a period when all important literary figures expressed themselves in the theatre he probably would never have written a play. His principal contribution to literature was due to his note-worthy scholarship and classical interests which enabled him to translate both the *Iliad* and *The Odyssey*. These facts were made memorable in John Keats' sonnet *On First Looking Into Chapman's Homer*. He brought Greek culture close to the English literary tradition. His principal plays show the effect of continental travel, particularly *Bussy d'Ambois* (1607) and *The Revenge of Bussy d'Ambois* (1613). *The Conspiracy and Tragedy of Charles, Duke of Byron* (1608) reflects contemporary French history. In addition he wrote *All Fools* (1605), *Monsieur d'Olive* (1606) and *Eastward Ho* in collaboration with Jonson and Marston. The latter was JOHN MARSTON (1575-1634) who wrote melodramas, impassioned, sensual, bloody and cynical. His best known plays are the trenchant and powerful *The Malcontent* (1605), *The Dutch Courtesan* (1605) and *What You Will* (1607), after which he abandoned the stage and took holy orders.

THOMAS DEKKER (1570-1641) was, next to Jonson, the best portrayer of his native London in this period. He excelled in his depiction of women and in his handling of street and tavern comedy. He worked largely in collaboration and on specific order for such acting companies as the Lord Admiral's Servants. He wrote *The Honest Whore* (1604) and *The Roaring Girl* (1611) with Middleton, *Westward Ho!* (1607) with Webster, *The Witch of Edmonton* (1621?, published in 1658) with Ford and Rowley. His most conspicuous success was *The Shoemakers' Holiday*, a delightful farce-comedy with strong democratic leanings and real social force, which plays better than most Elizabethan comedies in modern revival.

THOMAS HEYWOOD (?-1650) was for some years an actor, who played for Henslowe and Alleyn in 1598. After James I's accession, his name appeared in the lists of the Queen's Company. His first play was *The Four Prentices of London* (1596), which showed his sympathy with the poorer and middle classes. In the preface to *The Traveller* (1633) he claims to have had a hand in two hundred and twenty plays, of which thirty-five survive. *Edward IV* (1600) and *A Woman Killed With Kindness* (1603) are his best plays, and reflect the life of the bourgeoisie who had his sympathies. It is also worth noting that he wrote many of the pageants for the Lord Mayor's shows.

THOMAS MIDDLETON (1570-1627) wrote many plays in collaboration with Dekker, Rowley, Anthony Munday, Michael Drayton and Webster. Like Dekker, he was associated with the Lord Mayor's performances, wrote masques and seems to have had an abundant amount of civic consciousness. His plays reflect the rise of the importance of the City in English affairs, that is the rise of the moneyed class rather than the landed aristocracy. His comedies *Michaelmas Term* (1607), *A Trick To Catch The Old One* (1605), *A Game at Chess* (1624), and *A Chaste Maid in Cheapside* (1630) depict London life in a lively fashion. Of his serious plays, the most important are the tragedy *Women, Beware Women* (1612) and the psychological play *The Changeling* (with Rowley, 1621), which seems to have had a profound effect on his audience. Those men and women met on equal ground the challenge to their intellect of the effect of crime and illicit relations on human love and character.

JOHN FORD (1586-1639) was placed by Charles Lang, that devoted and appreciative critic of the stage, in "the first order of poets." Modern criticism does not rate him so high, except for the play *'Tis A Pity She's A Whore* (1626), which is a dramatic study of incest between brother and sister that frequently captures the imagination and powerfully affects the auditor. *The Broken Heart* (1633) and *The Witch of Edmonton* (1621?, printed in 1658), written with William Rowley, are the best of his other pieces.

CYRIL TOURNEUR (flourished 1600-1626) was originally called Turner but he changed the spelling of his name in 1611. He was primarily a poet but he wrote two intensely heavy tragedies *The Revenger's Tragedy* (1607) and the more bombastic *The Atheist's Tragedy* (1611). The former has been highly regarded in the past but modern reading, even with sympathetic eyes, does not seem to justify its high estate.

WILLIAM ROWLEY lived at the end of the sixteenth and the beginning of the seventeenth century. He was primarily a collaborator as is evidenced by the constant reappearance of his name in this chapter. He was responsible, alone, for four plays, *A New Wonder; A Woman Never Vext* (1632), *A Match At Midnight* (1633), his best known piece *All's Lost By Lust* (1633) and *A Shoemaker, A Gentleman* (1638).

There remain three principal Elizabethans and by now we are mostly concerned with the Stuart reigns. Gloomy JOHN WEBSTER (1580?-1625) was another of Henslowe's staff of playwrights. He indulged in frequent collaborations with Anthony Munday (1553-1633) who had a flair for plotting plays, Middleton, Heywood, Dekker, and Drayton. He was primarily a writer of melodrama but certain lyric qualities raised some of his writing to the tragic level. He is best remembered for the seldom revived, but essentially interesting, *The Duchess of Malfi* (1613-14), which is a fascinating study of evil and unhappiness. His earlier play *The White Devil* (1611-12) also has an Italian setting (in this respect he was like the greater Shakespeare) and is truly awesome. At least he succeeded in what he was trying to do, partly because he made full use of the ingenuity of the stage director and the transcendent ability of his actors. His other plays are unimportant. He has already been mentioned as a co-author of *Westward Ho!* (1607), and some say that he completed *The Malcontent* for Marston.

Due to the fact that he survived until after the Restoration, JAMES SHIRLEY (1596-1666) is usually called the last of the Elizabethans. This coincidence caused the incurably romantic Charles Lamb to acclaim him, not because he was inherently a good theatre man or even a passable dramatist, but because "he was the last of a great race." He had a certain felicity in writing and was fortunate in having an opportunity to draw on the wealth of what had gone before him in a great century. This was particularly true when one realizes that it was not considered unscrupulous to steal an idea, a method or even lines from another without even giving credit. Perhaps Shakespeare was particularly guilty of this. Shirley was educated at Oxford and Cambridge, became a Roman Catholic, gave up his clerical living, and taught. It has been said that an indifferent playwright came out of a first class schoolmaster. His best regarded play was *Love's Cruelty* (1640) a tragedy of sorts. Despite his loyalty to Charles and the fact that he was a favorite at court, it was a relief to many when he returned to teaching after the closing of the theatres in 1642.

The last of these great writers whom we must consider is PHILIP MASSINGER (1583-1640), who wrote many plays in collaboration with Dekker, Beaumont and Fletcher. Having spent four years at Oxford, he ranked as a scholar and one of the most powerful dramatists of his period. This latter characteristic may have been due to the remarkable tortures to which he exposed some of his characters, particularly in *The Virgin Martyr* (with Dekker, 1622). His interest in and perhaps conversion to Roman Catholicism, a characteristic of the later Elizabethans, is evidenced by the plays, *The Renegade* (1624) and *The Maid of Honor* (1632), which solves all problems by having the heroine take the veil. *The City Madam* (1632) was rated as a satirical comedy; but his most famous play, and the one for which he is remembered, is *A New Way To Pay Old Debts* (1625). This fame is largely due to the well-known character, Sir Giles Overreach, which for more than two centuries was considered as much a test of an actor's skill as Hamlet, Shylock and Lear. Robert H. Ball has made a masterly study of the portrayal of this character on the stage in *The Amazing Career of Sir Giles Overreach* (1939), which describes every important performance of the part. Massinger has been ranked only second to Shakespeare in the opening up and development of plot structure.

The time is drawing near for the Puritan triumph over the theatre, a theatre which allied itself with an unpopular cause. Before we reach that we have a most important theatrical development to consider, one in which scenic investiture reached a height only once or twice challenged and never equalled on the English stage. We refer to the Elizabethan, or rather the Stuart masque which claimed Jonson and Milton as its literary exponents and Inigo Jones as its supreme scenic master. It was a purely aristocratic form of entertainment introduced into England from the Italian courts and it attained popularity because it gave the nobility an opportunity to perform as actors in graceful representations of mythological and faëry themes.

In the full flush of her Fifteenth Century Renaissance, Italy had introduced the masque as a colorful variant and handmaiden to the pastoral comedy. The richness of the costuming and scenery, the mingling of music and dance with drama which was simple in detail, make a fascinating study.

Despite its physical beauty and frequent opulence it was essentially unsophisticated in plot: a group arrives masked, joins in a dance, pays some tribute or makes some offering—that is all that happens in most of these pieces. To a certain extent the masque can be likened to the dance dramas which may have preceded tragedy, but despite the naïveté in structure it was an essentially sophisticated form. This form can be traced through the induction scenes of such previously-mentioned plays as *The Arraignment of Paris* (1584) and *James IV* (1591), which were displayed in performances in London or in Elizabeth's progresses about the country. Certainly Shakespeare made some use of this form in portions of many of his plays, notably in *As You Like It, A Midsummer Night's Dream, The Winter's Tale*, and *The Tempest*. However, the chief literary champion was Ben Jonson, though one other in a single piece has capped them all from a literary point of view—John Milton in *Comus*, performed at Ludlow Castle in 1634.

However, the great English masques, costly though they were, came largely during the Stuart reigns. Charles didn't mind spending money but good Scotch thrift, or plain meanness, made James think twice before parting with a penny. In spite of his parsimony James allocated four thousand pounds for a single production. Multiply that by ten, because of the comparative value of money, and you will reach the equivalent of two hundred thousand dollars, the cost of an opulent Broadway musical. It must be remembered that this was for a production for a few favored guests for a single performance and there was neither intention nor opportunity to recover any initial expenditure. The next time you marvel at the prodigality of a New

York producer in spending a quarter of a million dollars for a *Jumbo* or a *Show Boat*, recall the thrifty James and the production of Jonson's *Oberon* in 1611.

Before mentioning some of the more important of these costly toys of a wealthy aristocracy that wished to have its eyes blinded by golden costumes gleaming in thousands of lights and scenes miraculously changing before them, we should examine briefly the methods of staging and the places of playing. It must always be remembered that when these elaborate imitations of France and Italy were being staged, the bareness of the professional theatre existed simultaneously. Perhaps the need for rich costumes for the actors at the Globe and Fortune came out of a desire to compete with these subsidized royal or noble performances in royal halls.

In London the scene of these triumphs was Whitehall Palace. The first Banqueting House was erected for Elizabeth in 1581. When it was determined in 1606 that it should be used for James' masques, it was reconstructed to accommodate these performances. After its destruction by fire in 1619, Inigo Jones designed a new one (1622), which still stands (October 1940), though its present ministerial use is far from the one for which it was planned. In his beautifully illustrated *Stuart Masques and The Renaissance Stage*, Allardyce Nicoll records that in 1637 Charles I, fearful of damage to the painted ceiling (from the candles, perhaps) commanded Jones to design a "Great new Masking Room," which was subsequently used in the few remaining years before the Civil War. The Great Hall was also used between 1619 and 1622 while the new banquet hall was being built.

Temporary seating had to be arranged which would not damage the walls or floor. The king's seat was on a platform which was called the "state" and was usually in the dead center opposite the stage and far enough back so that the elaborately arranged perspective was most perfect for the royal eyes alone; all others whether foreign ambassadors or nobles of the realm had to be content with a slight distortion of view. The royal party sat on the dais while the others were seated in tiers. Before them, to create the distance necessary for illusion and to permit the movements of dancers, was the well-carpeted dancing place. The masquers descended by stairs or ramp to dance with selected guests. It must not be forgotten that the performers were noble, even royal when the queen took part.

Various authorities, and the evidences of the scripts themselves, indicate a width of forty feet and a depth of twenty-eight. The front of the stage was six feet high while the rear was slightly more than seven feet; this permitted many of the scenic devices to be worked from below. Because of this height above the level of the hall the seating space for the spectators had to be proportioned in order to command a clear view. There was a forestage with wings and a stage proper with back shutters and back drop.

In this plan Inigo Jones imitated Palladio and Serlio, so that in general, what is said about the English masques also holds true for the Italian and French. All kinds of surprises, an important element in this type of performance, were effected through elaborate stage machines and trapped areas which permitted rocks to expand to mountain size and trees to grow before the delighted, startled eyes of the court. From above came the "glory," cloud machines which permitted the gods to appear and disappear, in essence the old *deus ex machina*. The *periaktoi* of the Greeks was most important as the extant eighteenth century scenery of the summer theatre at Sweden's Drottningholm displays. (A film has been made of this scenery in action which permits students of the theatre to see just how Louis Desprez, as a representative of the court designers, worked his elaborate effects.)

A separate stage front was often provided, in fact such authorities as Furttenbach and Sabbatini urged it strongly, as a place before the acting area in which the curtain might fall; to provide light and air for the mechanics working below the stage; and to permit unseen music. This advice was not always followed in the construction of the English masque stage.

The question of the curtain is an important one and since it is a problem in our own theatre, it would not be out of place for us to consider it here. This proviso for space between the edge of the stage and the acting area was to permit the disappearance of the curtain without further ado. This was particularly useful when the taut cloth dropped to the floor to permit that sudden view of the stage which many scenic designers considered most effective; a second device was to have the drapes drawn from either side and have them held by an actor in elaborate costume; another way was to allow the folds to festoon. The final method which obtains largely today was the regular up and down curtain which rose to disclose a scene. After several blasts on the trumpet, it had to be raised quickly and suddenly so as to startle the audience. A loud outpouring of music or song was frequently used to distract the audience when a rock had to open or a tree had to grow. The scenic effect was more real if the device which effected the miracle could not be seen.

The greatest scene designer and theatre architect that England produced was INIGO JONES (1573-1652). His was the only hand to uphold Albion when the Continent gloried in the beauty of its newly constructed theatres and the magnificence of its scenery and costumes. Jones made a thorough study of Roman ruins and even more particularly the work of the architect, Palladio, who created the Teatro Olimpico. James I recognized his talents and made him his architect and designer from 1605 to 1613. That he was employed by Charles I is equally well known because of Jonson's quarrel with him in 1631 (with whom did Jonson not quarrel?). The poet felt his lines were being smothered by Jones' scenery; the architect claimed he should have equal importance because his costumes charmed the eye and contributed to the pleasure of their noble audience. Certainly Queen Henrietta Maria favored him with all her love of the theatre and commanded him to design the scenery for Fletcher's *The Faithful Shepherdess* on Twelfth Night in 1634. This was but one of his many richly designed productions for the royal entrepreneurs.

The young noblemen and ladies who acted in these pieces were extravagantly gowned and the descriptions of their richly jewelled costumes, which were a far cry from nature, make it quite evident why these spectacles cost so much. The gentry were sometimes supplemented by professional players, for the records show sums of money expended for that purpose. One of the reasons for King Charles' growing unpopularity was his increasing demands for money, a considerable portion of which went into the production of these pieces which were performed until 1642.

Some of the most famous of these gracious masques are those of rare Ben Jonson, *Blackness* (1601), *The Hue and Cry After Cupid* (1608), *Queens* (1609), *Oberon* (1611), *The Fortunate Isles* (1625), and *Chloridia* (1631). Samuel Daniel, Master of The Queen's Revels, wrote *Tethys' Festival* (1610) in which the boy Charles I, made his debut; John Marston contributed the *Huntingdon Masque* (1607), and *Mountebanks* (1618); Thomas Campion wrote *Somerset's Masque* (1613); and James Shirley produced *The Triumph of Peace* (1633); Milton's glorious *Comus* has been mentioned before; Sir William D'Avenant, of whom we will have more to say when the Stuarts return to England, composed *The Temple of Love* (1635) and the famous *Salmacida Spolia* (1640). This is a constellation of the most brilliant theatrical splendor England ever saw.

England's greatest theatrical glory was cut short apparently by the grim, intolerant and bigoted Cromwell. Perhaps all the great dramatic talents were written out. Perhaps our eyes were still dazzled by the effulgence of Marlowe, Shakespeare, Jonson and blinded by the spectacular creations of Inigo Jones. Perhaps the Civil War came at the crucial moment. Whatever the cause, whatever the reason, the theatres of England shut their doors on a grey world in 1642 and never dared to open them *publicly* until popular reaction welcomed back the Stuarts in 1660.

⋞ IX ⋟

NEO-CLASSIC FRANCE

(1550-1700)

OUR last view of the French theatre was during the riotous days of the medieval *soties* in the latter half of the fifteenth and first half of the sixteenth century. It is not to be supposed that these farces died out. In fact they became even more popular as the populace became more conscious of the theatre.

This was a dark and warlike period with powerful nobles and religious and civil strife. France was in the hands of the Valois family which was closely connected with the Medicis of Italy. Strong minded Henri II had taken the devious and much debated Catherine de Medici as his bride for purely political reasons. He then proceeded to amuse himself with the handsome and intellectual Diane de Poitiers, who had been mistress to his father, Francis I. Catherine was a foreigner, disliked, put aside, but still and all she was the queen and, as the mother of three sons, her supremacy came later as one by one they ruled France at her behest.

The shortlived Francis II, who had married the beautiful Mary (later Queen of the Scots), soon died and through Charles IX and the pleasure loving Henri III, Catherine and the professional theatre in France began to come into their own. Her daughter Margaret was married to Henri de Navarre, who took part in the disastrous religious and civil wars which ravaged France until he, as Henri IV, restored unity. He, too, loved and encouraged the theatre.

It has been typical of France that in her darkest hours she has achieved a gaiety in her theatre. Perhaps half of this mood has been cynical and half a desperate need to forget political troubles in order to conquer her enemies by gentler, more efficacious means than men and guns.

The farces gave a needed release for energies that war and destruction had not set free. *Maître Pierre Pathelin* was still popular and is

121

the best known of these pieces. The secular drama flourished as the religious drama declined, and by 1548 the latter form of theatre was suppressed by law. This freed a growing opposition to the theatre on the part of the Church which had restrained its wrath and dislike of liberal ideas so long as it had any part in the dramatic performances. From this time on the clergy fulminated against actors and dramatists, denying them the sacrament of communion and Christian burial. In addition such secular groups as the Basochians and *Enfants Sans Souci* denounced the theatre.

The reason for the arbitrary decree of 1548 was curiously enough due to the Protestant Reformation. Apparently the protesting mind seems to find the theatre obnoxious. The excuse offered was that the Bible and religion were profaned by the enactment on stage of religious scenes for the instruction and pleasure of the people. This criticism filled the minds of the Huguenots and eventually enough Catholics became so uncomfortable that they began to wonder if it were a wise thing for people to know too much about the Bible. And so a combination of forces brought about the decree of 1548 forbidding religious performances. Instead of discouraging the theatre this acted as a stimulant for professional performances, but there were other obstacles to be overcome.

As a price for forbidding Church plays, the *Confrérie de la Passion* was given a renewed monopoly on performances in Paris or its vicinity. This meant that if a troupe wished to play it needed both the permission and the funds to pay the high rental fees demanded by the brotherhood.

All of these taboos tended to spur on a rediscovery of Sophocles, Euripides, Aristophanes and Menander. Just as in Italy and England, French scholars and literary men turned to translating and adapting the ancients for reading and performance. The *Pléiade* took the lead in this effort for a sincere appreciation of the classics and a desire to enrich their own native tongue. Jodelle, Du Bellay, Remi Belleau, Pontus de Thyard and Ronsard were active. Jodelle's *Cléopâtre captive* in 1552 was the first classical French tragedy, the preceding pieces being merely translations.

It is unusual that, as Sainte-Beuve has written, the trend was from the Mysteries of the Christian Church to Ancient Tragedy without any transition period whatsoever. The performance that introduced this innovation in French drama was held in private at the *Collége de Boncour* with the author, his friend and disciples playing the principal parts. It seems a pity that in turning back, French dramatists could not have caught the spirit of the ancient drama and set aside the artificial rules that a misreading of Aristotle brought into force. Had these plays combined the strength of earth and heaven found in the religious plays with the fire and exaltation of Greek tragedy, the French would have made this period of their theatre as great as England's.

It was in the colleges and universities that the new dramatic form arose and the *Pléiade* held its performances as well as received its stimulus. Just as Jodelle returned to the classics for his inspiration, so did Jean Bastier, whose pen name was LA PÉRUSE, from his native heath, with *Médée*, the distinguished Pierre de Ronsard with *Plutus* (1549), Jean de la Taille with *Saul* (1572) and *Les Gabaonites* (1573), Jean Antoine de Baïf with *Antigone* out of Sophocles and his highly important *Le Brave ou Taillebras*, a version of *Miles Gloriosus*, performed in 1567, and Jacques Grévin with his *Mort de César* (1560). Etienne Jodelle was also responsible for *Didon se sacrifiant*, a *Médée*, and *Antigone*. The latter piece followed the Greek in its simple action, few characters, short acts and a strict regard for the unities of time and place, but it lacked the grandeur of the ancients. In the unities action uncomplicated by a sub-plot must transpire in the time that it takes to perform the play, or not more than twenty-four hours in all and in a single place. It was this effort to restrict dramatists to these rigid requirements that made most Renaissance tragedy of little lasting value. It was really a misunderstanding of Aristotle which was responsible for this, because one has only to read Greek plays to realize how frequently the unities of time and place were violated by the masters themselves.

In the dining halls of the colleges with the undergraduates fresh from their reading of Greek and Latin, with the elixir of ancient learning in their veins, these plays were performed by student actors. Supervised by the playwright, these productions were exciting to the youths as they saw classical precepts carried out before their very eyes. These pieces, including the coarse classic comedy *Eugène ou la Rencontre*, by Jodelle, were all intended for the university audience and not for the public theatre.

These as well as other dramatists, Jacques de la Taille (1542-1562), with *Daire* and *Alexandre*, Charles Toutain who wrote an adaptation of Seneca's *Agamemnon* in 1555, were passed over when Robert Garnier (1534-1590) began to write. As we look back on him, he seems stilted and sententious, but he was so popular that his plays were reprinted year after year. It is well to remember however that Garnier represents an advance in style. There are many beautiful passages in his eight tragedies which include *Hippolyte*, *La Troade*, *Antigone*, *Les Juives* (this was his best and described the capture of Jerusalem by Nebuchadnezzar), and *Bradamante*, celebrated for having introduced the confidant to French drama and for having been the first tragi-comedy written in French.

The first concern may have been for tragedy but at the same time a healthy comic spirit was developing despite the efforts of state and ecclesiastical censorship. The previously mentioned Jean de la Taille, who wrote the critical treatise *l'Art de la Tragédie* (1572), was responsible for an adaptation of Ariosto's *Negromante*, as well as the latter's comedy of mistaken identity, *I Suppositi*, which should be compared with George Gascoigne's version, *The Supposes*. Greater interest in Italian drama was aroused by the first visit of the *Gelosi* to Paris in 1577, which inspired PIERRE LARIVEY (1540?-1612?), born in France of Italian parentage. Practically every incident in his life and lineage is disputed except the fact that his understanding of Italian prompted him to acclimate Italian comedy to France. Changing the names of characters and locale, he retained the type characters of the *commedia dell'arte*. His prose comedies were *written* however and by 1579-80 six of them had been published. His best known play was *Les Esprits*, which was an inspiration to Regnard for his *Retour imprévu*, and to Molière for *L'École des Maris* and *L'Avare*. Three more comedies were published by 1611 but we are ignorant as to whether they were actually performed.

For the sake of setting these plays in their proper niche in the theatre so that we will not exaggerate the importance of the dramatist, an easy thing to do because he is so vital to the theatre, we had best turn our attention to the playhouse. What kind of theatre, other than the college halls, would produce these plays, what professional actors would interpret the roles and thus bring inspiration to playwright and audience alike? And finally who would constitute their audience? It must be remembered that France was torn by civil and religious strife. The Huguenots fought the Catholic League which led Spanish politics and culture into Paris. This was anathema to the Protestants.

Earlier in the same year, 1548, which saw the ban on religious performances by the *Confrérie*, the first theatre designed for that purpose in Paris was built on the site of the ancient castle of the Dukes of Burgundy; hence its name, *Hôtel de Bourgogne*. Formerly the brothers had used the *Hôtel de la Trinité*. The new theatre was in the St. Denis quarter of the city on the corner of the *Rue Mauconseil* and the *Rue Française*. The streets still retain their names and are in the first arrondissement not far from the present *Halles Centrales* or the *Administration des Postes*. In contrast to the English theatres, this theatre had a roof. Unfortunately its interior was far from attractive. The stage extended well forward into the long, narrow auditorium which contained but few seats that were near the stage. These

were for the nobility and such ladies who would risk the embroil-
ments, quarrels and even riots which took place in the playhouse.
There were two narrow galleries along the walls, very much like
those seen in old churches in many parts of America. The stage with
its equipment was quite dissimilar to the ones already described because it had been built for the presentation of mysteries. Portions of
some of these were actually played after 1548, though they were announced as tragedies and even as farces. Thus they were able to avoid
the governmental ban on further production of religious plays. The
stage had extreme depth in addition to a deep fore stage, so that plays
requiring little in the way of scenic effects were acted before a
tapestried curtain which cut off the rear half of the acting area. The
ceiling of the auditorium was low. The hall's capacity was two thousand. Smelly candles in frequent need of snuffing were placed in the
footlights to illumine the down-stage area. Above the stage was a
great four-branched chandelier with huge tallow or wax candles
(Mantzius contends that only tallow was used except at court) which
gave a steady light and brightened the upper stage. The use of drapes
and tapestries soon led to Italian perspective. In the French theatre
this use was primarily temporary in its nature and not architecturally
permanent as it was in the *Teatro Olimpico*, which derived from
the Roman. The stage decoration was multiple, though there were
several distinct sections where various scenes might be played. This
was essentially a compromise as it was necessary to use the existing
scenery for there was no money with which to purchase new settings.
The intermissions were filled with musical interludes which called for
flute, drum and several violins. The musicians were placed in a side
gallery as Sylvia England points out in *An Unrecognized Document
in the History of French Renaissance Staging* (1935) and she, along
with others, makes it abundantly clear that the French stage was not
cluttered with spectators like the English until the latter part of the
sixteenth century.

Perhaps because of the roof, or because of the dim lighting this
playhouse has frequently been described as gloomy. The performances
began at two in the afternoon and even earlier in the winter so that
the audience might return to their homes before dusk and eventual
nightfall brought out footpads and other night marauders. Not that
the good burghers were entirely safe from unpleasant adventures
while they were in the theatre itself. Pickpockets were prevalent in
the dark corridors where they gathered to ply their unpleasant trade
and to gamble with those who preferred to support their immoral
lives by crooked cards or dice. These denizens won a bad name for
the theatre. We might be more sympathetic with the later years of

the *Confrérie*, which in the beginning had done really superb work in the production of mystery plays and in the stimulation of the religious theatre, if they had themselves policed their premises and helped to maintain its good name instead of waxing rich on rents. It has been said that it is the real estate interests which tend to stifle the proper expansion of the commercial theatre and this is merely an early example.

There was an important exception to the monopoly. It did not extend to the famous fairs which took place on the outskirts of Paris, as well as in certain designated districts within the walls. There, many traveling troupes of actors who normally wandered through the provinces of France achieved the height of their ambition when they could play for a Parisian audience and even for their king, Henri IV, who was fond of attending fairs. Frequently he was seen watching the actors, his gaunt figure towering over his subjects. There were numerous celebrated quack doctors, distinguished predecessors of the medicine show and its pitchmen, who employed actors to perform plays to attract the attention of the "doctors'" prospective customers. This gave employment to the large number of actors scattered throughout the country, those actors who had received their initial training in the magnificent performances of the mystery plays throughout the Middle Ages.

The most famous of these fairs was *La Foire Saint-Germain* where some of the provincial players had established a theatre. This did not come into any real importance until 1599 when another provincial troupe headed by Mathieu Laporte and his actress-wife Marie, first woman of the French stage, appeared there. Many of the comedians who were later to become famous on the stage of the *Hôtel de Bourgogne* or the *Théâtre du Marais* to which the Laportes were to transfer their allegiance. Jean Farine, Deslauriers, Guillot-Gorju (whose real name was Bertrand Hardouin) were among those comic actors and jugglers who were to win permanent fame on the stage. Farces largely made up the *repertoire* of these fairs but serious plays of superior literary merit were also performed.

To return to the playhouse we find that as early as 1578 whilst Charles IX still reigned, a year before the fateful Massacre of St. Bartholomew, the *Hôtel de Bourgogne* was rented to a professional troupe under the leadership of one Agnan Sarat of whom we know nothing more than that he and other French, Italian, English and Spanish troupes used to play there. In 1599 a native company headed by Valleran Lecomte and an Italian group played at the Court of Henri IV. Afterwards at the *Hôtel* the former referred to his men as the King's Men. By 1610 his company was established there as a permanent troupe. Three famous comic actors were included in this group, namely, Gros-Guillaume, who had formerly headed his own men, Gaultier-Garguille and Turlupin. Another of the mountebanks from the fair was Tabarin, who was well-liked but never achieved a permanent theatre post. The first three of these players were masters of dry humor and excelled in farce. The *Hôtel* wisely chose to emphasize this form because of its popularity among the populace. Turlupin played the broad parts of rascally personal servants. Gros-Guillaume was enormously fat, hence his name, with a mobility of expression which excited the mirth of the expectant audience. The thin and bow-legged Gaultier-Garguille had a salty wit and a flair for imitation which convulsed his spectators. Along with these farces which exploited the abilities of three such expert farceurs, melodramas and later tragic pieces were performed. The repertoire of this theatre was largely taken from Alexandre Hardy and other authors, whose plays were written by special contract with the management.

The King's Men received royal patronage in name only for Henri IV was as niggardly in this respect as the English Elizabeth, and the actors were ill-paid and frequently abused and assaulted. Many of the so-called nobility not only declined to pay their admission but vilified and even beat any manager who dared to insist that they pay for their entertainment, which was the pleasant privilege of the bourgeoisie and the artisans who frequented the playhouse.

Despite these discouragements and lack of financial and spiritual aid the troupe prospered sufficiently to maintain itself and to pay the *Confrérie* its rent. Relations remained amicable and for a long time the *Hôtel de Bourgogne* grew to be highly regarded in the affections of the Parisians. Unfortunately a variety of internal differences sprang up and in 1622 the King's Men decided to go on tour. In a panic, the *Confrérie* managed to persuade a provincial company to take over but with such poor results that these actors returned to the country. Paris, the heart of the nation and arbiter of things theatrical, was left with no playhouse. About 1622 a contemporary wrote,

> *"Tout divertissement nous manque;*
> *Tabarin ne va plus en banque;*
> *L'Hôtel de Bourgogne est désert."* *

That disgraceful state of affairs fortunately did not continue because Giambattista Andreini, son of the famous Isabella and her spouse brought his *commedia dell'arte* troupe to town and the people again could go to the theatre.

However, dependence on foreign talent was no answer to the problem so a new French troupe, the Players of the Prince d'Orange,

---

* We lack all entertainment,
  Tabarin goes no more to business,
  The *Hôtel de Bourgogne* is deserted.

took over in 1625. Lenoir was the leader and the group contained a number of actors who were to distinguish themselves on the French stage. Jacquemin Jadot, Alizon, Julien Geoffrin (better known as Jodelet) who played comic servants with consummate skill, and greatest of all, Guillaume Desgilberts, called Mondory by the theatre world, a virile actor of heroes. In 1628 their contract with the Brotherhood expired and the Royal Company (which had gone so far in its efforts to interfere with their rivals' success as to inspire riots near the playhouse to embarrass and annoy the patrons of Lenoir's men) hastened to return to the *Hôtel de Bourgogne*. From then on, they remained there with very considerable success, exile from Paris having made them more than willing to get on amiably with the demanding *Confrérie*. The latter however did not lose its fondness for the Prince d'Orange's troupe which was permitted to set up headquarters in the Berthault Tennis Court. The tennis courts which are frequently mentioned in French theatre histories were covered enclosures and only needed to have a stage set up at the end to convert them into adequate acting establishments. The next year saw another of these tennis courts turned into a theatre and the famous *Théâtre du Marais* was born. This constituted a formidable rival to the *Hôtel de Bourgogne*, which continued until the eventual weakness of the Marais brought about its absorption by the *Guénégaud* troupe, which had been Molière's men.

By 1634 the Royal Players were receiving real financial support from King Louis XIII, but the subvention was not offered to the Marais troupe, whose leadership was gradually being transferred from Lenoir to the principal actor, Mondory, a man of great ability. This was a period of consolidation rather than one of change. Valleran Lecomte had been succeeded as head of the Royal group by Pierre Le Messier, who acted under the name of Bellerose. Good-looking in a languid way, affected yet gallant, favored by women, he achieved his greatest success as a tragedian though he was admired in Corneille's comedy *Le Menteur* (*The Liar*), its characteristics naturally reflecting his own personality.

In contrast, the tragedian Mondory was violent in his playing and was considered coarse by many. His energies were enormous and were especially esteemed by Cardinal Richelieu who does not seem to have given him the financial support which would have enabled him to sustain himself against the King's raids on the Marais actors. These were occasioned by the rivalry between Louis and Richelieu. The King, finding it necessary to bow to his all-powerful minister in matters of state, took his revenge by ordering six of Mondory's actors to report to Bellerose for duty. These included, of all people, Lenoir and his wife, Alizon, Jacquemin Jadot, L'Espy and Jodelet.

Corneille's plays, however, constituted a great support for Mondory, who had acquired the Barons, parents of the famous Michel Baron. The *Marais* prospered until 1636 when, during a performance of Tristan's *Mariamne*, Mondory, who was playing Herod in his usual violent style, was stricken with apoplexy. He partially recovered and on February 22, 1637 played in *L'Aveugle de Smyrne* at the request of Richelieu. At his retirement after this performance he was granted a pension by his churchly benefactor. With his removal from the theatre, Richelieu's interest in the *Marais* was over. The best actors went to the *Bourgogne* and Corneille sent his plays there. The remotely situated *Marais* began to produce farces which were considered old-fashioned and beneath the notice of the court, though some years later with the return of Jodelet some of its former reputation and popular esteem returned.

These two theatres were the stage of Paris. Plays continued to be acted at court and Cardinal Richelieu built the present Palais Royal in his own palace; but more will be said of this handsome stage which passed into the hands of Molière many years later.

It is now time to turn back to the playwrights who provided the dramatic fare which served the actors and managers during their strenuous efforts to establish themselves in the minds as well as the affections of the court and public. Of these, the next in order can be passed over briefly; ANTOINE MONTCHRÉTIEN (1575-1621) followed the style of Garnier. Several of his tragedies were written for the *Hôtel de Bourgogne* and were successfully produced about 1600. His best known play *L'Écossaise* (1605) was concerned with Mary, Queen of Scots.

ALEXANDRE HARDY (1560-1631) was the most prolific writer of his time. His 1200 plays rivaled the fecundity of the Spanish playwrights. In addition to being official dramatist for the *Hôtel de Bourgogne* up to the time of his death, he was court poet to Henry IV. In contrast to the growing pseudo-classicist school of writing, Hardy endeavored to place his characters in his own time, and to have them think contemporaneously, despite his emulation of the five-act Senecan model. His forthright, honest, romantic workmanship and cleanliness of written speech attracted many people to the playhouse who had never gone before. His plays had action and he even introduced comic scenes into his tragedies. He disliked long-winded speeches and tried to keep his dialogue short and pithy. His best known piece was *Mariamne* (1610), though his constant flow of plays kept the Paris stage well-stocked for forty years.

Because they followed the tradition of Hardy, we can not ignore GEORGES (1601-1667) and MADELEINE DE SCUDÉRY (1607-1701), brother and sister, who were primarily novelists but who were responsible for a successful excursion into the theatre with the tragicomedy *Ligdamon et Lidias*. Scudéry unhappily allowed himself to be directed by Richelieu to undertake an attack on *Le Cid*. This provoked a tremendous controversy, which in its bitterness and insincerity can only be compared with the inspired attacks on Hugo's *Hernani* almost two centuries later.

Though JEAN DE MAIRIET (1604-1686) was a contemporary of Corneille, we had best discuss him briefly before going on to the great French dramatist. He was primarily an imitator of the Italian literary theatre, which certainly did not bear emulation though it was, because of its supposed classical inspiration, slavishly admired by the French and English of the sixteenth century. Mairiet was also involved in the attacks on *Le Cid*, but his neo-classic point of view would probably have forced him into the quarrel even if Richelieu had not prompted it. His own plays were influenced by his admiration for Spanish extravagance of expression, that Gongorism which swept over Western Europe, and Italian preciousness and affectation which Molière later was to ridicule in its French manifestations. Mairiet admired the Italians as did the Court (Marie de Medici as Queen had something to do with that), and his masterpiece *Sophonisbe* (1629) was unresolved, stuffy and dryly imitative.

In contrast to Mairiet, was that other follower of Hardy, JEAN DE ROTROU (1609-1650), whom Voltaire called the real founder of the French theatre. Certainly had his ideas triumphed, the stage would have been romantic rather than classical because he risked unpopularity and the anger of Richelieu by refusing to fall in line on the rule of the three unities. This was of course quite aside from his collaboration with four others on one of the Cardinal's play projects. His best known and most successful works were *La Bague de l'Oubli*, the comedy *The Ring of Forgetfulness* (1628), and the tragedy *Saint-Genest* (1649) which combined naïveté and profundity in a fashion which suggests Victor Hugo.

France had been a nation for eight hundred years before her first dramatist of first rank appeared and then within a single century came her three most important dramatists: Corneille, Racine, Molière. The earliest of these to appear on the scene was PIERRE CORNEILLE (1606-1684), who was born in Rouen. He was educated for the law and admitted to the bar in 1627. He practised with but slight success in his native town until Mondory's troupe arrived there for a performance. This was presumably on the occasion of Valleran Lecomte's resumption of the lease on the *Hôtel de Bourgogne* when the Prince d'Orange's company was turned out. Corneille's imagination and his naturally literary turn of mind were caught by the excitement of the theatre and by the excellence of the acting which had delighted Paris. He wrote a comedy *Mélite*, which he showed to Mondory who produced it and took it back to the metropolis where he staged it in 1629. Corneille went up to Paris for this production and remained there for a number of years carefully writing one play after another for the Marais troupe, for the Bourgogne and for the Cardinal.

Mélite came out of his own experience and therefore was realistic. He himself said that he used common sense and was guided by the plays of Hardy, though he did not intentionally flout the famous rules because he was entirely ignorant of them. He actually was writing a comedy of manners as he saw it and he achieved laughter without the introduction of the stock farce characters which the *commedia dell' arte* and the French imitations had made standard.

His next play, *Clitandre* (1632) followed the unities deliberately though he disliked the form; there is little else in the piece to interest any but the biographer of the dramatist. It is as worthless as he intended it to be. Next came a series of unimportant plays written whilst he learned his art, *La Veuve* (*The Widow*, 1633), *La Galerie du Palais* (*The Palace Gallery*, 1634), *La Suivante* (*The Follower*, 1634), *La Place Royale* (*The Royal Square*, 1634), *L'Illusion Comique* (1634). Despite his distaste for the unities which Richelieu, the supreme arbiter of good taste and good art, was enforcing, Corneille paid lip service to them. It must never be forgotten that he was a moralist and to achieve holy ends he was willing to sacrifice a small bit of incense to the gods so that he might privately worship as he chose.

The Cardinal decided that it would raise the level of the stage if the leading dramatists were to collaborate on plays though each was to be singly responsible for an act. The monstrosities thus turned out include *Les Tuileries*, *L'Aveugle de Smyrne* (*The Blind Man of Smyrna*), and *La Grande pastorale*.

Meanwhile in 1635 Corneille was writing his first tragedy *Médée* and preparing for his *chef d'oeuvre*, *Le Cid*. For this he went to Guillen de Castro's *Las Mocedades del Cid* for inspiration and plot. His treatment of the characters was entirely original. Heroism and grace were coupled with the beauty of his verse, and the highmindedness of his sentiments elevated this drama to a high place in dramatic hierarchy. To Richelieu's annoyance he disregarded the unities and the Cardinal urged the newly founded *Académie Française* 'to find' against the play in *Sentiments de l'Académie sur Le Cid* (1638) for these irregularities, though its beauties were acknowledged. The drama itself had been staged in the season of 1636-37.

Le Cid was the first, though the best known, of his four tragedies which include: *Horace* (1639), *Cinna* (1639) and *Polyeucte* (1640). These last three plays were noble and highminded. They also represent a structural advance over *Le Cid* with their rationalistic poetry. At the time of his death Racine, his rival, praised him highly before the Academy saying that he had found French poetry and the French stage disordered, irregular and chaotic and had reformed it and endowed it with *"raison,"* that quality beloved of the French.

In 1642 came *Le Menteur* (*The Liar*). Corneille's easy comedy and well-drawn portrait of a liar entitled him to be considered an important comic writer. However he was primarily a tragedian. *Rodogune* (1646), which many consider impressive and thrilling, almost equalled *Polyeucte*, the play in which the celebrated actor, Floridor, made a hit.

In 1647, after two unsuccessful attempts, the author was admitted to the Academy. From then on the dramatic and literary power of his work declined. He withdrew from Paris to Rouen to work on his verse translation of *Imitatio Christi* which was published in 1656?. He returned to the dramatic wars in 1659 with *Oedipe*, which was well received; in 1671 he collaborated with Molière and Quinault on the opera *Psyché*, which had many beautiful verse passages; his last play was *Suréna* written in 1674, just ten years before his death. Corneille was an eloquently vocal dramatist with high moralist intentions rather than a tragic writer of great power. His enemies said that much of his success was due to the excellence of the acting and the beauty of the mounting of his plays.

The furore of *Le Cid* brought him a following among the younger dramatists; but of these, only his younger brother THOMAS CORNEILLE (1625-1709) stands out. He wrote more than forty plays of which *Ariane* (1672); *Le Festin de Pierre* (1673); *Le Comte d'Essex* (1678), a treatment of the Elizabeth and Essex story; and greatest of all *Timocrate* (1656) stand out. This last play was given eighty-four times at the Marais, a phenomenon for that time. The actors tired of it before the audiences did, so the bored company stopped the run. Curiously enough it was never revived as far as we know.

Another contemporary of the Corneille brothers was PAUL SCARRON (1610-1660), the comic writer who was married to Françoise d'Aubigné who was later to be Mme. de Maintenon and wife of Louis XIV. He had a brilliant and scurrilous wit and his plays always had a *succès de scandale* as well as a more popular success. Perhaps part of this came from the serious accident which made him a paralytic and left him without any use of the lower part of his body. His famous burlesques included *Jodelet; ou le maître Valet* which depended on jocular quips, the equivalent of today's slick wisecracks, and the ability of the celebrated farceur, Jodelet himself, and *Les trois Dorothées, ou Jodelet souffleté* (*The Three Dorothys; or, Jodelet Insulted*, 1645); in addition he wrote a farce, *Scènes du capitaine Matamare et de Boniface pédant* (1647). His most decent and, curiously enough, best plays came after his marriage in 1651; *Don Japhet d'Arménie* (1653) which was dedicated to the King, *L'Ecolier de Salamanque* (*The Salamancan Scholar*, 1654) and *Le Marquis ridicule* (1656). There were also two plays published posthumously in 1662, *La fausse apparence* (*The False Appearance*), and *Le Prince corsaire*. Scarron's house was the center of scandalous gossip and witty intrigue as Corneille, Scudéry and his sister, Ninon de l'Enclos, Saint-Evremond and Marion Delorme were among those who gathered there. The income from his plays provided for this gathering place. A pension from his father and the Queen-Mother, Anne of Austria, supplemented it. In fact his establishment was said to have rivaled the *Hôtel de Rambouillet* in the brilliance of its conversation.

At this time CYRANO DE BERGERAC (1620?-1655) was also living in Paris. His own fame is inevitably eclipsed by Rostand's enormously popular drama which concerns him and bears his name. With his long, deformed nose and his superb ability as a swordsman his life was filled with the broiling exploits that we remember from the play. His tragedy about Sejanus, *La Mort d'Agrippine*, was attacked as irreligious and was a failure but he was consoled by the success of his comedy *Le Pédant joué*. This last play was produced at the *Hôtel de Bourgogne*, with the pompous Montfleury playing the fat part of the pedagogue. The actor's performance so displeased Bergerac that he ordered him not to play again for a month. Montfleury, astonished, did not take this command as seriously as Cyrano meant it and played the next night. Bergerac returned the next night and ordered him to leave the stage during the performance. Montfleury meekly withdrew. Such a man was Cyrano de Bergerac.

Though rather outside our province, it is worth mentioning that opera was introduced into France from Italy in 1645. *La Festa Teatrale della Finta Pazzia* was produced at the Petit-Luxembourg Palace at the behest of Cardinal Mazarin who aspired to be the theatrical arbiter and prime minister as Richelieu had been. Giacomo Torelli, the famous Venetian scene designer, had written the libretto as well as provided the *décor* and Giulio Strozzi had supplied the musical score. Since the French did not care for opera any more than they cared for Mazarin, the production was a complete failure. Torelli's coming had one beneficial effect however; he reformed scenic design and the whole principle of effective staging, by his introduction of proper stage machinery which could change heavy sets of scenery in a few seconds. So successful had he been in his native Venice that his machinery had been considered an invention of the devil and efforts had been made to assassinate him. He utilized this "sorcery" in an operatic production, Corneille's *Andromède* in 1650, just as earlier audiences had responded to the witcheries of Jacques Callot (1592-1635).

PHILIPPE QUINAULT'S (1635-1688) appearance on the scene was the occasion of the beginning of royalty payments to authors in France. Corneille had received two hundred crowns for each of his plays (Tristan commanded but a hundred). In 1653 he offered the *Hôtel de Bourgogne Les Rivales* and it was accepted at the usual rate but when he revealed it to be the work of Quinault, the actors refused to pay more than fifty crowns for it, despite the fact that they liked it. Then Tristan suggested that no down payment be made but that the dramatist should receive ten percent of the receipts for the first run of the play, after which the rights were to be vested in the company playing it. This proved satisfactory to all concerned and *Les Rivales* was produced. It was a huge success and the handsome eighteen-year-old author was more than satisfied. Quinault was nonetheless neither an important tragic nor comic writer but he eventually found his field in opera which had become popular with the coming of Lulli and the constant encouragement of the court. Between 1671 and 1686 he wrote the libretti for fourteen operas to Lulli's music; *Atys* (1676), *Proserpine* (1680), *Roland* (1685) and *Armide* (1686) were the most successful, the third having been taken from Ariosto and the last from Tasso.

Before we make way for Racine and Molière, we must take notice of FRANÇOIS TRISTAN L'HERMITÉ (? -1655), whose chief fame came from the success of *Mariamne* which was produced in 1636 at the Marais by the celebrated Mondory who acted Herod. His other plays were not of any considerable importance though they were reasonably popular then.

In point of time JEAN RACINE (1639-1699) belongs after Molière, whom he followed along the road to fame, but from the point of style, content, and attitude toward the theatre he is the successor of Pierre Corneille, whom he never equalled in originality but occasionally surpassed in facility. They both wrote what has been called polite tragedy. Though they thought it classic, with time on our side, we term it neo-classic. Any student of any period or any subject has always the interesting task of weighing the evidence which contemporary observation offers against the long view of scholarship.

Racine was born at *La Ferté-Milon* where his father was a well-to-do official of good family. Orphaned at four, he was taken in charge by his paternal grandparents. In his tenth year his grandfather died and his grandmother, who espoused Jansenism with a devoutness that this cause instilled, retired to the seat of the cult, Port-Royal. According to Catholic authorities this was a heresy that denied free will or the possibility of entering heaven by a reformation of character; the Protestants say that it was a revulsion from the casuistry of the Jesuits who were the bitter opponents of the Jansenists. Whichever is correct young Racine was thoroughly brought up in its teachings at home, then at the *Collège de Beauvais*, and at the religious retreat at Port-Royal where his grandmother and two aunts lived and taught until 1656. For four years he stayed there learning Greek from the sacristan and remarkable scholar, Claude Lancelot, and Latin and the humanities from Pierre Nicole. He learned Greek readily and began to steep himself in Hellenistic culture at the same time that he studied theology which he rejected at first but which he eventually adopted as his profession. Following this, he went for a year to the *Collège d'Harcourt* where he continued to read Greek, as some of his extant copies and the manuscript of his notes on the *Odyssey* in the *Bibliothèque Nationale* demonstrate.

Then, still with the Jansenist eye upon him, he went to live in Paris where he was under the tutelage of his cousin, Nicolas Vitart, intendant of the Duc de Luynes. He led a gay, though not dissipated, life with his new friends who included Abbé Le Vasseur and La Fontaine. His friendships were strong and endured through the long period before his marriage.

Racine began his literary career with a politic poem to Cardinal Mazarin and an ode, *La Nymphe de la Seine*, occasioned by the marriage of Louis XIV in 1660, when he was twenty-one and Louis but seventeen. On the recommendation of the critic, Jean Chapelain, the King granted him an annuity of a hundred *louis d'or* from the treasury. His next effort, *La Renommée aux Muses* (1663-4) was criticised by Boileau with such good sense and humor that it won Racine's heart and they became close friends.

All of this was but preparation for his theatrical career which began rather inauspiciously with *Amasie* (non-surviving) which was purchased by the *Hôtel de Bourgogne* but never produced by them. This venture so horrified his family that he was dragged from Paris and bullied into living with his uncle at Uzès and urged to seek living in the church. The only relief he obtained from the provincialities of this small town was in reading his beloved Greek and learning Italian and Spanish. He became so bored that he returned to the metropolis, where he came under the patronage of the Duc de Saint-Aignan, and soon met Molière, to whom he showed the script of *La Thébaïde*, which was enriched by Euripides and to a slighter degree by Seneca. The plot was simple and straightforward; he had rejected the examples of the two Corneilles and returned to first classic principles, an innovation which was always to be a characteristic of his writing. *La Thébaïde, ou les Frères Ennemis* (*The Theban; or, the Hostile Brothers*, 1664) was staged at the *Palais Royal* and though admired by many, was not a financial success. He followed this with another Greek subject in *Alexandre le Grand* (1665) which was first produced at Molière's theatre and was the occasion of the break between the two. Racine's vanity had been aroused by the intrigue of Floridor at the *Bourgogne* and he transferred his allegiance to that theatre. (Further details will be found in the Molière section of this chapter.)

Feeling that the *Bourgogne* had produced his play more satisfactorily (undoubtedly true), he continued to write for this troupe. His ingratitude to Molière was not the only unfortunate occurrence at this time. Pierre Nicole, his former master, in a controversy with Desmarets de Saint-Sorlin in January, 1666, said that writers of romances or plays were, from the point of view of Christianity, horrible. Racine, rightly or wrongly, took this remark as personal, so he launched a brilliant, unscrupulous and unsigned attack on Jansenism which is in regrettable taste to say the least. However, this was but an interlude in his theatrical relationships. He was busy writing *Andromaque*, his first important play, which was produced by the *Bourgogne* in 1667. This tragedy was based on Pyrrhus's love for Hector's widow and her agreement to marry him in order to save the life of her son. It is admirably written and represents an advance in psychological drama in spite of the fact that it never measures up to the standards of Euripides who first used the story as the basis for his deeply moving tragedy. In this piece, the beautiful Mlle. Du Parc, belovéd of Molière, appeared as Hermione. Racine persuaded her to enter Floridor's company, but it was not for long as she died the next year in 1668.

Perhaps to show that he had more than one string to his bow, he turned to comedy. Possibly this was in emulation of Molière, or of Corneille's *Le Menteur;* at any rate *Les Plaideurs* was staged in 1668. This lively and joyful satire was an acerb rewriting of Aristophanes' *Wasps*. It was not taken too seriously by its author who had written it in the famous tavern Mouton-Blanc, where the wits La Fontaine,

Chapelle, Furetière, and Boileau gathered. Nonetheless, it shows an ability to reflect contemporary life which is otherwise lacking in his work. Passing this piece off lightly, most of his preparation went into the composition of the tragedy *Britannicus*. He knew that his audience would be waiting to see whether he could produce as substantial a play as *Andromaque*, so he exercised all of his energies. The thirteenth of December, 1669 saw its première at the *Bourgogne*, with the elder and greater Corneille in a box. The plot was woven around Nero's desire for Junie, the affianced of his step-brother Britannicus; he murders him and seizes Junie, only to lose her to the vestals. Racine centered his attention on this small portion of the Emperor's career so as not to violate the precious unities. The play is exciting and its performance at Floridor's theatre, particularly that of Mlle. d'Ennebaut, was moving. The author himself said, in a preface to the play in 1676 in which he attacked Corneille by implication, that up to the time of writing it was the best received of his dramas both by court and people. This was not altogether true as the success did not come until *after* Louis had publicly admired it. This attack on Corneille, his overbearing manners, and his double dealing with Molière increased his unpopularity with many people in the theatre as well as in literary and, to a lesser extent, court circles.

Henrietta Maria Stuart, Duchesse d'Orléans, conceived the plan of sending the same project to Corneille and Racine, asking each of them to employ it in the construction of a play. It was to be concerned with the loves of Titus, Bérénice and Antiochus. Racine won the contest, but Henrietta Maria saw neither script for she had died in the meantime. The play had a deep tenderness and many fine passages. *Bérénice* was given an excellent production at the *Bourgogne* (1670) with Floridor as Titus, Champmeslé as Antiochus and his famous wife as Bérénice. Corneille's piece, *Tite et Bérénice*, was produced the same year.

Racine's next opus *Bajazet* (1672) had little to recommend it except that the part of Roxanne was an excellent vehicle for the beautiful Mlle. Champmeslé. *Mithridate*, which the author took from Plutarch's famous *Lives*, was produced in 1673 as a challenge of supremacy to the already defeated and aging Corneille, from whom he had borrowed in this tragedy, but it has little to say to us today. It was in this same year that the *Académie Française*, through Boileau, offered a vacant chair to Molière on the condition that he give up acting. To the amazement of the Academy and of Paris, the nearly dying man refused the offer, because acting was as much a part of his life as was writing. The Academy was so stupid as to fail to drop its

stipulation so that its annals lack the greatest name in French literature. The chair was then offered to Racine, who promptly accepted it.

His next play, *Iphigénie*, was performed at the court at Versailles
on August 18, 1674 and at the *Bourgogne* in the season of 1674-75
and is based on Euripides' *Iphigenia In Aulis*. This study of father-
love versus duty was given a happy ending because the author thought
a French audience would reject the Euripidean conclusion.

His enemies, who were numerous, formed a cabal against him and
trotted out PRADON (1632-1698) in an effort to defeat him. Pradon
tried hard with *Tamerlan, ou la Mort de Bajazet* (1676) which did
not even measure up to *Bajazet*, and *Phèdre et Hippolyte* which was
played at the *Théâtre de Guénégaud* under La Grange's management
at the same time that *Phèdre* was performed at the *Bourgogne*, but
went down in dismal defeat despite the temporary artificial "success"
claimed for it. His other plays *Statira* (1679), *Germanicus* (1694) and
Scipion l'Africain were even less effective.

But to return to Racine we find that in *Phèdre* perhaps, he produced his most lasting drama of passion and undying love. It never
measured up to the Greek original but it has provided such great
French actresses as Champmeslé (the originator), Adrienne Lecouvreur, Dumesnil, Clairon, Rachel, and Bernhardt with their most moving role. However, despite the heights he reached, Racine who had
wounded so many others, was deeply hurt by the Pradon episode—
so much so that he retired in 1677 to Port-Royal and Jansenism. He
thought of becoming a monk but his confessor discouraged him and
urged him to marry. He followed this advice and was very happy in
his domestic life. He wrote no more directly for the theatre, though
in 1689 Mme. de Maintenon (the former Mme. Scarron) persuaded
him to dramatize portions of *The Book of Esther* for her girls' school
at St. Cyr. He declined to allow *Esther* to be played in a public theatre but he wrote it with enthusiasm. Two years later his second biblical drama, *Athalie*, was staged under the same auspices. This play was
as simple and moving as the earlier drama and was enacted at Versailles.

Soon after this, he drew up a plan to relieve the poor who were
being taxed into starvation to pay for Louis' wars, and presented it
to the King. He was snubbed for his troubles and all but expelled from
court. This so angered Racine that he worried himself into his grave.

His plays command considerable respect. He drew his women characters better than any of his French predecessors or contemporaries;
in addition he achieved that sensibility, contraction of action and

compactness of plot which, coupled with a great deal of moving poetry, recommends itself to the minds of his compatriots.

Molière is the god of the French theatre and is so much a part of the life of his country that in 1940 her soldiers lived and died with well-read paper-backed editions of his comedies in their pockets. Jean Baptiste Poquelin, later called MOLIÈRE, was born on January 15, 1622 in Paris. He was the son of Poquelin, a prosperous uphol-sterer, and his wife Marie Cressé, a lady of taste, some culture and fortune, and a descendant of minor gentry. They lived in a house in the *Rue Saint Honoré* near the *Pont Neuf*. Jean's orderly mother died when he was eleven and his father remarried, but this second wife died three years later. Living in a busy quarter of Paris where the quack doctors set up their shops and displayed their dramatic and variety entertainments on platforms, the boy must have seen many French and Italian actors. This, together with the fact that his grand-father loved the theatre and frequently took him to performances, inculcated the virus at an early age and it grew to be a beloved pas-sion that never left him. The young Poquelin was hopelessly stage-struck.

The interest and connivance of his grandfather enabled the boy to escape from the career of court upholsterer for which his father in-tended him. He was sent to the *Collège de Clermont*, a large and highly regarded school run by the Jesuits. There the boy was thor-oughly inculcated with the logic and orderly thinking that the French call *raison* and he formed friendships with such men as Armand de Bourbon, Prince de Conti, Chapelle, poet and illegitimate son of Lullier the financier, Cyrano de Bergerac, François Bernier, and Hes-nault. Any detailed study of his life finds these names appearing over and over. Due to his father's illness in 1641, Jean assumed the parental post of *valet de chambre—tapissier* and travelled south with Louis XIII and his court. Upon his return he devoted himself again to the study of law and certain later contemporary references indicate that he may even have been admitted to the bar. However, this matter of passing the bar examination was more of a formality—even of an ex-change of money—than of any prolonged preparation for the legal profession. What is of greater importance is the fact that he was the pupil of Pierre Gassendi, the celebrated professor and adversary of René Descartes.

A tremendous stirring within himself soon forced him to abandon a legal career and he attached himself to the Béjarts' amateur dramatic group, *Les Enfants de Famille*, which was practicing in a small racket court. Every struggling theatrical organization in New York, London or the Paris and Vienna of old is indebted to the excellent precedent established by this group. Its very name is explained by the number of Béjarts in the list: Madeleine, Geneviève, Joseph, and in years to come Louis and the beautiful Armande. The leader Denys Beys, aided no doubt by the buffoon Du Parc (better known as Gros-René), guided the company from an amateur status to a professional one. Soon it aspired to larger quarters and a more resounding name. As *L'Illustre Théâtre* the group opened on January 1, 1644 in a remade tennis court near the *Tour de Nesle*. To save his family the disgrace of having its name appear on a playbill, young Poquelin blossomed forth as Molière for the first time. How we should like to know authoritatively of this venture, but the only available document is the scurrilous pamphlet *Elomire hypocondre ou les Médecins vengés* (*Elomire* [Molière] *the Hypochondriac; or, the Doctors Avenged*) published in 1670. The attack states that the venture was a failure and points out Joseph Béjart's stammering, Madeleine's red hair and far from spotless reputation (both of which were true), but since the anonymous author mixed his facts and was often as much as twenty years out of the way, it can not be taken too seriously. It does, however, establish the failure of the hopeful young group of whom the Parisians had expected great things. This may have been due to Molière's desire to produce and act tragedy, because neither he nor his troupe were satisfactory tragedians. So disastrous were the results that he was jailed for debt but was released a week or so later.

In 1646 *L'Illustre Théâtre* took to the road in order to learn technique and to build a repertory. This was not an easy task because of the keen competition of the twelve or more companies already touring the provinces. Perhaps the desperation of the opposition made them learn their craft so well that it became an art before they realized it. Scarron's novel *Le Roman Comique*, which describes a touring company playing country towns, is believed to have come in part from the author's having seen Molière's company play at *Le Mans*. They preferred touring the south and southeast sections of the country, that traditional home of troubadours and *trouvères*. Scarron's description of his hero, both in character and person, suggests Molière—he was above medium height, sturdily built with well-formed legs, dark of complexion with a large, bold nose, full, wide mouth and an extremely mobile face, with a gentle, kind and generous character, a keen sense of humor and a natural manner which was a direct contrast to the then fashionable concept of what manners should be.

During the ensuing twelve-year training period, not only were the acting abilities of the company being polished but their dramatist's

technique was being mastered with the help of actors and audience—
an expensive but superior method. Of the eleven farces then written
but two survive, *Le Médecin Volant* (*The Thieving Doctor*) and *La
Jalousie du Barbouillé*. They were primarily acting pieces, which in
their wittiness are known as the *baisers du rideau* of the Italian school.
Though in the author's words they "procured him some little reputation", he was not satisfied because he specifically aspired to emulate
that brilliant comedy of Corneille's *Le Menteur*, which had electrified
the Paris theatre a few years before.

At this period the company had prospered sufficiently to permit
additional actors. The leader, Denys Beys, had been replaced by
Charles Dufresne, who in turn was succeeded by Molière. The company included: Mlle. de Goila (later Mlle. Du Parc), Du Croisy, Louis
Béjart (later lamed in a stage accident) who played rascally servants.
La Grange alternated the part of the lover with Joseph Béjart, and
the de Bries. Mlle. de Brie (actresses, despite marriage or decency of
character, were never dignified with Madame) was born Catherine
Leclerc du Rozet and became the ill-used wife of Édouard Wilquin,
Sieur de Brie. His brutal treatment killed any love she might have
had for her husband so she devoted her life to the acting she loved so
dearly. Her delicate beauty and gracefulness were particularly orna-
mental in ingénue roles. Mlle. Du Parc was believed to have inspired
the love of Molière (he also had a long-lasting, if rather platonic, affair with the intelligent Madeleine Béjart), who proposed marriage
but was turned down because the ambitious actress sought what she
considered a *good* marriage. Attracted then by the attention and sympathy of Catherine de Brie, he fell in love with her and she became
his mistress. This connection was the beginning of the fame which
was soon to come to Molière.

For some time they had been playing at Lyons where in 1655
L'Étourdi (*The Blunderer*) was produced with great success. Its five
acts, based on Nicolo Barbieri's *Inavvertito*, were written in Alexandrine couplets. Without going into too much detail, perhaps we
had better define this form because it has been widely used in classical
French tragedy and comedy due to the fact that it is peculiarly suited
to the language. The couplets were in twelve-syllable lines with standard differences between the first or masculine couplet and the second
or feminine couplet. The first ended with a full vowel sound and the
second with a mute *e*, *es*, *ent*, etc.

To return to the theatre which had suffered during the civil war
between the King and *La Fronde*, this comedy introduced the clever
servant, Mascarille, a character based on the servants of the *commedia*

dell'arte which Molière admired and witnessed at every possible opportunity. The following year, 1656, *Le Dépit amoureux* (*Love's Tiff*) was performed at *Béziers*. This play continued to be popular long after its author's death and was imitated by Dryden in *Evening's Love*, by Vanbrugh in *The Mistake* and by Edward Ravenscroft, a Restoration dramatist, in *The Wrangling Lovers.*

Perhaps due to the influence of the Prince de Conti, various friends advised the company to move nearer Paris. The actors removed to Rouen, where the Duc d'Anjou, Philippe, younger brother of the King and later Duc d'Orléans, took them under his protection. From there it was not a difficult step to a royal command performance. On October 24, 1658 Louis XIV and his brilliant court assembled in the *Salle de Gardes* of the *Louvre* to watch this new troupe which had attracted the attention and patronage of his brother. Even the actors from the *Hôtel de Bourgogne* were there to see what the new rivals from the country had to offer. With that same obtuseness with regard to their ability to act tragedy, the company had decided to open with the minor Corneille play, *Nicomède*. The very stately lines sounded out of place on tongues used to the witticisms and sprightly dialogue of Molière. Sensing their failure to capture fully the admiration of the King the playwright had the wit to step forward and address Louis. Apologizing for his company's country manners, he asked leave to play one of his own pieces which had amused the provinces. Leave having been given, the performance of *Le Docteur amoureux* (*The Love-sick Doctor*), one of his earliest farces, was begun as quickly as possible. Slight though it was, the King and the court soon began to laugh and the bright, ascendant sun of success shone upon them.

With this recognition came a substantial guarantee of future support and permission to use the theatre in the *Hôtel du Petit-Bourbon*, which was shared three times a week with a first rate company of Italian players under the patronage of Cardinal Mazarin. These actors offered stiff competition because they had mastered French and played as well in that language as in their native tongue. In addition, Molière had to pay them fifteen hundred livres a year rent because they had prior rights in the theatre. However he could well afford it now because he was allowed to call his company the *Troupe de Monsieur*, from the King's brother, who was also supposed to grant three hundred livres a year to each member of the company. La Grange stated that the money was never paid but at least they possessed a name that was a valuable asset to a troupe fresh from the provinces. This honor brought the public clamoring to see their performances.

and the Poquelin family turned out in full force to welcome the successful return of the prodigal. All except one that is, his brother, who had drawn up a genealogical table out of pride in his mother's family and had neglected to include Jean's name because he was an actor.

Before going on to Molière's important plays it might be well to know the kind of theatres in which they were performed. The *Petit-Bourbon* was a theatre in a palace rather than a building especially constructed for that purpose. The stage was much shallower than that of the *Hôtel de Bourgogne* and the effect was much the same as the picture-frame stage we know today. Another theatre which the *Troupe de Monsieur* later occupied was the one in the *Palais Royal* which was a great contrast to their former home. This court theatre had been built by Cardinal Richelieu in his palace without any consideration of expense. The stage was magnificently equipped with every mechanical device of the Italian theatres that could be imitated together with the best work of the French machinists. The playhouse was intended for spectacular productions and was opened on January 14, 1641 with the politely applauded failure *Mirame*, written by the Cardinal himself. At Richelieu's death, the palace and its theatre passed into the hands of the King. By 1660 it had fallen into almost complete ruin but was turned over to Molière after he was deprived of the *Petit-Bourbon*, which had been pulled down to permit enlargement of the *Louvre*. After three months of repairs, it was reopened on the twentieth of January, 1661 with *Le Dépit amoureux* and *Sganarelle, ou le Cocu imaginaire* (*Sganarelle; or, The Imaginary Cuckold*).

Molière had established himself with the plays he had written in the provinces, but he brought out a new play, *Les Précieuses Ridicules* (*The Affected Young Ladies*) on November 14, 1659. This is a delightful satire on the affectation and obscurity of the so-called wit and high-flown conversation of the *Hôtel de Rambouillet*, as the circle of Madame de Rambouillet was termed. No one of this group was called by his own name, but by one which was chosen from a popular Oriental romance or novel of the moment such as Polixène or Aminte. This thinly veiled attack on a cult fashionable in court circles caused so many objections that the second performance was halted and the run not resumed until Louis, who liked to see his courtiers squirm, gave permission. Its bitterness was slightly disguised in the introduction to the printed play in which the author said that he was not attacking the *jeunesse doré* but their bourgeois imitators, as was plainly stated in his play. To save their faces they pretended to believe him and flocked to see it in such numbers that admission prices were doubled (an old Broadway custom not often used in these lean days) and it played twice a day for four months.

Molière's company was brilliant in his own plays but where were they to get others? The jealous tragedians at the *Bourgogne* and the comedians at the *Marais* declined to allow any of their dramatists to write for the *Petit-Bourbon*. Molière found it necessary to write more comedies in order to fill out his repertoire and so the whole world has gained from the pettiness of his rivals, the *Troupe Royale* and the *Troupe Marais*. *Sganarelle, ou le Cocu imaginaire* (*Sganarelle; or, The Imaginary Cuckold*, 1660), was a complete reworking of an Italian farce, *Il Cornuto per Opinione*. This was a direct descendant from such medieval farces as *Maître Pierre Pathelin*. It was a broad comic portrait of a bourgeois who believed his wife was making a cuckold of him; the part of Sganarelle was brilliantly acted by Molière himself. Its huge success helped to carry the troupe through the tragedy *Don Garcie de Navarre* (1661), which was a failure as were all his tragedies.

The next effort, *L'École des Maris* (*The School For Husbands*, 1661), was one of his most successful. It was based on Terence's *Adelphi*, a *novella* by Boccaccio, and Lope de Vega's *Discreta Enamorada*. Molière, like Shakespeare, did not mind borrowing from the classics or even more recent sources if the need arose. So few French plays receive a successful translation into English that it is a pleasure to recall the witty and graceful adaptation made by Arthur Guiterman and Lawrence Langner for the Theatre Guild in 1933. It was concerned with the efforts of two brothers to marry their wards; one was sensible and let his beloved have her own way; the other was naturally of a jealous disposition and imprisoned his, but in so doing, was duped into acting as a go-between for her young lover. It is a gay comedy of sense and charm and made the young Louis fonder than ever of his Molière, whom he felt he had discovered and whom he knew he fostered. The beautiful Armande Béjart, to whom Molière was already drawn, played the leading part with flirtatious charm.

It must not be forgotten that for the next century the King (*L'État, c'est moi*) and his court were the cynosure of all eyes. The nobles who had been reduced in power by Richelieu now fawned on their ruler and spent vast sums in order to make a good impression in Paris, at Fontainebleau, or whatever palace Louis chose as the center of his festivities. The balls, masques, pageants, operas and plays were extravagantly staged and the cost was terrific. Thus came about the evils of absentee landlordship. The vast sums required by an extrava-

122.   Julia and Pantalone.

123.   Scaramuccia and Columbina.

124.   Isabella and Pierrot.

*Commedia Dell' Arte Figurines in
Porcelain, Nymphenburg, Germany*

125. Commedia Dell' Arte, 18th Century. Showing Pierrot, Pantalone, and four soldiers.

126. Commedia Dell' Arte, France, 18th Century.

127. *Le Malade Imaginaire,* AT VERSAILLES. For Louis XIV, Molière's patron, who is seated in the center facing the stage.

La Salle du Bal donné dans le petit Parc de Versailles.

IV.

Aula frondibus et virgultis septa, ad saltationes et choreas ducendas parata, In Hortis Versalianis.

128. BALL IN THE LITTLE PARK OF VERSAILLES, 1678.

130. *Les Précieuses Ridicules.*

129. HARLEQUIN, MAKING-UP. 18th Century

131. CLOWNS. A beating scene.

132. *Le Malade Imaginaire.*

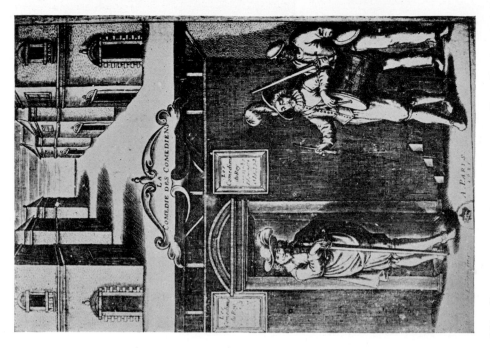

134. Frontispiece of *Comedy and Comedians*. De Scudéry. 1635.

133. Molière.

135.   DESIGN, BIBIENA, (attributed to Guiseppe). Hitherto unreproduced.

136. TEMPLE INTERIOR, BIBIENA SCHOOL.

137. PEN AND WASH DESIGN. GIUSEPPE BIBIENA. c. 1750   *Yale-Rockefeller Theatre Collection*

138. TRIUMPHAL ARCH WITH PERSPECTIVE. BIBIENA SCHOOL.

139. INTERIOR AND EXTERIOR COURT. GIUSEPPE BIBIENA, c. 1750. *Yale-Rockefeller Theatre Collection*

140. KITCHEN OF A PALACE. BIBIENA SCHOOL, c. 1750.

141. PALACE BOUDOIR. BIBIENA SCHOOL, c. 1750.

142. SETTING FOR THE *Teatro Regina di Pollonia,* Rome (c. 1710-1712) BY FILIPPO JUVARA (1676–1736).

143. STREET SCENE BY FILIPPO JUVARA, probably for same theatre as No. 142. Possibly for *L'Eraclio,* Act III, Sc. 3.   *Yale-Rockefeller Theatre Collection*

144. DESIGN BY SANQUIRICO FOR *Il Rivale de se Stesso*, 1818.

145. DESIGN BY SANQUIRICO FOR *L'Esule di Roma*.

146. A FRENCH STREET
THEATRE, 1572. A
performance of *Cas-
tro et Pollux.*

*Spencer Collection,
N.Y. Public Library*

147. STAGE OF THE ROYAL THEATRE AT NAPLES, 1749.

148. THEATRE AT BORDEAUX DESIGNED BY VICTOR LOUIS, 1773.

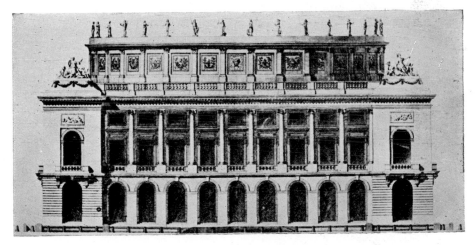

149. FACADE OF THE PROJECTED THEATRE FOR THE DUC DE CHARTRES.

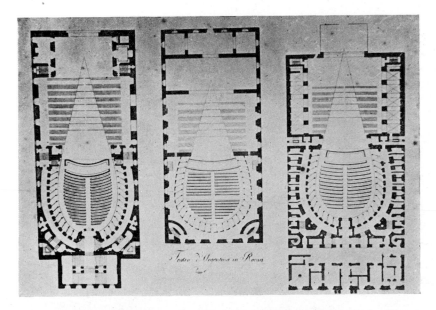

150. Note the perspective as well as the bad sight lines of the Teatro Argentina in Rome, which is still used.

151. 152. Louis-Jean Deprez. Designs for *Gustavus Vasa* at Stockholm, 1786.

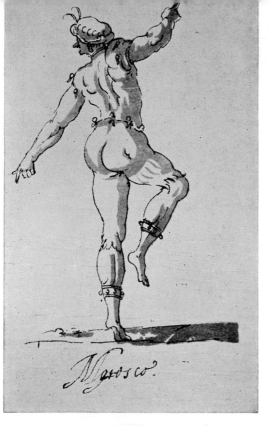

153. INIGO JONES. COSTUME DESIGN.

154. THE ACTOR ZANOTTI AS FABIO, BY CALLOT.

155. JUVARA. COSTUME DESIGN.

156. ARLECCHINO. DESIGN BY GIUSEPPE
MARIA MITELLI, 1634-1718.

157. Inigo Jones, Setting For Davenant's *Britannia Triumphans*, 1683.

gant king, his court and the numerous wars of conquest in the end caused the French Revolution. The theatre played an innocent part in the fact that it was one of the many enormous expenses attendant upon an extravagant monarch.

Molière's next play *Les Fâcheux* (*The Bores*, 1661) was commissioned by the great minister of finance Fouquet and was performed in the gardens at Vaux. This was most gratifying to Louis because it warranted the production of a pageant in which he and his court took so much delight. The setting called for a garden and one background, which was designed by Lenôtre and painted by Lebrun. The master machinist Torelli contrived a rock which turned into a shell that opened to reveal Armande Béjart who delivered the prologue. This was the most magnificent production that had ever been staged in France. The piece itself keenly satirized the pretensions of courtiers who considered themselves fascinating conversationalists, and musicians. It ridiculed also late-comers to the theatre, duelists and gamesters, and the bore who has been bored by a bore. What anger this aroused! What dismay the audience felt! But Louis was delighted, only Molière hadn't gone far enough so he suggested adding a portrait of a huntsman bore. Even the beauty of the scenery no longer interested the aristocratic audience. Their King had enjoyed a performance which was distasteful to them and since it had been dedicated to him, the courtiers dared not demur too loudly. This play constituted the beginning of a new dramatic form called either a *pièce à tiroirs* or a *comédie-ballet*. From a modern point of view it is valuable as a piece of social criticism. La Fontaine was so enthusiastic about it that he wrote the following to Maucroix the day after the performance:

> * "Nous avons changé de méthode,
> Jodelet n'est plus à la mode,
> Et maintenant il ne faut pas
> Quitter la nature d'un pas."

At the age of forty Molière decided he could no longer live without the lovely Armande so he unwisely married a girl twenty years his junior. Precedents and his natural powers of observation should have told him this was a mistake. Beautiful she was, but shallow, and though he trained her to be a fine actress, she never made him happy. In reality he found himself the jealous and betrayed older man about whom he had written and whom he had portrayed so well. She was the mother of his three children, only one of whom survived him.

---

* "We have changed methods, Jodelet is no longer in fashion, and now it is no longer necessary to depart a step from nature."

But she can be forgiven a great deal because of the eventual reconciliation which made his last years very happy.

The first play to be written and played after his marriage was the calm and lovely *L'École des Femmes* (*The School For Wives*, 1662). This aroused great enthusiasm among his friends, particularly La Fontaine and Boileau, and countered the increased opposition of the *Troupe Royale* at the *Hôtel de Bourgogne* due to the addition of the fine actress Mlle. Desoeillets who had formerly played in the provinces. The fact that the piece cast a doubt on the wisdom of a law which permitted guardians to dispose of their wards as they willed, gave the estranged courtiers an opportunity to declare the play immoral. This they promptly did, but Boileau came to the author's rescue and Molière defended himself in the brilliant pamphlet written in play form, *Critique de l'École des Femmes*, which so enchanted the King that he granted him a pension of a thousand livres despite the fact that he had been surprised when Boileau told him Molière was no mere entertainer but a great man. Score one good deed for Louis!

Though this piece was acted more than thirty times in succession, it was not enough for the King and he asked the playwright to bring his attackers onto the stage. This he did in *L'Impromptu de Versailles*, (*The Impromptu Performance at Versailles*, 1663) and it was performed in the new palace and was later transferred to the *Palais Royal* stage where the Parisians hailed it with delight.

Louis commanded two ballets, *Le Mariage forcé* (*The Forced Marriage*, 1664), in which he himself danced; and *La Princesse d'Élide* (1664) which was magnificently set but was not a success. Unfortunately the performance coincided with that sad day before the dramatist's son, Louis, died. In fact this whole period was marred by Armande's *amours*, either real or imagined. The troubles in his private life seemed to strengthen Molière as a dramatist because one of his three greatest plays came next.

Tartuffe (*The Hypocrite*, 1664), was played in a three act version as part of a court fête at Versailles despite the fact that its sombreness must have dampened the enthusiasm of those who had expected one of his lighter, less consequential pieces. It offended so many devoutly religious people, including the queen-mother, Anne of Austria, that she exacted a promise from her son that it should never be repeated. After her death in 1666 the King told him that he might produce the play again. It was performed on August 5, 1667 during the absence of the King at the wars. But Lamoignon, mayor of Paris, closed the play and would have arrested the author had it not been for the royal permission. It is important to remember that since 1665 the company had been under the King's protection and no longer under Monsieur's patronage. The company henceforth was known as the *King's Troupe,* as opposed to the *Bourgogne's Troupe Royale.*

In his attack on the hypocrite who hides in the clothing of the righteous, many of the devout as well as a vast number of bigots took it personally and waves of violent indignation swept over the court, the church and the bourgeoisie until Molière was scarcely safe from their rage. The company was especially suited to this performance. Du Croisy acted Tartuffe with Molière in the less rewarding part of Orgon; the dependable Madeleine Béjart as Dorine; and the gay, delightful Mlle. Molière, as the faithless Armande was called, in the role of Orgon's wife Elmire. A movement of antagonism toward liberal thought, emanating from the Jesuits, their rivals the Jansenists, and the Society of the Holy Sacrament, had arisen. Therefore the play was believed by them to be an affront to their privileges, an attack on their immunity to ridicule and an examination of their motives, which it was. Vigorously, if irregularly backed by the King, this thoughtful and well considered drama *Tartuffe* was permitted to be performed freely on February 5, 1669, nearly five years after the initial performance at Versailles.

The Molière company naturally had to find other productions to fill in while the *Tartuffe* affair was being fought out. Following up a series of three *Placets,* which defended his fine comedy of character with its strong social and religious implications, he wrote *Don Juan* (1665). Placing in the mouth of his title character sentiments which scarcely belong to a sensualist and seducer, he again attacked hypocrisy in brilliant style. Molière had become a vigorous antagonist as his enemies were discovering. It also allowed him the opportunity to satirize the haughtiness of the courtiers. Perhaps because of *Tartuffe,* perhaps because the Don Juan legend had been used by all the other theatres before the *Palais Royal* got around to it, this play though one of the author's finest, did not have the success it deserved.

L'Amour Médecin (Love Is the Best Doctor, 1665) was a comedy which had been written to amuse, and hold the King's respect at a time when his support was badly needed. However, he used it as an opportunity to score on another pretentious group, the ill-informed members of the medical profession, which suffered from another type of hypocrisy. The desire to hide their incompetency and venality in a mumbo-jumbo of Latin and medical jargon was galling to the social satirist Molière.

At a time when we are speaking principally of the dramatist and the actor, Molière the manager must not be overlooked. Due to the long postponement of *Tartuffe* and the comparative lack of success of *Don Juan, L'Amour Médecin* had been written and produced in five days. But it was necessary to find other plays for the company as the *Marais-Bourgogne* monopoly on playwrights was strongly felt.

Another dramatist of importance, Jean Racine, appeared on the horizon when Molière was at his zenith and Corneille was rapidly waning. Racine's first play having been taken and then rejected by Floridor's company, he offered his second, *La Thébaïde*, to the *Palais Royal* where it was produced in 1664 with but slight success. His next piece *Alexandre le Grand* (1665) was staged before a distinguished audience including Monsieur, his wife, the Great Condé and others for the *Palais Royal* could count on a brilliant following. The *Bourgogne* company recognized the talent of the rising dramatist and whispered in his ear that they could have performed his play much more brilliantly. To Racine's everlasting discredit he left the man who had given him his first impetus and took his script to Floridor who also mounted it immediately, so that both playhouses were running the same play simultaneously. Since it was a tragedy it is needless to say that Floridor, Montfleury and Mlle. Desoeillets played it better. Molière was naturally bitter for he had carried *La Thébaïde* at a loss and because he had believed in the future of the young author he had staged *Alexandre le Grand* against the advice of his company. He never spoke to Racine again.

But all this was but marking time before his next, and as some think, greatest play, *Le Misanthrope* (1666), produced in the fateful year of the great fire of London. In this play he created the character Alceste, played by himself, that took his audience by surprise. This comedy about a man who turns to misanthropy because of the heartlessness, insincerity and hypocrisy of the world, had much more depth than the general public particularly wanted; but it has always been cherished by lovers of great drama. Because Alceste's soul refused to be involved in the worldly way of living, he was the same detached character in the end that he was in the beginning, so the play lacked the resolved action that quickly touches popular imagination. The piece lacks all hope because Molière believed that society was so corrupt that there was no chance of reformation. Its detachment comes from the fact that he regarded the piece a comedy and Alceste as comic as everyone else. This was due to his mistaken idea that the world in which he lived was fixed and unchangeable.

For some reason it is traditional to think that *Le Médecin malgré lui* (*The Doctor in Spite of Himself*) was given as an afterpiece. Even Voltaire stated this unequivocally. Actually this highly theatrical and popular comedy was not produced until the sixth of August and was *not* combined with *Le Misanthrope* until the third of September. Satire, except for a few barbs projected into the hides of the medical profession, was in abeyance. Certainly some of his thrusts came because the tuberculosis from which he suffered was gradually wearing down his strength and the pretentious, learned doctors were unable to aid him. Sheer will-power kept him alive and he frequently had to be absent from his stage for long periods. The conspicuous successes of the last two plays were followed by three minor pieces written for *fêtes* given by *Louis Quatorze* at *Saint-Germain*. *Amphitryon*, an adaptation of Plautus' *Amphitruo*, was produced early in 1668 to flatter Louis and give him a classical excuse for his notorious affair with Mme. de Montespan. Next in point of production was the acrimonious *Georges Dandin* (1668) which recounted the adventures of a rich bourgeois who married an impoverished aristocrat and was betrayed by her. The public was undoubtedly unconscious of yet another attack on their nobility's lack of integrity.

This merely prepared the way for one of his great prose plays, *L'Avare* (*The Miser*, 1668), which was based on the satiric *Aulularia* of Plautus. Its eventual success was apparent from the reception of the first performance. Avarice was caricatured, though not so bitterly as in *Volpone*, and the character Harpagon was stupid and gullible. There are genuinely comic qualities that amuse rather than revolt the auditor. However it did not have a long run; it has been suggested that it was because it was written in prose. This disappointment was overlooked in the great news that at last Louis would permit *Tartuffe* to be performed publicly. Molière was at last vindicated in his long struggle and the acclaim which its performance on February 5, 1669 brought him, assured him that it was a true success, not a *succès de scandale*. It ran for forty-four consecutive performances and the company voted to pay the author double royalties for any future performances of it.

The years and his disease were closing in on him and he was still estranged from his wife who nevertheless continued to act leads at his theatre. Perhaps thinking of the need to keep his troupe going, he turned to pieces more likely to win the quick support of the public. The battle of *Tartuffe* had been won but the cost to his body and spirit was enormous. The slight, gay farce *Monsieur de Pourceaugnac* (1669) was followed by the spectacle *Les Amants magnifiques* (*The Magnificent Lovers*, 1670), and then by the much better play, *Le Bourgeois Gentilhomme* (*The Would-Be Gentleman*, 1670), performed at Chambord, with a ballet after each act. This delightful comedy returned to the favorite theme of the rich commoner who apes the aristocracy, scorns honest worth and is taken in by false values. The *Palais Royal* audience liked it immensely when they saw it a little later in the season.

Psyché was a ballet written on order in collaboration with Corneille and Quinault and was played in the *Salle des Machines* in the Tuileries on January 17, 1671. It has no theatrical importance but was personally important to Molière because it was at this time that his beloved Armande, inspired it is said by the pleadings of the loving Mlle. de Brie, returned to him penitently and his heart was overflowing. Boileau accused him of slipping and borrowing too easily from Terence's *Phormio* in constructing the very slight piece, *Les Fourberies de Scapin* (*The Escapades of Scapin*, May 1671). His next effort, *La Comtesse d'Escarbagnas* (December 1671) was even slighter and was introduced as an interlude in a mythological ballet at Saint-Germain. These were the days when Jean Bérain was designing his superlatively beautiful costumes and scenery.

Then came a comedy so fine as to rank with the author's best satirical work, *Les Femme Savantes* (*The Learned Ladies*, 1672). The precious ones had abandoned preciosity for an assumption of learning and he felt it was time to put them in their place again; this he did with his finest and most telling wit. But the end of his rich comic humor was in sight; tuberculosis was gaining so rapidly that there was time for but one more play, a satire aptly enough aimed at the doctors again, *Le Malade imaginaire* (*The Imaginary Invalid*, 1673). On the occasion of its fourth performance on February seventeenth, Molière, playing the hypochondriac Argan, had a seizure in the last scene but managed to play it out. A series of convulsions set in and a few hours later he died in the arms of a sister of mercy who had been sheltered in his house with a fellow-sister whilst they gathered alms in his section of Paris. He was denied the sacrament of Extreme Unction (though a more sensible priest came to his aid too late) and the Church forbade his burial in holy ground. Upon the insistence of his friend and patron, the King, the Archbishop of Paris finally relented and after four days he was buried without benefit of service. A further stipulation stated that the burial would have to take place at night; the procession was lighted by thousands of torches carried by his devoted friends from all classes of society. Thus ended the career of the greatest comic spirit France has produced and one of the precious few the world has ever known.

Leaderless, his company was destitute and it was then that La Grange, who had so long been helpful to Molière, turned out to be absolutely invaluable to the actors of the *Palais Royal*. Certain sentimental souls have criticized the troupe for having been in full swing within a week of his death. It was absolutely necessary for them not to stop their performances because Louis had at first thought they could not go on without their master and planned to amalgamate them with the *Bourgogne* troupe. Michel Baron, whose parents had once been at that theatre, joined the company in 1670 and was a favorite of Molière's. He learned the part of Alceste for *Le Misanthrope* and La Thorillière knew the part of Argan in *Le Malade imaginaire*. The success of these two plays enabled the company to continue. La Grange, who had always taken care of the accounts (his *Registre* has been of incalculable aid in all histories of this troupe), proved that they could operate profitably.

Their troubles were not ended however because Michel Baron, La Thorillière, Beauval and Mlle. Beauval transferred to the *Bourgogne* company. Lulli, who was always looking for a new theatre in which to produce his inevitable opera, wheedled the King into giving him the *Palais Royal*. In this crisis La Grange showed his first rate executive ability by securing the distinguished comedian Claude la Rose, known as Rosimond, from the *Marais Troupe* to take over Molière's parts. Three years before, the Marquis de Sourdéac had built a well-equipped opera house in the *Rue Mazarine* facing the *Rue Guénégaud*, but Lulli had managed to secure a monopoly on it for the production of operas. The *Marais Troupe* wanted the house but La Grange, with the help of money advanced by Armande, who was by then dignified as Mme. Molière, beat them to it. The theatre was opened July 9, 1673 with *Tartuffe*.

The beginning of the season was not too auspicious financially but a month later the weakened *Marais* company was suppressed and ordered to join La Grange and the *Guénégaud* theatre. This amalgamation strengthened both companies for the final struggle with the *Bourgogne Troupe* which went on for seven long years. The handsome Baron had become not only the finest tragic actor of the period, but an excellent comedian as well. His abilities were well balanced by the beauty and glorious voice of Mlle. Champmeslé, who had made her initial Paris appearance at the *Marais* in 1669. Her husband Charles Chevillet, known as Champmeslé, was a dramatist as well as an actor and so strengthened the *Bourgogne* that its company was superior to that of La Grange. The clever La Grange, however, first secured Thomas Corneille, whose *Circe* had been a success, and then enticed the Champmeslés to join the *Guénégaud* by an offer of an annuity in addition to two shares in the receipts. That was the final blow, and whether at La Grange's instigation or not, the King ordered the two theatres joined. The *Bourgogne Troupe* went over to act with Molière's company at the *Guénégaud*, and their old theatre was turned over to the Italian company. So in 1680 was created the *Théâtre Français*, the present-day *Comédie-Française*, the oldest national theatre in the world. Molière's ideas had triumphed. The French theatre was brilliantly established and a rich tradition was soon to be handed on to successive generations of actors.

X

UNRESPONSIVE EUROPE UP TO 1700

AUSTRIA AND GERMANY

AT A time when the English and French theatres had already reached the high dramatic point which they have yet to surpass in literature, though they have frequently done so from the point of view of staging, the rest of Europe was in a morass with hillocks of theatrical endeavor barely showing above the drab level of the general picture. Germany had produced no one since Hans Sachs who, in a sense, was the avenue from the Middle Ages into the Renaissance and the national development of the seventeenth century. This was of course understandable from a political point of view because the country was a mass of small states under the hegemony of Austria or whatever outside emperor might be elected for the Holy Roman Empire. Prussia was an unknown force and the Margrave of Brandenburg was still a petty princeling vastly exceeded in importance by Saxony, Bavaria, Hesse and Hanover.

Austria and Vienna were powerfully influenced by the inter-marriages of their rulers, and by the fact that their culture came from poor divided Italy who had still to develop a strong national theatre. Saxony and Dresden, Bavaria and Munich, looked south and west for that artistic stimulus which any country must have if she would survive as a nation. Deprived of it, any race becomes barbaric and its life is short in the long view of civilization. There was no drama of any importance. The chief artistic impulse from outside took its expression in music in which opera was the poor but only theatrical outlet. Painting had begun to come into its own but the theatre had a hard hundred years pull ahead. All cooperative artistic impulses, of which the theatre is the highest manifestation, had to await the end of that cruel wasting of human energies, the Thirty Years' War. This catastrophe destroyed the country and was the stimulus for the exodus of some of America's oldest and most valued citizens who left a troubled old world, tormented by the rigors of fratricidal and religious strife, to seek a peace beyond the waters which Europe, in its history as a continent of quarrelling nations everlastingly seeking a balance of power, has never been able to offer.

Theatrical development in Germany and the Netherlands followed the familiar pattern of the Renaissance. First came the Latin dramas and then the German and Dutch adaptations of such men as Gulielmus Gnaphaeus (1493-1568), Thomas Naogeorgus (1511-1563) who was strongly under the influence of Luther and wrote several bitter anti-Catholic plays, Jakob Wimpfeling (1450-1528) with *Stylpho* (1470), and the chief dramatist of this period, Nicodemus Frischlin (1547-1590) who wrote largely in Latin. His comic characters were his best though they were but imitations of the low comedians of the Roman farce. *Rebecca* and *Susannah* are his most important dramatic pieces. These plays were still being performed when the before-mentioned English companies went to play before the various courts of Germany.

The representations were highly realistic and in construction the stages more nearly approached the French than the English. Brunswick and Hesse were the two principalities which particularly welcomed these foreign companies who supplemented their meagre numbers with native actors and played in Germany. They introduced translations of such masterpieces as *Hamlet, King Lear, Romeo and Juliet* and Marlowe's *Doctor Faustus* which two centuries later was to influence Goethe's *Faust*. They made no attempt to start a school of native drama, though stirrings of talent were evident in many parts of the country.

Comedy was as enthusiastically received as tragedy and the English troupe is credited with having introduced the clown character *Hanswurst* (Jack Sausage as he was called) into Germany and he instantly became popular. Duke Heinrich Julius of Brunswick and Jacob Ayrer (1543-1605) incorporated him into their broad comic farces. He was sometimes known as *Pickelhering* and *Harlequin,* the latter name having been translated from the Italian of the *commedia dell'arte* troupes which had appeared at the principal courts of Austria and the other German states about 1670. Some of the pieces of the Italian company at the *Petit-Bourbon* had been printed in French about 1694 and the German actors had helped themselves to the outlines and stock characters. The Viennese, particularly, took kindly to these pieces as they had laughed heartily over crude jokes of any kind since the Middle Ages. As early as 1708, the Silesian Joseph Stranitzky established a theatre in Vienna where Italian farces were acted. He is credited with having established the standard costume of the peasant with a green peaked hat, in his playing of *Hanswurst*.

All culture couldn't remain in abeyance during the destructive

Thirty Years' War (1618-1648), so that as early as 1627 we find opera introduced from Italy where through the efforts of the *Camerata*, a group of Florentine nobles, it had had its inception in Florence. The first work was *Daphne*, by the composer Jacopo Peri and the librettist Ottavio Rinuccini, but it is no longer extant. The first surviving opera is *Eurydice*, by the same authors, and was written in 1600 for the marriage of Henry IV of France and Marie de' Medici. MARTIN OPITZ (1597-1639), who was responsible for the adaptation of many Italian operas, made a new version of *Daphne* with new music by Heinrich Schutz. It was performed in 1627 at Torgau, the court of the Elector John George I of Saxony, for the marriage of the ruler of Hesse with a Saxon princess. Opitz was responsible for the introduction into Germany of the Alexandrine couplet which had recently been inaugurated in France. He endeavored to introduce all kinds of foreign culture so as to strengthen the weak native drama. There were few productions of any kind except for rare performances of Italian operas by Italian troupes in their native tongue, particularly in Vienna, Dresden and Munich. These performances were enriched by handsome scenic investiture and later the plays themselves were mounted in the same extravagant fashion.

The man credited with the fathering of tragedy and formal drama in Germany was ANDREAS GRYPHIUS (1616-1664), who came from Silesia, that small province that saved Maria Theresa's face when she undertook the Seven Years' War. At first he imitated Senecan tragedy and then the stately and dull Alexandrines of France and at the same time introduced act divisions. Wedded to these were all the fustian and bombast the seventeenth century German mind could conceive; he out-blooded the goriest of the Elizabethans. In comedy he was more successful, though his pieces were heavy-handed and often grotesque in their striving after humor. His five baroque tragedies are too unimportant to name but his slightly more consequential comedies were *Peter Squentz*, a satire on the lower middle class (written 1647-1650, published 1657), and *Horrobilicribrifax*, a caricature of the noisy, boastful, brutal soldiers of his childhood (published 1660).

Much more important than Gryphius in the history of the German theatre was CHRISTIAN WEISE (1642-1708) who, though influenced by the older writer and the opera, was entirely willing to learn from the popular farces played by English actors and the native German clowns and farceurs. He introduced comic elements into his more than fifty serious and religious plays. Some of these pieces were similar to *schuldrammen* (school plays), which were didactic plays enacted in the monasteries and schools of Germany to inculcate the virtues and love of God. When he was rector at Zittau between 1679-

1688 and 1702-1705 nearly all of his plays were performed by his pupils. His dialogue was swift and he used prose for brevity and to heighten the dramatic effect of popular life. He had many imitators but none worthy of being enumerated.

At one time it looked as though Molière might have a beneficial effect on Germany. Five of his plays were translated and printed in 1670 and a German translation of his collected prose works was published in 1694. At the Court Theatre in Dresden a company headed by Magister Velthen included many of Molière's comedies in their acting repertoire from 1685 to 1692. Under the patronage of Duke Anton Ulrich, several French tragedies were produced in translation between 1691 and 1699. But this was a baroque period, the seventeenth century in Germany; the quiet beauty of the Renaissance was tortured into the highly ornamented, in architecture, design, painting and literature. This extravagance of expression was known as *schwulst* in Germany and corresponded to *gongorism* in Spain and *euphuism* in England. This and *Hanswurst* satisfied the Germans.

The Viennese stage, thanks to royal patronage, had begun to look to its physical improvement and adornment. LUDOVICO BURNACINI (1636-1707) became court architect and scene designer and is generally considered one of the scenic masters of all time. Among his numerous productions, that of *Il Pomo d'Oro* (1667) is characteristic of his work. In 1690 he designed the Imperial Theatre. A remarkably complete pictorial record of his work can be examined in the *Monumenta Scenica*.

ITALY

Opera was the most characteristic development of the seventeenth century in Italy. This was a natural growth because the chorus of Italian tragedy, introduced in imitation of the Greeks, was invariably sung. Pastoral dramas such as the lovely *Aminta* were accompanied with instrumental music and lyric songs were interpolated into the action. It was but a short step to the play written to be sung as a whole or to be recited to music. Ottavio Rinuccini and Jacopo Peri were responsible for the mythological pieces *Daphne, Eurydice* and *Ariana.*

CLAUDIO MONTEVERDE (1567-1643), frequently called the father of Italian opera, with his *Orfeo* (1607) bridged the gap between the early Florentine experimentalists and such literary librettists as Zeno and the eighteenth century Metastasio. APOSTOLO ZENO (1669-1750) introduced historical tragedy into opera by borrowing largely from the French tragedies which were greatly admired on the Continent. This Venetian poet wrote sixty operas, the most successful of which was *Iphigenia* and was taken lock, stock and barrel from Racine. Zeno ended his days in Venice whence he had gone from Vienna. There on the invitation of the Emperor Charles VI, of the famous Pragmatic Sanction, he had become poet laureate of the court opera from 1718 to 1728. On seeking his dismissal, he recommended Metastasio as "the best poet whom Italy possesses."

Zeno lived to see his fame eclipsed by one who was much greater, Pietro Antonio Domenico Bonaventura Trapassi, renamed the euphonious METASTASIO (1698-1782), whose position in the operatic field was unchallenged in his life time. He did not aspire to great dramatic heights. It was his aim to make use of his imagination, refinement of feeling, and expression to blend his country's poetry with the finest music of his collaborators and thus achieve an artistic whole. It has always been the contention of contemporary critics that he succeeded beyond belief in this admirable ambition. He was the most prolific Italian writer, having composed approximately eighteen hundred works, including twenty-eight grand operas, ballets, and other musical-literary pieces. Upon Zeno's retirement he became court poet at Vienna from 1730 until his death.

There was a quickening of the theatre pulse which brought about the building of two of Italy's most famous theatres, the *Teatro Olimpico* in Vicenza and the *Teatro Farnese* in Parma. The first was designed by Andrea Palladio (1518?-1580) though it was not completed until 1584. His son Silla and Vincenzo Scamozzi finished the work. The temporary architectural settings of canvas flats designed by Sebastiano Serlio (1473-1554) on principles derived from the study of Greek and Roman theatres no longer satisfied the demand for structural permanence in the Italian Renaissance. Palladio accepted Serlio's division of settings into three types, tragic, comic and satyric, but he wished to construct an enduring setting of solidly built houses with streets in perspective. This type of setting explains many contemporary dramas which permit actors to speak to the audience but to be literally unable to see each other. Every spectator could see down at least one street or alleyway.

The *Teatro Farnese* (completed 1618-1619) represents an advance over both Serlio and Palladio in that the proscenium arch is introduced. Though intended as a frame for the inner stage, it was soon utilized for special scenic devices that could be thus masked from view. The auditorium also was reformed, the classic semi-circle previously in use was restricted to the back central portion and the side seats stopped some distance from the stage. The whole modern development of the playhouse can be traced in the ideas embodied in the construction of these three theatres.

SCANDINAVIA

What held true for the Holy Roman Empire and Italy was in general true for Switzerland, Poland and the Low Countries, but the beginnings of drama in Denmark are exceedingly obscure. We know that English and French touring companies visited the Court and that the masses were believed to have been entertained by German clowns. The only native Danish dramatists who can be mentioned are Sthen, Peder Jensen Hegelund (1542-1614), Hieronymus Justesen Ranch (1539-1607) who wrote Biblical dramas and was the forerunner of Holberg, Mogens Skeel (1650-1694) whose comedies were remotely imitative of Molière. Sweden was considerably advanced beyond her southern neighbor though she shared the German influence in the introduction of the school play to teach the youth in the university, first in Latin and Greek and later in Swedish. The first author of this kind whom we know was Olaus Petri (1493-1552) who lived under the famous King Gustavus Vasa, celebrated in the play of that name. Petri wrote a *Tobiae Comedia* in verse. In the seventeenth century, however, these didactic dramas were sloughed off and replaced by such secular plays as: *A Merry Comedy by Name Thisbe* (1610) by Astopherus; a drama by Catonius about the fall of Troy; and *Judas Redivus* by Rondeletius which, despite its title, pictured the life of its time. This was a period of imperialism under Gustavus Adolphus and Charles XII and the Swedish people sought outside culture, particularly French, to bolster their pretensions to being an important kingdom. By the middle of the century the French influence was strong enough to introduce allegorical ballets, music, dancing and operettas at court. About 1660 Ruban Hjärne built a theatre in the castle at Upsala, where many school plays were performed. A company was established there later in the century and was then transferred to Stockholm where until 1690 it flourished as a national theatre. Isak Bork, who was an active member of this group, wrote several plays which had considerable success, particularly the *Tragedy of Darius*.

RUSSIA

Sweden's neighbor across the Baltic Sea, Russia, was similarly backward in developing her theatre though by the twelfth century some religious dramas (mystery plays) had been introduced from Poland, but they were strongly under Church influence. These pieces were called dialogues; the earliest of which, *Adam* (1507), survives in Latin. The earliest in Polish is *The Life of the Saviour From His Entry Into Jerusalem* (1533), composed by a Dominican friar of Cracow. Russia early employed marionettes in the production of what were called Vertep Plays from the three-storied booth (*vertep*) in which they were performed, at first in churches and later at fairs at Christmas time. In the beginning the subjects were religious, but by the middle of the seventeenth century they had taken on the form of broad, humorous caricatures of history and national life, including the tremendous schism brought about by the attempt to westernize the appearance and customs of the Russians. A "pitiful comedy" *Adam and Eve* was published in Kiev in 1675, the prologue of which was Biblical, and its four acts were concerned with Tsar Alexis Mikhailovich.

Tsar Alexis, second of the house of Romanoff, had heard of the famous companies at the court of Louis XIV and in 1660 he decided that it would enhance his prestige if he were to have a court theatre. But several attempts resulted only in failures because there were no professional actors in the country. In 1672 Alexis commissioned one Johann Gottfried Gregori, German Protestant pastor of Sloboda, the suburb of Moscow in which were centered all the western cultural interests of Russia, to write a comedy on the occasion of the birth of the Tsarevitch. A special wooden theatre was built in the village of *Preobrazhenskoe* (Transfiguration) and was opened with a production of *Esther and Ahasuerus*. This was followed by *Judith, Joseph, Adam and Eve* (all in German). In 1674 the ballet was introduced from France and for several years translations of German farces were played, as well as the first original play in Russian, *The Prodigal Son* by the Court Poet, Simeon Polotzki (1629-1680) who had come to Moscow about 1665. He was also responsible for *Nebuchadnezzar*, another religious drama.

Natalia Narychkine, second wife of Tsar Alexis and mother of Peter, was enamored of the theatre and made the actors welcome, even in the Kremlin. Her rival, Alexis' daughter, Princess Sophia Romanoff, was also a devotee of the theatre, having been trained in Gregori's acting school. Before her incarceration in a convent in 1689 she wrote the play, *Esther and Ahasuerus*, and is said to have made a translation of Molière's *Le Médecin Mal'gré Lui*, which was acted in her private apartments with Prince Vasili Galitzin in the cast.

Alexis was succeeded by his two minor sons, Ivan and Peter (the celebrated Peter the Great). Peter took as great an interest in the theatre as he did in everything artistic and scientific and endeavored to promote a permanent new theatre, but again the lack of actors hampered him so the court had to content itself with a German company playing in its native tongue. There were, however, reportorial plays like the "Living Newspaper," a technique claimed to have been invented by the Soviet theatre. These pieces crudely enacted in the Red Square were but the recounting of Peter's victories over the Swedes. These interludes and burlesques were also performed in private houses and sometimes took the form of criticisms of the Tsar's reforms. Inadequate as this all was, it instilled in the nobility and the people a love of the theatre which flowered into a real Russian drama in the eighteenth century.

XI

ENGLAND'S THEATRE REVIVES

1660-1710

Back to London with the triumphant restored Stuarts in 1660, went the English actors and playwrights who had observed the "polite tragedy" of France, as John Gassner puts it, and the theatre of Albion changed character. From the vigor and strength of the Elizabethans, it put on a Continental polish which only truly became it as comedy; when it was applied to tragedy it was rakish and false. Their comedy of manners has come down as truly brilliant. Modern reading and good staging make these pieces alive, witty and amusing even in our own time.

It must not be supposed that theatrical entertainment disappeared during the closing of the theatres, because many performances were given secretly in London. Outside of the capital where the Puritan control was not so predominant, troupes of actors managed a precarious living and "drolls" continued to be performed at the country fairs. In 1656, with the discreet winking of official eyes, Sir William D'Avenant was permitted to stage *The Siege of Rhodes*. This play showed the influence of Corneille and was the beginning of heroic tragedy, a form of drama the audiences of the next forty years were to esteem so highly. The scenic investiture of the production, for which John Webb, assistant to Inigo Jones, was responsible, drew attention to the keen interest in scenery. D'Avenant's devotion to the elder Charles was rewarded by a grant of authority from Charles II on November 15, 1660 to produce at the Salisbury Court Theatre under the name of the Duke of York's Company. At the same time, Thomas Killigrew (1612-1683) was established as the head of the King's Men at the Theatre Royal in Vere Street. This latter company transferred to Drury Lane in 1663 because their theatre with its bare Elizabethan stage had no provision for scenery.

This was not a period of enduring drama; but was a golden age of

English acting and a period of physical change and betterment in the playhouse. In 1663 the first great theatre in Drury Lane was built; it has been destroyed by fire several times only to be rebuilt. This playhouse established a theatrical tradition which even today holds us sentimentally, if not dynamically. The stage was like the Elizabethan in so far as the forestage (usually called the apron) extended far forward into the auditorium. Most of the action took place on this area; the upper stage being utilized only for scenic display. If, by any chance, the script required the discovery of an actor upstage he was required to come forward to the apron before speaking his lines. The proscenium wall was deep enough to permit of the traditional doors (two on either side), with boxes above which were sometimes used by spectators and occasionally by the actors themselves. The pit was still a gathering place for the vociferous gallants who kept up their chatter throughout the performance; in this they were imitators of the nobility to whom they were allied in bad manners. The court fops frequently caused trouble by forcing their way into the theatre, or by demanding their money back at half-time (the break between the two plays) if they wished to go to the other playhouse where they would be admitted for half-price. It was customary to charge a spectator for only one play if he came after the completion of the first play. Thus niggardliness was coupled with rowdiness and a general annoyance to others. This unruliness caused so much annoyance that the auditors, noble and otherwise, who came to see the plays, complained to the King. Charles II felt the disorders were so real and so unwarranted that in 1673 he issued a proclamation which was more or less successful in putting an end to this unpleasantness.

Killigrew set a very high standard of production at Drury Lane with his company that included such actors as the handsome Charles Hart (d. 1683) and Edward Kynaston (c.1640-1706), both of whom from boy "actresses" had grown into male leads and character parts; the dashing Michael Mohun (c.1620-1684); John Lacy (d. 1681), a fine comic actor who was the original immortal Bayes in George Villier's, Duke of Buckingham's *The Rehearsal* (1671), Teague in Sir Robert Howard's *The Committee* (1662), and was the author of several unimportant plays. These men were good actors and on January 3, 1661 were joined by the ladies with whom they played in Beaumont and Fletcher's *The Beggar's Bush*. D'Avenant did not enlist feminine charms until late in June of the same year, when he staged the second part of *The Siege of Rhodes*. Killigrew's ladies included the beautiful but far from able Mistress Margaret Hughes, Anne and Rebecca Marshall, the intelligent and dashing Mrs. Knipp (or Knep), and later the girlish Mrs. Boutel and pretty, witty Nell

Gwyn. This was a great advantage because the boy "actresses" had grown fortyish and had lost any feminine illusion they might have had.

Against this array JOHN RHODES (c.1606-1668), and later D'Avenant, who assumed sole leadership of the company, assembled the great Thomas Betterton (1635-1710); Robert Nokes (d. 1673); Joseph Harris (1661-1699), whose Wolsey in *King Henry VIII* and *King Henry V* was famous; the ugly, excellent low-comedian, Cave Underhill (c.1634-1710 or 1711), whose gravedigger in *Hamlet* was notable and of whom Cibber said he had never seen his equal as Sir Sampson Legend in Congreve's *Love for Love*. Rhodes' boys for a time included Kynaston; James Nokes (d. 1692-96) who played the nurse in Otway's *Caius Marius* (an adaptation of *Romeo and Juliet*) and appeared in Nevil Payne's *Fatal Jealousy* until the very end of his career; and William Betterton, young brother of Thomas. The actresses included Mrs. Davenport, Mrs. Davies, and Mrs. Saunderson, the future Mrs. Betterton who was to prove that a theatrical marriage could be happy and useful, and who was chiefly famous for the contemporary esteem of her Lady Macbeth.

D'Avenant's company of The Duke's Men was established in Lincoln's Inn Fields but the manager's weakness for spectacular productions encouraged him to build a new theatre. A site was chosen in Dorset Gardens which permitted an approach by water to the landing on the Thames. Unfortunately he did not live to see the theatre completed in 1671 and his interests passed to his widow and son Charles. It was there that the landscape painters Streater and Robert Agas designed settings which imitated the French stage. That they were not too successful and spent so much money that the D'Avenants could not continue their enterprise is evident. They had to accept the forced union with the Drury Lane company in 1682. From then until 1695 there was but one acting troupe in London. The King had given patents to the King's company and to the Duke's company which permitted a tremendous amount of leeway in the management of their theatres. Killigrew and D'Avenant had become managers in the modern sense and so great was their power that it is not until the reign of the Theatrical Syndicate that we find anything comparable. The old commonwealth system of sharing the financial returns passed out of existence and actors went on salary.

Of all the actors of the Restoration period there are but four who will bear discussion, three on their histrionic merits and one on her amatory accomplishments. Needless to say, this last is NELL (ELEANOR) GWYN (1650-1687) about whose life endless disputes have raged. Doubtless she was born in Herefordshire; certainly she came out of London's alleys; assuredly she was a voluptuously pretty woman with a sense of humor and some merit as a comic actress. She is chiefly remembered as one of the principal mistresses of Charles II and as the mother of the Duke of St. Albans was co-founder of one of England's proudest families. Her range as an actress was not great, but she had the ability to acquire knowledge and certain style without too much difficulty. Tradition places her as an orange-seller in the pit of Drury Lane but by the time she was half way through her teens, her pretty face had attracted Charles Hart who was a portrayer of young women and the lover of many of them in real life. He took Nell to his heart and coached her for the theatre. Her debut came in a serious role (she was never very successful in tragic parts for she had neither the figure nor the temperament for tragedy), Cydaria, in Dryden's *The Indian Emperor* in 1665. Her roguish recitals of prologues and epilogues were particularly successful. By 1668 the indefatigable raconteur and diarist, Samuel Pepys, saw that the King was paying her altogether too much attention and sighed over his prince's passion for pleasure. The next year Nell left the stage to become mistress to Charles. She had the wit not to survive him long, and despite her tremendous extravagance, the theatrically-inclined James saw that she was well provided for.

The three other outstanding names were THOMAS BETTERTON (1635?–1710), Elizabeth Barry and Anne Bracegirdle. The first was the foremost male actor on the English stage until his retirement in 1710. In 1661 he appeared at Lincoln's Inn Fields and continued with that company at Dorset Gardens after D'Avenant's death, when he himself assumed the managership. His Hamlet was guided by D'Avenant's memory of Joseph Taylor's performance in the character. Taylor was believed to have imitated Burbage and thus to have played the part as Shakespeare would have wished it played. Despite all this tutelage Betterton brought a freshness to the role that won the hearts of his audience. Pepys thought it "the best acted part ever done by man" and Betterton "the best actor in the world." He was a well-disciplined and sober actor with a melodious voice of great range, which Cibber said enchanted his audiences. Even the captious Tony Aston admitted that he had the power to enforce "an universal attention even from the fops and orange-girls." With the joining together of the actors in 1682, he went to Drury Lane where he played until the rupture of 1695. Then he moved over to the new theatre in Lincoln's Inn Fields until the first theatre in the Haymarket was built for him. He had had ample opportunity to examine scenery and methods of staging as well as Molière's writing technique when he was sent to Paris by James to inspect the French theatres. In addition to Hamlet, his most prominent roles were in *King Lear*, *Macbeth*,

Othello, King Henry VIII, Love for Love, The Provoked Wife and *The Way of the World*. His farewell to the stage was in *The Maid's Tragedy* on April 13, 1710 at which time he performed to a packed house in the theatre in the Haymarket which the wiseacres of a few years before had said was in the fields and too far from the center of things ever to secure a capacity audience. Betterton was the first great actor of the Restoration and was in the line of great Hamlets from Burbage to Gielgud.

The name in theatre annals which was coupled most often with Betterton's in a professional fashion was that of ELIZABETH BARRY (1658-1713). Her private life was far from spotless; her connection with John Wilmot, Earl of Rochester, was notorious, though it began innocently enough on her part. D'Avenant had endeavored unsuccessfully to train her. She was beautiful, dignified and intelligent but had no fire. The respectable daughter of a Colonel of Charles I's forces, it was not until her affair with Rochester that she blossomed forth as the greatest tragic actress of the seventeenth century. Between her debut at Dorset Gardens in 1673 and her final performance at the Haymarket in 1710, she had originated 112 characters. Of these her greatest were in *The Orphan* (she is always associated with "Ah, poor Castalio!" which so deeply moved the audience as she pityingly read this famous line); her "solemn and august" (according to Aston) Isabella in Southerne's drama *The Fatal Marriage; or, The Innocent Adultery* (1694), later altered by Garrick into *Isabella; or, The Fatal Marriage;* and her famous Belvidera in Otway's *Venice Preserved* (1682). She had great versatility as well, for she originated two such contrasting characters as Zara in Congreve's *The Mourning Bride* (1697) and Lady Brute in Sir John Vanbrugh's *The Provoked Wife* (1698). She held no formal farewell but played her last performance in Dryden's *The Spanish Friar* the day after Betterton retired. Thus the two whose stately presence had illumined the Restoration stage left it almost simultaneously.

The last great acting name of this period was ANNE BRACEGIRDLE (1663?-1748) who was well-known for her playing of comic parts, though she had considerable success in such dramatic roles as Portia, Isabella and Cordelia; but it was in such delightful roles as Araminta in Congreve's *The Old Bachelor* (1691) and Angelica in his *Love for Love* (1693), which the dramatist had composed especially for her, that she reached her heights. She was as well known for her virtue in a period when it was conspicuously lacking as she was for her abilities as an actress. In person she was attractive rather than beautiful and as her young charms dimmed she was piqued by the success of the delightful Mrs. Oldfield. And so in 1707 she withdrew and left the stage to her rival, though she emerged from her comfortable retirement to play Angelica for Betterton's benefit in 1709.

Tempting as it is to linger over the charms of the actresses and the striking qualities of many of the actors, we must give the dramatists their full meed of consideration. It was a time when histrionic ability supplemented and flattered the writing abilities of the dramatists. Their tragedies have never set the world afire for they were too conscious of the neo-classic example set by France, but their comedies gained in wit and polish from observation, first-hand or otherwise, of their Gallic confreres.

Naturally the first name on the roster is that of JOHN DRYDEN (1631-1700), who became Poet Laureate and Historiographer Royal under Charles II, though he had begun his career as a supporter of Cromwell. In 1659 he composed the *Heroic Stanzas on the Death of Oliver Cromwell*, but a year later found him celebrating the Restoration of the Stuart monarchy with *Astraea Redux*. His first success came with his collaboration with Sir Robert Howard on *The Indian Queen* (1664). Its great popularity arose not so much from its heroic verse, popular in France and introduced to England by D'Avenant in *The Siege of Rhodes*, as from its magnificent investiture. The Indian costumes and handsome scenery won the admiration of the audience. *Secret Love; or, The Maiden Queen* (1667) was principally noteworthy for Nell Gwyn's delightful acting of Florimel. *Sir Martin Mar-all; or, Feigned Innocence* (1667) was a coarsened adaptation of Molière's *L'Étourdi*. Dryden's coarseness was notable even in a far from squeamish age; it seems to have stemmed from certain qualities in his character. In *Tyrannic Love; or, The Royal Martyr* he did not serve the decorative Nell so well. As Valeria she was required to stab herself, come to life as she was being carried off the stage and speak an exceedingly funny epilogue. This piece coupled with *Almazor and Almahide; or, The Conquest of Granada* (1670) and the ridicule of the Duke of Buckingham's *The Rehearsal* (1671) managed in a large degree to give the quietus to this form of bombastic tragedy.

In 1678, he wrote one of his most important plays, *All for Love; or, The World Well Lost*. This piece was based on the story of Antony and Cleopatra and was in fact a new version of Shakespeare's great tragedy. He contracted the play by depriving Antony of his love of country and hope for the supremacy of the Roman Empire and Cleopatra of her bargaining qualities, which gave the Elizabethan piece its broader scope and wider application. This play was written in blank verse and was a retreat from the rhymed couplet whose monotony had excited such ridicule and general opposition.

Upon James II's accession to the throne, Dryden became a Roman Catholic. He has been accused of changing for political reasons. If this were true, it does not explain the fact that when William and Mary succeeded James, he retained his religion and so lost the post and salary of Poet Laureate and Royal Historiographer. Two years after the Glorious Revolution he produced the other play of importance for which he is particularly remembered, *Don Sebastian*. Some think this a better play than his drama about Egypt's queen, but though the characters of the former are better defined there is an heroic tendency that makes the piece bombastic. As was customary in his century he did much pamphleteering. He devoted the latter part of his life to translation, the most important author being Virgil. Dryden never had the assured living that many successful playwrights achieve and he was dependent on the gifts of noble and wealthy friends.

Dryden's successor as Poet Laureate in 1690 was THOMAS SHADWELL (1642-1692). He modelled his plays on those of Ben Jonson and dedicated himself to the effort of reproducing the *mores* as well as the literary and artistic characteristics of the London he knew so well. In the beginning he was a friend of Dryden, but his championing of the ardent Protestants in the personal scandalous attack *The Medal of John Bayes* caused Dryden to reply in his famous personal satire *MacFlecknoe; or, A Satire on the True Blue Protestant Poet, T.S.* (1682) and to castigate him as Og in *Absalom and Achitophel* (1681). Though Shadwell was the author of at least seventeen plays, only *The Sullen Lovers* (1670) is notable. His elevation to his post came largely through the lack of writers in the Whig Party rather than through any great literary excellence of his own.

A new constellation shone in the Restoration heavens for scarcely more than thirty years. THOMAS OTWAY (1652-1685) was gifted with an Oxford education and received some financial return from his work; nonetheless he was a bad manager and died in extreme poverty, despite the great success of two of his plays. His love of the theatre developed early and his initial connection as an actor was a miserable failure. After the indifferent reception of his *Alcibiades* (1675) he followed it the next year with a declamatory drama, *Don Carlos*, which was well received. Then came translations of Racine and Molière, but it was not until 1680, with *The Orphan; or, The Unhappy Marriage*, that he wrote his first important play. This has provided a rewarding acting part for England's actresses for a century and a half. *Caius Marius* (1680) is best left untouched, but in 1682 he wrote the play for which he is well remembered, *Venice Preserved; or, A Plot Discovered*. The three characters Pierre, Jaffier, and

Belvidera have kept this play alive despite its bombast and some long, dull passages. Mrs. Siddons who played the part a hundred years after it was written is always identified with her reading of the line, "Remember twelve." The love scenes between Jaffier and Belvidera were passionate in contrast to the great general pathos of the play whose characters were like puppets who moved through intense human suffering. Mrs. Barry appeared as Belvidera, and this but heightened Otway's unrequited love for her. But the burning love scenes were not for him and three years later, hounded by debt and extreme poverty, he died in utter destitution despite the fact that he was the principal tragic dramatist of his age.

The sprightly humors are upon us; the solemn tragedies and dull bawdry of Dryden and Otway are behind; and the Wits are next in line. Sir George Etherege (c.1634-1691) combined libertinism in his plays and in his life with perhaps a shade more emphasis on the latter. A handsome seducer and winebibber, he reproduced some of his wit in his writings. He was a distinct favorite of Charles II, as was his fellow roisterer Sir Charles Sedley who once distinguished himself by fighting a drunken duel naked in the streets of London. They were a charming pair, these two. Etherege had three comedies and several diplomatic missions to his credit, while Sedley had little but his handsomeness which bestiality soon reduced to a battered state and his plays have very little merit. Sedley's best play was probably *The Mulberry Garden*, a comedy based on Molière's *L'École des Maris* and published in 1668. His *Antony and Cleopatra* (1677), *Bellamira* (1678), and *The Tyrant King of Crete* (1702) are completely routine. During the first performance of *Bellamira* the roof of the theatre fell and injured no one but the author. Perhaps this was a perfect piece of unexpected dramatic criticism.

To return to Etherege, *The Comical Revenge; or, Love in a Tub* (1664) brought him forth as a dramatist with a play which combined favorite heroic verse, since discredited, with some fresh comedy scenes of genuine humor. He was the first writer to catch the light spirit of the fop, the wit and runner-after-women which are the chief characteristics of Restoration comedy. Had he been poorer he might have been more industrious; regardless of the finesse of his characterizations of Londoners he never achieved the insight into the soul that Congreve had. His plays were but an embroidering of his own life; his wenching and his state diplomacy were the truly important matters to which his fairly considerable energies were directed.

Despite the success of his first play, it was four years before he produced another and better one, *She Would If She Could*. So great was the interest in a new play by this author that a thousand people were turned away from the opening performance. It was an airy, fairy world of fantastic delights which he described, all centering on the pleasures of witty flirting and seduction by *bon mot*. His final play, *The Man of Mode; or, Sir Fopling Flutter* (1676) was the best comedy of intrigue written before Congreve. Its humor was more interesting to its contemporary audience because of the satirical portraits of Sedley as the erotic Dorimant; the exquisite Beau Hewitt as the preciously fashionable Sir Fopling Flutter who brought new chic from Paris; and the author himself as Medley. Notwithstanding the fact that it had an enormous vogue, Etherege wrote no more for the theatre but confined himself to diplomacy and erotic living in various places on the Continent and finally retired to Paris where he died as he had lived.

Though he wrote more than thirty plays THOMAS D'URFEY (1653-1723) is best known for his jokes and songs. Licentious, disreputable in speech and writing, a strong Tory and Protestant, Addison records that he was a boon companion of Charles II and that he had frequently seen the King leaning on Tom's shoulder humming his ribald songs, many of which were printed in 1719 as *Pills to Purge Melancholy*. One of his comedies, *The Bath; or, The Western Lass* gave Mrs. Verbruggen a delightful role in the season 1700-1701 and the piece seems to have intrigued its audience. That and *The Plotting Sisters* (1676), which Addison puffed in the *Guardian* with an account of D'Urfey's manifest eccentricities so as to increase interest in the author's benefit and so swell the coffers, were his only plays worth naming.

The comedy of manners was enriched by several brilliant contributions of WILLIAM WYCHERLEY (1640-1715) whose boldness in subject matter and choice of polite obscenity even exceeded that of Etherege. Because Cromwell still ruled England, this son of a "county" family was sent to France for his education at the age of fifteen. It was not long before he was to be found mingling with Molière's *précieuses ridicules* at the *Hôtel de Rambouillet*. Worshipping gentility and the fashionable, he turned from the Church of England to Rome, then back to Canterbury once more when he went to Oxford. However, under James II, Rome won him back. Such changeability suggests a worship of the correct thing rather than any profound religious convictions.

Coming down from Oxford where he had been exposed to a little polite learning rather than an acquisition of scholarship, he treated his profession of the law cavalierly. He lost no time in seeking out the pleasures of London and soon began to write for the stage. The appropriately named *Love in a Wood* (1671), staged at the Theatre Royal in Drury Lane, started him on a career which was to bring him everlasting fame. Pope said he had Plautus' wit. *The Gentleman Dancing Master* (1672), admired for its animal spirits, followed the bestowal of favors by the Duchess of Cleveland; Charles II's mistress felt the need of variety in her love affairs. The next year saw *The Country Wife*, which with *The Plain Dealer* explains his fame. His portrait of delightful Margery Pinchwife has been the pleasure of actresses from its creator, Mrs. Boutel, to its most recent brilliant revival with Ruth Gordon. When Garrick rewrote the piece under the title *The Country Girl* and modified its bawdiness for the sentimental eighteenth century audience he robbed the lines of much of their wit and sparkle, the play's *raison d'être*. Through this later version Mrs. Saunders, Mrs. Jordan and Ada Rehan have romped. In the suspicious cuckolded Pinchwife, Wycherley depicted the plight of all husbands, and by Horner's borrowing the impotency device from Terence's *The Eunuch*, the unscrupulous libertine is well drawn. Keenly written, this is one of the most successful comedies of manners in the history of the theatre.

His next and last play, *The Plain Dealer* (1674), partook of the bright comedy of his earlier work, but satire etched with vitriol tempered it. He painted a true picture of the heartlessness and viciousness of London living and exposed his honest hero Manly to the mendacity of false friends. A little like Molière was this telling attack on the legal profession. The cutting strokes appealed to Voltaire who had an acid wit himself, and who said that he knew of no comedy, ancient or modern, which had so much spirit. The success of the last play brought him a wife who caused him an endless amount of trouble. After having played watchdog to his morals for several years she died. The litigation over her estate so impoverished him that he was imprisoned seven years for debt. Charles had been so annoyed by his sudden marriage that he refused to help him; but James II, who had always admired the man and his work, paid his debts and Wycherley was once more free, though the brilliant phase of his career was over.

SIR JOHN VANBRUGH (1666-1726) belonged to two phases of the theatre, first as dramatist and second as architect. He was a bluff man of considerable social grace and was well-liked in society. This, together with his adoption of a military career, contributed to his rapid rise to fame. He turned his attention to writing and *The Relapse; or, Virtue in Danger,* a sequel to Colley Cibber's *Love's Last Shift,* was staged at Drury Lane in 1697 and won considerable attention for its bold and outspoken dialogue. This was successfully altered by Sheridan into *A Trip to Scarborough* in 1777 and a French translation as *Le Comte de Boursouflé* (1862) was brought out as a posthumous play of Voltaire to the amusement of contemporary English critics. Charles Montagu, later Lord Halifax, solicited his second play, *The Provoked Wife*, for Lincoln's Inn Fields in 1698. This play had two comic parts, Lord and Lady Brute, which were standard vehicles for all leading actors for more than a century; Garrick was particularly good in the role. After building Castle Howard for the Earl of Carlisle, and Blenheim for the Duke and Duchess of Marlborough, he turned his attention to building a theatre in which his plays might be acted. This was to have been a *bijou* of a house and it enlisted Congreve's enthusiastic support. As he worked on the new playhouse in the Haymarket, he let his imagination run wild and produced a large theatre with bad acoustics, though some unrecorded changes saved the fate of the house, and it was opened in 1705 with Italian opera. Three Molière plays and one that was considered Vanbrugh's best, *The Confederacy*, were produced the same year. This was followed by several unimportant pieces. At his death he left the unfinished play, *A Journey to London*, which Cibber completed and offered successfully as *The Provoked Husband* in 1728. This comic drama was played every season for the rest of the century and had several important revivals in the nineteenth century.

WILLIAM CONGREVE (1670-1729) wrote five plays and reached the high point of English comedy of manners which was rivalled by Sheridan and threatened by Somerset Maugham, though America's S. N. Behrman may yet reach a challenging position. Born at Bardsley near Leeds, his family removed to Ireland when his father was made Commandant of the garrison at Youghal and agent of the Earl of Cork. Young Congreve was educated at Kilkenny School, where the famous Swift (Dean-to-be) was a schoolmate; later he attended the celebrated Trinity College at Dublin. Like Wycherley, he began his career as a lawyer but soon devoted his energies to writing for the stage. Under the auspices of the former Poet Laureate, John Dryden who had many generous impulses, *The Old Bachelor* was acted in January, 1693 to almost universal acclaim. Its complicated action, skillfully woven around a central theme of credulous belief, was an extraordinary achievement for a young man not yet twenty-three. To prove that this was not a flash in the pan he offered *The Double Dealer* in November of the same year. This comedy about the deceitful advantages of truth-telling won extravagant praise from Dryden, who was more convinced than ever that a great master of comedy had arisen in England.

The laughter of Congreve found record in the first of his two best plays, *Love for Love* (1695), a brilliant comedy possessed of a wit that is still scathing in the twentieth century today, as was proved

when an indifferent revival held the brief attention of hasty New
Yorkers in a war-torn world. It shows a great structural advance over
his previous efforts and created the interesting characters of Valentine, Ben the sailor, Angelica and Miss Prue, which provide excellent
parts to challenge actors who can recreate the artificiality of seventeenth century acting. A tragedy *The Mourning Bride* was produced
in 1697 and was acted for a century but is seen no more. *The Way of
the World* (1700) was his peak in playwriting and is as near an
approach to the heights of Molière as any English comedy. This play
has a simple plot with brilliantly drawn characters. The delightful
Mirabel and Millament carry on an intrigue to marry despite the
efforts of the girl's aunt, Lady Wishfort, to prevent this union. The
urbanity of their lovemaking, their well-bred restraint and intellectual
understanding of one another provided the author with his best comic
lines and situations.

With the fall of the Stuarts and the accession of the Orange-Stuart
ménage, the middle class had achieved greater power than ever in
England and the bawdy wit of the Restoration writers had begun to
be frowned upon in no uncertain fashion. In 1698 the Reverend
Jeremy Collier published his notorious attack on the theatre, drama
and stage. *A Short View of the Immorality and Profaneness of the
English Stage* curiously enough was aimed at Shakespeare and the
Elizabethans as well as Congreve and Vanbrugh. The "noxious and
highly immoral play, *Hamlet*" was attacked while the boldness of
Wycherley went unrebuked, except in so far as he belonged to the
vile theatre of Collier's opinion. Congreve and others replied with
pamphlets and Collier answered and seems to have had the better of
the argument. Dryden actually went so far as to apologize and devoted
himself to government posts and to being the gentleman he was
born. Voltaire was extremely annoyed when he visited the dramatist
to discover that the "writer" was lost in the "gentleman." Congreve
spent the balance of his life in pleasant talk with Addison and Steele
in the famous coffee-houses of London, and because of his past literary
brilliance, Pope dedicated his translation of *The Iliad* to him. He was
buried in Westminster Abbey and his fortune was left to his friend,
Henrietta, Duchess of Marlborough, rather than to his own family,
who needed it; his intimate friend, the lovely Anne Bracegirdle,
received but £200.

The last of the great Restoration writers was the Irish born GEORGE
FARQUHAR (1678-1707) who, like Congreve, was educated at Trinity
College. Leaving there he joined a company of strolling players with
whom he played for a season. During this period he learned the rudi-
ments of the acting craft and the comparative effectiveness of dra-

matic construction. Next he appeared in Dublin, but thoughts of the countryside were still in his head, so when he came to write plays he took them from the streets of London into the green fields and inns of old England. An accident which had occurred while he was playing Guyomar in Dryden's *The Indian Emperor*—he had failed to exchange sword for foil in the fencing scene and had wounded a fellow-actor so severely that he nearly died—coupled with the fact that the handsome Irishman had become convinced that he was no actor, put an end to his career as a thespian and he went to London to write.

Love in a Bottle (1699) was produced at Drury Lane when he was but twenty and was so well received that it encouraged the budding dramatist. *The Constant Couple* the same year, benefited very largely from the acting of Robert Wilks as Sir Harry Wildair, a character later to become a "breeches part" in which Peg Woffington and Dora Jordan romped so charmingly that they bewitched their audiences. The audiences obviously wanted more so he supplied them with *Sir Harry Wildair* (1701), again with Wilks, and the lovely Anne Oldfield as Lady Lurewell. The sequel, as usually is the case, was not so good as the original and did not have the longevity of its predecessor. In 1702 he produced his version of Fletcher's *The Wild Goose Chase* in prose, under the title *The Inconstant; or, The Way to Win Him*. Perhaps this gave the clue to the charming lady who, as poor as he was, still wanted him so much that she caused a rumor to be circulated that she was a great heiress. He married her and found out his mistake. From that time, his financial affairs were even more disordered than they had been before. Dramaturgy seems to have paid him very little, despite the success with which his plays were greeted. *The Twin Rivals* (1702) and *The Stage Coach* (1704) were of little importance but his two best plays were yet to come as his brief life was ending. The first of these was *The Recruiting Officer* (1706) and dealt with the humorous side of the recruiting of men for Her Majesty's Forces in a small country town. His situation was well chosen and the plot was handled with facility, but the characters were slightly developed and never attained the depth of Congreve's. His last and most important play, written in six weeks as he was dying, was *The Beaux' Stratagem*, which is his brightest comedy and is known for its spontaneous good humor and rollicking spirits. The name of the character, Lady Bountiful, has become a synonym for ostentatious generosity. Farquhar lived to take his third night receipts (for this was the night on which all the receipts of the box-office were turned over to the author) and to receive an extra benefit the day he died.

Out of the large number of Restoration dramatists who practised dramaturgy more or less indifferently at times, there are two others who deserve mention. NATHANIEL LEE (1653-1692) wrote a number of tumultuous and bombastic tragedies with passages of considerable poetic beauty. His most important plays were: *Nero* (1675), *Sophonisba* (1676), *The Rival Queens* (1677) and, with Dryden, *The Duke of Guise* (1682). THOMAS SOUTHERNE (1660?-1746) was responsible for several plays, the best-known of which are: *Oroonoko* (1696), which was based on the South American Indian novel by Mrs. Aphra Behn and contains the famous line, "Pity's akin to love"; and *Isabella; or, The Fatal Marriage* (1694), which in Garrick's alteration was to become an acting vehicle for George Anne Bellamy, Mrs. Siddons, Eliza O'Neill and Fanny Kemble.

The seventeenth century not only saw the introduction of actresses but also women dramatists who earned their living by writing for the stage. The novelist and playwright APHRA BEHN (1640-1689), born to John and Amy Amis in Wye, with a childhood in Surinam, became the wife of a Dutch gentleman. Being of a generous mind and naturally of a loving disposition, she was called a harlot among other unpleasant names, but she seems merely to have lived a full life. She was attacked by the critics because she dared to be the first woman to earn her living by writing, instead of by the more usual courses of marriage or a less regular relationship. Her plays are of no great importance in the long view, nor are her novels, but they had a vogue in their day. She is of importance to us because she was a "first." Some of her plays would still be playable for audiences with strong stomachs; the best being *The Dutch Lover* (1673), *The Rover*, in two parts (1677 and 1681), *The Feigned Courtezans* (1679) and *The City Heiress; or, Sir Timothy Treat-all* (1682). The novel, *Oroonoko; or, The Royal Slave*, from which both Southerne and Garrick made plays, is best known to us and is the work with which she is usually associated. She has been the subject of several biographies, none of which are so revealing, nor so well-written as the brief and delightful life by V. Sackville-West.

Of the other ladies who had a hand in writing for the stage, Orinda (Mrs. Philips) was the first, but she did not support herself by her writing, so that our Aphra is unchallenged; the notorious Mrs. Manley, the gentle Mrs. Cockburn, and fat Mrs. Pix, and finally Mrs. Centlivre, whose plays still survive. SUSANNAH CENTLIVRE (1667?-1723) was born Freeman. After two husbands, she chose Queen Anne's cook Joseph as her third, and launched forth on a writing career after a brief time as an actress. Of her nineteen plays three are memorable: *The Gamester* (1705); the gay comedy *The Wonder; A Woman Keeps a Secret* (1714) with its significant humor, was later to supply Garrick with one of his best comedy parts; and finally her best play, *A Bold Stroke for a Wife*. This last was not particularly successful when it was first staged in 1718 at Lincoln's Inn Fields, but it has had a longer life than any of her other plays and the name of the character, Simon Pure, has passed into general English usage. Mrs. Centlivre was really a transition dramatist from the Restoration to the sentimental drama of the eighteenth century, as was Colley Cibber who more properly belongs in the latter century in so far as style and thinking are concerned.

Thus ends the Restoration which brought England a fine tradition of comic acting, several handsome playhouses, one dramatist of the first rank and several of the second. The theatre passed through a period of being the plaything of the Court and a time-passer for the nobility, but with the awakening of the middle-class, it broadened its base and widened its appeal though it lowered its dramatic standards for more than half a century. It suffered from the neo-classic blight of the French theatre but survived it, perhaps because exalted heights and false heroics were too much for the humor and basic common sense of the English.

XII

THE LEGENDARY EAST

NEAR EAST AND AFRICA

AT this point in our narrative of the theatre, we turn from the European stage which had achieved professional status, to those countries east and south of the Mediterranean whose culture had already been felt in Europe. The chronologies of the theatres of the Near East do not fit into the general scheme of things, so that we can only move gradually eastward without regard to strict historical order.

The Jews, who have done so much for the theatre since 1800, had no theatre in Judea. The very idea was anathema to the monotheistic who opposed with all their might and with terrific integrity the polytheism and anthropomorphism of the pagan nations which might have built a theatre for them as they did for Egypt, Greece, China, and Rome. In their divine literature, the Old Testament of the Holy Bible, there are at least two passages which drama-minded people mark out for their own. The first, of course, is *The Song of Songs*, which undoubtedly came out of the hymeneal songs sung at weddings. This beautiful passage of passionate love has been tolerated in the Bible because an allegorical meaning of God and His Church has been read into these sensuous and moving lines. It was never performed in a Jewish theatre but modern playwrights have transformed it for the stage, with little rearrangement. Professor Richard G. Moulton in the *Modern Reader's Bible* has divided the lines among the characters who he imagines took part. This is reasonable when one recalls that in early texts of the Bible, words were run together and were not separated by punctuation. Hubert Osborne adapted the poem, and it was successfully produced by the Department of Drama of the Carnegie Institute of Technology at Pittsburgh in the nineteen-twenties.

The other passage which has distinct dramatic content is *The Book of Job*. This might almost be said to be a five act drama, with prologue and epilogue. It has been called "closet drama," but that smacks of a literariness which the author of *Job* obviously did not desire. Perhaps it might be called a dramatic masterpiece that the obtuseness of its generation failed to call into being in the playhouse.

Outside the Holy Land, Jews were not so anti-theatrical. The colonists established in Alexandria undoubtedly wrote and performed plays which stemmed both from the Old Testament and Greek drama. They had become so completely Hellenized that they had lost their language and had adopted the Greek tongue and even required a translation of the Bible. There is too little left of their drama by which to measure its standards, but that it existed in the Greek theatres of Egypt is irrefutable.

Arabia, Turkey and Persia had a Shiah Mohammedan Passion Play tradition which did not come into being until Mohammed and his children were buried, and the complicated question of succession was settled. This settlement was only accomplished after terrifying cruelties. The heart-breaking sufferings of Hassan and Fatima were enacted so that the tradition of purification through agony grew up as it did in the Christian faith, but development came more swiftly among the followers of Mohammed.

This points to its purely religious significance that had only a slight and secondary theatrical meaning. The only reason for mentioning it is that for so long and so repeatedly it has been said that there was no theatre among those of Islam, and that they destroyed drama wherever they went. This still obtains in general; certainly the theatre in Spain disappeared under Saracen rule; and the Indian stage declined when the Mohammedans rode ruthlessly through that beautiful land in a series of invasions.

The sad story of Hassan and Fatima was made quite naturally into a passion play and is still enacted in the month of Muharram. The play continued for ten days with the audience becoming more and more worked up as it progressed. Being an intense people, they frequently broke out into disorders towards the finale for the real events which were responsible for the play produced a schism in the Islamic church which has yet to heal.

Both women and men were in the audience but all the parts were played by men. Many famous descriptions of this play have appeared, but none is more graphic than the account of S. G. W. Benjamin, first American Minister to Persia in 1882, which is given in full in volume three of Alfred Bates' *The Drama*. It first came into existence in the tenth century and has been performed ever since. During the short Deilamee dynasty, between about 933 and 986, the religious lamentations at the tomb of Hassan began to take form as drama, as episode after episode of the martyr's life was reconstructed. This has remained the principal dramatic contribution of Islam to this day, though the nineteenth century saw the development of quite unimportant secular drama in Persia.

In the Sunnite Mohammedan sect was found all the religious bigotry of the Semitic race which destroyed the theatre wherever it went; it was this section of Islam that swept over Egypt and Spain and crushed its dramatic culture. The only form of theatrical entertainment tolerated by this cult was the shadow-play (Karagöz) which was seen, and still is, in Turkey, Syria, North Africa, and Arabia.

In addition there were two other kinds of theatre in Turkey, *Orta Oinu* and *Meddah*. The first of these forms dates from the twelfth century, the beginning of the theatre in that country. It is like the classic mime and probably came from two sources, one being Byzantium, capital of the Eastern Roman Empire, and the other the *commedia dell'arte* by way of the trade and cultural routes from Venice. These simple plays were acted in the open, in a space thirty yards long and twenty wide, oval or quadrangular in shape. The women sat alone in a section opposite the single stage entrance and were shielded by a large veil from the vulgar gaze of the men. There were but two pieces of scenery, a chair or low screen stood near the entrance and a higher two-fold screen was placed at the opposite end of the stage. Doors, window, gardens, woods, castles, or whatever the scene was supposed to depict, were painted on sheets of paper pasted on these screens. This was intended to inform the audience of the play's locale. The two principal actors were *Pishekiar*, the leader, and the comic *Kavuklu;* in addition there was a female character, *Zenne*, as well as other minor parts. All the women of course were played by men. This theatrical form still continues in existence, but probably all of these purely Turkish types will pass with the rapid Europeanization of the country.

The second form *Meddah* (also famous in India and China) is the story-teller who relates characteristic tales of Turkish and Arabic folklore. Both of these play forms, together with *Karagöz*, were almost always permitted great license of speech. Many reforms of abuses, as in China, came through the invented tales or plays of the actors, whether human or puppet.

While it is not our intention to record in any detail the history of marionettes, puppets or shadow-plays, they must be mentioned where they are the *only*, or the principal theatrical activity. The Turkish *Karagöz* (called *Karakush* in North Africa) came out of the exploits of an historical figure who lived at the very beginnings of the Ottoman Empire. He is, like Punch in England, *Hanswurst* in Germany and *Petroushka* in Russia, a stupid, muddleheaded, good-hearted, sincere person. His companion *Hadshejvat*, is pretentious and interpolates many Arabic phrases into his speech. The shadow-play was undoubtedly borrowed from Java by the Arabs, though Indian influence is also apparent, and it was performed in good weather in a garden or courtyard. This was because the shadow figures were graven images and it was feared that the angel would not visit a house which was polluted by them. The devotees were so intent on watching the beautifully colored figures moving on the screen and listening to the amusing lines, slapstick business and snatches of songs, that they were totally oblivious to the abominable smoke of the lamps.

The primitive tribes of Uganda, Belgian Congo, French Guinea and many West African groups developed a type of drama which was based on their dead kings and which employed a medium to act out the ghosts' exploits or advice to the living. These rites, partly religious and partly theatrical are also to be found among the Indians of the Western World, the aborigines of Australia and many of the islands of Polynesia. These all should be compared with Egyptian drama.

INDIA

With the exception of the Chinese, and reservations are noted in a following chapter on that august theatre, there is no drama or stage in Asia so ancient as that of India. This enormously vast and wealthy country with its mingling of races and religions has produced great extremes of wealth and poverty, scholarship and downright illiteracy. The fact that there has always been and is starvation in the midst of plenty explains the difficulties of westernizing this great country. What is true now was vastly multiplied thirty-five hundred years ago when drama was first recorded there. Because of its cost, the theatre was primarily intended for the princes and their courts, though eventually dramatic art spread to the lowest castes of India.

Recent years have shown not only a great interest in the history and development of India's drama, but also a history of her stage which is an important segment of theatre. There has always been a tendency among the scholarly to concentrate on drama as literature and scorn the stage history of plays; which is why a certain type of scholarship has fallen into disrepute. It is the kind of hair-splitting one even finds in great libraries; drama should never be wrenched from its proper setting in the theatre, which is its only reason for existence. The reading of plays is a purely secondary ideal; they were meant to be performed on the stage before an audience, and it is only in the playhouse that we see theatre at its best and truest.

Brahma is supposed to have invented the theatre in India and to have commanded that the first playhouse be built so that Bharata, the father of Hindu drama, could produce his plays. It is significant that his name "bharata" has become one of the terms used for "actor." Nothing else is known of him nor of his plays, none of which survive. The earliest dramatic development known to us seems to have been the dialogue form employed in the Vedic hymns of the *Rig-veda* about 1500 B.C. The real beginnings came later however in the Epic Period of Hindu literature (500 B.C.-320 A.D.) when the two great Indian epics, *Mahābhārata* and *Ramayana* were composed. These are important to us because they were the great sourcebooks of the Hindu dramatists, just as *The Iliad* and *The Odyssey* were to the Greeks. It should of course be understood that the *Ramayana* was a literary epic, mainly the work of Valmiki.

It was long thought that the invasion of Alexander the Great may have created a Greek influence on the Indian theatre, through the introduction of traveling actors, but this has been generally discredited as it is pure supposition and no evidence can be found to substantiate it. The only dramatist of the Epic Period of whom we have any record was ASHVAGHOSHA (second century A.D.), a romantic poet and Buddhist teacher. Only short sections of three of his plays are still extant. *Shāriputraprakarana* was a story of the conversion to Buddhism of two young Hindus, Shāriputra and Maudgālyayana, in the very presence of Buddha himself. A second play, profane in character, had a courtesan as the heroine and the third was somewhat like a morality play, with abstract virtues as characters.

The outstanding work of the Hindu dramatists was accomplished during the Classic Period (320-800 A.D.) from which twenty-five plays still exist. This golden age came after a period of political turmoil which was followed by the succession of the Rajah Chandragupta in Northern India. The first playwright of this era was BHĀSA who apparently wrote about 350 A.D. because Kālidāsa, who lived about 400 A.D., mentions him in his drama, *Mālavikāgnimitra*. All but one of Bhāsa's plays were on epic themes. The single exception was *Daridra-chārudatta* (*The Poor Chārudatta*), a domestic piece which is probably an earlier version of *The Little Clay Cart*. His *Svapnavasavadatta* was the most admired of all of his romantic plays and was based upon the *Ramayana* and *Mahābhārata*.

Mrichhakatikā (*The Little Clay Cart*) was popularly credited to the legendary King Shudraka, mathematical genius and enormously successful lover, but probably was written by something less than the royal hand. The court poet Dandin has been assigned the role. It drew on Bhāsa's play, of which but four acts survive, but the ten acts of

The Little Clay Cart have even more definitely social implications than its predecessor. This play was successfully produced in an abbreviated version by Irene and Alice Lewisohn at the Neighborhood Playhouse in New York in 1924.

KĀLIDĀSA lived, according to Hindu tradition, at the court of King Vikrama at Ujjain during the first century B.C., but Western scholarship places him at the beginning of the fifth century A.D. He has been called the Hindu Shakespeare and the Bridegroom of Poetry. Like the others, he wrote in Sanskrit, which was a literary language understood only by the upper classes. Three plays and his beautiful lyric poem, *Meghadutā* (*The Cloud Messenger*), which though not a drama has often been recited on the Indian stage, are all that survive. Both Schiller and Shelley may have drawn on *Meghadutā* for some of their lyric work. *Shakuntala* (*The Fatal Ring*) was Kālidāsa's masterpiece, in fact it is the gem of all Indian drama. Its language is of surpassing beauty and combines grace and grandeur. Its seven acts contain humor of a superior kind in the motivation of this idyl of love. It was translated by Sir William Jones in 1789 and had a profound influence on Goethe.

Vikramonvashī (*Vikrama and Urvashi, The Hero and the Nymph*), translated into English in 1827 by H. H. Wilson, is on the whole inferior, though one of its five acts is very lovely. The admirable grace of this work is a quality which might be an excellent contribution to modern realistic drama if it were only realized by contemporary dramatists. Its influence, however, was largely felt in India rather than in Europe, which had been impressed by *Shakuntala*. *Mālavikāgnimitra* (*Mālavikā and Agnamitra*), a cynical romance based on a story of the Shungra Dynasty, is sometimes thought to be Kālidāsa's earliest play, though this is in doubt.

SHRĪ-HARSHADEVA (reigned 606 or 607-647 or 648), a king of northern India was also a playwright of some importance. *Ratnavālī* (*The Pearl Necklace*) resembled Kālidāsa's play about King Agnamitra and Mālavikā, and was notable chiefly for the resolving of the dramatic impasse of the plot by the use of a parrot as a principal character. His second play, *Priyadarsikā* (*The Lost Princess*) used the now well-worn device of a play-within-a-play. His best known piece, *Nāgānanda*, was a dance-drama (*nataka*) which was classical in language and was marked by decent restraint. It was a form of miracle play, in which the Buddhist hero-saint, Jimutavahana gave himself up to be devoured by the vulture Garuda, so that his people might be saved. A providential rescue gives it a happy ending through the convenient relenting of Garuda. Shrī-Harshadeva's plays have been translated into English, French, German, Italian and Swedish.

In the next century, another royal dramatist, Mahendravikrama-varman, wrote farces of little importance. The next playwright worthy of mention was BHAVABHUTI (late seventh-early eighth century), born a Brahman and termed by his fellows, the Sweet Speaking. He lacked the sense of humor which makes Kālidāsa particularly appealing to modern readers, and his style was much more rigid, for he seems to have been altogether too conscious of the growing rules of playwriting. *Mahāvīra-charita* (*The Story of the Great Hero*) was a dramatic rendering in reverse of the *Ramayana*, and *Uttarar-āma-charita* (*The Later Story of Rāma*) was a sequel to his first play. His best liked drama was *Malatimadhava* (*Malati and Madhava*, also known as *The Stolen Marriage*). This melodrama has been called the Indian *Romeo and Juliet,* though the analogy seems forced, particularly in view of the happy ending, which suggest a Restoration or an eighteenth century rewriting of Shakespeare. Though his style was over-elaborate he is highly regarded, and is the last of the Classic Hindu dramatists.

There were two other later dramatists of this period, Bhatta Nārā-yana (about 850) and Vishākhadatta (ninth century), represented in survival by a drama apiece. The first is credited with a six act play, *Venisamhāra* (*The Binding of the Braid of Hair*), which was taken from a story in the *Mahābhārata*. The other and more interesting work was by the later author and is an historical drama called *Mudrā-rākshasha* (*The Signet of Rākshasa*).

The Post-Classic Period (800-1000) boasted no great writers, though there are several worthy of mention. In the early part of the ninth century, Murari wrote *Anargharāghava*, which is his only play to survive; and towards the end of the century, Rājashekhara wrote four dramas: *Bālarā māyana*, in ten acts; *Bālabhārata* is incomplete, only two acts still exist; *Karpūramanjāri* (*The Cluster of Camphor Blossoms*), a four act *sattaka* (minor heroic comedy) composed in Prakrit; *Viddhāshalabhanjikā*, a light and graceful four act play which is similar in plot to his third work. In the next century Kshemīshvara wrote two plays of note, *Chandakaushika* (*The Angry Kaushika*) which in plot somewhat resembles *Job* of the Bible, and *Naishad-hānanda* which was taken from an episode in the *Mahābhārata*.

The Mohammedan invasions of India already referred to, coincided approximately with the Period of Decline (1000-1300). Early in the eleventh century Damodaramishra's rambling fourteen-act pretentious drama *Hanumānnātaka* or *Mahā-nātaka* (*The Great Play*) appeared. However, this was balanced by a play of real merit, *Prabod-ha-chandrodaya* (*Rise of the Moon of Intellect*), not unlike a morality play, and its six acts included such allegorical characters as Reason,

Error, Will, Exegesis, Revelation, Religion, etc. In this Krishnamishra had numerous imitators but none worthy of mention. *Gita-govinda* (*The Song of the Divine Herdsman*), written by Jayadeva in the twelfth century, was lyric rather than dramatic in form, though it has many theatrical attributes and has been called the Indian *Song of Songs*.

The Modern Period began in 1300 and has, with the exception of *Chitra-yajna* (c.1820), produced little that is of importance. This one play has a plot but the actors were expected to supplement the dialogue with improvisation such as is found in *commedia dell'arte*. Until the emergence of SIR RABINDRANATH TAGORE (1861-   ) there was no modern dramatist of any standing whatsoever. He is a Neo-Romanticist and is the Eastern equivalent of Maeterlinck with his mystic plays of poetic nature. *Chitra* (1894), *The King of the Dark Chamber* (1914) known as *Rāja* in the original (1910), and *The Cycle of Spring* (1917) are his most important symbolic dramas. He was awarded the Nobel prize for literature in 1913, and has had no successors of any renown.

Drama has never lacked criticism in India; by the tenth century dramatic theory had advanced to such a point that the *Dasarūpa* (*Ten Forms*) laid down precepts which were to be followed in composition. These were based on the principles enunciated in the plays of the Classical Period. There has always been a tendency to preciosity in these rules as 384 types of heroines are described. The Unity of Action was generally not observed; Unity of Time was usually limited to one year as far as an act was concerned though a longer time might pass between acts; Unity of Place was not known as there was no scenery, though locality was suggested by the speech of the actors.

The performances took place in a theatre that in form was not too far removed from our own. The stage was divided into a forestage, the sides of which were masked with wings, which was separated from the back-stage by a curtain which ran the full width of the proscenium. There was a decorated wall with doors at either side (hidden by the sightlines) leading from the greenroom. It was there that the actors dressed and made up, but they usually waited for their entrances in the wings. There was little attempt to introduce stage machinery though gods are spoken of as appearing from above, which suggests either a *deus ex machina* or an upper stage roofing over the up-stage area, but we have no exact evidence of this. The actors did not wear masks and the performances were intimate in nature, as the audience never numbered more than a thousand. The grandeur and size of Greek theatres required the use of masks but the

Indian stage developed a higher degree of subtlety due to the fact
that it was long a court theatre rather than a popular one. The diagram of Bharata's typical Hindu theatre in R. K. Yajnik's *The Indian Theatre* (1934) is particularly helpful in a volume which is
principally devoted to English drama on the Indian stage of the nineteenth and twentieth centuries. As this is but the transition of one
nationality to another, no mention of it is necessary here.

The shadow-play was as popular in India as in China, Turkey, Java
and other centers famous for their devotion to this theatrical form.
Methods of presentation do not materially differ but the subject matter varies according to the interests of the audiences. Though Sanskrit
authorities did not recognize the *chaya-nataka* (shadow-play) as
drama, there were at least seven which fall into this category. The
most important was the *Dutangada*, the earliest surviving play of this
type, and it was produced at the Dhooly festival, March 7, 1243. It
was based on the *Ramayana*, as were most of the other plays of this
type. The form soon spread to the islands off India, Bali, Burma, Cambodia, Thailand (Siam), China, Japan, Arabia, Asia Minor and North
Africa.

EAST OF INDIA AND THE ISLANDS

Several theatrical forms flourished in Burma. The shadow-play as
has just been noted had a great following. The Burmese developed a
drama, to be depicted by human actors, which like the Hindu was
based upon the Vedic epic, *Ramayana*, but which may have come
from India by way of Cambodia. There are highly religious dramas
of purely lyric character, as well as plays based on historical subjects.
And finally, there are the *Nat-pwes* (god-festivals) which are characteristic of Burma, though their theatrical importance is slight in
comparison with their religious significance. This acting out by female mediums of the decisions of dead *nats* (gods) is similar in character to the Ugandan tribal plays already mentioned. These plays are
acted in enclosures, the stage being upon the ground, usually covered
with mats. On three sides bamboo platforms hold the distinguished
guests in the audience, the crowd fills in the balance of the space on
the ground around the stage. There is always a small tree in stage-
center, either stuck in the ground or fastened to one of the poles supporting the roof. Earthen pots with petroleum-soaked flares serve as
footlights. A full orchestra is seated on either side of the stage and
masks are used in the performances.

Ruong-Eynao (*History of Eynao*) is a characteristic and popular
play of the Cambodian theatre, which like so many others is based on
the epics *Ramayana* and *Mahabharata*. The most outstanding of their

dramas is the *Roamke*, which is really only a poor translation of the *Ramayana* in dramatic form. The theatre of Cambodia is, and always has been, a combination of music, dance and pantomime. The pantomimic actions of the actor like the Roman mime, who in this instance becomes the dancer, are synchronized with the *Neac-con-crap* (*Ladies with the Two Pieces of Wood*), who beat time as they sing. The orchestra under the leadership of a mandarin of six degrees accompanies this performance. It recalls the experimentation in American and European theatres with dancing actors, hidden or visible seated singers, combined with musical accompaniment. This has been considered an advanced kind of opera-ballet in our theatre.

As late as 1883, performances were concentrated largely in Pnom-Penh because the Royal Theatre was the only one in the country. This was called *Rung-ram* (Dancing shed), which had a thatched roof, with all but one side open to the elements. Behind this single wall lies the greenroom for the actors, who are always women except when any of the plays based on the *Ramayana* are being performed. Then men are used. A mandarin without fixed salary is responsible for the administration of the Royal Theatre. The training, rehearsing and costuming of the company falls to one of the principal ladies of the court, who has a corps of female assistants who carry out the work under her general supervision.

What has held true for India and Burma, in general holds true for Thailand and the Malay Peninsula. Shadow-play and marionette performances are frequent here. Translations of western classics and pantomimes are performed but the native play, *mayong*, is, naturally, more usual.

Turning to the East Indies, we find that Java has a highly developed theatre based on the Indian mold. The other islands of the Indian and Pacific oceans have cruder variants of this theatre, but for the most part they are more nearly akin to the Burmese and the African, than to the sophisticated stage of Java. New Guinea is celebrated for its dance-dramas. In recent years Bali has become the mecca of designers, artists and other theatre folk which may presage an Oriental influence on the American Theatre. If it comes however it is likely to be a conscious use of forms and rhythms rather than a powerful influence developing out of inevitability. The Balinese theatre is akin to the Javanese and there are no strong differences between the two, lying as Bali does, all but touching the tip of Java.

The theatre of Java falls into three main forms, *wajang* (shadow-plays), *wajang topeng* (living actors with masks imitating marionettes) and *wajang gedog* (living, dancing, pantomimic actors). The first of these is traceable to the seventh century and may go even further back into antiquity through some possible connection with the Chinese marionette performances, but no one has been able to determine this definitely. The *wajang* performances are controlled by the *dalang* (leader), who recites the lines, frequently extemporaneously as he is familiar with all the plots. He operates the shadow-figures themselves and directs the *gamelan* (orchestra). These figures are flat and made of leather with grotesque features. It was once thought that the distortion was due to the Sunni Mohammedan abhorrence of images, but it has been proved that these grotesqueries antedate the infiltration of Islamic practices. The thin arms and long curved talon-like fingers and fingernails are operated by means of wooden sticks attached to the arms. The oral performance is called *lakon* (drama) and has had great influence on the written plays because the *dalangs* are often poets of native distinction.

Wajang topeng calls for actors to wear costumes and masks, which latter are held in place by an inside strap gripped by the actor's teeth. Naturally being unable to speak, their lines are recited by another whilst they dance. This dramatic form came into being in the eleventh century. Its plays are based on a Javanese *Ramayana* written at least as early as the thirteenth century and a prose translation of the *Mahābhārata* made about the tenth century. These two epics form the basis of Old-Javanese drama with its Sanskrit metre. The Middle-Javanese literature introduced a new metre known as *kidung*, which was employed in the famous Panji cycle of adventures. This is purely Javanese without foreign influence, though it spread beyond the confines of the country into Indo-China and the Malay Peninsula.

In the *wajang gedog*, actors performed without masks but still only in pantomime. This came in part out of the presence of the emperor when masks were not permitted. Due to western influence spoken parts have since been added and this new form is called *wajang orang*. One of the best known examples of the former type is *The Adventures of Dewa Sukma; or, How Petruk Becomes King of Madura*, which has a good deal of humor, though the plot is melodramatic.

The plays are performed in a playhouse known as a *pendoppo*. Like the Burmese theatre-building, it is open on three sides, though occasionally only on two. The pointed roof is supported by pillars. This theatre is intended for resident performances on state occasions but is also hospitable to the small touring troupes of comic actors who travel through the East Indies and along the Malay Peninsula.

Turning northward near the caravan route from India to China (once again in the public eye as the Burma Road), we enter the mysterious reaches of high and isolated Tibet. This country of which so little is known has supported an idealistic religious drama. Plays are largely influenced by the Hindu drama of India rather than by the neighboring Chinese stage, doubtless because of the introduction of Buddhism in the seventh century. During this same century, the sixth Tibetan Dalai lāma *Ts'angs-dbyangs rgyamts'o* wrote plays that were influenced by Hindu culture. Tibetan drama took a form somewhat similar to the medieval mysteries of the western world. Three of these have been translated and edited by H. I. Woolf, *Nansal, Djroazanmo* and *Tchrimekundan;* though they do not give us the full scope of a Tibetan performance because portions of the plays are improvised during the performance. Travellers have brought back colorful and romantic pictures of these great religio-dramatic festivals held in the spring and autumn and to which pilgrims come from afar to receive spiritual stimulus. The roles are acted by monks with professionals appearing in the feminine parts. The performances are classic in outline, with ballet and chorus. When the long narratives are concerned with Indian subjects, the leading role is acted by a Brahman, when Tibetan, by a *hunter*. The dance and music play just as important a part as do the costumes; the wide use of grotesque masks is calculated to awe the spectators; the constant blast of the silver trumpets is exciting and terrifying.

The Theatre of the East is a fascinating, if esoteric, subject for the Western student, and there is much to be learned from its formalism, its color, its elaborate embroidery of emotions, its devious pattern of dance, and its searching into the inner recesses of the soul.

XIII

INCOMPREHENSIBLE CHINA

EUROPEANS have almost always been puzzled by the Chinese Theatre. This is understandable because it has a form and tradition that is incomprehensible to the West. In the Hsia Dynasty (2205-1766 B.C.), establishing the Chinese theatre as second in point of world chronology, religious worship and celebrations of military successes transformed interpretive dancing into a dramatic form which might be said to be theatrical in kind. During the Shang Dynasty (1766-1122 B.C.) these dances included other ceremonies in honor of the deities controlling rain and drought, and the other two contrasts of famine and harvest. To heighten the dramatic effect, a stage was erected and the dances displayed upon it. Out of the ritualism of China, as in Egypt and Greece, came the chant which introduced speech to the theatre. It must, of course, be understood that there was no "theatre" in the accepted sense. These "performances" were religious in character and the "plays" were not intended for the people. The Emperor, the court and the priests were the "audience." It was not until centuries later that plays were performed for the people.

It might be well to mention that Wang Kuo-wei in his *The History of the Drama Under the Sung and Yuan Dynasties*, published in Shanghai in 1915 and not yet translated into an Occidental language, is a supporter of the theory that Chinese drama came out of ancestor worship; this source should be compared with Ridgeway's similar theories on the subject. His findings have been published in his brilliant, if frequently mistaken, work *The Dramas and Dramatic Dances of Non-European Races in Special Reference to the Origin of Greek Tragedy* (1915). In addition to the enacting of heroic scenes concerning their ancestors, the emperor wished lighter amusement and so employed dwarfs and others as court fools. Under the guise of humor these players had an opportunity to criticise, and frequently abuses in the administration of the country were pointed out in a short dramatic scene or in some aphorism. Sometimes this was taken in good part, but sometimes the ones who spoke or acted unpopular sentiments were executed. None other than the great Confucius (550 or 551-478 B.C.), in his capacity as minister of crime, felt it necessary to order such a death.

In the Chou Dynasty (1122-255 B.C.), sacred plays, *shen-hsi*, became essentially dramatic. During this same period an attempt was made to establish a popular theatre by an emperor about 700 B.C., but his successors so disapproved that we have no records concerning the attempt. Perhaps the failure was due as much to the number of rival rulers as to the inherent hostility toward poetic drama. During the next dynasty, that of Ts'in (249-210 B.C.) from which China took its name, the Emperor Ch'in Shih Huang (246-210 B.C.) divided the country into provinces, constructed roads and canals and erected handsome public buildings. Likewise he employed vast troupes of actors at his famous Ah Fang palace. These men who had been taken from the lower ranks of society sought the theatre as a means of advancement when all other professions were closed to them.

All of this was but preliminary to the real beginning of the Chinese theatre which came during the T'ang Dynasty (720-907 A.D.) under the leadership of the Emperor Hsuan Hsung, or MING HUANG (713-756) as he is posthumously called. This great artist and enlightened man was first sybaritic then, rejecting luxury, he destroyed his glorious costumes and ruled sternly. Falling in love with his daughter-in-law, Yang Kuei-fei, he raised her to a position next to his own. She had a great fondness for music and drama and through her influence, he indulged his natural theatrical instincts. In his pear garden at Ch'ang-an, he founded a school for actors, hence their name "Young Folks of the Pear Garden," which after all these centuries still persists as a name for actors. He has long been regarded as the patron saint of the theatre and before going on stage, actors burn incense to his image which stands in the greenrooms of all Chinese playhouses. The performances in the Pear Garden were of choral songs with a slight thread of story connecting, in fact a form of opera. They played in a pavilion in the orchard, where hundreds of boys and girls were trained. In these idyllic circumstances, Ming Huang established the tradition that is maintained today.

The invaluable A. E. Zucker, in his *The Chinese Theatre*, records that Wang reports 280 plays from the Sung Dynasty (960-1127) and 690 from the Chin Dynasty (1115-1234), without saying how many are extant. These were performed for the Imperial Court; the people had contented themselves with marionette performances, evidences of which extend as far back as the tenth century B.C. Such plays as

existed were composed in *Wen Li* (Classical Chinese). This enormously difficult language (there were five thousand ideograms) was
intended primarily for reading and constantly referred to other classical stories so that one would have to know the whole of literary writing to comprehend the slightest sentence. Nothing was ever simply
stated. A form of literary shorthand was set up, perhaps to confuse
the insufficiently learned reader. This pride in learning for the sake
of learning is always stultifying to great art; perhaps this is why some
scholars pervert the study of literature out of all recognizable meaning. The *précieuse*, the Classical scholar and even the modern wor-
shiper of the Ph.D. degree have much in common. The Chinese
scholar's scorn for the language of the people retarded any development in their literature just as the preference of Latin for Italian,
French and English long impeded any literary development in those
languages.

It took a great national disaster for China to change all of this. The
invasion of the Mongols under Kublai Khan set up the alien Yuan
Dynasty (1280-1368). Because the Mongol language had no literature
(and no alphabet until 1279) the overlords had no cultural background. For this reason there were no examiners qualified to test the
literary abilities of the conquered people for government posts. Their
livelihood removed, the scholarly Chinese found a means of expression in the despised drama. The great out-pouring of plays in this
period came as a direct result of political defeat. We have no way of
knowing how many dramas were written but 535 survived at the
beginning of the next Dynasty (Ming) and 116 exist today. There are
five names of dramatic writers which deserve mention: Mah Chih-
yuan; Pai Jen-fu, who composed fifteen plays; Ching Teh-hiu,
eighteen; Kao Wen-shieu, thirty; Kuan Han-ching, sixty. One of
Kuan's best known plays is *The Sufferings of Tou-E*, the style of
which is said to be natural and true; Chinese critics regard this
dramatist as the greatest of the whole Yuan school. These playwrights
belonged to two groups, the northern centering on Peiping (1225-
1280) and the southern on Hangchow in the years between 1280 and
1335.

The Yuan writers took many of their plots from the Sung dramatists but improved them by substituting dialogue and dramatic action
for the long poetic and narrative passages. This technique must have
made the Sung plays like fairy tales and in part explains the preva-
lence of story-tellers. Singing and music were an important accompaniment to the composition and performance of all Chinese plays.
These dramas took the place of the acrobats and jugglers whom
Marco Polo had described in the journal of his visit to the Great

Khan. Two of the best-known plays of the northern group are *Hsi Hsiang Chi* (*The Romance of the Western Chamber*) and *Chao Mei Hsiang* (*Intrigues of a Maid-Servant*). The former of these was the first to be translated and S. I. Hsiung, author of an arrangement of *Wang Pao Ch'man* (*Lady Precious Stream*), made a modern adaptation which was performed in England in 1938 and 1939. These pieces have more form to western eyes than is customary in a country where acting rather than dramaturgy is esteemed. Another drama of importance, *Hoei-Lan-Kin* (*The Chalk Circle*), was adapted into German by Klabund and has several times been produced in English in America. These as well as other plays have been frequently translated into European languages in the past two hundred years and so are more or less familiar to students of the drama and the stage. Practically all Chinese plays have some comic touches; true tragedy is unknown. The nearest approach is a melodrama with a happy ending, for the audiences like to be sent away from the theatre with a pleasant taste in their mouths regardless of logical character and plot development. Perhaps the best known of this type are *The Orphan of China*, made famous by Voltaire as *L'Orphelin de la Chine*, and *The Sorrows of Han*, which concerns itself with a princess who gives her life for the emperor she loves and the country she cherishes.

Eventually the Mongols were driven out of China and a native dynasty established. This Ming Dynasty (1368-1644) was also a period of considerable theatrical activity. We know of over 600 titles of plays of Ming authorship, 140 of which were major works. Kao Tse-ch'eng, T'ang Hsien-tsu and Wu Shih-chu were the best known playwrights. The most notable drama of the period, in fact of all South Chinese drama, was *P'i P'a Chi* (*Romance of a Lute*). Like so many of the literary plays of the Ming period this was enormously long, twenty-four acts in fact. Its lugubrious story of filial piety is rather sickening to the western mind. Though it is written in dialogue form and stage directions are inserted, it more nearly approaches the novel.

With the overthrow of the Mongol emperors, the old Chinese literary group was back in power and thirty, forty and forty-eight act dramas were introduced. Again there was no thought of true dramatic effect; the old idea of producing literary and poetic effusions was still pleasing to scholars. The length of these plays has been popularly disseminated to western audiences who believe that all Chinese plays are this long; this is manifestly untrue. Practically all plays produced today, whether new or old, are four act pieces. A performance lasts many hours, but this is due to the fact that many plays or scenes from plays are acted, not one play. To the nonunderstanding audi-

ence, it is difficult to tell where one play leaves off and another begins, hence this misconception.

The Ch'ing (Manchu) Dynasty was the last to reign over China.
From 1644 to the collapse from sheer inertia and internal corruption
in 1911, the Chinese were ruled by foreign Manchurian emperors.
Their management of the country was so vigorous in the beginning
as to produce a strong and united empire that has aroused the pride
of the Chinese.

There were 815 plays of some dramatic value among the pieces
produced by Ch'ing authors. The leading writers were K'ung Yun-
t'ing, Hung Fang-ssu, Chiang Shihchuan and Li Yu, who was a dramatic critic in addition to being the author of fifteen plays. Most of
his work was published about 1672, during the Restoration period in
England and almost at the end of Molière's great life in France.

During the years between 1870 and 1880, a new dramatic form (*Pi-
huang*) came into being. It began as provincial drama in the Hupeh
locality but gradually spread over the entire country and is considered representative of modern drama. Since the outbreak of the
Sino-Japanese war there has been great communal activity, influenced no doubt by the infiltration of communism. These patriotic
plays are intended to incite resistance to the Japanese invader and as
such are performed by the soldiers as well as by the civilian population including even children. They are concerned with Japanese
atrocities, the bombing of civilian populations, the murder of children
and other refinements of war, whether European or Oriental.

The greatest actor known to us is the living player Mei Lan-fang,
famed for his female impersonations. His tours from Moscow to New
York have won him world-wide acclaim. For the most part acting is
the privilege of men, though women have flourished in male and
female roles at various times in the past and present. Their banishment
from the stage was due to their extra-curricular activities of marrying and otherwise consoling eligible nobility and officials. On their
most recent return to the stage, they found it necessary to imitate
the conventions of the female impersonators if they were to win the
applause of the populace.

As one would expect, the entire technique of acting in the Chinese
theatre is artificial to such an extreme that it becomes laughable, when
it is not downright dull, to western eyes. This attitude wins the ire
of Orientalists and their sympathizers. Certainly it is necessary to put
aside any ideas of customary European acting and to adopt the conventions of a highly symbolic art.

Everything depends on the acting, the singing, the music, and the
extraordinary richness of the costuming. There is no scenery and

only the barest necessities in the way of properties. The last consist of a chair or table, a fan, an umbrella, a whip, a pole and other similar objects and are all that is necessary to convey the meaning to the audience. Once the gestures are understood they are extremely eloquent. A fan held beside the face indicates that one is standing bareheaded in the sun; a character holding an umbrella indicates a severe rainstorm; white paper falling from a red umbrella or being tossed into the air by a stage hand in sight of the audience indicates a snowstorm; an actor walking with hands outstretched, feeling to right and left or carrying a lamp, indicates that it is dark and he can not see his way. This is no more ridiculous than some of our own conventions. Our stages are seldom dark longer than a moment or two for dramatic effect; this heightens the illusion of darkness before the footlights and spotlights are brought up enough to illumine the action. We then depend on the words of the character who tells, directly or indirectly, that the scene is a dark one.

For the Chinese the closing of a door is signified by bringing the hands together when extended to arm's length. Passing a sleeve in front of the eyes to denote weeping is an equivalent of our placing a handkerchief to the eye, silently shaking the shoulders to denote grief. Lifting the foot indicates crossing a doorsill, and lifting the feet high in several steps suggests going up stairs; for climbing a hill or a wall, the player mounts a chair or table. A single actor carrying a banner indicates that there are a thousand soldiers; the Chinese and Elizabethan conventions of indicating an army are similar and the text always calls for individual combats rather than mass action. A man carrying a whip indicates that he is on horseback; lifting the foot indicates mounting, while the reverse action plus handing the whip to an attendant, informs the audience that he has dismounted. The fights which abound in military plays are masterpieces of acrobatics, but the actor is never touched by the weapon of his adversary, the maneuvering being accompanied by wild military music. The defeated warrior leaves the stage first. Sometimes a spear is thrown and an actor catches it, sinks to the floor to indicate that he is killed and then quickly runs off the stage. In civil life, a suicide is indicated by leaping off a table and, if possible, landing on one's back. If the act of self-destruction involves drowning, the actor performs a long leap and exits running.

During the early part of the third century A.D. masks were said to have been introduced by the noted actor, Lan Lin-wang. Later the face of the actor was painted and the character of the individual was indicated by the colors used, as had been the custom in Greece and Rome. The dead white face indicates evil and cunning, frequently dignity as well, as would be natural to the Chinese for villains are almost invariably extremely dignified. Red means vigor, faithfulness, virtuousness and loyalty; whilst black denotes fierceness and frequently coarseness; blue indicates cruelty; purple is not so sanguine nor so loyal as red. Gods have golden or yellow faces, and devils are green. The faces of women characters are decorated only with simple cosmetics so that they will be more attractive to the onlooker.

The acrobatic art has been developed to superlatively high standards. Only the most expert western tumblers and jugglers could hope for any success in competition with them. This accounts, of course, for the great popularity of the military plays whose battle scenes employ these powers to the utmost.

The lack of scenery and the visible property men and musicians with their casual attitude toward the play, have a completely disconcerting effect on non-Oriental spectators. It is not true that the Chinese are casual about the matter. Being realists, they recognize the fact that dramatic entertainment is pretense in essence. Nature is observed but not imitated. If the audience must pretend that the action which they see is real, why not exercise the imagination a step further and imagine the background, the physical appointments and the elaborate properties necessary for the spectacular scenes of the western theatre?

This point of view bears close scrutiny on all except one point; the Chinese can discard all realism in the theatre except in their costumes. They demand rich and authentic costumes; occasionally they are richer than reality so as to dazzle the eyes of the spectators and thus draw more customers to the playhouse. This is as arbitrary as the property man who, wearing black, moves (supposedly unseen) through the action, placing tables and chairs, arranging pillows under a swooning actor, handing out or receiving whips, swords or other personal properties at appropriate times in the play's action.

The actor's standing in the community is very low, and only occasionally has he raised his head above this level. MEI LAN-FANG (1894-   ), with his enormous following in his own country and the homage yielded him by such masters as Stanislavski and the theatrically great in England and America, is the most conspicuous example. In 1919 he played with the Japanese Imperial Theatre; this was the first time a Chinese actor had appeared on a foreign stage. Of the storytellers, the lowest form of acting art in China, Liu Pao-chuan, now in his seventies, commands a tremendous following. Actors have to accommodate themselves to strict gradations among themselves in the greenroom, in their sleeping quarters and in their traveling arrangements. Those playing emperors or members of royalty or nobility are favored above others. This is in contrast to the Mystery Plays of Medieval Europe, when Pontius Pilate and Herod were better paid than Jesus.

In the present century, and even before, drama is regularly divided into three classes: *Fun Pan Hsi,* is the oldest in point of development and is concerned with reverence of ancestors and patriotism; *Jin Pan Hsi* deals with civil and military subjects and differs somewhat in methods of singing and acting; *Fun Min Hsi,* the most recent class, admits colloquial dialects in the place of classical Mandarin speech.

Since the beginning of the Chinese theatre, plays have been performed on a platform extended out into the auditorium and faced on three sides by the audience. The same was true in the Elizabethan theatre just as it was in the semi-circular staging of early Greece. There is no curtain; the actor hides his face as he gives the prologue to the play. A change of scene or act is indicated by the actor's movements about the stage. There are two doors in the center of the back wall; entrances are made through the one at the audience's right, and exits through the left. Usually there is a mirror up center for the convenience of the actor in changing or altering his costume. The properties are outside the acting area, where the property men sit. The musicians, four to eight in number, sit on stools facing the audience. Chinese music has melody but no true harmony and conforms largely to the pentatonic scale. To western ears, the sounds are harsh and sharp, though occasionally slow and plaintive, and even so acutely agonizing to the auditors that sometimes they are forced to leave the theatre.

This in brief is the Chinese theatre which today, as it has for hundreds of years, entertains some four hundred millions of peoples involved in a horrible war. Outside of China, playhouses have been established wherever considerable numbers of Chinese are domiciled, but their theatre has had little direct influence on the Occidental stage. In addition to the exceptions previously noted George C. Hazelton and J. H. Benrimo with their play *The Yellow Jacket* (1913), Eugene Vakhtangov with his production of *Turandot* in Moscow in 1922, Okhlopkov with his staging at the Realistic Theatre, and Thornton Wilder with his *Our Town* (1938) have been conspicuously successful in drawing on the principles of the Chinese and Japanese stage.

XIV

KOREA AND JAPAN

KOREA

Out of the temples of religion came the Korean theatre, developing from the Buddhist processional chants, which in turn became secularized into a form of historical drama. Many of its literary sources were Chinese, in fact some plays were written and acted in that language. Korea's own first plays which are still performed, were moralities known as *Sokiungkok* and dealt with ancestor worship, an Oriental characteristic. These were declaimed in epic style by a single actor playing the most important parts in succession. The other actors merely assisted while the lead recited written lines or improvised on a theme. This naturally called for a performer of distinction with literary tendencies. The performance took place in a simple playhouse that was frequently temporary, set up with poles to hold the mats which constituted the roof. A small platform was placed at one side and low benches or mats served to seat the audience.

In the serious drama, which resembles the *Nō* plays of Japan, a great many pieces were performed and took several hours, sometimes a whole day for presentation. Korea flourished under the Silla Dynasty (57 B.C.-935 A.D.), which was a period of political expansion into Manchuria and Siberia. The next Dynasty, Koryu (918-1392), bore the fruits of this increase in political power and there was a corresponding cultural growth. During the tenth century this was coupled with the state's persecution of the Buddhist monks, which drove many of the priests into the mountains to live as hermits. The reputed political corruption and immorality of the monks was depicted in the theatre by a series of propaganda plays. This turned the masses against the monks and made easier the destruction of their authority and influence. Realizing its possibilities for wide-spread influence some of the monks devoted themselves to dramaturgy. This interest in the theatre continued and music and theatre were greatly encouraged by Pyun-wun-wang and again in the fifteenth century under

King Sejong who ordered a study made of the situation so as to develop new forms. He was also responsible for the removal of women from the stage, so that the female impersonator has been firmly established ever since.

The Korean drama is difficult to translate because of the many puns and innumerable plays upon words. A stage performance is known as a *kuk*; tragedy is *pikuk* and comedy is *hikuk*. Under western influence the civil and military plays have yielded to a new division of drama.

Some of the more important dramas are the fifteenth century *The Adventures of Hong Kil-dong*, dramatized from a novel written by the monk Kasan; *The Adventures of Kyong-op*, also written by a monk, Ha Jong; an adaptation of Yi Munjong's novel *The Frogs* was produced in the eighteenth century; *The Adventures of Yi Ha-ryong* was also staged in the same century. Classical dramas included the well-known *Chunhiangchon* (*Story of Chunhiang*), written in Korean in the sixteenth century by Lie Kiuhiung, and *The Story of Sim Chung*, another of the Eastern plays celebrating an almost unhealthy filial devotion and which glorified the endurance of suffering and death for one's parents.

JAPAN

The Japanese have always been an acquisitive and imitative people. We are particularly conscious of that in the days these pages are being written, but this has ever been a characteristic. Theatre came into Japan out of China by way of Korea, but not until the end of the sixth century did it actually exist. According to tradition, a man of Chinese extraction, Hada Kawatsu, was commanded to devise entertainment for the whole country, and he contrived thirty-three dramas which were the foundation of the Japanese theatre. Whether or not this is authentic, the essential truth is established; Japanese drama came out of the Chinese, and has always been envious of its parent.

The inhabitants of Nippon have advanced the theory that their drama was based on a ritual dance (*Sambāso*) employed as propitiation to stop a volcanic eruption in 805. At the beginning of the twelfth century Iso-no-Zenji, known as the Mother of Japanese Drama, was performing dances in male attire. Japan's classic period ended with this century, but one of her most significant dramatic literary movements was begun in the fourteenth century. It was at this time that the famous *Nō* drama, which is not always understood in world history, came into being. Along with it arose the supplementary and relieving *Kyogen* (comic interludes).

This classic and composed *Nō* form was compounded of poetry and prose coupled with music and the dance and was no longer than the average one-act play. It is supposed to have developed out of the religious *Kagura*, a pantomimic dance of legendary origin which arose from the Shinto worship. An eighth century sun-goddess, disgusted with the actions of her brother, retired into a cave until the aid of another goddess was enlisted to remove her; the deistic lady danced upon a tub, thumped her heels and created a rhythm which, according to tradition, is the origin of the fixed beat of this dance form. This came out of Buddhism but despite the fact that many monks began to write plays of this kind it won adoption by the military and aristocratic classes of Japan.

One of the priests, Kwanami Kiyotsugu (1333-84), is credited with having been the first to write *Nō* dramas. He was soon taken under the protection of his ruling Shogun, Yoshimitsu. Fifteen of the surviving 235 examples of this literary form are accredited to him. Theatrically, he is more important as being the father of the brilliant Seami Motokiyu (1363-1444).

Yoshimitsu made himself responsible for the education and advancement of Seami, who revised the *sarugaku* (literally "monkey music," from the character of the monkey). *Dengaku*, a pantomimic dance, was added to *sarugaku* to form the true *Nō* (art). The theatre in which this was performed undoubtedly arose from the *kagura* dancing stage attached to the Shinto temples. Seami, who was also an actor and therefore vitally interested, increased the dignity of this form, which is its leading characteristic to this day, and introduced human elements which won the hearts of his audience in a way that no temple drama had been able to do. He had achieved what he considered the drama *par excellence*, the epitome of theatrical form, for he composed the music as well as the libretti. He was responsible for over a hundred of these plays which are still extant, the best known being *Ama* (*The Fisher Girl*), *Hachi-no-Ki*, *Hagoromo*, *Isutzu*, and *Ominameshi*.

The *Nō* play began with one actor, *Shite*. The second actor, *Waki*, was added and has almost surpassed the first in importance. Each of these is accompanied by other actors who are called *Tsure*, or by a boy called *Ko-kata*. If five *Nō* are given, at least three *Kyogen* must be played to supply comic relief from the ghostly action of the serious pieces. The relationship is similar to that in the Greek theatre when the three tragedies were followed by a satiric play. *Nō* actors are masked and there is musical accompaniment; both masks and music are lacking in the *Kyogen*. Of these latter which reflect the social life of the times, some 250 are still in existence.

The first theatre to be opened at Yedo (*Tōkyō*) was established by Saruwaka Kanzabusō in 1624. The playhouses in which the *Nō* are acted are built according to extremely exact formulae. The stage is wooden, eighteen feet square, open to the audience on three sides, with a narrow extension on the stage-left for the chorus or singers, and another at the back for the prompter and the musicians. The pointed roof over the stage resembles that of a Japanese temple. This is supported by four pillars, each of which has a name and a special significance in the staging of these plays. *Shite-bashira* is the First Actor's Pillar by which he enters from the bridge, and is the point where he begins his performance. Directly in front of this is the *Metsuke-bashira*, the Mark Pillar, which the *Shite* uses as a mark in his performance. Diagonally opposite the First is the Second Actor's Pillar, the *Waki-bashira*. Behind that is the *Fue-bashira*, the Flutist's Pillar, by which the flute-player sits. The actor enters the stage by the *Hashi-gakari* (*bridge*), which is an open corridor with railings on either side. At the furthest stage right of the bridge is a five-colored curtain which the actor lifts with two bamboo sticks when he enters from or exits to the greenroom. This is also called the mirror-room (*Kagami-no-ma*) and is utilized as a dressing-room. There is a ladder leading down from the front of the stage, but it is not used in the action. In front of the bridge are *Ichi-no-matsu*, *Ni-no-matsu* and *San-no-matsu*, meaning First, Second and Third Pine Tree. These potted trees are symbols for heaven, earth and humanity and mark the position when an actor is playing on the bridge. A large pine tree is painted on the back wall of the stage. The acting area is separated from the audience by a pebble path.

The acting is highly stylized and the movements are carefully rhythmical. The thumping of the feet on the wooden floor coupled with the music enhances the ghostly quality of these performances. The stereotyped expressions of the masks (there are fifteen standard kinds) can never change. They are carved of wood and many are really sculptured in quality. The voice is pitched abnormally high or low to serve as contrast to the musical background of the *Samisen*. The gait is artificial, as it is imitative of marionettes, but the movement from one pose into another is a studied part of the performance. An actor signifies the end of his playing by tapping the stage floor with his foot. The use of the fan is an important adjunct of acting technique. The costumes are extremely rich. Sometimes during the dance, the outer garment is slipped off and a more handsome one appears. Since women never appear in the *Nō*, the actors who impersonate them wear wigs (*katsura*). Property men are dressed in black so as to be invisible and it is quite true that the audience never notices them.

The *Joruri* began about the middle of the fifteenth century during the *Muromachi* Period (1338-1565) as the recital of a single actor, whom tradition names as Uda, a blind chanter of *Monogatari*. This theatrical form is based on the miracle of his having been given back his sight by the Healing Buddha, who dwelt in Joruri land, the Land of Bright Purity. When puppets were introduced to enact the plot and pantomime of the play, the libretto was referred to as *Joruri* and the entertainment itself as *Ayatsuri* (manipulation, from the working of the puppets by their handlers).

The puppet is carried on to the stage by four puppeteers; one holds the body, whilst the others manipulate its head, arms, and legs. The play is read and acted with vocal inflection; the reader stands at one side of the stage and uses as many voices as the script calls for. The manipulators are entirely covered in black so that the audience will not notice them; an illusion which we are bound to say is completely effective. The carved figures are so remarkable that after the first seeing the puppeteers seem to disappear.

Some of the foremost practitioners of this art were Satsuma-no-jo (end of the sixteenth century) and his son Satsuma Joun; Inoué Harima (1631-1685), who composed as well as read these pieces (the author is subordinate to his acting ability); Uji Kaga, also known as Kadayu, who performed mostly in Kyōtō; Gorobei (1650-1714), who later took the name of Takémoto Gidayū, performed at Dotombori in Ōsaka, the busiest quarter, being so skilful in manipulation as to give his name, *Gidayū*, to reciters.

Most of the success of this last practitioner was due to the fact that the famous Chikamatsu wrote for him. He retired in 1705 and his theatre, which like all of these playhouses was called *Ningyo Shibai* (doll theatre), was taken over by Takeda Izumo (1688-1756). He carried on the traditions of his master and, as a memorial, kept the name (*Takémoto-za*), which has continued down to the present moment of writing.

In 1702 a rival to Takémoto appeared in the ambitious Toyotaké Wakatayū (1680-1764), who set up in the same quarter an independent theatre known as the Toyotaké-za. Toyotaké secured the services of Ki-no-Kaion (1663-1742), who became a leading dramatist and the chief rival of Chikamatsu in the writing of puppet-plays. Nishizawa Ippū (1665-1731), an Ōsaka bookseller, in collaboration with Yasuda Abun and Namiki Sōsuké (1694-1750), succeeded Kaion and wrote twelve *joruri* for this theatre. There have been numerous other writers down the years because this is still one of the most popular forms of theatrical entertainment in Japan.

What the *Nō* drama was to the aristocratic classes, the *Kabuki* (popular theatre) was to the masses. According to well-substantiated tradition, the inventor of this form was a renegade priestess, O-Kuni, from the celebrated Shinto temple at Izumo. Up to that time, *Taiheiki* (public recitations with music from a three-stringed guitar supplemented by the tapping of a fan), were the general public's theatre. O-Kuni danced to the music of a little bell and sang innocent religious lyrics. She attracted the attention of the handsome *Kyogen* actor, Sanzaburo from Nagoya, who became her lover, manager and author. He taught her to sing popular songs of his own composition and to dance in a more abandoned fashion, hence the term *Kabuki* indicating the art of song and dance. Her performances first took the name *Onna* (woman) *Kabuki*. She often played in men's dress and gathered about her a troupe of women and children, as well as men who habitually wore women's dress. O-Kuni reached the height of her popularity in 1603-04, even being invited to perform before the Imperial Court. Her success spread and numerous imitation *Kabuki* troupes consisting of male and female prostitutes sprang up. This caused such a public scandal that in 1609 the *Onna Kabuki* were relegated to the outskirts of the cities and in 1629 were suppressed.

As early as 1617, Dansuke, perhaps foreseeing what would happen, gathered together a troupe made up of young men who had appeared in the *Onna Kabuki* together with some of the disreputable youths of the town to form the *Wakasha Kabuki*. To make up for the lack of women, great attention was paid to costume. The prohibition of women from the stage, however, did not wipe out immorality, in fact it only changed its channel, and vice became even more prevalent. In 1644 young boys were denied the privilege of acting in these troupes because the morals of the warrior class were being undermined. This second form of *Kabuki* was finally prohibited in 1652.

Encouraged perhaps by the success of the *Ayatsuri*, some of the more mature men of the last *Kabuki* reorganized it on a higher literary basis, suppressing the elements which had previously destroyed it. This was known as *Yara Kabuki*. These players attracted a better class of dramatist to write for them and segregated the women's parts to a small group of female impersonators known as *onnagata*. Though the rule against women appearing on the stage had been relaxed by the middle of the nineteenth century these mimics still play the female roles. They have so perfected their art of impersonation that they wear women's clothes off-stage, cultivate a high and artificial voice and assume the mincing walk of tightly bound feet common to Oriental women.

The methods of staging *Kabuki* varied considerably from earlier production methods as the plays did themselves and the class of audience differed from the classic *Nō*. Instead of the bridge, the *Hanamichi* (Flower-way) was developed for the entrances of the actors. A similar device has been used in modern western staging; Reinhardt employed it for the entrance of large crowds through the audience and up steps onto the stage, first in *Sumurun* and later in *The Miracle*. A variant was used during the heyday of obscenity and nakedness in American burlesque houses of the nineteen-thirties when runways were built out into the auditorium for the pleasure of the audience (though the burlesque houses had taken it from such legitimate theatres as the Winter Garden).

Masks are not used in the *Kabuki* and the performances are long, frequently lasting all day and sometimes until late in the evening. The plays begin as early as nine in the morning, but of course the audience does not necessarily sit through all of it. If they do, their meals are served to them just as if they were at home. In this fashion they approach the "theatre-restaurant" which was a form of cabaret entertainment very popular in New York during the depression following the Wall Street Crash of 1929.

Many great actors developed in the *Kabuki* theatre. Some of the early ones were the realistic Sakata Tōjūrō (1645-1704), the *onnagata* Segawa Kikunojó (1691-1749), and the founder of *Aragoto* (school of exaggerated acting), Ichikawa Danjūrō the First (1704-1760), of the Ichikawa family, who act under the name of Danjūrō. This was a period dominated by the actor because few if any established dramatists would write for the popular theatre where their work would be ignored by the court and the ruling classes. It wasn't until the second half of the eighteenth century and the beginning of the nineteenth that important writers contributed to the success of the *Kabuki*.

The one conspicuous exception to this rule was the man who has been called the Japanese Shakespeare, CHIKAMATSU MONZAYÉMON (1652 or 53-1724) but his puppet plays were overshadowed by his writing for the *Kabuki* theatre.

Chikamatsu was born Suginomori Nobumori, but is believed to have taken his *nom du théâtre* from the name of one of the Buddhist temples in which he was educated for the priesthood. Through all of his writings runs a rich vein of Buddhist lore. By the time he was nineteen, he was living in Kyōtō and had contributed a *haiku* ode to an anthology of poetry written by residents of that city. He is believed to have entered into the service of one Lord Ogmiachi, who in addition to his noble birth, was celebrated for the comic pieces which he wrote for Uji Kaga, the chanter of *Joruri*. At this time Chikamatsu must have made the acquaintance of Gidayū, pupil of Uji Kaga, and for whom he later wrote many plays when they were both famous.

In 1677 he burst upon the literary scene with a play for the *Kabuki* theatre at Kyōtō and it was produced by Sakata Tōjūrō under the title of *The Evil Spirit of Lady Wisteria*. Though he probably wrote earlier plays which have since been lost, this piece established him as a dramatist. He is believed to have written more than a hundred plays of which we are certain of at least fifty. These were full length plays, as long or longer than those of Shakespeare with whom he has been compared. He had wide variety as a writer, combining as he did comedy and tragedy, realism and romance. Despite the unrealistic conventions of the theatre, the Japanese like extreme realism in their scenes of cruelty. Murder, torture and suicide must be displayed naturally to a people who are well-versed in these matters. The conventions of the western theatre which spare the feelings of its auditors would never be tolerated. In his masterpiece, the wildly melodramatic *Kokusinya Kassen* (*The Battles of Kokusinya*), a Caesarean operation is performed on stage. Just last season a New York audience found the childbirth scene in Gustav Eckstein's *Christmas Eve* difficult to bear. In contrast the love scenes of the Occidental theatre would horrify an Oriental audience.

After 1699 he wrote exclusively for the *Ayatsuri* stage and in 1705 he moved to Ōsaka where he supported himself by writing for Takémoto. One of his best known historical plays is the romantic *Fair Ladies at a Game of Poem-Cards*. He introduced Chinese stories into Japanese drama and is credited with initiating *Shinju* plays (plays of double suicide for love). So popular did these become and so suggestible are the Japanese that a wave of these suicides is said to have swept over the country and that they have since become an institution. Whether this is truth or poetry, certainly *The Love Suicide at Sonezaki* and other plays of this genre had a very considerable influence on the audience. So rapidly did he write (he is credited with having written a play in a single night), that two weeks after a certain suicide took place in 1703, the drama based on it was produced. This was surpassed by the somewhat similar domestic play, *The Love Suicide at Amijima*, and like other similar pieces was based on an actual occurrence and was a simple well-observed drama of ordinary people.

The long artistic partnership with the actor Gidayū ended with his death in 1714. His respect for his interpreters, whether in *Kabuki* or *Joruri,* and a real understanding of their powers explains a good deal of his own success. A full knowledge of the limitations and extensions of the medium is what makes a successful dramatist such as Shakespeare, Molière, Goethe, and Japan's best, though not in the same class, Chikamatsu. Gidayū's death caused a schism in his company because it was his last wish that one of his younger pupils, Masatayū, should succeed him. Many of the older students were jealous of this favor and withdrew from the *Takemoto-za.* Appreciative of Masatayū's ability and respecting his collaborator's dying decision, Chikamatsu wrote *The Battles of Kokusinya* for him. This was produced in November 1715 and ran for seventeen months thereby establishing Masatayu's reputation and saving the theatre from ruin. Realizing the limitations of his voice, this actor skimmed over the narrative passages usually stressed, and emphasized the characterization and dialogue in which the dramatist excelled, so that both gained from the collaboration. This partnership continued to be popular until the death of the playwright, which came on November 22, 1724, not long after the production of his last play. Rumor had it that the piece prophesied the destruction by fire of a large section of Ōsaka, which actually happened soon after. The play was banned from repertory, and disappointment and chagrin may have hastened Chikamatsu's death.

TAKEDA IZUMO (1688-1756) is the only other outstanding Japanese dramatist before modern times. He was the greatest collaborator of his period, having participated in such joint-efforts as required five or six authors. This was worked somewhat on the principle of the Hollywood Conference, famed in satire and wisecrack. A committee was set up with a president who assigned the subject. Each author worked out a treatment of it, and these were discussed at subsequent meetings. The work thus went on harmoniously and nothing was accepted for the play that didn't receive an unanimous vote. One of Takeda's best known efforts had three collaborators and was known as *History of the Transmission of the Art of Calligraphy by Sugawara,* in five acts.

In 1701 the historical incident took place which is the basis of all plays about the forty-seven Ronins. Asano, entrusted with receiving an important diplomatic delegation, sought the advice of the nobleman Kira. Asano, a warrior, was not familiar with court etiquette. Kira insulted him and Asano slashed him across the face with his sword. Such an act of violence in sacred precincts required that Asano commit *harakiri,* suicide by stabbing the abdomen, which he did. All of his lands were taken from his family and his followers were disbanded, thus becoming wave-men, *Ronins* (wanderers without a home or lord). Oishi, the principal follower, with the aid of forty-six others, determined on revenge. They stormed Kira's castle and offered him the privilege of *harakiri*, but he was too cowardly to accept, so they slew him, cut off his head and placed it on Asano's grave. Because of this act they were required to commit suicide, which each did separately and alone. This story stirred the imagination of Japanese dramatists and other writers. Chikamatsu made a five-act arrangement as *The Story of the Forty-seven Ronins*. Finally this version no longer found favor with audiences so Takeda Izumo, with two collaborators, made a new eleven-act play on the theme called *Chiushingura; or, The League of Faithful Retainers*. This drama is the most famous of the more than forty plays on the topic and was the author's best work. In general he followed Chikamatsu's style though he was more concerned with improbabilities in his plots than was the older man.

There were a number of lesser playwrights including Chikamatsu Hanni, who chose his name out of respect for the great Chikamatsu; Sakurada Jisuké (1734-1806); Segawa Jokō (1738-1794); Namiki Gohei (1745-1808); Kawataké Shinshichi (1746-1794); Tsuruya Namboku (1755-1829); Kawataké Mokuami (1815-1893), all of whom were *Kabuki* writers.

In the nineteenth century a great Shakespearean scholar, Tsubouchi, arose to bring western ideals into Japanese drama. He wrote a version of *Julius Caesar* for the *Joruri* playhouse, which involved descriptions woven into the text. In addition he composed a trilogy of which the seven-act *Maki no Kata* published in 1897, is the best. This is largely in dialogue form. It increased the influence the West has had on Japan. In addition to Shakespeare, translations of Ibsen, Strindberg, Maeterlinck, Wilde, Shaw and O'Neill have been admired. Some Japanese writers have composed in the western tradition, but the bulk of the public considers this a precious effort of the younger generation and prefers the epical dramas to which they have been accustomed. Dr. Tsubouchi assembled a formidable Shakespearean library at Waseda University in Tōkyō, where he was a professor until his death in recent years. During his lifetime a group of his devoted students raised funds for a theatre museum, now known as the Tsubouchi Memorial Museum, which is the center of theatrical research in Japan.

Since the return of women to the stage in the middle of the nineteenth century, 1881 to be exact, there have been almost no actresses of the first rank. Perhaps the best known was Ichi Kawaga, who was the head of the theatre for women, for there were and are playhouses where only women may act. The ninth descendant of the famous

Dānjurō, the nineteenth century Kori Koshi Suguru, was definitely in favor of having good actresses in plays. Whenever possible he used them in his productions, despite the fact that he was adept at playing feminine roles himself. This was not his specialty and he should not be considered an *onnagata*. He acted principally in the plays of his close friend, dramatist and critic, Genichiro. Both he and Sadanji acted at the Meijiza in Tōkyō. Leading actors of the present century include Uzaemon, Shikwan, Danyenon at the Kabukiza as well as Baiko at the Teikokuza, the Imperial theatre erected in 1911.

The theatre in Japan is enormously successful. The *Nō* theatre is still aristocratic rather than popular, but the *Kabuki* and *Ayatsuri* stages have a tremendous following among the people. At a time when schemes to revive the popular influence and financial well-being of the western theatre are on the tip of the tongue, the Japanese stage has never been more affluent. News dispatches as late as the autumn of 1940 attest to its importance and popularity in the midst of the financial strain of a great war which is trying the nerves and resources of the whole Japanese people.

DANCE BEFORE DEATH
FRANCE IN THE EIGHTEENTH CENTURY
(1700-1830)

THE age of Molière and Racine did not end neatly with the seventeenth century, however convenient that might make it for history-making. Beaumarchais in the third quarter of the eighteenth century is part and parcel of Molière, while Voltaire was an often acrimonious and occasionally witty extension of Racine. It is for that reason we offer no apology for placing JEAN FRANÇOIS REGNARD (1655-1710) at this point. He is usually considered the most important comic writer after Molière, though he never wrote a comedy that could be mentioned in honest comparison. His life was highly romantic and was by far the most exciting thing about him, involving as it did a steadfast love for a married woman, with whom he was captured by the Turks. After a long confinement, they were released only to discover that the husband they thought was dead, was alive. She returned to him and Regnard went to Sweden, explored northern Lapland, visited John Sobieski, King of the Poles, returned to Paris, and found the lady's husband really dead and the lady about to enter a convent. His pleas were in vain and she took the veil.

After that his dramatic efforts seem tame. He wrote several plays for the Italian troupe at the *Hôtel de Bourgogne*, who had been given permission by the King to play in French. The first of these was *Le Divorce* (1688), which was at first a failure but when Evaristo Gherardi chose it the next year for his debut, its success was assured and it continued to be played for a long time. *La Coquette* (1691) was the best of the eight prose comedies which were added to the repertory of the Italian troupe, but it was suppressed in 1697 when *La Fausse Prude*, which Mme. de Maintenon shrewdly suspected was aimed at her was announced.

Regnard transferred his allegiance to the *Comédie-Française* at the *Théâtre Guénégaud* with *La Sérénade* (1693), a light one-act comedy in prose which had some of the gayety and wit of Molière. However in 1695 the *Bourgogne* company acted *La Foire Saint-Germain,* one of his livelier pieces. Toward the end of 1696 appeared *Le Joueur,* the partly autobiographical study of a gambler, which showed his brilliant character study of a youth who sacrifices everything to gaming. P. L. La Thorillière shone as Hector, the valet. *Démocrite* (1700), which suggests the *Don Quixote* theme, had so much originality that it is remembered despite the great faults in its construction; Regnard was an over-hasty writer. He imitated Plautus in *Les Ménechmes* (1705) and though he changed the plot considerably it was still an extremely amusing comedy. His last and most important play, *Le Légataire Universel* (1708), was the most delightful comedy of a dramatist who considered it was his duty to amuse. His characters were veritable thieves and it was in this development that he came nearest the mordant and castigating wit of his great predecessor.

What Regnard was to the comic aspects of Molière's genius, FLORENT CARTON DANCOURT (1661-1725) was to the farce-producing side. He was of less importance than Regnard and some histories of drama might ignore him completely, in fact they do, but as he wrote steadily for the stage between 1685 and 1718, he has a contribution to make to a history of the theatre. He lacked the soul-searching that makes his master's plays so cauterizing; he took the husk for the substance and like Regnard sought but to amuse. As Petit de Julleville so admirably puts it, *"Il ne fait pas le portrait de la société; il en fait la caricature; il indique le trait saillant des hommes et des choses en l'exagérant."* * His plays as their titles suggest give a contemporary view of Paris and its environs; and include *La Foire de Bezons, Les Vendanges de Suresnes, Le Moulin de Javelle* and *La Foire Saint-Germain.* Most of his farces are in a single act and reflect the social life of the times. He pictures the financial ruin of many of the nobles and the growing wealth of the bourgeoisie. It is for this reason that these pieces have an interest for the humanist if not for the dramatic critic whose high standards preclude commenting on the merely popular and casual.

CHARLES RIVIÈRE DUFRESNY (1654-1724) was both a playwright and novelist. His novel *Les Amusements Sérieux et Comiques d'un Siamois* (1707) reflects not only contemporary life in Paris but the developed consciousness of the Orient which was beginning in France and elsewhere in Europe. His plays do not contain this same interest for they are concerned with the small doings of his own world and that of local society. Therein lies their value and not for any character which they created. Dufresny's plays are but the eight comedies which

* *Le Théâtre en France.* Paris. *Librarie Armand Colin:* 1921.

he wrote for the *Comédie-Française* of which *L'Esprit de Contradiction* (1700) and *La Joueuse* (1709) are the best remembered.

Regnard was regarded first as the successor of Molière but that honor soon passed to ALAIN RENÉ LE SAGE (1668-1747) when he produced his satiric comedy *Turcaret* (1709). This play exposed and angered the financiers so successfully that they tried to bribe the author to withdraw this comedy which showed them enriching themselves out of the taxes for the government which they were collecting. But Le Sage declined to be bribed. His only other play was the farce-comedy *Crispin Rival de Son Maître* (1707), the sources of which lie in the comic servant of the *commedia dell'arte*. It is a distinct loss to the French theatre that he wrote no more for the *Comédie-Française*, but turned his attentions to the novel. This was partly due to the unsatisfactory arrangements of the production of *Turcaret*, which caused him to allow his plays to be performed by the actors at the fairs. These were the only performers who by various tricks managed to escape the royal edict that there should be but one troupe in Paris. They played in the outskirts of the city so that citizens who wanted more amusement than the *Opéra* or *Comédie-Française* offered could find it in the musical pieces and farces performed there.

But to return to Le Sage, *Le Diable boiteux* (*The Devil on Two Sticks*, 1707) was his first novel. The first part of his well-known *Gil Blas* was published in 1715. This was completed in 1724 and 1735, and finally printed as a whole in the year of his death, 1747.

David Auguste de Brueys (1640-1723), who was greatly overrated by Voltaire who said his *Le Grondeur* was superior to the Gallic naïveté of Molière; Jean Palaprat (1650-1721) who collaborated with Brueys; and Marc-Antoine Legrand (1673-1728), a light comic playwright and poor actor whose pieces were acted by the Italian troupe which has escaped the ban, by the *Théâtre Français* and by the company at the *Opéra*, were all minor dramatists. Legrand in *Cartouche ou les Voleurs* (1721) has his thief say of his profession "*à prendre et n'être pas pris*." This charming saying finds expression in the celebrated *Robert Macaire* a century later.

Just as the brilliant Restoration drama of England had passed into the Sentimental Comedy, a French equivalent appeared in *La Comédie Larmoyante* (tearful comedy, and appropriately called). Louis XIV had died in 1715 after a period of dullness—through the respectability of his second wife, Mme. de Maintenon. During the Regency established during the childhood of Louis XV (1710-1774) and under the leadership of the Duc d'Orléans, there was a period of stock-taking, which blossomed forth later into a cruder imitation of the dissoluteness of *le grand monarque*. The young Louis was declared of age in

SHAKESPEARES

COMEDIES,
HISTORIES, &
TRAGEDIES.

Published according to the True Originall Copies.

Martin Droeshout sculpsit London

LONDON
Printed by Isaac Iaggard, and Ed. Blount. 1623.

159. BEN JONSON.

Theatre Collection,
N. Y. Public Library

160. RICHARD BURBAGE, POSSIBLY AS HAMLET.

161. RECONSTRUCTION OF AN ELIZABETHAN STAGE.   *Yale-Rockefeller Theatre Collection*

At the Theatre Royal in Drury-Lane,
This present MONDAY, May 27, 1776,
Will be prefented a TRAGEDY, call'd

KING RICHARD the THIRD.

King Richard by Mr. GARRICK,
(Being his Firft Appearance in that Character thefe 4 Years)
Richmond by Mr. P A L M E R,
Buckingham by Mr. JEFFERSON.
Treffel by Mr. D A V I E S,
Lord Stanley by Mr. B R A N S B Y,
Norfolk by Mr. H U R S T,
Catefby by Mr. P A C K E R,
Prince Edward by Mifs P. HOPKINS.
Duke of York Mafter PULLEY, Lord Mayor Mr GRIFFITHS,
Ratcliffe by Mr. WRIGHT, Lieutenant by Mr. FAWCETT.
King Henry by Mr. REDDISH,
Lady Anne (Firft Time) Mrs. SIDDONS,
Dutchefs of York by Mrs. JOHNSTON,
Queen by Mrs. HOPKINS.
To which will be added

The D E V I L to P A Y.

Sir John Loverule by Mr. VERNON,
Jobfon by Mr. MOODY,
Lady Loverule by Mrs. JOHNSTON,
Nell by Mrs. WRIGHTEN.
Ladies are defired to fend their Servants a little after 5 to keep Places, to prevent Confufion.
The Doors will be opened at Half after FIVE o'Clock.
To begin exactly at Half after SIX o'Clock.   Vivant Rex & Regina.
To-morrow, (by particular Defire) BRAGANZA, with Bon Ton, or High Life above Stair.
{Being the laft Time of performing them this Seafon.}
And Dancing by Mr. SLINGSBY and Signora PACINI.

162. PLAYBILL FOR GARRICK IN *Richard III*.

By *Subfcription*.

AT THE

QUEEN's THEATRE

In the *Hay-Market*:
On *Wenfday* next, being the
Second Day of *March*, will be
prefented,

A New OPERA, call'd,

CLOTILDA.

The Boxes to be open'd to the Pit.   And no Perfon to
be Admitted, but by the Subfcribers Tickets; which
will be delivered on Tuefday and Wenfday Morning
next, at Mr. *White's Chocolate-Houfe* in St. *James's-ftreet.*

Boxes upon the Stage 15 s. Firft Gallery 5 s. Upper
Gallery 2 s.

To begin exactly at Six a Clock.

And by Command. No Perfon to ftand upon the Stage,

Vivat Regina.

163. PLAYBILL FOR *Clotilda*, 1709.

Theatre Collection, N. Y. Public Library

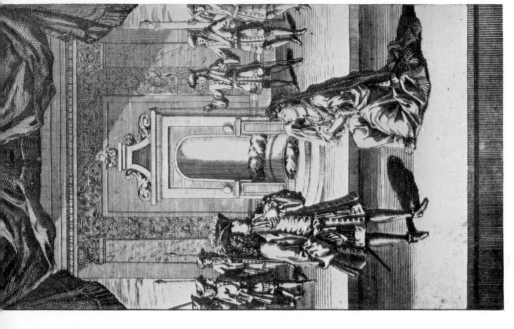

164. HAMLET. The closet scene, with Betterton as Hamlet and Mrs. Barry as the Queen.

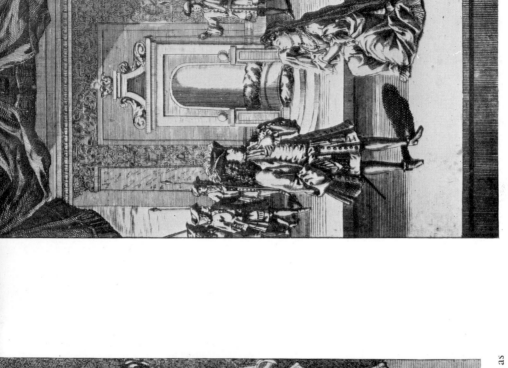

165. MEASURE FOR MEASURE. This and plate number 164 show methods of Restoration staging.

Rowe's Collected Works, 1709

Charles R.

Hereas Complaint hath often been made unto Us, That divers Persons do rudely press, and with evil Language and Blows force their way into Our Theatres, (called the Theatre Royal in Bridges-street, and the Dukes Theatre in Dorset-Garden) at the time of their Publick Representations and Actings, without paying the Price established at both the said Theatres, to the great disturbance of Our Servants, Licenced by Our Authority, as well as others, and to the danger of the Publick Peace: Our Will and Pleasure therefore is, and We do hereby straightly Charge and Command, That no Person of what Quality soever, do presume to come into either of the said Theatres before and during the time of Acting, and until the Plays are quite finished, without paying the Price established for the respective Places. And Our further Command is, That the Money which shall be so paid by any Persons for their respective Places, shall not be return'd again, after it is once paid, notwithstanding that such Persons shall go out at any time before or during the Play; And (to avoid future Fraud) That none hereafter shall enter the Pit, First, or Upper Gallery, without delivering to the respective Door-keeper the Ticket or Tickets which they received for their Money paid at the first Door.

And forasmuch as 'tis impossible to command those vast Engines (which move the Scenes and Machines) and to order such a number of Persons as must be employed in Works of that nature, if any but such as belong thereunto, be suffer'd to press in amongst them; Our Will and Command is, That no Person of what Quality soever, presume to stand or sit on the Stage, or to come within any part of the Scenes, before the Play begins, while 'tis Acting, or after 'tis ended; and We strictly hereby Command Our Officers and Guard of Souldiers which attend the respective Theatres, to see this Order exactly observ'd. And if any Person whatsoever shall disobey this Our known Pleasure and Command, We shall proceed against them as Contemners of Our Royal Authority, and Disturbers of the Publick Peace.

Given at Our Court at *Whitehall* the Second day of *February* in the Twenty sixth Year of Our Reign.

LONDON,

Printed by the Assigns of *John Bill* and *Christopher Barker*, Printers to the Kings most Excellent Majesty. 1673.

61?

166. Proclamation of Charles The Second Relating to Theatre Prices, One of the Earliest Known Legal Documents Pertaining to the Theatre.

Theatre Collection, N. Y. Public Library

167. WILLIAM CONGREVE.

168. COLLEY CIBBER.

169. NELL GWYN. A reputed portrait.

170. ANNE OLDFIELD.

171. Peg Woffington.

172. Mrs. Jordan.

173. Elizabeth Barry.

174. Mrs. Bracegirdle.

Theatre Collection, N. Y. Public Library

175. DAVID GARRICK AS ABEL DRUGGER
IN *The Alchemist.*

This is the JEW.
That SHAKESPEARE drew.

176. CHARLES MACKLIN AS SHYLOCK; NOTE THE
ACCOLADE, ATTRIBUTED TO POPE.

Theatre Collection, N.Y. Public Library

Jean Racine
de l'Academie Françoise

178. Jean Racine.

PETRVS CORNELIVS ROTHOMAGENSIS
Anno Dni 1643

177. Pierre Corneille.

179. John Philip Kemble As Hamlet.

180. Harry Woodward As Mercutio.

Theatre Collection, N. Y. Public Library

181. INTERIOR OF THE DRURY LANE THEATRE DURING ALTERATIONS.

182. CARICATURE OF EDMUND KEAN, AS RICHARD III,
CARRYING THE DRURY LANE UPON HIS SHOULDERS.

183. THE THIRD DRURY LANE.

Theatre Collection,
N. Y. Public Library

184.   THE OLD PRICE RIOT AT COVENT GARDEN IN 1763, DURING A PERFORMANCE OF
Artaxerxes BY THOMAS ARNE.

185.   CARICATURE OF MRS. SIDDONS AND CHARLES AND JOHN PHILIP KEMBLE AFTER THE
COVENT GARDEN FIRE, 1808.

186. EMPEROR MING HUANG, SO-CALLED FOUNDER OF THE CHINESE THEATRE, ESTABLISHED THE
FIRST DRAMATIC SCHOOL IN EIGHTH CENTURY, A.D.   *Collection, John Adams Reeves*

187, 188, 189. Scenes From the Modern Kabuki, Unchanged in Its Traditions and Forms.

190. GANGIRO AS GENZO.

191. UZAYEMON ICHIMURA.

192. BAIKO IN *Sukeroku*.

193. BAIKO.

194. TAMAEYEMON.

195. MORITA KANYA.

196. KIKUGORO AND A CHILD.

197. SUMIZO ICHIKAWA.

198. GANGIRO NAKAMURA.

ACTORS OF THE MODERN KABUKI.

Courtesy of Louis Ledoux

199. A Kabuki Stage. Note run-way into audience.

200. A Typical No Stage.

1723 and in 1725 was married to Marie Leczinska of Poland. He was a pleasure-loving, vain and extravagant ruler. His policies together with those of his ministers, Orléans and Bourbon and through his mistresses the majestic Pompadour and the flamboyant Du Barry, were invariably short-sighted. They led to the wide discontent, heavy taxation and grinding poverty of his people and brought about the French Revolution under his unhappy successor, Louis XVI. He was however somewhat interested in the theatre, at least the ballet and spectacular court productions in many of which he himself figured as an actor and dancer. To him we owe the encouragement of such ballet masters as Jean Georges Noverre (1727-1810), and such painter-designers as Daniel Marot (1663-1752), François Boucher (1703-1770) and Louis Jean Desprez (1743-1804).

But these elegancies were to come later; first France had to survive the lachrymose drama. The charms of this sentimental form were expounded chiefly by Marivaux, La Chaussée and Destouches. PIERRE CARLET DE CHAMBERLAIN DE MARIVAUX (1688-1763) has been known abroad largely as a novelist and for his sentimentalities and meticulous writing, for which the French have coined the revealing term *marivaudage*. He was extremely conscious of his effects as he wrote. There was nothing spontaneous about him except the purity of his language and what was then regarded as high moral tone. This latter seems somewhat lacking in *Les Fausses Confidences* (1732) in which Dorante, a handsome but poor young man, sets out to make his rich mistress fall in love and marry him. He succeeds, and in the succeeding falls in love with her himself. This seems to have removed the dubiousness of the morality, at least in the eyes of the author's contemporaries. That he was a follower of Racine and the neo-classicists is evident in the fact that it was in the morning that Dorante entered Araminte's service as her manager and by evening had won her hand in marriage.

In *Le Jeu de l'Amour et du Hasard* (*The Game of Love and Chance*, 1730), he introduced the daring situation of a nobleman asking the hand of a maidservant in marriage, and this some years before Jean-Jacques Rousseau and long before the Revolution. Though this is softened by the fact that the audience knows the maid is really a lady in disguise and that the nobleman pretends to be a valet, makes it none the less interesting as a sign of the change to come.

His other plays include: *La Surprise de l'Amour* (1727), which contained a favorite role of Adrienne Lecouvreur; *L'École des Mères* (*The School for Mothers*, 1732), in which Sarrazin played Argant; *Le Legs* (*The Legacy*, 1736); and *L'Epreuve* (*The Test*). Of his novels, the most celebrated is *Mariamne* (1731-1736).

PIERRE CLAUDE NIVELLE DE LA CHAUSSÉE (1692-1754) is always

associated with *la comédie larmoyante*. His plays were composed in verse and were filled with virtuous women who had to undergo countless misfortunes in order to woo the sentimental tears of the audience. La Chaussée's most highly regarded pieces are: *La Préjugé à la mode* (*Fashionable Prejudice*, 1735), which relates the story of a man who would like to be a faithful husband but fashionable life demands he be a libertine; and the highly romantic *Mélanide* (1741), which is woven around the unhappy circumstances of a woman whose husband is alienated from her. He becomes the rival of his own son and is about to fight a duel with him but she stops it and wins him back.

PHILIPPE NÉRICAULT DESTOUCHES (1680-1754), the son of a well-known and wealthy family, also contributed to this popular dramatic form. Disappointed in love, he left his father's house to join a troupe of traveling actors. In the course of time he turned to writing for the stage and his first work, *Le Curieux Impertinent* (1709), was displayed with success. He had a pleasant talent that expressed itself in such quotable lines as "*La critique est aisée, et l'art est difficile.*" Many think his first play was his best. It was followed, with comfortable success, by a series of pleasantly elaborated comedies concluding with *L'Obstacle Imprévu* (*The Unforeseen Obstacle*, 1717). About that time he was sent to England on a diplomatic mission and it was not until 1727 that he had another play produced, *Le Philosophe Marié*. He achieved his greatest success with *Le Glorieux* (1730), which excited Voltaire's admiration. This is a tragi-comedy that combined romanticism with tenderness and pure pathos. It was written with Quinault-Dufresne of the acting Quinaults in mind, and that young man acquitted himself extremely well in the vain and showy part.

Two plays that have no significance for us now but which attracted considerable attention at the time (and, with *Le Glorieux*) were considered the most important comedies of the first half of the eighteenth century in France. *La Métromanie* (1738) by Alexis Piron (1689-1773) was concerned with the mania of writing poetry; and *Le Méchant* (1747) by Jean Baptiste Louis Gresset (1709-1777) showed how a wicked man through perverse pleasure could upset a comfortable and respectable household.

It must not be thought that all of France was laughing through its tears at the comic effusions of Marivaux and *les comédiens larmoyants*, for the formal tragedy also continued its neo-classic and sterile tradition which was unlikely to provoke any tears at all. PROSPER JOLYOT DE CRÉBILLON (1674-1762) was the only one who could be called worthy of being the opponent of Voltaire. He specialized in horror plays and it was his intention to move his audience to pity and terror, but never to offend their refinement nor their propriety. A father kills his son in *Idoménée* (1705); he drinks his son's blood in *Atrée et Thyeste* (1707); a man kills his mother in *Electra* (1709); a father kills his son and commits suicide in *Rhadamiste et Zénobie* (1711) the most successful play. The circumstances are romantic and frequently these bloody happenings occur without either party being aware of their relationship. It is by that means that Crébillon shields the decorum of his auditors. His last two plays, *Catalina* (1742) and *Le Triumvirat* (1754) were written in competition with Voltaire.

The mere mention of the names of some of the other tragic writers of this period is sufficient; it is a roll call of tragic mediocrity which includes: Dormont de Belloy (1727-1775), Charles Pierre Colardeau (1732-1776), Jean François de la Harpe (1739-1803), Guimond de la Touche (1725-1760), Antoine Marin Lemierre (1733-1793), Jean François Marmontel (1723-1799), Jean Jacques Lefranc Pompignan (1709-1784), and Bernard Joseph Saurin (1706-1781).

The man who dominated the first three quarters of the eighteenth century in France was François Marie Arouet, called VOLTAIRE (1694-1778). Born into some wealth, he retained his father's name until the success of *Oedipe*, when he chose the name by which he was to be known, but there has always been controversy as to its origin. His contribution to the theatre certainly does not lie in the enduring quality of his plays nor in his literary pronouncements which were frequently no more reliable than his calling Shakespeare an inspired barbarian, a singularly unfortunate statement. It was made, however, with sincerity because Shakespeare has always been too untrammelled for the neat rules of French classicism, which is a purely artificial form and should not be confused with true classicism which stems from the great tradition of the Greek drama. Classicism is really a sense of responsibility on the part of the dramatist towards his characters and his plot, and does not come from any artificiality which arises from setting up rules. This holds true for short-sighted dramatic critics from Aristotle to the present day. The healthiest thing about the living theatre of the western world is the willingness of its critics and its audience to accept experimentation and to reject the mechanically constructed play, whether contrived by Aristotelian dogma or the *Académie Française*.

Voltaire was really a social reformer and his particular hatred was for the clergy who he felt stultified intellectual and political life. He was far from outraged by regal tyranny and absolutism, as his four-year "honeymoon" at the court of Frederick the Great attests. However, even this became too much for him and he fled from Potsdam in 1753 only to be ignominiously arrested at the borders of Prussia. Frederick had worshipped at the shrine and hoped Voltaire would bring an air of fresh French culture to Berlin, but he demanded such flattery and servility from the philosopher and dramatist as to sicken him.

But this is to get ahead of the story of his connection with the theatre. For so-called libel in 1717 (not his first offence), he was imprisoned in the Bastille. There he polished his first play (originally written when he was nineteen, according to his account). *Oedipe*, a version of the Oedipus legend, was produced in 1718 by the *Comédie-Française* and ran for forty-one performances. It was a slavish imitation of Corneille and Racine, particularly the latter. He knew their plays so well that it was natural he would turn out a play that resembled theirs. *Artémire* (1720) and *Marianne* (1724) were in the same tradition.

Following an assault upon his person by the servants of the Chevalier de Rohan he took fencing lessons to avenge himself upon the man who had resented his epigrams in this fashion. Hearing of this, the authorities again confined him in the Bastille. On his release in May, 1726, he went to England where he was received with highest honors both by the social and literary world. It was then that he met Congreve, Addison, Steele and the other wits of Albion. He came under the influence of Shakespeare, whom he aspired to refine, but he was certainly more affected by Addison's *Cato;* cold formalism would naturally seem the higher art to him. Alexander Pope, Dean Swift and John Gay were among his friends. He was impressed by the handsome new London theatres and the fact that the dramatist and actor had a greater social position than they did in his own country. The personal political freedom and comparative liberality of thought was entirely sympathetic to him. He returned to France in the spring of 1729 determined to write a new series of plays on Roman subjects.

He arrived just in time to find that the body of the distinguished Adrienne Lecouvreur was not only denied the rites of the Church but burial as well. The body of the greatest tragic actress of France had been wrapped in cloths and carted away in the night to be buried no one knows where. When one considers the magnificent funeral of Mrs. Oldfield at Westminster Abbey not many months later, one can understand the horror and aversion with which Voltaire was afflicted. He endeavored to reform the French stage, to help raise the standards of acting and improve conditions in the playhouse, particularly the barbarous custom of seating spectators on the stage. London had rid itself of this absurdity but Paris had long declined to do it because it was thought the stage would appear too *empty* with only actors upon it. One might ask, where was the scenery of the magnificent seventeenth and eighteenth century productions? It was at court for the specially invited few. The public audience contented itself with an architecturally painted backdrop and a few simple wings that would not interfere with the view of the nobles seated on the stage. In the end, Voltaire had his way, the actors gave up the benefit of selling expensive seats on the stage and through the generosity of the Comte de Lauragais ironed out the financial difficulties. The changes cost 60,000 francs and the theatre was dark for three weeks. On April 23, 1759 the *Théâtre Français* was reopened with a production of *Le Legs* in which Préville and Mlle. Marie Anne Dangeville delighted the audience. The innovator who had labored thirty years for this reform was pleased to have won out at last.

Brutus (1730) and *Zaïre* (1732) and *La Morte de César* (1735) were the three most important of his plays to follow his visit to England. *Zaïre*, which took its jealousy motif from *Othello*, has long been considered his best play but despite the fact that France's leading actors have long declaimed its stately lines, it leaves us completely cold in the reading and seeing in the present day. His play about Caesar does not indicate that the Roman dictator had any great intelligence as the conspiracy is contrived almost under his nose. The play has nothing to offer to the list of dramas on this subject.

Of *Alzire* (1736), *Zulime* (1740), *Mahomet* (1741) and *Mérope* (1743), the most important by far is *Mérope*. For this play Voltaire announced that he had returned to the first Greek principles, but what he really meant was that he had eliminated love scenes. Mlle. Dumesnil made a very considerable success in it. The enemies of Voltaire resuscitated old Crébillon and applauded his plays so as to annoy the historian-philosopher, who countered with a number of unimportant plays on classical subjects. In 1755 he went much further afield and chose China as the subject for *L'Orphelin de la Chine*, which demonstrated a recurring interest in the Orient. It was not until *Tancrède* (1760) that he again produced a play that is worthy of attention. But it is hard to find what his contemporaries saw in this drama of the Middle Ages. Eight more plays, two of which were not acted, followed in the next eighteen years. The ninth, the feeble *Irène*, was performed by the *Comédie-Française* along with his *Nanine* on March 30, 1778. This was the occasion of a brilliant *première* with all the Royal Family, except the pouting Louis, who was hostile to the dramatist, in the audience. The production commemorated Voltaire's triumphant return from his long self-imposed exile in Switzerland. When he left his seat in the box to go on stage between plays he was crowned with a laurel-wreath; all the *sociétaires* (members) of the company were grouped around a statue-bust of him which had also been wreathed in laurel. Mme. Vestris, the former Marie Josephe Dugazon, recited a poem to the man who had championed the cause of freedom when it was most unpopular. When he left the theatre the demonstration began all over again. Two months later he was dead, but not before he had received the greatest acclaim ever given any one in the theatre of France.

His long efforts to improve the acting standards of his beloved company had at least been achieved in part; the personnel of the company was finer than when he had first become associated with it; bombastic acting was on the decline, and his cooperation with Mlle. Dumesnil, Mlle. Clairon and Lekain had elevated the *Théâtre Français* to the first place in the theatre of the Continent. It was so regarded by the other European nations and even Garrick, who the next year received a public burial in Westminster Abbey, had chosen to learn from his French colleagues. Germany, Denmark, Sweden and Russia received their acting inspiration from France; French comedies and tragedies were played everywhere, at court and in the public theatres for such citizens as had the price of entry.

The building in which these performances took place was not the *Guénégaud* theatre but a new one built by the *sociétaires* themselves. Lagrange's company had been driven out of the old theatre by the authorities of the Sorbonne who had proposed to establish a college in the neighborhood. This august body thought the morals of the students would be undermined by the close proximity of a theatre. The order had come first in 1687 but its execution had been delayed until 1689. The *sociétaires* determined to erect their own edifice and so protect themselves against hypocritical attacks on their leases. The clergy was another stumbling block because it tried to intimidate those who were willing to sell ground to the actors.

The theatre cost two hundred thousand livres (roughly forty thousand dollars, the equivalent of at least two hundred thousand) of their hard-earned money and was located in the *Rue des Fossés, Saint-Germain-des-Prés*. It was oldfashioned in shape, being long and narrow, and had no seats in the pit. There were three tiers of galleries and the stage, encumbered by the audience, only allowed some fifteen feet across and eleven in the back for the actors to perform. The rear was left free for them to enter and so that the scenery might be seen. It is obvious that no very high degree of theatrical production could survive these obstacles. The company occupied the playhouse until 1770 when its ill-repair caused them to move into the *Salle des Machines* in the *Tuileries*.

There was little or no attention paid to historical details in costuming and the actors wore huge Louis *Quatorze* wigs even after the fashion changed. Three-cornered hats, gilt armours, lace cuffs were the style; just as below, a round wickerwork frame with a short skirt attached which reached below the knees, was customary. It is easy to see why naturalism in acting could make little headway. Gloves, high red heels, and in the hands always a fan, a dagger, a wand or some other small property. This naturally led to the bombast and *rodomontade* of typical Parisian acting. These costumes cost thousands of francs and the actors could never have survived the financial strain had it not been for the patronage of the nobles who gave them their dresses and brocaded suits after they had been worn but a few times. The make-up was a mere painting of the face as no characterization would have been possible. The actresses wore jewels supplied them by their admirers, the actors might have rings presented by ladies of the nobility and there was a good deal of amatory fraternizing; it was not unusual for a titled woman to take an actor for a lover. In this respect, eighteenth century France was like Restoration England.

It was a period of heights and depths in acting and with an increase in the importance of the individual protagonist, a brief account of a few that were outstanding, as well as those who were typical, might not be out of place. ADRIENNE LECOUVREUR (1692-1730) was a celebrated tragic actress who had the wholesome task of eradicating the memory of Mlle. Duclos (1670-1748), who with Pierre Trochon de Beaubourg (c. 1662-1725), had elevated bombast and false emotion to absurdity. Baron's easy approach to a part was lost but Lecouvreur re-established it; or at least she was successful for herself and set a powerful example to the others. It is difficult for the present day reader to imagine the degree of pathos possible. If he recalls the declamatory style of French public speaking of the twentieth century and then considers to what length a pompous actor might go in seeking the applause of an insincere audience, he may get a rough idea of the kind of playing Lecouvreur was attempting to overcome. It was this pathos that Voltaire, for all his adherence to artificiality found abhorrent. If one were to consider *that* the normal approach to life and the theatre, one can be less critical of the neo-classicism of the dramatist-reformer. After nine years of acting in the provinces, beginning in Lille in 1708, Lecouvreur made her debut March 27, 1717 with the *Comédie-Française* in the name part of Crébillon's *Electre*. She made her way because of her ability to project her innermost being into her playing. She had great ability in making the most of her vocal and general physical equipment, but it was her integrity, her very soul, that made her acting believable. She excelled in Racine's characters and originated Artémire and Mariamne for young Voltaire. Outstanding among her comedy roles were Elmire in *Tartuffe* and Célimène in *Le Misanthrope*. It is to be regretted that she played most often in La Motte's appallingly bad tragedy *Inès de Castro*. Her romantic life was the subject of the play *Adrienne Lecouvreur* by Scribe and Legouvé.

It would be nice to be able to say that the excellence of this really noble woman had inspired a fine male actor to achieve the heights with her, but honesty and accuracy forbid. That is not to say that QUINAULT-DUFRESNE (1693-1767) fell into the faults of Beaubourg, for whom he was *double*. That means that he was an understudy, but not that alone; if one played at court, then his *double* acted at the theatre. It must have been difficult for the rest of the company because their styles of playing were at the extremes of acting. If Beaubourg shouted, Dufresne crooned and that pleased the ladies mightily. Though an important step in the right direction, it did not really bring Quinault-Dufresne into the forefront of great acting. At least Lecouvreur must have been happier when she played with him rather than with the shouting Beaubourg. The younger man was an affected player who had hoped to equal or surpass Baron but all recorded reactions to his playing tend to confirm our feeling that he was at best a mediocre actor.

MARIE ANNE BOTOT DANGEVILLE (1714-1796) was the most fascinating *soubrette* of her century. She began as a child of eight on the *Comédie-Française* stage, appropriately enough as La Jeunesse in *L'Inconnu*, and won instant acclaim, continuing to play children's parts until she appeared in Destouches' *Le Médisant* in January 1730. She played a wide variety of comedy parts in plays by Molière, Marivaux and even such tender parts as Hermione in Racine's *Andromaque*. Voltaire offered her the part of Tullie in his *Brutus* but she rejected it, feeling that comedy was really her line. Her uncanny ability to forecast the success or failure of a piece when it was in rehearsal was so amazing that authors brought their plays to her to read and they followed her advice. She was never proved wrong and we wonder how the theatre managers could have been so stupid as to allow her to retire in 1763.

There were two tragic actresses of note to follow Lecouvreur, Dumesnil who conformed to some of her precepts and Clairon who held opposing views on the subject of acting. Marie Françoise Marchand, known as Mlle. DUMESNIL (1713-1803), after a provincial career as an actress, appeared for the first time as Clytemnestra in Racine's

Iphigénie, August 6, 1737. She was soon noticed by Voltaire who in 1740 cast her as Zulime in the play of that name. The sensation she created in *Mérope* was such that the author graciously credited the acclaim to her acting. Her playing of this and other similar parts was violent to an extreme. She felt the emotion she was playing so much that her performances were subject to heights and abysmal depths if she were unsuited to the role, or if it did not appeal to her. She had great warmth, more than the great Lecouvreur, and was an almost diametrical opposite of the studied Clarion.

Claire Hippolyte Josèphe Léris de Latude (1723-1803) adopted the name of Mlle. CLAIRON for acting purposes. She was as famous for her amours as Dumesnil was for her quiet life and love of drink, and it was due to these affairs that she turned up in Paris after a brief provincial career. She appeared first in 1743 at the *Académie Royale de Musique* as Venus in Danchet's opera *Hésione*. Not long after, the indifferent singer but pretty little actress was given an opportunity at the *Théâtre Français*. To everyone's amazement she chose *Phèdre* for her debut and scored a complete success. Her playing of Dido, Clytemnestra and Melpomene was long admired. She succeeded Dumesnil in the critical affections of Voltaire, for her artificiality and carefully studied effects were in keeping with his own. She managed to create the illusion of a character by technique without ever feeling the part as did Dumesnil. The latter actress was most generous towards her young rival and was her only friend when she first entered the company. Clairon's playing was never so exaggerated as Mlle. Dulcos' but there was a grandiloquence from which Voltaire was never able to free her. Later in her career she was able somewhat to simplify her performances. As a protest against the steadily increasing interference by the courtiers in the conduct of the theatre, she retired in 1766.

Henri Louis Caïn (1729-1788), called LEKAIN, was the protégé and discovery of Voltaire whose precepts in acting he followed. He urged him to retain his amateur status but finally, realizing that it was meat and drink to the boy, he set out to help him become a professional. Lekain's physical unattractiveness, except for his large and expressive eyes, was a serious handicap in a day when the actor seen close-to needed to be handsome whether natural or made up. Mlle. Clairon especially disliked his appearance but after he had demonstrated his remarkable acting abilities her attitude softened, though they never became real friends. This may have been due to the fact that Lekain who was a born mimic, used to take-off Clairon's stilted and grand style to the amusement of their mutual friends, if not of the lady herself. He made his debut on September 14, 1750 as Titus in Voltaire's *Brutus* with the author's vigorous encouragement.

As anything that the playwright did was greeted both with violent approval and disapproval, so did the younger generation wax enthusiastic over Lekain, while the elders looked down their noses and made caustic remarks about the state of acting. He provided a good balance for Clairon during the next sixteen years though a more violent player than she was. He perhaps felt his role more, as Mlle. Dumesnil did. He was highly regarded in Voltaire's *Semiramis* (first staged in 1748) and attracted particularly favorable attention in *Zaïre* and *L'Orphelin de la Chine*, in which plays he simplified his costumes somewhat so as to permit freer acting. Oedipe, Mahomet and Orosmane, all Voltairean characters interested Frederick the Great when Lekain performed at the Court Theatre, but the king found him somewhat exaggerated in style. Talma records that in his last years he sloughed that off and played at his best in the tragic roles he greatly preferred. Despite his mimic talents, he never acted comedy.

Of the comedians, the wittiest was certainly the new type of comic represented by Pierre Louis Dubus (1721-1799), whose *nom du théâtre* was Préville. Up to his time, the pot-bellied buffoon with drink-swollen face was characteristic of this type of actor and the audience was amazed when Préville first took over the role of the sly valet in Regnard's *Le Légataire Universel*, but they soon grew accustomed to his smart playing and admired it. He had great variety as an actor and certainly was not a *type*, for he acted high comedy as well as the blunt humor of the Miller in *La Chasse de Henri IV* and the wily trickery of Figaro in *Le Barbier de Séville*. There are several pictures extant of his acting with François René Molé (1734-1802), who was the perfect *jeune premier*. Their style of playing suited each other and the *Comédie* was fortunate in having them both at the same time. Molé's popularity with the ladies, and even with men, was enormous, particularly as Beverley in Bernard-Joseph Saurin's drama of the same name written in imitation of Lillo's *The London Merchant*. He was not a great actor but his facile technique and personal charm held the interest of the spectators in roles which were not too demanding.

It is not to be thought that all of Voltaire's attentions were attracted to the professional theatre for about the middle of the century a most distinguished amateur theatre had come into being upon which Voltaire advised. The Marquise de la Pompadour, but recently become Louis XV's mistress and later to be chief adviser on matters of state, felt the need of extending her hold over the King. Knowing that she possessed a pleasant voice and some acting ability and feeling that the setting of the stage would enhance her physical charms, she caused a small theatre to be built in one of the galleries, *Le Théâtre des Petits Appartements*. This is not to be confused with the larger stage erected by Louis XIV for professional productions, which was still occasionally used. Mme. de la Pompadour's theatre was to be a *bijou* and she was to be its chief ornament.

On the occasion of the marriage of the Dauphin to Maria Theresa of Spain in February, 1745, Voltaire had been commissioned to write a comedy-ballet for the occasion, *La Princesse de Navarre*. De la Popelinière added some lyrics and Jean Philippe Rameau composed the music. The ballet was not particularly successful but Voltaire had attracted the attention of Mme. de la Pompadour who had but recently been elevated to the position of the King's mistress. After Louis XV's return from winning the battle of Fontenoy in the same year, the Historiographer Royal was commissioned to write an heroic ballet in which Pompadour was to appear. *Le Temple de la Gloire* represented the King as the character Trajan and Pompadour was the goddess who crowned him. Her singing and acting enchanted him as much as her beauty and her enslavement of him was now complete. For the next four years, she frequently used her play-box at Versailles.

Though their performances were separated by thirty years, Marie Antoinette, who had been coached by Dugazon, finally won the King's consent to act and used the stage of her tiny theatre at the *Petit Trianon* also at Versailles, rather than Pompadour's or the state theatre where Louis XVI infrequently brought the professional actors; it was all a part of the aristocratic dallying with the theatre. The masses were willing to accept the fact that the mistress of their King appeared as an actress, but it was another thing when the Queen staged and took part in private theatricals. Her brothers and sisters-in-law acted with her, but they were the first to circulate insinuating and scandalous anecdotes about the young Austrian's frivolity. Much as you may condemn her extravagance and blind defiance of an etiquette which she did not understand and which irked her, thus hastening the *débâcle*, you have but to pity her the malicious attacks on her private amusements. She played, however, with political dynamite when in 1785 she chose to act Rosine in *Le Barbier de Séville* and to invite Beaumarchais to the performance. This was done after Louis had banned the performance of *Le Mariage de Figaro* for five years (it was first publicly performed April 27, 1784 at the *Comédie-Française*). Beaumarchais' plays had criticised the nobility and it had been on those grounds that the King had forbidden the presentation of *Figaro*. The people had been shamelessly overtaxed for generations and the display of such bad taste plus the cost of theatrical extravagance at that time whipped up the public rage against her.

This leads us back naturally to the professional theatre of Beaumarchais, but first a few words must be said of JEAN FRANÇOIS DUCIS (1733-1816) who is principally known for having translated and introduced Shakespeare, though in a sharply altered form, to the French stage. All of the English barbarism was removed and most of the drama as well. He heightened the love-interest between Hamlet and Ophelia; reduced the action to a single day to fit into the neo-classic and sacred unities; and turned Elizabethan blank verse into Alexandrine couplets. The mangling he contributed was perhaps no worse than some of our renditions from the French, but the liberties taken seem more severe. *Hamlet* appeared first in 1769; it was followed by *Romeo and Juliet* (1772); *King Lear* (1783), in which the gentle Pierre Brizard was seen with Talma; *Macbeth* (1784); *Othello* (1792). It was not until Alfred de Vigny (1799-1863) that more exact translations of Shakespeare were made. Ducis' labor of love was badly executed; his own plays are of no importance.

Though principally remembered as a philosopher and the leading editor of the monumental and much needed *L'Encyclopédie* (1751-1780), DENIS DIDEROT (1713-1784) also wrote for the theatre. As a critic and friend of many of the dramatists, he had much to contribute to dramatic progress, but he was not content to let it rest with that. He wrote *Le Fils Naturel* (completed 1757, acted 1771) and *Le Père de Famille* (completed 1758, played 1761) which were neither pure tragedy nor comedy but domestic tragedy, *drame bourgeois*. His other plays were mostly translations from English and have no permanent value. He was totally unable to create a character in the theatre; his heroes always turned out to be Diderot, despite the earnestness and reasonableness of many of his dramatic theories.

Pierre-Augustin Caron (1732-1799) took the name of BEAUMARCHAIS and it is by that name that the most celebrated comic talent of France after Molière is known. His life paralleled in chronology that of the founder of the United States, George Washington. The American colonies did him a great dis-service, for he was not paid for his shipments of munitions and supplies during the American Revolution, because of which he spent an old age in partial penury. Those who feed revolutions usually are destroyed by them. His situation in France was none too tenable and he almost went to the guillotine along with the aristocrats whom he had attacked and made laughably ignoble in his two most famous plays.

He began as an imitator of Diderot in trying to write of family affairs. *Eugenie* (1767) is the story of the domestic life of a gently born English girl who hopes to marry a great English nobleman, Lord Clarendon; the false ceremony, the seduction, and her eventual marriage after Clarendon asks her pardon. Its banality does not imply that it is uninteresting for there is a great deal of movement. *Les Deux Amis* (1770) added nothing further to his reputation, but five years later he had written a comedy, which in one form or another is familiar to the whole reading world as well as the theatre, *Le Barbier de Séville*. Beaumarchais borrowed liberally from the Spanish comedy of intrigue as well as from Molière, though his characters were French rather than Spanish, but the form in which they appeared excuses the plagiarism just as it does all plays of the first rank. His comedies cannot be disassociated from his life; he was a social reformer, a liberal at a time when that was dangerous, yet he was a bourgeois at heart. He hoped to see a bloodless change of régime, or at least a modification of the existing order, which would bring about democracy.

Assailed on all sides and falsely accused of forgery at the very time he was writing *The Barber of Séville*, it was four years before he was cleared of the accusation and the play finished and produced. At the last moment he made the mistake of expanding it into a five-act drama by amplifying the dialogue but this only weighed down the original. Louis XVI having removed his ban of the year before, it was first performed on February 23, 1775. Préville played Figaro; Mlle. Doligny, Rosine; Molé, Almaviva; and Dugazon, La Jeunesse. It enjoyed one of the most brilliant openings ever accorded a play on the Parisian stage. The disappointment and criticism suggests the analogy of Sheridan's initial failure with *The Rivals* just a month before. The next morning Beaumarchais turned up with his corrections and met a chilly reception from the actors at the theatre who had so hoped for success. Reducing it to its original four-act length and removing the padding of the comedy, the sparkle and brilliance returned and the piece had the enduring powers which had been hoped for it, just as Sheridan's play had.

These were bad times for theatre people. Both Louis XV and his grandson, the stubborn and stupid Louis XVI, practised a severe censorship. The censor was naturally repressive but even his worst strictures did not please the King who often went over his head and banned plays which had already been approved. Through certain court officials, he interfered constantly in the management of the playhouse in the *Rue des Fossés*. The dramatists were having the worst time of all. Beset by censorship on the one hand, they found the actors altering, refusing, or mangling their plays as they saw fit.

Finally, under the leadership of Beaumarchais, the authors decided to revolt, intending to withhold their pieces until the actors should give satisfactory guarantees that they would not tamper with their scripts. The pieces were to be acted for the author's benefit until the receipts fell below an arbitrarily set mark and then were to be owned by the company. (This is like the stop-limit clause in the rental of a Broadway theatre.) The author's vanity might be tickled by the number of representations his play received, but there would be no further royalty for him. Many authors were not willing to become involved in the controversy because they affected to consider money beneath them, or, like Diderot, were living comfortably in the country and were not concerned with their rights or with the rights of others.

In the general excitement the actors chose an unfortunate time to quarrel among themselves. Mme. Vestris, secure as the mistress of the Duc de Duras, seized the roles she coveted from Mlle. Saint-Val. When the audience learned of this it hissed the usurper and Vestris offered to return some of the roles if Saint-Val would share them with her. This was completely unfair but Saint-Val had been so indiscreet as to publish the correspondence she had had with the Duc de Duras on the subject and so, after worse punishments were threatened, she was banned from Paris. She was heaped with praise on her provincial appearances in a wave of anti-royalism, and the presence of her younger sister in a play at the *Théâtre Français* brought about a favorable demonstration obviously aimed at Vestris. Marie Antoinette also entered the controversy by bringing Mlle. Raucourt back to Paris. (Françoise Raucourt [1756-1815] had been a very popular actress but after her liaison with the Duc d'Aiguillon her fame had passed despite the fact that she was an unusually fine actress. Then, perhaps because of sexual aberrations, she had felt public displeasure.) But the Queen had merely made bad matters worse. At the same time the *Comédie Italienne* (revived in 1716), which was only supposed to perform pieces with music, sought to secure some of the authors of the *Comédie-Française*.

In 1780 after months of controversy during which the theatre was being desperately injured and the nobles were paying more attention to theatricals in their private theatres, or at the *Petit-Trianon* with the Queen instead of going to the professional playhouse, the King intervened. This was surprising because Louis cared little about the stage. His only interest had been to see that republican sentiments were not expressed. The terms of the agreement drawn up by the Council of State to be signed by Gerbier for the actors and Beaumarchais for the playwrights were disliked by both. The authors got less return than they had previously received unless the play had a real run. The actors had to keep books open and available, and more money had to come into the box office for the dramatist to retain his right to his play. Both parties signed it because they were worn out by the struggle. This was also the outcome of a recent controversy between the Dramatists' Guild and the League of New York Theatres over a not dissimilar matter. Authors were too busy fighting to have enough plays ready for Broadway production; the Paris of 1780-81 saw a similar dearth of new plays.

Beaumarchais was luckier in this respect than some of the others. He had a draft of *Le Mariage de Figaro* written and he quickly finished the play. It was read by Lenoir, a lieutenant of the police, and referred to Louis for examination. Mme. Campan read it aloud to him and Marie Antoinette. The King decided to veto it though the Queen was favorable toward it. Among other things it was a satire on arbitrary police measures. When the public heard about it they were willing to back up the author who declared that he would see the play produced at the *Théâtre Français*. He capitalized on the growing intolerance of tyranny in many quarters and, recalling Molière's struggle to get *Tartuffe* publicly presented, he sought to have his play discussed as much as possible. Despite the fact that most of the nobles were enemies of reform, they encouraged him to read the play at their salons because of the novelty and great interest in the play's fortunes. Partly through the connivance of the Queen and Comte de Miromesnil, a plan was made to present the play to an invited and noble audience at the *Théâtre des Menus Plaisirs* June 13, 1783. Louis finally got wind of the plan and to the great annoyance of the audience which had assembled, forbade the performance.

After even further complications, the play was eventually given at the *Comédie-Française* on April 27, 1784, and for seventy-five nights thereafter. Dazincourt played Figaro; Molé was Almaviva; Mlle. Saint-Val, the Countess; Mlle. Olivier, Cherubin; and the great Préville satisfied himself with the minor part of Brid'oisin, because he did not trust himself to undertake Figaro again. The success was overwhelming. The theatre was crowded for hours before curtain time. Many of the nobility dined in the theatre so as to be sure of their places and also sure of their dinners. The audience was amazed to hear such revolutionary sentiments at such a time, but to our ears the lines seem scarcely dangerous. Nonetheless, they had their effect and were an influence toward the coming popular outbreak.

The French Revolution brought horror and chaos and it brought some of the poorest plays the theatre has ever seen. They came near being equalled during and after the Russian Revolution. Politics and the theatre do not mix well. When the stage is used as deliberate propaganda without thought of its artistry, drama suffers and scenery, machinery, and popular sentiments do not take its place. The first evidences of the Revolution came in the demand for a poor play, Chénier's *Charles IX;* the populace clamored for it because it was anti-clerical and they knew Louis was opposed to its performance. The company declined to play it until the Commune directed them to do so; this they did, and after great difficulty the name part was cast with Talma. Danton and Desmoulins were in the audience and led the applause for a truly great performance. However dissension in the company grew because there was strong royalist sentiment. Eventually Talma was expelled. Gaillard and Pierre Dorfeuille who were the managers of the *Théâtre des Variétés Amusantes* on the *Rue de Richelieu* near the *Palais Royal* offered him a home there. He was followed by Dugazon, Mme. Vestris (whose republican sympathies had come to the fore in the past few years), Mlle. Desgarcins, Grandmenil and others. They were called the *Théâtre Français de la Rue de Richelieu* and opened their season with anti-royalist Chénier's *Henri VIII.* Fleury, Molé, Mlle. Raucourt and Mlle. Joly headed the original group in the *Rue des Fossés,* now known as the *Théâtre de la Nation.*

FRANÇOIS JOSEPH TALMA (1763-1826) was one of France's most celebrated actors, a brilliant performer and innovator who introduced many reforms to simplify acting. This was quite necessary as the innovations of Voltaire had been forgotten and bombast had returned to the stage. His Othello, Hamlet, Neron and Oedipe were particularly admired. His later friendship and admiration for Napoleon did not prevent his continued fondness for England, where he had spent his early youth and to which he returned in the second decade of the nineteenth century to be present at the dinner in honor of Kemble's farewell.

But for the moment we must return to the streets of Paris where the blood-thirsty stomped singing and jeering in their search for a man or woman marked out for execution. These *tapes-dur* went to the theatre and their jeers and dirty appearances were a feature of every performance. Naturally the old theatre was marked for their special attentions as its sympathies had been royalist and certainly moderate. On January 3, 1793 Fleury brought out Louis Laya's *L'Ami des Lois,* which was a protest against the extremists and the Jacobins endeavored to howl down the first performance, but they were drowned out by the applause of the rest of the audience. However, the radicals invoked official power to suppress the piece. No matter how much revolutionists deride censorship when it is aimed at them, they never seem to be able to take unfavorable criticism. They demand the protection of the law until they are in a position to change those laws and persecute their political enemies. By some miracle Laya survived their rage to write other plays, but none whose timeliness brought forth such praise and extravagant blame.

FRANÇOIS DE NEUFCHATEAU (1750-1828) wrote *Pamela ou la Vertu Recompensée* because his sympathy with the Revolution had come to an end at the arrest of the King on August 10, 1792. Feeling that matters had gone too far, he wrote a seemingly innocent piece which was passed by the censor. Its literary merits were weakened because he stacked the cards against his enemies. But with the lovely Mlle. Lange playing Pamela, despite the effort of the actors not to underline the meaning of the play, it was all too apparent what was meant. Preferring not to arrest them at once, the Jacobins allowed them to play during August before they interfered. The actors resumed in September with a blue-pencilled script but the playhouse was closed after the first performance and the actors were arrested and thrown into prison.

While the parent house was having political difficulties, Talma's off-shoot which had scored with Ducis' version of *Othello*, turned to producing the kind of revolutionary tracts (called plays) which line the shelves of the *Bibliothèque de la Ville de Paris* today with hundreds of titles. They yielded to public demand because the sentiments of the pieces certainly went far beyond any left-wing sympathies the actors had possessed originally. The classics were re-written to include republican sentiments, or restaged to emphasize those that were already contained in the play. It recalls the close parallel of the sovietizing of Shakespeare and other dramatists to give communistic meanings unthought of by their authors. It is notable that one of the greatest successes of the Russian stage of recent years has been Stanislavski's restaging of Beaumarchais' *Le Mariage de Figaro*, which a hundred and fifty years ago had caused so much furore at another troubled time in the history of the world.

The famous counter-revolution of the 9th Thermidor saved the lives of the *Comédiens Français*, who reappeared on the twenty-second of the month in the refurbished and newly named *Théâtre de l'Égalité*. (This was the new theatre to which they had moved in 1782.) The boxes were removed and the tricolor prominently displayed. Talma and others from the *Rue de Richelieu*, ignoring the quarrels of the past, generously went over to congratulate them. The old company led a pillar-to-post existence; their playhouse in the *Faubourg St. Germain* was too far from the center of things for the public to come to its productions and the theatres were centering on the *Palais Royal*. Part of the company went down to act for the commercial manager Sageret, at the subsequently named *Théâtre de la*

Réaction, but others, notably Mlle. Raucourt, held aloof. Eventually and fortunately a reunion of the scattered older group was effected with the younger. The dramatists opposed a house with a monopoly on the playing of drama, but they were willing to aid the *Comédie-Française* in its reunion and on May 30, 1799 it was consummated with the happy combination of *Le Cid* and *L'École des Maris*. Napoleon had become the First Consul and the *Comédie* was a favorite of his so its future looked hopeful as the eighteenth century ended.

We can not leave France and Paris, which represents the stages of the whole country, without some comment on the expansion of the theatre in the past hundred years. In 1701 there were three companies in Paris: the *Comédie-Française* for dramatic performances; the *Académie royale de Musique* for opera; and the *Comédiens du Roi de la troupe italienne* for performances in Italian, slight pieces with music, and of course *commedia dell' arte* which continued until as late as 1780.

By the time of the Revolution there were at least twelve outstanding theatres of one kind or another operating in the city of Paris. These included the *Théâtre de la Republique* (Talma's group in the *Rue de Richelieu*), the *Opéra*, the *Opéra-Comique*, the *Théâtre Feydeau* (Sageret's *Théâtre de la Réaction*), the *Théâtre de l'Égalité* (the original *Comédiens du Roi*), the *Théâtre de la Montagne*, the *Théâtre des Sans-Culottes*, the *Théâtre Lyrique des Amis de la Patrie*, the *Théâtre du Vaudeville*, the *Théâtre de la Cité*, the *Théâtre du Lycée des Arts* and the *Amphithéâtre d'Astley* for the circus.

The amazing thing is that all of these theatres were crowded both during and after the Reign of Terror. The stage was in a more flourishing condition than it had been under the monarchy when the private theatres of the court and the nobles seriously interfered with the audiences of the professional stage. The gorgeous *fêtes* at court and royal theatricals removed many of the aristocracy from the public playhouses. Thus by default, they turned them over to the bourgeoisie and during the Revolution to the proletariat, though the bourgeoisie were never absent even though their lives were in danger when they ventured forth. Since that time the French stage has continued in the same hands, though Napoleon was to dominate it as he did Europe but his reforms were for the lasting good of the theatre.

During the Napoleonic era there was no appreciable change in the characteristics of the French theatre. In fact it might be said with almost exact truth that there was no real change until 1830, when *Hernani* revolutionized the French stage a good half century after Lessing's work was finished. The melodramas which had begun towards the close of the century continued into the nineteenth. The short sketches called *vaudevilles*, which had begun as pastoral farces, were sharpened by the technical excellence of Scribe, who was to revolutionize plotting in dramatic technique.

Napoleon whose passion was organization, could not forbear to provide a new set-up for the *Théâtre Français*. He was interested in the theatre as a means of extending the glory of France. Several of his mistresses had been leading actresses, notably the beautiful Mlle. Georges and the lovely singer of *La Scala*, Giuseppina Grassini; so after a fashion he probably qualified as a dramatic critic. While in Moscow during the fateful Russian campaign, he promulgated the *décret de Moscou* October 15, 1812. This decree laid down the rules under which the French national dramatic theatre was to operate and these in essence are still in effect at the moment of writing (for the playhouse has resumed performances since the German occupation of Paris). A subsidy of 100,000 francs a year was provided; during the period of the Revolution there was none and under the monarchy only 12,000 annually.

Napoleon very much wanted a great tragic poet for France and had encouraged such mediocre talents as Baour-Lormain, Alexandre Duval and the scholarly François Marie Raynouard. None was forthcoming.

Several of the leading players had passed their prime and it was time for a new crop of actors to appear. There are three ladies of really considerable ability who began their stage careers at about the same time, Duchenois, Georges and Mars. They continued acting into the period of romanticism, in fact both Mlle. Mars and Mlle. Georges have been associated with that movement. Catherine Josephine Rafuin was known on the stage as Mlle. DUCHENOIS (1777-1835). She came of rather disreputable surroundings, having been the daughter of a woman who was the keeper of a shady inn and her husband, a traveling horse-trader. Duchenois, extremely plain, worked in the kitchens of taverns and was a prostitute. She had, however, an excellent figure and after she came to fame she was fond of playing the title role in Voltaire's *Alzire* for it permitted her to appear almost nude.

Like the passionate Mlle. Dumesnil, she had a real personality which enabled her to project her soul through a not too attractive exterior. People were surprised when she chose *Phèdre* for her debut, but once they had seen her performance they forgot other actresses who had played the role. The unhappiness of her early life made her appreciate the sorrows of the characters she portrayed; their grief in her voice and her mobile face touched her audiences. Her passionate nature complemented Talma whose art had grown in maturity and she played opposite him until his death. The elder Dumas said that most people preferred her playing of Lebrun's *Marie Stuart* to that of the great Rachel.

Marguerite Joséphine Weimer, Mlle. GEORGES (1787-1868) was the much younger rival of Mlle. Duchenois, being but fifteen when she appeared in the full-blown part of Clytemnestra in Racine's *Iphigénie*. Mature for her years and possessed of a classical beauty, she benefited from the rigorous coaching of Mlle. Raucourt (who had been bewitched by her the first time she saw her) and so triumphed in the part. The claims of Georges and Duchenois were violently argued by their partisans. Attracted by Georges' voluptuous appearance Bonaparte made her his mistress, so Mme. Bonaparte (the Empress Joséphine to-be) championed the older and plainer actress. Mlle. Georges only played at the *Théâtre Français* until 1808, when she fled to join a Russian lover and to act with the French company in St. Petersburg. In 1813 she came back to her old theatre but, with the restoration of the Bourbons, she was too outspoken a Bonapartist and so was forced to leave France in 1817. Talma and Mlle. Mars were similarly Napoleonic enthusiasts, but their hold on the public was too secure for the government to dare to harry them. Later we hear of Mlle. Georges as the heroine in the dramas of Victor Hugo.

Anne Françoise Hippolyte Boutet, Mlle. MARS (1779-1847) was the illegitimate daughter of Jacques-Marie Boutet (known on the stage as Monvel) and the lovely provincial actress, Jeanne Marguerite Salvetat. She began her theatrical career with Mme. Montansier's children's company, but was slow to develop her acting powers after her official grown-up debut in 1799. It was not until that fine comedienne and teacher, Louise Contat took her in hand that she began to improve. Beginning as an *ingenue*, she progressed to an *amoureuse* and, with Mlle. Contat's retirement, she succeeded to her roles, those worldly young women, those *grandes coquettes*. It was apparently her ability to suggest glorious youth and the sprightliness of mature young womanhood which won her such a reputation. Mantzius records that Oehlenschlaeger saw her at thirty-eight, Fru Heiberg at fifty-seven, and Eduard Devriant at just past sixty, yet they all saw a young and lovely girl playing. Fru Heiberg said to her husband that one could learn to speak French by merely listening to her speech. Mlle. Mars was primarily a comedienne but she undertook some of Victor Hugo's romantic heroines, albeit a bit reluctantly but nonetheless successfully.

The Romantic movement is beginning to crowd upon us. Talma, who at Napoleon's behest had played the neo-classic *Mort de César* for an audience of crowned heads at Erfurt in 1808, felt the new wine coursing through his veins. Meeting young Hugo at a dinner in 1826, he discussed *Cromwell* with him and expressed his desire to create the role; but illness and death were upon him and he did not live to undertake it. The dust of pseudo-classicism which had endured for two hundred years was about to be swept out the door by Hugo's romantic broom. But for that welcome change we must wait until we return to the France of 1830 and the fall of the Bourbon kings.

XVI

DECORATIVE EIGHTEENTH
CENTURY ITALY
(1700-1815)

THE last time that Italy was mentioned we were concerned with the development of the opera, which naturally included the eighteenth century Metastasio, whose libretti were famous throughout Europe. Despite a certain facility of expression and the admirable ability to be sung, these plays have no particular merit as drama. Opera is really a separate form and belongs to music. At its best it is a bastard art and at its worst, it is incomparably dull. The scenic investiture of opera and ballet comes into our scheme of things because the technique and the artists are the same.

But enough of these operatic affairs. We have three dramatists to consider whose business is primarily theatrical. The first of these is the fabulous CARLO GOLDONI (1707-1793). He was a Venetian of the Venetians and his plays reflect the gracious and romantic living of the celebrated republic of the Northern Adriatic. It was a republic in the sense that there was no king, but there was a *doge* (an elective office) and a hereditary nobility. Despite the prosperous tradesmen class and a wide interest in commerce, there was no democracy as we understand the word. Goldoni came out of the bourgeoisie and it was primarily the aristocracy which he satirized in his innumerable comedies. He upheld women at a time when their equality with men was completely unthinkable. He admired the medical profession and his portraits of doctors are among his most kindly; lawyers shared this dispensation from criticism as a class, for it was the legal profession for which he was educated. Individual doctors and lawyers who practiced only for their selfish ends were castigated in no uncertain terms. He has been called the Italian Molière and justly so because he took the Frenchman as his model and endeavored always to emulate him. A kindly disposition, together with state censorship and a natural disinclination to be unduly harsh, as much as his own lesser talent, prevented his equalling the master of French comedy. The fact that Goldoni has reached the prominence he has in the history of the Italian theatre is due to the lack of competition from contemporary authors as well as from subsequent dramatists. He was not a writer of the first rank, but in the Italian scene he ranks as first. Pirandello is the only name which might conceivably challenge his, but it is too soon to determine whether this dramatist was truly metaphysical or whether his entertaining psychological audacities were shallow or not sufficiently felt.

Goldoni was a prolific writer; even the number of his plays is unknown. It has been set as high as three hundred, which is probably an exaggeration as some of his plays were acted under different titles in France and Italy and therefore were counted more than once. He took a most active part in writing for the *San Samuele* (1734-35), *Sant' Angelo* (1748-1753) and *San Luca* (1753-56, 1762) theatres of Venice and the *Tordinona* Theatre (1758-59) of Rome. The bitter criticism of the aristocratic Carlo Gozzi who hated him, eventually drove him out of Italy. In 1762 he accepted an offer which had been made him the previous year to write for the *Théâtre Italien* in Paris and he continued to turn out plays for this company until the playhouse was closed in 1780. By 1769 his work had so impressed Louis XV that he was granted an annual pension of 4,000 livres, which he received until the Revolution deprived him of it. His declining years were spent in writing plays, planning a magazine and otherwise trying to eke out an existence. He died in utter want on February 6, 1793, leaving his widow penniless. Chénier went to the National Convention to beg for the restoration of the dramatist's old pension, and an annuity of 1,500 livres and a benefit performance of *Le Bourru Bienfaisant* was granted her.

His best known play is *La Locandiera* (*The Mistress of the Inn*), which was produced December 26, 1751 at the *Sant' Angelo* in Venice with the attractive Coralina in the leading role. This so annoyed the wife of the theatre owner, Mme. Medebach, that Goldoni writes in his *Memoirs* "she took to her bed again with a new series of fits, which completely exhausted the patience of her mother, husband, relations, and servants." * This delightful comedy of intrigue has much of Molière in it and thanks to Helen Lohman's translation and Eva Le Gallienne's Civic Repertory Theatre, it is entirely familiar to us.

It must not be forgotten that it was his disgust with the verbal indecencies of the *commedia dell' arte* which caused Goldoni to become a playwright. It was his desire to write clean plays reflecting the social customs of his country and at the same time correct some spe-

* *Memoirs of Carlo Goldoni: Written by Himself.* Translated by John Black, edited by William A. Drake, N. Y.; Alfred A. Knopf. 1926.

cific abuse of power or morals. He damaged the improvised comedy so much that all of Gozzi's efforts to rebuild it were in vain and its popularity waned to the vanishing point. As Goldoni had no great writer in Italy to turn back to, he naturally found Molière an inspiration in his reformation of the Italian theatre. His plays continue their popularity even today and their author is called "Papa Goldoni."

Un Curioso Accidente (*A Curious Mishap*, 1755), one of his most successful pieces, is a comedy of domestic intrigue, having a well-drawn portrait of a scheming young woman. He condemned war in *La Guerra* (1756), and *l'Amante Militare* (*The Military Lover*, 1752), and duelling in *Il Cavaliere e La Dama* (*The Gentleman and the Lady*, 1749). His first great success in France was *Le Bourru Bienfaisant* (*The Surly Benefactor*) which was played in Paris on November 4, 1771 and the following day was presented with equal success for the Court at Fontainebleau. Préville, Mme. Préville, Bellecoeur, Molé and Mlle. Doligny headed the brilliant cast. *Il Servitore di Due Padroni* (*The Servant of Two Masters*, 1740) has a modern reputation because of Max Reinhardt's rollicking production which was seen in America, Austria and Germany. These and countless other light pieces are the contribution of the author who, in the seriousness of youth, had begun his theatrical career with the successful tragi-comedy *Belisarius* on November 24, 1734.

Count Carlo Gozzi (1720-1806) was the bitter antagonist of Goldoni because he upset tradition. Loving his class the more passionately because his well-born family had fallen on poverty-stricken days which had not reduced a jot their pretensions to grandeur, he resented criticism. Ill-clad and ill-fed, the Gozzi children amused themselves at their country villa where they had fled when they could no longer afford to live in Venice. There they acquired an early taste for the theatre by writing and acting plays satirizing their neighbors. Quarrels among themselves were frequent and later Carlo and his brother Gaspare, who had become manager of the *Sant' Angelo* theatre, indulged in mutually recriminatory pamphlets that showed wittiness but an appalling lack of taste. In his endeavor to ridicule Goldoni and Chiari, a contemporary dramatist, he composed *fiabe* (stories or fables). These were written in dramatic form and were an endeavor to restore *commedia dell' arte*, so recently banished by Goldoni's plays. With characteristic fickleness, the Venetians welcomed back the old forms and accepted Gozzi's exaggerated fairy-tales. These pieces abound in extravagances, which both resemble the English Christmas pantomime and Arabian Nights' Entertainments. In the first, *L'Amore delle tre Melarance* (*The Love of the Three Oranges*, 1761), he ridiculed both Goldoni and Chiari. The bombast of the latter was made for parody. The overwhelming success of the performance by the fine Sacchi troupe (Sacchi performed the role of Truffaldino, with Darbes as Pantalone) influenced Goldoni in his decision to leave his country and go to France. In October of the same year came *Il Corvo* (*The Raven*) which was equally pleasing to the Venetians. *Turandot* (1762) a long and pretentious piece, is notable chiefly for its study of the development of the name part character. It soon bored the Italians, but it has had considerable influence outside of his own country. The Germans accepted it as a welcome retreat from French neo-classicism and it was a source of inspiration to Goethe. Eugene Vakhtangov used it as the basis of his last brilliant production (1922). The Provincetown Players performed it in New York in 1926 in an adaptation of Vakhtangov's version. Four years sufficed for Gozzi's connection with the theatre; he withdrew in 1765, preferring to end his theatrical career while his plays were still interesting to the Venetian public. The rest of his long life was spent in reviling and resisting change. The introduction of tri-colored republicanism by the French and the capture of his beloved Venice all but destroyed his mind and he remained unhappy and embittered to the end. His life was the subject of the play *Carlo Gozzi* by Renato Simoni, distinguished dramatic critic and collector of Milan.

Before turning to Alfieri, we should mention the Marchese Francesco Scipione di Maffei (1675-1755) who under the influence of the French, wrote *Merope* (1715), the only tragedy of any importance before Alfieri. There is a certain simplicity about this drama which won the hearts of its auditors and it remains the greatest Italian tragedy. It first won the admiration, then the scorn but finally the imitation of Voltaire, when he wrote his piece of the same name. What was of even more importance was his attempt in his native Verona to establish an Italian National Theatre. He enlisted the aid of Luigi Riccoboni, the actor and later stage historian; they revived the old Italian plays and Riccoboni made a tremendous success in *Merope*. This experiment preceded by some years the efforts of Gottsched and Carolina Neuber in Leipzig and the much later Hamburg venture of Ackermann, Ekhof and Lessing. Beyond this and the mediocre talents of the Bolognese Pier Jacopo Martello (1665-1727), who imitated the tragedies of Corneille with little success, there was no serious drama in Italy.

The coming of the third important writing talent of the eighteenth century, COUNT VITTORIO AMADEO ALFIERI (1749-1803), lifted the general level of writing. Other than the principal dramatists there were many minor playwrights, such as the humorous Albergati, the comic Avelloni, the sentimental Gualcetti, the farcical Federici, the light di Rossi, the classic Conti and the tragic Verri. Alfieri led an ill-disciplined and passionate life, as reflected in his plays. His tremendous love of liberty and hatred of tyranny was the dominant theme of five of his dramas. He wrote historical plays without real knowledge of history or the patience for careful research. His characters exhibit unnatural passions, and love and hate are equally harsh. "Fiery" (*calda*) was his favorite adjective. Between 1775 and 1779, twelve of his nineteen plays were begun and by 1789 were in definitive form. *Agamemnon* and *Oreste* were the first of his classical plays and, though as always, he portrayed the characters as he imagined them without regard for reality, he was successful in his handling of these themes. Where Racine translated the Greek characters into seventeenth century Parisians, Alfieri kept them the noble beings envisioned by Sophocles and Euripides. *Merope* measured up neither to Maffei's nor to Voltaire's play. *Virginia* was taken from the classic Roman story of the father who killed his daughter to save her from dishonor; another treatment of this theme was made by Lessing in *Emilia Galotti*. His first play *Filippo* was the story of Philip II of Spain and his unhappy liberty-loving son, Don Carlos. This subject naturally attracted him, just as it did Schiller in Germany. These ideas were fermenting in the two, as yet disunited countries of Europe.

Saul was his masterpiece. It has pathos, emotional appeal and the ability to move audiences when interpreted by such as Ristori, Italy's great actress of the nineteenth century. *Mirra* was another favorite vehicle of hers and one of Alfieri's finest dramas. This play of incest had a dark grandeur which is stirring despite its moral ugliness. All of his plays were written to encourage his fellow Italians to rise and throw off their petty princelings and create a great and united Italy.

VINCENZO MONTI (1754-1828), handsome Italian poet and lover *par excellence*, entered the theatre as a follower and imitator of Alfieri. His dramatic contributions were minor but his personality swept all before him. His first play *Aristodemo* (1786), though a great success, was a pallid piece of classicism. The oratorical *Caio Gracco* (1825) was better constructed but its chief interest has been to actors wishing long speeches and showy parts.

GIOVANNI PINDEMONTE (1751-1812) was perhaps more famous for his affairs of the heart than he was as a playwright. He was a bitter anti-cleric which showed in his highly correct classical tragedy, *I Baccanali* (*The Bacchanals*, 1788) and even more strongly in *Adelino e Roberto*, better known as *Auto da Fé* (1807). His best play was *Ginevra di Scozia* (*Ginevra of Scotland*, 1796) but its bloody story of supposedly Scottish intrigue is not as appealing as the noble character of Cincinnatus in *Cianippo* (1806). Pindemonte's brother, Ippolito

(1753-1828) was responsible for the dull and classic tragedy *Arminio*.

NICOLO UGO FOSCOLO (1778-1827), half-Italian and half-Greek, was blessed by and suffered from the ardors of both races. Women were his problem. He couldn't leave them alone and his red hair and amorousness attracted them so that his life was one affair after another. Despite this, he managed to write several plays of contemporary importance and compose a few poems which are still remembered in Italy. His *Trieste* (1797) was written in imitation of Alfieri and dedicated to that distinguished dramatist. *Ajace* (*Ajax*, c.1809) was heroic, metrical and lofty in tone but rather dull in performance. His masterpiece and the play for which he is known, *I Sepolcri* (*The Tombs*, 1807), is a lofty imperial dream of his native Greece conceived on an epic scale.

The plays of Goldoni, Gozzi, Alfieri and Monti were performed at a time when there was a large amount of theatrical activity and acting standards were high. Handsome theatres such as the *San Cassiano* in Venice, the *Teatro Filarmonico* in Verona, the *San Carlo* in Naples were being built all over the peninsula and attention to scenery and magnificence of costume were at their highest point. Just as Burnacini, Bernardo Buontalenti (1536-1608) and Alfonso Parigi the younger (d.1656) in the previous century, the Galli-Bibiena family, who for all the eighteen-hundreds were engaged in creating baroque theatrical designs, were the highest exponents of this art. Filippo Juvara (1676-1736), Giovanni Niccolo Servadoni (1695-1766), Vincenzo Re (flourished eighteenth century), Giovanni Battiste Piranesi (1720-1778), Pietro Gaspari (1720-1785), Bernardino Galliari (1707-1794), Fabrizio Galliari (1709-1790), Lorenzo Quaglio (1730-1804), Lorenzo Sacchetti (1759-1829), and Mauro Braccioli (1761-1810) are the great names of the period. Their projects were many and varied; their work colored the whole Italian scene and spread into Austria, Germany, France and faraway Russia, where Pietro Gonzaga (1751-1831) went to design a theatre for the Empress Catherine II.

Venice was the center of a school of light and graceful design. Bologna, the home of the Galli-Bibienas, Parma and Pisa were famous for the baroque. Naples, as might have been expected, was florid. Florence and Rome were famous for their magnificent carnivals and *fêtes* to which they bade the great designers come and decorate, for they had produced no outstanding scenic artists within their own ranks. The influence of the designers of northern Italy was felt everywhere and it is in this field of art that she was best equipped to contribute to the theatre.

The end of the century blended into the nineteenth as Bonaparte and the French set up the Cis-Alpine Republic and controlled the political, cultural and artistic destinies of Europe. Not again until Hitler are we to see so thorough an infiltration of foreign culture into so many countries. Plays expounding the virtues of liberty and its French interpretation, were popular and French actors were to be seen everywhere. Italians, Austrians, Prussians and Russians received their stimulus from the French by warlike means, just as the seventeenth century culture of Racine and Molière had spread by peaceful conquest. Only England remained remote from all of this. This was largely due to political reasons as she was at war with France for most of the period. There were reflections of the Revolution, but these disappeared with the rise of Napoleon Bonaparte and French Imperialism. Italy was to feel its influence until the debacle of Waterloo and the restoration of the hodge-podge of small Italian states.

XVII

THE EMERGENCE OF GERMANY

(1700-1830)

THE eighteenth century found Germany still a sterile promontory on a continent where the theatre flourished; efforts to improve her dramatic status were yet to be made in any force. Plays were not being printed and for the most part only existed in manuscript and prompt-copies. As is usually the case, most of them were lost or destroyed. In all probability there was nothing of literary value among these pieces, but our ability to check for ourselves is gone. The plays that were performed in the latter half of the seventeenth and well into the eighteenth century were known as *Haupt- und Staatsaktionen* (Chief and State plays). These were not necessarily a type of drama as was long thought, but were merely the principal pieces to be performed and were so named to distinguish them from the after-piece, *Nach-komoedie* or *Nachspiel*. Karl Mantzius, distinguished Danish actor-historian, gives a remarkably clear picture of acting conditions in this period in his monumental, if often-disputed, six volume *History of Theatrical Art*. As he states, the longer and more important plays of Molière, such as *Tartuffe*, would be *Hauptaktionen*, while *Georges Dandin* or *Les Précieuses Ridicules* would be considered for the shorter *Nachspiel*. However with the passage of time, absurd and bombastic military plays with dragons and obscene clowning by *Hanswurst* were immensely popular with the dull-witted and frequently uncouth audience, and came to be considered the usual *Hauptaktionen*. The subjects of these pieces were the criminal deeds of England's Jack Shepherd or the military exploits of General Wallenstein with grotesque harlequinades mixed in to draw an audience. As has been said, almost none of the scripts survived, so that we must depend on the greatly detailed playbills of the period, the earliest we find being dated 1702. This is from Hamburg, an early outpost in the history of the theatre, later to be made famous by Lessing and Schroeder.

Despite the lack of established theatres and the general poverty of the country, which was to feel the results of the Thirty Years' War for another half century, there were a number of acting troupes travelling about the country. Although this was an expensive procedure, it was done because there was no city in greater Germany, not even Vienna, capital of the Holy Roman Empire, large enough to support a popular theatre longer than a few months. There was no royal or noble patronage of these players worthy of note. They sometimes were granted the right of using high-sounding names, but the all important subsidies were lacking. Such expenses could be ill afforded by the myriad of small German courts, which were largely served (if at all), by English, Italian, Dutch and French companies. Italian opera and magic were given preference at the Imperial Court of Vienna, in the middle of the century, and even such German patriots as Frederick the Great could only bear to hear French spoken on the stage or at court because they considered their native tongue uncouth and ill-mannered.

JOHANNES VELTEN (1640-c.1693) was the first educated actor-manager to have come from the middle class, rather than from the ranks of barbers or veterinarians. He apparently began with the troupe of Carl Andreas Paulsen (flourished during the middle of the seventeenth century). After Velten's death the company passed into the hands of his widow, Catharine Elisabeth, who frequently played in Copenhagen. It later became the Denner-Spiegelberg Company; was taken over by the famous Neubers; and later emerged as the Koch and Ackermann Troupes, finally ending in the hands of the great Friedrich Ludwig Schroeder in 1771 after one hundred and twenty years of existence. While Josef Anton Stranitzky, who had formerly been a member of the Velten players, was holding forth in *Hanswurst* pieces in Vienna, Christian (or Johann) Spiegelberg (d.1732) was the leading actor-manager of the touring companies.

With no German dramatic literature worthy of the name, and no great theatre to foster it, a fortunate circumstance took place. Friedrich Wilhelm I of Prussia, a military bully and the worst domestic tyrant of the period, was forcing his male (if tall enough) Prussian subjects into an army that he hoped would some day conquer his neighbors. One of the young men he sought to impress into his service was the Prussian JOHANN CHRISTOPH GOTTSCHED (1700-1766) who escaped to Leipzig in the Polish-Saxon kingdom. He was a born organizer, but lacked tact and creative ability as well. In the beginning he acted as the saviour of the German theatre and, despite his efforts to regiment it in Prussian fashion, he did it a great service. He was a professor at the University of Leipzig, which enjoyed a little literary renaissance during the eighteenth century and the city was eventually to be called "little Paris" by Goethe. If taste was to be improved in the theatre some model needed to be found and the rigid neo-classicism of France naturally appealed to the professorial mind. He translated numerous tragedies into German, Alexandrine couplets and all. Unhappily, he chose such poor examples as Pradon's *Régulus*, but Corneille's *Le Cid* and Racine's *Iphigénie* were also added to the repertory he was building. But where was he to find the actors to collaborate on such a theme? A providential coincidence took care of that.

In 1697, Frederika Carolina Weissenborn was born of good family in Reichenbach, Saxony. This tall, handsome blonde was to become the illustrious CAROLINA NEUBER (1697-1760) and Gottsched's collaborator. Cursed, or perhaps in this case blessed, with a cruel and tyrannical father, she ran away at the age of fourteen with a childhood sweetheart. Recaptured and thrown into jail, she was later returned to her father's house for five years of beatings and other efforts to break her spirit. Her next escape came at nineteen, but this time she had two arrows in her bow, having taken two young men with her. They turned up at Weissenfels where Spiegelberg was playing in 1717 and were taken into his company. A handsome, intelligent girl would be a distinct addition to such a troupe.

Though Johann Neuber, whom she married the next year, was an indifferent actor, he seems to have been well-educated and of good breeding from the evidence of his letters, and to have handled the successful portion of his career with tact and ability. The second young man, having served his purpose, disappears nameless from history.

Neuber and Carolina learned their profession with Spiegelberg and a few years later were to be found among the members of the Haak Company, another off-shoot of the Velten actors, founded by Elinson, whose widow married first Haak and then Karl Ludwig Hoffmann who took over the management. In addition to this excellent actor, there was the talented Friedrich Kohlhardt. In 1724 the group was playing in Leipzig, where they were first noticed by Gottsched in what was probably the original theatrical critique of Germany, *Die vernuenftigen Tadlerinnen* (*The Reasonable Censors*), in which he praised their efforts. Frau Elinson-Haak-Hoffmann died in 1725; quarrels broke up the company and Hoffmann went to St. Petersburg for the Russians spent more *rubles* on the theatre than the Germans spent *gulden*.

In 1727, the Neubers took over the management of the company for which they secured the privilege of calling themselves the Royal Polish and Electoral Saxon Court Comedians, to give them the English version of their complicated name. The stately Carolina was thirty and at the height of her powers. Gottsched was twenty-seven and had already vigorously begun his efforts to reform the theatre. The three joined forces to carry through this much needed reform. Literature had at last deigned to notice, even to consort with the lowly stage.

Frau Neuber wanted to raise the standard of her profession, to rid it of the obscenities of *Hanswurst* and to play only regular comedies and tragedies. This she did for some years, though it cost her a large part of her audience. Though it was a long time before the reform was accomplished, she trained her actors to memorize their lines and to depend no more on improvisation. She insisted on rehearsals, carefully planned stage business and as good scenery as the Neuber purse could afford. Whether they had more than a castle set painted in perspective with wings, a forest set and a simple interior of a peasant's hut is doubtful, but they were always fresh looking. Costumes were her great extravagance; she could never resist furbelows and this was likely to be true in her acting as well. She also tried to improve the moral status of the actor, by insisting on the young girls' living in her house. The younger actors took their meals there, and she ran a kind of training school and settlement house for the aspiring thespians.

They enlarged and strengthened the company with Gottfried Heinrich Koch (b.1703), who was adaptable and learned easily the affected and elocutionary Neuber style, made translations for them from the French, and painted scenery; the serviceable Johann Friedrich Schoenemann (b.1704); his charming wife-to-be, Anna Rachel Weigler; and finally the elegant "Little" or "Handsome" Suppig, who joined them in 1731 and rumor hath it became Frau Neuber's lover, though this may well have been mere scurrilous gossip. In addition to Gottsched's ponderous translations, his pathetically constructed *Der sterbende Cato* (*The Dying Cato*) and Koch's adaptations, Frau Neuber herself wrote plays. These *Vorspiele* (*curtain-raisers*) took the form of allegorical dialogues in which she pleaded her theatrical reforms. It was in one of these that she celebrated the death of *Hanswurst*, but the stubborn devil wouldn't die and, due to financial difficulties, she had to invoke him herself; this must have been a bitter dose for the theatre's foremost innovator to have to take.

By 1738, the Schoenemanns had left Carolina to form their own troupe. She was for some time a favorite in Hamburg, whilst Leipzig was occupied by her former fellow-actors. Gottsched took a fancy to them and turned his critical pen against his old collaborator, which she unfortunately answered from the stage, as actresses have been known to do. The professor believed in reforming historical costume and in playing Greek and Roman characters in something at least remotely resembling their true dress. This struck the Neubers, as well as others, as funny, so they played *Der sterbende Cato's* third act exactly as the author wished it costumed. That is, they seemingly burlesqued the costumes, wearing fleshlings under their Roman togas to the hilarious delight of the audience. This infuriated the critic and the battle waged fast and furious and unhappily destroyed them both.

Lessing and Goethe were intolerant of Gottsched's pomposity. They ignored his very real accomplishments in the hard struggle to establish a literary German theatre. They could only see his stodginess and held that his classic French rules were restraining the proper development of the stage. They castigated him and his power was broken. Lessing, however, paid tribute to Carolina Neuber's acting powers and was obligated to her for his first production, *Der junge Gelehrte* (*The Young Scholar*) in January, 1748. That was the same year that Koch left the company to act in Vienna and dissolution set in.

Carolina's remaining years were sad ones of trying to placate creditors; her theatre was taken away by Schoenemann; Koch secured her Saxon acting patent by asserting she was no longer capable of managing a company. This ingratitude from two men whom she had aided, destroyed her pride and self-reliance. As late as 1753 she acted in Vienna as a member of another company, but tastes had changed and her declamatory style and always fussing manner of costuming were declared in insufferable taste. The Neubers would have starved to death, had it not been for the kindness of old friends and acquaintances. The Seven Years' War deprived them of their refuge, Johann died in 1759 and poor Carolina lived less than a year longer. Due to the kindness of an utter stranger, she received burial in a remote corner of the churchyard (though this had been denied her by the Church) in the hamlet of Laubegast near Dresden. Here in 1776, a monument was erected in her honor but not on hallowed ground as the Church still stupidly refused to permit it.

Having waited so long for great actors, Germany found herself with a number in the same century which saw a national dramatic government organized in an as yet disunited country. Due to the genius of three dramatists, a dramatic critic and half a dozen actors, a stage, which has since challenged the world, was firmly established. So entrenched was it that the ridiculousness of the so-called romantic movement between 1830 and 1848 could not destroy it. As frequently happens, it was the actors who came into prominence first, along with the critic Gottsched. After Carolina Neuber the next to step into the first rank was KONRAD EKHOF (1720-1778), who is chiefly famed for earnestness, sincerity and honest restraint; his fitness to challenge the greatest of all acting art can scarcely be conceded except by the most biased and nationalistic of critics. In 1738 he became a member of the Schoenemann company at the same time as the attractive and intelligent Sophia Schroeder, mother of "the Great Schroeder", Friedrich Ludwig. Also in the company was Konrad Ackermann, whom Frau Schroeder was to marry. After many years in this and other companies, Ekhof joined forces with Ackermann in 1764, who, with the Schroeders, was conducting the most famous theatrical organization in the country. He was never altogether happy in their group because of the sarcasm and unpleasant manner of Schroeder towards him. Later he was to leave the Ackermanns and eventually end his days in pleasant charge of the theatre at Gotha. During the next year (1765) however came the beginnings of that remarkable experiment, the Hamburg National Theatre.

Ackermann, whose finances certainly could not stand the strain, erected a new theatre on the site of the old and crumbling opera house on the *Gaensemarkt* which had stood for eighty-seven years. His company included besides himself in the comic parts: Ekhof in the principal tragic parts (though he often insisted on playing comedy, which he outrageously overacted); Frau Hensel, a good actress of colossal height and commanding beauty, but a schemer who destroyed all unity by her avidity for praise and the principal parts; young Schroeder was the incomparable French valet and danced cleverly in the ballets; his mother, now Frau Ackermann; the enchanting Karoline Schulze, the Hamburgers' idea of the ideal Juliet; Dorothea and Charlotte Ackermann played children and young girls.

However, the greatest reason for its present importance is the fact that Gotthold Ephraim Lessing was associated with the venture. He was offered the post of stage poet; that is the playwright whose duty it was to write new pieces for the playhouse, to make translations, and compose prologues and epilogues for special occasions. This he declined to do, because he felt that he could not turn out plays frequently enough to suit their purposes. However, the group were so anxious to have his name associated with theirs, as well as to obtain the acting rights of *Minna von Barnhelm*, that they employed him at a salary of eight hundred thalers a year (about nine hundred dollars), which was a good stipend. But how was he to help? Johann Friedrich Loewen (1727-1771) was acting as theatre manager, so that place was filled. Abel Seyler (the power behind the throne) and Adolf Sigmund Bubbers also stood by to assist in that way if necessary. Loewen conceived the idea of a journal with Lessing as a dramatic critic to criticise their efforts. Seyler agreed, at first grudgingly, but later was enthusiastic over the periodical's success. This was a bold idea, but one that worked.

Criticism can and should be constructive as well as destructive. This function of the critic which well became Lessing is frequently ignored by modern criticism. Today Brooks Atkinson in New York and St. John Ervine in London are respected for their efforts to improve drama and from their knowledge of the past to guide playwrights and actors in their reviews. This is stimulating on both sides of the footlights, at a time when a wisecrack passes as criticism.

This *Hamburgische Dramaturgie* is one of the world's leading examples of fine dramatic criticism and has led many writers to term Lessing the world's greatest stage critic after Aristotle. Perhaps this is unkind to such French theorists as Diderot, Voltaire and Marmontel, not to mention the English, who had preceded him. In this field, Gottsched and Johann Elias Schlegel had been the initial critics. The form was determined in part by the *Biblioteca teatrale italiana* (1762-1765) by Ottaviano Diodate, but Lessing had a completely free hand. The first issue did not come out until April 22, 1767, the day of the opening of the *Nationaltheater*. Ackermann's enterprise had been taken over by a *consortium* of twelve businessmen of the city, with a triumvirate of Seyler, Bubbers and Johann Martin Tillemann, Seyler's business partner. But in practice, it was a one man affair, as Seyler dominated all. The acting services of Ackermann and his two daughters were retained for sentimental reasons, but he played rarely and had little to do with the theatre of which he disapproved. Their greatest error however was in not retaining Ackermann's brilliant stepson, Schroeder.

Despite all its faults and the inevitable mistakes, the venture was the most brilliant yet to be undertaken and provided for two years (there was a hiatus of several months when poor attendance forced them to close) a repertory of plays that was distinctly above the average. Molière, Lessing, Voltaire, Loewen, Destouches, Quinault, Marivaux, La Chaussée, Schlegel, Weisse, Thomas Corneille and Régnard are representative of it. The group was attacked for producing too many French and too few German dramas; but where were the native plays to be found? Lessing, Loewen, Schlegel and Weisse were the best the country had to offer. The venture came to an end in 1769 and poor, pushed aside, harassed Ackermann had to be won back and persuaded to take over the theatre so that Hamburg might have a theatrical season.

Acting and managerial affairs make exceedingly complicated history and it is not our intention to penetrate too deeply into any specific phase of the theatre, but to tell a connected story as clearly as the events and our ability will permit. For that reason we must leave the painted thespians and journey into the lives and minds of the writers who provided the lines for these actors to declaim so well or so badly.

GOTTHOLD EPHRAIM LESSING (1729-1781) was born at Kametz in Saxony and was educated at the University of Leipzig, where he was destined for theology, but preferred philology and literary criticism. He was particularly influenced by the philosophical discourses of A. G. Kaestner. While still a student, his *Der junge Gelehrte* was staged at the theatre of Carolina Neuber. In the same year, 1748, he went to Berlin against the wishes of his parents. There he made a poor enough living with reviews, translations and an occasional poem. He met Voltaire in 1750 not long after the distinguished Frenchman had come to Potsdam, and was employed by him to make translations. The boy interested him so much that he is said to have had him in his house every day. This association was a valuable one for Lessing, though he rejected many of Voltaire's ideas. Unfortunately they quarreled, as was the philosopher's habit. Certainly Lessing had been indiscreet in showing his copy of *Le Siècle de Louis XIV* in advance of publication and its author suspected him of dishonorable motives. This estrangement rose to plague him in 1766 when he was refused a post in the Royal Library at Berlin because Frederick the Great recalled Voltaire's angered remarks concerning Lessing's youthful indiscretion. He turned to criticism and the composition of plays, *Der Freigeist* (*The Free-thinker*), *Die Juden* (*The Jews*), both of which preached tolerance and were included with *Der Misogyn* (*The Misogynist*) in volumes published in 1753 and 1754. Then came his rewriting of Plautus' *Trinummus* in *Der Schatz* (*The Treasure*, 1750), published in 1755, the same year that he wrote his first tragedy *Miss Sara Sampson*, which was a reworking of the Medea story in a middle-class English setting. In this he was influenced by Lillo's *The London Merchant*, which had changed the trend of English drama. Lessing's play was an example of the *tragédie bourgeoise* against which Voltaire fulminated in his most pontifical manner. It had great influence in Germany and replaced French neo-classic tragedy. In 1756 he went to Leipzig where he remained until he became secretary to the Governor of Breslau in 1760, which post he held until 1765. It was at this time that he contemplated writing a play about Faust, but the project never advanced further than a sketch of his plan. His reason for doing it was to reconnect literature with the old *Hanswurstiades*, and the career of the magical Dr. Faustus seemed a way to restore in new form what Gottsched and Carolina Neuber between them had destroyed.

In 1766, he published his art criticism under the title of *Laokoon*, and the following year came the play for which he is best remembered, *Minna von Barnhelm*, which has been called the first contemporary drama of Germany. This is a tender, serious comedy and has been regarded as a tribute to German womanhood and the Prussian army, which is why it has long held the stage, even into the 1939-40 Berlin season. This was given a good production at Hamburg, but its reception was more brilliant in the capital of Prussia. In the spring of 1770, he was offered and accepted the post of librarian at Wolfenbuettel. This kind of work was very pleasing to him, particularly as it afforded him the opportunity to continue his compilation of works of bibliographical nature. Many of the treasures he found in the archives he supervised were described by him for the benefit of scholarship. His next play was *Emilia Galotti* in 1772, in which Ekhof made a great hit as the tragic Odoardo. This was a retelling of the Virginia story from Roman times with a contemporary background of Vienna. It was seven years later that he wrote his final, and many think best play, *Nathan der Weise* (*Nathan the Wise*) which again pleaded religious tolerance. Disliking clumsy German Alexandrines but wanting to use poetry he introduced blank verse, that is rhymed iambic pentameters. This play is particularly famous because of his masterly use of the parable of the three rings representing Christianity, Judaism and Mohammedanism to illustrate his play of intellectual enlightenment and toleration of both the minorities and those with whom we disagree. This play appeared in German repertory all over the country for more than a hundred and fifty years, but is seen no more because of its embarrassing teachings.

Lessing was the first German dramatist of importance but he is not of the first rank; he served as an introduction to the great Goethe. His principal contribution to the theatre was his clear critical thinking as expressed in the *Hamburgische Dramaturgie* and other volumes of dramatic opinions. He believed that all art is but a reflection of nature and that any formal pseudo-classic rules which interfere with this are false. Sophocles and Shakespeare were his two dramatic gods and were the yardstick by which he measured his contemporary German playwrights. His standards were so high that it was only in his criticism that he attained the literary status to which he aspired; none of his plays could pass his own test of a great play. He succeeded in freeing native drama and leaving it in a plastic state for the more expert hands of the revolutionary poet Schiller, and the genius of Goethe.

There were a number of minor dramatists of this period who contributed to the theatre. Among them was FRIEDRICH GOTTLIEB KLOPSTOCK (1724-1803), who was primarily known as an ardent uncompromising republican poet, but was responsible for plays that were both religious and nationalistic. His earliest work was his best and he never lived up to his youthful poetic promise and was still an adolescent when he died in his eightieth year.

CHRISTOPH MARTIN WIELAND (1733-1813) was the exact antithesis of Klopstock, standing as he did for enlightened absolutism. His own plays were worthless, but his interest for us lies in the fact that he translated twenty-two of Shakespeare's plays, and so made them available for the first time in German, barring some rough translations of certain scenes by the English comedians in the late sixteenth and early seventeenth centuries. *Hamlet* was reputedly acted in Hamburg as early as 1625. It was played in Vienna in 1773, but so badly that it resembled a burlesque of itself. It remained for Schroeder to give it its proper première on September 20, 1776. Wieland's prose translations were polished by Eschenburg and were acted during Schroeder's eight great years at Hamburg. They did service until August Wilhelm Schlegel, famous for his slightly romantic and anti-French but nonetheless indispensable *Lectures on Dramatic Art and Literature*, made highly effective poetic versions. Sixteen of these were published between 1797 and 1801; an additional instalment was issued in 1810.

EWALD CHRISTIAN VON KLEIST (1715-1759) was best known as a poet; *Der Fruehling* (*Spring*) was his masterpiece, and was published in 1749. At the suggestion of Lessing, Kleist, who was a major in the Prussian army which he so much admired and was to die for, turned to dramatic poetry. He was stationed at Leipzig when Lessing went there and he thus benefited from the keen criticism of his friend in preparing his tragedy, *Seneca*. This had more poetic than dramatic value, so his mentor was probably wrong in urging him to turn his lyric talents in the direction of the theatre.

CHRISTIAN FELIX WEISSE (1726-1804) was another friend of Lessing's who belonged to the Leipzig school of playwrights. He was a voluminous but unimportant writer, who never developed in any field except that of *singspiel* (*operetta*) which was introduced into the country in 1741. In 1752 he made a new version of Charles Coffey's *The Devil to Pay*, which had first been translated by Herr von Brock, with new music by Staudfuss. This *operetta* turned up again in 1766 with melodies by Johann Adam Hiller. The new form was firmly entrenched on the German stage.

Sturm und Drang (*Storm and Stress*) represents the literary revolution in Germany. Chivalry and revolution were in the air simultaneously. Both religious and political ends were sought; the political was against the established authorities, and the religious was a reaction to the free-thinking generation which preceded. Both ends were unachieved, but a great deal of writing was let loose, some bombastic and ridiculous, some fiery and inspired. The movement took its name from the drama, *Sturm und Drang* by FRIEDRICH MAXIMILIAN VON KLINGER (1752-1831), which appeared in 1776. Some of the inspiration for the play came out of the American Revolution, which caught the imagination of the young and free spirits everywhere; the hero of this piece actually ran away to take part in our national struggle. Jean-Jacques Rousseau played an important part in acting as a stimulus for this group, as he did for Beaumarchais in France. *Die Zwillinge* (*The Twins*), in the same year, was probably von Klinger's most powerful play, concerned as it was with the crime of fratricide. JAKOB MICHAEL REINHOLD LENZ (1751-1792) was another of the *Sturm and Drang* group of young geniuses. Of this group he was perhaps the most outrageously extravagant in expression and ended his life insane, in Russia, whence he came of German-Russian parentage. *Der Hofmeister* (*The Tutor*, 1774) deals with the problem of the poor, educated young man who must earn his livelihood as a tutor in noble German society where he is subjected to slights and insults and treated as a servant. His *Die Soldaten* (*The Soldiers*, 1776) is concerned with the arrogance, licentiousness and brutality of the military class in Prussia. In this he pursued the same subject as HEINRICH LEOPOLD WAGNER (1747-1779) in his *Die Kindermoerderin* (*The Infanticide*, 1776), where a young girl is betrayed and tormented by an officer until she kills the child she has had by him. HEINRICH WILHELM VON GERSTENBERG (1737-1823) was best known as a poet, but like others of the period who believed they were influenced by Shakespeare, he turned to drama. His *Ugolino* was a five-act attempt to imitate the great dramatist but it was doomed to failure. The German people were ready for Shakespeare and Elizabethan verse and wanted no more dilutions of the original.

JOHANN WOLFGANG VON GOETHE (1749-1832) was to Germany what Molière was to France, Shakespeare to England and Ibsen to Norway. Despite his austere power, he was not theatrical enough to reach the technical heights of the English and French masters. This has surprised many of his admirers because he was master of a playhouse for years and was in a position to observe the rules of dramaturgy most likely to be effective in staging. Shakespeare, Molière and Ibsen had the same advantage and made use of it. *Faust*, Goethe's greatest drama, seems formless. The first half bears more relation to the playhouse than the second, which contains some of his noblest writing, but which is less frequently acted because of its weakness of dramatic structure.

Lessing understood backstage conditions thoroughly, as Brander Matthews, distinguished American critic, professor and founder of the Brander Matthews Dramatic Museum at Columbia University, states so ably. He asserted that Lessing was the first dramatist to provide for changes of scenery during the act intermission rather than between scenes, an innovation which did not retard the progress of the play so much. Insignificant perhaps, but it shows a playwright who is knowledgeable of backstage problems. The great George Pierce Baker, founder of the 47 Workshop at Harvard, and later of the Department of Drama at Yale, always contended that every budding dramatist should go through the production mill, so that he would realize the technical problems he was posing. So long as he lived, his students of dramatic technique were required to build, paint, and handle scenery, as well as to act and direct. This is a point of view that mystics of the theatre abhor, but Goethe was no mystic in that sense of the word, and his disregard of theatrical limitations is the more puzzling.

He was born at Frankfurt-on-Main of good family; educated first by tutors, later at the University of Leipzig and finally at Strassburg, where he came under the influence of Johann Gottfried von Herder (1744-1803). Only five years older than Goethe at the time (1770), Herder had already accomplished a great deal with his poems and his compilation of an anthology of folk poetry. He was the center of attraction for a number of young men and it was from him that Goethe got his appreciation of Diderot and Rousseau. Shakespeare had already begun to influence him, but his mentor's comments made him all the more conscious of the English dramatist.

This was also the period when he learned to dislike Voltaire, though he was later to praise him, and became interested in Gothic architecture. Herder treated the young playwright with such scorn and disdain that he dared not show him either his beautiful songs nor his first plays, *Die Laune des Verliebten* (*The Caprices of a Lover*) and *Die Mitschuldigen* (*The Accomplices*), both of which were written in Alexandrines. On the other hand, he was enormously stimulated by his association with Herder and though he frequently resented his treatment he continued to return for more. Georg Brandes in his brilliant biography says: "He was exceptionally fortunate to know in his early youth a mind that was so much more completely developed than his own and so much more comprehensive. This is indeed an experience which everyone who hopes to accomplish something unforgettable in the domain of art must undergo. Even the genius needs a mentor; and no one needs to a greater degree than a genius that particular sort of emancipation which fructifies."

His first important play *Goetz von Berlichingen* came in 1771, and told the story of a sixteenth-century robber-knight who had some of the characteristics of Robin Hood. It was based on Goetz's autobiography and interlarded with bits from Tasso, who had an early influence on his writing, as well as from popular German romances.

Chivalry was undergoing a renaissance in literature, especially in France, and the young writer had but recently been living in Strassburg which was then a part of France. This was all background, however. The technique was that of a Shakespearean historical drama, clowns and comedy were introduced into tragedy. Proud of his results, he sent the play to Herder who returned it with the comment, "Shakespeare has quite spoilt you." Then Lessing's *Emilia Galotti* appeared, which with all its faults had the virtue of being original in treatment, or so it seemed to Goethe, who revised his own work along the lines of this play. In this rewritten version it appeared in the summer of 1773 and was hailed with delight. It had answered that need the audience felt for Shakespearean spirit translated into German thought and concept. However, it marked the end of imitation on Goethe's part, though *Faust* and *Egmont,* which were both planned about the same time, show the swift change of scene which was an Elizabethan characteristic. His other pieces assumed the eighteenth century idea of the kind of play that was produceable.

It must not be forgotten that he had been educated for the legal profession and during his work on old Goetz had been admitted to the bar. In addition to being a poet and dramatist, he was a lawyer, art critic, theatre manager, philosopher, scientist, and even a statesman. Several of his minor pieces came next; they were influenced by Lessing, who in turn was influenced by the French. The operettas *Erwin und Elmire* and *Claudine von Villabella* were written in 1775, revised in 1787, and came at the beginning of the Weimar period, which extends from the former date until the beginning of his friendship with Schiller in 1794. His novel, *Die Leiden des jungen Werther* (*The Sorrows of Young Werther,* 1774) had a tremendous influence on the youth of Germany as well as all of Europe, and for a while it was fashionable for young men to dress themselves in Werther's blue coat and yellow breeches, to shoot themselves with a copy of the book in hand, or at least to threaten to take their lives in this fashion. Such a vogue recalls the influence in Japan of *The Love Suicide at Sonézake.* In his two middle-class tragedies, *Stella* and *Clavigo* in the year before he went to Weimar, he further enhanced his contemporary reputation, without adding anything to his present fame. This transference of abode to the capital of Thuringia came at the oft-repeated invitation of the young Prince Karl August. This noble youth of seventeen, with a clear, simple, vigorous mind and quick-witted manner attracted the playwright of twenty-six. The vivacity, liveliness, and excellent conversation of the latter was most appealing to the prince. Goethe, in a sense, stood in relation to Karl August, as Herder had earlier stood to him. This analogy can not be forced too far however, but he did become the counselor of the young man who had just acceded to the position of reigning Duke of Weimar.

It was in 1774 and 1775, that *Faust* was first drafted. Stemming from Marlowe, this version is now called the *Urfaust (Original Faust)* and is much simpler than the final result. He had come under the influence of Hans Sachs and purified the older dramatist's realistic doggerel. This he utilized in this play and in a series of minor pieces which were written during the same period, though he accomplished little of enduring merit during his first ten years at the Duke's Court. The constant love affairs, which had been a necessity for him since he was fourteen, continued. He wrote four minor dramas, worked on *Egmont*, experimented with a prose version of *Iphigenie* in 1779 and one of *Torquato Tasso* in 1780. Orestes with the diseased mind and the noble and pure Iphigenia are beautifully drawn in his tragedy derived from the Greek and completed in 1787. Whereas he did not rise to the heights of the Athenian masters, he did surpass Racine in freedom and originality, not that these were conspicuous characteristics of the French playwright. The tragedy of the sensitive poet-dramatist Tasso would naturally appeal to one of Goethe's temperament. He saw a parallel between the Italian's sojourn at Ferrara and his own life at Weimar, and certain portions of the play are autobiographical, certainly some of the characters are drawn from Lenz, Duke Karl August and himself. The monumental iambic verses were finally completed in 1790, nine years after the play had been first begun. The reason for working on this doubtless came out of his own long visit to Italy in 1786-1788.

It is necessary at this point to consider *Egmont* which he had worked on for so long, but which was finally completed in 1788. It is lacking in conflict and is far from being dramatic; its principal charm lies in an idyllic depicting of love against a background of war. The scene is laid in Brussels at the time of the Duke of Alba's campaign against the Flemish rebels. He created one of his most delightful characters in the maiden, Claerchen, whom Egmont adores and from whom he declines to flee even when Alba enters the city and he knows that he must die.

The lives and literary careers of Goethe and JOHANN CHRISTOPH

FRIEDRICH VON SCHILLER (1759-1805) were so irrevocably intertwined, that perhaps it would be best to introduce the younger dramatist at this point in our narrative. He was born at Marbach in Wuerttemberg, the son of an officer in the service of Duke Karl Eugen. As a boy he was forced to attend the military school newly established by his father's master despite his total lack of interest in a soldier's career. In 1778, while still a student, he began working on the play which was revealed in 1781 as *Die Raeuber* (*The Robbers*). This piece like all of his early work is part and parcel of the *Sturm und Drang* period. It is as highly melodramatic as his *Fiesco* (1783) and *Kabale und Liebe* (*Intrigue and Love*), the next year. This was due to the contrivances of plot which forced unnatural decisions upon his characters. In these three plays he wished to depict certain of the nobility or military class as despicable, so he invented arbitrary situations which were foreign to proper character development. Despite this, the plays were popular. His first effort was produced with much *éclat* at the *Nationaltheater* at Mannheim. *Kabale und Liebe* held the stage for a long time and was one of the principal "theatre pieces" in the repertoire of the noted contemporary producer, Max Reinhardt. Schiller's characters are largely outward show rather than full of inward meaning. They are passionate leaders of revolts, great patriots, and avengers of oppressed persons.

Schiller had incurred the displeasure of Duke Karl Eugen by his plays, partly because of their revolutionary sentiments, and partly because the Duke, who had chosen a military career for him, did not care to have his subject choose another one for himself. The situation grew so desperate that he was imprisoned but was released in 1783. He was offered and accepted the post of theatre poet for the *National-theater* at Mannheim where he remained until November 1784, when he left the principality. For the next three years he visited with friends while he was composing the romantic *Don Carlos* which was published in 1787. The theme of this was similar to Alfieri's *Filippo*, but he abandoned the prose of his earlier efforts for iambic pentameters. He also forsook his revolutionary period and was content with the possibility of improving social conditions by more gradual means. It was for long a prime favorite in his native land but its political sentiments have made it *non grata* there.

Through Goethe's influence he was awarded a professorship in history at the University of Jena where, between 1788 and 1793, he wrote *Geschichte des Abfalls der Niederlande* (*The Revolt of the Netherlands*) and *Geschichte des Dreissigjaehrigen Kriegs* (*The History of the Thirty Years' War*), which served as the background study for his monumental *Wallenstein*. This teaching appointment was not a tribute to Schiller's ability but merely represented Goethe's desire to get him out of the way when he came jobless to Weimar. Goethe's unfriendliness toward him had been a bitter disappointment to Schiller. On the strength of his new post, he married Charlotte von Lengefeld in February, 1790, and it was in January of the next year that he suffered his first violent tubercular attack.

Schiller and Goethe were finally drawn together early in 1794 and through the kindly machinations of Schiller's wife, who had known the great dramatist all her life, a real and lasting friendship ripened. It was not exactly a friendship between equals for Goethe's age, fame and rank were always a curtain; however the younger man gave him the much-needed stimulus and incitement to work; and he in turn dealt out his large stock of ideas to his friend. He was naturally slow in construction and composition, whereas Schiller was fiery and drove himself as hard as he could. It is said that when he knew his years and months were numbered he wrote most of the night, immersing his feet in icy water to keep himself awake.

At the beginning of their association they were not writing for the theatre; Goethe was writing novels and ballads, and Schiller, with the help of his friend, was organizing various literary and musical journals which were not financially successful. It must not be forgotten that for some time Goethe had been a theatre manager for whom the noted Ekhof had appeared on at least one occasion. By 1791 he had turned his attention to the management of the new Court Theatre which the Duchess had ordered built. The playhouse was officially opened in May, 1791 with the production of *Die Jaeger* (*The Marksmen*), by the virtuoso actor-dramatist August Wilhelm Iffland. Iffland went to Weimar in 1796 as leading actor, but to the regret of all (though he was not Goethe's ideal) he soon left for Berlin, where he headed the royal house until 1814.

In 1797 Karoline Jagemann, the actress, singer and mistress of the Duke, came into great prominence and dominated the Weimar stage until Karl August's death in 1828. She demanded constant attentions, privileges and her own way in everything, and was a thorn in Goethe's side. He tried desperately to rid himself of the managership in 1808, but the Duke, instead of releasing him, willingly granted him more power. The climax came in 1817 when Karoline insisted on the performance of *Der Hund des Aubrey de Mont-Didier* (*The Dog of Montargis; or, The Forest of Bondy*). This piece of trivia from the French had, as the title suggests, a canine for a hero; Goethe had no intention of accepting such a desecration of the Weimar stage which occurred in his absence from the city. When he learned of it he offered his resignation and this time the Duke accepted it.

But to return to Schiller, the encouragement of Goethe enabled him to finish his trilogy on the career of Wallenstein in 1799. The previous year he had given up his teaching in Jena and had settled in Weimar where, when his health permitted, he assisted in the direction of the theatre. He was gentle and friendly with the actors, while Goethe was more distant and more severe. They served to balance each other; they sought the same end for drama, the classical stage where the actors appeared in perspective and did not stand out unduly. In other words, the playwrights' stage, not the actors'. Their classicism however was leavened with romanticism. For that reason there was no need for a romantic revolution in the 1830's, as there was in France.

The trilogy of *Wallenstein* contains *Das Lager* (*The Camp*), *Die Piccolomini*, and *Wallensteins Tod* (*Wallenstein's Death*). The character of the great general is one of the outstanding pieces of German literature. Masterly in style and impressive in conception, the huge canvas unfolds graphically to reveal idealism at a time of horrible civil and religious war. The whole of the play was revised for publication in 1800.

Knowing that his time was growing short, Schiller worked all the harder in the next few years to get as much written down as he could. *Maria Stuart* (1801), like *Don Carlos*, marks a return to the problem of Catholicism influencing governments. In the latter play he was bitterly anti-Catholic, but by the time he was ready to write the history of Scotland's unhappy queen, a return to those wars was unthinkable. He had become a more tolerant man who was interested in making his leading character attractive to the audience regardless of their religious or political convictions; but he was determined to be as impartial and removed as he was in *Wallenstein*. At Goethe's suggestion, he staged the play himself and seems to have been successful.

Goethe's *Palaeophron und Neoterpe* (1800) was a slight but clever allegory contrasting modernity with ancient times and youth with age, and was composed as a festival piece to be played with masks in celebration of the Dowager Duchess Anna Amalie's birthday. In 1802 he wrote another allegory, *Was wir bringen* (*What We Bring*), on the occasion of the opening of the new theatre at Lauchstaedt. That same year, Schiller wrote what he called a romantic tragedy, *Die Jungfrau von Orleans* (*The Maid of Orleans*). This drama is operatic in its general set-up and Joan's speeches are frequently written almost as arias. It is somewhat sentimental and certainly does not measure up to Shaw's *St. Joan*, with its heart-rending inquisition scene. But for a century Schiller's drama was a favorite with such actresses as

Rachel, Ristori and Janauschek. *Die Braut von Messina* (*The Bride of Messina*) was modelled after Sophocles' *Oedipus Rex*. Schiller usually based his plays on historical incidents or on some tradition, but having always wanted to write a play on classic lines, he chose this story of fratricide and near-incest. The rivalry of brothers hearkens back to his first play, *Die Raeuber*, but his character development is much finer and his dialogue is greatly improved. He liked to use crowds, so the chorus took their place, but its relationship to the play was not the same as in Greek tragedy. He also departs from the ancient ideal by permitting a death to take place *on* stage. His last play, *Wilhelm Tell*, was the only one which ended on a happy and upward note. It was a poignant defense of liberty and the homely virtues, and was produced in March, 1804. Almost at once he began his truly last, but uncompleted, drama *Demetrius*, which had a Russian locale but was similar to *Die Jungfrau von Orleans* in the advancement of an idea in which the hero was almost victorious until assailing doubt appeared to defeat him in his inner mental struggle. He had finished the first act and was just beginning the second, when death, in the shape of his old adversary, tuberculosis, defeated him in May, 1805. He was in the prime of his life and many more plays of the highest standard might have been expected from him. Handsome, gentle and beloved, he stood for that fine romantic classicism which he and Goethe sponsored. The older man was terribly hurt by his death. He felt very much alone, as there was no one who even approached mental equality about him.

There is but one of Goethe's major dramatic works to be discussed, *Faust*. This was naturally the *chef d'oeuvre*, to which he devoted a large part of his attention from its inception in 1775 until the publication of the second part in his *Posthumous Papers* in 1833, the year after his death. *Faust, Ein Fragment*, which was printed in 1790, represents a reworking of the *Urfaust* (the manuscript of which did not turn up until half a century after he died). Not satisfied with either of these versions, he began a complete new play on the subject in 1797, the first part of which was published in 1808. It is this first part that is the best known to the world as it is the more conventional half, and the section most readily playable. His translators have done him disservice, for his masterpiece has yet to be turned into an English version which truly reproduces the spirit and masterly qualities of the original German. The second half seems formless, and contains sections that are neither related to the practical limitations of the stage nor to the limitations of the minds of his audience, whether in the playhouse or in the library.

Goethe's character of Faust was a poet-dreamer and idealist; Marlowe's Dr. Faustus wanted unlimited power; Goethe's sought the divine, the ability to understand the inner workings of nature and the mystery of living, the greatest mystery of all. This high ideal is mingled with a sensual, feminine fullness and a rich inner life, which makes for fascinating contradictions in style. All of his own life and experience went into this play, which is to German drama what *Hamlet* is to the English and *Electra* to the Greek. The second part of *Faust* is a paean of praise to the wondrous workings of civilization. All of the pettiness of isolation and selfishness and mean negation are wiped out in a glorification of the individual who finds salvation in the fine performance of collective tasks. The individual civilization is submerged in the greater civilization of all humanity at its finest and most honest moment. Every step of Faust's inner life, every experience leads him to the higher and more complete life. A free people living in a free land in sincere love of the finest spirit in life. This is what makes this a great play, despite many dark, muddy and ill-understood passages that confront us. Like all great drama it ennobles those who study its meaning and truly apprize its catharsis.

Goethe's long life ended in 1832 after he had created a great dramatic literature and German culture had attained its highest point. There has been no giant since to challenge him, though the latter half of the nineteenth century was to bring a group of writers, stirred by Ibsen, that colossal intellect of the North, which would produce a drama and theatre that Goethe might have admired, no matter how much he might have deplored its realism.

Before we consider some of the lesser dramatists who followed Schiller and Goethe, or who were writing contemporaneously with them, we had perhaps better return to the stage where these dramas were being performed. The names of Schroeder and Iffland stand out among the thespians. Hamburg had become a great theatrical center. Vienna, with the natural advantages of being one of the important capitals of the world, had founded the *Burgtheater*. This playhouse still stands and produces today despite a series of wars that have been disastrous to Austria, involving in the end the loss of her status as a nation and her reabsorption into the German Reich, which once she had so proudly headed.

The Great Schroeder had returned to Hamburg after the collapse of the Hamburg National Theatre and the resumption of its management by poor, tired Ackermann, his step-father. The latter died on November 13, 1771. With his mother as financial guarantor, he undertook the management of that playhouse and set out to give the city its most exciting performances with such productions as *Emilia Galotti* which had just been published, Lenz's *Der Hofmeister*, and *Goetz von Berlichingen* which was staged by him for the first time in 1774. But his admiration for the genius of Shakespeare, which he undertook to transmit to the good burghers of his city was more intense than his regard for the German masters. His performance of *Hamlet* has already been observed. His choice of this play was fortunate, because the problem is universal and the setting in Denmark was near enough and familiar enough to the audience to make its reception easy. He was less fortunate in his staging of *Othello* for it was a complete failure. Then came *Macbeth*, *The Merchant of Venice*, *As You Like It*, *King Lear* (his own greatest role), *King Richard II*, *King Henry IV*, *The Comedy of Errors*, *Much Ado About Nothing*, *The Taming of the Shrew*. There were eleven of Shakespeare's dramas presented in the eight years he managed the theatre. All of the critics of Germany and nearby countries, who were fortunate enough to see his Lear, have written rhapsodies about it. As he omitted the first three scenes of the first act, he avoided any idea of senile madness, playing the character as a straight, noble, old man; a man, but always a King. His height and fine figure certainly enhanced the part in the eyes of his contemporaries.

Schroeder was the first stage manager of Germany to work for unity of performance in his direction. He always read the play to the assembled company and as he had remarkable ability to characterize the parts as he read, they learned much from him. By insisting that they adhere within reason, to the style and manner set by him, he was able to achieve ensemble effects which were much admired.

However, all was not going so well for him financially. The theatre was making excellent money, but his mother was exceedingly niggardly, and was still paying her distinguished son but sixteen thalers a week. Probably he might have had more had he cared to press for it, but his was a nature which could not ask for things. Besides he was annoyed at the attitude of the citizens of Hamburg who blamed him for the supposed suicide of his half-sister, the lovely and popular Charlotte Ackermann. He was supposed to have been such a severe taskmaster, that she became too unhappy to live. Whether this was true or not, his audience thought so and made it quite clear. There was also a lot of dissension and grumbling in the company about his strictness. All of these things added up and were making his life intolerable, so he boldly decided to close the theatre and dismiss the company, an autocratic decision if ever one was made. For four years the insufficiently appreciative actors had to struggle under five inefficient managements, one of whom was the poor, unlucky Seyler, until Schroeder returned.

Schroeder and his wife went to Vienna to the *Burgtheater* which had been established in 1741. Despite the presence of his friend and pupil, the noted Brockmann, the management was most anxious to secure Schroeder and as always, Frau Schroeder was taken because of him. He had married Christina Hart, a pretty, young blonde dancer in 1773. Like many husbands, he forced his wife forward when it would have been a great deal better for her to have remained at home to be the graceful and charming hostess which she really was. In addition to Brockmann, the Burg Company included his old admirer Bergopzoomer, as well as the popular attractive tragic actress Johanne Sacco who had worshipped at his shrine when she was Fraeulein Richard. There were also the older Stephanie brothers and J. F. Mueller, who welcomed him with much more reserve, as was proper towards a rival and not an old friend. The younger Stephanie made a certain amount of trouble for Schroeder as he was dictatorial as usual, forgetting that he was a member of a company ruled by a group of actors along the lines of the *Comédie-Française*, rather than the great actor-manager. He was paid exceedingly well and acted principal parts from his enormous repertory of seven hundred roles. German companies, whether in their own country or in German playhouses abroad, have prided themselves quite justly on their extensive repertoire. Four years of this republican regime was enough for Emperor Schroeder and his mind turned back to his former empire. His audience, court and public alike as well as Joseph II, urged him to remain. The Emperor even talked to him in an effort to dissuade him, by recalling that he had tired of Hamburg twice before, and would again, if he persisted in returning. When this happened, he was to return to Vienna and the Emperor's favorite theatre.

Before trudging over the bad roads of Germany to the great Free City and seaport, we must take notice of Brockmann, who from 1778 was a leading actor at the Burg until his death in 1812. Born JOHANN FRANZ HIERONYMUS BROCKMANN (1745-1812) in the Austrian city of Gratz, he became the apprentice of a barber. Having a natural inclination toward the theatre, he turned to Hamburg, where he received instruction from Schroeder. He created Hamlet, whilst the greater actor contented himself with the role of the Ghost in 1776, though later he played the title role, as well as Laertes and the First Gravedigger, on subsequent occasions. When Brockmann acted with Schroeder, he restrained his natural inclinations to overact, but it has been said that he always needed a stronger personality to advise him.

Before returning to Hamburg, Schroeder was determined to assemble a new company and whip it into shape. The season of 1785-86 at Altona, Luebeck and Hanover sufficed for this purpose. Shortly after Easter, 1786, for the theatrical year began at Easter, he returned to the management of the Hamburg playhouse and for twelve years was the acknowledged autocrat of that stage. He made a great deal of money, lived in a handsome house and did much to raise the estate of actors. He was treated more or less as one of the great burghers and this in turn reflected on all actors, so that people in general had a higher regard for them.

His company had become the best in the Empire, and the repertory was a sound one, though it lacked the brilliance of his earlier regime. He himself is said to have considered the theatre not so much his love of loves but as the means to achieve the comfort and tranquillity which he desired. He coldly dissected his own acting and said he never lost himself in a role.

Unfortunately he never played many of the plays of Goethe and Schiller, though he admired the latter very highly. Before Schiller went to Weimar, he tried to persuade him to go to Hamburg and act as theatre-playwright, but this the dramatist never did.

In 1798 Schroeder retired to his estate in Holstein, though he still owned the theatre and received rent for its use. Beyond an unsuccessful return to management in 1811-12, when theatrical affairs became so precarious that he had to return, he had no further connection with the stage and died happily in the country in 1816.

He was, without qualification, the leading German actor of his century and accomplished a great deal towards the establishment of acting and directing standards which for many years after his death were without equal. He was also a playwright of no special merit, having borrowed most of his plays from English comedies in an effort to record the private life of the German middle class with whom he associated. Certainly AUGUST WILHELM IFFLAND (1759-1814) never measured up to him as an actor, though he made a tremendous contribution to the development of the Berlin stage at the end of the eighteenth and the beginning of the nineteenth century. Again to call on Karl Mantzius' excellent account of acting in this period, he was associated with two actors who, though better than the average, never equalled his abilities. These men were the plump and jolly actor-playwright, Johann David Beil (1754-1794), and the amiable, tall and thin Heinrich Beck (1760-1803). Though he usually acted the lover, he played Schnaps in Goethe's unpretentious *Der Buergergeneral* (*The Citizen General*) at Weimar in 1793, which in its minor farcical way reflected the French Revolution. All of these men came under the influence of Ekhof and acted at his Court Theatre at Gotha during the last year of his life; he must have been greatly esteemed by these three youths just entering the acting profession.

Iffland was a good-natured, childlike person. He was vain, fond of money and somewhat of a snob at the same time. His adulation of royalty was as slavish as the regard of Mr. Collins for Lady Catherine de Burghe in Jane Austen's delightful *Pride and Prejudice*. His acting was that of the virtuoso rather than that of the great ensemble player as was Schroeder's. He was an admirer of Ekhof and modelled his playing on him. His physical control was admirable and he moved easily on stage, despite his ever-increasing weight; his voice lacked power and frequently became shrill when he endeavored to stretch it, and was monotonous in the lengthy speeches which were characteristic of the plays of the period.

Ekhof died in 1778 and the following year the theatre was abandoned and the company was transferred to the *Nationaltheater* at Mannheim under the able leadership of Baron Wolfgang Heribert von Dalberg (1750-1806). Though this aristocrat had the best interests of the theatre at heart, he was somewhat over-influenced by contemporary French taste. Iffland, Beil, Beck, Johann Michael Boeck and Frau Boeck were the leading players, with Boeck playing the lover and the younger hero, though he was older than the triumvirate who had started out together. That pleasant friendship lasted between Iffland and Beil, but Beck dropped out some time after playing in the original production of *Kabale und Liebe*. Schiller's association with Dalberg brought about the initial performances of *Die Raeuber* and *Fiesko*, which was not liked as well as the first play. It took a great deal of daring for Dalberg to risk the staging of a revolutionary work in the Germany of his day, and Schiller does not seem to have been particularly grateful for it.

It may be recalled that Goethe, amazingly enough, opened his career as a theatre manager at Weimar with a play of Iffland's, but the actor had quite a good contemporary reputation as a dramatist, principally among those who preferred his realism to the romanticism of Schiller and Goethe. His pieces might be termed somewhat realistic, affecting and sentimental, with characters that reflected the good German burghers. *Die Jaeger* (*The Marksmen*) was probably his best work and is reputed to have been aimed at the later inseparable dramatists. His other plays include: *Dienstpflicht* (*Official Duty*), *Die Advokaten* (*The Barristers*), *Die Muendel* (*The Ward*). and *Die Hagestolzen* (*The Old Bachelors*).

In 1792 Iffland became stage manager at Mannheim, but his mind was set on securing the same post at the Royal Theatre in Berlin. He was also offered the directorship of the flourishing stage at Munich in 1796, but he declined it. We know that Goethe tried to secure him for Weimar and that he went there to act principal character parts that year, but declared himself unwilling to accept a permanent position.

After the death of Frederick the Great, who had not been interested in German acting, his nephew, Friedrich Wilhelm II succeeded to the throne. He dismissed the French company and allowed the German troupe to move into the theatre on the *Gendarmenmarkt,* with Karl Theophilus Doebbelin as director. This was not successful, so J. J. Engel the critic-playwright, and Ramler the learned professor, took over at the King's behest. The gifted, if uneven, actor Johann Friedrich Ferdinand Fleck (1757-1801), who had created the part of Wallenstein, was made stage director; and though he was soon replaced by Iffland, he continued as an actor until the end of his life the briefness of which was a severe artistic loss to the theatre.

Friedrich Wilhelm III had even more interest in the theatre than his father and granted Iffland's request for a new building which was to house both drama and opera. The Royal Theatre was opened on the first day of the nineteenth century, and it was destroyed by fire in 1818. A new structure was begun in 1819 under the direction of the great architect-designer Karl Friedrich Schinkel (1781-1841) and was completed in 1821. Iffland, who was a natural royalist, was happy; he was most graciously received by the King and the famous Queen Louise who admired his work. Royal director at last, he conducted the affairs of the playhouse on a sound, if not brilliant basis until his death in 1814.

Before we can take leave of this eighteenth century dramatic movement, which through the longevity of some of its protagonists, continued until about 1830, there are several other playwrights who deserve mention. These were men who were contemporaries of Schiller and Goethe and were strongly influenced either by them or by the other numerous playwrights of the *Sturm und Drang* period. The earliest of these was August Friedrich Ferdinand von Kotzebue (1761-1819) who wrote historical, fairy and social problem plays. Though these are generally ridiculed today for their falsity and insincerity, they passed as important dramas in his day. They were translated into all Western European languages and were particularly popular in London; no less a person than Sheridan borrowed *Pizarro* from *Die Spanier in Peru oder Rollas Tod* (*The Spaniards in Peru; or, the Death of Rolla*). In 1789 he brought out *Menschenhass und Reue* (*The Stranger*) which enormously impressed his contemporaries. Of his more than two hundred plays the best known to us is his first piece, largely because it was one of Mrs. Siddons' favorite acting parts. Towards the end of his career, his plays frequently became more licentious and often obscene, but always in the guise of inculcating morality and virtue.

Some mention should be made of the Schlegel brothers who were a part of the Romantic School. The elder, AUGUST WILHELM VON SCHLEGEL (1767-1845) wrote one unsuccessful play *Ion* (1803), which was based on Euripides; but it was as the translator of Shakespeare, Dante and Calderón de la Barca that he is best known. He was a learned man who wrote in four languages and translated from Icelandic and Sanskrit; in fact he and his brother were instrumental in introducing Oriental culture into Europe. He traveled extensively on the Continent in the company of Mme. de Staël, and delivered lectures on the drama in France, Italy, Austria and Sweden, where as secretary to Crown Prince Bernadotte he was ennobled in 1818. His most important and enduring work was his previously mentioned *Vorlesungen ueber dramatische Kunst und Litteratur* (*Lectures on Dramatic Art and Literature*) published 1809-11. His lesser known brother KARL WILHELM FRIEDRICH VON SCHLEGEL (1772-1829) made his primary contribution as a lecturer and critic, though he composed one play *Alarcos* (1799) which had no success.

ERNST THEODOR AMADEUS HOFFMANN (1776-1822) was a minor dramatist and writer of ghost stories, whose principal offerings to the theatre were his slight *Nachspiele* (after-pieces), his outstanding musical direction and his scenic decorations for the theatre of Warsaw, the Polish capital, which was flourishing in the early years of the nineteenth century in the difficult days after the Austro-Prussian-Russian partition of the country. Most of his work however was done in Berlin, where his brilliant conversational wit was buoyed up by alcohol until his mind refused to respond to this artificial stimulation. This bright humor does not seem to have been translated into his dramatic pieces, comic though they were. Other dramatic notables of the period whose work was of some slight contemporary importance were: Ludwig Joachim von Arnim (1781-1831), Georg Friedrich Philipp von Hardenberg known as Novalis (1772-1801), Friedrich Fouqué (Baron de la Motte, 1777-1843), and Heinrich Joseph von Collin.

A man of higher standing than any of these was that protagonist of the *Sturm und Drang*, LUDWIG TIECK (1773-1853) who bridged the gap with Goethe into the nineteenth century. He wrote a number of comedies with fairy-tale titles including *Blaubart* (*Bluebeard*), *Der gestiefelte Kater* (*Puss-in-Boots*) and *Prinz Zerbino*. His first play was the fatalistic *Charles de Berneck* (1793). Among his other pieces were *Leben und Tod der heiligen Genoveva* (*The Life and Death of St. Genevieve*) and *Kaiser Oktavianus* (*Emperor Octavian*). When the elder Schlegel abandoned his translations of Shakespeare, Tieck undertook the completion of the work in 1825. From 1823 to 1827 he was associated with the theatre in Dresden for which he wrote dramatic criticism à la Lessing, the results of which were published as *Dramaturgische Blaetter* (*Dramatic Leaves*). Like the brothers Schlegel, his greatest contributions were his criticisms and translations, rather than his original creative work, though he achieved some renown for his lyric poetry, his novels and shorter stories.

Little has been said about the Austrian stage because no dramatist of lasting importance had arisen. Farce and *Hanswurst* still were most popular. This stock character was cherished by the actor and author of *Hanswurstiades*, GOTTFRIED PREHAUSER (1699-1769), whilst a rival character, *Bernardon,* was put forth by the author-actor-director JOSEPH FELIX VON KURTZ (1715-1784). This unhappy state of affairs existed largely because the Court, which might have been expected to encourage serious dramatic production, turned its entire attention to Italian opera and French dramas enacted in French, and Metastasio ruled the Austrian theatre. Gottsched's reforms in the German theatre had made little headway in Vienna, despite the fact that many members of Neuber's company, including the tragedy queen herself, had appeared there, but that wasn't until 1747. The *Burgtheater* itself was occupied from 1752 until 1772 by a French company supported by the Court. With the rising influence of the young Joseph II, son of the devout Italian-loving Maria Theresa, a German company was installed in the Burg, but to retain the interest of the nobility, they found it necessary to model their repertory on the French. Out of their own ranks, they produced a playwright who patterned his comedies and tragedies strictly on the Gallic pattern, CORNELIUS HERMANN VON AYRENHOFF (1733-1819), and whose *Die Postkutsche* (*The Stage Coach*) was the most pleasing.

Prince von Kaunitz, Prime Minister of Maria Theresa and Joseph II, had long had an interest in things German. He commissioned J. F. Mueller, one of the principal actors of the new German company at the *Burgtheater* which was now also regarded as the Court and National theatre, to assemble a more experienced company. To carry out this commission, Mueller traveled throughout Germany and sought advice from Lessing. He was able to enrich the company, by adding new talent to the ranks and when the great Schroeder came to join Brockmann and the others, a first class troupe was established. The repertory was enlarged to include Shakespeare (whose *Hamlet* had been so badly played before the reorganization of the theatre), Schiller, Goethe and Lessing; Mozart's operas were added to Gluck's and the preference for Italian music-dramas declined.

Whilst the real drama was being played at the *Burg*, farce had retreated to the *Leopoldstadttheater* founded in 1780 by Karl von Marinelli. These burlesques, utilizing the transformation machinery familiar in English pantomime, ridiculed the Hungarians and Bohemians to the delight of the Viennese; *Hanswurst* who had become Harlequin was in turn transferred into Kasperl, an awkward, stupid young Austrian peasant who was always the servant of the hero.

The staging also improved and a number of native designers developed to supplement the great Italians who had formerly predominated in Austria. In the seventeenth century Burnacini had reigned supreme at the Court of Vienna and the eighteenth century finds such illustrious names as: Ferdinando Galli-Bibiena (1657-1743), "First architect and painter of Festivals and Theatres of Vienna"; Giuseppe Galli-Bibiena (1697-1756) was stationed in Vienna; Bernardino Galliari (1707-1794) worked both at Innsbruck and Olmuetz; Vincenzo Mazzi (1748-1790); and Lorenzo Sacchetti (1759-1829) were at the Austrian capital; Antonio de Pian (1784-1851), though born in Venice, so identified himself with the Viennese theatre as to be considered a native designer; the Bohemian Joseph Platzer (1756-1806) designed for the Austrian and Bohemian stages; and Norbert Bittner (1786-1851) who was a native Austrian artist contributed largely to the Viennese stage of the early nineteenth century. Some idea of the kind of work being done in the capital can be found in the twelve magnificent volumes *Denkmaeler des Theaters* published by the Friends of the *Nationalbibliothek* in Vienna, and better known as the *Monumenta Scenica*. Just in this year, three handsome portfolios entitled *Theatrical Designs from the Baroque through Neo-Classicism* were issued by H. Bittner and Company of New York and add valuable unpublished illustrative material to the history of the Austrian theatre.

Let us leave Vienna and return to Berlin, where the genius of HEINRICH BERNT WILHELM VON KLEIST (1777-1811) burned without the good Berliners ever being sufficiently cognizant of the fact. So neglected was he that he was reduced to penury and, despondent over his ill-success, killed himself just as Ferdinand Raimund had done. He was a dramatist of horror and his psychological values are considerable, though they have not as yet been as thoroughly examined as they deserve. His first play, *Die Familie Schroffenstein* (1803), was a powerful piece written in Switzerland, where he had gone with the idea of becoming a farmer in the country which had given birth to the man whom he admired so much, Jean-Jacques Rousseau. In 1807 he wrote an *Amphitryon* and the following year brought out the tragic *Penthesilea*. Superficially, this last play was the story of the

Amazon queen who destroyed the man she loved because he had conquered her, but in reality it was the exposure of his own soul which sought to learn the whole truth only to find it was beyond the compass of the human mind. The play so shocked his publisher Cotta, that he was unwilling to advertise it. His work was always doomed to failure and disappointment; the chivalric drama *Das Kaethchen von Heilbronn* (1810) was the only one to receive any attention during his lifetime. *Der zerbrochene Krug* (*The Broken Jug*, 1811), a really good realistic comedy which has been compared with the genre of Dutch painters, was a failure when produced at Weimar. *Die Hermannschlacht* (*The Battle of Arminius*) and *Der Prinz von Homburg* were published after his death, attention having been drawn to them by Ludwig Tieck. The first of these plays was inspired by his passionate hatred of the French and the latter by his love of the Hohenzollerns. They were not so narrowly nationalistic as many German critics and historians would have us believe, but present an honest love of country in the study of a hero who becomes terrified by the idea of death, demeans himself and eventually recovers his moral equilibrium. Of himself the dramatist said, "Hell gave me my half-talents, heaven bestows a whole talent or none." Goethe who paid tribute to him in several poems said that Kleist "seemed to him like a human form beautifully planned by nature, but infected with an incurable disease." This does not fully go to the seat of the conflict which so disrupted the mind of Kleist, but does indicate something of the nature of the struggle which finally drove him to double-suicide with his sweetheart, Henriette Vogel, on November 21, 1811.

As Kleist's own plays indicate, this was a period of intellectual gloom. The drama of fate arose from this feeling in which free will was denied and all good and evil came because it was predestined. There was no escaping your doom, innocent or guilty though you might be. The arch-priest of this school was FRIEDRICH LUDWIG ZACHARIAS WERNER (1768-1823), whose *Der vierundzwanzigste Februar* (*The Twenty-fourth of February*, 1809) was the father of many fate dramas. This one-act piece piled horror on horror and coincidence followed coincidence until the effect was lost (to us, not to early nineteenth century Germans). This play over-balanced such better work as his *Martin Luther oder Weihe der Kraft* (*Martin Luther; or, The Consecration of Power*, 1806), in which Iffland was particularly successful in Berlin. Like all Germans of the period he wrote an anti-Napoleon play, *Attila* (1807), a tendency which finds its modern counterpart in anti-Hitler drama in the non-totalitarian countries. However, it was his one-act play which produced the profoundest effect upon his audience and his contemporaries. Inspired by this the great imitator ADOLPH MUELLNER (1774-1829), who formerly followed Kotzebue slavishly, wrote the similarly titled *Der neunundzwanzigste Februar* (*The Twenty-ninth of February*, 1812). In this chilling play which began with incest, death struck every Leap Year until all of the offending family were murdered. So successful was it, that he followed it with a similar drama in four acts, *Die Schuld* (*Guilt*, 1812). Not only did he and Werner fool the public with this trash, but they took in the critics as well and were deemed successors worthy of Schiller.

Turning now to Vienna we begin with JOSEPH SCHREYVOGEL (1768-1832), whose own plays have largely perished, but whose influence as a stage director was important. He was manager of the *Burgtheater* from 1814-1832, coming into power shortly after the death of Brockmann, and director of the *Theater an der Wien*. He advocated the classical theories of Lessing and only appreciated Goethe and Schiller when their plays were written along those lines. He had been befriended in Weimar by Goethe but his abhorrence of romanticism made him resist any vestiges of the movement, regardless of personal loyalties. He had however a profound influence on the development of the leading Austrian playwright of the nineteenth century, FRANZ GRILLPARZER (1791-1872), to whom he gave great encouragement.

This playwright had a thorough command of dramatic technique as did the psychological Heinrich von Kleist. Unlike Kleist, Grillparzer avoided the horrible and catered more definitely to popular taste, but he cannot be said to have achieved so high a dramatic ranking in the long view. Though a great deal of this was due to his own lack of talent, some of it must be set down to the rigors of the petty censorship installed by Prince Metternich in 1815. Fearful of any new ideas and endeavoring to save their precious thrones, the Austrian and German sovereigns, as well as the restored Bourbons, set up a reign of intellectual terror that only ended with the revolutions of 1848.

These were the days of the Holy Alliance which purposed to maintain the *status-quo* and to restore everything to the pre-Napoleonic days. It was their attempt to interfere in Latin America that prompted the United States' declaration of the Monroe Doctrine. If the iron hand sought to stifle the Americas, it is easy to understand how rigorous would be a censorship in the very capital of Metternich, the messiah of this unholy order. Heine was hampered, the famous Grimm brothers and others were dismissed from the universities, and all intellectual life was trammelled in a fashion that only the days since 1933 recall. During these thirty years, many of the most learned Germans, as well as the democratic and unliterary, emigrated to America where they were welcomed.

But to return to Grillparzer, he managed to have a few of his plays produced, though *Koenig Ottokars Glueck und Ende* (*The Fortunes and Death of King Ottokar*, 1825) was "lost" in the Censor's Office for two years. *Die Ahnfrau* (*The Ancestress*, 1817), a drama of fate, was successful but its author received little financial return from it (he published it on Schreyvogel's advice as they both felt the critics misrepresented the drama). The trilogy, *Das goldne Vliess* (*The Golden Fleece*, 1821) which told the tale of Jason and Medea; *Des Meeres und der Liebe Wellen* (*The Waves of Love and of the Sea*, 1831), which was about Hero and Leander; *Der Traum ein Leben* (*Dream is a Life*, 1834); and the successful Merovingian comedy, *Weh dem, der Luegt* (*Woe to Him Who Lies*, 1840) were, in addition, his principal dramas. Several of his tragedies were kept unpublished until after his death, partly because of censorship. On the whole, he was a well-liked dramatist who might have achieved more had he lived in a less bureaucratic state at a different time.

FERDINAND RAIMUND (1790-1836) was an excellent actor and writer of dialect farces of fairy-tale qualities, who doubtless would have risen higher but for a most imperfect education. As an actor he frequently rewrote his part to improve it, then he began to add scenes and occasionally new songs; from there it was an easy step to writing his own farces. The first of these, *Der Barometermacher auf der Zauberinsel* (*The Barometer-Maker upon the Magic Island*), was composed for one of his own benefits in 1823. He was a master of Austrian dialect and through his own knowledge of peasant life he tried to humanize the characters in his fairy farces. Realizing his inability to rise to the first rank of writers and suffering from a persecution mania, he killed himself in a fit of insanity.

A contemporary of Goethe's later years as well as of the dramatist-critic Ludwig Tieck, was the fantastic writer, CHRISTIAN DIETRICH GRABBE (1801-1836). He seems to have been inspired with braggadocio for his very first play, *Herzog Theodor von Gothland* (*Duke Theodore of Gothland*, 1822), was apparently not played at all. Then he wrote two historical dramas, *Kaiser Friedrich Barbarossa* (1829) and *Kaiser Heinrich VI* (1830), the conception of which was so grandiose that the resultant plays seemed like unfinished buildings. This was even truer of his most important play, *Napoleon oder die hundert Tage* (*Napoleon; or, The Hundred Days*, 1831). In this he demanded whole battlefields to be represented upon the stage and went clear out of the playhouse with his dramatic demands. This may have had something to do with his increasing alcoholism which entirely spoiled his last plays and brought about his early death. He was an opponent of the Shakespeareanism which Tieck was advocating in his lectures and reading.

There is no definite break between the eighteenth and nineteenth centuries in German-Austrian theatre. The tendencies begun with Lessing continued to function with Schiller, Goethe and Kleist until the beginning of Naturalism and the rise of Hauptmann towards the end of the nineteeth century. Nevertheless the men who wrote and the stage directors who functioned after Goethe's death were inspired by a new movement of "young Germanism." For that reason we had best postpone any consideration of these nationalistic writers until a later chapter. From then on all the motivation is clearly directed toward an end which was sterilized and deprived of fecundity by the Nazi Revolution of 1933.

XVIII

THE THEATRE IN NORTHERN AND EASTERN EUROPE

(1700-1800)

SCANDINAVIA

THE greatest name in this period came out of the little town of Bergen in Norway, which was then united politically with Denmark, and both nations have a claim upon his fame. LUDWIG VON HOLBERG (1684-1754) has rightfully been called the "Molière of the North," but he did not achieve that flattering title without a struggle of many years and such hardships as fall to few of the great. He was so much imbued with the life of the people about him, particularly of his adopted home, that the noted nineteenth century dramatist Oehlenschläger said of him: "He has known how to paint the *bourgeois* life of Copenhagen of his time so faithfully that if this city were to be swallowed up and if at the end of two hundred years the comedies of Holberg were rediscovered, from them one would be able to reconstruct the epoch just as from Pompeii and from Herculaneum we know the times of ancient Rome."

He was the son of a lieutenant-colonel in the army, who had risen from the ranks and was hardly in a position to afford the twelve children he fathered. As the youngest child, Ludvig was destined for a military career, but his early predilection for learning was so pronounced that this plan was abandoned and he was sent to the Latin School in Bergen and later to the University of Copenhagen. Financial difficulties forced his withdrawal, so he took a job as tutor in the family of a Norwegian parson. As soon as he was able, he returned to the capital where for the next few years he alternately studied, taught and lectured in order to pay for his education at Oxford, where he all but lived in the great Bodleian Library. He traveled over a large part of Europe in his young years, so that when at last he returned to Denmark, he had accumulated the experience which was of so much assistance to him during his later years of writing.

His first work was a comic epic, *Peder Paars* (1719-20), which parodied the form and style of the great Homer and the literary Virgil, but drew for satire on the superstitions, pedantry and stupidity of his own people and his own time. A tremendous outcry arose against the poem and King Fredcrick IV was asked to suppress it. The State Council met to consider the matter and decided that it was an innocent and not indecent work written to amuse, but advised the author not to continue composing poems of this kind. He followed their advice.

In 1720, Etienne Capion, member of a French touring troupe which had been playing at the palace, obtained permission to erect a permanent theatre in the city of Copenhagen. After two years of French and German traveling companies, René Montaigu, also a French actor, was granted the right of arranging and producing plays in the Danish language. The Royal Theatre was opened on September 23, 1722 with a translation of *L'Avare*. The troupe wished, however, to have native work to present, so they turned to the author of *Peder Paars* who is said to have composed five plays in the first year and to have completed almost twenty by 1724.

In 1728, after several years of not very lucrative theatre business, the city was badly damaged by fire and soon the puritanical Christian VI ascended the throne in 1730. The theatre was then closed and Holberg is credited with having written the *Funeral of Danish Comedy* for that occasion.

Holberg wrote voluminously on other subjects; and in 1730 he became Professor of History at the University of Copenhagen, where he had begun as a teacher of metaphysics in 1718. But with the accession of Frederick V to the throne, the playhouse was reopened in 1747 and Holberg was asked to supply more plays, but the quality of these was not up to that of his earlier work. The Baron's considerable fortune was left to reopen and support the Soro Academy, which had been closed since 1665.

Several of his comedies are worth special mention from the thirty-three plays he wrote. *Mester Gert Westphaler Eller Den Meget Talende Barbeer* (*The Loquacious Barber*), *Den politiske Kanderstöber* (*The Pewterer Politician*), *Den Stundeslöse* (*The Busy Man*), the extremely funny *Erasmus Montanus*, *Barselstuen* (*The Lying-in Room*), the social-minded *Jeppe paa Bjerget* (*Jeppe of the Mountain*), *Jacob von Thybo*, *Den Vaegelsindede* (*The Fickle Woman*) are his best known. All of these are satirical and ridicule the provinciality, snobbery or meanness of mind or purse of those about him; his broad humor and swift strokes quickly delineate character. He chose such subjects as Molière and Goldoni used, but his way of handling them was original. Whatever he borrowed he made his own and this is the principal reason why his comedies still delight Scandinavia.

The next playwright to be mentioned, JOHAN HERMAN WESSEL (1742-1785), is also common both to Norway, where he was born in the parish of Vestby, and Denmark, where he attended the University of Copenhagen after elementary school work in Christiania; but he chose to live and die in Copenhagen. He supported himself by teaching modern languages and in 1778 was made translator for the Royal Theatre. The Norwegian Society, which was founded in 1772 by those who were dissatisfied with the union with Denmark, found an ardent ally in Wessel. Though the society was pro-French and anti-German, the dramatist did not hesitate to satirize the absurd and stilted qualities of the slavishly admired neo-classic French tragedy. *Kjaelighed uden Strömper* (*Love without Stockings*, 1772) was an hilarious parody, though its first audiences were unfortunately so inured to bathos that they didn't know whether to laugh or cry.

The Danish Society, the opponent of Wessel's Norwegian Society, included JOHANNES EWALD (1743-1781) among its members. This playwright was a lover of adventure, who, as a child, had been greatly influenced by *Don Quixote* and *Robinson Crusoe*. He ran away to Prussia to fight in the Seven Years' War but seems to have ended up as a drummer boy and then a non-commissioned officer in the Austrian army. Certainly this love of Germany shaped his writing, for *Sturm und Drang*, Klopstock, Iffland and Kotzebue all took their toll. His first play was the religious and poetic *Adam og Eva* (*Adam and Eve*, 1769), but his fame had been established by his funeral ode on the death of King Frederick V in 1764. He drew the attention of other writers to the rich source material to be found in the folklore and legends of Scandinavia; the prose tragedy, *Rolf Krage* (1770) was based on the Saxo Chronicle of Danish legends. *Balders Dod* (*Balder's Death*, 1774) was the first Danish drama to be written in iambic pentameters. It was based on another tale of Saxo and was composed in the beautiful little village of Rungsted, to which the author retired friendless, abandoned by his relatives and broken in health. Eventually the government recognized his claims to national gratitude by granting him a pension; this enabled him to live in comfort in Copenhagen where he again found friends. In 1778 he wrote the play for which he is best remembered, *Fiskerne* (*The Fisher-*

men); it is a dramatization of the life of the men in the fishing village where he had lived. Some of his best lyric poems are contained in this play; the most notable being *Kong Kristian stod ved Höien Mast (King Christian Stood by the Lofty Mast)*, later the Danish anthem, which was translated into English by Longfellow.

Ewald had imitators in Thomas Thaarup (1749-1821) and Ole Johan Samsöe (1759-1796), whose work was outstanding, though not enduring. The former wrote *The Harvest Feast* and *Peter's Wedding*, both of which were popular at the time because of their simple, homely style. In addition to Samsöe's tales based on Scandinavian legend, his historical drama *Dyveke* was a promise of better plays to come, but his untimely death cut short what might have been a successful writing career. Oluf Christian Olufson, Christian Magnus Falsen, Christian Levin Sander and Charlotte Dorothea Biehl were other minor Danish playwrights. Of the Norwegian writers, the only one worthy of mention is Nordahl Brun (1745-1816), but he is better known as a writer of hymns than of plays. In 1772 he was responsible for two plays, *Zarine*, based on the lines of classical French tragedy, and *Einar Tambeskielver*, which is credited with being the first historical Norwegian play. Both of these were produced at the Royal Theatre where Nils Bredal had become director.

Scandinavia has always been famed for its critics. One of the first in the dramatic field was Knud Lyhne Rahbek (1760-1830), editor of *The Danish Spectator* as well as director of the Royal Theatre in Copenhagen. He and the poet-playwright Christen Hendriksen Pram (1756-1821) avoided politics and wrote comedies of very slight importance. In 1809 Rahbek wrote his famous treatise on dramatic technique and it was published as *Letters of an Old Actor to His Son*. Jens Baggesen (1764-1826) was as well known as a critic outside his native Denmark as within its narrow borders. He derided the writers and the manner of living in his homeland, both of which seemed sterile, bigoted and niggardly. Certainly they were frugal and bourgeois, whatever else might be said about them. Admiring Voss, Klopstock and Wieland, the translator of Shakespeare, he fell in love with the *Sturm und Drang* movement. He was a lifelong friend of Lenz, but it was to Schiller that he poured out his highest worship and to whom he wrote several affected verses in German. His satiric writing directed against the French, after his earlier admiration for Voltaire's plays, did a great deal to free Danish letters from neo-classicism.

While Baggesen was writing in Europe, little Iceland, which since 1262 had been under the domination of Denmark, produced its first dramatist, Sugurdur Petursson (1759-1827), whose comedies have

little lasting merit but are noteworthy as an evidence of theatrical
interest in that tiny and sparsely settled island.

During the time that Norway, Denmark and Iceland were producing some worthwhile drama and variously flourishing playhouses,
Sweden was lagging behind. It was only through royal insistence that a theatre existed at all; due to the large number of wars
which drained the country of its resources and culture in the first
half of the eighteenth century. What dramatic fare there was, was
frugal. A theatrical revival came about through the king, Gustavus
III (1746-1792), who was a poet, playwright, and *entrepreneur*. In
his youth, the rationalist historian Olof von Dalin (1708-63) acted
as his tutor and he naturally turned his pupil's mind not only to French
rationalism, but to the French theatre which he sought to emulate
when he took the throne in 1771. It was he who founded the National
Theatre in Stockholm in 1782, the Academy of Music, the Academy
of Fine Arts and the Swedish Academy in 1786, all on French lines.
Gustavus enlisted the aid of the dramatist Johan Henrik Kellgren
(1751-1795) to assist in his writing; their collaboration produced
Gustavus Vasa which was based on the life of the king's ancestor.

One of Gustavus' most enduring works was his stimulation of production at the delightful court theatres at Drottningholm and Grips-
holm, though the former was the more important of the two. With
the collaboration of Louis-Jean Desprez (1743-1804), who went to
Stockholm from Paris in 1784 to act as designer, he devised a series
of ballets and French pieces for this theatre. It was erected in 1766
at the Drottningholm Palace on the Island of Lofö in Lake Mälar,
and was designed as a royal plaything, with everything centering on
the thrones of the king and queen. The nobility and the palace staff
could be admitted if desired, for the auditorium could be enlarged
or diminished by a series of drapes. The elaborate machinery was
handled in full view of the distinguished audience so that the scene
transformations and stage effects might be watched. The scenery was
designed as an artificial extension of the auditorium, thus suggesting
that the actors were in the same room despite the picture-frame proscenium. This theatre has been preserved and today under the direction of Agne Beijer it houses a theatrical museum and occasional performances under royal patronage.

KARL GUSTAF LEOPOLD (1756-1829) wrote unimportant dramas
that were much admired at the time. *Virginia* and *Oden eller Asarne
Invandring* were pseudo-classical tragedies; for the latter the dramatist was rewarded by the king with a laurel wreath from the grave
of Virgil. Carl Israel Hallman (1732-1800) wrote a number of fashionable parodies. Of these comedies the best was *Opportunity Makes*

201. HANS SACHS.

202. BEAUMARCHAIS.

03. ELIZABETHAN STAGE, FROM FRONTISPIECE
OF *Roxana*.

Folger Shakespeare Library

204. PULCHINELLA. COMMEDIA DELL' ARTE
FIGURE, MILAN.

Yale-Rockefeller Theatre Collection

206. ADRIENNE LECOUVREUR.

205. TALMA.

Theatre Collection, N. Y. Public Library

207. EXTERIOR OF THE THEATRE AT FONTAINEBLEAU.

Pfnor, Monographie du Palais de Fontainebleau

209. Lucien Guitry as Pasteur.

Crosby Gaige Collection, N.Y.P.L.

208. Victor Hugo.

210. Opening Night of *Hernani*, 1830, *Comédie-Française*.   *Dubech*

211. Lorenzo Sachetti, Caricatured By a
Student.

212. Caricature By Tiepolo.

Courtesy of Janos Scholz

213. Carlo Goldoni.

214. Carlo Gozzi.

Theatre Collection, N. Y. Public Library

Monte di Parnaso fatto in firenze nella festa a Cauallo
per la uenuta del Serenissimo Principe d' Vrbino
Si uedeua nella piu alta parte del Monte Rouere Arme
del Ser.mo Casa d'Vrbino le Muse e Pallade stauano
alla sua Ombra ueniua Coronate delle frondi
dell'istessa Rouere erano sparsi per il Monte tutti
quei letterati che nomina il Cortigiano con l'istessa Corone in
in testa, ueniua lafama sul minor Giogo del Monte et apud la
seguiuano Cento Settanta de sui ministri. anno 1616

215. DESIGN BY ALFONSO PARIGI THE YOUNGER, D. 1656; ENGRAVED BY JACQUES CALLOT.

216. DESIGN BY LORENZO SACHETTI (1759-1829).

218. Design By Lorenzo Sachetti.

217. Design By Bodenchi, 1665-1749.

219. SETTING FOR *Teodosio il Giovane,* ACT III, SC. 1. BY JUVARA, 1711.

220. SETTING, *Teodosio il Giovane,* ACT III, SC. 3. BY JUVARA, 1711.

Yale-Rockefeller Theatre Collection

221. FESTIVITY IN THE *Place de L'Hôtel de Ville,* PARIS, IN HONOR OF THE MARRIAGE OF THE DAUPHIN TO MARIE JOSEPH DE SAXE, FEB. 13, 1747. *Spencer Collection, N. Y. Public Library*

222. Setting For *Teodosio il Giovane*, Act III, Sc. 4. By Juvara

223. Setting For *Il Ciro*, Act II, Sc. 2. By Juvara, 1712.

224. SETTING BY LORENZO SACHETTI.

225. SETTING BY GIULIO QUAGLIO, 1746-1801.

226. SETTING FOR *Quinto Fabio* BY ANTON DE PIAN (1784-1851).

227. SETTING BY KARL SCHUTZ, 1746-1800.

228. DESIGNS BY JOSEPH PLATZER (1756-1806).

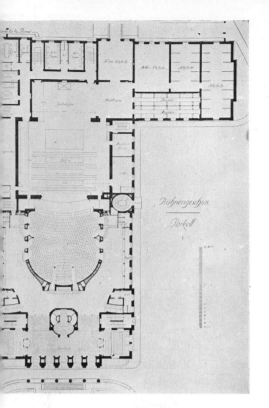

229, 230. GOETHE'S THEATRE AT WEIMAR. Floor
plan of the present structure.

*Littmann, "Das Grossherzogliche
Hoftheater in Weimar"*

231. *Hamlet*, FROM A PAINTING BY BENJAMIN WEST.

Cincinnati Art Museum

239. EDMUND KEAN AS SHYLOCK.

240. SARAH SIDDONS, ORIGINAL UNPUBLISHED WATER
COLOR BY HARGREAVES.

241. CHARLES KEAN AS RICHARD III.

Theatre Collection, N. Y. Public Library

242. RICHARD BRINSLEY SHERIDAN, FROM A
PORTRAIT BY JOSHUA REYNOLDS.

244. Madame Ristori as Lady Macbeth.

243. Coquelin as Cyrano de Bergerac.

245. Ernesto Rossi.

246. Tomasso Salvini as Othello.

the Thief, to which Carl Michael Bellman (1740-95) contributed some attractive lyrics and music which are still popular. Olof Kexel (1748-1796) wrote a number of extremely broad farces; *Kapten Puff* and *Michel Wingler* are probably the best. Johan Magnus Lannerstjerna (1758-1797) and Karl Envallson (1756-1806), who wrote more than eighty comedies, were associates of Bellman and are grouped with him. The only other playwright of any note was that follower of *Sturm und Drang*, Bengt Lidner (c.1757-93), who was responsible for *Erik XIV, Medea, The Death of Countess Spastara* (1783) and *The Last Judgment* (1788). Sweden's only important woman writer of this period was the poet Anna Maria Lenngren (c.1754-1817) who wrote anonymously for many years. She translated a number of contemporary dramas into Swedish and when her identity became known she was honored by the Swedish Academy.

RUSSIA

We left the Muscovite Empire with Peter the Great just back from his travels about Western Europe and ready to begin his reforms which were to transform a backward nation into one of the greatest nations of the world, a position from which she has since receded for only brief intervals. Individual names of authors began to stand out, the first being FEOFAN PROKOPOVITCH (1681-1736), who was a religious writer as well as a composer of verses and plays. Though these last were not published until after his death they were played in various parts of Russia during his lifetime. *Vladimir*, a tragi-comedy, was staged in Kiev in 1702 and in 1705 was played in the Red Square in Moscow. This play, politically enough, has many references to Peter's military exploits and was acted in Russian, probably by the German group headed by Johann Kunscht of Danzig. This company also acted translations from the contemporary German drama, *Hauptaktionen* and *Hanswurstiades*, which would have permitted the introduction of recent historical events into their action. The next writer to appear on the scene was a non-Russian, the Moldavian prince ANTIOCHUS DMITRIEVITCH KANTEMIR (1708-1744), whose name would not merit inclusion in a history of the theatre if he had lived at any other period. His plays were satires (the first having appeared in 1729), but he was better known as a translator and composer of satiric poetry.

VASSILI KIRILLOVITCH TREDIAKOVSKI (1703-69) was born in Astrakhan, the son of a local pope. While still a student at the Slavo-Graeco-Latin Academy, he wrote two plays, *Jason* and *Titus*, which were acted by the students. He translated Boileau's *L'Art Poétique*, Fénelon's *Télémaque;* Horace's *De Arte Poetica.* His real contribution came in philology and grammar; but Pushkin was the first Russian to recognize that fact. Trediakovski resented the advent and success of Lomonosov and Sumarokov and criticised them bitterly because he was jealous of anyone's impinging on his orbit. MICHAEL VASSILIEVITCH LOMONOSOV (1714-65), a poet and indifferent writer of tragedies, encouraged the German influence on Russian literature. Like Trediakovski, he aided in developing a literary Russian language, of which the first important name was that of ALEXIS PETROVITCH SUMAROKOV (1718-77), who has been called "The Father of the Russian Theatre," and who, with characteristic immodesty, referred to himself as the "Racine of the North." Perhaps the one thing that he did best was praise himself and complain about others' ill-treatment and disparagement; no doubt this was but a natural reaction to his excessive vanity.

Sumarokov was born and educated at St. Petersburg (the present day Leningrad), where by order of Peter the Great, plays had to be represented at least twice a year in all schools. Not only native religious plays and interludes were given, but translations of foreign work of which Molière seems to have been a great favorite. This was considered the most efficacious method of teaching students to apply themselves to modern literature. One of the most brilliant of these pupils was Sumarokov, whose compositions were considered worthy of publication at the school's expense. Upon leaving in 1740, he naturally turned to playwriting; his plays were primarily an imitation of those protagonists of polite tragedy, Racine and Voltaire. Having been educated for the Cadet Corps, literature was only an avocation until one of his tragedies was acted by fellow-members of his corps and won him some reputation. The Empress Elizabeth, like the Empress Anna Ivanovna, who doted on Italian actors and *commedia dell' arte*, was passionately fond of the theatre, and demanded on pain of punishment that her entire court attend the Russian interludes which were acted on Sundays. One of Sumarokov's plays won her attention, and she became interested as well in Volkov, the son of a tradesman from Yaroslav. The latter was so inspired that he returned home and converted a building into a theatre and began producing plays; first with amateurs, then professionals. His reputation soon spread to the Russian Court and he was summoned to St. Petersburg. A theatre was built at the capital and opened in 1756 with Sumarokov as director. But the playwright's bad disposition and complaints about real or imaginary slights, caused his removal to Moscow in 1760. He continued to write and produce and at the same time wrote recriminatory letters to the Empress, then the brilliant Catherine the Great. This would seem to have been a dangerous habit in the Russia of absolute imperialism, but he died in his bed, a victim of alcoholism and debt.

His *Hamlet* bore no relation to Shakespeare's beyond the first act soliloquy, and though it was his conceit that it was an adaptation, he actually took it from a poor German translation. He patterned his work on Corneille, Racine and Voltaire, but it lacked their polish and the purity of their verse; his historical plays which he claimed were based on Russian subjects bore little more than libelous resemblance to their originals. The best known of his tragedies are *Khorev*, *Demetrius the Pretender* and *Semiera*, but they are extremely artificial. He contended that his comedies, the best of which, *The Usurer*, *The Guardian*, and *Tressotinius; or, The Pedant*, were based on Molière, though it is doubtful if that gentleman would have recognized the fact.

Interestingly enough, the handsome and intelligent CATHERINE II (1729-96) found time outside that which she had allotted to lovers, cruelty, or the extension of her empire to compose a number of plays and operas. These were naturally flattered far beyond their importance but she managed to preserve more than a customary amount of detachment as an author, certainly as an autocrat. Her plays have no lasting importance but in their day they won praise from no less a person than Diderot, who was often in attendance at her court. Due to the collaborators she chose, the merit of the pieces varied considerably and they usually fell into disfavor. The mild liberalism which she had favored in the beginning was eventually routed by her vigorous censorship and increasing fear of western ideas. Performances took place at the beautiful little court theatre in the Hermitage Palace in which the marble seats were arranged as an amphitheatre. Needless to say, the audience was as brilliant as that of any New York or West End first night.

Her first published play was the comedy *O Tempora* (1772), in which the personages bore the names of the characteristics they resembled; the same year *Mrs. Grumble's Birthday* caricatured the educated classes and their affectations; sections from *The Merry Wives of Windsor* went into her "translation," *A Pretty Basketful of Linen*, in which Falstaff became Polcadoff, which might be translated as Half-Ton. *Rurick*, to quote the title page, was "modelled on the historical plays of Shakespeare without observing the ordinary rules of the classical drama." At any rate, it was an historical drama concerning Rurick, Russia's first grand-duke.

DENIS IVANOVITCH VON VISINE (1744-92), or Von Viezin to give it the German spelling, was one of the brightest dramatic lights of Catherine's time. At fourteen he had been taken to the theatre and to quote him, though the entertainment was poor, he "nearly went mad with joy"; but it was the beginning of a love that lasted all his life, though he wrote only two memorable plays, the humor of which has been compared not too unfavorably with that of Gogol, particularly *Revizor*. The first, *The Brigadier* (1766), was a comedy that enjoyed a very great success, though it lacks any subtlety, being entirely in black and white. After living abroad on his wife's money he wrote *The Minor* (1778), his other comedy, which showed a good deal of structural advance over the first play but when it was performed, Potemkin is said to have called out to the dramatist, "Die now, at once!—or never write again!" He followed the latter half of the advice.

Several minor playwrights came next. JAKOV BORISSOVITCH KNIAJNINE (1747-91) was a highly imitative writer whose work, like Sumarokov's, copied French and Italian originals. His *Dido* was based on Metastasio, and *Rosslav* and *Vadim* which brought down Catherine's wrath upon his head as she considered it too liberal, were neo-classic. VASSILI IAKOVLEVITCH KAPNIST (1757-1824) had the good fortune to survive the Empress; she had forbidden the performance of his *Chicanery*, which attacked the abuse of Russia's judicial power and the general venality of judges. Paul I liked the piece so much that he permitted its performance in 1798, to the vast entertainment of its audiences. VLADIMIR IGNATIEVITCH LOUKINE (1757-1824) endeavored to introduce middle-class comedy into a country which did not enjoy a true *bourgeoisie*. He was much influenced by Marivaux, Diderot and Beaumarchais, but he did not have enough talent to reproduce the effectiveness of their work in his native tongue.

Though GABRIEL ROMANOVITCH DERJAVINE (1743-1816) did not write any original dramatic work until he was past sixty, we include him because he was one of Catherine's collaborators. Not long after he wrote the ode *Felitsa*, which celebrated Catherine's charms, he was severely reprimanded by the Empress, because as her second secretary, she complained that he was too free with his hands. *Dobrynia* (1804) was an attempt to establish a drama based on that of Greece, but it was doomed to ignominious failure. Derjavine enjoyed a high contemporary reputation, but he never recovered from the castigation given him by the critical Pushkin.

Another collaborator of Catherine's, NICHOLAS IVANOVITCH NOVIKOV (1744-1818) has produced enough to stand on his own feet. He was a critic and journalist who was associated with the Empress in the production of a literary journal *The Drone*, which she ordered suppressed when she grew bored and annoyed with it. He was a it is for this reason that he has been compared to the great Tolstoi.

CATHERINE ROMANOVNA, PRINCESS DACHKOV (1743-1810), who was primarily interested in science and politics, was commanded by the Semiramis of the North to write a comedy. The political aspect of Russia interested her intensely, and upon her return from a two-year sojourn abroad, she was inclined to return to politics rather than the theatre. Catherine forestalled any such decision by offering her the presidency of the Academy of Science, which, albeit somewhat reluctantly, she accepted and held for twelve years.

Certain other writers who began their work in this century belong more properly in the period of transition from the so-called classical to the so-called romantic school. The status of the stage and acting was not particularly high despite the smiles cast upon the theatre by Catherine or by Paul I. Russia was at least a century behind other countries and theatrical conditions reflected that status.

POLAND

Mention has been made in the last chapter of Russia's indebtedness to a country which has been oppressed again and again, and no longer exists as a nation (1940). The Poles have always been receptive to the call of the Roman Catholic Church, so that mystery plays were a natural part of their theatrical beginnings. Despite the difference, which was as wide as the ideological gulf between the Greek and Roman churches, some of these plays were transmitted to their fellow Slavs across the precarious border. The first recorded secular play was *The Return of the Greek Ambassadors* by Jean Kochanowski in 1578.

French influence was predominant in Poland at a time when all Europe was feeling the Gallic influence; ever since Henry III of France was the elective king of Poland there had been a strong bond of sympathy between the two nations. In 1661 *Le Cid* was played in a Polish translation by André Morsztyn. Plays were performed at court or in the palaces of rich nobles but the people never had a chance to glimpse them and it was not until the 19th of November, 1765 that the first public playhouse was opened. Performances were given not only in Polish but in French, English, German and Italian as well.

It has been said that the Polish theatre had two fathers, the King, Stanislaw-August Poniatowski, who footed the bills for the first public theatre in the country, and a young military officer, ADALBERT BOGUSTAWSKI (1760-1829), who quitted the royal service in 1778 in order to indulge his love for the theatre. He was an actor, opera singer, director, head of the dramatic school, translator and playwright. This jack-of-all-trades, or man of genius, depending upon your estimate of his ultimate worth, handled Polish theatre affairs as sole director of the official theatre from 1783 until 1814. In addition to assembling a really respectable company of actors, he persuaded such literary men as Count Alexander Fredro to write for the stage. His thespians included the tragedians Owsinski and Szymanowski, the comic players Hempinski and Zolkowski, as well as Mme. Truskolawska and her daughter Ledochowska, who has been called the Polish Mrs. Siddons. So the Polish theatre was begun and was a flourishing enterprise up until September, 1939. Now the actors and authors as well as all the people of that unhappy country are scattered.

XIX

ENGLAND AND THE BRITISH THEATRE

IN EXTENSION

(1710-1815)

THE theatre in North America emanated from England and Ireland. Actors and dramatists traveled backwards and forwards across the Irish Sea. For a long time there was only one-way traffic from England to America but in the century to follow, the nineteenth, America was to begin to pay her cultural debt to Britain.

We resume our story of the British theatre when fat Queen Anne was on the throne and Marlborough ruled England through his duchess, Sarah, who ruled the Queen. The large theatre in the Haymarket was open, the wits were gathering in the coffee houses, French dramatists were visiting England and witnessing the wondrous court productions with their handsome settings, and the actors of Albion were more respected than they had ever been. Theatrical matters were changing for the better because the size of the new Vanbrugh playhouse in the Haymarket was recognized as a mistake and the expectation of large profits was not realized. Its location in present-day Piccadilly Circus proved satisfactory but the trouble arose over the fact that there were not enough regular playgoers to support a theatre of that size. Other managers recognized this fact and built small theatres in the Haymarket, Lincoln's Inn Fields and Goodman's Fields. There it was possible to enjoy a performance, to hear the lines and see the small and telling business of the actor. The real days of bellowing came with the huge theatres of the next century.

As was indicated in the last English chapter the character of the audience was changing. Queen Anne cared nothing for the theatre and the first of the Georges could not have understood the actors had he attended. Since the nobles had become less affluent, their places in the theatre were being taken by the well-to-do tradesmen in a conscious effort to ape their so-called betters. Some of them had married into aristocratic families and so found their places in the play-house quite naturally. This had the inevitable effect of emasculating (or refining, depending on your point of view) Restoration comedy and transferring the emphasis to sentiment. Except for Otway, tragedy had amounted to nothing since the closing of the theatres, so the vulgarizing had no chance to pervert its nobility.

The Augustan Age (so-named out of flattery of George I) in the theatre covers the first half of the century and one of its principal names was that of COLLEY CIBBER (1671-1757), whose career began in the Restoration but whose influence and importance came later. He was the son of the Danish sculptor, Caius Gabriel Cibber, who settled in England where he became a wealthy and celebrated artist. Colley began his career as an actor with Betterton's company at Drury Lane in 1690 but soon turned to playwriting as well. His first comedy was *Love's Last Shift; or, The Fool in Fashion* (1696), of which Congreve said that it had "a great many things that were like wit in it." Vanbrugh honored it by writing a sequel, *The Relapse*, in which Cibber also played the lead and established himself as a come-dian of merit. Then came the delightful *She Wou'd and She Wou'd Not; or, The Kind Impostor* (1702) which he followed with his best play, *The Careless Husband* (1704), written for Mrs. Oldfield and himself.

During the course of the next thirty years Cibber was prominently identified as an actor and manager both at the Haymarket and at Drury Lane, but it was a period of complicated lawsuits and con-stant shifting of personnel. The only peaceful element was the con-stant good humor, tact and friendliness of Cibber who declined to allow anyone to quarrel with him, always bowing and lifting his hat even when his opponent would not speak. In the end, the dispute was always settled in favor of Colley. He saved his anger for the newspaper critics who he declared, "took upon them very often to censure our management, with the same freedom and severity as if we had been so many ministers of state." This remark was not only typical of his thoughts but of his literary expression as well. Among his collaborators in theatre management were the actors Robert Wilks, Thomas Doggett, Barton Booth and the writer Sir Richard Steele.

In 1717 Cibber stirred up a hornet's nest with *The Non-Juror* (adapted from Molière's *Tartuffe*) because he made the leading char-acter an English Catholic priest who was fomenting rebellion, and dedicated it to George I. The king was so pleased by this attention that he granted the author two hundred guineas. With an abusive prologue by Nicholas Rowe, the play ran for eighteen nights to the annoyance of the Jacobite and Catholic factions in national politics. The sentiments of the play pleased the Whigs, and that undoubtedly was responsible for his appointment as Poet Laureate in 1830.

Two years before this he had returned the courtesy shown him by Vanbrugh with the completion of the latter's last play *The Provoked Husband* (1728). Saddened by the deaths of Mrs. Oldfield and Robert Wilks, he sold his share in the theatre in 1732 and rarely appeared afterwards on the stage. He published his famous and delightful *An Apology for the Life of Colley Cibber, Comedian . . . with an Historical View of the Stage during his Own Time* (1740). Modern scholarship has confirmed the judgments of Horace Walpole, Oliver Goldsmith and even his grudging enemy, Samuel Johnson, for there is no more acute analysis of English acting than that provided by the amiable and sharp-witted Colley Cibber.

Lovely ANNE OLDFIELD (1683-1730) was the deftest comedienne of her century. She had been apprenticed to a seamstress but could often be heard reciting verses from plays to her family. One day George Farquhar happened to pass by while she was performing. He was so charmed with her voice and manner that he brought her to the attention of Christopher Rich, who engaged her in 1700 for Drury Lane. It was not, however, until 1704 that they realized what a treasure they possessed for, like Mrs. Barry, her powers were slow in revealing themselves upon the stage. Cibber however studied her work and believed that she could carry the part of Lady Modish in *The Careless Husband*, which she played so brilliantly as to win the town; in fact she is even credited with many of the play's best lines. High comedy was her forte; her walk, her carriage or the glance of her eye was enough to provoke a judicious chuckle or even a laugh. She avoided tragedy when she could, but her portrayals of such roles as Cleopatra and Semandra in *Mithridates* were successful. Despite her alliances with Arthur Mainwaring and Lt. General Charles Churchill, by each of whom she had a son, she was respected in her private life, for she was the friend and intimate of many ladies of quality. When she died her body lay in state and she was buried in Westminster Abbey with half of London in tears.

BARTON BOOTH (1681-1733) was as distinguished in tragedy as Mrs. Oldfield was in comedy. He was a Shakespearean actor of note and also played the pseudo-classic or pathetic tragedies which came into vogue shortly after the turn of the century. Of these, by far the best was Addison's *Cato* (1713), which established Booth as the leading serious actor of the country. Like so many of England's best actors, he began in Dublin, for in those days there were close ties between the royal playhouses of London and Dublin. (The Irish showed an earlier and warmer appreciation of the stage than the northern Scottish capital where minds were still overly influenced by the strictures of John Knox.) His London debut was at Lincoln's Inn Fields in 1700 as Maximus in *Valentinian*, and he remained there for four seasons before going over to Betterton from whose training he profited from 1705 to 1708. That year he transferred to Drury Lane where he stayed for twenty years. His best tragic parts were Cato, the Ghost in *Hamlet*, Hotspur and Brutus. In comedy he shone as the gay Lothario in Rowe's *The Fair Penitent* in the Drury Lane production of 1714. He, too, won the nation's admiration and respect and was buried in Westminster Abbey.

A gayer partner for Mrs. Oldfield was ROBERT WILKS (1665-1732), that lively Irishman whose work in Dublin won him a letter of introduction to Betterton, who persuaded Rich to take him on. But he did not advance very rapidly and so, at the advice of the older actor, he returned to the Irish capital where he made such a reputation that Rich begged him to come back to London. The native audiences were so anxious for him to stay in Ireland that the Duke of Ormond, Lord Lieutenant of Ireland, issued a warrant to prevent his leaving the country. However, he and his wife managed to slip out with Farquhar, who was on his way to London and writing fame. He produced *The Constant Couple* for Wilks who repaid him by playing Sir Harry Wildair so delightfully that London audiences were ecstatic and the dramatist's reputation was assured. The actor's gayety was supported by his careful study of a part and his judicious attention to detail. In comedy he was brilliant; and in tragedy, natural, if not inspired. The other roles in which he excelled were Mirabel, Archer, and Don Felix in Mrs. Centlivre's *The Wonder*. In his time there was never a man who loved acting more. If he did not play every night he was unhappy, and he occasionally disrupted the company by his demands to play. His modesty, however, was proverbial and his generosity great. When Farquhar died he left the care of his two young daughters to the actor who justified his friend's implicit faith in him.

To most people the name of JOSEPH ADDISON (1672-1719) at once conjures up that famous periodical, *The Spectator*, and Sir Roger de Coverley, one of the most famous characters in English letters. It is to be regretted that he never attempted the transfer of this delightful gentleman to the stage, though his accomplishments in that medium do not suggest that it would have been successful. During his later twenties he spent some time in France where he absorbed the pseudo-classical mode of tragedy, with the result that his most famous work, *Cato* (1713), is a carefully composed but cold drama. It was puffed into great success both by the Whigs, with whom its author was aligned, and by the Tories, who wanted it known that they were just as patriotic as their rivals. His only other play *The Drummer; or, The Haunted House* (1716) was an indifferent comedy and a failure. Addison was more of a politician and scholar than dramatist.

The Irish-born SIR RICHARD STEELE (1672-1729) was the other half of the literary partnership of which Addison was the stronger from a literary point of view. However, there was no comparison between the two men in the theatre as Steele had real and deserved success with several of his own comedies and later was part of the management of Drury Lane. (In fact the theatre was once closed for three days to show political displeasure at some measures he was opposing in Parliament.) His *The Funeral; or, Grief à la Mode* (1701) was fresh, clean fun and marked the turn from the prolonged indecency of the Restoration writers. The lively Mrs. Verbruggen gave one of her best performances in this play which gave great impetus to the sentimental comedy which was to have so much success throughout the century. *The Lying Lover; or, The Ladies' Friendship* (1703) was based on Corneille's *Le Menteur* and was moral in tone. Steele's hatred of duelling, which arose from an injury he had inflicted on an opponent in 1695, is prominent in the gaol scene of this play. *The Tender Husband; or, The Accomplished Fools* (1705) presented the author's sentiments on successful marriage. It achieved such success that Mrs. Oldfield was asked again and again to play Biddy Tipkin. Years later Steele admitted that Addison had written several of the best scenes; he could do successfully for another's play what he could not do for his own.

Steele's last and best play, *The Conscious Lovers*, was produced in 1722 and boasted an excellent cast headed by Barton Booth as Young Bevil and Mrs. Oldfield as Indiana. The sufferings of the latter are said to have caused army officers to weep but Wilks quipped that the officers would fight none the worse for it. The dialogue was good and the characters were carefully depicted in well-thought-out situations.

In contrast, NICHOLAS ROWE (1674-1718) failed at comedy in his one effort, *The Biter* (1704), which is said to have amused only the author when it was staged at Lincoln's Inn Fields. His tragedies met a better fate; *The Ambitious Stepmother* (1700); *Tamerlane* (1702), which was supposed to suggest the struggle between William III and Louis XIV; and *The Fair Penitent* (1704) based on Field and Massinger's *The Fatal Dowry*, which won the admiration of the renowned Dr. Johnson. In the latter play Mrs. Oldfield was excellent as Calista and Booth's Lothario was so famous that the name was adopted into the language as a synonym for rake. Rowe's most successful play was

The Tragedy of Jane Shore (1714), better known simply as *Jane Shore*, in which Mrs. Oldfield, as the unhappy heroine, carried the run to nineteen nights at Drury Lane. In 1715 Rowe succeeded the playwright Nahum Tate as Poet Laureate. His principal claim to lasting fame, however, came from his editing of the first modern edition of Shakespeare's plays in 1709. Unfortunately he based his edition on the corrupt Fourth Folio but his knowledge of the stage and play construction permitted him to divide the plays reasonably into scenes, and to note actors' entrances and exits. His notes on production and Shakespearean traditions were gathered for him from Stratford sources by none other than Thomas Betterton. The illustrations in Rowe's edition are in all probability drawn from contemporary actors and staging, and present a clear picture of production methods.

The essayist, poet and critic ALEXANDER POPE (1688-1744) advocated pseudo-classicism in tragedy. The theory was carried out by such men as JOHN DENNIS (1657-1734) with his *Iphigenia* (1700), *The Comical Gallant* (1702) and *The Invader of His Country* (1720). CHARLES GILDON (1665-1724) wrote *The Roman Bride's Revenge* (1697), *The Patriot* (1703) and *A Life of Mr. Thomas Betterton* (1710). AMBROSE PHILIPS (1675-1749) adapted *The Distrest Mother* (1712) from Racine's *Andromaque* (called a good translation by William Hazlitt) which held the stage for more than a century with Mrs. Cibber, Mrs. Barry, and Mrs. Siddons in the lead. CHARLES JOHNSON (1679-1748) also drew on Racine but his best known play is *Coelia* (1732), a domestic tragedy. AARON HILL (1685-1750) drew *Zara* (1736) and *Alzira* (1736) from Voltaire after borrowing *The Fatal Extravagance* (1721) from *The Yorkshire Tragedy* and seeking inspiration in English history for *Elfrid; or, The Fair Inconstant* (1710) and *King Henry the Fifth; or, The Conquest of France by the English* (1723). More successful than any of these in the pseudo-classical school which followed the precepts of neo-classicism in France was JAMES THOMSON (1700-1748), a disciple of Addison. He turned to classical subjects with a vengeance during those years when every new season produced its complement of Greeks and Romans. After the success of his series of poems, *The Seasons*, he turned to the stage with *Sophonisba* (1729), which has the priceless line, "O Sophonisba, Sophonisba, O." This play was so parodied that he had to rewrite it. Although Aeschylus was the source for his *Agamemnon* he peopled it with characters out of contemporary life. Walpole's efforts at censorship were obviously attacked in this and as a result, Thomson's next play was proscribed. *Edward and Eleanora* (printed 1739) drew on *Alcestis* but its principal interest is that Lessing found inspiration in it for his *Nathan der Weise*. He collaborated with David Mallet on the masque *Alfred* (1740), which contains the song "Rule Britannia," for which Thomas Arne wrote the music. Thomson's final play *Tancred and Sigismunda* (1745) owes much to Le Sage and *Gil Blas* and though it is largely smothered with pseudo-classicism, it contains some hint of the coming romantic movement.

Ballad operas, masques, and pantomime were all dramatic forms that required music and enjoyed much vogue in the eighteenth century British theatre. The master of the first was JOHN GAY (1685-1732) whose lesser work is completely overshadowed by the delightful satire *The Beggar's Opera* (1728), staged at Lincoln's Inn Fields under the management of John Rich. It is said to have made "Rich gay and Gay rich" from its sixty-two performances which were brightened by the lovely Lavinia Fenton (soon to be Duchess of Bolton) as Polly and Thomas Walker as the gallant and fascinating highwayman, Macheath. (Quin had declined the part, and Cibber was afraid to produce it at Drury Lane.) The play was political dynamite as the bribery of Sir Robert Walpole was caricatured. He was present at the opening and when people turned to see how he was taking it, he brazenly called out "Encore." He had his revenge, however, because *Polly* (1729) was forbidden performance by the authorities. This scandal brought fame and money to Gay because everyone rushed to buy a copy of the printed play. It was not until 1777 that it was staged in England by George Colman the Elder when he was manager of the Haymarket, but it did not measure up to its predecessor. None of Gay's other plays are of either literary or theatrical value.

English pantomime, which was musical and contained topical songs almost from its inception, is not to be confused with the true meaning of the word, which is dumb-show. Its beginnings are not altogether clear for the form came in part out of *commedia dell' arte* and from the dances utilized in the masques, which were rarely given after the withdrawal of royal support. Satiric songs, dancing and music answered the tragic Italian opera, already opposed by ballad-opera.

Colley Cibber records what must have been the first pantomime, though Genest (stage historian) has no information concerning it. Cibber says that there was a mimic story about Mars and Venus told in dance and gesture. Genest records John Thurmond's *Harlequin Dr. Faustus* (1723) at Drury Lane, to which John Rich answered with *The Necromancer; or, History of Dr. Faustus* in December of that year. Though Rich, who became a celebrated harlequin, had been associated with *Harlequin Executed* (1717), he had to fight a difficult battle with Drury Lane in the early days. For that reason he welcomed an opportunity to exploit his own talents in order to bring people to Lincoln's Inn Fields and later Covent Garden (which he built in 1733). Meanwhile, the older theatre employed William Pinkethman, as harlequin. The pantomime was used as an afterpiece to the tragedy and there was no incongruity in the mind of the spectator. After all it must be recalled that this form had been introduced with Otway's *The Cheats of Scapin* (1677), an English version of Molière's *Les Fourberies de Scapin*. They have continued to exist down to the Christmas of 1939, for they have become a holiday tradition in England.

After Rich, the most noted exponent of this theatrical form was Joseph Grimaldi (1779-1837), whose memory will ever be associated with the celebrated production of *Mother Goose* in 1806. This style of entertainment was just as popular in Ireland, Scotland and the English provinces as it was in London. It was played in America before the Revolution but never caught the public's fancy. An equivalent type of musical extravaganza which might be called the American version of pantomime came into being about the middle of the nineteenth century, in the manner of *The Black Crook* in 1866.

Now we must turn to the man who introduced domestic tragedy and who was responsible for the first serious drama having as its hero a man who was not a member of the nobility. GEORGE LILLO (1693-1739) with *The London Merchant; or, The History of George Barnwell* (1731) thus changed the whole course of English tragedy, though none of his plays seem to have great merit today. His first play was the ballad opera, *Silvia; or, The Country Burial* (1730) and was followed by the aforementioned middle-class drama which had real kinship with *A Yorkshire Tragedy*. Then he produced a murder play, *Fatal Curiosity*, which in plot resembles Werner's *The Twenty-fourth of February* and Rupert Brooke's *Lithuania*. In addition he was responsible for a masque, *Britannia and Batavia* (1734); *The Christian Hero* (1735); a tragedy, *Marina*, an adaptation of *Pericles* (1738); and the posthumously produced tragedy *Elmerick; or, Justice Triumphant*.

HENRY FIELDING (1707-1754) famed as a novelist had much more in common with Gay than he did with Lillo. He began his literary career as a playwright and continued as such until the Licensing Act of 1737 cut short his work just at the time when he might have been expected to turn out plays that would have endured. None of his plays has much value except perhaps *Tom Thumb* (1730), which he reworked as *The Tragedy of Tragedies* (1731) along the general lines of Buckingham's *The Rehearsal* in which he burlesqued the weakness of tragedy and the lack of literary invention afflicting the English stage. It was only in his lively burlesques that he had anything special to offer the theatre. *Author's Farce* (1730), *The Grub Street Opera* (1731), *The Covent Garden Tragedy* (1732) and *Pasquin, A dramatick Satire on the Times* (1736), which belabored the corrupt practices of Sir Robert Walpole and his followers, were all burlesques. The daring of the last-named piece was surpassed by *Historical Register for the year 1736* (1737).

As a result of these attacks, Walpole persuaded Parliament to pass the Licensing Act of 1737, which theoretically limited the playhouses by making Covent Garden, Drury Lane and the Haymarket the only legal theatres. All other houses had to, and did, produce illegally. They called their plays concerts and concentrated on pantomime and other subterfuges. But the real reason for the bill was the creation of a licensing system for plays which insured censorship at the source. In 1788 the law was amended to permit performances in other than patent houses for periods not exceeding sixty days, and all pretense of restricting the number of theatres was wiped out by the Theatres Act of 1843.

The right of the Lord Chamberlain to censor plays was retained and still is in effect. Many people contend that this is the reason for so much puerility in English dramatic writing. This is probably an unjust accusation for the law does not breed childishness, though occasionally it does prevent the production of really important plays. As is characteristic of Britain, however, such plays are produced by clubs for audiences made up of members and no tickets are sold. Therefore, most of the banned plays have been performed anyway, though their audiences have been small and select and the wide British public has been denied them. Due to increased democracy brought about by the Second World War, so much cumbersome British tradition is passing that perhaps the government will discover that its citizens are adult and can be trusted to pick their own dramatic fare. It would be ironic if German air raids were to bring about freedom from theatrical censorship.

But to return to the eighteenth century and Fielding, the Licensing Act ended his connection with the theatre for he had been acting as manager of the Haymarket. He wrote only one more play, at the request of David Garrick, and that was merely the reworking of an old piece.

HENRY CAREY (d.1743) after writing indifferent farces, turned to burlesques. His most famous was *Chrononhotonthologos*, or to give it its full title, *The Tragedy of Chrononhotonthologos: Being the most Tragical Tragedy, that ever was Tragediz'd by any Company of Tragedians* (1734). It is celebrated for its tongue-twisting opening in the antechamber of the palace, to which Rigdum-Funnidos and Aldiborontiphoscophornio enter. Rigdum-Funnidos speaks, "Aldiboron-tiphoscophornio! Where left you Chrononhotonthologos?"

It would have been a pleasure to have seen this play performed in Dublin and to have heard the jaw-breaking and tongue-twisting names emerge with a rich Irish brogue. There is no record that JAMES QUIN (1693-1766), with all his fondness for jokes, ever played it. But Quin was not an Irishman anyway, even though, as a young man, he was a popular actor at the Theatre in Smock Alley.

This playhouse had quite a history for it had been founded in 1662 and had been the scene of two shocking disasters in thirty years. The galleries fell during a performance of *Bartholomew Fair* in 1671 and again in 1701 when the scandalous Shadwell's *The Libertine* was being played. One wonders if the audiences were not a little suspicious of the underpinnings, but the blue-nosed element said it was a judgment sent from heaven as a warning. Fortunately for Quin, the house was torn down and a new theatre on the same site played host to him when he appeared as Abel in Sir Robert Howard's *The Committee* in 1710. After several seasons in Ireland, he returned to London to Drury Lane and in 1715 made a hit as Bajazet in Rowe's *Tamerlane*.

In the following season he went over to John Rich's company at Lincoln's Inn Fields, where his Hotspur was much admired. His own hot temper (he killed two men, though the first time was during a duelling scene and was therefore called an accident) was balanced by his generosity and good nature. His sarcastic tongue was balanced by his readiness to help others. When several drunken noblemen rushed back stage in 1721 to kill Rich, Quin and a fellow-actor were able to head them off. This incident was the cause of a series of riots against the activities of the aristocrats to which the king put a stop by stationing a guard of soldiers at each playhouse, a practice which continued for more than a century (doubtless because nobody remembered they were no longer needed).

Quin's slow and portentous speech and his gravity undoubtedly suited some of his roles but became ludicrous in others. His most successful performance took place on the night of November 14, 1746 at Covent Garden when he acted Horatio to Susannah Cibber's Calista and Garrick's Lothario in *The Fair Penitent*, the applause growing so tremendous as to disconcert the actors. He and Garrick rivalled each other in *King Richard III*, but the latter's performance was preferred. Quin's Falstaff in *King Henry IV* was preferred to Garrick's Hotspur. The modernity of Garrick won out, though the two became close and lifelong friends.

CHARLES MACKLIN (c.1697-1797) was Irish born though it was at Bristol that he made his debut as Richmond in *King Richard III* after an adventurous youth. He was called a wild Irishman, probably with justice. He was loved and hated and no two people ever agreed about his personality but all agreed on one thing: he was the greatest Shylock since Shakespeare's day (though Doran claims that no one could have been better than Edmund Kean) for he restored the character to its serious meaning after it had been played as farce-comedy for more than a century. It was in 1741 that he absolutely electrified his audience with his performance (he had kept the manager in ignorance for fear he would forbid it, so he merely walked through the rehearsals). Pope saw it the third night and immortalized it with "This is the Jew that Shakespeare drew." His performance as Sir Archy Macsarcasm in his own comedy, *Love à la Mode* (1759) and as Sir Pertinax Macsycophant in his *The Man of the World* (1780) were both notable.

Born in London with the good Irish name of Raftor, CATHERINE CLIVE (1711-1785) made her debut in *Mithridates* in 1728. In 1731 she made a great hit as a comedienne and singer in Charles Coffey's *The Devil to Pay*. Kitty Clive played mostly at Drury Lane. She was an original member of Garrick's company from 1747 when he took over the management of the house and she was the only actress of whom he stood in awe. She had a sharp tongue but a kindly nature, and this showed in her playing of all types of comic characters from buxom chambermaids to affected fine ladies and natural old women. Her work and her blameless life (she had separated from Mr. Clive soon after her marriage) won praise from Fielding, Garrick, Goldsmith and even the irascible Dr. Johnson. She was particularly delightful as Lucy in *The Beggar's Opera*.

SUSANNAH MARIA CIBBER (1714-1766) was a sister of the composer Thomas Arne, and in 1734 became the wife of the worthless Theophilus Cibber, actor-son of the beloved Colley. Living with him was impossible and she soon left him. As Zara in Aaron Hill's *Zara* (which had been adapted from Voltaire), she made her reputation as a tragic actress. In 1753 she became Garrick's leading lady and by the precept of his more conversational readings, he helped her rid herself of a singsong manner of speaking. She remained with him, to the delight of his audiences, until her death.

MARGARET WOFFINGTON (c.1714-1760), better known as Peg, was Dublin-born and made her debut during childhood as Polly in a children's company production of *The Beggar's Opera*. Possessing beauty and an incomparable figure, she attracted great attention in her native city as Sir Harry Wildair in *The Constant Couple*. This won her a London engagement where she was adored for her "breeches parts" as long as she chose to play them. Her elegant fashionables, such as

Lady Betty Modish and Lady Townley, were among her most successful parts. During the fifth act of a performance as Rosalind in 1757 she suffered a paralytic stroke and, despite a brave effort, was unable to go on and fled from the stage screaming with terror. Brave and beautiful, loose in her living, kind to almost all, caring little for women, generous even in her dying, Peg was one of the real ornaments of the British stage.

We have now come to that fine actor and manager, but indifferent playwright, DAVID GARRICK (1717-79), whose career in the theatre lasted forty years. He began as a playwright with the performance of his *Lethe; or, Aesop in the Shades* (1740) at Drury Lane, but the real sensation was to come the following year when he made his acting debut at Goodman's Fields as Richard III. His natural manner of playing won enthusiastic applause from his audience as it followed along the lines established earlier in the same year by Macklin as Shylock. The town was mad about the new style of playing and packed the theatre every night to see him as Richard; Lear; and Pierre, in *Venice Preserved*. Horace Walpole wrote that "there was a dozen dukes of a night at Goodman's Fields."

His success was so great that the managers of Covent Garden and Drury Lane became alarmed and invoked the 1737 law to force the theatre to close. After a summer season in Dublin, Garrick played for Fleetwood at Drury Lane and stayed with that company, until April, 1745. Then he returned to Ireland for a year or more as joint manager with Thomas Sheridan of the Smock Alley Theatre. After a short season with Rich at Covent Garden, 1746-47, the last he was to play under another's management, he and Lacy bought Drury Lane together with a renewal of the patent. In September he opened with the strongest company he could secure: Spranger, Barry, Macklin, Mrs. Pritchard, Mrs. Cibber, Mrs. Clive and Mrs. Woffington, with whom he had conducted a long affair. When the Woffington affair ended in 1749 he married the lovely dancer Eva Maria Speigel, known on the stage as Mlle. Violetti, and pretty Peg went over to Rich at Covent Garden.

Garrick's company was brilliant and London flocked to see them though some of the older actors looked down their noses at the new-fangled playing. Barry was one of the finest actors of the town and he and his manager played in friendly rivalry at Garrick's theatre. Garrick's Hamlet outdrew Barry's Macbeth but in many of the plays they appeared together, including *Othello* with Garrick in the title role and Barry as Iago; *The Fair Penitent* with Garrick as Horatio and Barry as Lothario; *King Henry V*, with Barry as the King and Garrick as the Chorus; Samuel Johnson's feeble *Irene* (1749), with

Barry as Mahomet and Garrick as Demetrius. Garrick's Benedict to Mrs. Pritchard's Beatrice in *Much Ado About Nothing* delighted the public. However, Barry countered with Romeo to Mrs. Cibber's Juliet with such success that it was not repeated, much to Barry's disgust. Another season was enough and he went to further fame at the rival house, where he could act Romeo as much as he liked and his audiences were only too glad to pay to see him.

At least twenty-four revivals of Shakespeare took place under Garrick's management. However, despite his admiration for the Bard of Avon, he did not hesitate to alter the scripts, giving Macbeth a dying speech and hacking *Catherine and Petruchio* from *The Taming of the Shrew* and *Florizel and Perdita* (in which foolish, lovely Mary "Perdita" Robinson was adored in 1762) from *The Winter's Tale*. He was astute in the management of his theatre for the audiences liked the "refinements" of his versions. Year in and year out, he gave them what they wanted; some years the company was better than others for his temper was sharp and feelings were hurt. Even Mrs. Cibber left him for several years but returned before she died. He produced most of the good new scripts but he was so ill-advised as to reject John Home's romantic *Douglas* (in which the excellent Anne Barry made a tremendous hit as Lady Randolph in 1757) and Goldsmith's *The Good Natur'd Man*. He provided one or two plays himself, notably *The Clandestine Marriage* (1766) which he wrote with the elder Colman and so provided many with the successful role of Lord Ogleby. His identification with Townley's *High Life Below Stairs* (1759) has led various writers to ascribe the play to him and an edition was so assigned under the title of *Bon Ton; or, High Life Below Stairs* (1776).

In 1776 he sold his share in the theatre to Richard Brinsley Sheridan whom he kindly advised in the conduct of the management. A popular call was made for Garrick to act a round of his characters before he took formal leave of the stage, as he had appeared but seldom since 1769. Among others he played Hamlet, Richard III, Lear, Benedict, Abel Drugger in *The Alchemist* (one of his best roles), Kitely in *Every Man in His Humour*, Archer in *The Beaux' Stratagem*, Sir John Brute in *The Provoked Wife* and ended successfully with the youthful Don Felix in *The Wonder*. He died in 1779 and was buried in Westminster Abbey while the nation mourned.

Garrick, as well as the other London managers, took many of the modern plays in his repertory from four popular writers. SAMUEL FOOTE (1720-77) wrote the satirical farces *The Knights* (1749), *The Orators* (1762), the witty farce *The Minor* (1760), and *The Maid of Bath* (1771) which slandered Elizabeth Linley, later Mrs. Sheridan.

ARTHUR MURPHY (1727-1805) wrote the more sentimental *The Way to Keep Him* (1760) and *All in the Wrong* (1761). GEORGE COLMAN the Elder (1732-94), whose plays have quite a sting to them, wrote *Polly Honeycombe* (1760). *The Jealous Wife* (1761) and collaborated in *The Clandestine Marriage* (1766). HANNAH COWLEY (1743-1809) wrote more than twenty plays of all kinds but is best recalled for her comedies; particularly *A Bold Stroke for a Husband* (1783) and *Who's the Dupe?* (1779).

OLIVER GOLDSMITH (1728-74) attacked the sentimental comedy of HUGH KELLY'S (1739-77) *False Delicacy* (1768), and RICHARD CUMBERLAND'S (1732-1811) *The West Indian* (1771). This attack took the form of an essay, as well as the play *The Good Natur'd Man* (1768), which was considered somewhat ungenteel by its audiences, though that did not prevent their laughing at it. Despite the fact that this was not a great play, nor in some respects even a good play, it had real humor and excellent characterization. Goldsmith shed his faults in *She Stoops to Conquer; or, The Mistakes of a Night* (1773), a play that is fully deserving of all the contemporary and posthumous praise it has received. It has been said that it suggests the romantic comedies of Shakespeare. This may have come out of the revival of interest in the great dramatist about the middle of the century. Tony Lumpkin and the Hardcastles are exceptionally well-drawn people, keenly observed and rich in humor.

The Irishman RICHARD BRINSLEY SHERIDAN (1751-1816) is the man about whom more has been written than any other eighteenth century British dramatist. Handsome, lovable, able, reckless, spendthrift and brilliant, he was a true son of his country. His mother was the playwright and story writer, Frances Sheridan (author of *The Discovery*, 1763), and his father was the pompous conceited Dublin actor and elocutionist, Thomas Sheridan. Two of his plays are nearly perfect; *The Rivals* (1775), which drew slightly upon his mother's *A Journey to Bath*; and *The School for Scandal* (1777), the latter being termed by many the most brilliant comedy of the English stage. This may be too high praise but certainly it is worth setting side by side with Congreve, Jonson, and even Shakespeare. It is from the first two that Sheridan drew much of his inspiration. Along with Fielding's mock-tragedy of *Tom Thumb* and Villier's *The Rehearsal; The Critic; or, A Tragedy Rehearsed* (1779) takes its place among the immortals in this satiric form. Sheridan was both too lazy about writing and too occupied with social, managerial and political problems to write as much as he might have. He purchased Drury Lane in 1776 and for a time thoroughly enjoyed all of the endless problems of management. but eventually he grew bored with it and unfortunately sent for his father to run it for him. He had many successes but the poor old theatre was made to supply the money for his houses, his entertaining and his political aspirations.

By 1791 the playhouse had fallen into such disrepair that Sheridan decided to rebuild it rather than attempt to alter it. He was partially financed by his composer father-in-law, Dr. Linley, but expenses went so far beyond what had been anticipated that they were more pressed than ever, and it was not until 1794 that they were able to reopen. However, though he was then in Parliament, he gave the management more attention and was able to pull the theatre out of the hole and make it a paying proposition again, thanks largely to the great acting of Mrs. Siddons and Kemble whom he treated rather shabbily. In 1809 the building burned. Undaunted he set out to raise the money to rebuild again, though he had nothing to do with the management of the new house (the present theatre). It was opened in 1812 by his wife's cousin, Samuel Whitbread acting for a group of bankers. Sheridan was so slightingly treated that he sold out his interest in the enterprise.

He wrote only three other plays, *St. Patrick's Day; or, The Scheming Lieutenant* (1775), the ballad-opera *The Duenna* (1775) and *A Trip to Scarborough* (1777) which was only a cleaned-up version of Vanbrugh's *The Relapse*. As well as for his contribution to the theatre, Sheridan will also be remembered for his two magnificent speeches at the impeachment trials of Warren Hastings (they had more theatrical artifice than sincerity if eye-witnesses can be believed). Sheridan truly ends the Augustan age. He was brilliant in his keen perception of where sentiment should and should not be placed.

The actress who brilliantly created the role of Lady Teazle was FRANCES ABINGTON (1737-1815), a comedienne of charm and ability. She made her debut at the Haymarket in 1755 as Miranda in *The Busybody*, but her real success came in Ireland where she played for five years. It was only upon the insistence of Garrick that she returned to the company at the Drury Lane. She excelled in such comedy parts as Miss Prue in *Love for Love*, Biddy Tipkin, Lucy Lockit and Miss Hoyden, but was no less admired for her Ophelia, Desdemona, or Portia.

Another Irish actress of reputation was DOROTHEA JORDAN (1762-c.1816) who created a considerable reputation in that country and in the north of England before taking London by storm in 1785 with her playing of Peggy in *A Country Girl* (Garrick's reworking of Wycherley's play). Her acting of "romp" parts was delightful and she remained at Drury Lane until 1809, though she had been the mistress of the Duke of Clarence (later William IV) and bore him ten children who were ennobled under the name of Fitz-Clarence. Her Rosalind, Lady Teazle, Imogen and the "breeches part" of William in *Rosina* were favorites with her audiences.

The outstanding English tragic actress was SARAH KEMBLE SIDDONS (1755-1831), the daughter of Roger Kemble, a provincial actor-manager and founder of an acting line which is still represented on the English speaking stage by the Kemble-Coopers. She was of majestic mold; her classic beauty, height and presence aided in her portrayal of tragic roles, though at times her performances were almost overpowering. A legend was current about her frightening audiences into fits by her character-rages and it is undoubtedly true that she frequently awed the spectators. She managed to combine a successful marriage with a theatrical career. Her husband was the indifferent young actor William Siddons, the alliance with whom her parents tried to discourage, but Sarah was a strong-willed woman and went her way in this as in her professional life.

After having been admired in the provinces for several years she was sent for by Garrick and played for him at Drury Lane during his last season, 1775-76, but she was so nervous that her performances were awkward and she was a failure. Discouraged, she returned to the country and played for five years at Bath until Drury Lane again asked her to go back to London. Her second debut on October 10, 1782 as Isabella in Garrick's version of Southerne's *The Fatal Marriage* was a resounding triumph. She reached the pinnacle, however, as Lady Macbeth in 1785, a role which was to remain her finest and the one with which she bade farewell to the stage in 1812. Other parts to which her talents were particularly suited include: Queen Katharine in *King Henry VIII*, which John Kemble so magnificently revived in 1788; Volumnia in Kemble's version of *Coriolanus*; Elvira in *Pizarro* (Sheridan's adaptation of Kotzebue's play); Mrs. Haller in Kotzebue's *The Stranger*; Zara in *The Mourning Bride*; and Lady Randolph in *Douglas*, in which she made her last appearance on the stage in 1819 for the benefit of her younger brother Charles and his wife. Her performances were always carefully studied and though sometimes stiff their proportions were always symmetrical. She lacked Rachel's passion but her playing was dignified and finished.

Sarah's name is always associated with her famous brother JOHN PHILIP KEMBLE (1757-1823), who was educated for the Catholic priesthood but soon discovered that he had no vocation for the church and turned to the stage like other members of his family. He made his debut at Wolverhampton in 1776 in the title part of Lee's *Theodosius* and two years later joined the great Tate Wilkinson who managed the York theatre circuit. Dublin took him to its heart as Orestes in *The Distressed Mother* in 1781 and he continued on to such fame that Drury Lane called him to appear as Hamlet on December 30, 1783. Audiences were never excited by his interpretation of this role but the critics were interested and admired its studied qualities. Two seasons later his Macbeth gave him a popular following which he held until the end. He appeared with his sister in Moore's *The Gamester, King John, Othello,* Cumberland's *The Carmelite* and *Macbeth,* in which Mrs. Siddons is given credit for firing his imagination. His regularity, precision, and detailed performances were also well suited to *Coriolanus* and Addison's *Cato.*

Kemble became manager of Drury Lane in 1788 and retained that post until 1796 when he was arrested for a bill which Sheridan had neglected to pay. His post as manager enabled him to satisfy his desire to present revivals that were more historically correct than the customary presentations of Hamlet and Othello in knee-breeches, silk stockings and peruke. Sheridan persuaded Kemble to resume the management in 1800-01 but the following year he severed his connections with Drury Lane for ever. He went over to Covent Garden as manager and he and Mrs. Siddons held the boards until the devastating fire of 1808 which wiped out the theatre. This all but ruined him and had it not been for the generous loan (later turned into a gift) of ten thousand pounds by the Duke of Northumberland, he would not have been able to rebuild. This accomplished, he opened the new Covent Garden (which was to be destroyed again by fire in 1856 and rebuilt as the present home of opera in London) in 1809. To recoup his losses he raised the admission prices a fraction, including an extra sixpence on the pit. This provoked the famous O. P. Riots (Old Price), which devastated performances for three months. The audience danced the O. P. dance in which they pounded their feet, sang and shouted and prevented the actors from being heard. Their rage was directed at Kemble and Mrs. Siddons, whom they accused of taking exorbitant salaries while the poor were forced to pay for rebuilding their playhouse. The people finally won in the compromise agreement, which reduced pit prices (the extra premium on the boxes was upheld) and wiped out a lot of other objections that had annoyed the vociferous London audiences. English stolidity seems to have been just as non-existent in this case as it had been during the famous Half-Price Riot of 1762 which occurred at Covent Garden during a performance of Dr. Arne's *Artaxerxes.* Kemble managed to regain his popularity and only the growing fame of Edmund Kean (whom he unwisely challenged to rival performances) brought about his gradual eclipse. He retired from the stage in 1817 with a final performance of *Coriolanus.*

While the Kemble-Siddons family which also included Charles, Elizabeth (who as Mrs. Whitlock made a tremendous success in America and played before President Washington), and Marie Therese De Camp (Mrs. Charles Kemble) had stood for fine acting, playwriting reached almost its lowest depths in the history of the English theatre. There were but three writers whose heads were briefly lifted above the general level of mediocrity. THOMAS HOLCROFT'S (1745-1809) best known work was the sentimental comedy *The Road to Ruin* (1792). ELIZABETH INCHBALD (1753-1821) found French and German problem plays fascinating, so she strove to emulate them in English. Showing an unusually fine command of dramatic technique, several of her plays demand respect; namely, the satirical *I'll Tell You What* (1786), *Such Things Are* (1788), which was a plea for the correction of prison abuses, and her *Lover's Vows* (1798). GEORGE COLMAN the Younger (1762-1836) inherited some of his father's writing ability and this, together with his own native wit and a fine sense of humor, enabled him to write several amusing comedies, farces and musical shows. Three of the many pieces which stand out are *Inkle and Yarico* (1787),*The Heir-at-Law* (which contains the celebrated Dr. Pangloss, 1797), *John Bull; or, An Englishman's Fireside* (1803) and *Who Wants a Guinea?* (1805).

What held true of theatrical fare in London held true for all of England and Ireland. In London, public taste was shaped at the three major playhouses but occasionally one of the short-lived minor houses captured the public's fancy. Edinburgh, and curiously enough Dublin, were long hostile to the theatre. However, by the latter half of the seventeenth century the stage had captured a large band of adherents which it has retained until the present day. Dublin fathered a literary renaissance during the twentieth century and is now a stronghold of drama. Of the provincial cities, the high theatrical standards of Liverpool, Birmingham, Bath and York stand out. All actors went on tour so that even the smallest country towns saw first-rate acting.

THE COLONIES AND THE NEW AMERICAN NATION
(1598-1815)

Nine years before the English settlement at Jamestown, Virginia, the first play to be given within the confines of the present borders of the United States was performed in what is now New Mexico. In April, 1598 the explorer Onate reached the shores of the Rio Grande and took possession of this territory on the last day of the month. Mass was followed by a sermon "and in the evening, the performance of an original comedy written by Captain Farfan, on a subject connected with the conquest of New Mexico." This, however, was in Spanish. In 1606 a French masque by Marc Lescarbot was given in Port Royal, Acadia. In 1640 there were dramatic performances and in 1647 a ballet, in Quebec. The first play in English seems to have been an amateur performance in Accomac County on Virginia's Eastern Shore in 1665. Three young men, Cornelius Watkinson, Philip Howard and William Darby were ordered to appear in court to answer charges which declared that they had acted *Ye Bare and Ye Cubb* on August twenty-seventh. They were directed to bring the lines of the play (unhappily not preserved) and the costumes which they wore. They were found "not guilty of fault" and the informer Edward Martin was ordered to appear at the next court "to show why he should not pay ye charges wch accrued."

In 1684 Increase Mather inveighed against "gynecandrical dancing." In 1699 Richard Hunter petitioned John Nafan, Lt. Governor of the New York colony, for the right to present plays but we can find no evidence that he took advantage of the permission. But in the winter of 1703-04, Anthony Aston, the actor and carping critic, came to New York and acted, according to the preface to *The Fool's Opera; or, The Taste of the Age.* He fell in with Jack Charlton, his "old acquaintance, Fencing Master—and Counsellor Regnieur, sometime of Lincolns-Inn," who was his partner and fellow-actor. Whether Hunter had any part in this enterprise is not recorded. In 1709 the Governor's Council passed an act forbidding "play-acting and prize-fighting"; just at whom it was aimed is not clear for Aston had returned to England.

In 1714 *Androboros* was attributed to Robert Hunter, Governor of the New York Colony; this farce satirized the citizenry but most authorities doubt that it was ever performed. An advertisement in the *New York Gazette* for March 16-23, 1729 suggests the possibility of a performance of *Romeo and Juliet* at that time, but such a specialist as G. C. D. Odell (author of the monumental and scholarly *Annals of the New York Stage*) doubts it. Professor Odell reserves the honor of the true establishment of a local stage for *The Recruiting Officer*, December 6, 1732.

Virginia was not so backward, for a "pastoral colloquy" had been acted by the students of the College of William and Mary in Williamsburg in 1702, and in 1716 a playhouse was erected for Charles and Mary Stagg, who were to secure their supporting cast, music and scenery from England. Charleston, South Carolina saw Otway's *The Orphan* on January 24, 1736 and Philadelphia entertained the Murray-Kean company in 1749. These cities, then, were the theatrical capitals of America.

Thomas Kean and Walter Murray opened their engagement on March 5, 1750 at the Theatre in Nassau Street, New York, with *King Richard III*, with Kean probably in the name part. Response was not particularly cordial; many people thought play-acting was sinful and the gentry did not support it consistently. The company was probably ineffectual, though its repertory included such plays as *The Spanish Fryar, Love for Love* and *The Beaux' Stratagem.*

A better company soon arrived with the Hallams, who opened a tour at Williamsburg September 5, 1752 with *The Merchant of Venice.* Upon reaching New York Lewis Hallam, Senior, was dissatisfied with the barren nature of the playhouse, so he built a second one on Nassau Street. This was opened with *The Conscious Lovers,* in which his handsome son Lewis made his debut.

Despite the fact that the newspapers printed statements to the effect that acting aroused passions, the John Street Theatre was opened on December 7, 1767 with *The Beaux' Stratagem;* young Hallam played Archer and his mother, then Mrs. Douglass, spoke the epilogue. The settings were simple and shabby for it was fifteen years since new equipment had been imported from England and no native designers had as yet appeared; lighting consisted of candlelight and oil lanterns.

During the American Revolution the principal American seaports were occupied by British troops who entertained themselves with amateur productions as all professionals were far away in warm Jamaica. Female roles were at first played by the officers, but before long some of the ladies of the town were inducted into the mysteries of acting. We know that Major André, who was later executed as a spy, both designed sets and appeared as an actor.

When the theatres reopened, it was customary for them to have a resident stock company which played a repertory of tragedy, comedy and farce with occasional musical interludes or pantomimes. There were the John Street Theatre in New York, the Southwark Theatre in Philadelphia, the Theatre in East Baltimore Street in the Maryland metropolis, the Dock Street Theatre in Charleston and others which were available. No city could afford a company the year round so the companies divided their time between two or more playhouses. Increasing numbers of the actors were native-born, or Englishmen domiciled in America, so that the establishment of these acting troupes was no longer the problem it had been during the middle of the eighteenth century.

In addition to English repertory, American dramatists were beginning to raise their heads. Many of these pieces were written to arouse feeling against British injustice in the years before the Revo-

lution. The honor of contributing the first play written by an American is shrouded in doubt and controversy, though it seems in all
probability to belong to THOMAS GODFREY (1736-1763) of Philadelphia with his *The Prince of Parthia* (printed 1765) which was not
acted in the author's lifetime. He had added two hundred new lines
to James Thomson's *Alfred* which had been produced during the
Christmas holidays of 1756-57 at the College of Philadelphia. Godfrey's play saw actual professional production in 1767. It was only
by a fluke that this was the first play by an American to be produced
in America, for Colonel Thomas Forrest's *The Disappointment; or,
The Force of Credulity* (1767) was withdrawn from production by
the American Company at the Southwark when it was discovered
that it caricatured various living Philadelphians.

In the meantime, Major Robert Rogers had published his play
Ponteach; or, The Savages of America, the first play written by an
American on an American subject. A fellow-writer of Massachusetts,
Mrs. Mercy Otis Warren (wife of General James Warren, sister of
James Otis, and friend of Samuel Adams, John Adams and Thomas
Jefferson) was very much concerned over political conditions in the
American colonies. Because of this, she wrote the thinly disguised
political satires, *The Adulateur* (1773) and *The Group* (1775). The
young Hugh Henry Brackenridge, whose feelings were akin to those
of Mrs. Warren, contributed *The Battle of Bunkers-Hill* (1776) and
John Leacock wrote *The Fall of British Tyranny; or, American
Liberty Triumphant* (1776). These were answered by the Tory sym-
pathizers with the anonymous *The Battle of Brooklyn* (1776), and
The Blockheads; or, Fortunate Contractor (1782), a comic opera.
The British General Burgoyne (also a playwright) contributed *The
Blockade of Boston* (1775-76), but its performance was interrupted
by an American attack on the city.

It was the Boston-born ROYALL TYLER (1757-1826) who wrote the
first play worthy of consideration from a theatrical or literary point
of view. *The Contrast* (1787) was in many ways a delightful comedy
of American social customs and was performed at the John Street
Theatre on April 16, 1787 by a company including Hallam, John
Henry, Thomas Wignell and Mr. and Mrs. Morris; the strongest cast
which could be assembled at the time. The play had a great success
and when it was published in 1790 President Washington headed the
subscription list. None of Tyler's other plays are noteworthy and
most of them have not survived.

Washington was quite a play-lover. His attendance at the performance of *Darby's Return* in 1789 has frequently been noted. This
play which was based on a character from O'Keefe's *The Poor Soldier,*

was concerned with an Irish soldier who returned to his native land to describe his adventures in America (these included seeing Washington). WILLIAM DUNLAP (1766-1839) was its author and is still regarded as the most important man of the theatre to have come forward up to that time. He was playwright, manager, stage historian, painter and public-spirited citizen of New York. His first play, *The Modest Soldier; or, Love in New York* (1787), was not acted. His first production was *The Father; or, American Shandyism* (1789). He translated or adapted nearly sixty foreign dramas, including a number of Kotzebue's, all of which were serviceable to him as co-manager of the American Company with Lewis Hallam and John Hodgkinson (an English actor who had come to America in 1792). Articles of agreement among the three were drawn up in 1796, the same year that saw the birth of dramatic criticism in this country. In his frequently unreliable but entertaining *History of the American Theatre* (1832), Dunlap tells us that John Adams' son Charles, John Wells, Elias Hicks, Samuel Jones, William Cutting and Peter Irving used to meet after the play to write opinions which were published in the newspapers.

Since the John Street Theatre was too small and too shabby for the rapidly growing New York, a new and handsome playhouse was erected on Park Row across from the City Hall. (This same City Hall still houses our municipal offices.) The Park Theatre was opened January 29, 1798 with a performance of *As You Like It*. During the first season, Dunlap's best play, the tragedy *André* (with Hodgkinson as André and the brilliant English actor Thomas Abthorpe Cooper as his friend) was performed with much success. It was high time that New York had a decent theatre. Boston had replaced her New Exhibition Room with the handsome and imposing Federal St. Theatre in 1749, and Philadelphia, in the same year, had opened the Chestnut Street Theatre, which was modelled on the beautiful Theatre Royal in Bath.

From then on theatrical enterprises blossomed forth continually and much of the old moralistic opposition disappeared. There were occasional recrudescences of this feeling due to such mishaps as the burning of the Richmond Theatre in 1811, when seventy-one people lost their lives. However, the road was opening up and the managers bethought themselves of the advantages of introducing important foreign stars to attract more money to the box office. The resident companies would support them much as they did in Germany and England during the same period and in the same way the summer theatres of America support guest-stars today.

The first of these was JAMES FENNELL (1766-1816) who came to

America in 1793 and attracted considerable attention in Philadelphia. He subsequently claimed that he acted in that city for thirteen weeks for which his receipts were thirteen thousand dollars. In light of the changing monetary values, this return was enormous. After his success other players began to think of the advantages of starring tours, which were eventually to damage the theatre of the entire country both financially and artistically. In the beginning, however, they may have had some good effect by causing stock actors to strive to emulate the visiting stars.

The first really fine English actor to settle in this country, THOMAS ABTHORPE COOPER (1776-1849), decided to discard the fixed stock system for starring tours. He had received his training under Stephen Kemble at Edinburgh. In 1796 he came to this country to act for Wignell in Philadelphia, after a short preliminary season in Baltimore. His fellow-passengers to America included John Bernard and the first William Warren; and it was not long before every ship was depositing English actors on our shores in the hope of winning good American dollars. Cooper was by far the best of the lot. His only rival was the older actor George Frederick Cooke. Cooper made his debut as Macbeth at the Chestnut Street Theatre in 1796 and two seasons later, on February 28, 1798, he first performed *Hamlet* at the Park Theatre where he was to win considerable fame. Not being satisfied with his salary (Mrs. Merry was getting three times as much) he returned to London where he made a brilliant success at Drury Lane, in 1803, as Othello to Cooke's Iago and Charles Kemble's Cassio. This so increased his prestige that when he returned to New York he received $750 a night. From 1808 to 1815 he was associated with Stephen Price in the management of the Park. When they dissolved partnership Cooper took to the road and it has been said that he played one hundred and seventy-six characters in sixty-four theatres, traveling upwards of twenty thousand miles. The Park had become fashionable and Price continued as manager until he went to England to take over the management of Drury Lane, but he did not abandon his American enterprise. In this respect he might be likened to Augustin Daly or Gilbert Miller.

GEORGE FREDERICK COOKE (1756-1811) was a London-born actor, whose principal work was done in England, though he spent the last two years of his life in America. He had played for nearly twenty years before his powers were truly appraised by Dublin, in his performance of *Othello*. In 1801 he triumphed in London as Richard III (his most extraordinary performance), Shylock, Iago and Sir Giles Overreach. He was considered Kemble's only formidable rival, and acted both with him and Mrs. Siddons. Alcohol made such a slave of him that he could not be counted on for his performances. When he did appear, he was likely to be too drunk to act and more than once was so hissed by his audience that the curtain had to be lowered.

Cooper, who had gone to England to look for talent, persuaded Cooke to return to America regardless of the risks involved. When he was sober enough to play, he created a furore in New York, Boston, Philadelphia, Baltimore and in Providence, where on July 29, 1811 he played his last performance. He died in New York in September and was buried in the "strangers' vault" in St. Paul's Church. When Edmund Kean was playing here he erected a monument to him in the churchyard, the first monument to be erected to an actor in America.

From this time on, drama in the United States and the British Isles moved in separate channels. American drama still continued to receive its chief sustenance from England as well as the Continent, and English and Irish actors were more than welcome, but the character of the theatre became nationalistic. America had erected its own dramatic structure and was able to maintain it.

XX

AMERICA'S AGE OF ACTORS

(1815-1905)

THE tendencies noted in the immediately preceding chapter continued for some time to come. No dramatist worthy of serious consideration was to arise during the century, but acting flowered. Perhaps there will never again be such an age of actors in America for currently our interest in the theatre comes largely from the content and style of the play rather than primarily from the actor's part. Previously the classics and a repertory of minor trash were offered over and over again. New plays were not frequently produced and audiences attended the playhouse to judge the relative merits of the acting. It was the era of rivalries. As they judged Forrest by Macready so, a generation later, they were to evaluate Booth by Forrest. Actors attracted an individual following which is only comparable to the fans developed by the films today. Hostilities were far from unknown among the adherents of rival thespians and disorders in the playhouse were an all too common occurrence.

JOHN HOWARD PAYNE (1791-1852) was both an actor and a playwright of some reputation. He is known the world over as the author of *Home, Sweet Home* (music by Sir Henry Bishop) which occurred in his musical play, *Clari, the Maid of Milan* (1823). His melodrama *Julia; or, The Wanderer* (1806) was staged at the Park Theatre. Afterwards he attended Union College but abandoned it in favor of the stage. He made his debut as Young Norval in *Douglas* for Price and Cooper at the Park, on February 24, 1809. He showed talent and was well received. He acted Octavian in *The Mountaineers;* Tancred, and Romeo. He then went to Boston (where he had prepared for the stage) to appear even more successfully at the Federal Street Theatre. Upon his return he acted Rolla, Edgar and Hamlet, playing in Philadelphia, Baltimore and Washington, Richmond, Norfolk, and Charleston during the 1809-10 season. Also in 1809 his second play, *Lover's Vows*, reworked from Mrs. Inchbald's and Benjamin Thompson's version of Kotzebue's *Das Kind der Liebe*, was published.

Though he was successful as a road star, Cooke and others blocked his progress in New York, so that when his friends raised a purse of two thousand dollars, he was glad to sail for England in 1813. Despite the fact that England and America were at war, after a preliminary internment, he made his debut at Drury Lane as Young Norval. He repeated his London triumph in Liverpool and Dublin and then went to Paris during Napoleon's famous Hundred Days, in 1815. Making a friend of Talma, he was granted the freedom of the *Comédie-Française*, which enabled him to begin the study of French plays which were to influence greatly many of his own.

His best tragedy was *Brutus; or, The Fall of Tarquin* (1818), which was a success at Drury Lane with the great Kean in the title part, though Payne's financial returns from the play were insignificant. Of his adaptations of French melodramas, perhaps *Therèse* (1821) was the best. Certainly it paid his debts, for he had been imprisoned after making a failure of the management of Sadler's Wells.

Charles the Second; or, The Merry Monarch (1824) adapted from Alexandre Duval's *La Jeunesse de Henri V* was his best comedy. Washington Irving, his close friend, is said to have been a silent collaborator in this and other of Payne's plays. It secured a real success both in England and America. Charles Kemble was a particularly happy choice for the title role.

When Payne returned to America in 1832, a benefit was arranged for him in the new Park Theatre with all the leading theatrical talent rallying around. *Brutus, Charles the Second* and *Catherine and Petruchio* were the plays chosen to honor him. Charles Kemble, Fanny Kemble, Edwin Forrest, Thomas Abthorpe Cooper and J. W. Wallack were the leading actors who volunteered. Seven thousand dollars was raised at five dollars a ticket throughout the house except for the gallery at one dollar. The Boston benefit the following spring did not raise so much though the *Boston Transcript* states that as many as twenty-five plays from his pen were performed in each season in that city. His benefit in New Orleans, at the Camp Street Theatre in 1835, in which the first Tyrone Power participated, was Payne's last connection with the theatre. He went into the American consular service and died in Tunis where he was serving his country. In 1883 his body was brought back to America and buried in Oakhill Cemetery, in Washington.

While Payne was turning to European sources for his plays Mordecai Noah, and JAMES NELSON BARKER (1784-1858), found their inspiration in native themes. Barker seems consciously to have attempted to provide an American drama because he felt it to be an important part of the cultural life of any nation. His first play to be produced was *Tears and Smiles*, March 4, 1807 at the Chestnut Street Theatre in Philadelphia, with the strongest cast that could be assembled in that city: The first Joseph Jefferson and his wife, the first William Warren (the manager) and his wife, William Wood and his wife, and Mrs. Melmoth. The author recorded this in his own words, as given in Dunlap's history; also stating that it was acted "to a brilliant audience and with complete success." * This comedy of manners evidently derived from Tyler's *The Contrast*, though the manners ridiculed have become French in Barker's play about Philadelphia life.

His second play dealt with the subject of the Embargo Bills of 1807 08 forbidding American ships to engage in foreign trade (an interesting parallel with the present day Neutrality Act). *The Embargo; or, What News?* (1808) was successful, though the man who had suggested the topic to Barker, the actor Blissett, took the script to Baltimore with him to act it there and the author never saw it again. It was not printed and no promptbook has survived.

The first produced play about Indian life by an American was Barker's *The Indian Princess; or, la Belle Sauvage* (1808). Another version of the drama was staged in London at Drury Lane as *Pocahontas; or, The Indian Princess* (1820). This play dealt with Pocahontas, John Smith and John Rolfe. Its importance was increased by the fact that during the first half of the century many plays glorifying the Red Man were partly inspired by Barker's drama.

Scott's novel, *Marmion*, in Barker's dramatization, was played with considerable success in 1812 and continued to be acted for the next forty years, being twice printed. His last play was his best and in this he returned to American history for a subject. *Superstition* (1824) dealt with the regicides who fled to New England to escape punishment by Charles II as his father's murderers. This is woven into a plot about Indians, and Puritan fear of witchcraft, in a sometimes absorbing drama. Barker made a real contribution to the theatre of his day.

MORDECAI MANUEL NOAH (1785-1851) also employed native themes in his plays though his first two dramas, *The Fortress of Sorrento* (1808, not acted) and *Paul and Alexis; or, The Orphans of the Rhine* (1812) were of European extraction. In 1819 he wrote *She Would Be a Soldier; or, The Plains of Chippewa*, for Catherine Leesugg (later the wife of J. H. Hackett), which was based on an incident of the War of 1812. The American Revolution inspired *Marion; or, The Hero of Lake George* (1821), which was performed by the

* Dunlap, William, *History of the American Theatre*. 1832.

Park Theatre company. Sympathy for the cause of the Greek revolutionists prompted *The Grecian Captive; or, The Fall of Athens* (1822).

The Siege of Tripoli (1829) came out of American trouble in the Mediterranean. After its third performance for Noah's benefit, when the audience had left the house, a fire broke out and ruined the theatre. He donated his returns of four hundred dollars toward the relief of the company, for actors were able to accumulate so little financial reserve that disasters of this kind wiped out their costumes and often reduced them to penury. Noah's sympathy and aid were symptomatic of his sense of responsibility toward distressed humanity. He was not an important playwright but his plays enjoyed real success on the American stage.

The most important contributions to culture, however, were still English importations, particularly actors. The first great name after Cooper was that of Junius Brutus Booth (1796-1852) who made his American debut in Richmond in 1821 as Richard III, in which role he had triumphed in London, at Covent Garden, in 1817. He was greeted with enthusiasm and was engaged for the Park in New York, where he opened on October 5, 1821 to tumultuous applause. The money taken in at his benefit seems to have been the nucleus of the funds used to purchase his farm near Bel Air, Maryland, which was to become his permanent home and the birthplace of his celebrated children.

His Iago was noted as were his Hamlet, Lear, Shylock and Sir Giles Overreach. Walt Whitman, writing fifty years later, said that his Richard was magnificent and that no actor so well understood the value of a stage-wait as did Booth. Drink and growing eccentricities imperilled his acting and made the lives of his family a burden. His spirited fencing as Richard and Hamlet was occasionally carried to such length as to require the actors playing Richmond or Laertes literally to fight for their lives. The early career of his more famous son, Edwin, was saddened by his efforts to take care of his father and keep him in shape so that he could continue to act.

Booth's great rival, Edmund Kean (1787-1833), is principally identified with the stage of his native land but his American engagements brought forth almost hysterical praise. He was the finest actor who had yet visited this country when he opened as Richard III, in November, 1820, at the Anthony Street Theatre. Like many English actors of the period he made the mistake of involving himself in a dispute with the press and public. This occurred during his second visit to Boston, which came in June, 1821, when so many people were out of town that he had a poor house his third night and declined to play, even when the manager who had warned him against playing so late in the season, sent for him and told him that the house was filling. He paid for this outburst of temper both in England and in America, when he returned for his second and last tour in 1825. Despite the fact that he apologized for his previous ill-nature, he was hissed and was even the target of missiles hurled by a still unforgiving house. He never came back to America again.

The next English actors of note to appear were CHARLES KEMBLE (1775-1854) and his daughter, Fanny, FRANCES ANNE KEMBLE (1809-93). Their visit had been occasioned by the fame of his daughter's Juliet, which had taken London by storm in 1829. The news of this success spread to America. Our audiences wanted to see for themselves and so, in 1832, the Kembles were engaged to appear at the Park Theatre. Fanny appeared as Bianca in *Fazio* and won the hearts of her auditors, though it was her Juliet that completely captivated them. Her father's noble appearance impressed the spectators and the Kembles became the rage from Boston to New Orleans. This happy state of affairs continued for two years when Fanny surprised everyone by losing her abolitionist heart to a Southern planter, Pierce Butler, and marrying him. Living in the south and being unable to interfere with the slaves proved most trying to her, despite her children, and she left him. They were not divorced until 1849, but she returned to the stage in 1847.

America, however, was beginning to produce its own actors of importance. JAMES HENRY HACKETT (1800-71) made his debut in New York on March 1, 1826. He duplicated his American reputation in England in the part of Falstaff, which he had first played in Philadelphia in 1832. He became the most famous American interpreter of this role, a reputation which he retains today. His Yankee character, Nimrod Wildfire in James K. Paulding's *Lion of the West* (1831), was acclaimed. He was the first player of Rip Van Winkle, and the father of the American romantic actor James K. Hackett (1869-1921), who played in such confections as the *Zenda* series.

EDWIN FORREST (1806-72) was the next celebrated American actor to appear on the scene. His first appearance was in 1820, at the age of fourteen, in his home town of Philadelphia. He played at the Walnut Street Theatre, which was erected in 1809 and which, with its raked floor, still serves the theatre. His New York debut came eight months after Hackett's, in 1826, as Othello at the Bowery Theatre, where he always remained a favorite with the gallery gods. His performances were more and more enthusiastically received, so after ten years of establishing himself as America's foremost actor, he went to London in 1836 to challenge England's best. He met a biased criticism, mostly deprecating the idea of any American daring to set himself beside the august actors of England. Kean had praised him highly and Macready pretended a kindly deference toward an American cousin while never missing an opportunity to undermine his career. The papers were frequently nasty-nice or praised only to sneer. This attitude on the part of the English hurt poor Forrest deeply and he had suffered much before he so injudiciously hissed Macready from a box in Edinburgh in 1845. He had been hissed as Macbeth shortly before and he suspected his English rival of prompting it. This may have been true, but more probably it was merely discourtesy and bad manners.

The affair had most unhappy repercussions. Macready appeared in New York in 1849 and public hostility towards him had grown since Forrest, with unhappiness in his heart, had told his friends about the treatment he had received from the fair-play-loving English public. This, coupled with the natural antagonism of Irish-born Americans who had seen their country destroyed economically by the English, prompted a demonstration against Macready so violent that the Governor of New York called out troops to protect him. The crowd inside the theatre and the mobs outside were extremely abusive, and a stupid officer gave the command to fire. So many were killed that a venial press tried to suppress the number of dead and injured, and even today it is still impossible to arrive at a fair figure because of the exaggerated claims made by both sides. Macready escaped the back way and fled the city. The Anglophile citizens of New York were so shocked, and so desirous of placating Macready and honoring England, that they tendered apologies and a dinner to the actor. Obviously both sides of this controversy between two actors went too far, but it is cited at this length to show the tremendous popular hold on the emotions which actors secured in the last century.

It is only fair to say that Forrest's connection with the outrage has never been proved. He went on to new fame and all went well with his career until it encountered the rising genius of young Edwin Booth, but of that we will speak later. He went through an unpleasant divorce suit with his wife, Catherine Sinclair, which alienated much of his public and soured his own disposition. He played last, in 1871, in Boston and when he died he left his considerable fortune to establish a home for aged actors near the city of his birth.

Forrest's bitter rival, WILLIAM CHARLES MACREADY (1793-1873), had already created a considerable reputation for himself before he came to America, in 1826, for his first tour. Strongly influenced by Kean, none of his performances truly stand out save his Lear, though he was a popular actor in his day. He played both with and in competition to Forrest in his first English season and in 1843 and 1844 he made a successful American tour before ever-widening audiences. His last return in 1849 met the reception already described.

That brilliant scholar of the American drama, Arthur Hobson Quinn, has warned against falling into the easy assumption that ROBERT MONTGOMERY BIRD (1806-54) and the Philadelphia school of playwrights constituted a romantic movement in America such as Hugo and the elder Dumas had established in France. Nonetheless, up to a certain point, the similarity is evident. Bird, like others of this school, competed for the thousand dollar prize offered by Edwin Forrest to stimulate American playwriting and to provide himself with native vehicles. Two plays by Bird won the prize and both bear mentioning. The first was the enormously popular *The Gladiator* (1831), which was reputedly played more than a thousand times in the author's lifetime, and which survived both Bird and Forrest, for John McCullough and others played it. It was a hardy, romantic melodrama, at which London lifted noses when Forrest first played it, but which reads well enough today. *The Broker of Bogota* (1834) was more complicated in structure and perhaps more finished but it never achieved the success that the Roman drama did.

JOHN AUGUSTUS STONE (d.1834) was an actor who had so little success in his life that he drowned himself in the Schuylkill River because his play *Metamora; or, The Last of the Wampanoags* (1829), made so much money for Forrest and brought its author so little. That actor's dealings with all of the young playwrights who wrote for him were niggardly, to put it mildly, and in some cases downright dishonest. Another of the men who supplied plays for Forrest was ROBERT T. CONRAD (1810-58) whose best known work was *Jack Cade* (1835), which has real power today. This story of the Kentish rebellion against injustice, in the fifteenth century, was ready-made for an actor of Forrest's physical proportions and voice. Conrad also wrote *Conrad, King of Naples* (1832), for a rising young tragedian, James E. Murdoch, who became one of the great road stars.

Another member of the Philadelphia school of playwriting was RICHARD PENN SMITH (1799-1854) who managed to pick up the characteristics of all the other playwrights of the period including Barker, Payne and Dunlap. None of his plays has much dramatic interest but one of them, *Caius Marius* (1831), had considerable use on the stage beginning with Forrest. Verse dramas were certainly the tradition in the City of Brotherly Love, and one after another flowed from the pens of their creators. Among the most famous was *Francesca da Rimini* (1855), by GEORGE HENRY BOKER (1824-90), which was first performed by that fine actor, E. L. Davenport, and subsequently by Lawrence Barrett and Otis Skinner. Many other authors have written Francesca plays, but Boker's drama stands up as well as its rather stilted verse form permits. This type of drama had no lasting hold on the American stage because it was always foreign to it. It was a European medium that did not transplant well. Only when a later writer such as Maxwell Anderson could find inspiration in the people about him did we have poetic drama deserving of any claim on our audiences.

Before we progress further into the century, there is a characteristic native theatre form which should be introduced—the Negro minstrel. Though a Negro, in the person of William Bates, had set foot upon the stage as Sambo in Murdock's *Triumph of Love* in 1795, and a Negro band existed in Boston, there were few efforts to use Negro rhythms or his ebullient personality upon the American stage. Exception should be made of IRA ALDRIDGE (1810-66) who was born in the same little town of Bel Air, Maryland, where Edwin Booth was to see the light of day. He aspired to the theatre after becoming the valet of Edmund Kean and eventually attracted considerable attention, particularly in England and Russia, for his performances in such dissimilar roles as Othello, and Mungo, in Bickerstaffe's *The Padlock*.

The introduction of Negro minstrelsy has generally been credited to THOMAS D. RICE (1806-60) though it would be more correct to say that he popularized it, as its beginnings are various and are scattered over a wide range of territory. Even the stories of Rice's beginning are fabulous. According to one version he began in Cincinnati having borrowed the clothes of a Negro stage driver and also his song:

> "Turn about an' wheel about an' do jis so,
> An' every time I turn about I jump Jim Crow."*

While the nearly naked Negro hid behind the scenes, the audience roared its glee so loudly that Rice did not hear the Negro calling that the steamboat was coming and he had to have his clothes back. Finally he became so excited that he emerged in his undraped condition shouting: "Massa Rice, Massa Rice, gi' me nigga's hat—nigga's coat—nigga's shoes—gi' me nigga's t'ings! Massa Griffif want 'im—STEAMBOAT'S COMIN'!"

Whether this account of the 1828-29 season is correct, or the story that Louisville or Pittsburgh was the scene of Rice's triumphs and Jim Crow's home, the important thing is that a new stage character was created. Rice popularized the black-face Negro minstrel over the United States and took England by storm. The audiences at the

---

* Robert P. Nevin, *Stephen C. Foster and Negro Minstrelsy*, Atlantic Monthly, vol. XX, p. 608, Boston, 1867.

Bowery Theatre in New York begged for more, which Rice provided in the farces *Bone Squash* and *The Virginia Mummy*. James Roberts and George Washington Dixon probably preceded Rice, but with nothing like his popularity or artistry.

Troupes were formed at once. The first consisted of Daniel Emmett, Frank Brower, William Whitlock, and Richard Pelham who appeared February 17, 1843 at the Chatham Theatre in New York and were known as The Virginia Minstrels. Though they claimed to have organized in 1842, it was 1846 before Christy's Minstrels began at the Mechanics' Society Hall on Broadway near Grand Street, where they remained until 1854. Edwin P. Christy was the founder, but his famous successor, George Harrington, took the *nom de théâtre* of George Christy and was known as such on two continents. There were innumerable troupes playing every city, town and village of this country right up to the time of the First World War, when increased railroad rates and the interference of cheap motion pictures cut the road to pieces. The most famous of these troupes included Bryant's Minstrels (with the famous Dan Bryant); the San Francisco Minstrels; Lew Dockstader's company; and that most enduring troupe, Thatcher, Primrose and West's.

Vaudeville, under the name of Variety, had its inception in this country in the early part of the nineteenth century. The beginnings are misty but in 1926 this theatrical form, which had become an industry, celebrated its centenary. Acrobats, musical turns, juggling, topical songs had long existed in the theatre and before the Civil War had come to be played as a series of acts for a lower class public. For a long time women rarely went to see this form of entertainment because the jokes were considered off-color and the crowds were often rude and noisy. The famous "444 Broadway" was its home. Variety changed its name to vaudeville (taken from the French term, which bore no resemblance to what he meant by Variety) when John W. Ransome used it to describe a touring specialty company in the eighteen-eighties.

Tony Pastor cleaned it up and offered it as an entertainment for women and children as early as 1865. However, its national development as a commercial form of entertainment extending into every city and town came largely through the efforts of such men as B. F. Keith and F. F. Proctor. Both the "two-a-day," as it came to be called, and later the three, four, five and even more performances, made it into continuous vaudeville and contributed, in the end, to its decline. Almost every singer and dancer, native or foreign (as well as actors, who appeared in "dramatic sketches" of low theatrical or literary merit) joined the trained seals, dog and pony acts, acrobats, tumblers and jugglers who made up the cast of these performances. Some of the men associated with vaudeville in a managerial capacity were the operatic impresario Oscar Hammerstein, F. F. Albee, John J. Murdock, Sullivan and Considine, Alexander Pantages, Sylvester Z. Poli, Charles E. Kohn and Marcus Loew.

The ranking theatre of the entire vaudeville field was, of course, the Palace Theatre in New York, the topmost pinnacle of "big-time." Its Monday afternoon openings were crowded with all the theatre-wise on Broadway and managers looking for talent frequently found it there. In front of the theatre, and around the corner on Forty-seventh Street, were congregated all vaudevillians who were "rest-ing" or "at liberty." A combination of motion picture competition and the increasing tendency to book the same act over and over again, with no new jokes, no new faces, and worn and dirty costumes, killed vaudeville.

To return to the more legitimate branch of the theatre, such dramatic stars as Mlle. Céleste, the Mathews (father and son), Mme. Vestris, Mme. Malibran, Tyrone Power, and the great Rachel came to America frequently, during the period before the Civil War, with real success except for the last named. Her single American tour, in 1855, was a failure due in part to the exorbitant prices which were charged, and the fact that not one American in twenty had any knowledge at all of French. Even though the prices were reduced and the receipts were good, the enormous expense of the productions made a loss inevitable. She then went on to Boston and afterwards back to New York for a second engagement. In those days the heating of large theatres was extremely difficult and expensive. To save money, her too canny brother, who was her manager, neglected to heat the Walnut Street Theatre in Philadelphia where she was playing. She caught pneumonia but recovered sufficiently to sail to Charleston where she gave one performance of *Adrienne Lecouvreur*, her last on any stage. Her brother's niggardliness eventually cost her her life as the tuberculosis from which she suffered was aggravated and advanced by her illness in America.

More successful was CHARLES ALBERT FECHTER (1824-79), who in his youth had played with Rachel in Paris, despite his English birth. His English always had a French accent but his voice was musical and his appearance youthful. His build was like that of Forrest. Fechter's principal innovation was his playing of Hamlet as a blond Nordic with flowing hair. This was well received by London, and the United States when he came here in 1870. His playing had magnetic glamour rather than innate intelligence. He spent his remaining years in this country, though he played little after 1876 when he had broken his leg in a fall on the ice. He became a farmer and lived in retirement in Bucks County, Pennsylvania until his death.

The first native American actress to reach the heights was CHARLOTTE CUSHMAN (1816-76), who began her career on the operatic stage as the Countess Almaviva, in *The Marriage of Figaro*, at the Tremont Theatre in Boston, in 1835. While playing at the St. Charles Theatre, in New Orleans, she lost her fine contralto voice. Then she turned to the drama and appeared first as Lady Macbeth at the Bowery Theatre, New York, in September, 1836. This was always her most successful role. Henry Austin Clapp, Boston critic and stage historian, said that he had never heard a voice so saturated with anguish as hers when in the third act she realized that all her crimes had been committed to no avail. This was the play in which she took her leave from the stage in 1875. She had a regal bearing and her approach to a part was dignified. She had something of the Kemble stateliness which was particularly helpful to her in her Katharine in *King Henry VIII*. However, her most popular role was that of Meg Merrilies in a dramatization of Scott's *Guy Mannering*. Nancy Sykes was another of her best parts. Curiously enough she was extremely fond of playing men's parts, of which the best were her Romeo, to her beautiful sister Susan's Juliet, and Cardinal Wolsey; she also acted Hamlet and Claude Melnotte.

One of the freshest talents to rise in the American theatre was the actress-playwright, ANNA CORA MOWATT (1819-70), who was born Ogden, in Bordeaux. At fifteen she married a wealthy banker. Threatened by tuberculosis at eighteen, she went abroad, where in London and Paris she had ample opportunity to examine social customs. This served her in her later plays, particularly *Fashion*, which was the first American social comedy. Her really delightful *Autobiography* (1854) tells in considerable detail of her European trip as well as of her theatrical triumphs and road tours. In 1840 she wrote her first play *Gulzara; or, The Persian Slave* which was intended for her amateur group in Flatbush. Accordingly there were no mature male characters, making it unsuitable for professional production, though it was published. When Mowatt lost his money through speculation she turned to public readings and wrote articles for periodicals.

Then came her famous *Fashion; or, Life in New York* (1845) which is still an excellent acting vehicle if played straight without efforts to make it "quaint." It had a most successful run after its opening on March 24th. As a result of this Mrs. Mowatt was offered a starring role as Pauline in Bulwer-Lytton's *The Lady of Lyons*, June 13, 1845 at the Park Theatre. No less discerning a critic than Edgar Allan Poe praised her grace, "her own sense of art" and her "rich and natural elocution." She was enthusiastically received in Charleston, Mobile, and New Orleans ending with a brilliant season at Niblo's Garden in New York. E. L. Davenport became her leading man and she wrote *Armand, the Child of the People* (1847) with their acting abilities in mind. This romantic drama has not worn so well as *Fashion,* but the audiences of the day liked it. She and Davenport went to England where they made a very favorable impression, first in *The Lady of Lyons* at the Olympic in London, and later in *Armand* for twenty-one nights at the Marylebone Theatre. They were held over for the next season and *Fashion* was produced with violently differing critical reactions. After playing in Dublin, in 1851, she returned to America. Following several tours as far west as St. Louis, Mrs. Mowatt retired from the stage in 1854 to marry William F. Ritchie, publisher of the *Richmond Enquirer;* she passed the rest of her life in a charming cottage on North Eighth Street in Richmond. In 1855 she brought out a volume of short stories, depicting life behind the scenes, which attracted considerable attention and has since proved invaluable to students. *Mimic Life; or, Before and Behind the Curtain* to a certain degree reflected her own life. These books, together with her own taste and refinement, went a long way toward dispelling the prejudice popularly held about the loose lives of actresses. Thus her influence on the theatre of her day was threefold.

Boston-born E. L. DAVENPORT (1816-77), who was one of the most scholarly and tender of Hamlets, began his career on the stage in Providence, in 1836, in support of Junius Brutus Booth. He attracted sufficient attention to be rewarded with the role of William in Jerrold's *Black-eyed Susan,* in Newport, and from there went to the Tremont Theatre in Boston where he stayed for two years. He played in stock at the Walnut Street Theatre in Philadelphia for three years and then went to the Bowery in New York. In 1846 he appeared at the Park as Romeo, Fazio and Benedick and then began the profitable association with Mrs. Mowatt. When she returned to America, he stayed on in England, where he had considerable success, until 1854. In 1856 he made his most celebrated appearance as Hamlet at Burton's Theatre, with Burton and Palcise as the grave-diggers; Mark Smith as Polonius; Charles Fisher as the Ghost; and Mrs. Davenport, of the English acting family of Vinings, as Ophelia (one of the strongest casts to be assembled in that period). His Brutus, William, Sir Giles Overreach and Benedick were among his best regarded roles. He was the founder of a distinguished theatrical family including his daughter, Fanny (1850-98), celebrated portrayer of Sardou roles; his son Edgar L.; his daughter May, who married William Seymour, long manager of the Boston Museum and father of May Davenport Seymour, curator of the theatre collection of the Museum of the City of New York; and his son Harry, a character actor of reputation.

EDWIN BOOTH (1833-93) was probably America's greatest actor, if contemporary criticism can be believed together with the word of men and women still living who saw him play and who are competent to judge. His first appearance was at the age of sixteen when, on September 10, 1849, he played Tressel to his father's Richard III. Neither his father nor the other actors thought that this lithe, curly-headed, graceful youth with expressive and luminous eyes would turn into one of the finest portrayers of Hamlet from Burbage to Gielgud. His first New York appearance was at the National Theatre, September 27, 1850, as Wilford in *The Iron Chest*. He substituted for his father as Richard III a year later, when the older man was taken ill, without arousing enthusiasm (it was never one of his best parts). Between 1852 and 1856, like all the other best actors, he appeared in San Francisco (which has always been one of the best theatre towns in this country), as well as in Hawaii (then the Sandwich Islands), and Australia. Upon his return to New York, his performances were matched against Forrest's, Booth playing more quietly, with a gentler artistry of classic proportions, while Forrest kept to the older tradition which is often referred to as rant (a term which is merely relative and is usually saved for the generation immediately preceding the critic). The partisans of the two actors were violent and some of Booth's were so ill-advised as to influence a venial press to give the palm to him. Whether that charge was true or not, certainly their criticism was so highly personal as to wound Forrest and to drive him to the road. Booth, who was one of the kindest of men, would certainly have preferred to triumph solely on his merits as an actor. His Sir Giles Overreach was a successful addition to his repertoire and his Hamlet and Richelieu were now acclaimed. In 1862 he became manager of the Winter Garden, where from 1864 to 1867 he produced Shakespeare in the magnificent fashion which Charles Kean had attempted at the Princess in London. In 1864 with his brothers, Junius Brutus, Jr., and that fine actor and hothead, John Wilkes Booth (assassin of Lincoln), he produced *Julius Caesar*. This was the only occasion when all of them appeared in the same production. On November 26, 1864, Booth appeared as Hamlet in his production which ran for one hundred nights and set a mark honestly broken only by Barrymore and Gielgud in this century.

He went into retirement after Lincoln's death when there were innumerable insults and even violence offered to members of the Booth family. When he returned, January 3, 1866, as Hamlet, he was cheered by his devoted followers. In 1869 he built the magnificent Booth's Theatre at the corner of Sixth Avenue and Twenty-third Street, which he opened on February 3rd with *Romeo and Juliet*. Mary McVicker, daughter of J. H. McVicker, prominent Chicago theatre manager, and soon to be his second wife, was his Juliet. He followed this after ten weeks with *Othello*. Later he produced *Much Ado About Nothing* and other plays but in 1874, despite the artistic success of the venture and all the money which was taken in, he became bankrupt and had to surrender the theatre. It was then that he launched the various tours which carried him into almost every town in the country. He played with such foreign stars as Salvini, in *Othello*, and with the distinguished Ristori. His triumphant tours with Lawrence Barrett, in 1887-89, and Modjeska in the latter year were dear to the hearts of his audiences. In 1861, 1881 and again in 1882, he had appeared successfully in London. The second engagement was with Sir Henry Irving. On April 4, 1891, he played for the last time at the Brooklyn Academy of Music, appropriately enough in his most famous role, Hamlet. He converted his handsome house on Gramercy Park into a clubhouse for actors, The Players, retaining only an apartment for his own use, where he died June 7, 1893.

There were several productions which influenced the American theatre quite aside from the literary value of the pieces played. Perhaps the outstanding one was *Uncle Tom's Cabin* (1852), which was dramatized by the actor, George L. Aiken, from Harriet Beecher Stowe's anti-slavery novel. It ran for three hundred performances in New York, an unprecedented run, and was to be seen in stock and touring companies throughout the entire country for the next fifty years. Little Cordelia Howard was the most famous Little Eva, but every child actress for several generations cut her teeth in the part. It was even played with two Little Evas and two Topsys. It still holds the stage today, when played to the hilt without burlesque, as in the Players' revival of 1933 with genial Otis Skinner as Uncle Tom.

Jean Margaret Davenport's translation of *La Dame aux Camélias*, as *Camille*, in 1853 was the first presentation in this country of the Dumas *fils* play. Matilda Heron's superior version later became so popular that everywhere audiences were weeping over the woes of Marguerite Gautier. Almost all the great ladies of the American theatre through Ethel Barrymore, Eva LeGallienne and Lillian Gish, have appeared as the unhappy courtesan. One of the most delicate and carefully considered productions was that in which Miss Gish appeared under the direction of Robert Edmond Jones. The production reopened the old Opera House in the mining town of Central City, Colorado, in 1932, and was later brought to New York.

Mrs. Henry Wood's *East Lynne* (1863) opened at the Winter Garden Theatre with Lucille Western as Lady Isabel and tears were shed from Maine to California by the same kind of audiences that today weep over the cinema and radio serials. It pandered to the most sentimental taste which was generally rampant throughout the country. It was played by every stock troupe and every touring star from Miss Western to the least conspicuous tent show announcing *"East Lynne* tonight," until it became a by-word.

Musical shows have always had an attraction for the American people and have become one of the most characteristic facets of our theatre. In the beginning we imported our ideas from Europe (or pretended that we did) and certainly introduced most of our dancers from there. We were soon to take the lead in this field and eventually London, Berlin, and Paris were importing our ideas and our artists. The first production to indicate our supremacy in this form was *The Black Crook* (1866), which was considered so wicked that merely to look upon it would consign one to the flames of hell. The ministers in their pulpits fulminated against it. Moral people would have none of it. Ladies, if they went at all, appeared heavily veiled so that their eyes might not be too dazzled by such an exposure of feminine pulchritude undraped for masculine eyes. When Christopher Morley revived the piece at the Lyric Theatre in Hoboken, in 1929, it had become quaint and over-dressed in our eyes, but its loveliness remained.

The Black Crook came into existence when the managerial team of Jarrett and Palmer imported a number of artists and much complicated scenery for a ballet, *La Biche au Bois*, which they planned to produce at the Academy of Music. The destruction of that theatre led them to ask William Wheatley to take over the production. He added an absurd melodrama by Charles M. Barras to the ballet to give the dances continuity and progression, thus creating what would be called today a "book show." The stage of Niblo's Garden was completely reconstructed. The *Times* for September 3rd, 1866, reports: "Such a stage was never seen in this country before. Every board slides on grooves and can be taken up, pushed down or slid out at will. The entire stage may be taken away; traps can be introduced at any part at any time, and the great depth of the cellar below renders the sinking of entire scenes a matter of simple machinery."

Such actors as G. C. Boniface, J. G. Burnett and the English importations, George Atkins, Rose Morton and Milly Cavendish headed the cast. The ballet for which it was famed included Marie Bonfanti, Rita Sangalli, Rose Delval and the Rigl sisters. This was an extravaganza cast the like of which America had not seen before. The

Tribune for September 17th says: "Niblo's Garden opened in a literal blaze of glory on Wednesday evening. The audience assembled on that occasion was so large that it filled the house in every part, overflowed into the lobbies, and, in the shape of frequent and large detachments, extended to the street and pervaded the neighborhood. Great enthusiasm prevailed before the curtain, and great excitement behind it. A livelier scene than was thus presented could not well be imagined. 'The Black Crook' was played by easy stages, from 7¾ o'clock until 1¼. Most of the auditors remained until the gorgeous end. . . . The scenery is magnificent; the ballet is beautiful; the drama is—rubbish. . . . The last scene in the play, however, will dazzle and impress to even a greater degree, by its lavish richness and barbaric splendor. All that gold, and silver, and gems, and light, and woman's beauty can contribute to fascinate the eye and charm the senses is gathered up in this gorgeous spectacle."

The Black Crook ran for four hundred and seventy-five performances, closing on January 4, 1868—New York's longest run up until that time. The later extravaganzas of the Kiralfy brothers and eventually the magnificence of the *Ziegfeld Follies*, the *George White Scandals* and the *Earl Carroll Vanities* stemmed from Wheatley's stupendous production at Niblo's Garden in 1866.

These were the days of outstanding theatre managers. The incomparable PHINEAS TAYLOR BARNUM (1810-91) controlled his American Museum and imported or manufactured stars with all the fervency of his bold imagination. From Jenny Lind, to General Tom Thumb, and the original Siamese Twins, Cheng and Eng, he chose his attractions. His menagerie was famous and tourists from all over the country considered a visit obligatory. In 1881 he merged his aggregation with that of J. A. Bailey to form Barnum and Bailey's Circus and so passes out of the scope of our history.

Edwin Booth has already been mentioned. Henry C. Jarrett, A. M. Palmer, Augustine Daly, and Lester Wallack were all powerful men. Among them they controlled the principal theatres of New York exchanging stars and lesser players with other managements in the east such as W. E. Burton and Mrs. John Drew in Philadelphia, John T. Ford in Richmond and later in Washington and Baltimore. In the west and deep south were Sol Smith, Noah M. Ludlow, Sam Drake, father and son, among others. These managers developed stock companies which varied from year to year and exchanged stars. So a semi-permanent set-up was provided which gave stability to theatre traditions and provided excellent training for actors, young and old.

Perhaps this was responsible for the splendid acting of the century and the general improvement of standards. This continued as touring attractions became increasingly lucrative in the last third of the nineteenth and the first two decades of the present century. Yet paradoxically this condition, more than anything else, caused deterioration for there were not enough good actors to go around when players were engaged for the run of a play and all its financial possibilities were milked from it in a New York run and in endless duplicating companies up to ten or twenty in number. Inferior actors were used and people in many sections of the country began to complain that the productions sent them were inferior. Thus fifty years saw the rise and fall of the road. Further reasons for its decline, as mentioned in the case of vaudeville, developed after the First World War with increased railroad rates and subsequent heavy competition from inexpensive motion pictures and free radio and television.

But we are anticipating events, for the cycle has but just begun to run its course. The invention of the touring system *per se* has been credited to none other than the prolific Irish-American dramatist and actor, DION BOUCICAULT (1822-90). Before he was twenty he had his first successful play, *London Assurance*, March 4, 1841, produced at Covent Garden with a brilliant cast including Charles Mathews, Mme. Vestris and William Warren. This play was an instantaneous hit and provided many excellent acting parts as all his plays were to do. Such literary values as Boucicault's pieces may have lacked were made up for, in their own day, by fat roles. After *Old Heads and Young Hearts* (1844), at the Haymarket, he went to France where he lived for the next four years. It was there that he formed that acquaintance with French drama which was to aid him substantially in the construction of his own plays, many of which were translations or adaptations of Parisian successes.

He came to America in September, 1853, after his first wife died. With him came Agnes Robertson, adopted daughter of Charles Kean and Ellen Tree, who apparently was only his common law wife. (This became evident at the time of his marriage to the beautiful young actress Louise Thorndyke, in 1888, for which public abuse was heaped upon their heads, for he thereby rendered illegitimate his children, Dion, Aubrey and Nina, all of whom acted and were prominent on the English stage.) Agnes Robertson was the original heroine of many of his plays.

His first outstanding play written here was produced in New Orleans, in 1855. *Grimaldi; or, The Life of an Actress* dealt with the attitude of society towards women who have gone on the stage, and boasted a brilliant cast including the Boucicaults, J. G. Burnett and Mr. and Mrs. E. A. Sothern.

Before turning to his next play he demonstrated his loyalty to the country of his adoption by joining the movement, which playwrights such as Bird and Boker had begun some years before, to protect the legal rights of authors in their plays. In the eighteen-forties Bird had endeavored to secure the passage of a copyright law, which would prevent the stealing of plays. He was unsuccessful, and Boker tried again in 1853. In 1856 Boucicault secured the passage of a law which entitled the dramatist "along with the sole right to print and publish the said composition, the sole right also to act, perform, or represent the same."* Though this law failed to achieve all the results hoped from it, or to protect his plays from pirating, Boucicault sent out several companies to act them. This inaugurated the "road" as we understand the term. That it was abused because of the avarice of managers and actors does not prevent us from realizing that at its inception, it was basically a good idea. The old days of the touring star who might move on, each day or two, and so force stock companies to perform new pieces from three to six times a week were definitely over. This worked out to the advantage of the theatre as a whole.

The Sidewalks of New York (also called *The Poor of New York* and in an English version, *The Streets of London*, 1857) was taken from *Les Pauvres de Paris* (1856) by Edouard Brisebarre and Eugène Nus. Boucicault omitted much of the moralizing and sentimental effusions of the French and by his local allusions made it seem a purely American play. The famous panic of 1857 was introduced, as well as a fire scene, which drew on the numerous fireman plays of the previous decade such as *The New York Fireman and the Bond Street Heiress* (1850). *The Sidewalks of New York* has the real sense of theatrical values characteristic of all his plays.

In ignorance of Dickens' authorship he based his next important play on a French version of *The Cricket on the Hearth*, which had been produced in Paris as *Le Marchand d'Enfants*. Discovering the real facts, he renamed his characters and entitled the play *Dot* (1859), and it was staged at the Winter Garden theatre with Agnes Robertson in the title part and Joseph Jefferson as Caleb Plummer (one of his best performances). In the same year Boucicault turned his hand to an American problem in that study of Negro character, *The Octoroon* (1859), which lies between the Abolitionist propaganda of Mrs. Stowe and the naturalism of *All God's Chillun Got Wings* and *In Abraham's Bosom*. The validity of the characters compensated for the melodramatic action, and the brilliance of the cast, which included George Holland, A. H. Davenport and the Boucicaults (who with-

* *Copyright Enactments of the United States*, Washington, 1906, p. 43.

drew after a week because of a monetary dispute) made the performance so much more thrilling to the audience.

Next he turned to the Irish subjects which made him particularly famous and for which, because of his birth, he had a special aptitude. Irish characters had begun to sprinkle American plays as the Irish immigration increased their representation in our audiences. Boucicault was led by his promise to provide a play for those Irish-American actors, Mr. and Mrs. Barney Williams. *The Colleen Bawn* (1860), adapted from Gerald Griffin's novel, *The Collegians*, was not played by them because Laura Keene's theatre business was in bad shape and needed a new play to stimulate attendance. Of this piece no less an authority than Arthur Hobson Quinn says that, "For the first time real Irish life was placed upon the stage."*

The next important piece was *Arrah-na-Pogue* (1864) performed first in Dublin and the following year in New York. It is largely notable because two of its characters, Colonel Bagenal O'Grady, a fine type of Irish gentleman (acted by John Brougham) and Shaun the Post (created by Boucicault). He transferred a French original to an Irish setting in *Daddy O'Dowd* (1873) and improved the characterization of *Les Crochets du Père Martin* (1858). The best of these plays with Gaelic setting was *The Shaughraun* (1874) in which several of his most interesting and sympathetic characters appeared— Robert, Irish gentleman and Fenian; the essentially decent Molyneux, English officer; and Conn, the Shaughraun, whom the program describes as "the soul of every fair, the life of every funeral, the first fiddle at all weddings and parties." This was one of Boucicault's best acting parts, which he played for years. The drama, first produced at Wallack's Theatre, was long current and brought a fortune to its author (which later reverses dispersed).

His *Rip Van Winkle* (1865) was one of a series of adaptations of Washington Irving's story and, with Joseph Jefferson's later alterations, was probably the best. For the next forty years it held the stage to the delight of countless audiences everywhere in these United States as well as in the British Isles, where this piece of Americana was much relished.

The man who is most widely associated with the play was the third of his name, JOSEPH JEFFERSON (1829-1905), son of the man who had played Rip in an earlier version. Young Jefferson made his debut at the age of three as the boy in Sheridan's *Pizarro* and later had the advantage of Junius Brutus Booth's coaching for Marrall in *A New Way to Pay Old Debts*. His first part to attract attention, after many years of playing in various parts of the country, was that of Dr.

* Quinn, A. H., *A History of the American Drama*. N. Y.: F. S. Crofts. 1936.

Pangloss, in Colman's _The Heir-at-Law_, at Laura Keene's theatre in 1857. Without losing the original humor of the role, he invested it with understanding and a certain amount of pathos which broadened the character and rendered it more sympathetic.

A part that he made very much his own was that of the young Yankee, Asa Trenchard, in Tom Taylor's _Our American Cousin_ in 1858. He drew the materials for his conception from our own New England, so that the accretions to the role had validity without ever becoming eccentricity. The play had been neglected and had found no English production. It was drawn to Jefferson's attention who saw the possibilities in Asa, as did Laura Keene when he pointed out the play's virtues. Sothern, who was cast as the silly ass Lord Dundreary, was much dissatisfied with his part. After kidding the part for a couple of weeks and doing one outrageous piece of business after another to show his dislike of the role, he found the audience responding and laughing heartily. By the end of the first month he had evolved a first rate character out of Taylor's sketch which was to serve him for the remainder of his career upon the stage and to bring him a fortune.

Though Jefferson's Bob Acres was one of his most successful parts in later years, it was not one of his best. It is Rip for which he is likely to be remembered as long as there are those who have heard his name. At the Royal Adelphi Theatre in London he created the role, in Boucicault's version, and for one hundred and seventy nights he continued to reduce the English audience to laughter and tears in a thoroughly lovable characterization. His pauses became as famous as those of Irving for he had both dignity and repose. His pantomime in the last act was so nearly perfect that no words were necessary.

John Johnstone Wallack, known to the public as LESTER WALLACK (1820-1888), was the son of that Anglo-American actor-manager James William Wallack who came repeatedly to America after his debut in 1838, settling here in 1852 for the rest of his life. The father took over Brougham's Lyceum at Broadway and Broome Street in the same year and called it Wallack's. Subsequently he built a house at Thirteenth and Broadway which bore the same name. His son, who in 1847 had made his American debut under the _nom de théâtre_ of John Lester in Boucicault's _Used Up_, took over the management of the theatre in 1861. He remained there with one of the smoothest and most brilliant companies on our stage, though it was perhaps too apt to look to England for its inspiration. In 1882 he opened the third house of the same name at Broadway and Thirtieth Street.

Lester Wallack's romantic and light comedy parts were his best; Charles Surface, Benedick to Rose Eytinge's Beatrice, and Elliott

Grey in his own *Rosedale; or, The Rifle Ball* (1863). When he retired from the theatre a monster benefit was organized at the Metropolitan Opera House by A. M. Palmer, Augustin Daly, and others
on May 21, 1888. Twenty-one thousand dollars was raised which
Wallack declined to accept though his wife was willing. The play
was *Hamlet*. All the famous actors who had not secured parts walked
on in the scenes requiring supernumeraries. Booth was Hamlet;
Modjeska, Ophelia; Lawrence Barrett, the Ghost; and Joseph Jefferson and W. J. Florence, the Grave-diggers. Probably no production
of the play in this country has ever boasted such a cast as occasioned
by the love and affection of the profession for this distinguished
actor-manager.

AUGUSTIN DALY (1838-99) began writing dramatic criticism in
1850 for the New York *Courier*, which connection he kept for ten
years. But he soon blossomed as a playwright with one of his most
successful pieces, *Leah the Forsaken* (taken from Mosenthal's *Deborah*), which opened with Kate Bateman at the Howard Athenaeum
in Boston, December 8, 1862 and then moved on to Niblo's Garden
in January, 1863. (This role became Kate Bateman's as much as Isabel
had been Lucille Western's.) After several more adaptations, Daly
brought forth his first original play, *Under the Gaslight* (1867), in
which he at least succeeded in his painting of local color. The audiences recognized the New York background, a familiar device in
melodramas of the forties, fifties and sixties. The big scene came when
the wounded soldier Snorkey, who has been bound to a railroad track,
is rescued in the nick of time by the heroine, Laura. In *After Dark*
(1868), Boucicault used the same situation and Daly went to court
where he was awarded the exclusive right to its use in the United
States (Boucicault's play being first performed in England).

Daly adapted more than ninety plays, usually from the French or
German drama or from English and American novels. Most of these
were theatrically successful when performed at his New York
theatres but none of them retain much literary value except in so far
as they catch some feeling of the original. However, they served his
managerial ambitions and launched several popular actresses who appeared under his direction. Clara Morris, an emotional actress of
merit, made a reputation for herself in *Man and Wife* (1870), Daly's
adaptation of Wilkie Collins' novel. In the same piece one of the best
comediennes of the second half of the century, Mrs. G. H. Gilbert,
made a great hit as Hester Dethridge. Miss Morris followed up this
success with Daly's *Divorce* (1871), the idea of which was borrowed
from Trollope's novel *He Knew He Was Right*. It ran for two hundred performances at Daly's Fifth Avenue Theatre. The cast included

the fine comedian, James Lewis as well as W. J. Lemoyne, Fanny Davenport, Mrs. Gilbert, and Linda Dietz.

Daly opened his new Fifth Avenue Theatre with *Pique*, December 14, 1875, which survived for two hundred and thirty-eight nights. In this John Drew played his first comedy part and Fanny Davenport was launched as a star. In *Frou-Frou* (1870), taken from the drama by Meilhac and Halévy, Agnes Ethel created a powerful impression, as did Fanny Davenport in Daly's adaptation, *Article 47* (1872), taken from Belot's *L'Article 47*.

In 1879 Ada Rehan, the young woman who was to become one of America's leading portrayers of comedy, came to Daly's where she was seen in a variety of parts. Of these, her two outstanding roles were Mrs. Osprey in Daly's *The Railroad of Love* (1887) and the Baroness Vera in his *A Test Case* (1892). However, it was in Daly's notable Shakespearean revivals that she made her real reputation. Her Viola was irresistible; her Rosalind took all-time high rank; her Peggy, in *The Country Girl*, was perhaps as fine as Mrs. Jordan's; but it was her Katharine, in *The Taming of the Shrew*, for which she will always be remembered. In that part she had few if any peers; certainly none in her own time. Daly must be given credit for this, for it was he who restored the play to its full Shakespearean significance, re-inserting the portions which Garrick had deleted.

He took his company to England, first in 1884 and again in 1886, when a Berlin season was undertaken, and also in 1888 when his version of the *Shrew* won high praise. Paris was only mildly enthusiastic but English critics recognized the value of his restorations and the company was well received. So warm was the response that he built a theatre in London, Daly's (1893, torn down in 1939), which became one of the most popular theatres in the British capital. His delightful production of *Twelfth Night* saved it financially after his second show, Tennyson's *The Foresters* (1893), had succeeded only mildly. He maintained his two playhouses in New York and London up to his death. Many of his later years were spent in building up a magnificent theatrical library.

Daly was responsible for the encouragement of a man who was a much better playwright than himself; one who succeeded in establishing professional playwriting in America. BRONSON HOWARD (1870-1908) proved that American plays on native themes could be successful at a time when Boucicault and Daly were flooding the field with adaptations. The latter produced *Saratoga* (1870) at his own theatre. This is a mildly amusing farce-comedy with a very likeable character in Bob Sackett and is enhanced by sprightly dialogue. His next important play was *The Banker's Daughter* (produced in Chicago as *Lillian's Last Love*, 1873). It was brilliantly produced by A. M. Palmer at his Union Square Theatre with Sarah Jewett, Charles Thorne and W. J. Lemoyne, in 1878. This was a realistic drama of some merit. The same year saw his delightful one-act play *Old Love Letters* at the Park Theatre, with Agnes Booth and Joseph Whiting, in which he deftly handled a stock situation. In *Young Mrs. Winthrop* (1882) Howard popularized a theme which became a commonplace in American plays, that of a husband and wife who drift apart because of the husband's absorption in business.

The melodramatic *The Henrietta* (1887) was a play of financial tycoons and their "big business" ways which have gone out of fashion as theatrical fare. As played by William H. Crane and Stuart Robson at the Union Square it drew almost half a million dollars in sixty-eight weeks and made the author's fortune. With the combination of Howard's talents and these splendid actors it played for years on the road and was quite deservedly successful.

His most popular play was *Shenandoah* (1888), though it was at first a failure when produced by Montgomery Field at the Boston Museum. This stirring play of the Civil War, however, attracted the attention of Charles Frohman. His production at the Star Theatre in 1889 launched him on his successful career as a manager, which was to continue with his fine productions at the Empire (opened in 1893 with *The Girl I Left Behind Me*) until his death in the sinking of the *Lusitania* in 1915. The cast included many actors who went on to further fame such as Viola Allen, Henry Miller, Wilton Lackaye and Effie Shannon.

Perhaps the most significant contribution Bronson Howard made to the theatre was his formation of the Society of American Dramatists and Composers to protect their rights in their dealings with unscrupulous or reactionary managers. This developed into the present day all-powerful Dramatists' Guild of the Authors' League of America which treats collectively with both producing managers and the much more powerful film interests which now recognize their tremendous stake in the preservation of a theatre which their past activities almost completely wrecked.

Steele MacKaye (1842-94) made his principal contribution to the theatre in his imaginative staging and his introduction of advanced scenic devices. In the Madison Square Theatre he installed an elevator stage and overhead lighting, which Thomas Edison personally installed in 1880. The general improvement of playgoing comfort was enhanced by the addition of folding seats in the auditorium. MacKaye had studied in Paris with Delsarte and Régnier and he imported many of their acting theories. In the popular mind, however, he will always be associated with his play, *Hazel Kirke* (1880), a quiet, natural domestic drama. His production of this play at the Madison Square Theatre ran for two years and for the following thirty was to be seen on every English speaking stage.

JAMES A. HERNE (1839-1901) may be said to have practiced art for truth's sake, for he was an uncompromising moralist. He believed in the improvement of his audience and despite his melodramatic means, he tackled the job unflinchingly. He began with *Hearts of Oak* (1879), in collaboration with David Belasco; a melodrama of the *East Lynne* variety, in which he and Mrs. Herne acted, off and on, for some years. He progressed from this to *Margaret Fleming* (1890). a truthful drama with little popular appeal yet the one play which today seems to have real merit. It is a character study of a cultivated American woman, developed with real perspicacity and an insight into feminine psychology which had hitherto been lacking in American drama. *Shore Acres* (1892) is as much a character study, though of a more serious nature, as Denman Thompson's *The Old Homestead* (1886), or the rollicking *The Widow Bedott* (1880) which David Locke (Petroleum V. Nasby) fashioned for Neil Burgess.

Herne's two remaining plays were *Reverend Griffith Davenport* (1899), a character study of a man who put his principles above everything else, and *Sag Harbor* (1899), which bears a strong resemblance to the earlier *Shore Acres*.

Two writers of comedy stand out, Hoyt and EDWARD HARRIGAN (1845-1911), the latter also a comic actor of great talent. His fame was established by his series of *Mulligan* plays in which he and Anthony Cannon, known on the stage as Tony Hart, appeared. The team of Harrigan and Hart is still remembered, though it only endured from 1872 to 1885.

In 1890 the Harrigan Theatre was built, was leased to Mansfield in 1895, and as the Garrick, was the mother house of the Theatre Guild from 1919 to 1925. It was the last stand, in 1929, of the Provincetown Players and has since been torn down. Harrigan continued as an actor in the plays of others, and in 1909 made his last appearance at a public Gambol of The Lambs at the Metropolitan Opera House.

Harrigan created genre pictures of Irish and German immigrants in New York. Mulligan and his wife Cordelia (played by Hart) are well drawn persons, whose lives were of considerable interest to New York theatre-goers of their day. Mulligan's rival, the German butcher, Lochmuller, is introduced to dramatize the natural antipathy between these two national groups in this country, which makes up much of the comedy in these plays. Rebecca and the Reverend Palestine Puter represent the Negro race. *The Mulligan Guard* (1873); *The Mulligan*

Guards and the Skidmores (1875); *The Mulligan Guard Picnic* (1878); the particularly famous *The Mulligan Guard Ball* (1879); *The Mulligan Guard Chowder* (1879); *The Mulligan Guards' Christmas* (1879); *The Major* (1881); and *Cordelia's Aspirations* (1883); are among the plays in this series. His best plays, other than these, are probably *Old Lavender* (1877), *Squatter Sovereignty* (1882) and *Reilly and the Four Hundred* (1890), which are based on a sound understanding of comic art and have delighted countless American audiences. The Harrigan family is today represented by two of Edward's children, both actors, William, and Nedda (widow of that genial character actor, Walter Connolly).

CHARLES HOYT (1860-1900) wrote many broad farces which were convulsing in their day largely because of the talents of a group of fine farceurs. In his first success, *A Bunch of Keys; or, Where There's a Will, There's a Play* (1882), he had the collaboration of Willie Edouin (as actor and writer) and such highly trained comedians as James T. Powers and Julian Mitchel. In 1884 he wrote *A Parlor Match* for Charles E. Evans and William F. Hoey, which burlesqued spiritualism and hunts for buried treasure. Then came one of the long-run plays of all time, *A Trip to Chinatown* (1891), which ran for six hundred and fifty performances at his Madison Square Theatre with Harry Conor as Ben Gay (who acted the role for eleven years). In a more serious vein Hoyt satirized hypocrisy in *A Temperance Town* (1893), which perhaps has more value than his other plays. Then he turned to the wide subject of national politics in *A Texas Steer* (1894) in which Caroline Miskel (Mrs. Hoyt) appeared.

WILLIAM GILLETTE (1855-1937) was also a popular playwright but was better known as an actor. He adapted the plays of others to provide himself with acting parts. The best known of these were *Esmeralda* (in collaboration with Frances Hodgson Burnett, 1881), *The Private Secretary* (adapted from Moser's *Der Bibliothekar*, 1884), *Too Much Johnson* (1894), *Secret Service* (1896) and *Sherlock Holmes* (1899).

In addition to Booth, John S. Clarke, Davenport, and that fine tragedian John McCullough, the leading actor of serious roles in the second half of the century was LAWRENCE BARRETT (1838-91). He was known for the purity of his elocution, his enthusiasm for the parts he played and the intensity of his feeling. His Cassius (to E. L. Davenport's Brutus and Walter Montgomery's Antony, in a revival of *Julius Caesar* at Niblo's Garden in 1870), was one of his finest characterizations. His playing of Yorick in William Dean Howell's *Yorick's Love* (1878), his King Arthur in William Young's *Pendragon* (1881), and his Lanciotto in Boker's *Francesca da Rimini* (revived in 1882), were perhaps his best known non-classic roles. His Shakespearean tours with Booth have already been mentioned. Today his family is represented on the stage by his granddaughter, Edith Barrett, who has made a reputation for her playing of whimsical parts.

These were the days of many fine actors: the comedians, Mr. and Mrs. W. J. Florence (in *The Mighty Dollar*, 1861); the tragic Janauschek; beautiful Mary Anderson; the Shakespearean acting team of lyric and lovely Julia Marlowe (first with Robert Taber) and E. H. Sothern; the excellent character actor, John Gibbs Gilbert; Rose Coghlan; E. M. Holland; Sarah Cowell Lemoyne; Georgia Cayvan; the comedienne, Maggie Mitchell; the darling of the mining camps, Lotta (Lotta Crabtree), in *Little Nell and the Marchioness*, 1866; the comic Marie Dressler; the glamourous Lillian Russell; the burlesquers, Weber and Fields, who have appeared on the stage, screen and radio since 1882; John T. Raymond (famous as Col. Mulberry Sellers in *The Gilded Age*, 1874); Sol Smith Russell; Nat Goodwin and all his wives; Ida Conquest; Blanche Walsh; Carlotta Nillson; the beautiful Sadie Martinot; De Wolf Hopper and the many actresses whom he married; Olga Nethersole, that emotional actress whose *Sapho* (Fitch's version, 1899), drew police interference; Mary Shaw, who was served likewise for her acting in *Mrs. Warren's Profession*, 1907; Virginia Harned; Odette Tyler; Annie Russell (who had a theatre named for her at Rollins College); the comic May Irwin; Julia Arthur; striking Elsie De Wolfe (present Lady Mendl); Nanette Comstock; William Faversham; Melbourne MacDowell; James O'Neill (in his starring vehicle *Monte Cristo*, first played by him in 1883); Margaret Illington (who was later married to Major Edward Bowes of radio fame); Percy Haswell; George Fawcett; May Robson, who has become the best trouper of all through her work in the films; and the finest living character actor, Otis Skinner, who is also author of such outstanding volumes as *The Last Tragedian* (a study of Edwin Booth, 1939), *Mad Folk of the Theatre* (1928), and his delightful autobiography, *Footlights and Spotlights* (1924). This is an embarrassment of riches, for many of these excellent actors have continued to appear even into our own time.

It is difficult to select any who deserve mention above those just named. However, any consensus would be likely to agree that Minnie Maddern Fiske, Richard Mansfield, Maude Adams, and the Drew-Barrymore family should be given special attention.

Minnie Maddern Fiske (1865-1932) was born Mary Augusta, daughter of the western theatre manager, Thomas W. Davey, and Lizzie Maddern, favorite southern actress. She made her first New

York appearance at the age of four, with J. K. Emmet, and later played Prince Arthur in an all-star revival of *King John* at Booth's Theatre in 1874. She starred in Charles Callahan's *Fogg's Ferry*, in 1882, and *Caprice* (1884), which Henry P. Taylor wrote for her. Upon her marriage to Harrison Grey Fiske (editor of that fine theatrical paper, the *New York Dramatic Mirror*) in 1890, she retired from the stage until 1896. After that date she returned and revealed herself as a serious actress of great merit. Her Nora in *A Doll's House*, in 1894, was a considerable success, as was her Tess in *Tess of the D'Urbervilles* (1897), both of which helped to establish her as the leading American actress. Among the other important plays in which she appeared were the highly successful *Becky Sharp* (1899); *Leah Kleschna* (1904); Langdon Mitchell's witty comedy of divorce, *The New York Idea* (1906), with George Arliss; *Rosmersholm* (1907); *Salvation Nell* (1908); *Pillars of Society* (1910); *Hannele* (1910); Philip Moeller's *Madame Sand* (1917); St. John Ervine's *Mary, Mary, Quite Contrary* (1923); and *The Rivals* (1925). Though often called an Ibsen actress, in her later years she turned almost entirely to comedy at which she was probably the deftest hand in the American theatre.

RICHARD MANSFIELD (1857-1907) began his successful stage career with an amazing *tour de force* as Baron Chevrial in *A Parisian Romance*, in 1883, after several years of minor singing roles in Gilbert and Sullivan and other comic operas in England and America. His triumph came over night. This was followed by the charming and sentimental title part in *Prince Karl* (1886). His acting of the dual roles in Thomas Russell Sullivan's adaptation of Robert Louis Stevenson's *Doctor Jekyll and Mr. Hyde* (1887) added to his reputation. Probably the only acting of a dual role in recent years with which it might be compared would be that of Basil Sydney in Woollcott and Kaufman's *The Dark Tower*, in 1933. Mansfield's *King Richard III* production in London and New York in 1889 resembled the arrangement later used by John Barrymore in that both included a portion of *King Henry VI, Part III*. This was always one of his most brilliant roles. Then came the famous *Beau Brummel* (1890), which Clyde Fitch had written, with some advice and an occasional line tossed in by the actor. This became one of Mansfield's most highly regarded performances, as did *Cyrano de Bergerac* (1898), in which he rivalled Coquelin. In his last season, 1906-07, he appeared in *Peer Gynt*. His interest in this play may have stemmed from the enthusiasm of Beatrice Cameron (Mrs. Mansfield, 1868-1940), who was one of the prime forces in the early Ibsen movement in this country, having played *A Doll's House* for special matinees during the season of 1889-

90. In 1894 Mansfield introduced that follower of Ibsen, George Bernard Shaw, to the American stage with *Arms and the Man* (1894). and also acted in the world première of *The Devil's Disciple* (1897) in Albany, New York. Mansfield was one of the most brilliant actors on the American stage.

In the long view MAUDE ADAMS (1872-   ), daughter of the character actress Annie Kiskadden, will probably have no special importance, but if the pleasure she gave to audiences, particularly in performances of Barrie's plays, is considered the scales will tilt deservedly in her favor. Her first appearance of importance came in De Mille and Belasco's *Men and Women* (1890). She became John Drew's leading lady in *The Masked Ball* in 1892. Under Charles Frohman's management she played in *Rosemary* in 1896. On September 27, 1897 she appeared in the starring role of Lady Babby in Barrie's *The Little Minister* (one of her greatest hits); then came *L'Aiglon* (1900); and *Quality Street* (1901). Probably her most enduring success was *Peter Pan* (1905). Then followed *What Every Woman Knows* (1908); *The Legend of Leonora* (1914); and *A Kiss for Cinderella* (1916). She was then absent from the stage, during which time she experimented with her hobby, stage lighting, until her reappearance for a transcontinental tour (though she did not appear in New York) with Otis Skinner, in *The Merchant of Venice*, in the season of 1931-32.

The DREW-BARRYMORE family in this country was founded by John and Louisa Lane Drew. However, it was Mrs. Drew (1820-97), with her indomitable management of the Arch Street Theatre in Philadelphia, who was truly responsible for the establishment of their fortunes in America. Mrs. Malaprop, in *The Rivals* (she played in two famous revivals), was her best part. She was not a subtle actress but she had authority and genuine humor.

Her son, JOHN DREW (1853-1927), was one of the most polished comedians on the American stage. His acting of social comedy, particularly comedy of manners, was of a very high order. His daughter Louise, an actress, married the actor John Devereaux; their son is a leading juvenile, his best role to date being in *Life with Father* (1939). Old Mrs. Drew's actress-daughter Georgie married that splendid, if eccentric, and handsome actor Maurice Barrymore (real name Herbert Blythe, 1847-1905). They had three children who have been called, with others of their kin, the royal family of Broadway. As such, an apocryphal play, *The Royal Family* (1927) by Edna Ferber and George Kaufman, celebrated some of their supposed exploits. Lionel Barrymore (at present a film actor) did his finest work in *The Copperhead* (1918) and *The Jest* (1919), but his *Macbeth* (1921), in Robert Edmond Jones' exciting settings, will probably be longest remembered. John Barrymore has had a more varied career, perhaps, than any of the family. Some of his performances led critics to acclaim him the finest American actor but for some years now he has been unable to live up to his high rating. His best performances were in *The Affairs of Anatol* (1912), *Peter Ibbetson* (1917), *Redemption* (1918), *The Jest* (1919), *King Richard III* (1920), and *Hamlet* (called one of the truly great portrayals of the role, 1922). After long activity in the cinema, he returned to the stage in *My Dear Children* (1939), a drama which seemed partly autobiographical.

ETHEL BARRYMORE (1879-   ) is probably the most consistently excellent artist in the whole family (of which only the most outstanding members have been mentioned). She created a sensation in her first starring role in Fitch's *Captain Jinks of the Horse Marines* (1901); her performance in *Alice Sit-by-the-Fire* (1905) was delightful; her acting was considered naturalistic in *The Silver Box* (1907); she was brilliant in the title role of Somerset Maugham's *Lady Frederick* (1908). She appeared in Edna Ferber's *Our Mrs. McChesney* (1915); *Rose Bernd* (1922); as Ophelia, to Walter Hampden's Hamlet (1925); in *The Constant Wife* (1926); *The Kingdom of God* (1928), which opened the theatre named for her; and *The Ghost of Yankee Doodle* (1937). Her playing of the one hundred and one year old lead in *Whiteoaks* (1938) received considerably higher praise than the play itself. Miss Barrymore is still one of the vital actresses of our theatre.

It is necessary to turn back almost half a century to consider the situation of the theatre in our country at a time when the road was so flourishing a proposition that a group of men sought to control it as a group of speculators might attempt to corner a market in Wall Street. The prime movers in this were the firms of Klaw and Erlanger, Liebler and Company, Charles Frohman, Nixon and Nirdlinger, and others. It was their ambition to control the booking of every production which toured in America. They seem to have been largely responsible for lowering the standards of the road in America despite the fact that they boasted of managing Duse, Réjane, Eleanor Robson, Viola Allen, and others. The truth was that any theatrical offering was bluntly excluded from the Syndicate's distribution channels if it failed to meet with approval, or could not meet the terms they demanded. Naturally there was opposition. David Belasco and Mrs. Fiske fought the Syndicate up and down the land; Sarah Bernhardt played in a tent through Texas rather than yield to its demands.

This leads us naturally to the actor-producer-playwright DAVID BELASCO (c.1854-1931), who was born in San Francisco. Though his first appearance on the stage may have come earlier, we are sure that he acted the Duke of York in 1868 in Charles Kean's production of *King Richard III*, in Victoria, British Columbia. Soon he was acting in San Francisco and his first play *Jim Black; or, The Regulator's Revenge* was acted on the road when he was only twelve. His was an amazing career. None of his plays have any literary importance; a point in which he resembles his rival manager and playwright, Augustin Daly. However, many of them made stage history. What he wrote, alone or in collaboration, always came out of his experiences as an actor in his early youth, or his later directing and producing. He became stage-manager of the Madison Square Theatre in New York in 1880, after serving in a similar capacity for Baldwin's Theatre, the Grand Opera House, and the Metropolitan Theatre, in San Francisco. After staging Howard's *Young Mrs. Winthrop* (1882) he became associated with Daniel Frohman, in 1886, at the Lyceum Theatre on Fourth Avenue and his rise was steady from that moment. In 1887 he joined playwriting forces with HENRY C. DE MILLE (1850-93), who was playreader at the Madison Square Theatre. They produced four hits in a row, *The Wife* (1887), with Herbert Kelcey and Georgia Cayvan; *Lord Chumley* (1888), for E. H. Sothern, had overtones of Lord Dundreary, his father's famous role; *The Charity Ball* (1889) in which that fine character actress, Mrs. Thomas Whiffen, appeared to great advantage; and *Men and Women* (1890), with one of Frohman's casts: Sydney Armstrong, Maude Adams, Frederic de Belleville, William Morris and Orrin Johnson.

Between the second and third plays, Belasco staged Sophocles' *Electra* at the Lyceum Theatre in 1889, in which he made the first extensive use of the artistic stage lighting for which he was to become famous in later years. It was then, in all probability, that he realized that his real forte in the theatre lay in direction and production. Nevertheless he almost always had some hand in the plays he produced, whether his name appeared on the program as co-author or not.

He was anxious to become an independent producer, so in March, 1890 he severed his connection with the Lyceum and blossomed forth with *The Ugly Duckling* (1890) and *Miss Helyett* (1891), with the handsome Mrs. Leslie Carter, whom he trained as an actress and eventually established as a star. During his long career in the theatre he was responsible for the development of several actresses as stars; he had the uncanny knack of recognizing hidden potentialities and bringing them to the surface. He was like Reinhardt in this respect, for his stars did not always retain their seeming importance when they passed into the hands of less sympathetic, less understanding producers. It would be impractical to list all of Belasco's productions. They resembled each other only in so far as they stood for realism in the theatre. He was accused of overdoing naturalistic effects in staging, not in writing; however, it must be borne in mind that when he came into the theatre only Steele MacKaye cared anything for the artistic essentials of production. Other managers were willing for their actors to appear in front of such settings as had done service for the past two hundred years, without any real attempt to assimilate new ideas of staging. Because of an abhorrence of this Belasco probably went too far when he reproduced a Childs restaurant behind the proscenium in *The Governor's Lady* (1912). In spite of criticism he had accurately calculated some of the effects which attracted audiences. He rarely had a financial failure once his battle with the Theatrical Syndicate was won.

Besides Mrs. Carter, for whom he produced *The Heart of Maryland* (1895); *Zaza* (1899); *Du Barry* (1901); and *Adrea* (1905); he brought out Blanche Bates, in *Naughty Anthony* (1900); *Madame Butterfly* (1900); *Under Two Flags* (1901); *The Darling of the Gods* (1902) with George Arliss; *The Girl of the Golden West* (1905), with Frank Keenan; *The Fighting Hope* (1908); and *Nobody's Widow* (1910), with Bruce McRae. He took the Jewish comedian, David Warfield, out of Weber and Fields' act and made a dramatic star of him in *The Auctioneer* (1901); *The Music Master* (1904), which ran in New York and on the road for nearly four years; *A Grand Army Man* (1907); *The Return of Peter Grimm* (1911); and *The Merchant of Venice* (1922). He presented Henrietta Crosman in *Sweet Kitty Bellairs* (1903), in which that talented actress Jane Cowl made her first appearance. He trained Frances Starr who appeared in *The Rose of the Rancho* (1906); the serious drama, *The Easiest Way* (1909); *The Case of Becky* (1912); *The Secret* (1913); *Marie-Odile* (1915); and *Tiger! Tiger!* (1918), among others. Mary Pickford, who appeared in *The Warrens of Virginia* (1907), was starred in *A Good Little Devil* (1913), with Lillian Gish and Ernest Truex; Lenore Ulric, the most emotional actress under his management, appeared in *The Heart of Wetona* (1916), and *Tiger Rose* (1917). He also produced *The Son-Daughter* (1919), for which Albertine Randall Wheelan created beautiful costumes; *Kiki* (1921); Charles Mac-Arthur's and Edward Sheldon's *Lulu-Belle* (1926), with Henry Hull; *Mima* (1928); and *Ladies of the Evening* (1924), with the last of his stars, Beth Merrill.

In 1902, during his fight with the Syndicate, he took over the Republic Theatre (which he renamed the Belasco) in order to have a playhouse where he could let his productions be seen. He built the Stuyvesant Theatre (the present day Belasco) and opened it in 1907 with *A Grand Army Man* in which David Warfield appeared. He was one of the leading American managers and perhaps did more to train young actors than any other producer. He was sometimes associated in management with his son-in-law, Morris Gest. The latter was entrepreneur for such productions as the *Chauve-Souris* (1922), The Moscow Art Theatre (1923), *The Miracle* (1924), *Wonder Bar* (1931), and *Lady Precious Stream* (1936). In addition he managed the intimate musical shows at the Princess Theatre with F. Ray Comstock during the second decade of the century.

There are but two other writers who must be mentioned, before 1906. These are Clyde Fitch and AUGUSTUS THOMAS (1857-1934). Thomas was primarily interested in American themes, largely of a sectional nature. He was more of a newspaper reporter than a dramatist. He frequently took his titles from states as in the sentimental *Alabama* (1891); the political melodrama *In Mizzoura* (1893); *Arizona* (1899), in which honor and ethics are considered against a background of the army, cowboys and Mexicans. His best farce was *Mrs. Leffingwell's Boots* (1905), which had a successful run. His two most important plays were *The Witching Hour* (1907), a psychological drama about a gambler who discovers that his "luck" comes from mind reading; recognizing this he is able to conquer himself and to turn his abilities into more legitimate channels; and finally *The Copperhead* (1918), a serious drama about the Civil War in which Lionel Barrymore appeared to great advantage.

CLYDE FITCH (1865-1909) was the first writer of social comedy in this country to take unmistakable rank in world theatre. He borrowed much of his technique from Scribe, and his plot manipulations were expert. But beyond this lay a real feeling for the value of dialogue in the theatre. He unfortunately had a tendency to sacrifice the integrity of his plays for sure-fire effect. Had he been less successful, he might have been a better writer. He required less of actors in the way of interpretation than any man writing in the last days of the last century or the first decade of the present one. Unfortunately he was not so close to life, in the broad sense, as he might have been. Because of this, those of his plays which attempt to face facts are his least impressive.

Fitch always loved the theatre, acting as a child and in his college years at Amherst. There he designed scenery and costumes and learned the mechanics of the stage. This stood him in good stead when he wrote *Beau Brummel* (1890) for Richard Mansfield, theatrical but highly effective both as a play and as a film. *The Moth and the Flame* (1898, revised from a one-act play *The Harvest*, 1893) was his next original long play, a well-sustained melodrama. He turned to American history in *Nathan Hale* (1898), though he made little use of actual events. This play introduced a schoolroom scene, which has been a favorite device of American playwrights ever since. He took a thrilling Civil War legend for his even more successful *Barbara Frietchie* (1899); and in *The Cowboy and the Lady* (1899) he was one of the first to introduce the cowboy play, a vivid drama with a good basic situation and many excellent scenes.

As the delightful opera singer, Mme. Trentoni, Ethel Barrymore delighted audiences in one of Fitch's best comedies, *Captain Jinks of the Horse Marines* (1901). He revealed the machinations of toadying businessmen and society-loving women in the moralistic *The Climbers* (1901). The sentimentality of *The Stubbornness of Geraldine* (1902) came as a boon to Weber and Fields, who promptly burlesqued it as *The Stickiness of Gelatine* (1902), just as they had done with *Barbara Fidgetty* (1899). One of his most interesting plays was *The Girl with Green Eyes* (1903); the central character of which, in her jealous obsession, suggests the hopeless liar of *The Truth*. He has balanced the suspicious woman with a husband who, incapable of jealousy, finds it difficult to understand his wife's problem. However his decent reticence saves him. Fitch weakens his play by giving it a so-called happy ending out of deference to the supposed wishes of his audience. Some of his best scenes appear in the intensely emotional, well-wrought melodrama, *The Woman in the Case* (1905), which has genuine theatrical vitality. He exploited some of the characteristics of the German-American, as Harrigan had done, with *Her Great Match* (1905). His dramatization of Edith Wharton's fine novel, *The House of Mirth* (1906), was unsuccessful. His best comedy undoubtedly is *The Truth* (1907), that remarkable study of a woman who is a natural liar and who cannot help herself. Not only the character of Becky, but Roland and Mrs. Crespigny are exceedingly well drawn. The play was written with such smoothness that the critics did not grasp its real importance and, with Clara Bloodgood in the lead, it was a failure in New York. In April of the same year, Marie Tempest made a tremendous hit in the play in London. On the strength of this the play was sent on tour in America the next season and continued successfully until Miss Bloodgood shot herself in Baltimore. It was revived with critical and popular approval in 1914 by that excellent comedienne, Grace George, whose deftness as an actress has long been admired on our stage.

Fitch's final play *The City* (1909) was not produced until after his death and was, in many respects, his strongest work. In this he deals with the effect of city life upon a family who come to it from the small town in which, for generations, they have always been the leading citizens. The author's New England nature shows itself in this grim study of their disintegration. However, he does not blame the city, for it is his thesis that the good or bad in people can be brought out by the larger urban life, according to the seeds which are within them. It is as a student of character, in his better plays, that he will be remembered.

The tradition of the nineteenth century continued into our present era and did not die until the world cataclysm of 1914-18, when America emerged as a great nation, a world power, a stronghold of democracy. The beginnings of that awareness were foreshadowed in the theatre by the poet-dramatist William Vaughan Moody.

XXI

ROMANTICISM AND NATURALISM—
TO THE FALL OF PARIS
(1830-1940)

IT WAS a young and vigorous French manhood that swept in romanticism as it was sweeping out the Bourbons. It was a period of ardent excitement, hot enthusiasms and extreme partisanship. The French have always been noted for their liking for new literary and artistic movements, for which they find apt names. From romanticism to surrealism this has been true, and when there is a free France, and a new cultural enthusiasm sweeps its people, there will be more new movements and new names for them. This period is notable because for the first time art and literature were synonymous in the minds of their adherents. England had far outstripped France, as had Germany, and young Frenchmen felt that a new renaissance had come to them. It was in their blood; it was in the air; it swept everything before it.

Painters and sculptors wrote, poets painted; all composed music, while musicians were writing poems. The excitement was tremendous. Such men as Delacroix, Delaroche, Auber, Meyerbeer, Hugo, Gautier, Mérimée, Berlioz, David, Lamartine, Musset, Halévy, Dumas *père* were the new artists who could and did do everything. Charles X had been overthrown, Louis-Philippe, with his umbrella, had been made a citizen-king. The latter mistake was not corrected until 1848, but the artists kept freedom alive and thrilling.

There is another difference about this movement, which did not obtain in earlier theatrical developments in France. It received its inspiration in part, perhaps largely, from outside the country; from the German examples set by Goethe and Schiller as reported by Mme. de Staël in *De l'Allemagne* (1810), as well as from the visit of an English company to Paris in 1827. Headed by Charles Kemble they acted *King Lear, Othello, Macbeth* and *Hamlet* for the first time in a form

337

which might be said to represent Shakespeare truly to Parisian audiences. With these glowing performances in mind, VICTOR HUGO (1802-85) wrote the famous preface to his lengthy, unacted (and really unactable) drama, *Cromwell*. It was in this play that the son of a Napoleonic general and nobleman and a royalist mother, declared his defiance of classicism in the theatre. He had originally intended the play for production, but after death had removed Talma from the scene, this involved and repetitious drama about England's puritan dictator was left to the purely literary field. The principles of romanticism, derived in part from Jean-Jacques Rousseau, demanded a return to nature through its reflection in art.

After *Cromwell* (1827) came the characteristic *Marion Delorme* (1829) in which a morally soiled heroine (played originally by Marie Dorval) redeems herself through love. The play was considered indecent by the censor and its performance was forbidden. It was not until 1831, after the departure of Charles X, that the play was acted. Thus the honor of opening the campaign at the *Théâtre Français* was reserved for *Hernani*, which made theatrical history. The classicists were there to hiss it, for some of them had listened at the door and, catching single lines, had practiced caricatures of them. A burlesque version was acted before the play itself. Hugo had a hard time of it, fighting the censor at each step for each line. When the great night came, he announced that he would dispense with the paid claque, a device then in use in all the theatres and opera houses of the world. He knew he could count on the artists of Paris for his claque. Hugo was their god. His name was on every lip. The watchword was *Hierro* (iron) and on the night of the opening, February twenty-fifth, the architects, musicians and poets were there to battle for the cause, with flowing hair, velveteen breeches, and generally picturesque costumes.

The opening was bedlam. Scarcely a line could be heard that night and for a hundred nights thereafter the tumult continued. The classicists took boxes and left them unfilled. They turned their backs on the stage. They shouted and talked. But night after night the young adherents went back to the playhouse and cheered the lines of *Hernani* as though they had never heard them before. Their *esprit de corps*, their devotion to an ideal, was a magnificent thing. Seeing or reading *Hernani* today, we are likely to wonder, in the line from George M. Cohan's *The Tavern*, "What's all the shooting fer?" For all of Hugo's faults (as well as his special virtues) are apparent in this drama. The characters violate their own integrity, *point d'honneur* is raised to the absurdity of the Spanish drama and beyond it, the ending is contrived and unnatural. Yet, with all this, there is a lyric poetry in the piece, a music in the lines, which still charms us. Despite its own faults and the opposition of the classicists, the play was a success and opened the way for other romanticists to enter the playhouse.

In 1832 came *Le Roi s'amuse*, which was banned after a single performance because of its references to Francis I. In this powerful, but uneven, poetic drama the author throws off early royalist sympathies to adopt republicanism. It is perhaps best known to present day theatregoers in the form of the libretto of Verdi's opera, *Rigoletto*.

Having built his reputation upon his poetry (and his novels, for which he is now best remembered), Hugo found that Alexandre Dumas was having more success with his prose dramas than with his verse. Probably because of this he too turned to prose for his next three plays, *Lucrèce Borgia* (1833) with Mlle. Georges; *Marie Tudor* (1833); and *Angelo* (1835). It was an unfortunate move for his melodramas stood as what they were: stark, implausible, contrived. They were as bad as any of the strivings for a thrill which have infused this form since its inception in the last century. Hugo's poetry is all that stands between him and what used to be called "ten, twenty, thirty," the crudest melodrama of all.

Realizing his mistake, he returned to verse, albeit an individual poetic form which he had contrived in his earlier work by breaking up the rigid Alexandrine couplets traditional in the French drama. *Ruy Blas* (1838) has a better constructed plot, though it depends on a series of coincidences that sound ludicrous when repeated. Its character development is extraordinary as everyone develops in a kind of reverse fashion. However, this shoddy thinking, coupled with some really beautiful poetic passages, has made this play almost as popular in France as *Hernani*, and in England it was more so, particularly when Fechter appeared in it. Mlle. Mars' playing of Doña Sol gave the part tremendous vitality while Lemaître as Ruy Blas swept his audience off its feet at the *Théâtre de la Renaissance*.

With the failure of his trilogy, *Les Burgraves* (1843) Hugo realized that the playhouse was not for him. Poetry, novels and politics occupied the rest of his long life. This failure revealed something else and that was a change in the public response to the more extreme forms of romantic drama. The way was being paved for the entrance of realism, but we shall speak more fully of that later in this chapter.

Out of the boulevard melodramas of the celebrated Guilbert de Pixérécourt, with his popular *Victor ou l'Enfant de la Forêt* (1798), came the impetus which swung the romantic novelist, the quadroon ALEXANDRE DUMAS (1802-70), into the theatre with his *Henri III et sa cour* (1829). Dumas was one of the most prolific writers in France, having practiced the "speed-up" before it was thought of in Russia or the United States. He was accused of employing collaboration in a kind of literary factory. This system produced his novels *The Count of Monte Cristo*, *The Three Musketeers*, *The Queen's Necklace*, and many other works.

Henri III had a real success at the *Comédie-Française* and its excellent and telling plot, together with its introduction of justified illicit love, had a great deal to do with the popularization of the romantic movement. He followed this up with *La Tour de Nesle* (1832) with Mlle. Georges at the *Porte-Saint-Martin*. This play was destined to become hugely popular because of its use of all the tried and true melodramatic devices, some of which were new in Dumas' day. He understood that the important thing about a melodrama was that it should reach the unthinking audience, which wished to be amazed. Not having experienced either such exalted life or such degraded existence as is commonly portrayed in this form, even in the politer versions we know today, they were willing to risk all on faith. It was that quality in his audience which Dumas understood and of which he never lost sight in his three hundred volumes of plays, novels and stories.

One other play by Dumas should be mentioned before we leave him. The drama of passion, *Antony* (1831), reflects the middle-class life of his time and in a sense foreshadows the rise of realism even in the midst of the romantic. Nonetheless it is Byronic, for the English poet-dramatist had a strong hold on the imagination of Europe in the twenties and thirties of the last century.

The theatre which Hugo's plays ousted is typified by CASIMIR DELAVIGNE (1793-1843), a classic lamb among romantic wolves. He made some effort to inoculate his classicism with the romantic virus with but slight success. He is remembered today for that hoary actor's vehicle of the nineteenth century *Louis XI* (1832), in which Pierre Ligier created the title role. After the initial success of his classical *Les Vêpres Siciliennes* (*Sicilian Vespers*, 1819), he was sufficiently won by the new movement to violate the unity of action with the introduction of comic scenes into his serious play, *Marino Faliero* (1829).

The poet ALFRED DE VIGNY (1797-1863) belongs in a study of this kind for two very good reasons. The first is because he translated Shakespeare (the father of French romanticism) in a manner which was close to the spirit of the English dramatist. He chose but two, *Le More de Venise* (*Othello*, 1829), and *Le Marchand de Venise* (written but not acted, 1828). The second reason for Vigny's inclusion is the charming *Chatterton* (1835), in which his simplicity seems almost classic when placed beside the effusions of Hugo.

ALFRED DE MUSSET (1810-57) is still a delightful dramatist in the theatre despite the fact that he wrote but one drama to be acted, *La*

Nuit Venitienne (1831). This having failed, he wrote no more for the playhouse, but left a printed treasure trove in *Comédies et Proverbes* (1840) reprinted from the short pieces printed in the *Revue des deux mondes*. Many of these charming plays later found their way to the stage; some, in his lifetime. His finest serious play was *Les Caprices de Marianne* (1833), which was one of the best productions of the *Comédie*. Louis Delaunay (1826-1903) was particularly fine in this play from the first time he acted it, in 1851, until his retirement in 1887. It was restored to repertory in 1906. Musset's best comedies, which always have an underlying fatality, despite their brilliance, were *Il ne faut jurer de rien* (1836, acted at the *Théâtre Français* in 1848); *Un Caprice* (1837, acted in 1847); and *Le Chandelier* (1835, played at the playhouse established by Dumas, the *Théâtre Historique*, 1847). These are among the most successful and delightful of the modern productions of the *Comédie*. Musset's most nearly Shakespearean drama was *Lorenzaccio* (1834). As time has passed, the plays of Musset have increased in importance until now he seems to be the finest playwright of the first half century in France as well as a poet of the first rank.

At the same time that the romantic movement was at its height (1827-43), another popular element in drama arose which made much better sense to the average playgoer than the poetic grotesqueries. Its father was EUGÈNE SCRIBE (1791-1861) who, having been enormously successful in his own day, passed through a period of being completely neglected and under-rated. Today we can see that his great knowledge of plot manipulation was valuable to many more important writers. None other than Ibsen learned much of his technique from the man who was said to write a hundred plays a year, at the rate of ten a month, with two months' vacation in the summer. This was only possible because of the enormous number of collaborators he employed. He always gave them full credit and a share of the profits from his play-factory.

He won his audience with his well-plotted comedies of intrigue. Taking the *vaudeville* form, which was halfway between a play and a musical comedy, he made a real comedy or drama or even tragi-comedy from it. In the comedy form he is a blood relation of Beaumarchais, though without any of the latter's feeling for character. That was his weak point and perhaps is the greatest reason why his plays do not survive on the stages of the present day. The Russians, since the Revolution, have found his plots valuable as an exposé of *bourgeois* morality with the result that many more of his plays are to be seen in Moscow than in Paris.

Scribe invented the well-made play of which we hear so much in histories of dramatic theory and criticism. His disciple Sardou merely took the precepts of the master to heart and with the assistance of such accomplished players as Bernhardt and Fanny Davenport popularized them not only in Paris but in the whole of America in the last quarter of the century. It was Scribe who was the father of the historical comedies which have been more than a casual, if unacknowledged, inspiration for the wave of so-called "debunking" biographies and novels which swept over us shortly before and after the First World War. He it was who, in his best known play, *Le Verre d'Eau* (*A Glass of Water*, 1842), stated unequivocally that all the famous affairs of history have been determined by a petty motive. A wasteful European war was begun because Louis *Quatorze* criticized the design of a window in the *Trianon* which was defended by his Minister of War, Louvois. It is the ignoble motive in man which Scribe, the narrow realist, believed always dominated his actions. This theory was embodied in the plays he poured forth during the years that he was official dramatist for the *Gymnase*. His best known plays include *Bertrand et Raton ou l'Art de Conspirer* (1833); the appealing historical drama *Adrienne Lecouvreur* (written with Gabriel Legouvé in 1849), and the technically brilliant *La Bataille de Dames* (1851). The collaborators, other than Legouvé, with whom he worked most frequently were Jean Henri Dupin, Germain Delavigne, Delestre-Poirson, Marc-Antoine Desaugiers, Xavier Santine and A. H. J. Duveyrier who wrote under the name of Melesville.

The actress who created the role of Adrienne was none other than the distinguished Elizabeth Felix, known as RACHEL (1821-58). Born a Swiss Jewess, she was so poor that she sang in the streets until the musician, Alexandre Étienne Choron, took her under his protection until his death in 1833. Then she was entered at *St. Aulaire's Conservatoire de Musique*. After a beginning at the *Gymnase* in 1837, she went on to her debut at the *Comédie*, the twelfth of June the next year, in *Horace*. Then followed *Cinna, Andromaque, Tancrède* and *Iphigénie en Aulide* and by autumn she was famous. Her Phèdre was perhaps her greatest acting performance to which she brought such vigor and naturalness that she came to be regarded the most awe-inspiring actress of her time. Once she sensed her power, however, she bullied the *Comédie* and became the most money-grubbing person perhaps ever to have graced the French stage. This caused her to be disliked intensely but her acting was so superb that she was forgiven actions that even the great in any field can seldom afford to give vent to and still retain people's regard.

We can not leave this period without some mention of JEAN GASPARD DEBURAU (1796-1846), the most famous Pierrot of French pantomime, who was celebrated in Sacha Guitry's *Deburau* (1918). Associated with the *Théâtre des Funambules*, home of acrobats and variety turns, he played in a series of mimes in which the name of the character appears. When he was in his prime there came along VIRGINIE DÉJAZET (1798-1875), one of the most charming actresses of the nineteenth century, who played light farces and breeches parts. Her appearance in gay musical pieces and several short plays by Sardou was the delight of Paris for many years.

In contrast there was the actor, called the nineteenth century colossus of drama, FRÉDÉRIC LEMAÎTRE (1800-76). His beginnings are more suggestive of Deburau or Mlle. Déjazet than of a serious dramatic actor. He appeared as the lion on all fours in a pantomime, *Pyrame et Thisbé*, at that intimate theatre, the *Variétés amusantes* (fourth of the name). His first real success came at twenty-four in the tearful *L'Auberge des Adrets* at the *Ambigu*, in which he created the celebrated role of Robert Macaire. From then on, as far as the public was concerned, anything he did was to be admired. His romantic playing was excellent as this indicated and as *Ruy Blas* was to make certain. He created a number of characters including Don César in Dumanoir and D'Ennery's *Don César de Bazan* (1844), and Toussaint in Lamartine's *Toussaint-Louverture* (1850), in which he appeared in black-face.

The people did not long retain their taste for romantic dramas. With the failure of Hugo's *Les Burgraves* in 1843, and with the ascendant star of Scribe, other writers in the prose field were turning their attentions toward a more realistic drama, though the versifiers still clung to the romantic, as was natural. Rachel's success at the national dramatic theatre had certainly increased the recurring interest in the classics when FRANÇOIS POINSARD (1814-67) turned out *Lucrèce* (1843). This was more classic than romantic, and it came at the psychological moment to capture the public. He followed with the pathetic *Agnès de Méranie* (1846); *Charlotte Corday* (1850); the verse-play, *L'Honneur et l'argent* (1853); the drama of the Revolution *Le Lion amoureux* (1866), and the anti-clerical *Galilée* (1867).

There are several writers of dramatic verse to be mentioned before we return to the main current of prose in French drama. HENRI DE BORNIER (1825-1901) was educated in the classics and served as a librarian in, and later director of, the *Bibliothèque de l'Arsenal*, home of several of the finest theatre collections in France. His first play *Le Mariage de Luther* (1845), was accepted by the *Comédie-Française* when he was but twenty. The play for which he is remembered is a classical tragedy which could never have been written if the romantic movement had not existed. *La Fille de Roland* (1875) is an heroic drama which touched the imagination of its audience and was genuinely successful. His *Mahomet* (1888) was forbidden production because of the interference of the Turkish ambassador.

Though he was not yet born when the romantic dramatic movement was already dwindling, the poetic FRANÇOIS COPPÉE (1842-1908) was not insensible to it, in spite of living in a realistic era. He wrote in the Hugo tradition of florid poetry combined with some of the lyricism of Musset. His first play was in the latter genre, the one-act *Le Passant* (1869) staged at the *Odéon* (Sarah Bernhardt contributed to its triumph). So, also, was that incident of the Commune, *Le Pater* (1889), the performance of which was forbidden by the government. Of the first group the best, and probably his masterpiece, was *Pour la Couronne* (*For the Crown*, 1895), a serious verse drama. In this a man is about to betray his country and is killed by his son to save him from dishonor. Being unable to live with himself after this parricide, he falsely confesses to his father's crime so that he may die. It is a highly moving play. Both *Severo Torelli* (1883) and *Les Jacobites* (1885) are harsh and unpleasant. He did not have sufficient dramatic skill to master their themes.

In a sense JEAN RICHEPIN (1849-1926) might be compared with the poetic nature of Coppée. His *Le Chemineau* (*The Wayfarer*, 1897) constitutes a poetic link with Rostand as well as the earlier writer.

HONORÉ DE BALZAC (1799-1850) is so well known as a master of the novel that his plays are usually overlooked. Claimed both by the romantic and realistic movements, he belongs on the whole to the latter, despite his lifelong admiration for Sir Walter Scott who certainly, in the beginning, influenced his work. He will always be known for his analytical sketches which made up the great *Physiologie du mariage* (1829) and the long series of novels comprising the monumental *Comédie Humaine*. A dramatization of themes from these novels was produced by the Vakhtangov Theatre in Moscow, though only the most superficial aspects were touched upon in what was essentially an effort to discredit the French *bourgeoisie*. Three of the best known of his pieces written expressly for the theatre are *Pamela Giraud* (staged at the *Gaîté*, 1843), *La Marâtre* (*The Stepmother*, at the *Théâtre Historique*, 1848) and the penetrating *Mercadet* (*The Jobber*), successfully acted at the *Gymnase*, 1851, after having been completed by D'Ennery. It was eventually added to the repertoire of the *Comédie* in 1869.

It was not Balzac who was destined to inaugurate the realistic school of drama but ALEXANDRE DUMAS *fils* (1824-95), though there are those who claim the honor for Augier. Inasmuch as Augier first wrote in the old poetic form he is rather the consolidator of the claims staked out by Dumas than the actual prospector. Nonetheless his point of view undoubtedly influenced Dumas when the latter turned his own novel, *La Dame aux Camélias*, into a play in 1852 and condemned thousands of audiences to tears, for more than half a century, over the cruel fate of that good-hearted *fille de joie* of the higher class, Marguerite Gautier. The author certainly had no sentimental end in mind when he created the piece. He was concerned with painting a picture of French society. That he drew liberally on Hugo's play *Marion Delorme* was probably not intentional. He wanted to reform social conditions in France, forgetting that the world he saw was but a small part of the moral and social structure of the nation.

Following *Diane de Lys* (1853), which depended primarily upon its plotting, his third play, *Le Demi-Monde* (1855), was certainly his best and showed a great advance over the play popularly called *Camille* (usually played under that title in this country). The expert plotting of Scribe had its influence on Dumas. His depiction of character shows a keen perception and his method of advancing the plot by gradually lifting veils that cover the past is unusual and highly effective. In *La Question d'Argent* (*The Money Question*, 1857) he chose a subject out of the stock of Augier though the inadequacies of his early education denied him the knowledge to write the play he might have written. Its interest today lies largely in its witty dialogue. In *Le Fils Naturel* (*The Natural Son*, 1858), he considers, from first hand observation, the problems of illegitimacy. In this he clearly establishes for the first time the thesis play, *pièce à thèse*, for which he is remembered. He pleads the need for a change of law and social attitude toward the illegitimate child.

Of his other plays the most important are perhaps the puritanical *La Femme de Claude* (*Claude's Wife*, 1873); *Monsieur Alphonse* (1873), which in part anticipated the tough comedy of the *Théâtre Libre* movement; and that foreshadowing of the psychological method, *L'Etrangère* (1876), which employed a star-studded cast including Bernhardt, Coquelin, Got, Fèbvre, Mounet-Sully, Sophie Croizette and Madeleine Brohan.

ÉMILE AUGIER (1820-1899) began, as has been said, as a writer of verse plays which ill accorded with his solid, well-to-do *bourgeois* background and attitude toward life. His morality restrained the lyric enthusiasm of his verse and it was not until he turned to prose that he really achieved dramas of enduring merit. The play for which he is best remembered is *Le Gendre de M. Poirer* (*The Son-in-law of M. Poirier*, 1854) which was written in collaboration with Jules

Sandeau. This, as are his other plays, was rooted in the soil of France and stands for the fundamental virtues which were dear to his heart. Their defence could always command his pen. Marriage was a sacred thing; fidelity after the ceremony was not sufficient; one must prepare for it by keeping one's thoughts and deeds worthy of it. This was no frigid moralizing but emanated from a passionate love of virtue. Augier, alone or in collaboration, is never cold.

It is woman who unites the opposing ideologies of the nobles and the *bourgeois* in his collaboration, which was based on Sandeau's novel, *Sacs et Parchemins*. The satisfactory mingling of these ideals and points of view was vital to France at this period because the old and new aristocracy was being wedded to the *bourgeoisie* to provide a new social backbone for the country.

Le Mariage d'Olympe (1855) was an answer to Dumas' elevation of the courtesan, a view which he rejected so strongly as to have her killed on stage in his own play. This violence alienated his audience and the play was a failure. Somewhat similar in tone and in its general type of character was *Les Lionnes pauvres* (1858) written in collaboration with Edouard Foussier. In this, wives that sell their favors, and the moral dangers of luxury, are dealt with severely.

The three plays which, because of the continuity not only of ideas but of characters, constitute a trilogy are *Les Effrontés* (*The Shameless*, 1861); *Le Fils de Giboyer* (*Giboyer's Son*, 1862); and *Lions et Renards* (*Lions and Foxes*, 1869). The best and strongest of these is probably the second, which was anti-clerical in tone, for Augier's *bourgeois* ideas made him bigoted and unfair toward the Jesuits. Because of the political connotations of the drama, it required the direct intervention of Napoleon III to insure its production. *Les Fourchambault* (1879) was his last play because he was afraid that the work of his old age might not measure up to the standards of dramaturgy he had set for himself. Leading a blameless, happy and what he termed an uneventful life, he was anxious that if he were to be remembered it should be for the highest expression of his ideals.

At the time when Dumas *fils* and Augier were dealing with the thesis play, the out-worn French farce was undergoing rehabilitation in the capable hands of EUGÈNE LABICHE (1815-1888) who was the outstanding dramatic humorist of the nineteenth century in France. Some of his admirers foolishly claimed that his work was on a par with Molière, while detractors openly wondered how much was the contribution of his numerous collaborators. The latter point can perhaps best be answered in the words of Émile Augier, "The distinctive qualities which secured a lasting vogue for the plays of Labiche are to be found in all the comedies written by him with different collaborators, and are conspicuously absent from those which they wrote without him."

He began as a writer of *vaudevilles* with *Monsieur de Coislin ou l'homme infiniment poli* (*M. Coislin; or, The Infinitely Polite Man*, 1838), which introduced the low comedian, Paul Louis Auguste Grassot, who remained a favorite with the public for the rest of his life. This piece had the collaboration of Marc Michel and was performed at the *Palais Royal*. However, his plays in general can be divided into those whose primary purpose is to amuse and those in which philosophical thought is mingled without lessening the entertainment. Of the first class the best known is the hilarious *Le Chapeau de Paille d'Italie* (1851), which has known numerous adaptations in English, the best being *The Italian Straw Hat* and the most recent, *Horse Eats Hat*, adapted for a spirited production by Orson Welles and John Houseman under the aegis of the Federal Theatre. In this the farce formula which involves the search for something that only turns up after a chase lasting until five minutes before the final curtain, is employed to great advantage. Of the second class the best are *Le Voyage de M. Perrichon* (1860); *La Poudre aux Yeux* (*Dust in the Eyes*, 1861), both written in collaboration with Edouard Martin; and *Le Misanthrope et l'Auvergnat* (1852), which inaugurated his thoughtful farces.

While Labiche was a farceur EDOUARD PAILLERON (1843-99) contributed at least one play to thoughtful comedy that is a brilliant example of nineteenth century comedy at its best. Neither his first one-act play, *Le Parasite* (1860), nor the pathetic full-length *Les Faux ménages* (*The Hypocritical Households*, acted at the *Gymnase*, 1869), won the success achieved by his brilliant one-act drama, *L'Etincelle* (*The Star*, 1879). However, it is for *Le Monde où l'on s'ennuie* (*The World of Boredom*, 1881) that he is remembered. This is a delightful satire on the Parisian intelligentsia with whom he was thrown in contact not only as a playwright but as part proprietor of the *Revue des deux mondes*.

To return to the main thread of realistic French drama we come to VICTORIEN SARDOU (1831-1908), to describe whose work George Bernard Shaw invented the apt term *Sardoodledum*. He began his career with an insecure existence editing dictionaries and other works. Most of his plays could not secure a hearing and such as did were utter failures. He made quite a reputation for himself as an unsuccessful playwright before writing *Les Pattes de Mouche* (*A Scrap of Paper*, 1860), a drama of intrigue which attracted overwhelming popular support. From then on all went well with him and he became the most popular dramatic writer in France. He catered to his audience, adding every ingredient to his plays that experience had taught him would be relished. He was essentially a man of the theatre. He found opportunity in everything. Divorce supplied him with the subject of his salacious *Divorçons* (1880), which shocked and delighted his public. He wrote many of his plays for stars, to be employed by them as vehicles for their abilities or their charms, which is a heavy handicap for a dramatist to impose upon his playwriting. Mlle. Déjazet was the first; then Bernhardt, for whom he wrote the romantic *Théodora* (1884), operatic *La Tosca* (1887), the mediaeval Greek *Gismonda* (1894); and finally Sir Henry Irving, for whom he created *Robespierre* (1902) and, collaborating with Émile Moreau, *Dante* (1903).

Sardou was at his best in composing broad historical dramas of strong national feeling, such as *La Patrie* (*Fatherland*, 1869), which combined intrigue, passions, comedy (always a characteristic of his writing), imposing stage effects, good use of crowds which really participated in the lines as well as the action (thus anticipating the practice of Saxe-Meiningen, Reinhardt and other experts at mob scenes), as well as touches of melodrama. It is easy to see that everything the popular audience might fancy is thrown in. He did not advance dramatic technique, borrowing liberally from Scribe and every other nineteenth century dramatist, but he popularized the playhouse among a wide audience. His plays were scarcely less successful outside France than in Paris. Bernhardt triumphed in his historical dramas which gave her the opportunity to display her lively beauty in a series of magnificent costumes. In America Bernhardt and the emotional actress, Fanny Davenport, daughter of that fine player, E. L. Davenport, vied for public favor with rival productions of the same plays. Miss Davenport had the advantage of playing in English but Bernhardt's French was compensated by her exoticism and a magnificent gift for publicity. Sardou sat in Paris, wrote plays and made a vast sum of money together with a reputation which has since almost completely disappeared.

In the poular mind Rosine Bernhard, SARAH BERNHARDT (1844-1923) is naturally associated with Sardou because her world-wide reputation was achieved largely in his dramas. Her first success came at the *Odéon* as Cordelia in *King Lear*, and the queen in *Ruy Blas* in 1867, followed by Zanetto in Coppée's *Le Passant* (1869). Returning to the *Comédie-Française*, where she had had little success in her debut (1862), she covered herself with glory in *Phèdre* (1874) and as Doña Sol in *Hernani* (1877). Her vitality was amazing and endured until the very end for she all but died upon the stage. Her emotional power, her tremendous magnetism, the pathos of her death scenes, and above all her glorious voice, her *voix d'or*, made her one of the most memorable actresses of all time. Duse was her rival and for many years was considered inferior in ability (certainly in popularity). In the long view we are inclined to give the palm to the Italian actress but that does not necessarily minimize Bernhardt's own great position.

She was a sculptress of considerable ability and her work was admired, winning honorable mention in the Paris Salon in 1876. It was shown again in 1881. Her best known work was the bust of Sardou. She was also a painter and even composed a drama, *L'Aveu* (*The Confession*, 1888), but without much success. She did better in the reworking of old scripts for her own use and in the advice she was able to offer the men who composed vehicles for her talents.

After her break with the *Comédie*, occasioned by unfavorable criticism of her performance in Augier's *L'Aventurière* (1880), which she contended was insufficiently rehearsed, she began her tours. After London, she went to Denmark, Russia and America. From 1880 to 1881 she appeared almost every other season in some foreign country, including both Americas and Australia. Her American tours brought her fabulous sums but the repeated announcement of her "farewell tour" became scandalous and then amusing. Her last appearances were during the First World War to raise funds for French war charities.

Among her notable productions were Jules Barbier's *Jeanne d'Arc* (1890); Moreau's *Cléopâtra* (1890); Lemaître's *Les Rois* (which opened the *Théâtre de la Renaissance* in Paris in 1893); Rostand's *La Princesse Lointaine* (*The Faraway Princess*, 1895); Sudermann's *Heimat* (1895); Rostand's *La Samaritaine* (1897) and *L'Aiglon* (written for her, 1901). In 1899 she essayed the role of Hamlet, both in Paris and London, with a very mixed reception. She made a motion picture, *Queen Elizabeth*, in 1912. When she died, in 1923, the whole world mourned her passing.

Even Bernhardt had lesser rivals within her own country, of whom the most important was Jeanne Alfrédine Tréfouret, known on the stage as JANE HADING (1859-c.1934). She began her career in Algiers, in 1873, then played *coquette, soubrette* and *ingenue* parts at the Khedival Theatre in Cairo. Her voice showed promise and she returned to France, appearing in various operettas, but it was as leading woman for the Coquelin company that she became best known. Her outstanding performances were in Lavedan's *Prince d'Aurec* (1892), Capus's *La Châtelaine* (1902), and Donnay's *Le Retour de Jérusalem* (1903).

GABRIELLE RÉJANE (born Réju, 1857-1920) was one of the most versatile actresses ever to appear on the French stage. She began as a *soubrette*. Her first hit came in Henri Meilhac's *Ma camarade*

(1883) and soon she was known for her great emotional power, creating a reputation for herself in such dramas as Porto-Riche's *Amoureuse, Ma Cousine* and *Germinie Lacerteux.* The role of Catherine in Sardou's *Mme. Sans-Gêne* (1893) established her as the foremost comedienne of France, and she had particular success in New York in this play. *Zaza* and *La Passerelle* were two of her greatest triumphs. She was known for her vivacity, animation and lovely voice.

The greatest French actor of the latter half of the last and beginning of the present century was BENOÎT CONSTANT COQUELIN (1841-1909), known generally as Coquelin *aîné.* He made his debut at the *Comédie* in 1860 as Gros-René in Molière's *Le Dépit amoureux* following it the next year with an overwhelming success as Beaumarchais' Figaro. Until 1886 he remained at this theatre, creating role after role. Some of these were in Augier's *Paul Forestier* (1871); Dumas *fils' L'Etranger* (1876); Pailleron's *Le Monde ou l'on s'ennuie* (1881); and Erckmann and Chatrian's *Les Rantzau* (1884). After a disagreement with the theatre management over his right to make provincial tours, he resigned as *sociétaire* and toured Europe and America with great success. He returned to the *Comédie* in 1890 but split with them again in 1892, this time permanently. In 1897 he became director of the *Porte-Saint-Martin* where he won great acclaim in Rostand's immortal *Cyrano de Bergerac* the same year. He will always be identified with this role. In 1900 he toured the United States with Bernhardt and after their return appeared opposite her at the *Théâtre Sarah Bernhardt* in *L'Aiglon.* He was rehearsing the production of Rostand's *Le Chantecler* (1909) when he died. Two other members of the family who never reached the sublimity of Coquelin *aîné* were ERNEST ALEXANDRE HONORÉ COQUELIN (1848-1909), known as Coquelin *cadet,* and JEAN COQUELIN (1865-   ), who created the role of Ragueneau, in *Cyrano de Bergerac,* in his father's fine production.

Before Rostand created his furore in the theatre there was the naturalistic movement in France, emanating from Ibsen and Hauptmann and culminating in the *Théâtre Libre.* The names associated with naturalism are those of Zola, great novelist but indifferent playwright; Antoine; Daudet; but above all, as a writer, HENRI BECQUE (1837-99). He was an unimpassioned writer with a fondness for slipping in some of his best lines almost unnoticed. Violent as a person, always looking for affront, he even brought suit against a manager who refused one of his plays. None of this temperament went into his unaccented dramas, of which the best are *Les Corbeaux* (*The Crows,* 1882); and *La Parisienne* (1885). He achieved the natu ralist's aim, "a slice of life," without form and with little or no plot. In the earlier play a family of miserable people are being closed in upon by a number of completely unprincipled people who take advantage of the death of the father to get what pickings they can from the carcass of the unhappy family. Nevertheless theirs is no conscious villainy. All of the vultures are perfectly natural and behave with complete normality. Therein lies Becque's artistry, for he has foreseen his situation, the kind of characters appropriate to appear in it, and the pattern of their actions.

The technique is, if anything, firmer in *La Parisienne*, as the situation and characters are more concentrated. The perfect wife is also the perfect mistress. Enjoying a well-ordered life in both her capacities, she is tempted to change lovers. This will advantage her husband and make her lover realize her desirability in the event that he might be becoming surfeited. The change in pattern offends her and the even way of her existence is violated. Unable to bear the new arrangement she discards the second lover and resumes her relations with the first, her husband remaining undisturbed throughout. The picture is complete. It is a perfect example of the *comédie rosse*.

The novelist Émile Zola (1840-1903) had a real passion for the theatre despite his difficulty in adjusting himself to it as a writer. His theorizing is much more significant than his application of it. He swept the comedy of intrigue and mere plotting off the stage, just as he did the *pièce à thèse*. The action was to arise from character; the logic from "sensations and sentiments," not from facts; conflict, and the plot, from life with the introduction of no foreign, artificial stimulus. This is very close to the best dramaturgy as we understand it today. He had his greatest success in his first play *Thérèse Raquin* (1873), the first tragedy of the naturalistic theatre in France. *Thérèse* and her lover, Laurent, decide to murder her husband. This they do by drowning him. But they have not sufficient strength to profit by their crime. The night of their marriage they commit suicide. Neither *Les Héritiers Rabourdin* (1874); nor *Le Bouton de Rose* (*The Rose Bud*, 1878), adapted from a story in Balzac's *Contes Drôlatiques*, are of genuine significance.

Another writer of fiction was drawn into the theatre, Alphonse Daudet (1840-97), but he never achieved the impersonality necessary for full success. Only in *L'Arlésienne* (1872), out of his beloved and native south, does he achieve in the theatre the fine documentation on which he prided himself. It was a complete failure at its first performance but when revived in 1885, during the full flush of the naturalist movement, it was extremely well received and has remained ever since as one of the bright spots in the repertory of the *Odéon*.

GUY DE MAUPASSANT (1850-1893), the superb short story writer of deserved fame, attempted the theatre three times. The first was in an untitled piece given at *Étretat* privately on two occasions, in 1873, before an audience which included Turgeniev, Meilhac and Flaubert. In this, Maupassant acted the role of a woman. It was twenty years before he returned with another drama, *Musotte* (1891), in collaboration with Jacques Normand, which though interesting does not reveal the wonderful powers of observation for which he is famed. Upon his death, a two-act comedy, *La Paix du Ménage* (*The Peace of the Household*, 1893), was discovered.

The man who was responsible for properly transferring the plays of naturalism to the stage, and who gave encouragement to the movement by providing an assured, uncensored audience, was ANDRÉ ANTOINE (1858-1943). His reputation is world wide and even twenty years ago people had the feeling that anyone so famous should be dead. Nothing he did in his subsequent career as a fine director of the *Odéon* could measure up in any way to his brilliant eight years, between 1887 and 1894, at the *Théâtre Libre*. He was an obscure clerk working for the gas company in Paris, an amateur actor in his spare time. He had no money, except for his small salary, but out of this he financed the whole project, renting a tiny hall, assembling a company and persuading an audience to attend that bill of one-act plays, which on the night of March 30, 1887, launched a theatrical experiment that in time was to influence the *Freie Buehne*, The Moscow Art Theatre, and many years later The Theatre Guild, in New York. The plays were received indifferently that first night, only Léon Hennique's *Jacques Damour*, an adaptation from a novel by Zola won attention. Two months later the second bill was made up of the three-act comedy, *La Nuit Bergamasque* by Émile Bergerat, and the one-act *En Famille* by Octave Méténier. From that performance the success of the venture grew. Antoine was taken seriously in his efforts and he began the second season with thirty-seven subscribers to his performances, which were private (thus eluding the censor), and a debt of several thousand francs. During these years he gave a hearing to such men as Curel, Brieux, Courteline and Ancey. The distinguished *doyen* of the critical corps, Francisque Sarcey, was hostile; and Jules Lemaître misunderstood Ibsen, thus missing the whole idea of the movement. Nonetheless Antoine gave almost the first hearing to such important foreign dramatists as Tolstoi, Ibsen, and Hauptmann. Though not openly associated with this theatre, Georges de Porto-Riche, Henri Lavedan, Maurice Donnay, Paul Hervieu, and even the critical playwright Lemaître, profited by the moral and intellectual awakening promoted by Antoine.

It has long been popular to say that the poetic theatre, in *La Princesse Lointaine* and *Cyrano de Bergerac* sounded the death knell of naturalism, but this Rostand himself denied. Naturalism passed easily into realism in France as it had elsewhere. The Free Theatre had done more than introduce naturalism, it had changed the whole concept of staging and acting in Paris, the stronghold of conservatism in the theatre. Antoine reformed the oratorical tradition of acting, though it persisted at the *Comédie* down to Edouard Bourdet's management in the nineteen-thirties. It is admired by the French and is hard to uproot. The "natural" directors probably went too far, with their low-pitched voices, and actors with their backs consistently to the audience, but at least they gave themselves and others a new concept of acting and direction.

These were not the only experimental theatres of the time, though many of them tarried but briefly. A whole study of the movement might properly be made in its relation to the little theatre movement of the present day. Perhaps the most interesting was the *Théâtre d'Art*, organized by Paul Fort in 1891 and joined by ALEXANDRE LUGNÉ-POE (1869-1940), who had spent two years' apprenticeship (1888-90) under Antoine. In 1893 the *Théâtre l'Oeuvre*, founded by Lugné-Poë, opened with such plays as *Pelléas et Mélisande* and *Rosmersholm*. It can be said to have carried on the experimental productions of the *Théâtre Libre* when that organization expired. Lugné-Poë championed Ibsen, who became a symbol with him, as well as all outstanding foreign dramatists. He was always most hospitable to Hauptmann, Schnitzler, Tolstoi, Wilde, d'Annunzio, Synge, Kaiser, and such pieces from the Orient as *The Little Clay Cart* and *Sakuntala*. Later in his career, in the nineteen-twenties, he staged Crommelynck's *Cocu Magnifique;* Natanson's *L'Age Heureux;* Orna's *L'Égoïste*, and the work of other contemporary writers. In addition to direction, which was his principal concern, he was a fine actor and toured widely.

The most important writer to come out of the *Théâtre Libre* was EUGÈNE BRIEUX (1858-1932), a reformer in the shape of a dramatist. His plays have become outmoded with the passage of time, but between 1890 and 1920 interest in him was enormous not only in his own country but upon the Anglo-Saxon stage as well. The reason why this preacher's work has been so largely discarded lies in his journalistic attack upon a problem. There is too little poetry and too much didacticism. However, he said a great deal that needed saying and a reading of his plays gives as accurate a picture of social conditions in France, in those years, as do Ibsen's dramas for Norway.

Ménages d'Artistes (1890) and the more important *Blanchette*

(1892), at Antoine's theatre, began the important part of his writing career. The second play is concerned with the problem of the young woman who wants to teach. He considers the problems of philanthropy in *Les Bienfaiteurs* (*The Philanthropists*, 1896); the ill effects of marriages of convenience in *Les Trois Filles de M. Dupont* (1897); the perversion of justice under the French legal system in *La Robe Rouge* (1900); the need for legal birth control in *Maternité* (1903); the problem of venereal disease in the modern world in *Les Avariés* (*Damaged Goods*, 1902); superstition and religion, against an Egyptian background to disarm criticism, in *La Foi* (*Faith*, 1909); and the situation of a young woman compelled to work in competition with men in *La Femme seule* (1912). Brieux lacked the traditional wittiness of the French but he made up for it in earnestness and he undoubtedly made people think. As that, after all, was his intention, he succeeded at it; so perhaps we should not quibble about his artistry. There were several who followed in his footsteps; ÉMILE FABRE (1870-   ) offers, in *La Vie publique* (*Public Life*, 1902), his most characteristic work, a study of political compromise and moral defeat.

In contrast to Brieux stands the work of that serious dramatist FRANÇOIS DE CUREL (1854-1928). His plays are more esteemed now than when they were first produced under Antoine's direction. He led the life of a literary amateur and composed dramas when the artistic spirit moved him. He was far from the naturalism of the movement with which he was at first identified, being spiritual in concept and almost romantic in approach. The development of character seemed to him the most interesting contribution to dramatic literature and most of his plays do not fit conveniently within the proscenium arch. They have been little acted outside of their own country because few of them were commercial successes and his dramaturgical weaknesses seem emphasized in translation. He was a psychological dramatist with a strong interest in unusual situations in which he searches out the dark and hidden motives of human conduct. Each of his plays is different from the others so that it is hard to select a typical one to represent him. Perhaps his best are *Le Repas du Lion* (1897, but rewritten in 1920); *La nouvelle Idole* (published 1895, acted 1899); and what is perhaps his masterpiece, *La Fille sauvage* (*The Savage Girl*, 1902). This symbolic drama, which relates the whole spiritual history of mankind, strongly shows the influence of Ibsen which is apparent in a number of his plays.

GEORGES DE PORTO-RICHE (1849-1930) began as a poet and this quality is inherent in all his work no matter how seemingly realistic it became. Love was the subject which most interested him, along

with Donnay, Bataille, Pierre Woolff, Romain Coolus, Francis de
Croisset, and others. He really wrote but one play and created but
one character, for all of his later plays are in one way or another an
elaboration of his first (long) play and his best, *Amoureuse* (1891).
His single character is always a woman in love, whom he describes
wittily and with light detachment. *Amoureuse* is one of the finest high
comedies of the modern theatre. Its huge success doubtless carried
the Parisians back to see his later plays, which grew longer and
longer. *Le Vieil Homme* (1911) reached four hundred printed pages.
Neither that nor *Le Passé* (*The Past*, 1898) touch the heights. He
wrote less and less, but polished and repolished, and lengthened his
plays until they reached the absurdity of *The Old Man*.

MAURICE DONNAY (1859-1945) preached the right to love and, in
contrast to Curel and Porto-Riche, turned out many plays for the
Paris boulevard theatres. He understood the interests of his public and
supplied what it wanted, albeit with considerable artistry. He prepared an excellent adaptation of *Lysistrata* in which Réjane appeared
in 1892. With *Amants* (*Lovers*, 1895) he appeared in the front rank
of sophisticated drama. This ironic play of free love has remained
his best despite the success of the long line which followed it. The
problems of earning a living or adjusting oneself to social conditions
never emerge in the witty pastries which Donnay concocts. *La
Douleureuse* (1897) and *L'Affranchie* (*The Free Woman* (1898)
are perhaps his best plays after *Amants*.

HENRI LAVEDAN (1859-1940) is undoubtedly the most outstanding
of the worshipers of the gentle passion in modern French drama. His
boulevardism, however, did not prevent his writing several realistic
plays of much interest. *Le Prince d'Autrec* (1892) is a character
study which has been likened to *Le Gendre de M. Poirier* because
an aristocratic family is ruined by the extravagances of a young prince
only to be saved by his bourgeois mother. At best he was a trivial
writer, with a large popular following, as is evidenced by such exposés
of the vices of the social world as *Viveurs* (*High Life*, 1895); *Le
Nouveau Jeu* (*The New Fad*, 1898); *Le Goût de Vice* (*The Taste
for Vice*, 1911) and other similar plays.

HENRI BATAILLE (1872-1922) is another devotee of love who composed innumerable triangle plays in almost every possible combination. To read one after the other is enough to make a man ascetic
but he succeeded in his purpose which was to provide every season,
or almost that often, a new piece for the boulevards. One play is
rather like another, but a variant of the situation piqued a prurient
curiosity in his public each time. *Maman Colibri* (1903), is the story
of a middle-aged woman who has an affair with a friend of her son.

La Femme nue (*The Naked Woman*, 1908, acted in English as *Dame Nature*) is concerned with an artist who offers marriage to his model, only to repent of it because he wants to marry a wealthy Jewess who is married, in turn, to an elderly prince. He offers to divide his time between the two women, the husband in the case being complacent so long as he does not lose his wife's money. *Les Flambeaux* (*The Torches*, 1912) is blessed with a scientific background but the passion of a famous research specialist for his young secretary, and the wife's efforts to defeat it, prove similar to his other plots.

PAUL HERVIEU (1857-1915) is probably the most representative of all the French dramatists of this period because he never seems to have a thought which is not characteristic of his nation. It is only in his lack of wit that this rational writer is un-French. Several of his plays are devoted to proving a thesis in the most logical manner possible. In these his structure is bare and the characters scarcely filled out, which weakens them in the theatre. An example of this is *La Course du Flambeau* (*The Passing of the Torch*, 1901) in which he matches maternal against filial affection with the former outweighing the latter. This would seem more natural if it were not for the fact that the woman in this case is faced by the alternative of saving her daughter's life at the expense of her own mother's. The outcome seems far-fetched and remote.

In *Les Tenailles* (*The Nippers*, 1895), he considers the situation of a woman who wishes to divorce her husband. The husband declines to permit their incompatible marriage to be severed, so she deceives him with another and has a child by her lover. Several years later the husband is willing to grant her a divorce, after she has told him in a quarrel that the child is not his, but now she refuses in order to protect her son. *Connais-toi* (*Know Thyself*, 1909), is a plea for tolerance in marriage, a rejection of the rule which requires the unfaithfulness of wives to be punished, in the case of a husband who loves his wife and wants to forgive her. *La Dédale* (*The Labyrinth*, 1903) shows his concern for children as alienated parents are brought together at the sickbed of their child. *Les Paroles restent* (*Words Remain*, 1892) shows the evil which slander can cause and is reminiscent of Echegaray's *El gran Galeoto* (*The Great Galeoto*). *La Loi de l'homme* (*The Law of Man*, 1897) is again a thesis play, for a woman denied divorce has left her husband but is forced to return to him in order to insure the happy marriage of her daughter. Hervieu was primarily a moralist as his plays show.

There is no French dramatist who has been held in higher esteem in the past half-century than EDMOND ROSTAND (1868-1918). The high enthusiasm for his masterpiece, *Cyrano de Bergerac* (1897) has faded somewhat and there is a tendency to minimize its standing in the long view of dramatic effect. But it is impossible to underestimate its popular appeal even after forty years. Rostand stands for poetry and romance, which is always an underlying strain in drama, though sometimes the blood stream becomes so anaemic as to make us think it has dried up, and there is no more. But even if there are only two works of genuine quality in a century that is quite enough to keep alive the soul of the theatre.

Rostand can be said to have really begun his dramatic career with *Les Romanesques* (*The Romancers,* 1894). This delightful comedy was much acclaimed at the *Théâtre Français* where it was produced. It drew on *Romeo and Juliet,* as well as *A quoi rêvent les jeunes filles* by Alfred de Musset, and has been called a burlesque, which seems a somewhat doubtful classification. The next year he produced *La Princesse Lointaine* (*The Faraway Princess*) for Sarah Bernhardt. This portrays the high idealistic love of Joffroy, the troubadour, for the lovely princess, Melisinde; it has great pathos and real lyric beauty. This was followed by another drama for Bernhardt which exhibited an advance in dramatic technique.

Then came that highly colored, brilliant romance *Cyrano de Bergerac* based loosely on the almost legendary seventeenth century figure. The première has been compared to that of *Le Cid* or *Hernani,* which is really an error for the latter plays inaugurated schools of dramatic technique whilst *Cyrano de Bergerac,* at best, reaffirms romantic thought. It is Rostand's top flight, though he did not descend too far in his later plays.

He followed this great success with another, though *L'Aiglon* (1900), cannot compare with *Cyrano.* The very nature of the historical subject precluded that. Nevertheless it provided a vehicle for Sarah Bernhardt, Maude Adams and others. His next play, *Chantecler,* was a fantasy employing only animal characters. It was presumably stimulated by his retirement to the country and a first hand observation of nature. Its lyric satire was merely a curiosity on the stage, for this is a complex play that must be read with care to be appreciated. The characters are sometimes animals, refined to a high point; sometimes they are human beings pretending to animal nature. Coquelin's death delayed its production until Lucien Guitry could be secured for the role of Chantecler. Mme. Simone played the Hen-pheasant. Rostand's last play, which was not quite finished when he died, *La Dernière Nuit de Don Juan* (*The Last Night of Don Juan*), was not published until 1921 nor played until 1922. It added nothing either to the Don Juan legend or to its author's reputation.

Several writers remain to be mentioned who are either remembered or cherished for a single play or who have developed a style so characteristic that one play can answer for all. In a country as prolific in playwrights of real ability as France in the late nineteenth and twentieth century, some compression is necessary.

The French stage maintained a remarkably high literary level until immediately after the First World War. There were brilliant revivals in the twenties, and again in the middle thirties, but there were too few new talents arising. The post-war theatre was largely a muster of dramatic abilities which had already been in harness before 1914. The stage was dying at its roots despite a surface brilliance that was deceptive. Whether new shoots will grow up around the old stump, which is all the Second World War has left of the tree, is too speculative for any except the clairvoyant. We can but hope.

There are many writers who have achieved fame of a sort, whose names can merely be mentioned. Of these the most outstanding are: Henri Meilhac, Ludovic Halévy, Alexandre Bisson, Edmond de Goncourt, Octave Feuillet, Octave Mirbeau, Émile Moreau, Georges Ohnet, Pierre Véber, Pierre Loti, Catulle Mendès, Oscar Méténier, Georges Mitchell, Gaston-Armand de Caillavet, Alfred Capus, Michel Carré, Robert de Flers, Georges Feydeau, Paul Bourget, Tristan Bernard, Paul Nivoix, François Porché, René Fauchois, Jean Sarment, Boussac de Saint Marc, Charles Vildrac, Gabriel Marcel, Paul Demasy, Denys Amiel, Jean Victor Pellerin, André Birabeau, Jacques Natanson, Marcel Achard, Jacques Deval, A. P. Antoine, and Jean Cocteau. This list could be extended almost indefinitely and many of the men who are merely mentioned have much to offer. The farces of Flers and Caillavet have been played everywhere. Goncourt is one of the great literary figures of the mid-nineteenth century. Detailed studies of these and others may be found in the numerous histories of the French theatre. The closer we come to the present day, the more the problems of compression are encountered, so that we can select from the vast array of talent in each country only the most significant or influential names.

Romain Rolland (1866-1944) is so much better known as a novelist than as a dramatist that there is always a chance, not only of overlooking his plays, but also his very original thoughts about the theatre. Being unwilling merely to contribute to the commercial stage, he was connected with the people's theatre movement and wrote a most informative and provocative book on the subject, translated into English by Barrett H. Clark as *The People's Theater* (1918).

Rolland was inspired by Shakespeare and the philosopher Renan, but he never reached even remotely near his gods. He tried to write for the masses but his plays are not such as to appeal to them despite his conscious striving, or rather, because of it. He was a pacifist before the First World War and transferred his residence to Switzerland when his views clashed with those of his countrymen. This, coupled with his fondness for the Germans, explains perhaps the remarkable popularity his *Danton* (1899) and *Le quatorze Juillet* (1902) had in post-war Germany. These plays are intended for large and popular production, the latter calling for audience participation in the singing and dancing which ends the play. *Le Jeu de l'amour et de la mort* (*The Game of Love and Death*, 1925) also is derived out of the French Revolution as is *Les Loups* (*The Wolves*, 1898). Rolland's plays are filled with rhetorical speeches and high-flown oratory. Occasionally, however, he came down to earth in a scene which was drawn from within his characters and was also of high theatrical effect, as in the short scene between Courvoisier and Carnot in the second act of *The Game of Love and Death*. In its New York production, played by Frank Conroy and Claude Rains, it electrified an audience which had been lulled almost to sleep by the long-winded speeches preceding it.

Rolland found a disciple in GEORGES DUHAMEL (1884-   ), a Parisian doctor, at least three of whose plays possess real dramatic power. His protagonists are real characters, but in a sense they are all the same person. His women are never clearly defined, despite the fine acting of his wife, Blanche Albane, in the feminine leads. *La Lumière* (*The Light*, 1911) was produced by Antoine at the *Théâtre de l'Odéon* in 1912. Symbolism, irony, tenderness runs through this as it does through *Dans l'ombre des statues* (*In the Shadow of the Statues*, 1913) and *Le Combat* (*The Combat*, 1913).

Though PAUL CLAUDEL (1868-   ) wrote a number of plays, it is for *L'Annonce faite à Marie* (*The Tidings Brought to Mary*, 1912) for which he will be remembered. A descendant of Maeterlinck, and Mallarmé, there is a symbolism and allegory about this, as in his other plays of religious nature, that are touching. There is something of the mediaeval mystery in its quality of simple, saintly resignation. He also received considerable acclaim for *L'Otage* (*The Hostage*, 1911).

HENRY BERNSTEIN (1876-   ) is a writer of astonishing versatility. Just when you think it is safe to dismiss him as a mere boulevard writer, he turns out a play of some merit. When you expect the most of him, he is the least rewarding, as a general rule. His tendency is to follow the fashion. His most recent play, *Elvire* (1940), was anti-Nazi and was running when Paris fell. Needless to say it was hastily closed and its author is now in America. He is a highly Semitic writer and many of his plays have either rebuked anti-Semitism or gloried in the accomplishments of his race. His best known play is an improbably contrived and heavy drama, *Le Voleur* (*The Thief*, 1907); but *Le Détour* (1902), *L'Elévation* (*To the Heights*, 1917); and *Mélo* (1929) have attracted considerable attention for their dextrous stagecraft.

Two other writers for the commercial stage have attracted a fairly extended following because of their wit, Sacha Guitry and ALFRED SAVOIR (1883-1934). Savoir was much more than a mere farceur, though his comedies were light and amusing. There was a bitter savagery about some of his work, such as *Le troisième couvert* (*The Third Cover*, 1906); *Baptême* (*Baptism*); and *L'éternel mari* (*The Eternal Husband*, 1911). His comedies possessed unusual wit and retained it even in translation, as in *La huitième femme de Barbe Bleue* (which was graced with a scintillating performance in America by Ina Claire as *Bluebeard's Eighth Wife*, 1921); *Banco* (1922); and *La Grande duchesse et le garçon d'étage* (*The Grand Duchess and the Waiter*, 1924). His *Lui* (*He*, 1929); and *Le Dompteur* (*The Lion Tamer*, 1925) were symbolical, and his historical comedy, *La petite Catherine* (1931) was a brilliantly malicious portrait of the Russian empress.

SACHA GUITRY (1885-   ) was born into the theatre, having a distinguished actor-father in Lucien Guitry, for whom, in 1919, he wrote his best play, *Pasteur*. Though *Nono* (1905); and *La Prise de Berg-op-Zoom* (*The Taking of Berg-op-Zoom*, 1912), were gay successes before the war of 1914-18, he did his best work afterwards. Besides *Pasteur* he wrote other biographical plays, *Deburau* (1918); *Beranger* (1920); *Mozart* (1925); and *Charles Lindbergh* (1928). Of his later comedies *Jean de La Fontaine* (1922) and *Le nouveau testament* (*The New Will*) are perhaps the wittiest. In addition, he is probably the best high comedian on the Paris stage where he has been idolized with his successive wives. Of these, Yvonne Printemps (present wife of Pierre Fresnay) is best known.

The best of the older group of serious playwrights are Paul Raynal, Paul Géraldy and HENRI RENÉ LENORMAND (1882-   ). Lenormand is the master dramatist of the unconscious desires and weaknesses of humanity. Among his fifteen or so plays, the most outstanding are *Le temps est un songe* (*Time is a Dream*, 1919) which explores the possibility of the simultaneousness of time; *Simoun* (1920) contemplates both the psychology and physiology of a growing incestuous love of a man for his daughter, of which he is unconscious almost to the end; and *Les Ratés* (*The Failures*, 1920), his masterpiece. This study of weaklings against a theatrical background is relieved from any melodrama by the accurate observation of character and the detailed exposition of weakness which is drawn with such sincerity as to win our affectionate interest.

PAUL RAYNAL belongs both to the psychological school of Lenormand and to the new school of tragedy which he heads. In the first group undoubtedly his best play is *Le maître de son coeur* (*The Master of His Heart*, 1920), which studies the destruction of the friendship of two men by a woman who is jealous of it. This play has since been added to the repertory of the *Comédie-Française* as worthy of future survival. His tragedy *Le tombeau sous l'Arc de Triomphe* (*The Tomb beneath the Arc de Triomphe*, 1924, acted in this country as *The Unknown Warrior*) is a poignant study of a soldier in wartime and his last moments of happiness with his sweetheart and his father before he goes to a death of which he is certain.

PAUL GÉRALDY treated the problems of sex as a serious psychological study rather than reducing them to the formula of farce or light comedy. Though he is inclined to be overly introspective about his characters he is nonetheless a sound and thoughtful writer. His best plays are probably *Les noces d'argent* (*The Silver Wedding*, 1917) which is concerned with the ingratitude shown parents by their children; *Aimer* (*To Love*, 1921) is a character study of a woman who is tempted to take a lover but thinking over the situation and recalling her dead child, she pulls up short, and puts the temptation aside; and *Robert et Marianne* (1925), a two-character drama, presented at the *Comédie-Française*, which examines the marriage relationship from a purely intellectual point of view.

JEAN GIRAUDOUX (1882-), who won recent notoriety by his conduct of French military censorship in the Second World War, is known principally for two plays. *Siegfried* (1928, adapted from his novel) deals with the situation of a French soldier who suffers from amnesia as the result of war wounds. He is nursed back to health by a German woman and believes himself to be a German. He rises to power within the state, but when through the political schemings of an enemy his memory is returned to him, he disappears to become a Frenchman again. In *Amphitryon 38* (1929), an independent study of the Amphitryon legend, he presents his most brilliant play. Its wit and gaiety were scarcely suggested by the brief adaptation prepared by S. N. Behrman for Alfred Lunt and Lynn Fontanne.

JULES ROMAINS (1885-), whose reputation as a dramatist is obscured by the magnitude of his monumental series of novels known as *Les Hommes de Bonne Volonté* (*Men of Good Will*), has provided at least two provocative dramas. *Knock* (in English *Dr. Knock*, 1924), in its satire, is a worthy follower of Molière, while *Donogoo* (1930) is principally interesting for its curious use of cinematic technique, which proved that the post-war French theatre was not entirely dead to dramatic experiment.

JEAN-JACQUES BERNARD (1888-   ), son of the humorous writer, Tristan Bernard, has written a number of half-realized novels of intelligence and artistry but has only reached the heights once. *Martine* (1922), brilliantly staged by Gaston Baty, is a simple and completely naive drama of the heartbreak of a country girl and the complete waste of her life through a passing (for the man) love affair from which she never recovers. Bernard has here examined a woman's soul with great penetration and understanding.

EDOUARD BOURDET (1887-   ) was director of the *Comédie-Française* when war broke out in 1939. He had given the national house of drama one of its liveliest directorates during the thirties. He is best known for his character studies as well as for his slick portrayals of present day society. *La Prisonnière* (*The Captive*, 1926), which studies homosexual love with both sympathy and penetration, is restrained and never offensive in its portrayal, though it brought about a revival of censorship upon its American production in 1927. *Le Rubicon* (1910) and *Le Sexe faible* (*The Weaker Sex*, 1929, acted in New York with the punning title of *The Sex Fable*), a gay comedy of manners, are also among his best plays.

MARCEL PAGNOL (1895-   ) burst on the scene in a blaze of sensation in *Les marchands de gloire* (*Merchants of Glory*, 1924), in collaboration with Paul Nivoux. Though uneven in writing this drama of war profiteers is brutal in its impact. His ironic comedy, *Topaze* (1928) is a masterpiece of satire in its study of unscrupulousness. His local studies of Marseilles characters in *Marius* (1930) and *Fanny* (1931) are keenly observed.

SIMON GANTILLON is truly a man of one play, *Maya* (1924), which is a study of a prostitute who believes herself to be a kind of Mother Earth. In this she might be compared with Cybel in O'Neill's *The Great God Brown*. The New York police thought it merely an extremely salacious play when it was brilliantly presented by the Neighborhood Playhouse and required its closing under pain of prosecution, thereby robbing America of one of the most interesting of modern dramas.

STÈVE PASSEUR is the most mordant writer of the post-war period. His work, however, is extremely uneven and he has been both condemned for prolixity and ranked with Racine for the purity of his line. His work is frequently grotesque and almost always bitter. His most typical play is *L'Acheteuse* (*The Woman Buys*, 1930), in which a perverted middle-aged spinster buys a lover. It is sadistic in its unpleasantness. Passeur was introduced to the Paris stage by Lugné-Poë, who has been responsible for giving so many young writers their first opportunity.

JACQUES COPEAU (1878-   ), like Lugné-Poë was an innovator in the theatre. In 1913 with five friends, Louis Jouvet, Charles Dullin, Gaston Gallimard, Charles Paquement and Jean Schlumberger, he opened the *Théâtre du Vieux Colombier*. It was a success from its inception and has been compared with Antoine's *Théâtre Libre* in its influence. Out of it grew *La Compagnie des Quinze* of which Pierre Fresnay and Michael St. Denis were the best known members and André Obey's *Noë* (*Noah*) the most significant play. Out of the latter group came the *Théâtre des Quatre-Saisons*, which has performed in Paris and New York, and numbers André Bakst and André Barsacq among its leaders. Copeau foresaw the influence his theatre might have but he could not know that 1914 would bring war and the disbanding of his company just after a real start had been made to offer a thoughtful theatre at the *Carrefour de la Croix Rouge*. There, in a playhouse seating less than four hundred, he had given Shakespeare, Molière, Heywood, Musset, Paul Claudel's *L'Echange* (*The Exchange*), Jean Schlumberger's *Les Fils Louverne*, Henri Gheon's *L'Eau de Vie*, and above all *The Brothers Karamazov*, which he adapted for the French stage. With the company scattered, Copeau went to visit Gordon Craig at Florence where, with Suzanne Bing, they projected a dramatic school, which Craig and Copeau were to realize separately. In 1917 and 1918 he lectured in America and with the artistic and financial encouragement of Otto Kahn, and the cooperation of the French government, he reassembled his company in New York at the Garrick Theatre, even securing Jouvet and Dullin from the army. They did not have a popular success in America because a foreign-language theatre is always an exotic one unless there is a large group within the country speaking the same language. French theatres have always failed popularly in New York.

After the war Copeau returned to Paris and built a permanent architectural stage which has excited the envy and admiration of theatre workers ever since for, in its simplicity and usefulness, he secured the maximum of flexibility at the minimum of expense. There he staged such modern French plays as Vildrac's *Le Paquebot Tenacity* (*S. S. Tenacity*), *L'Oeuvre des Athlètes* (*Athletes' Work*, by Georges Duhamel which Henri Bordeaux admired), François Porché's *La Dauphine*, Anatole France's *Au Petit Bonheur* and *Saül* by André Gide.

Among the theatrical producers who welcomed foreign talent, probably none stand higher than JACQUES HÉBERTOT. Among his *régisseurs* he has included Theodore Komissarzhevski and Georges Pitoëff, as well as Jouvet. He has entertained such companies as the Kamerni, Moscow Art, and Zacconi's during their Paris seasons. He controlled the *Théâtre des Champs-Elysées;* the *Comédie des Champs-Elysées*, which he founded in 1913; and in 1923 the two-hundred seat *Studio*, which has housed many experimental productions including Sarment's *Facilité;* Henri Ducernois' *Le Club des Canards Mandarina;* and Strindberg's *The Dance of Death;* Denys Amiel's *Voyageur (Traveller);* Gantillon's *Cyclone,* and Pellerin's *Intimité (Intimidated),* among others equally interesting. These were produced by Gaston Baty at *La Chimère.* He had formerly worked with that fine director FERMIN GÉMIER (1866-1934) at the *Comédie des Champs-Elysées.* When Gémier went to the *Odéon* to breathe new life into the work of the national playhouse, GASTON BATY (1885-   ) emerged as a director of the first rank. After a year as scenic director at the *Odéon* he went to the *Studio* to produce the previously mentioned plays and later to the *Théâtre Montparnasse.*

The year before the *Studio* was opened CHARLES DULLIN opened his experimental *Atelier* after a preparatory period of work in the country with his group. Dullin is essentially a man of the theatre and so Goldoni, Pirandello, and Calderón are writers who have interested him. He has introduced two younger writers, Jarl Priel and Bernard Zimmer, and such designers as Lagier, Valmier, Touchagues and André Foy.

Among the most successful producers in Paris were GEORGES PITOEFF (1896-1939) and his wife Ludmilla (1896-   ), who acted with him after 1917. He was born in Tiflis and managed a company in St. Petersburg from 1912 to 1915 when he went to Switzerland. They both acted in Paris after the war, being most successful in such plays as Pirandello's *Henry IV,* Shaw's *Saint Joan,* Schnitzler's *Reigen* and Andreyev's *He Who Gets Slapped.*

Paris, like New York and London, is a city of innumerable theatres dating from the nineteenth century. Other than the state theatres the *Comédie, Odéon, Opéra* and *Opéra-Comique,* there were such houses as the *Sarah Bernhardt, Renaissance, Porte-Saint-Martin, Ambigu-Comique, Antoine* and many others of real importance which no general history of the theatre can even name, much less enumerate their repertoire. The most modern and handsome theatre in the city was the *Théâtre Pigalle* built at the foot of Montmartre hill by Baron Henri de Rothschild (who under the pen name of André Pascal wrote *La Rampe,* 1909 and *Le Caducé,* 1921), and his son Philippe.

Now exiled from France, they created, in 1929, one of the greatest theatres, structurally and scenically, ever to be built. Sacha Guitry created *L'Histoire de France*, (1929), in many scenes, to show off its adaptability.

The French theatre has raised its literary standards consistently. Its acting has been notable and the last three generations have shown a great advance in the techniques of production. All of this is now in abeyance, but we can only trust that the boulevardism into which the French theatre slumped can be rooted out some day along with the conquering German troops and all their ideologies. These now occupy the beautiful capital, Paris, the City of Light. Paris, the home of Corneille, Racine, Molière, Beaumarchais—may she again be intellectually and spiritually free!

XXII

THE DYNAMIC NORTH,
LAND OF DRAMATISTS

FROM the moment that you round the corner of the nineteenth century and Scandinavia is mentioned Ibsen is the one name that comes to mind, so profound was his influence, so great his dramatic power. Following close after his are the names of the Norwegian Björnson and the Swedish Strindberg, with the antecedent Danish Oehlenschläger well in the rear. Denmark, through this romantic dramatist and through its philosopher Kierkegaard strongly influenced the early Ibsen and so for that reason should be considered first. The arrangement of the theatre by countries may seem arbitrary as the drama spills over from one to the other thanks to neighborliness and a common vision and intellect. Perhaps we can best point out the peculiar virtues of each stage and its literature and the development within borders by this method of presentation, but the pervading influence of the great men must be taken for granted. As Ibsen influenced the theatre of the entire western world the impact of his power at close range can not be underestimated.

DENMARK

The greatest dramatist, and with the critic Edvard Brandes, one of the two outstanding men in the Danish theatre, was ADAM GOTTLOB OEHLENSCHLAGER (1779-1850). As a son of a superintendent of the Frederiksberg Castle, he was brought up with that beautiful palace as a playground; in the summer the sight of lovely court ladies and handsome uniformed officers were among his earliest memories. Thus was the basis laid for his later romanticism as a writer. He studied in Copenhagen until he was stage-struck at sixteen, and then made his debut as an actor. After two years of acting he realized he was a failure and returned to his studies, later matriculating at the University of Copenhagen. Coming under the influence of Henrik Steffens.

young Oehlenschläger found inspiration in the German romantic movement and in 1803 published a volume of poems which included the lyric drama, *St. Hansaftenspil (St. John's Eve)*. This poetic play promoted a bitter controversy because of its bold challenge to the conservative rationalists. He followed this with the romantic *Aladdin eller den forunderlige Lampe (Aladdin; or, The Wonderful Lamp, 1805)* and the much more interesting and impressive tragedy *Hakon Jarl (Earl Hakon, 1807)* in which he contrasts Christianity with heathenism as extolled through the principal barbaric character. This was written in Halle where he was visiting Steffens, later going to see Goethe in Weimar. While he was in Paris he wrote his second historical tragedy *Palnatoke (1807)* which was based on northern mythology; then he turned to the Middle Ages for the amorous *Axel og Valborg (Axel and Valborg, 1808)*. While visiting Mme. de Staël in Switzerland he composed the biographical *Correggio (1809)* in German as he aspired to literary position in Germany as well as in Denmark, though he never achieved his aim; nor was he able to fix the attention of the Danes on their southern neighbors because irresistibly they looked to their blood-brothers to the north.

Returning again to love as a theme he wrote *Hagbart og Signe (1815)* which dealt as well with the northern subjects that had characterized *Staerkodder (1811)*. If his hold on the affections of his countrymen might have slipped a bit it was because much of his writing was careless and uneven after his return from abroad in 1809, but he recaptured it with the idyllic drama *Den lille Hyrdedreng (The Little Shepherd Boy, 1818)*. From then on he turned more and more attention to epic poetry and wrote no more for the theatre. In the Lund Cathedral during the summer of 1829, Esaias Tegner the Swedish poet, crowned him "the northern king of song," which also betokened stronger bonds of unity among the Scandinavian countries.

BERNHARD SEVERIN INGEMANN (1789-1862) was better known as a writer of historical novels in the style of Sir Walter Scott than as a playwright, but several of his plays should at least be mentioned. Like Oehlenschläger, he was primarily of the romantic school; this form was particularly prominent in *Masaniello (1815)* and *Blanca (1815)*. The two best known of his plays were the comedy *Magnetismen i Barberstuen (Magnetism in a Barber Shop, 1821)* and the mythological *Kampen for Valhal (Struggle for Valhalla)*.

A prolific historical dramatist and novelist of the same school was JOHANNES CARSTEN HAUCH (1790-1872), and though he was born in Norway and died in Rome, he is considered Danish, for most of his life was spent in Copenhagen where in 1851 he succeeded Oehlenschläger in the chair of aesthetics at the University. Among his earlier plays, *Tiberius* (1828), *Bajazet* (1828) and *Gregory VII* (1832), were primarily studies of character. Feeling that the historical novel might be a more satisfactory medium, he wrote several after 1834, but returned to the theatre in 1841 with *Svend Grathe*. The best of his later dramas were *Sostrene paa Kinnekullen* (*The Sisters of Kinnekullen*, 1849), *Aeren tabt og vunden* (*Honor, Lost and Regained*, 1851) and *Tycho Brahes Ungdom* (*Tycho Brahe's Youth*, 1852). His contemporary CHRISTIAN HVID BREDAHL (1784-1860) also carried on the romantic tradition in a great number of monologues and duologues, though strictly speaking they were not true dramas.

Comedy and the short *vaudeville* form gained a great deal from the pen of the playwright and editor, JOHAN LUDVIG HEIBERG (1791-1860). He was the son of that dramatist Peter Andreas Heiberg whose satires violated the press laws in 1799 and forced him to flee to France where he lived the remainder of his life. The younger Heiberg was educated in Copenhagen, taking his doctorate at the University in 1817. Of his early plays *Don Juan* (1813) was written for marionettes. In 1819 he went to Paris to visit his father and remained for three years while developing a taste for creating vaudeville sketches. Among the best of these were *Kong Solomon og Jorgen Hattemager* (*King Solomon and Jorgen the Hatter*, 1825), *Recensenten og Dyret* (*The Critic and the Beast*, 1826) and *Aprilsnarrene* (*April Fool*, 1826). In 1828 he wrote the long national drama *Elverhöi* (*Elf Hill*), which won him the post as stage-poet for the Royal Theatre, which he held until 1836. When he returned to that playhouse in 1849, it was as sole director, a position he held until 1856. He edited several literary journals including *Den flyvende Post* (*The Flying Post*) of Copenhagen, to which Hans Christian Andersen, Carl Christian Bagger and Thomasine Christine Gyllembourg (Heiberg's mother) contributed. Not a little of his dramatic success was due to the talents of the actress Johanne Luise Heiberg, his wife.

A follower of Heiberg was HENRIK HERTZ (1798-1870) who wrote lively comedies and vaudeville sketches as well as some romantic plays. His first successful comedy was written in verse, *Amors Genistreger* (*Amor's Clever Pranks*, 1830). This was followed by *Emma* (1832) and his more realistic *Sparekassen* (*The Savings Bank*, 1836). Probably *De Fatiges Dyrehave* (*A Park for the Poor*) was his best known vaudeville and *Kong René's Datter* (*King René's Daughter*, 1845) his best romance.

HANS CHRISTIAN ANDERSEN (1805-75) is always so closely identified with fairy tales for children that it is difficult to remember that this was the least of his literary interests. It was his hope that he would

248. JOHAN AUGUST STRINDBERG.

247. HENRIK IBSEN.

THEATRE.

By the Old American Company.

On *Monday Evening*, the 19th Inst. will be presented,
A COMEDY, called,

The RECESS:
Or, The Mask'd Apparition.

Muſicato,	Mr. HALLAM,
Don Guzman,	Mr. HENRY,
Don Ferdinand,	Mr. MARTIN,
Don Pedro,	Mr. HAMMOND,
Lazarillo,	Mr. RYAN,
Octavio,	Mr. ROBINSON,
Alguazil,	Mr. WOOLLS,
And, Don Carlos,	Mr. HARPER.
Donna Marcella,	Miſs TUKE,
Donna Aurora,	Mrs. HAMILTON,
Leonarda,	Mrs. GRAY,
And, Beatrice,	Mrs. HENRY.

DANCING by Mr. DURANG.

To which will be added, (the Fifth Night, by Deſire)

The PRISONER at LARGE:
Or, The Humours of Killarney.

Old Dowdle,	Mr. HENRY,
Lord Eſmond,	Mr. HARPER,
Jack Connor,	Mr. MARTIN,
Tough,	Mr. HEARD,
Father Frank,	Mr. WOOLLS,
Fripon,	Mr. RYAN,
Frill,	Mr. ROBINSON,
Landlord,	Mr. VAUGHAN,
Mons,	Mr. HALLAM.
And, Adelaide,	Miſs TUKE,
Mary,	Mrs. HAMILTON,
Landlady,	Mrs. GRAY,
And, Rachel,	Mrs. HENRY.

PLACES in the BOXES may be taken of Mr. *Faulkner* at the Box-office, from *Ten* to *Twelve*, A. M. and on Days of Performance from *Three* to *Five*, P. M. where also Tickets may be had, and at Mr. *Gaine's* Book-Store at the Bible in *Hanover-Square*.
Ħ Hallam & Henry respectfully inform the Public, the Doors will be opened at a *Quarter* after *Five*, and the Curtain drawn up precisely at a *Quarter* after *Six* o'Clock.

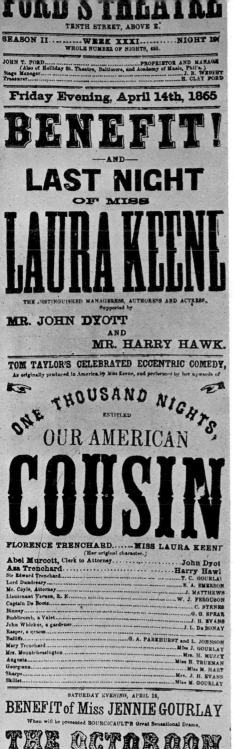

MANAGER, ... MR. W. STUART.
STAGE MANAGER, ... MR. J. G. HANLY.

BOOTH BENEFIT

FOR THE

SHAKESPEARE STATUE FUND

FIRST SONG TIME OF THE BROTHERS BOOTH
ON THE SAME STAGE

Mr. Stuart has pleasure in announcing that, owing to the generous zeal and untiring devotion of Mr. Edwin Booth, a performance will be given at this Theatre, on

FRIDAY EVENING, NOV. 25, 1864

Mr. J. S. Clarke having kindly ceded that evening for the occasion, for the Benefit of the Fund to raise a Statue to Shakespeare in the Central Park, being the second benefit for that object at this Theatre.

The evening will be made more available by the appearance in the same piece of the three sons of the great Booth.

JUNIUS BRUTUS
EDWIN AND
JOHN WILKES

"FILII PATRI DIGNO DIGNIORES."

Who have come forward with cheerful alacrity to do honor to the immortal bard, from whose works the genius of their father caught its inspiration, and of many of whose greatest creations he was the best and ripest illustrator the stage has ever seen.

The play selected for the occasion is the tragedy of

Julius Cæsar

JUNIUS BRUTUS BOOTH as . . . . **CASSIUS**
EDWIN BOOTH as . . . . **BRUTUS**
JOHN WILKES BOOTH as **MARC ANTHONY**

Julius Cæsar, 1st appearance	Mr. E. Varrey
Casca, 1st appearance	Mr. C. Kemble Mason
Octavius Cæsar	Mr. C. Walcot, Jr.
Trebonius	Mr. C. K. Chester
Decius	Mr. J. W. Burgess
Metellus	Mr. T. S. Cline
Titinius	Mr. C. S. Thomas
Cinna	Mr. J. Duell
Varro	Mr. D. Johnstone
Pindarus	Mr. E. Post
Soothsayer	Mr. P. Evans
Popilius Lenas	Mr. N. Decker
Servius	Mr. W. F. Burroughs
Flavius	Mr. B. F. Williams
Lucius	Miss Fanny Prestige
1st Plebeian	E. A. Eberle
2nd "	O. S. Fawcett
3rd "	A. E. Anderson
4th "	S. F. Oliver
Portia	Mrs. F. S. Chanfrau
Calphurnia	Mrs. C. Walcot, Jr.

Guards, Lictors, Matrons, Virgins and Plebeians.

Mr. Stuart trusts those of the public who have paid high prices for their seats will remember that in addition to the value they receive in intellectual enjoyment, they are contributing to a great national work, and not to the personal advantage of any individual.

The Orchestra, under the direction of Mr. Robert Stœpel, will perform

Overture, "BEATRICE," Bellini; Selections from "LA JUIVE," Halevy; "STRUENSEE," Polonaise, Meyerbeer; Grand March from "LOHENGRIN," R. Wagner; "DINORAH" Mazurka, Meyerbeer.

SATURDAY, Nov. 26, OPENING NIGHT of the engagement of EDWIN BOOTH.

Mr. Stuart begs to announce that on Saturday Evening, Nov. 26th, Mr. EDWIN BOOTH will make his first regular appearance this season, in the play of HAMLET.

The piece will be placed on the stage under the immediate direction of Mr. Booth, by Mr. J. G. Hanly, stage manager, in a style, it is hoped, combining splendor of production with strict historical correctness. The play has been in active preparation for the last three months, and no expense of effort has been spared in the endeavor, by a more strictly pictorial arrangement of the ordinary stage resources, and by the ability and superior execution of the several means of scenic illusion to carry out the spirit of the play into the most minute details, and thus advance the drama as a branch of national literature and art. The scenery, music, costumes, properties and machinery will be entirely new, and, to give a perfect completeness to the cast, engagements have been made with Miss J. W. WALLACK, Jr., one of the most gifted actresses who ever graced the stage; Mr. EDWIN VARREY, Mr. CHAS. KEMBLE MASON, and the eminent comedian Mr. THOMAS PLACIDE, all of whom will make their first regular appearance for many years on the New York stage on this occasion.

Seats may now be secured for Saturday and every eve

252. PLAYBILL OF THE ONLY PERFORMANCE IN WHICH THE THREE BOOTHS APPEARED TOGETHER. *Theatre Collection, N.Y. Public Library*

251. PLAYBILL FOR THE PERFORMANCE AT WHICH LINCOLN WAS SHOT.

254. THOMAS ABTHORPE
COOPER.

253. THE RESTORED
DOCK STREET
THEATRE, CHARLES-
TON, S.C.

Courtesy of Dock St. Theatre

255. IRA ALDRIDGE
AS OTHELLO.

256. EDWIN BOOTH AS HAMLET.
Theatre Collection, N. Y. Public Library

257. THE BOSTON MUSEUM IN 1876.

258. E. L. Daven-
port as Brutus.

259. Fanny Davenport as Fedora.
Museum of the City of New York

260. Southern and Marlowe in
Romeo and Juliet.

262. Edward Harrigan, in
*Reilly and the Four
Hundred.*

261. Dion Boucicault in
The Shaughran.

263. Edwin Forrest as

264. MRS. FISKE AS TESS OF THE D'URBERVILLES.

265. OTIS SKINNER IN *Kismet.*

Theatre Collection
N. Y. Public Library

266.

RICHARD MANS-
FIELD AND
BEATRICE
CAMERON
IN *Richard III.*

267.

JOE JEFFERSON
AS RIP VAN
WINKLE.

268. SKETCH FOR CORONATION PROCESSION IN *Der Jungfrau Von Orleans*, SAXE-MEININGEN
PRODUCTION.

269. SET FOR SAXE-MEININGEN PRODUCTION OF *Miss Sara Sampson*.

270. SCHILLER's *Fiesco*. SAXE-MEININGEN PRODUCTION.

271. *Prinz Von Homburg*, SAXE-MEININGEN PRODUCTION.   *Yale-Rockefeller Theatre Collection*

273. SAXE-MEININGEN PRODUCTION OF *The Pretenders.*

272. *Jungfrau Von Orleans.* MEININGEN.

274. COSTUME, *Jungfrau Von Orleans.* MEININGEN.

275. COSTUME, *The Pretenders.* MEININGEN.

*Museum of
Modern Art*

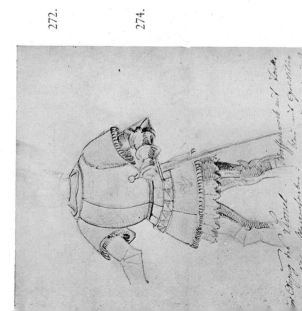

276. ADOLPHE APPIA. SETTING FOR *The Valkyrie.*

277. ADOLPHE APPIA. SETTING FOR *Little Eyolf.*   *Museum of Modern Art*

279. Design for a Shakespearean Play. *Craig, "The Art of the Theatre"*

278. Gordon Craig. Setting for *Electra*.

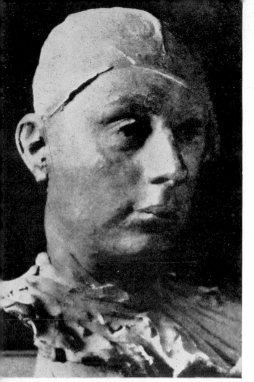

283. **Jacques Copeau**, in *Le Carosse du Saint-Sacrement*, at *Le Théâtre du Vieux Colombier.*

280. **Bust of André Antoine, as Pierrot.**
Dubech,"Histoire Illustrée du Théâtre"

281. *The Wild Duck. Le Théâtre Libre.*

282. **Characters From** *The Wild Duck. Le Théâtre Libre.*
Henin Collection, N.Y. Public Library

284. PUSHKIN.

285. GOGOL.

286. TURGENIEV.

287. COUNT LEO TOLSTOI.

289. V. I. Nemirovitch-Danchenko.

288. Constantin Stanislavski in *The Lower Depths*.

291. Maxim Gorki.

290. Anton Chekhov.

292. OUSPENSKAYA IN *The Cherry Orchard.*

293. KACHALOV IN *The Lower Depths.*

294. KACHALOV AS HAMLET.

295. OLGA KNIPPER-CHEKHOVA IN *The Cherry Orchard.*

296. MICHAEL CHEKHOV.

297. TAIROV.

298. PLAYBILL, MOSCOW ART THEATRE FOR *The Cherry Orchard,* 1905.

OUTLINE FOR A FAMILY TREE OF THE
MOSCOW ART THEATRE

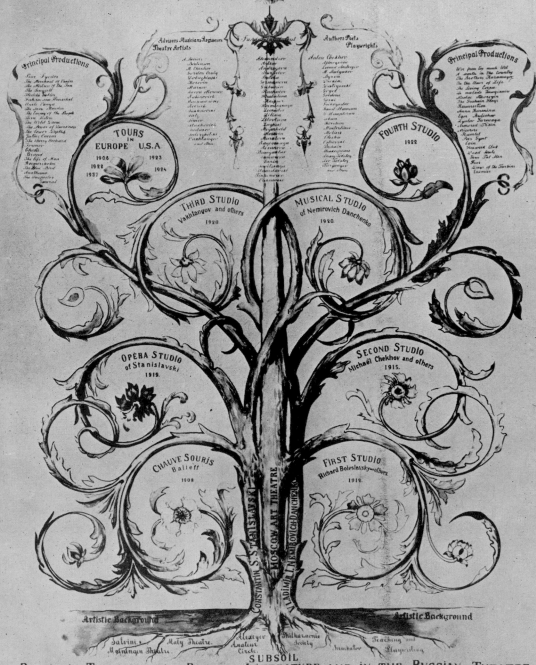

299. FAMILY TREE OF THE MOSCOW ART THEATRE, DRAWN BY IVAN DJENEEF. *Courtesy Ivan Djeneef*

be remembered for his dramas but his talents and the opinion of the world decided otherwise. His plays had some of the same delicate humor and wonder that made his fairy tales so beautiful, but he never quite mastered dramatic technique so that his plays were uneven and appeared ill-finished. Perhaps his best was *The New Lying-in Room*, which was brought out anonymously and won high praise. The fact that it was well-received lends some credence to Andersen's contention that much of the bitterest criticism was directed at him personally and not at his romantic dramas and novels.

FREDERIK PALUDAN-MULLER (1809-1876) was a poet and not primarily a theatre man, though he wrote the romantic drama *Kjærlighed ved Hoffet* (*Love at Court*, 1832) and the lyrical *Amor og Psyche* (*Love and Psyche*, 1834). He then turned to the composition of such dramatic poems as *Venus* (1841), *Dryadens Bryllup* (*The Dryad's Wedding*, 1844) and *Tithon* (*Tithonus*, 1844). Some people claim his famous narrative poem *Adam Homo* (1841-48) was dramatic, but this seems rather far-fetched. Later he added *Kalanus* (1857) and *Tiderne Skifte* (*Times Change*, 1874) to his list of plays.

The BRANDES brothers, Georg Morris Cohen (1842-1927) and Edvard (1847-1931), were largely responsible through their criticisms for the introduction of realism into the Danish theatre. The elder brother was the author of the monumental *Hovedstrømninger i det 19de Aarhundredes Literatur* (*Main Currents in Nineteenth Century Literature*, 1872-1890), which examines European literature from a dramatic point of view. These six volumes were based on his lectures given at the University of Copenhagen, though he did not remain there because his anti-clerical views offended the Regents. He was also the author of critical biographies of Shakespeare, Goethe, Ibsen and Voltaire. His brother Edvard was a dramatic critic and theatre historian in a country where such standards were very high. Under the influence of Ibsen he wrote the plays *A Visit* (1882), *En Politiker; Fortaelling* (*A Politician*, 1889) and *Young Blood* (1899).

A contemporary of Brandes was GUSTAV WIED (1858-1914), who was perhaps the most controversial man in the Danish theatre. He was a rank individualist who at times seems a mere opportunist. Wherever he may have differed with realists, it certainly was not on grounds of sentimentality for he took the greatest pleasure in rending the feelings of the sentimentalists. In his thirty volumes of novels and plays, of which the most important, *The Weaker Sex* (1900), *Dansemüs* (*Dancing Mice*, 1904), *Et Φpgr* (*The Reckoning*, 1904) and *Ranke Viljer* (2 × 2 = 5) are the most coruscating. Ernest Boyd says that, "Wied is the personification of Danish wit."

The leading playwright of the present century is HJALMAR BERG-

STROM (1868-1914) who had strong interest in social problems and the welfare of his fellow men in their efforts to adjust themselves to living. However all of his plays do not reflect this outlook because he himself admitted his inability to tie himself to a program and keep to it unrelentingly. Of the dozen dramas he wrote perhaps the most interesting are *Möntergaard 39* (*Thirty-nine Mönter Street*, 1904), *Lyngaard & Co.* (1905) and *Karen Borneman* (1907) which was suppressed because it was believed to be an attack on morality. The case was taken to the *Rigsdag* (parliament) but permission for its performance was not given until a new administration was elected. It is a fascinating study of family relationships and happenings, all of which have taken place in the past and come out one by one.

HELGE RODE (1870-   ), with the pessimistic *Dansen Gaar* (*On with the Dance!* 1898), *Bartholins Glaedesdag* (*Bartholin's Day of Joy*, 1905) and *Grev Bonde og hans Hus* (*Count Bonde and His Castle*, 1912) and KAJ MUNK (1898-   ) are the principal living dramatists. Munk is realistic and his viewpoint is hopeful. His principal plays are *En Idealist* (*An Idealist*, 1928), *I Braendingen* (*In the Surf*, 1929), *Cant* (1931), *Ordet* (*The Word*, 1932) and *De udvalgte* (*The Elite*, 1933). A revival of *En Idealist* in 1939 proved most successful with Valdemar Moller and Ulla Poulsen in the principal parts. KJELD ABELL, author of *Anna Sophia Hedvig* (1939), is one of the most promising of the younger writers.

As Denmark is a small country, there can be little specialization; an actor must play a tremendous variety of parts and because the runs are short he must frequently serve as director. In this way actors and producers understand each other's point of view more readily. For the past century, the three families Poulsen, Mantzius and Neiiendam have dominated the stage. At the present time, the critic and theatre historian, Robert Neiiendam controls the Theaterhistorisk Museum, which he organized in 1922 in the Christiansborg Palace, and Fru Neiiendam is perhaps her country's leading character actress. Johannes Poulsen headed the Royal Theatre and was a distinguished actor. His father, Emil Poulsen, was the most famous portrayer of Ibsen roles, and his grandfather was also a leading light on the stage. It is a small and friendly circle which will some day perhaps be permitted to attend to its own small and comfortable affairs.

NORWAY

In the little seaport of Skien in southern Norway was born the man whose vigorous mind, clear social thinking, and forceful dramaturgy changed the whole course of world theatre. That man of course was HENRIK IBSEN (1828-1906). His early life was spent in most comfortable circumstances for his father was a well-to-do lumberman and his mother of German descent was of an artistic and retiring disposition. When the boy was eight years old, his father was declared bankrupt and the family retired to the country where they still had a house at Venstöp; there they remained until Henrik was fifteen. As he was the eldest child it was up to him to look for work and he became apprenticed to a druggist in Grimstad. He was a solitary youth and took little or no interest in gossip, banter and flirting; the small town atmosphere of low-grade mediocrity bored him and the people about him thought him odd and unsociable. So he was.

While reading for his examinations at the University at Christiania (present day Oslo), he was so moved by Cicero's orations and Sallust's history that he wrote his first play, *Catiline* (1850). This was a romantic drama containing surprising force for one so young, but it was weakened by the revenge motive of a violated vestal virgin. Some of the author's suppressed annoyance at the smugness of his surroundings and a flash of his indignation which was in a few years to lash the world, crept into this otherwise immature drama.

Soon after he went to Christiania the play was published, thanks to financing by his friend of Grimstad days, Ole Schulerud. Schulerud and C. L. Due, his two real friends, had preceded him to the city and, as in the past, they were ready to stand by him in his need. There he met Björnson and Jonas Lie, the novelist and dramatist to-be, and wrote for various publications.

In September 1850, his short saga which had faint overtones of Oehlenschläger, *Kaempehojen* (*The Warrior's Tomb*) was staged with slight success. Just when matters were financially at their worst, Ole Bull the violinist who had founded a theatre in Bergen, invited him to be its poet and stage manager. This was a wonderful opportunity for Ibsen, and from November 1851 until 1857 he was associated with the enterprise. It gave him an opportunity to get his plays staged and to learn his technique and his art at the same time. In 1852 he was granted a stipend to travel abroad for four months. Though the amount was small, he made it go as far as possible and made contacts with Henrik Hertz and Johan Ludvig Heiberg and others, and saw for the first time the plays of Shakespeare, Holberg and Scribe, all of which were to influence his later development.

The Frenchman undoubtedly influenced him in developing his own technique for in his six years at Bergen he staged one hundred and forty-five plays, a large number of them by Scribe. Those were industrious years, for he drove himself and every one who came in contact with him. He was accused of being ill-tempered, and it is probably true. Björnson who succeeded him, worked just as hard with less ill-feelings, but obviously Ibsen was not a tactful person. He was too forthright and people who loved him, loved him for his integrity and his honest and pure mind, not for his social grace, which was practically non-existent.

His early and unimportant plays were staged there. They are hardly worth studying as dramatic literature unless one is keenly interested in the structural and ideological development of a great playwright. *St. John's Night* (1853) was in his nationalistic period as befitted a man who composed it for the Founder's Night of *Det Norske Teater*, Bergen's effort to steal Christiania's national thunder. William Archer says that the play is "a sort of half-way house between *A Midsummer Night's Dream* and *Peer Gynt.*" * The first play that really shows promise was *Fru Inger til Ostraat* (*Lady Inger of Ostraat*, 1855) which, despite its highly complicated and insufficiently organized plot, marks the beginning of the inventiveness that was to carry him far. It was a romantic historical drama dealing very freely with sixteenth century Norwegian characters, though showing the influence of *Adrienne Lecouvreur.*

Gildet paa Solhaug (*The Feast at Solhaug*, 1856) was a romantic play filled with ballads of the type created by Hertz. Many persons pointed out Ibsen's indebtedness to the Danish writer and he rejected it in his preface to the second edition, but the metrical form used is telling evidence. On the next Founder's Night, January second, in his last year at Bergen Ibsen presented *Olaf Iiljekrans* (1857), another nationalistic drama, in the hope of following up the popular success of *The Feast at Solhaug*. The new play was much weaker and failed to impress either his critics or his audience.

He was to have more discouragement in the next seven years, but they were brightened by two events of supreme importance. In 1858 he married the faithful woman to whom he was devoted for the rest of his days. In 1863, after numerous applications for a travel allowance from the state, it was granted and he was permitted to travel in Germany and Italy, to write and to broaden his theatre knowledge. These made up for the disappointments attendant upon *Hermaendene paa Helgeland* (*The Vikings at Helgeland*, 1858), which drew on the Norse sagas, German mythology, Hebbel's *Niebelungen* and other sources. This was an excellent acting piece and, though strong and harsh, it managed to be romantic. It was rejected both by the Danish company playing at the Christiania Theatre and by Heiberg at Copenhagen, who disliked it intensely. Finally Ibsen was reduced to producing it himself at the small and struggling Norwegian The-

* Introduction to *Lady Inger of Ostrat*, The Collected Works of Henrik Ibsen, Vol. I, London, William Heinemann, 1910.

atre to which he had been appointed director, an ill-paid post, in 1857. The first night in November, 1858 brought no immediate success but the play has stood the test of time well and was staged in Bergen in 1859, at the Christiania Theatre (by then more Norwegian) in 1861, Copenhagen and Stockholm in 1875, Munich, Dresden and Vienna in 1876, Berlin in 1890, Moscow in 1892 and London in 1903. Ellen Terry appeared in the lead at the Imperial Theatre and her son, Gordon Craig, staged it and contributed beautiful designs, which Shaw said did not properly represent the spirit of the dramatist. Blanche Yurka appeared in the play in New York in 1930 and Thomas Wilfred projected a moving background by means of his color organ, the clavilux.

In 1862 Ibsen enraged the conservative element with *Kjaerlighedens Komedie* (*Love's Comedy*), which introduced a clergyman on the Norwegian stage and pitilessly satirized the social lies concerning love and marriage. There is much genuine comedy in his first play to be located in a contemporary locale, though its exuberance has bitterness at heart. Once the good burghers accustomed themselves to it, it became a favorite and was still being played in repertory at the time of the beginning of the Second World War.

Not having received public encouragement to go on in the style of *Love's Comedy*, he returned to the historical drama. *Kongsemnerne* (*The Pretenders*, 1864) is written in prose with but few poetic passages. It is more highly concentrated in form than his earlier plays and the attention of the audience is never permitted to flag. He undoubtedly profited from his experience as stage director and designer, for all superfluousness was removed. Some years before he had read a pamphlet on dramatic construction, *Das moderne Drama* by Hermann Hettner, which dwelt on the necessity for authors to look to the psychological development of their characters whether they were composing contemporary or historical pieces. Ibsen put these principles into practice for the first time in *The Pretenders*. This essay into the Norwegian civil wars of the thirteenth century proved to be his first truly significant drama. From then on his work built to a climax which held for more than a decade and then inevitably weakened until there was mystic darkness in the last few years of his long life.

Ibsen felt nothing but bitterness towards his native land as he left on his travels in the month that *The Pretenders* was produced. Björnson had been able to raise from friends some donations to supplement the 400 specie-dollars (about 350 dollars in our currency) which the government allowed him, but only the strictest economy permitted him, his wife and son Sigurd, to travel in Denmark, Germany and Italy, which was his final destination on this trip. In addition, he was extremely touchy on money matters so that Björnson had to exercise the utmost tact to persuade him to accept additional monthly stipends. He could only bring himself to accept the help of his friends by considering it as a debt due a man writing a great drama. He was sincerely naive, not pompous, in this assumption. It was from the warmer clime of Rome that he sent back his great dramatic poem *Brand* (1866), which was published in Copenhagen. In this he drew on the philosophy of the Danish preacher, Soren Kierkegaard. Like him, Ibsen attacked the meanness of the age, the pettiness of spirit and the inevitable compromise which marred every work. To him, the Devil was compromise. It was this feeling which the poor minister Brand felt when he declined an appointment in a warmer climate and allowed his child to die because of winter's rigors. He felt that if he accepted he would be compromising his faith so long as the people of his frigid parish needed moral sustenance. Over and over again he takes the hard way, only to meet death in an avalanche and hear the Voice cry out, "God is Love."

The faults in national character which inspired *Brand*, were the source of another lyric drama *Peer Gynt* (1867). Opposed to the resoluteness of the preacher-hero of the last play, he set up vacillation, tepidness and amiable thoughtlessness in Peer, who stood in Ibsen's mind for the whole Norwegian nation. He created a character which has fascinated audiences ever since, for it is impossible not to be extremely fond of him. Muddle-headed, morally irresponsible and supremely selfish as he was, he appealed to popular taste.

The last play of the poetic period did not come until 1873, though he had been writing it since 1870. *Kejser og Galilaeer* (*Emperor and Galilean*) was a two-part drama including *Julian's Apostasy* and *Julian, the Emperor*. It was a study of the conflict between paganism and Christianity, with Ibsen's idea of a combination of the two which he hoped the future would bring into existence. The magnitude of the drama is impressive. Not until Hardy's *The Dynasts* or O'Neill's *Lazarus Laughed* do we find anything comparable. It was not staged in Norway until 1903 though the Germans performed it in 1896, and again in 1898 in Berlin for the celebration of his seventieth birthday.

Just before this he began his first realistic drama and his first exclusively prose work in *De Unges Forbund* (*The League of Youth*, 1869), which was a political comedy, noted for its trenchant dialogue. It assassinated the local politicians, liberal and conservative alike, and excited the wrath of the liberals at the première. *Samfundets Stötter* (*Pillars of Society*, 1877) vividly and realistically pictures the corruption inherent in small town life. The portrait of character disintegration in Consul Bernick constitutes an indictment of all bourgeois society. The author rather stacks the cards against his principal, but he wished to simplify the problem so that his reforming spirit would be clear in the minds of the audience.

Related to this play, because the need for freeing women from the economic and spiritual bondage to which they had been subjected is common to both, he wrote *Et Dukkehjem* (*A Doll's House*, 1879). This created a furore that is hard for us now to picture. The home had been destroyed, children abandoned and the nobility of marriage wrecked by this vile writer Ibsen. It appears now that he was at fault in a number of respects in the construction of his plot. In his desire to make it clear that a woman who is allowed no life of her own, can develop no protection against the world, he chose the device of Nora committing forgery to aid her husband and then being blackmailed because of it. It is difficult to believe that the reasonable creature the wife is represented to be would not realize that forgery was a serious offense, regardless of her husband's treatment of her, or of her upbringing prior to her marriage. It doesn't seem that she has anything to gain by leaving her husband and children, for how is she to live? Can she really bear not to see her children again? Will she not perhaps return? These are all unanswered questions but there is no doubt that when Nora dashed out of the house and slammed the door, she slammed it on a great deal of shoddy thinking and that her gesture fanned the revolt of women already stimulated by John Stuart Mill and various women pioneers.

Two years later he wrote the play which probably stands the longest chance of survival in the socially realistic group of his dramas, *Gengangere* (*Ghosts*, 1881). Despite the fact that syphilis can be mentioned today in polite society without its being masked under the euphemism of "social diseases," this play holds its own; there were those who said that it was written to be smutty and would soon die. The problems of inherited disease, insanity and euthanasia are still as great as they were sixty years ago. The survival of the play does not rest so much on its subject matter as on its masterly depiction of one of the greatest feminine characters in the annals of the theatre, Mrs. Alving. This woman, unlike Nora, did not leave her husband and finds her middle age saddened by the plight of her son whom his father's dissipation and ignorance of medical precaution and cure has doomed to insanity. It is a masterpiece of writing and plays extremely well. Its last revival with Alla Nazimova in New York in the 1935-36 season proved its most successful in this country. Agnes Sorma, Eleanora Duse and Mary Shaw increased their reputation by their performances in this drama.

En Folkfiende (*An Enemy of the People*, 1882), despite its air of personal indignation, has proved one of his most successful plays. A good doctor discovers that improperly drained sewers are polluting the waters in the local bathing establishment. Innocently he points the fact out to the town corporation expecting gratitude and praise only to be branded an enemy of the people; the municipality does not wish to tear down the baths which had but recently been erected. It is in this play that the typical Ibsenism occurs, "A minority may be right—a majority is always wrong." It was chosen by the French as the play with which to honor him on his seventieth birthday; Ermete Novelli triumphed in it in Italy; Sir Herbert Beerbohm Tree played it for years in England and America; and Walter Hampden has revived it more than once in New York.

His most appealing play came next, *Vildanden* (*The Wild Duck*, 1884). This in part reflects Ibsen himself in the self-mocking portrait of Gregers Werle. It is indeed a reflective and retrospective play. The dramatist's skill in unravelling events that have happened in the past makes it fascinating to a modern audience. First a suggestion here, then another there, and finally truth is seen in all its beauty. He created two beautiful characters in the wife Gina, and the little daughter Hedwig, who was drawn from his own sister whom he loved so dearly in his youth. Grandfather who pretends to being a hunter, is the spiritual parent of Odets' old Jacob in *Awake and Sing*. Hjalmar Ekdal, the father, the idealistic failure, is a masterly portrayal. This play quickly proved a great theatrical success everywhere though its lack of a starring role prevented its being performed as often as *Hedda Gabler* or *A Doll's House*. That which was formerly considered a weakness has proved an attraction in the last generation because, if directed with sympathy for its spiritual qualities, it permits a well-balanced ensemble to act it successfully.

Rosmersholm (1886) was still in the realistic vein, but poetic and mystical elements were creeping in, as instanced by the white horses of Rosmersholm. It is a tale of the emancipated woman Rebecca West, who has become poisoned by her new learning. James Huneker declares, "As cunning as Becky Sharp, as amorous as Emma Bovary, as ambitious as Lady Macbeth, Rebecca West is the most complete portrait of a designing woman that we know of; she is more trouble-breeding than Hedda Gabler." * The struggle between the liberal and the conservative elements in religion is weighted on the conservative side because of the ruthless character of Rebecca. She wants the liberal minister Rosmer, and drives his wife Beata to suicide in the hope of gaining her ends. Convinced that he is a moral coward and cannot

* Huneker, James Gibbons, *Iconoclasts*. N. Y.: Scribner's, 1907.

measure up to her expectations, she reveals her guilt to him and they seek suicide together. It is a confusing play, but one that is occasionally rewarding if studied closely enough.

Fruen fra Havet (*The Lady from the Sea*, 1888) is the first of his symbolic dramas which, though written in prose, are poetic in nature. This is a psychological drama of a woman who is freed of her love for a stranger when her understanding husband permits her freedom of action; granted it, she elects to remain with him. However the plot is deeper than that, for Ibsen had begun to explore the unconscious, that fruitful source of latter-day novels and plays

This theme he followed further in *The Master Builder* and *Little Eyolf* but abandoned in perhaps his best play, *Hedda Gabler* (1890), which is a character study pure and simple. Hedda is a hypersensitive woman who has made herself unhappy by always wanting what she does not possess; she is restless and bored because she does not receive all the attention she craves. The sensual side of marriage distresses her and she considers her husband George Tesman a dull dog (which he is) and is fascinated by the brilliance of Lovborg. When, however, she finds that Mrs. Elvsted is helping him to overcome his weakness for drink and to achieve a real position in the world, she is consumed with envy and nothing will satisfy her until she has destroyed his work and driven him to suicide. Because she realizes that her handi-work is known to lascivious Judge Brack and that the only way she can silence him is by giving herself to him, she chooses to shoot her-self. The role of Hedda has attracted almost every ranking emotional actress the world over. Some of the most famous have been the (original) German Frau Conrad-Ramlo, the Danish Fru Hennings, the Norwegian Constance Bruun, the French Marthe Brandès, the Italian Eleanora Duse, the English Mrs. Patrick Campbell, Laura Cowie and Jean Forbes-Robertson, the American Elizabeth Robins (the first to play it in London), Mrs. Fiske, Nance O'Neil, Alla Nazimova, Emily Stevens and Eva LeGallienne.

Bygmester Solness (*The Master Builder*, 1892) was the first of his last four dramas. These were written in Christiania where he had re-turned with the idea of putting his house in order, though he was to live for fifteen more years, the last six of which counted for nothing in the way of creativeness because by 1900 he had lost his power as a writer. In *The Master Builder*, the rebel who had left Norway be-cause he hated its hypocrisies, returns to his native land to explore the inner mysteries of living and the depths of his own soul. It is almost entirely a duologue between Solness, the architect, and the young girl, Hilda, to whom he pours out his soul, his past and hoped-for achievements. The fault of the play lies largely in the utilization of a symbolic struggle when the actual one was really more dramatic.

The girl is a somewhat irritating young woman who presumably stands for the younger generation egging its elders on to perform tasks beyond their strength. The characters are obviously based on personal observation, as the excellent introductions to William Archer's edition of the collected works indicate in detail. Young girls and women flocked around him; partly because he was a genius, partly because of his celebrity, but largely because he was an ardent advocate of feminism. They wearied Fru Ibsen but never alarmed her.

Iille Eyolf (*Little Eyolf*, 1895) continued the symbolism of the previous drama but instead of ending on a defeatist note it stopped with the hope that if nothing new might be accomplished at least the unhappy past might be conquered. The mysticism is inclined to be frail and misleading. Had Ibsen written this play in his great period it might have been an exciting drama instead of an occasionally interesting one. There was more vigor in his next play, *John Gabriel Borkman* (1896), which was a study of middle age in its relations with the younger generation. The hero was an unscrupulous man whose ends were Utopian; he sacrifices every decent feeling to achieve vast power. His prototype can be found in men like Ivar Kreuger or Samuel Insull, though the purity of *their* motives is open to question. It leaves its audience feeling a terrific weight of depression, which was doubtless the emotion it evoked in its creator. The final drama was *Naar vi Doede vaagner* (*When We Dead Awaken*, 1900). The same slavery which the desire for power caused in Borkman is repeated in the sculptor Rubek's terrific lust for supremacy in art. The whole play is a plea for the happiness of man and a protest against the forces which stand in its way.

Ibsen's influence is incalculable; we know that it spread to every theatre outside the Orient, and that some of his plays were translated and acted in faraway Japan. However he can not be said to have been a strong influence in the eastern world any more than any other dramatist including Shakespeare. Our own theatre has felt Oriental influence but it has been largely superficial. The two great civilizations find very few tangent points.

There is no question of Ibsen's abilities as a dramatist for he raised dramatic structure to the high position it now holds in the modern world. He was a social-minded man but was not a reformer using his plays as tracts in the Brieux sense. He hated compromise both in life and in the theatre and so lifted standards by referring all problems back to the soul of the individual. He denied having a philosophy and because of this denial he enforced his ideas all the more vigorously. His was the thinking mind in the modern world with all the ramifications that statement implies.

There was but one man in the Norwegian theatre who could be placed beside Ibsen, even though the place be lower. That was BJORNSTJERNE BJORNSON (1832-1910), Ibsen's friend, benefactor, co-worker and rival. Their development as dramatists was not dissimilar and as they grew, the standards of Norwegian literature were raised. They both stood for Norwegian independence of cultural over-lordship by Denmark, though they both sympathized with her in her struggle against rapacious Germany, when all liberals felt that Sweden and Norway should have gone to the assistance of their smaller brother.

Björnson lived in Copenhagen and in Rome during a part of Ibsen's most difficult period and so felt all the more strongly that writer's desire to free himself from the local rut. Nonetheless he returned to Christiania and was on hand when financial assistance was needed by his friend. His first play was a one-act piece, *Mellem Slagene (Between Battles*, 1857) and followed his initial success with peasant novels and short stories. It was written during a sojourn in Copen-hagen where he was under the influence of Oehlenschläger. It was one of the saga-dramas which included *Halte Hulda (Lame Hilda*, 1858), *Kong Sverre (King Sverre*, 1861) and the trilogy *Sigurd Slembe (Sigurd the Bastard*, 1862), the first act of which was in verse, the remaining eight in prose. This romantic historical drama raised its author to the forefront of European dramatists. After his already mentioned management of the theatre at Bergen from 1857 to 1859 and his long European tour, he became manager of the Christiania Theatre in 1865. There he staged *Maria Stuart i Skotland* and his really excellent study of young married people *De Nygifte (The Newly Married*), both in the same year.

For the next ten years he wrote very little for the theatre, being largely immersed in managerial problems and in local politics, where he was a liberal distinctly on the side of the Left. He then returned to Italy to write two social plays, *En Fallit (A Bankruptcy*, 1875) and *Redaktoren (The Editor*, 1875). The first attacked modern bourgeois business ethics and the latter was concerned with the venial press. The former has been compared not too unfavorably with *Pillars of Society* which it preceded.

Leonarda (1879) is about a woman with a past who renounces the man she loves so that he can marry her pure and unspoiled niece. For some reason this play stirred up a tremendous local controversy far out of proportion to its powers. None of his other plays, which include *Kongen (The King*, 1877), *Geografi og Kjaerlighed (Geography and Love*, 1885) and *Naar den ny Vin blomstrer (When the New Wine Blooms*, 1909), are really important. *En Hanske (A*

Gauntlet, 1883) deals with a modern-minded young woman who, demanding the single standard, breaks off her engagement when she discovers the badly soiled past of her fiancé. This so shocked theatre managers that they would not produce it, except in a modified form which weakened its strength considerably.

His dramatic masterpiece, *Over Evne (Beyond Human Power,* the first part of which came in 1883 and the second in 1895), is a struggle between good and evil. The first part is concerned with a righteous pastor who endeavors to cure by faith and succeeds in the church but not at home. The second, which bears only the most superficial resemblance to the first, delves not very deeply into the relations between capital and labor and is another study of those who strive to go beyond human powers. Because of this drama and a number of really first class novels, he was awarded the Nobel Prize in 1903. Though he provided Ibsen with competition for a time, he is distinctly inferior in dramatic power.

There were several minor Norwegian playwrights who should be mentioned in passing: ALEXANDER KIELLAND (1849-1906), who was an advocate of naturalism both in his novels and plays, the best of the latter being *Tre Par (Three Couples,* 1886), *Betty's Guardian* (1887), and *Professoren (The Professor,* 1888); the novelist JONAS LAURITZ EDEMIL LIE (1833-1908) who wrote the poetic drama *Faustina Strozzi* (1876) and the fairy-like *Lindelin* (1897); MONS LIE (1864-   ), son of the former, wrote *Tragedier om Kjaerlighed (Tragedy in Love,* 1897), *Lombardo og Agrippina* (1898) and *Don Juan* (1900); GABRIEL FINNE (1866-99) was primarily a novelist but his one drama *The Owl* (1893) was a weird piece which showed the strong influence of Maeterlinck; SIGURD IBSEN (1859-1930), son of the great Ibsen, was responsible for one drama which achieved some reputation, *Robert Frank* (1914); GUNNAR HEIBERG (1857-1929) was a link between the nineteenth and twentieth centuries with his political comedies and social dramas, the best of which include the comedy *Tante Ulrikke (Aunt Ulrikke,* 1884), the satirical *Kong Midas (King Midas,* 1890), the poetic *Balkonen (The Balcony,* 1894) and the lyric *Kjaerlighedens Tragedie (The Tragedy of Love,* 1904); KNUT HAMSUN (1859-   ) is a great novelist and won the Nobel Prize in 1920, but his plays *At the Gates of the Kingdom* (1895), *The Game of Life* (1896), and *Sunset* (1898) are faulty; HANS WIERS-JENSSEN (1866-1925), whose *Anne Pedersdotter,* a play of witchcraft, attracted world-wide attention when adapted by John Masefield as *The Witch* (1910); JOHAN BOJER (1872-   ), the novelist who turned to the theatre in *Theodora* (1902), *Brutus* (1904) and his best drama *Sigurd Braa* (1916) among others; and in addition

Suomen Kansallisteatteri (Finnish National Theatre), which was organized in 1887. There, modern and nineteenth century native as well as the best contemporary foreign plays are performed by a well-rounded and enthusiastic company. The manager of the theatre, Einó Kalima, is alert and sensitive to his country's needs for most of the people are Finnish-speaking Finns. Many of the wealthier class belong to the Swedish group, whose theatre culture is of longer standing. These find their entertainment and dramatic stimulus in the *Svenska Teatern* (Swedish Theatre) in Helsinki, like its Finnish brother a few streets away. Nicken Rönngren, its director, has specialized in the importation of foreign plays; O'Neill has been of particular interest to him as he is to all Scandinavians. Two of their most outstanding productions have been *Mourning Becomes Electra* and Robert E. Sherwood's *Reunion in Vienna*, both of which were brilliantly acted.

The earliest Finnish dramatist worth mentioning is the son of a village tailor, ALEXIS STENVALL (1834-72), who employed Kivi as a *nom de théâtre*. His interesting and well-constructed comedy of peasant life, *The Parish Cobblers* (1864), was the first important drama to be written. He is best known, however, for his novel *Seitseman veljesta* (*Seven Brothers*, 1870). Among the playwrights who were his contemporaries were KAARLO BERGBOM (1843-1906) who was better known as the founder and first director of the Finnish National Theatre; J. H. ERKKO (1849-1906) who wrote patriotic dramas based on themes taken from the national epic, the *Kalevala* (made familiar to us by Longfellow's translation); PAAVO CAJANDER (1846-1913) who was responsible for the translation of several of Shakespeare's dramas into Finnish; E. F. JOHNSON (1844-95); EINO LEINO (1878-1926), who translated Goethe's *Iphigenia* into poetic Finnish; TENVO PAKKALA (1862-1925), who wrote of the small town working class; OTTO MANNINEN (1872-) who is responsible for the adaptation of several of Molière's comedies; MARIA JOTUNI (1880-) who wrote humorous realistic dramas; HILJA MADETOJA (pseudonym L. Onerva, 1882-), playwright, novelist and poet; and the contemporary HELEN WUOLIJOKI who has perhaps more to say than any other dramatist of her country. She is particularly interested in feminism and social justice and these are the subjects of *The Women of Niskavuori, Justine* and *Hulda, Daughter of Parliament*.

The man who has done more than anyone to systematize the theatre in Finland is the distinguished dramatic critic, YRJO HIRN (1870-), professor at the University of Helsinki. His critiques on Shakespeare and the drama of Finland have been widely read. He was responsible for the establishment of a theatre collection in the University Library and for the encouragement which led the resident theatres to establish archives of their own.

There have been several outstanding Finnish nationals writing in Swedish, the first being JOSEF JULIUS WECKSELL (1838-1907), whose tragedy *Daniel Hjort* (1862) was the leading nineteenth century drama of this group. KARL AUGUST TAVASTSTJERNA (1860-98) introduced realism in his play *Affärer* (*Affairs*, 1890), a tradition which was carried on by MIKAEL LYBECK (1864-1925) whose dramas felt the outside influence of symbolism and are known for the depth of their psychological perception. Other writers of merit are: GUSTAF VON NUMERS (1848-1916); ARVID MORNE (1876-   ) who is also responsible for much activity in social and political affairs; NINO RUNEBERG (pseudonym Alceste, 1874-   ); and RUNAR SCHILDT (1888-1925), whose plays are frequently compared favorably with those of Lybeck as being the best work done by the Swedish writers in Finland.

Finland has a most active little theatre movement, which, attached to schools and in municipalities as well as in the strictly rural districts, is doing work which in extent and scope probably lies about half way between the amateur movement in little Iceland and the vast United States movement.

SWEDEN

Following in the footsteps of the eighteenth century dramatists Bellman and Lidner, came ERIK JOHAN STAGNELIUS (1793-1823), whose mysterious death added romance to his name. His dramas have some of that same quality, particularly *The Martyrs* (1821), the posthumously published *The Bacchantes* (1822) and *Sigurd Ring*. Not long after his death another writer came on the scene who was destined to become the first poet of Sweden by the middle of the century. JOHAN LUDVIG RUNEBERG (1804-77) composed a little comedy *Friaren fran Landet* (*The Country Lover*, 1834) which was unsuccessful, though it was laid in the charming Finnish country where he was born. It was a long time before he returned to the theatre with his comic *Kan ej* (*Can't*, 1862) and his much better received tragedy, *Kungarne pa Salamis* (*The Kings at Salamis*, 1863).

AUGUST TEODOR BLANCHE (1811-68) was the dramatist who was the most popular with the audiences of the first half of the nineteenth century. He called his comedies and farces pictures of real life, but they would not be accepted by the true realists though they came at a period when this movement was stirring in Germany. The most successful were *Magister Blackstadius* (1844), *Rika Morbror* (1845) and *En tragedi i Vimmerby* (1848). FREDRIK AUGUST DAHLGREN

(1816-95) created the national opera *Värmlandingarne* (1846), as well as translated many of the plays of Shakespeare and Calderón de la Barca into Swedish.

However, the man for whom the Swedish theatre is known and whose fame still endures is JOHAN AUGUST STRINDBERG (1849-1912). At one period in his life he went into a sanitarium to correct a nervous condition, which forethought permitted a cure. Afterwards, however, he was a split personality as his realistic historical dramas and his dream fantasies show. These deviations combine to make him one of the most puzzling personages in the theatre. He is distinguished for a frantic and almost fanatic hatred of women, despite or perhaps partly because of his three marriages. This tendency showed in his early stories before he turned to the stage as a career. Poverty forced him to interrupt his studies at the beautiful old University of Upsala, though he was able to resume his education in 1870. He tried the teaching and acting professions before turning to journalism. His short stories based on student life and later newspaper experiences provoked wide controversy and brought him a good deal of fame.

His first play was a classical drama, *The Declining Hellas* (1869) for which he received favorable mention by the Swedish Academy. However his reading in such widely varying writers as Byron, Schiller and Oehlenschläger, as well as from the romantic period of Ibsen and Björnson affected his style. He too fell under the influence of the philosopher Kierkegaard. Then came the minor dramas *in Rome* (1870), which was performed by the *Kungliga Dramatiske Teatern* (Royal Dramatic Theatre) in Stockholm; *The Free-thinker* (1870); and his first consequential work, *Oväder* (*The Outlaw*, 1871). When the Royal Dramatic Theatre performed this latter play in the fall of 1871, it won the favorable attention of the aged Charles XV who rewarded him with a pension, but bad health and the death of the king robbed him of this. *Mäster Olof* (1872) which was rejected for performance was a romantic historical drama that supposedly dealt with Gustavus Vasa, the reformer Olaus Petri and Gerdt the Anabaptist, but it was modern in the sense that they are made to stand for the forces of liberalism and reaction. It was not until he had made repeated revisions that it was accepted for the stage in 1878. Between his dramas and his stories, Strindberg built up public hostility to such a degree that it was not until nearly the end of his life that the whole world had recognized his great powers of psychological observation and his high importance in the theatre; then popular taste changed and he received adulation instead of jeers and criticism of the harshest kind.

In 1874 friends procured an appointment as amanuensis for him at the Royal Library. The latitude allowable in that institution permitted him the time to acquire sufficient knowledge of Chinese to catalogue the manuscripts in that language in the library's possession. In 1879 his learned monograph in French on the relations between Sweden and the Orient was read before the *Académie des Inscriptions* in Paris, for there has always been cultural sympathy between France and Sweden.

He turned to medieval subjects for *Gillets hemlighet* (*The Secret of the Guild*, 1880) and *Herr Bengt's Hustra* (*Bengt's Wife*, 1882). His next play *Lycko Pers resa* (*Lucky Peter's Journey*, 1882) bore the imprint of *Peer Gynt* and was received very favorably when it was staged in 1883. Its satire on social customs was delightful and was well received by the audience, for a change. That same year he and his family left to travel in Denmark, Germany, France and Italy where he continued to write stories and novels which probed deeply into social and marital relationships.

These were the years in which he persistently criticized the *status quo*. Ibsen had seen fit to defend womanhood from man's injustice but Strindberg felt that the ladies had been so much encouraged that they wished to substitute feminine for masculine domination of the world. He held that in marriage one party had to be the master and that men could be counted on to be fairer than women could. This thesis he made abundantly clear in a series of plays of which the magnificent *Fadren* (*The Father*, 1887) was the first. This is perhaps the most widely performed, as well as widely read, of his dramas, probably because the thesis is stated in clearly dramatic terms which are understandable to an audience at any time and in any clime. The feminine alliance of the wife, her mother, and the old nurse to oppose the will of the father in the matter of the education of his daughter, reaches such tyranny as to have him declared insane so that they may gain their way. This is not so extreme as it sounds for Strindberg has constructed his drama logically and carefully. The wife is a delightful and seemingly reasonable person in every relationship but that with her husband, whose natural anger causes him to do and say things that need be twisted only slightly to persuade an outsider that he is truly as insane as they claim. The scene in which his old nurse tricks him into the strait-jacket is heartbreaking because she so obviously believes that she is only doing her duty for her poor boy. As *Le Père* it was performed first at Antoine's *Théâtre Libre* in Paris in 1887 and in 1890 the *Deutsche Freie Buehne* staged it in Berlin. Lugné-Poë's production at the *Théâtre l'Oeuvre* in 1894 was in honor of Strindberg's visit. Its first Swedish production came in Stockholm in 1901, but not until 1911 did London see it with Warner and Edith Oland, who repeated it the next year in New York. Its most notable revival in this country was given by Robert Loraine in 1931.

In *Fröken Julie* (*Miss Julie*, 1888) he exposes an upper-class woman who is tormented by her hatred and contempt of men and her intense physical desire for them. It is true naturalism in its ugliness and one has but to read it to understand the whole case for naturalism in literature. Its power and remarkable character depiction render this one-act drama one of the finest examples of this play-form.

Kamraterna (*Comrades*, 1888) deals with another husband and wife relationship such as we find in *The Father*, only this time it is the New Freedom with which the author is concerned. The husband has granted his wife comradeship in marriage only to have her take every advantage of it to belittle and destroy him. Awakening at last to the situation he leaves her, saying that he can find comradeship outside the home but there he expects to find his wife. His long one-act play *Creditors* (1888) deals with a similar situation, but the dramatic culmination of this sexual duel really did not come until *The Dance of Death* (1901, in two parts). In this remarkable drama the wife is far from blameless but it is the husband who is the tyrant. It is their mutual hatred which holds them as strongly as intense love might have done.

Medeltidens bonde (*Mother-Love*, 1892-93) and *The Link* (1892-93) also probe the marriage problem in its relation to children. His own divorce problem entered into the writing of the touching hold children have on a man and a woman even when they loathe each other and are seeking to free themselves of a hateful connection.

His dramas move in two directions from this point on because of his mental split. On the one hand he wrote clear and logical historical dramas which were greatly admired in Sweden and neighboring countries, while on the other he composed highly subjective dramas that seem to have no connection with reality except in their persistent symbolism. These plays make fascinating reading and are of interest to the theatre laboratory but do not make their way in the commercial playhouse; they did, however, father the expressionist movement in the world.

His historical pieces include *Gustavus Vasa* (1899), *Erik XIV* (1899), *Gustav Adolf* (1900), *Engelbrecht* (1901), *Charles XII* (1901) and *Gustavus III* (1903). He turned towards religion in his mystical *Till Damaskus* (*Toward Damascus*, 1898-1904) as he had indicated he might do in the poetic and legendary *Himmelriketsnycklar* (*The Keys of the Kingdom of Heaven*, 1892). Among the symbolical plays, which act best in the mind, are *The Dream Play* (1904), *Spogelses-Sonaten* (*The Spook Sonata*, 1907), and his swan song of faith, *The Great Highway* (1909). *Easter* (1900), though symbolical, acts better than the others. Harriet Bosse, who played in this became his third wife, neither of his first two marriages to non-professionals having proved satisfactory, His last did not work out well either but at least the separation which came in 1904 was entirely amicable.

A few months before his death, Strindberg was honored as no Swedish writer had been before or has been since. Thousands of people united to do him honor with a torchlight procession, speeches, cheers and a considerable sum of money, which was almost entirely given to public charities. Celebrities from everywhere united to do honor to the man who almost all his life had been excoriated as a dangerous madman and a fanatic by the conservatives, whose opinions and actions he attacked so ably in his great dramas, novels and short stories. His influence throughout the world has been very considerable, more so than the production of his plays would indicate. His anti-feminism, to put it mildly, offends too greatly too many of the theatre's patrons, women, and since they support the box-office they might be said to call the tune. His greatest disciple and one who bids fair to surpass him by far is Eugene O'Neill, our greatest living dramatist.

The combined influence of Ibsen and Strindberg has kept the general dramatic standard high in Scandinavia both during and after their lives. There are a few writers whose works stand out in the general run of affairs without even remotely approaching the heights. Of these the best known are: FRU AFHILD AGRELL (1849-   ), a novelist-playwright who, inspired by Ibsen's feminism, wrote *Rescued* (1883); like the former, ANNE CHARLOTTE EDGREN-LEFFLER, Duchess of Cajanello (1849-1893) wrote plays under the stimulus of Ibsen, though she was better regarded as a novelist; HARALD JOHANN MO-LANDER (1858-1900) was successful in Finland as well as in Sweden; his most successful play was probably *Rococo* (1880); TOR HEDBERG (1862-1931) steered a clear course between mysticism and sheer naturalism in several plays, of which the idealistic *Johan Ulfstjerna* (1907) and *Borga Gård* (1915) are the best; PER HALLSTROM (1866-   ) has written a number of plays of which the serious *Bianca Capello* (1900), the comic *Erotikon* (1908) and the historic *Charles XI* and *Gustav III* in 1918 stand out; GUSTAV AF GEIJERSTAM (1858-1909) was brutally naturalistic in *Criminals;* HJALMAR SODERBERG (1869-   ) depicted Stockholm life; HJALMAR BERGMAN (1883-1930) was highly popular in his time, *Maria Jesu moder* (*Mary Mother of Jesus*, 1905), *Parisina* (1915) and *Swedenhielms* (1925) being his best pieces; the Swedish-American HENNING BERGER (1872-1924) is best known for *Syndafloden* (which was successfully adapted into English as *The Deluge* (1922) in which Pauline Lord made a hit).

Among contemporary writers are PER LAGERKVIST (1891-) who is both a symbolist and, to a lesser extent, an expressionist in his *The Last Man* (1917), *The Eternal Smile* (1920), *The Way of the Man Who Is Happy* (1921) and *The Hangman* (1935), which created a powerful impression in London in 1935; and the sophisticated Ragnar Josephson as well as Sigfrid Simertz.

PER LINDBERG (1890-) is perhaps the best known director in Sweden. He regularly stages plays at the Royal Dramatic Theatre, though at one time he managed a private theatre with the great actor-producer Gösta Ekman (1890-1938). He has been guest-director in Norway, Denmark and England. In addition he has written several theatre critiques, and is as well known for his acting as for his direction. He played everything from dandies to Shylock; Peer Gynt, Fyodor in *Redemption* and Hamlet are his most successful roles. Another producer of great experience is PAULINE BRUNIUS, director of the Royal Dramatic Theatre in Stockholm, an honor which had never before been granted a woman. From 1926 to 1931 she managed the *Oscars Teatern* with John Brunius and Ekman. She is also an actress of note whose Hedda Gabler, Julie Cavendish (*The Royal Family*) and Marguerite Gautier are outstanding. Per-Axel Branner (1899-) is a prominent stage and film director, though it was as an actor that he achieved his first fame. He has been head of the Swedish Actors Association and his recent staging of *Our Town* was acclaimed. Torsten Hammaren (1884-) is both an actor and a director at the Town Theatre in the seaport of Gothenburg. *Journey's End* and Ernst Toller's *Hoppla wir leben* are among his most interesting productions. Olof Molander (1892-) preceded Fru Brunius as director of the Royal Dramatic Theatre, the standards of which he raised to their present high level. One of the younger directors in Stockholm, Sandro Malmquist (1901-) manages the *Nya Teatern* (New Theatre), which has staged classical, modern and experimental plays. Harry Roeck Hansen (1891-) with his wife Ester uses the *Blanche Teatern* as a testing place for budding talents.

Sweden's outstanding scene designer and one of the best in Europe is Isaac Grunewald (1889-), who is highly regarded as a painter as well. Among the plays and operas for which he has designed scenery are Schiller's *Fiesco, Antony and Cleopatra, Sakuntala, Cavalleria Rusticana* and *Samson et Delilah*. John Jon-And (1889-) is principal designer for the *Kungliga Teatern* (Royal Opera House). Otte Sköld's sets for the productions of Euripides' *Medea* and Masefield's *The Faithful* were outstanding. Sven-Erik Skawonius (1908-) has been admired for his beautiful designs for *Mäster Olof, Lysistrata, Cenodoxus* and Marc Connelly's beloved *The Green Pastures*.

Sweden has built up a fine acting tradition with such men as the typical Anders de Wahl (1869-), who interpreted Strindberg to Swedish audiences. Lars Hanson (1886-) is known abroad because of his silent film appearances with Lillian Gish and other stars of American films. In Stockholm and at the Royal Dramatic Theatre he created Orin in *Mourning Becomes Electra* and took the principal roles in plays by Shakespeare, Schiller, Ibsen and Strindberg. Karl Gerhard (1891-) is really a one-man theatre for he acts, writes and produces witty, political satires. Marta Ekstrom is probably the leading actress of Sweden today, having to her credit such various roles as Irene in *Idiot's Delight* and Lavinia in the O'Neill trilogy. Among other actresses who are noteworthy are Tora Teje, Inga Tid-blad, Signe Hassa who played Manuela in *Girls in Uniform* and Muriel in *Ah! Wilderness*, and Greta Garbo (of the films).

This live and active theatre still carries on in wartime, making films, producing plays, keeping up the spirits of a nation surrounded either by enemies or cowed friends. It has been a theatre of fine and uplifting thoughts and careful technique rather than greatness; there is but one exception to that, poor, splendid, bedeviled Strindberg.

XXIII

THE GOLDEN AGE OF
RUSSIAN LITERATURE
1800 TO THE REVOLUTION

RUSSIAN literature developed largely despite official influence rather than because of it. Various tsars and court officials did offer financial rewards which sometimes were lifesavers for artists and writers exhausted by the struggle of creating literature and obtaining a living at the same time. This is why we so often find their names listed as being government employees in *sinecures*, which gave them freedom for writing. Quite often the Russian libraries were opened to them and they worked on library time, often treating their jobs with contempt, which may have something to do with the utter chaos in those reservoirs of learning and culture.

The century began dismally with the despotism of Tsar Paul I (despite his wave of liberalism while still heir-presumptive to the throne) when he succeeded his mother Catherine as ruler in 1796. He was assassinated in 1801 and his son, Alexander I came to the throne and though he was soon involved in the Napoleonic Wars, he tried to retain a liberal spirit; he was in fact far ahead of his time and his own people politically. He took it out in dreaming however and like so many of his family, died by assassination. This atmosphere was certainly not the best for creation and the rigid and reactionary censorship maintained by the government for fear a breath of liberalism might blow in, made writing a most precarious and unsatisfactory task, especially writing for the stage where the censorship was the most rigorous. Despite this fact, a truly great dramatic literature was built up and the world's finest acting theatre was established. The repressive measures of tsarist censorship did not prevent great writing, but curiously enough the vigors of Soviet restraint of public opinion has successfully eliminated any first class dramatic talent.

However this analogy can be pressed too far; it may be that all the great Russian writers but Gorki were dead before the Bolshevist Revolution of 1917 and there has not been time to develop a new group.

The nineteenth century did not begin very auspiciously in its first writing talent, because VLADISLAV ALEXANDROVITCH OZIEROV (1769-1816) was still looking backward to the French models, rather than to the English and Scottish writers who were so much to influence Turgeniev and the other novelists and dramatists. *Iaropolk and Oleg* (1798) was a tragedy based on out-moded models and was destined to failure, as was *Oedipus at Athens*, which he modelled on Ducis of all people. Then he looked to the British Isles and Macpherson for *Fingal* (1805) which shared the fate of his earlier efforts. His one success, *Dmitri Donskoi* (1807), arose from his drawing his leading character from Alexander I and from Napoleon who appeared as Mamai. It was probably the worst of his tragedies, but 1812 seemed to make his play prophetic after the French retreat from Moscow, so that his reputation grew without reason. Certainly the subsequent *Polyxena* and *Medea* destroyed whatever fame he had achieved, and he died insane, or very nearly so.

Neither VASSILI ANDREIEVITCH ZHUKOVSKI (1786-1852), who claimed the honor of having introduced romanticism into Russia and who was the author of the indifferent plays *Camilla; or, Rome Delivered* and *Paul and Virginia;* nor IVAN ANDREIEVITCH KRYLOV (1768-1844) can claim the honor of being the true founder of Russian drama. Krylov attained fame and eventually some wealth from his fables, which had been inspired by La Fontaine, but his dramatic productions were really slight. By the time he was fourteen he had written a comic opera, *Kofeinitsa* (literally, *Fortune Teller by Coffee Grounds*), which many critics feel was the best of his plays. When he was nineteen or twenty he wrote two sad failures, *Philomena* and *Cleopatra*. He also was responsible for a translation of Schiller's *Die Jungfrau von Orleans*. It has been stated that the comedies *The Rogues* (1793) and *The Author* (1794) were merely adaptations and not original with Krylov at all. Krylov was one of the librarians who neglected his duties in favor of indifferent dramaturgy, though his fables seem, after re-reading, to deserve their fame.

One can't help but feel that all this was but marking time, waiting for the great Romantic poet and dramatist, ALEXANDER SERGEIVITCH PUSHKIN (1799-1837) to make his appearance. Grandson of a free Negro and well connected with Russian families, he is claimed by both races. Byron in England is the closest analogy we can find for this brilliant young writer who was certainly influenced by him, though Pushkin's fame in Russia was undimmed by the competition of Shelley or Keats, and so seems more outstanding. Pushkin is better known as a poet than as a dramatist, as relatively little of his writing was intended for the stage, though almost all of it is either dramatic in feeling or structure. His greatest work for the theatre was *Boris Goudounov* (1825), which has great theatricality as well as flights of poetic genius. His characters are well-resolved in this prose-drama, which was written after he had come under the influence of Shakespeare and cast off the early French influence which his upbringing and education at the newly-opened college at *Tsarskoie-Selo* had made most natural. *Boris* was not published until 1831, and few of his contemporaries recognized its power. *Eugene Onegin* was a poem not intended for the stage, but its dramatic form and revealing portraiture of Russian character charmed the composer Tchaikowski, just as it has countless others. To him however it suggested beautiful melodies and formed the inspiration for his opera of the same name. Isaac H. Rabinovitch's setting for the famous duel scene in the snow, celebrated as one of the most beautiful stage settings ever conceived by a scenic artist, is in the magnificent production placed in the repertory of the Bolshoi Theatre in Moscow since the Russian Revolution. Tchaikowski chose the novel, *The Queen of Spades*, as the libretto for his comic opera which has been played around the world; *The Covetous Knight* was set to music by Sergei Rachmaninov.

His other plays include: *Angelo*, which was a reworking of portions of *Measure for Measure; The Stone Guest*, which is a comparatively slight telling of the Don Juan legend, the dénouement being more or less the same as Mozart's *Don Giovanni; Rusalka*, also known as *The Water Nymph*, which was left unfinished at the time of his death. There were also short plays of one or more scenes: *The Feast in the Time of Plague*, which was borrowed from John Wilson's *The City of Plague;* and *Mozart and Salieri*, a bitter story of talent's envy of genius. Despite the favor shown him by Tsar Nicholas I and his personal popularity, there was a tendency to disparage his work and to underestimate his standing in Russia. On the occasion of the unveiling of a monument to him in 1881, Dostoyevski paid him homage; since then criticism has taken its cue from the distinguished novelist. In *Eugene Onegin*, Pushkin gave his country a national poem which became a classic and an inspiration.

ALEXANDER SERGEIEVITCH GRIBOYEDOV (1795-1829) wrote the first and last true comedy of manners to be composed by a Russian. The variously-called *The Misfortune of Being Clever, Woe from Wit, Wit Works Woe* and *Intelligence Comes to Grief*, depending on your translation of the transliteration *Gore ot ouma*, paints a satiric portrait of social life in Moscow in the 1820's. Because of the censorship, it could not be published and the manuscript was passed from hand to hand to be read and was even acted in private houses; bits of it were played by students in the streets at carnival time. It was finally acted in a mutilated version in 1831, two years after Griboyedov's assassination in Teheran where he had gone on a diplomatic mission; but it was not until 1869 that it was acted in an uncut version. Ever since its publication in 1833 it has been considered the wittiest comedy of the Russian theatre. In writing it, he was influenced by Molière's *Le Misanthrope*, though his character Tchatski is more the annoyed young man than an Alceste who has left life behind him. Pushkin, who was irritated at the success of a rival, nonetheless put his finger on the weakness of Griboyedov's satire, when he asked, *"Who* is clever?" The answer of course was Griboyedov. In this he fell into some of the same temptations to be witty that beset Oscar Wilde. The tragedy *The Georgian Night*, which he brought back from Persia with him in 1828, was inspired by Shakespeare but was not at all up to his earlier piece.

Before we can turn to Gogol, whose name is frequently linked with that of Griboyedov, we must consider the poet Lermontov and ALEXIS STEFANOVITCH KHOMIAKOV (1804-1860). Khomiakov's tragedies, *Yermak* and *The Mock Demetrius*, were rhetorical and full of enthusiasm for ancient Russia; this Slavophile movement was absurd, as most literary turnabouts are likely to be, whether they have political connotations or not. France went through one in the sixteenth century with a certain Swiss named Hotman, who wanted to return to ancient Gaul; the Southern Slavs underwent a wave of Illyrianism under the leadership of Louis Gay; the Germans have had various waves of Germanophilism, the most recent being Hitler's *Nibelungenliedism* inspired by Richard Wagner. (It has been said that it is a pity that the German *fuehrer* had not been inspired by a passion for Bach rather than Wagner.)

MICHAEL IOURIEVITCH LERMONTOV (1811-1841) was more famous as a poet than as a dramatist. *The Demon* (1838) has strong dramatic qualities and is his most noted poem. Curiously enough, he seemed to feel that he wanted to try everything that Pushkin did and invaded the field of the Afro-Russian on more than one occasion; he was also influenced by the Germans. *The Spaniards* (1830) to a certain extent reflects *Nathan der Weise* and *Kabale und Liebe*. From Shakespeare's *Othello* he took his inspiration for *Masquerade* (1835), which in 1917 was one of the great Meyerhold's most outstanding productions at the Alexandrinski Theatre in what was then Petrograd; it was a thrilling pageant of color and sense. The influence of the brilliant German writers caused him to title another play in a foreign language, *Menschen und Leidenschaften* (*Men and Passion*).

NICHOLAS VASSILIEVITCH GOGOL (1809-1852) is a name to conjure with, for he wrote one of the great comedies of all time, as well as one of the finest of novels, *Dead Souls*, the first part of which was printed in 1842; the second part he burned just before his death so that all we have is a fragment; and the third was merely sketched, not written. His entire life was a battle with the censor and many of his pieces were never completed because he realized that they could not be acted. All of his plays were written between 1832 and 1837, with the exception of the one-act *The Gamblers*, which did not reach its final form until 1842. His first play was either *Marriage* (in an earlier version it was entitled *The Suitors*) or a play which he abandoned after deciding that it would never pass the political censorship, *The Order of Vladimir of the Third Class*. This last named drama was concerned with the machinations of a government official who, disappointed in his ambitions, goes insane; portions of it remain in *The Lawsuit*, *The Servants' Hall* and *A Fragment* and the central theme was utilized in his story, *A Madman's Diary*. His truly great piece was the *Revizor* (*The Government Inspector* or *The Inspector General*, depending on the adaptation). The vaudeville nature of its theme has caused a certain amount of carping from the critics. This play about a town (any Russian town) with venial officials, centers on the discovery that the supposed *revizor* is visiting the city and no one has covered up the bad administration's corruption. The man who is mistaken for the government official takes advantage of the situation most thoroughly. After his disappearance, the bilked citizens hear that the real inspector-general has just arrived and is at the inn awaiting the presence of the municipal authorities. The idea for the play was suggested to Gogol by Pushkin. The amazing thing is the fact that it was permitted production; this was due to the championing of the dramatist by Vassili Zhukovski, who took the play to Tsar Nicholas. He was so entertained by it that he ordered it staged; and it has been acted frequently ever since, both in Russia and other countries. Meyerhold's production of it was one of his most scintillating; his use of skeleton stairs and a semicircle of doors is known wherever men study the theatre. Gogol established native comedy with *Revizor* for it certainly is a humorous masterpiece.

The great novelist IVAN SERGEIEVITCH TURGENIEV (1818-1883) also contributed to the theatre, though his principal gift to his native country was his imperishable style which won him tremendous acclaim inside and outside Russia. His masterpiece was the novel *Fathers and Sons* (1862), which Maurice Baring has said was "as beautifully constructed as a drama of Sophocles." * The Russia he wrote about was chiefly the country and gentry of his childhood for he spent a great portion of his mature years in Baden Baden and France where he won the accolades of Flaubert, Taine and George Sand. In his novels *On the Eve* and *Virgin Soil*, he endeavored to describe a new generation which would solve social problems and not just accept them as inevitable, as in *Rudin* and *The Diary of a Superfluous Man*. Unhappily he had little confidence in his ability to write plays, thinking of them largely as work to be read rather than acted. Certainly *A Month in the Country* (1855) is a perfect example of his mistaken judgment for it was and is one of the most finished productions of the Moscow Art Theatre, having been added to its repertory in 1909 and successfully recreated from that presentation by the Theatre Guild in New York in 1930. This psychological piece was strongly influenced by Balzac's melodrama *La Marâtre* (*The Stepmother*), though the double suicide was removed and the play made into a domestic comedy. However, despite his indebtedness to Balzac, he made it essentially Russian; in fact he used the central situation again in his novel *Virgin Soil*. Many of his plays were inspired by other writers: *Steno*, a romantic drama written when he was quite young, stemmed from Byron; his short play, *Lack of Caution*, undoubtedly came from Mérimée. This he followed with several short vaudeville sketches, which was a curious characteristic of otherwise serious Russian dramatists, notably Chekhov. *Lack of Funds, Lunch with the Marshal of the Nobility*, the highly revealing portrait of society, *A Conversation on the Highway*, *Broke*, a delightful caricature of the indolence and lack of essential integrity in the upper classes, and *An Amicable Settlement*, are of this genre. Then he came under the influence of Alfred de Musset and wrote "dramatic proverbs," such as *Cloth Tears Where It Is Thin, An Evening in Sorrento* and *A Provincial Lady*. His best work undoubtedly lay in the psychological field, of which *The Parasite* and *The Bachelor* are examples. The latter is a delicate and refreshingly gentle comedy which has much to commend it. However *A Month in the Country* is his dramatic masterpiece, but it was not acted until 1872. It is unfortunate that the censorship and his own lack of confidence in his ability to write plays prevented him from doing more direct work for the theatre, for he had undoubted talent if not genius.

ALEXANDER NIKOLAIEVITCH OSTROVSKI (1823-1886) had the distinction of being the only leading Russian writer who was a playwright by profession. Coming from a lower middle-class Moscow family, his work is primarily devoted to the portraiture of the middle

* *An Outline of Russian Literature* by Maurice Baring, New York, Henry Holt.

class of the cities. This ability endeared him to his people, though his work is seldom acted outside his native land. Since the Revolution, his plays have been especially popular because of his sharp portraiture of the trading class. The Mali Theatre, the oldest producing organization in Moscow, has been particularly successful with its production of his masterpiece, *The Storm.* Of his forty-one plays, that and his really fine realistic comedy of the bourgeoisie, *Enough Stupidity in Every Wise Man* (one of the Moscow Art's most popular productions), are outstanding.

From 1846, he wrote steadily for the theatre, though for many years the censor forbade the performance of any of his plays; it was not until 1861 that his first full-length drama, *It's a Family Affair We'll Settle It Ourselves,* was staged though it had been published in 1850. After the success of his comedy *Keep Out of a Stranger's Sleigh* in 1853, his plays were steadily produced. 1859 was a great year for Ostrovski because a collection of his plays was published and *The Storm* was staged. This moving play is an excellent characterization of a wife who, under the influence of a terrific thunder storm, confesses her unfaithfulness to her husband. Though she was driven into the affair by the domination of her mother-in-law and the husband's neglect, he cannot forgive her. The parting scene between the wife and her lover is noteworthy for its restraint and pity. This and the year following saw an appreciation of his work written by the critic Dobrolyubov in *The Realm of Darkness* and *A Ray of Light in the Darkness.*

Ostrovski's plays are frequently and purposefully unresolved; he had no interest in the well-made play. This seeming formlessness that he and Chekhov adopted has often puzzled and annoyed western critics who expect the path of the plot to be well marked. *Poverty Is No Crime; The Snow Maiden,* on which Rimsky-Korsakoff based his opera; *A Protégé of the Mistress; The Poor Bride,* which is another play of a young woman hemmed in and finally destroyed by her environment; *Wolves and Sheep* (1875), which is more neatly made than most of his pieces, are perhaps the most outstanding of this type of play. In 1874 he organized the Society of Dramatic Authors and Composers; in addition he was co-director of the Imperial Theatre in Moscow and was responsible for the establishment of the Russian Academy of Dramatic Art; and it was through his efforts that the monopoly on performances granted to the state-supported playhouses was removed. He was a playwright who, despite obvious lack of theatricality, was nonetheless of the theatre. His perceptions, his acuteness of observation and his reality were couched in terms understood in the playhouse. He continues to be acted and appreciated today and he has had considerable influence on later dramatists; and though his fame is local rather than international, he was one of the greatest of Russia's theatre men.

ALEXIS FEOFILAKTOVITCH PISEMSKI (1820-1881) was a novelist who endeavored to earn his living by writing. He came of a very distinguished, if impoverished and down-at-the-heel, noble family; his education like that of Gogol and Dostoyevski was meagre. His first novel, *The Times of the Boyars*, was inspired by George Sand's *Indiana* and celebrated free love, but was banned for publication by the censor. Then came *The Muff*, and in 1858, with the lifting of the ban on his first story, his best novel, *A Thousand Souls*, which is partly concerned with the theatre in that a provincial actress is the heroine, was published. Then in 1863 he turned directly to the stage by writing *Cruel Fate* (sometimes called *A Hard Lot*, or *A Bitter Fate* from the transliteration *Gorkaia Soudbina*). This popular tragic drama treats of the life of the serfs and was the first of its kind to achieve success; it has inevitably been compared with Leo Tolstoi's *The Power of Darkness*, though it is distinctly inferior to it. The enforced seduction of the serf's wife by the landlord, the husband's return and murder of the child and his banishment to Siberia has a crude and grim power, without much exploration of his characters' inner life. He was interested in plot and was successful in its construction. *Usurpers of Law* discusses the tyranny of provincial landowners in the eighteenth century, but is not so well-written nor was it so well-received as *Cruel Fate*.

ALEXANDER VASILEVITCH SUKHOVO-KOBYLIN (1817-1903) was not particularly interested in the theatre and it has been said that he would probably never have turned to dramatic creation if he had not been involved in a criminal action. This focussed his attention on the scandals for which his country has always been famed, one of which he chose to immortalize in *Krechinski's Wedding* (1855), which was performed one hundred and ninety-four times in the theatres of Moscow and still remains a favorite in the repertory of provincial stages. In *The Affair* (1869) he wrote a criticism of judicial procedure which was held up by the censors until 1882 when the legal practice referred to had already been abolished. This method of suppression of a play is not entirely unknown to any city which has a corrupt political regime. It may be recalled that in 1932 George Sklar and Albert Maltz wrote a play airing the Tammany scandals and specifically referring to James J. Walker, then Mayor of New York City. When *Merry-go-round* was to be moved from the Provincetown Playhouse into a Broadway house, various structural faults not previously noted were discovered by the city inspectors. It was some time before the theatre could be made "safe" for an audience and, as perhaps foreseen, the demand for tickets had subsided when the management was allowed to reopen it. In the Russia of the Tsars or Soviets it is not necessary to go through such an elaborate hocus-pocus to prevent a performance which the authorities dislike or mistrust. The author's last play, which was not unlike *The Bankrupt* of Ostrovski, *Tarelkin's Death* (1869, acted in 1900) completed his contribution to drama, but *Krechinski's Wedding* was his *chef d'oeuvre*.

A cousin of the great Tolstoi, COUNT ALEXEI TOLSTOI (1817-1875) was responsible for three plays which were successful at the time of writing and which continue to be acted, probably because of the brilliance of the Moscow Art Theatre's staging of the trilogy. *The Death of Ivan the Terrible* (1867), *Tsar Fyodor Ivanovitch* (1868) and *Tsar Boris* (1870) constitute the whole of this poetic drama. Tolstoi was primarily a poet, however, and these pieces were his only contribution to the theatre. Their picturesqueness and color have long been attractive to foreigners who see the Russia they imagine in the lines of his plays.

FYODOR MIKHAILOVITCH DOSTOYEVSKI (1822-1881) never wrote for the stage, though his name is always associated with it because of the successful dramatizations of several of his novels. *Crime and Punishment* (1866), *The Possessed* (1871-1872) and *The Brothers Karamazov* (1881), which was left unfinished at his death, have all been successfully dramatized and the first has several times been filmed. When the adapters came to Dostoyevski's own dialogue, they found that they were scarcely able to alter a line, so well constructed are his speeches. The last novel has been especially powerful on the stage; Jacques Copeau's version performed by his own *Théâtre du Vieux Colombier* and subsequently, under his direction, by the Theatre Guild in New York in 1927 proved one of that worthy organization's most penetrating performances, though the *succès d'estime* did not turn into a popular hit.

COUNT LEO NIKOLAYEVITCH TOLSTOI (1828-1910) was a great realistic novelist, playwright and reformer. He was didactic in his approach to his art for he sought to improve, even to reform society and social conditions. It is regrettable that he did not turn to the drama until he was almost sixty and the great period in which he wrote *War and Peace* (1870) and *Anna Karenina* (1875) was behind him. Then had come a break with literature in the artistic sense of the word for he wrote *My Religion* and a series of pamphlets along religious lines. His admirers were sorely tried for they felt that he had so much to give to literature that his energies should not be wasted on social reform. Even his rival, Turgeniev, on his death-bed,

took time to send him a poignant message begging him to return to
his first love, the novel. Fortunately this request was heeded and the
flow of stories was resumed. In 1887 he wrote his first important
play, *The Power of Darkness*. This was a remarkable study of
peasant life in all its naturalistic details; though the story and its
protagonists pass through the mire in order to show the power of
moral regeneration, it goes far beyond the realism of Ostrovski in its
Christian enlightenment. True humanitarianism had at last come to
Russian drama. His championship of the under-dog soon caused his
own noble class to regard him as a betrayer; this did not disturb his
plans to arouse society to its responsibilities.

The First Distiller (1887) was a delightful short piece attacking
alcoholism among the peasants. Two years later appeared that forceful comedy *The Fruits of Culture*, which satirized the upper classes
in their dealings with their tenants. The fury his sly wit aroused in
these landlords was naturally humanly pleasing to its author; and it
so influenced Shaw that he paid tribute to it in the preface to *Heartbreak House*. *Redemption* (*The Living Corpse* as it is sometimes
named), was unfinished at the time of his death and was not published
until 1912, the same year in which another uncompleted drama, *The
Light That Shines in Darkness*, was issued. *Redemption* is a thesis
play, frankly attacking the evils of Russian marriage laws. It is a fine
acting play vehicle in which Moissi and John Barrymore have given
notable performances of Fedya. The second play was in a sense autobiographical, treating as it did a nobleman who tried to live as Christ
would have wished him to, but his wife so resisted his efforts that
domestic discord arose. However, the dramatist was somehow unable to make his man really believable and thereby weakened an
otherwise noble drama. Tolstoi was the epitome of Russian realism
and though he has long stood in the forefront of the world's great
novelists, his plays have never won him that admirable distinction.
Nonetheless, he contributed a humanitarian spirit to the literature
of his country when it was sadly needed. His honesty, nobility and
fine spirituality are to be cherished and respected.

The whole century had provoked an interest in acting that will be
discussed in the next chapter of the Russian theatre, which is concerned more with problems of staging and techniques of acting than
with dramaturgy. The very censorship so often alluded to, had caused
those who were timid about daring the relentless law of the tsars
to experiment with acting technique as a solution of their creative
urge. Exile could not come out of planned direction and ensemble
acting, but a play considered politically undesirable might provoke

an arrest which was unanswerable and to which no defense might avail.

With this in mind, we will turn from the development of the Mali, Bolshoi and Alexandrinski theatres, to say nothing of that great acting ensemble the Moscow Art Theatre, to consider the next and probably greatest dramatist of all, ANTON PAVLOVITCH CHEKHOV (1860-1904). He was the master of the indirect approach, the apostle of the inner development of character regardless of the seeming lack of outer form. His plays are as satisfying as those of Gorki, Strindberg, O'Neill and O'Casey in our present century. He and Gorki represent a changing social order; their influence in their own country and throughout the world has been considerable. Whether this would have been true of Chekhov had his work not been combined with the complementary genius of Stanislavski is debatable. The perfect combination of the ensemble work on his stage refined the extraordinary character portrayal of the dramatist, and once seen, the effect is haunting. Because of the world-wide influence of the so-called Stanislavski method of acting, the genius of Chekhov has been brought home to innumerable audiences.

He was the grandson of a serf and was reared in the tradition of the small educated middle-class whose problems he understood so well. His preparation for and practice of medicine made him conscious of the influence of physical make-up on people's minds and on their psychological development; but he never lost sight of their humanity as do so many medical men. It was this feeling of having the well-being of the underprivileged at heart that gave him that great compassion for which he is revered.

Combined with this ability to comprehend the petty tragedies of the small and unimportant, was a broad sense of humor which expressed itself in the vaudeville farces which have caused so much hearty laughter in the theatre. When the world seemed to rebuff his tragedies and serious comedies, he always turned back to these stage pieces with relief, because in them he knew he was successful in his own time—a very satisfactory feeling. They are perhaps more generally familiar in Anglo-Saxon countries because little theatre and college groups have produced them over and over; they are literally actor-proof and the audience is well rewarded.

The Bear (sometimes called *The Boor*, 1888), *The Marriage Proposal* (also known as *The Proposal*, 1889), *The Wedding* (1890) and *The Anniversary* (1892) are four completely delightful vaudeville sketches; they are farcical comedies of Russian family life with their gallery of quarrelling lovers, boorish creditors, canny widows and snobbish bridegrooms and are representative of the amusing side of the life this modest doctor saw as he visited his patients. He took pride in his profession and carried succor to those stricken with typhus during a plague. The more serious elements in his greater work were mostly derived from his professional life; his hundreds of short stories are vignettes of life in the latter half of the nineteenth century. Like Schiller, he was cut off in mid-career by the deadly enemy, tuberculosis, so that he left but four major works for the theatre he so passionately loved. Considering the great finish he imparted to his last work *The Cherry Orchard*, which was produced just before he died, his very best work would have obviously come in the next ten or fifteen years.

Except for his vaudeville sketches, he used the short play form somewhat sparingly, though two of his best known pieces belong to the one-act genre. *On the High Road*, written in 1884 and first presented to the public in 1885, is a somber study of the down-and-outers, whether from internal or external causes. The pathos of the degeneration of the landowner, Bortsov, who has taken to drink after the death of his wife; the unhappiness of the tramp, Merik, who was betrayed by the girl he loved, are graphically delineated. The rough sympathy of others toward these two is touching and in this Chekhov showed his understanding and appreciation of common people perhaps better than in any of his other plays. The censor suppressed the piece because it showed a facet of life which might have set people thinking about righting the manifest inconsistencies in the make-up of their national life.

Next came *Ivanov* (1887), his first full-length play which, according to Nemirovitch-Danchenko who perhaps admired Chekhov more than any one else did, is not so much a play as the draft for a play. This is true but it demonstrates the power of his characterization and gives us a hint of what is to come. It was produced at Korsh's theatre in Moscow in 1887 and in St. Petersburg in 1889; its failure has been ascribed to the fact that the actors did not know their lines. This lack of preparation was the cause of much dissatisfaction with the nineteenth century Russian theatre. It has been said that plays were produced with only two days of rehearsal in order to rush in new pieces for an audience which constantly demanded novelty. It is hard to credit such carelessness to Korsh who was a conscientious manager. It may have been due to the fact that *Ivanov's* leading characters are not sufficiently resolved to be theatrically effective. What success the Art Theatre had with it when it was revived after Chekhov's death was due to the naturalistic acting of the secondary characters. However, in all of his great works it is the poetic quality which should be stressed; Gorki, in an article on the playwright, records that P. O.

Morozov said, "Chekhov's plays should be staged as lyrical dramas."

The *Wood Demon* (1888) was one of his less effective pieces which he abandoned when it failed to impress his warmest advocates. Next came *That Worthless Fellow Platonov*, which was written in 1889 but it was long lost and has only recently turned up. It adds very little to the Chekhov heritage because it is so over-written and its horrors laid on too thick. Discouraged by these failures, and perhaps a little by his own inadequacies in mastering the full-length play structure, he turned back to vaudeville and to his short stories, where his technique was established and admired. It was not until 1896 that he returned to the long play in *The Sea Gull*, which was performed at the Imperial Theatre in St. Petersburg, better known as the Alexandrinski. Though a failure in the beginning, it was later produced in a new incarnation by the Moscow Art Theatre in 1898, to win undying fame for itself and the great producing organization.

Chekhov's theory of tragedy was far from the conventional approach of either classicism or romanticism. There are no heroic deaths in his plays; life wears away slowly and unhappily and there are no providential endings. Occasionally a suicide takes place, as in *The Sea Gull*, where, due to outside exigencies of duty and frustration, young lives are cut off in their prime. It is a subtler kind of writing that he developed. For all its seeming aimlessness, his plays have a secret direction which preserves their integrity of purpose. It takes a master hand to achieve this kind of drama, just as it takes a special kind of acting to bring out its full values. Just as the Stanislavski theatre brought into fruition the Chekhov style, the Group Theatre of New York has caught the spirit of their fine dramatist, Clifford Odets, who in essence is a follower of Chekhov. Sometimes the actor comes first, sometimes the playwright, but there has to be harmony between the two to produce great theatre. From Sophocles through Shakespeare and Molière to Chekhov and Gorki, the greatness of their work has been largely determined by that initial combination, despite the approval which later reading and understanding provided.

The Sea Gull has since been performed successfully in many languages; in English it has attracted such translators as Isabel Hapgood, Constance Garnett and Stark Young among others. Its most successful, if not necessarily its most artistic, production in America came in 1938 with a combination of the Theatre Guild and Alfred Lunt and Lynn Fontanne, and was later included in their repertory on tour. This is a study of the vanity of an actress, the idleness of a fashionable novelist who dabbles in love, the hopelessness of the actress' unloved son, and the young girl he adores who is seduced by the novelist. Young lives are frustrated at every turn. This submission to environment is peculiarly Russian; a young American would have reacted so differently that no American dramatist utilizing such a situation in his own country would have arrived at anything like Chekhov's conclusion, regardless of comparative literary merits.

Returning to the plot of *The Wood Demon,* he took what would serve best and turned it into *Uncle Vanya* (1897), the play in which he created one of his most lovable characters. It is in this remarkable sense of characterization that he particularly excelled; his novelist's instinct stemmed from the great line which had produced Turgeniev. Vanya is a frustrated man who deserved more from life and people than he got; everything was sacrificed to keep a mediocrity afloat which represents the particular futility inherent in the plot. All of Chekhov's literary life was a protest against the sacrifice of decency, honesty and genius at the altar of mediocrity; it is this injustice that has fired many minds in the theatre.

It was not until 1901 that *The Three Sisters* was produced by the Moscow Art Theatre. This play was successful on its initial appearance and has remained one of the author's most produced works. It has been staged in New York by Eva Le Gallienne and her Civic Repertory Theatre, by the Surrey Players and other organizations. The play is concerned with the circumscribed lives of three girls immolated in a provincial town, whose greatest ambition is to go to Moscow which is their symbol of freedom but it is a wish that is never fulfilled. The sisters represent the leashed energies of the Russian people kept in severe restraint by the tsarist régime, which were not to be released for a generation. Even then the people were to find that the government they created circumscribed their freedom of action and thought just as the earlier one had done. The tragedy of Russia has been the constant betrayal of her people by the government, which by now should certainly be expected to reflect their will.

His masterpiece was *The Cherry Orchard* written in 1903 and produced in 1904 with his wife Olga Knipper-Chekhova (1870-   ) as Mme. Ranevski, a role which thirty years later she was still playing. In this Chekhov has shown the passing of the wealth and power of the landed classes through their own weakness, a total disregard of their responsibilities and an unwillingness to accept a changing order. It is sad to reflect that in all history the ruling class or opinion is always unwilling or unable to read the handwriting on the wall. Every visible evidence of the broadening of the popular base of government and power from Lafayette and Garibaldi to Franklin Roosevelt is met with an opposition which fails to recognize an effort to save the whole basis of a system on which their well-being depends.

This is because they distrust or dislike any democratic widening of the economic base of their country. In Chekhov's play the symbol he chose was the cherry orchard, which for sentimental and artistic reasons Mme. Ranevski and her highly intellectualized brother, Gaev, wished to preserve at the expense of their whole system of living. Olga Knipper-Chekhova, Edith Evans and above all Alla Nazimova have made this extravagant, worldly, lovable woman a living character in the theatre. This play, perhaps more than all the others, has cemented Chekhov's strong hold on the imagination of the entire twentieth century theatre world. Shaw felt his influence in *Heartbreak House;* our own Odets shows it in every play that he has written; England's Rodney Ackland has chosen him as his literary inspiration in *Musical Chairs* and other pieces. Chekhov and Stanislavski together have changed the whole current of modern dramatic thought.

MAXIM GORKI (Alexei Maximovitch Peshkov, 1868-1936) is claimed by Soviet sympathizers for their group of playwrights. This is despite the acknowledged fact that the first of his two great plays was written for the pre-revolutionary theatre. It is quite true that his sympathies always lay with the poor and downtrodden people of his country, but that he really accepted the narrow ideology of Lenin and Stalin is certainly to be doubted. He held himself aloof and lived abroad for many years before he was won back by concessions granting him personal and intellectual freedom and because he was impressed with the fact that it was his patriotic duty as a Russian and a great revolutionary to return to bolster national prestige.

In 1900 Gorki was still writing short stories and novels, when Chekhov sought Gorki's literary aid. At the time, the Art Theatre was on a southern tour playing in Sevastopol and Yalta, where their leading dramatist was endeavoring to conserve his health; Chekhov had been won over by Stanislavski in spite of their previous disagreements which have since been minimized or censored. There they planned to rehearse their new plays in May in order to secure his cooperation and he invited Gorki, who was also in the Crimea, to come and watch the bad temper of rehearsals as the best way to learn the technique of playwriting. The older writer criticised his work and aided him in the construction of his play, *The Smug Citizen* (sometimes translated as *The Middle Class* or *The Petty Bourgeois,* 1901). This bitter picture of middle-class life was poorly constructed, but it contained a number of interesting types which would recommend it to a company devoted to ensemble playing. Nemirovitch-Danchenko and Stanislavski played it in St. Petersburg, where it very nearly became a *cause célèbre* because its author had just been dismissed from the Russian Academy and the youth of the city were so enraged that they threatened a demonstration.

Shortly before Gorki produced his first great play, *The Lower Depths* (also known as *A Night's Lodging, At the Bottom* and *Down and Out*, 1902), a schism took place in the ranks of the Art Theatre. Meyerhold, who had differed strongly on fundamentals of production with Stanislavski, left the troupe with ten other actors and actresses who went their own artistic ways. The main company went on, however, with the financial backing of S. T. Morozov, the fabulously wealthy Moscow millionaire whose house was so magnificent that it inspired the curiosity of grand dukes, who backed a number of revolutionary movements and supported Nemirovitch-Danchenko and Stanislavski whom he so much admired. They busied themselves with the new work which the former tramp, great raconteur and real humanitarian was preparing for production. This piece is quite formless as measured by the standards by which the people were accustomed to judge plays before Chekhov. In fact from the murder of Kostylov at the end of the second act, the drama went down hill as far as the plot was concerned, and became a series of incidents related to a fascinating gallery of characters assembled in a slum house. Luka, the philosopher tramp; Nastya, the prostitute, brilliantly played by Olga Knipper-Chekhova; the dying Anna, wife of Kleshtch the locksmith; and Satine, the tubercular and alcoholic thespian, are among those who gather in a cellar owned by the fence, Kostylov. Luka is a wandering philosopher who brings a kind of philosophy and hope wherever he goes. The play is not entirely one of degradation and filth for it ends on a note of hope. It was a success and remains today one of the outstanding plays of the century.

It would be pleasant to say that Gorki moved on from fine play to fine play, but strict regard for the truth makes us admit that it was thirty years before he wrote the second drama for which he is remembered. One play followed another; though they were not equal in power, they had certain fine qualities that attract us. *Summer Folk* (1903) satirizes those who behave as though they were "summer people" in their own land; *Children of the Sun* (1904, acted in 1905) is a drama which, according to Nemirovitch-Danchenko, shows the proletariat's supreme distrust of the intelligentsia; and which certain Stalinists refer to as a play of pseudo-science, was produced during the abortive Revolution of 1905. The description of its opening night recalls nothing so much as the efforts to continue production during the Reign of Terror in Paris. A proper evaluation in Russia of Gorki's work is always mixed up with communist ideology; if it is not again mentioned that does not mean that conflicting statements are not made about most of his plays.

After this production Gorki separated from the Art Theatre and did not even offer his next pieces to them. It has been suggested that they were scarcely worthy of the tremendous energy which that organization poured into its productions; they probably were not, to judge from the results. These included *The Barbarians* (1905), *Enemies* (1906) which has been popular in the Soviet régime because it relates the enmity between the owners of a factory and its workers who had killed the manager, *The Last Ones* (1908), *Odd People* (1910), *Vassa Zheleznova* (1911), *Children* (1912), *The Zykovs* (1912), *The False Coin* (1913) and *The Old Man* (1915) which was translated by Marie Zancvski and Barrett H. Clark as *The Judge* (1918).

Always a revolutionist, he chose Maxim Gorki (Maxim the Bitter) as his *nom de plume;* with the coming of actual revolution, he threw himself into the midst of its activities. The theatres were used for revolutionary meetings and the plays were transformed into tracts to glorify the cause. However, the excesses of the Civil War disgusted him and he ventured to protest to Lenin, who reminded him that eggs must be broken to make an omelet, or some such homely simile. However, as has been recorded, the great writer went to Germany to live where he remained until the partial return to normality of the first Five Year Plan won him back and he watched hopefully over the development of young dramatists, though mostly in vain. By 1932 he had completed his second famous drama, *Yegor Bulychev and Others*, which is a masterly study of the moral disintegration of the great merchant class at the time of the beginnings of the Revolution of 1917. This piece was performed by the Vakhtangov Theatre under the direction of Vladimir Dmitriev, with Boris Shchukin (1894-1939) in the leading role. Peace having been restored with the First Art Theatre, it was also staged there with Vasilii Kachalov (1875-   ) as Yegor. Thus audiences have had an opportunity of examining the merits of two methods of staging, the first which followed Vakhtangov's precept, "Each play should have its own style," and the second the traditional naturalism and ensemble performance of the First Art Theatre. *Dostigaev and Others* (1933) was a sequel to *Yegor Bulychev* but never reached its heights except in the humorous passages in which the play excels. Upon Gorki's death, his name was given to the Art Theatre which is now officially called the Moscow Art Academic Theatre of the Union of Soviet Socialist Republics in the name of Maxim Gorki, though it is unlikely that posterity will ever refer to it other than as the Moscow Art, or within Russia as the First Art Theatre.

It is necessary now for us to go back thirty years to the days when that selfsame theatre was looking for other dramatists to fill the gap left by the death of Chekhov and the defection of Gorki. One of the men to whom they went for plays was LEONID NIKOLAYEVITCH ANDREYEV (1871-1919), who was the first symbolist in the Russian theatre, having been strongly influenced by Maeterlinck. He wrote in prose, but lacked the poetic genius of ALEXANDER ALEXANDRO-VITCH BLOK (1880-1921) who led the fight for symbolism in poetry. Though he contributed but one play of importance, *The Rose and the Cross* (1912), which was concerned with chivalry in France of the Middle Ages, he wrote a number of lyric dramas and several of his poems were dramatized. Andreyev's technique was cruder and though several of his works have undoubted power they have not proved to be lasting. He wrote *Savva* in 1906 which was an attack on religious superstition. He intended to model his leading character on a young man who had been captured while involved in a plan to blow up the ikon of the Virgin of Kursk but Gorki persuaded him not to, for he felt that a clinical study of the workings of this man's mind would libel his character. Gorki later used him as the basis for his character of Nils in *The Smug Citizen*, which was a highly sympa-thetic portrayal. His gloomy plays *To the Stars* (1905), *King Hunger* (1907) and *Black Maskers* (1908) were so overshadowed by *Savva* that they were almost unnoticed. In contrast to his former symbolism, *The Days of Our Life* (1908) was highly realistic. All his life he alternated between the two styles, though his preferences were toward realism. He was a gloomy man of gloomy mind who fitted well into the blackest period of Russian reaction following the Revo-lution of 1905. *The Life of Man* (1906) was strongly influenced by Poe and its mysteries were distinctly jejune. Despite the fine produc-tion given it by the Moscow Art Theatre, it remained a very nearly worthless, if pretentious, play. *Anathema* (1909) is concerned with the Christ-like Jew, Leiser, who gives his millions to the poor and when he has no more to give is stoned to death by them. The thirtieth performance was examined by the censor on the grounds that the play was irreligious but was absolved of that charge. Not long afterwards the management was obliged to withdraw the play on political grounds. Nikolai Evreinov staged this as well as *Anfisa* (1909), a play of semi-incest, and *Gaudeamus* (1910), a comedy of prostitutes and student life, at Komissarzhevskaya's theatre.

One of his most important plays was *Professor Storitsyn* (1912), which deals with the bankruptcy of the intellectual classes. On the surface it is a realistic tragedy of a noted teacher who can inspire his students, but whose relations toward his family are brutal to an extreme; the idea of the failure of aesthetics in a country of grinding poverty and cruel governmental tyranny represents the symbolical. *The Pretty Sabine Women* (1912), a Shavian comedy of the teetering policies of some liberals, and *Katerina Ivanova* (1912) are his best known plays until *The Waltz of the Dogs* appeared in 1915. This is a study of the degeneration of man overwhelmed by the loss of his fiancée and his brother's efforts to murder him. The abnormal and subnormal always fascinated Andreyev. The moral deterioration of a woman unjustly accused of infidelity by her husband, who decides to become what she has been called, was described in *Katerina Ivanova*. There were elements of schizophrenia in *The Black Maskers*. There is less abnormality in *He Who Gets Slapped* (1916), which tells the story of a man who joins a circus as a clown because he was betrayed by his wife. It satisfies one side of his nature to be the one who is slapped, but the other side is complimented by his ability to serve out home truths to the audience. He contributed nothing more to the theatre and left the country after the Treaty of Brest-Litovsk, which he denounced as a Bolshevist sell-out of his country.

NIKOLAI NIKOLAYEVITCH EVREINOV (1879-   ) was perhaps the most original of the dramatists to arise after Chekhov, though he was not a writer of the first rank. He belonged to the symbolist group along with Andreyev and Blok and was especially interested in the drama of the soul and all the workings of the inner mind. Before the appearance of his first plays *The Rehearsal* (1900), *Fools as Blind as Idols* (1900), *The Foundation of Happiness* (1902), *Stepik and Manyurochka* (1905) and *The Handsome Despot* (1906), he had been an actor and circus performer. Then he directed plays for the Antique (or *Starinny*) Theatre of St. Petersburg for the season of 1907-1908, returning there for 1911-12 in an effort to restore the historical stage. In 1908 Vera Komissarzhevskaya called him to her theatre as *régisseur* to replace Meyerhold who had resigned. In the spring of the following year he and Theodore Komissarzhevski founded the Gay Theatre for Grown-up Children in the same city in which he produced his own *Gay Death*. He became interested in presenting nudity on the stage in his performance of Fyodor Sologub's *Night Hops;* then followed his absorption with the monodrama which he claimed to have introduced. *The Representation of Love* (1910) and *The Theatre of the Soul* (1912) were examples of this form, which he felt would explain the soul, for he believed theatrical expression to be a primitive urge along with the basic instincts of self-preservation and sex. He was kaleidoscopic in his beliefs and went quickly from one to another, expounding each brilliantly for the brief time he believed in them. Then like Pirandello, he became fascinated with illusion and produced his major work, *The Chief Thing*. Amusingly enough he wrote this in 1919 after the materialistic Soviet regime had come into power. It was produced in Petrograd in 1921 and was played by the Theatre Guild in New York in 1926. He is far from being a sound playwright and though still alive at the time of writing (or at least no news has come out of Europe of his death), he is a part of our theatrical past as surely as if he were dead.

VLADIMIR VLADIMIROVITCH MAYAKOVSKI (1894-1930) was a futurist like Marinetti in Italy and was utterly opposed to the symbolists. They endeavored to poetize all drama, whilst the futurists sought to give the language and all dramatic expression new vigor through their use of street slang like Parisian writers of the same period. They endeavored to shock and surprise their audience. Certainly Mayakovski reciting his poems and plays in a woman's yellow blouse with green stripes pencilled on his face was not likely to give many people much confidence. Sometimes it is only by buffoonery that certain ideas can be put across but futurism has failed wherever it has been tried; it has perished as have dadaism and as will surrealism and all other aesthetic movements that have no true basis in life or human experience. They amuse for a while as does Salvador Dali whose portraits of the Marx brothers and others as well as his extraordinary ballet designs succeed really because he is an excellent draftsman as well as a clown. Mayakowski's *Mystery-Bouffe* (1921) is his best known play.

Other dramatists of the pre-revolutionary period include Anatoli Vasilevitch Lunacharski (1876-1933) who wrote *The Temptation* (1896), *The King's Barber* (1906), *The Magi* (1918), *Vasilisa the Wise* (1919), *Ivan in Paradise* (1919), *Faust and the City* (1920), *The Chancellor and the Locksmith* (1921), *Oliver Cromwell* (1921), *Thomas Campanella* (1921), *The Emancipated Don Quixote* (1922), *The Bear's Wedding* (1924), *Poison* (1925), *Velvet and Rags* (1927), *Napoleon Intervenes* (1931) and for whom the great Leningrad State Theatrical Library in the Alexandrinski is named; S. Naidenov (1863-1923), who wrote *Vanyusha's Children* (1901), *The Rich Man* (1903), *Avdotya's Life* and *The Prodigal Son* (1904), *Walls* (1906-07), who some critics think had much of the genius of Chekhov and much more knowledge of dramaturgy; Eugene Nikolayevitch Chirikov (1864-1932), the realistic author of the pro-Semitic *The Jews* (1905), which was acted in New York as *The Chosen People* by Paul Orleney and Alla Nazimova the same year, *The Legend of the Ancient Castle* (also known as *The Black Death*, 1907), *After Glory*, *The Friends of Publicity* and *In the Rear House* (1902), *Ivan*

Mironych, The Peasants (1905), *Red Lights* and *Marya Ivanovna* (1907), *The Provincial Lady* (1908), *The Witch, At the Bottom of the Court* and *The Mysteries of the Forest* (1909), *The Lord of Nature* (1910) and *The House of the Kochergins* (1911). Chirikov's sympathetic attitude toward the Jews along with that of Chekhov and Gorki, was responsible for the emergence of such Yiddish playwrights as Ansky (*nom de théâtre* for S. A. Rappaport, 1863-) with his *Father and Son,* written in Yiddish and translated into Russian in 1906. Scholom Asch (1881-) wrote in Yiddish, but his plays have been translated into Polish, Russian, English, German and other languages, as he has something universal to say. Perhaps his most important drama is *The God of Vengeance* (1907). D. Y. Ayzman (1869-) is the author of several pieces, the most interesting of which is his tragedy, *The Thorn Bush* (1907). The highly polished Dymov (also known as Kain, really O. Perlmann, 1878-) came under the influence of Meyerhold early in his career so that there is a strong strain of symbolism in his writing. He has been principally concerned with Jewish problems, particularly those having to do with intellectual connection with Russian thought and culture. *Every Day* (later renamed *Nyu,* 1907) was acted first in German. It is the story of a libertine who wreaks havoc upon all women he meets, because they cannot resist his appeal. There were other Yiddish writers, but these are the principal names.

Those dramatists whose work lies mainly in the Soviet period will be considered in the chapter devoted to the stage and to changing acting and directing techniques in the Russian theatre. There is no playwright in that group who can rank with the great lights of the Golden Period. Perhaps it is too much to ask for genius or even superior talent in a quarter of a century of effort, where most of the energy has gone to build a new social order. Nonetheless more might be expected from a dramaturgy the brilliance of which has been reflected in the minds of everyone connected with the theatre everywhere in the world. Perhaps the great days are over and the new political religion has destroyed the Russian genius. The bitter persecutions of the tsars were unable to stamp this out because there was faith and hope in the future, which anti-religion has now impaired. It was a great century which produced such giants as Pushkin, Gogol, Turgeniev, Ostrovski, the great Tolstoi, Chekhov and Gorki. Not since the Elizabethan period in England has there been such a flowering of dramatic genius. It is this that gives one hope that some day in other ways and times this may come again. Perhaps but one pyrotechnic display is permitted to a nation for Greece, France and England have never reached their heights but once.

THE REPUBLICAN COUNTRIES,
WITH AND WITHOUT KINGS
(Belgium, Holland and Switzerland)
(1815-1940)

THE theatres of Belgium and Holland naturally enough have been very much influenced by each other and by their neighbors. Belgium has had a checkered political career, being dominated by France, Spain and Austria among others. Holland has been overrun by Spain and France. They have been separate countries and joined together. Belgium is bi-lingual and has been influenced by the Flemings and the French. Germany and England have strongly influenced the Dutch. Switzerland, since the heroic struggle for freedom from Austria in the fourteenth century, has remained independent. It is divided roughly into German, French and Italian sections, as the language and habits of those cantons conform somewhat closely to their neighbors. Though Switzerland has kept her integrity and maintained her borders, her division of culture has perhaps been responsible for the lack of a Swiss literature.

The thrifty and money-making Hollanders whose descendants after several centuries of money and position have provided New York with its aristocracy of family, and America with two of its most distinguished presidents, have patronized theatres but have created no important drama. In the beginning they depended on English and German actors to perform Elizabethan works and *Hanswurstiades* (one of the character's names, *Pickelhering*, came from Holland). Then the court theatres established their own companies who played in French and German. However by the time that Napoleon had been defeated, actors were generally to be heard playing in Dutch in the few playhouses of this small country.

It was not until near the end of the nineteenth century that a dramatic literature worth mentioning developed, though the Dutch have honored the dramatic art as they have all arts. Of the playwrights' names, Frederik Van Eeden, Jan Fabricius, Hermann C. J. Roelvink, J. H. Speenhof, Geert Teis (*nom de plume* for Geert W. Spitzen), Mrs. J. A. Simons-Mees, Mrs. Roland Holst, are outstanding in the nineteenth and twentieth centuries.

There is beyond all others, however, one name, HERMANN HEIJERMANS (1864-1924) who deserves consideration in any history of the theatre. He belonged to the school of Naturalism and was one of the principal followers of Hauptmann. His first successful play was *Ahasuerus* (1893) which came directly from life and the author's experience; *Ghetto Tooneelspel in drie bedrijven* (*The Ghetto*, 1898), deals with Jewry's dislike of inter-marriage with Christians, and though family background is well drawn in this, the protagonist is not sufficiently resolved to provide the contest of wills that this kind of play requires. Some of his other plays are concerned with militarism, industrial problems and bourgeois hypocrisy. His *Uitkomst* was close to *Hannele* in its unrealistic study of a poor delirious child, while *De Meid* (*The Maid*, 1905) tells the story of a young domestic who is so unhappy and frustrated by life that she takes sadistic pleasure in tormenting her mistress by blackmail. In *Allerzielen* (*All Souls*, 1904), Heijermans deals with an unmarried mother who is taken into the household of a minister. She is entirely unrepentent of her sin and goes off with her lover when he returns, regardless of the fate of the clergyman who has lost his post for his Christian act. *Eva Bonheur* (1916) depicts another ungrateful woman, who in this play is heedless of her father's happiness. His one-act play, *Der Brand in de Jonge Jan* (*A Case of Arson*, 1922), was chiefly notable because of the protean *tour de force* of the actor, de Vries, who played the seven characters who are witnesses of the crime.

Op Hoop van Zegen (*The Good Hope*, 1900) was his *chef d'oeuvre* and is one of the ranking dramas of the last half-century, having been played in almost every country. Outside its own land, where it was acted more than a thousand times, it has been particularly successful in the productions given it by Eva LeGallienne at the Civic Repertory Theatre in 1926, by the First Studio of the Moscow Art Theatre, and by the Stage Society of London in 1903. Like *The Weavers*, it is a group play and depends for its effectiveness on ensemble playing. It is the story of an unscrupulous, greedy syndicate which sends out an unseaworthy ship. This play has stood the test of time and is worthy of revival in the professional theatre, as well as in the educational field where it has been remarkably successful. It is to be hoped that in some future day other writers will take up where this fine, humane artist left off.

In turning to Belgium, one name stands out so preeminently as to overshadow all others including Henry Kistemaeckers and Émile Verhaeren. That name of course belongs to MAURICE MAETERLINCK (1862–   ), whose world-wide influence cannot be disputed. He has stood for symbolism, and many writers and theatres have come under his banner for a time at least. In his middle twenties he went to France where he was under the influence of Arthur Rimbaud, Paul Verlaine and Stéphane Mallarmé, the symbolist poets, and contributed two volumes of poetry to that school. In 1889 he turned to drama with a near-Elizabethan tragedy, *La Princesse Maleine*, which was received with raptures, as all his plays were to be greeted for the next forty years. His dramas, many of which he labelled for marionettes feeling that living actors could not portray them, depict the inner life in a timeless world. Some of them have become so familiar that they have passed into popular literary lore and language. His short plays *L'Intruse* (*The Intruder*, 1890), *Les Aveugles* (*The Blind*, 1890), *L'Intérieur* (*Interior*, 1894) perfectly picture the inner existence in simple terms which can be understood, and in language which is beautiful. In these plays, as in *Pelléas et Mélisande* (1892), later made into an opera by Claude Debussy, *La Mort de Tintagiles* (*The Death of Tintagiles*, 1894) and *Aglavaine et Sélysette* (1896), he went as far into spirituality as drama can go. Having basically a healthy and vigorous mentality, he realized that he was pushing toward intellectual attrition. He himself said in 1896 that he intended to renounce his mysticism and turn to what was more human, less brilliant and more true. This was beginning to be evident in *Aglavaine et Sélysette*. With *Monna Vanna* (1902), he moved toward conventional practice and followed this with the plays for which he is best known, though his influence on others undoubtedly came from his early mystic series of dramas rather than from his more realistic writing. In *Monna Vanna*, he took a variation of the plot which Shakespeare had used in *Measure for Measure*, that of the woman who offers her virtue to save others. In this, Maeterlinck abandoned the theme of fate controlling all actions and permitted a character to determine his own destiny.

In 1908 he wrote the play for which he is known everywhere, *L'Oiseau Bleu* (*The Blue Bird*) which was given its première by Stanislavski at the Moscow Art Theatre. This fairy tale of happiness is entirely lacking in the sentimentality which has too frequently marred his work. In this tradition he follows the line of the early nineteenth century dramatist, Ludwig Tieck, whose fairy-like plays were long acted in German theatres. Maeterlinck's allegory written for children has had wide adult following and was produced successfully in this country by Winthrop Ames at the New Theatre in 1910. The sequel to this, *Les Fiançailles* (*The Betrothal*, 1918) has less general appeal and has never been so successful as the earlier piece.

Soeur Béatrice (1910) was the touching, if sentimental, drama of a nun who forgets her vows of chastity, leaves the convent and goes out into the world. Long afterwards she comes to the realization of her sin and returns to her post to find that the Blessed Virgin has taken her place and her absence was never discovered. This poetic drama recalls the philosophy of the Mary Plays in Mediaeval France, where the Virgin frequently assisted those who were negligent or sinful. Vollmoeller expanded the play into his popular spectacle *The Miracle*. *Marie Magdeleine* (1910) is of this same general group. A Roman tribune offers to save the life of Jesus if the Magdalene will yield herself to him. Having cast her voluptuous life aside, she refuses and Christ is pleased at the resoluteness of her decision and goes willingly to His self-appointed doom.

There remains but one major work to be discussed, *Le Bourgmestre de Stilemonde* (1918). This drama concerning the heroism of Belgian men and women during the German invasion of their country in the First World War has been much admired for its restraint and lack of chauvinism; the Germans evidently did not appreciate Maeterlinck's point of view so the aged dramatist was forced to flee his home in France and seek haven in America in 1940. Undaunted, still highly respected for his important contributions to modern drama the great Belgian writer, in his own words, still seeks "a new theatre, a theatre of peace, and of beauty without tears." Written in earlier and happier years, these sentiments are still his and his courage still holds.

The literary genius of Belgium turned toward poetry. Maeterlinck's early work was in this form and his dramas have always been poetic in form and usually in content. ÉMILE VERHAEREN (1855-1916) was primarily a poetic rather than a dramatic writer. His beautiful poem, *Les Flamandes* reflects life in the quiet Belgian countryside. Subject matter for some of his plays came from his deep sensitiveness and his appreciation of his country and its culture. Writing in French, he is frequently grouped with dramatists of that country along with Maeterlinck and Kistemaeckers. His first important play *Les Aubes* (*Dawn*, 1898) was given its initial performance in Prague, where it was hailed, as everywhere, as a powerful impressionistic play about universal peace. Set in Oppidomagne (read Paris) as the invading armies (read Prussians) envelop the city, the popular leaders on both sides decide there shall be peace, no matter how much the officers clamor for war, so the defenders take the provisions stored away against a siege and banquet the invaders. When the officers try to interfere, they find the soldiers' guns turned on them, and in desperation the defending military rulers murder the foreign leader who has offered peace, and his funeral oration is delivered by the popular leader of the forces which had been opposing him. This play won almost universal popularity and Meyerhold's production of it was one of his best.

Verhaeren's other plays completely lack the power and importance of *Les Aubes*. *Le Cloître* (*The Cloister*, 1900) was pale and far from absorbing. It was staged in Brussels and Paris and in 1921 was produced in New York by Emanuel Reicher for the Theatre Guild for two subscription performances without awaking any special enthusiasm either from critics or public. *Philippe II* (1904) and *Hélène de Sparte* (1912) are little known outside Belgium and France.

HENRY KISTEMAECKERS (1872-1938) really belongs to the French theatre despite his Belgian birth, for he is a follower of Sardou and Scribe. He is primarily a theatrical writer, being more concerned with plot development and the intricacies which would catch the attention of his audience, than with the logical building of his characters. For this reason many of his plays such as *L'Occident* (1913), *The Woman of Bronze* (written in collaboration with Eugène Delard and adapted into English by Paul Kester, 1919) were dated soon after they were written. A notable exception to the rule was his *La Flambée* (*The Spy*, 1912), which manages to avoid the more obvious scenes of plays of this kind and to concentrate on the human element. A French colonel, about to be divorced by his wife, who is in love with a government minister, seeks a loan from a foreign banker. The financier suggests that in return for the money, certain military secrets be revealed. In the fight that follows the banker is killed unintentionally. Revealing his secret to his wife, the protective instinct is aroused and she elects to stay with him. His rival suspects what has happened and threatens the officer with exposure but he counters with the unanswerable question of what the government official would have done under the same circumstances. Moved both by patriotism and by an awakened realization of the husband's worth, he tactfully withdraws from the situation and agrees to remain silent. The husband and wife are then reunited, forever we hope. Reduced to an outline, the play seems sentimental and banal but it represents a successful attempt on Kistemaeckers' part to analyze his characters and to paint an honest picture of real people.

There are a number of lesser Belgian playwrights, whose work is little known outside of Belgium and France including Charles Van Lerberghe, whose work has been likened to Maeterlinck's early plays,

François Léonard, François-Charles Morisseaux, Henri Liebrecht, Georges Rodenbach, Sylvain Bonmariage, Henri Davignon, Horace Van Offel and Paul Spaak. GUSTAVE VANZYPE (1869-   ) has written a number of plays, two of which have been translated into English as *Mother Nature* and *Progress*.

The writing team of FRANZ FONSON (pen name for Jean François), and FERNAND WICHELER (1871-   ) is chiefly known for the light and charming comedy *Le Mariage de Mlle. Beulemans* (1910), which was turned into an operetta in 1913. C. Haddon Chambers adapted the play as *Suzanne*, the same year it was staged in Paris. The pair were also responsible for *Le feu de la Saint-Jean* (*The St. John's Day Fire*, 1912), but Fonson alone wrote *La Demoiselle de magasin*, which Holman Day adapted into English as the reasonably successful *Along Came Ruth* (1914).

After Maeterlinck and Verhaeren, probably the best known Belgian writer is the eccentric FERNAND CROMMELYNCK (1888-   ), whose first play is his best known and most successful. *Le Cocu magnifique* (*The Magnificent Cuckold*, 1920) was staged at Lugné-Poë's *Théâtre de l'Oeuvre*, that Paris house where many of the most interesting experimental productions have been made in this century. Lugné-Poë's acting, the play's satiric qualities and a first act that was truly remarkable, redeemed some of the incoherence and grotesqueness which afflict it. Perhaps the fact that Meyerhold played it without any sexual emphasis, so different is the Russian and the French feeling toward that subject, that the play seemed more exciting in Moscow than in Paris. Cuckoldry has never been a particularly pleasing dramatic subject in English and American drama; the Restoration rather wore out Anglo-Saxon patience. This may explain why the play has never been presented in this country, though it has frequently been announced. There are several magnificent acting parts which have proved tempting but not sufficiently so to overcome the reluctance the subject causes in American minds. However the brilliance of the drama at once established Crommelynck as a dramatist to be reckoned with, though no play he has written since has quite measured up to it. That may be because the bypaths of dramatic technique have interested the author rather than the straightforward attack which can readily be understood and measured without esoteric qualification.

Not long after, *Les Amants Puérils* (*The Childish Lovers*, directed by Fermin Gémier) and *Tripes d'or* (1930) appeared at the *Comédie des Champs Elysées* without advancing his dramatic standing, in fact they lowered his prestige. *Carine, ou la jeune fille folle de son âme* (*Carine; or, The Young Girl Frantic about Her Soul*) followed, and though its central scenes are still incoherent, there was a lyrical symbolism about the play that was attractive to its audiences. His play which has the widest universal appeal is *La femme qui a le coeur trop petit* (*The Woman with Too Little Heart*, 1934). It is concerned with Balbine who has not enough heart to take part in the vicissitudes and joys of the world. She marries a widower, just verging on old age, and sets out to make his home attractive, and though her domestic virtues are admirable, they are not enough to bring happiness to her nor to those around her. All of the household, the step-daughter, the brother-in-law, the farmer-overseer, the servants are involved in love affairs, real or imaginary, which give them release. Balbine alone cannot give herself and she combats what she considers their lunacy with her morality and domesticity. Only her husband loves her, so by using some of the methods of Petruchio in *The Taming of the Shrew*, he widens her heart. The drama is mixed in style and alternately lyric, realistic and symbolic. The scenes seem to have been placed in helter-skelter juxtaposition, but the effect of the whole is exciting.

It must not be thought that because Belgium produced no drama of note before the last quarter of the last century, that there was no theatre in that country. From mediaeval times there were amateur mystery plays sponsored by the Church; during the Renaissance, just as Holland received English and Dutch troupes, French traveling companies visited the cities and castles of Belgium. When reigning monarchs visited Bruges or Ghent a festival was held in their honor, and beginning with a triumphal entry and a dramatic pageant of welcome, they were followed by a ball or balls, where masques and other dramatic festivities were held. These could be and were handsome and elaborately expensive occasions. Festival books picturing these marriages, entries or even funerals were printed and to this day are the best evidence of the beauty of the occasions.

Frequently when French kings visited their military camps companies of actors were dispatched from Paris to entertain the monarch, his generals and other officers who were sometimes drawn from the nobility of that section now known as Belgium. With the coming of her independence and the establishment of the national capital at Brussels, the famous *Théâtre de la Monnaye* was founded and operas and plays were performed. Many of the finest French actors were trained and polished in this playhouse which upholds the oldest traditions of the country. After the war experimental theatres which had a kinship with Jacques Copeau's *Vieux Colombier* were established. René Moulaert and Jules Delacre directed in Brussels at the *Théâtre du Marais* and Johann de Meester was the director of the nationally conscious Flemish People's Theatre.

Switzerland on the other hand has no such imposing background. Plays were performed in the Middle Ages and traveling troupes from Germany or France made their appearance in the beautiful little Swiss cities, but no literary movement sprang up and there were no large and important theatres. Perhaps because of this the amateur or little theatre movement has caught on more strongly there than anywhere on the Continent, with the possible exception of Russia. In this, Switzerland has been like those sections of America where the professional theatre to all intents and purposes has died out. The people themselves, feeling the need, have established their own theatres where they act and produce for themselves.

In the twentieth century these peoples' theatres and popular dramatic festivals have grown up as a group dramatic expression. When historical or patriotic subjects are portrayed it is actually considered part of a man's duty as a citizen to take part. These performances take place in Basel, Lausanne, Zurich and other parts of the country, sometimes attracting audiences as large as twenty thousand people for a single occasion. The theatres for out-of-door performances are so well planned that the acoustics are excellent and the actors' voices can be heard as distinctly as if they were singing. The direction naturally has to be simplified and gestures enlarged or reduced to a minimum. Long speeches must be avoided in writing for this type of audience, as the words have a tendency to become monotonous unless it is possible to break them up with physical movement. Nonetheless, *Julius Caesar* was enormously effective, because a portion of the city of Rome could be shown and the action could become as continuous as in a passion play such as the one at Valenciennes or Mons or present-day Oberammergau.

French stock companies have settled in Geneva, and Zurich has played host to a German company at the *Schauspielhaus*, which since 1933 has become truly important because of distinguished non-Aryan actors and directors, or others who were not in sympathy with fascism. It was under the direction of Ferdinand Rieser until the fall of 1938 when Oskar Wälterlin, a Swiss director, succeeded to the management. Here such plays as Carl Zuckmayer's *Bellman* and *Talleyrand und Napoleon* by the German-born dramatist Hermann Kesser (now a Swiss national) have been given their first performances. The veteran Albert Basserman played Talleyrand and Karl Paryla was Napoleon. This theatre has become isolated in the Second World War and many of its finest workers are in this country.

The most conspicuous talent to be given to the theatre world from this ancient republic was of course, Adolphe Appia. This great scenic designer and innovator received his training at Bayreuth with Wagner, and is discussed in a chapter on Germany, where his ideas found fruitful soil and he found employment. He cooperated with Jacques Dalcroze in an experimental dance and drama playhouse at Dresden. Appia's greatest contribution to the theatre lay in his writing which freed the energies of designers the world over and gave justification to their scenic efforts which could even be understood by Philistines.

XXV

THE MIDDLE EAST OF EUROPE

(1815-1940)

THE population of the smaller countries in the East and South of Europe consists of a mixed Slavic and Latin blood, an interesting combination which has provided the people with several outstanding dramatists and a lively and active theatre. As has been suggested this theatre had its beginnings in the Renaissance. Hungary developed no true drama until the close of the eighteenth century. It depended on the French and German companies who played in Budapest and toured the principal cities and towns thoughout the country. Czecho-Slovakia, a Wilsonian creation, was a part of the Austrian empire; Yugoslavia was part Austrian and, like all the other Balkan countries, had been a part of Turkey, which had a severely limited theatre. Doubtless *Karagoz* and the shadow-players were known in the western reaches of the Ottoman Empire.

POLAND

By the beginning of the nineteenth century, the final partition of Poland by Russia, Austria and Prussia had already taken place and the Poles were a subject people. COUNT ALEXANDER FREDRO (1783-1876), whom Bogusławski had induced to write for the theatre, turned out many comedies imitative of Molière, the best known of which is *Maiden's Vows*. In his satiric quality he was exactly the opposite of the serious and moving ADAM MICKIEWICZ (1798-1855), who was revered as the first important dramatic poet of Poland. His tremendous prophetic poetic drama *Book of the Dead* chanted the theme of enslaved Poland which would rise again. Intended to be read, it was more lyric than dramatic.

The gloominess of Mickiewicz was unpalatable to the handsome JULJUSZ SLOWACKI (1809-1849), who was the leader of Romanticism. His patriotic play *Kordjan* preaches armed revolution in contrast to the sacrifices demanded by the older dramatist. Słowacki was willing to offer his blood and his life if dying would help his country. His next two plays were highly romantic, *Balladine* and *Lilla Weneda*. Then he began to be influenced by Shakespeare and to form his plays on an Elizabethan model. His best known piece, *Mazeppa*, and *Horsztynski*, which has been called the Polish *Hamlet*, were both written at this point in his career. Perhaps it was the introspection of this tragedy or perhaps it was the sad fate of his native land which caused him to turn to mysticism in the three lyric plays *Father Mark*, *The Silver Song of Salomé* and *Samuel Zborowski*, which drew on a religious background though they still embodied his nationalist spirit.

Writing at the same time as Słowacki was the comic dramatist KORZENIOWSKI (1791-1853) who composed comedies of manners in contrast to Count Fredro's character comedies. Korzeniowski's plays reduced his characters to types instead of real people, suggesting somewhat remotely, Wycherley and Congreve of the English Restoration. His best play was *The Carpathian Mountaineers*.

The dramatic poem which was the Polish masterpiece of the nineteenth century was *The Profane Comedy* (1835-48) by COUNT ZYEMUNT KRASÍNSKI (1812-59). Tinged with Byronism and carrying overtones of Goethe's *Faust* this represents the titanic struggle between the aristocracy and the masses. In the end both champions are killed and the common people are benefited. When the abortive revolt of 1863 was quelled, the playwright Swietochowski advocated what would be called a policy of appeasement but NARZYNSKI (1839-72) bitterly attacked this defeatism in a hotly written drama, *The Positive Ones*. His *Epidemic* demonstrated the difficulty the nobility had in adjusting themselves to money matters, a subject which the leading comedy writer of the period, BLIZÍNSKI (1827-93), treated humorously in *Mr. Damazi*.

Another comic talent of the century was that of MICHEL BATUCKI (1837-1901) who wrote savory comedies of the Galician section of old Poland, which he celebrated in such gay and picturesque pieces as *Bachelors' Club*, *A House Where One Is Received*, and *Big Hats*. CASIMIR ZALEWSKI, a contrasting writer of the same period, found his inspiration, like many of the lesser German writers, in the dubious quarters of Dumas, *fils*, and later in Sardou. Nevertheless he achieved considerable success with his vigorous drama *The Veteran of Marriage*.

Ibsen reached across the Baltic Sea to touch STANISLAW PRZYBYSZEWSKI (1867-1928), who prided himself on his individualism. He was concerned with the attitude of people whose souls were facing the infinite. His most successful plays *For Happiness*, *The Golden*

Fleece and *Snow* were called by the critic Larentowicz a dance of love and death with remarkable tragic power.

About the beginning of the present century a new hope of independence arose in the hearts of the Poles and a literary movement called The Group of Young Poland was inaugurated which embraced not only writers, but artists and actors. Any movement no matter how *sub rosa*, nor how innocuous it seemed or was, stood a strong chance of immediate suppression. The Russians, then as now, suppressed the liberties of the Poles and lived in constant fear of insurrection. They were quite correct in their assumption for there were several major uprisings after the partition. The Russian efforts to remove the people from their land and to substitute Russians suggest a parallel with the German efforts to destroy Polish nationality today. It is easy to see how an intensely patriotic people would seize upon any excuse to inculcate a spirit of resistance to oppression.

Przybyszewski was also a member of the Group of Young Poland, but its shining apostle and the greatest theatrical talent his country has produced was that of STANISLAW WYSPIANSKI (1867-1907). He was a dramatist, a scenic and costume designer, a director, a critic, in fact an all-round man of the theatre. He was even more, for he was a painter, a poet and a town-planner. He wavered between the church and the stage, as have many others, finally choosing the latter as the means of expressing his artistic impulses. In addition he adorned the interiors of churches with paintings and stained glass windows; he designed the interiors of public and private buildings, even designing furniture for them so that the whole might be perfect.

Wyspiánski came under the influence of the great Greek dramatists as well as Shakespeare. In fact he wrote a critical treatise on *Hamlet* in which he shows his evident intention to write a play of this kind which would show the soul of Poland to the world. Because of the pull between Sophocles and the Elizabethans, his plays are mixed in style. *November Night* was a dramatization of the November Revolt of 1830, in which he set forth the rhythm of revolution and sacrificed his story to attain this end. He designed his own settings for the production but they have since been attacked as overclassical for so flaming and intense a drama. *Les Noces* (*The Wedding*, 1901) was written at a time when Shakespeare exerted his strongest influence upon him. Just as Banquo's Ghost appears in *Macbeth*, so did individuals from a woman's memories people the scene of a remarkably composed peasant wedding.

Due to censorship, his first plays were published in Paris. These included *The Legend* (1892), *Meleager* (1894), *The Varsovienne*

(1898), and *Lelewel* (1899). His enthusiasm for Greek subjects and his strong feeling for classicism were apparent in such plays as *Meleager, Ulysses' Return, Achilles, Anathema* and *The Judges.* He used a Greek background, however, for some of his plays with Polish subjects, such as *Acropolis,* or introduced classic figures into a national background as in *November Night.* His use of crowds created a large part of the dramatic effect in many of his pieces, notably in *The Legion.* Polish critics consider *The Wedding* and *Boleslaw the Bold* as his finest dramatic works, so filled are they with passionate understanding of the history of his country, together with his power to depict its problems and to mingle archaic and popular forms.

The Group of Young Poland did not begin and end with Wyspiánski and Przybyszewski. It enlisted a number of other talents, most of whom survived the First World War and were alive to see that amazing resurgence of the theatre which took place between 1919 and 1921. GABRIELLE ZAPOLSKA (1860-1921) was identified with the Red Theatre, which was the Polish equivalent of the *Théâtre Libre.* In *Madame Dulska's Morals,* she attacked bourgeois standards. THADDEUS RITNER (1873-1921) wrote ironic and well-constructed plays though slight in content. *Wolves in the Night, James the Simple* and *The Little House* were his chief works. WLODZIMIERZ PERYNSKI (1878-1930) wrote social comedy which attacked various middle-class sins and was tolerant of hypocrisy. His best plays were the realistic *Smile of Fortune* and *The Prodigal Sister.* He was also a novelist like the well-known STEFAN ZEROMSKI (1864-1925). Zeromski wrote a number of plays to be read and not acted, with the laudable intention of pointing the way for his younger contemporaries, though some of them were performed with considerable success. Among these were *The Rose* and the tragedy, *Sulkowski.* As a result he was encouraged to write directly for the stage such pieces as the melodramatic *Whiter Than Snow, Tourogne* which dramatized the Galican peasant insurrection of 1846, and *The Little Quail Has Run Away from Me.* This last depicts his favorite type of character, the socially-minded idealist who sacrifices his own happiness to the common good of all.

Numerous dramatists began writing in those days after the successful conclusion of their war with Soviet Russia, 1920-21. Anyone desirous of learning about this resurgence will find much of interest in the account written by Wladyslaw Zawistowski, Polish critic and historian, in the excellently planned and executed *The Theatre in a Changing Europe* (1937), edited by that scholarly lover of the theatre, Thomas H. Dickinson. Among the playwrights who came to the fore were JERZY SZANIAWSKI, who wrote such poetic, charming and weak pieces as *The Sailor, The Bird and The Bridge;* ZOFJA NALKOW-

SKA, the novelist, contrived wordy, psychologically successful dramas such as *House of Women* and *The Day of His Return;* and the politically inclined ADOLF NOWACZYNSKI before the First World War covered his polemics with historical disguises in *Frederick the Great, Tsar Dmitri the False,* and *Pulaski.* In the period after the war when dissimulation was no longer necessary, he still placed his plays in the past, notably *The Springtime of People in a Quiet Spot,* which depicts a small town during the Insurrection of 1848.

KAROL HUBERT ROSTWOROWSKI was essentially a man of the theatre. He was highly regarded before the war for the humanity of his historical dramas *Caligula* and *Judas.* With the change in dramatic fashion he offered an expressionistic play *Charity,* which in subject matter was keyed in with his earlier work. Not satisfied with this form however, he returned to realism in a trilogy *The Surprise, Moving Day* and *At the Goal.*

Like the novelist Zofja Nałkowska, MARJA JASNORZEWSKA-PAWLIKOWSKA brought psychological values to the stage. Turning from poetry she wrote a number of socially useful plays including *Mamma's Return, Egyptian Wheat* and *Heavenly Lovers.* There were numerous other writers whose importance it is impossible at the present time to estimate, so scarce have become the records of the Polish theatre. Merely to list their names and the titles of their plays would be of little use to the student. The fact that a theatre was established in Warsaw merely to act native drama and by so doing to encourage young writers, will give some idea of the extent of modern dramatic literature. From 1919 to 1924 The Masque Theatre (*Redouta*) performed only such plays. In direction and acting it patterned itself on the Moscow Art Theatre; the directors Juljusz Osterwa and Mieczysław Limianowski followed the lead of Stanislavski. After 1925 it became a touring company with its base at Vilna, ancient capital of Lithuania, formerly an independent state and now a part of the U.S.S.R.

In addition to government-supported theatres in Warsaw, there were a number of other theatres in the country, notably at Cracow, where the producing standards before 1914 were much higher than elsewhere. This was because Austrian rule was not so intellectually vicious as the Russian, and more personal freedom was permitted. When the citizens of Warsaw wished to see plays that censorship had not rendered completely innocuous, it was necessary for them to go to Cracow in Galicia. The Germans were considerate of the stage in Poznan, though they discouraged anything nationalistic. The Russian government supported several state playhouses in Warsaw, but upon its withdrawal the municipality took them over and operated them together with the municipal theatre. The few private playhouses were generally swallowed up by the cities and towns where they were located. A notable exception to this was the Polish Theatre (*Teatr Polski*) which was founded in Warsaw by Arnold Szyfman in 1913 and conducted as a channel for the entrance of foreign plays and new theatrical ideas into Poland. He might be compared in this respect with Alexander Tairov of the Kamerni Theatre in Moscow and Lugné-Poë with his various theatrical enterprises in Paris.

The Variety Theatre (the pre-war *Teatr Rozmaitosci*), where the plays of Wyspiánski were given, was renamed the National Theatre (*Teatr Narodowy*). This was a municipal playhouse as there were no more state theatres after the Russian withdrawal.

Leon Schiller, formerly a director of the Polish Theatre, with Wilam Horzyca, took over the management of the playhouse that had been named for the founder of the Polish stage, the Bogusławski Theatre. They added an additional director, Alexander Zelwerowicz, began a series of bold and provocative productions showing their strong interest in the social welfare of the general public, and experimented with scenic devices which followed no set rule. If this theatre can be said to have had a blood brother, the Vakhtangov in Moscow might be cited. Both held to the principle that each play requires its own style of production.

A great number of fresh directing talents sprang up during this period of prolific production. Notable among them were Karol Borowski, Ivo Gall, Wacław Radulski and Zbignew Ziembiński. These producers had active cooperation from the best painting talents in the country. After the great Wyspiánski, perhaps the most important designer was Wincenty Drabik (died 1933), noted for his eclecticism and his ability to adjust himself to various *régisseurs*, as well as for his intolerance of the conventional and the cheap. To this standard, Karol Frycz, who was primarily a realist, also subscribed. Andrzej Pronaszko created settings at the Bogusławski Theatre as well as in Lwow, when Leon Schiller transferred his activities there. Three scenic artists who also deserve mention are Stanisław Sliwiński, Stanisław Jarocki and Władysław Daszewski.

Poland has always been famous for her actors as well as for her beautiful women. Literature, the novel and the drama alike, has been peopled with mysterious, dark Polish beauties. It is generally agreed that the greatest Polish actress was HELENA MODJESKA (1844-1909). Born in Cracow she acted in her native country for sixteen years before coming to the United States. Her best-known tragic roles include Juliet, Desdemona, Mazeppa, Maria Stuart, Ophelia and Princess Eboli. She and her husband Count Bozenta Chlapowski, a critic, went to California where they attempted to found a colony. In 1877 she returned successfully to the stage in San Francisco in an English adaptation of *Adrienne Lecouvreur*. From then on she continued to act successfully in America with an occasional sojourn in London. Her popularity had become so great that in 1905 a monster testimonial performance was arranged for her at the Metropolitan Opera House. Following this appearance she retired to her farm near Los Angeles.

Among the men, Kazimierz Kamiński, an actor who used the inductive approach, and the highly external performer, Mieczysław Frenkiel, stand for the two main schools of Polish acting.

What the future of the Polish theatre may be, no one can say. Observation of the terrific nationalism of the Poles and their ability to hold to it through more than a century of persecution in the past, suggests that the Polish culture will persist.

HUNGARY

The beginnings of drama in Hungary are of comparatively recent date, although in 1550 *The Marriage of the Priests*, a Protestant tract, succeeded the anonymous mystery and morality plays which appeared wherever the Roman Church had a foothold. In 1696 the writer Georg Felvinczy organized the *Berufs-Schauspielgesellschaft* (Professional Players Society) which staged plays both in Latin and Hungarian at Siebenbuergen and Kolozsvár.

There was a barren stretch until KATONA (1792?-1830), after much reading of Shakespeare, offered his drama *Bánk Bán* in 1818. This patriotic tragedy passed with little notice when it was first produced; it was not until 1834, after Katona's death, that the famous actor Gabriel Egressy made the play popular. The *Nemzeti Szinház* (National Theatre) was organized in 1837 in Budapest and soon constituted a strong nationalizing force for the Hungarian theatre. Following this, SZIGLIGETI (pen name of Joseph Szatmáry) is popularly credited with the establishment of folk-comedy. He may perhaps have borrowed, consciously or unconsciously, from the Austrian Raimund or the later Anzengruber. Among his numerous comedies were *Marna, Female Rule, The Three Matrimonial Commands, Stephen Dalos;* his tragedies included *The Shadows of Light* and *The Pretender;* and among his folk-pieces were *The Deserter, The Foundling* and *The Pretender*. Szigligeti had a real knowledge of stagecraft which he coupled with genuine wit and an understanding of the peasants of his country, creating strongly nationalistic plays.

The romantic drama of the aristocratic IMRE MADÁCH (1829-1864), which is to Hungarian drama what the not dissimilar *Faust* is to the German stage, bears the resounding title *Az ember tragediája* (*The Tragedy of Man*, 1862). This overwhelming piece envisages the ignoble end of humanity as a sort of pageant revealed by Lucifer to Man to induce him to adopt a negative attitude in this world.

Among the mid-nineteenth century writers whoses names alone require mention are Sigismund Czako, Charles Obernyik, Ignatius Nagy, Count Ladislas Teleki who wrote *The Favorite*, and Charles Hugo whose *Banker and Baron* was so successful he dared not write a second play. However it was not really until the twentieth century that Hungarian drama began to take its proper place in the European scene. The aristocracy was cultivated and appreciated the best so long as it did not require too much mental exertion and amused them sufficiently. In this they were aped by the comfortable middle class, which is likely to form the backbone of an audience for the commercial theatre in any country.

The first internationally known dramatist in the Hungarian theatre was FERENC MOLNAR (1878-   ) who was born of a well-to-do Jewish merchant family. He definitely stands for the depicting of life through rose-colored glasses, and a pleasant sentimentalizing of values. Many of us enjoy this deception when the sardonic ones are not too relentless in pointing out our own illusions. There are as many levels of sentimentality as there are persons, which is only another way of saying that one man's meat is another man's poison. There is certainly no instance in which the adage is more apt than in playgoing tastes.

Molnár started off innocuously enough with *The Attorney-at-Law* (1902) and followed it with a psychological study of children who had become maladjusted through the wealth and over-solicitousness of their parents. In *The Devil* (1907), which demonstrates his cynicism, the dress-suited Satan deliberately rouses an old love affair only to chuckle when he destroys marital happiness.

In 1909 he wrote the play for which he will long be remembered and for which his earlier plays scarcely prepared his audience. *Liliom* is the story of a handsome tough, who is kept by the proprietress of a Budapest amusement park where he is the barker. Julie, an honest little serving girl, loves him and he goes to live with her. She supports him in idleness until he learns that she is to have a baby. Upon learning this he goes out to rob a bank messenger in order to secure the funds to take care of her. Cornered by the police he stabs himself and is carried, dying, to Julie. He begs her to marry the old carpenter who is in love with her. He dies and is taken to the Heavenly Police Court where, as a suicide, he is offered the opportunity of returning to earth to do the good which he had left undone. Liliom, consistent in character, scorns the offer and is led off to his punishment. Fifteen years later he is given one day off to redeem himself by a single good deed. Unchanged from the good-for-nothing that he had always been, he steals a star to take to his child. She is frightened by him and turns away when he wants to kiss her. Angered by her refusal he slaps her in his stupid, rough fashion and the Heavenly Police have no choice but to take him away again. Julie, alarmed by her daughter's cry, rushes out in time to see him and to be startled by the resemblance to the man she loved, the graceless rascal Liliom.

The tenderness and understanding that went into this drama have never been equalled by Molnár, though he approached it in *The Glass Slipper* (1924). In this, the little drudge in a boarding house loves the star-boarder, a middle-aged cabinet-maker, but he marries the land-lady who, in turn, carries on an affair with a young roomer. Irma tries to warn her idol but he will pay no attention and in desperation she goes out to sell herself in a house of ill-fame as a spiritual way of kill-ing herself. She is arrested in a police raid, but something of the purity in her soul at last awakens a response in her middle-aged hero. Dis-gusted and unhappy over his unsuccessful marriage, he decides to divorce his wife and go away with Irma, making her blissfully happy at last.

The Guardsman (1924) is an elegant trifle about a jealous actor-husband who tests his wife's love by masquerading as a guardsman and making love to her. She flirts with him and he sets out to consummate the affair, knowing that if she rebuffs him he will be everlastingly happy; if she yields, at least he will be the one to possess her. He se-cures a half-confession from her but when he resumes his guardsman's disguise, she merely laughs at him and tells him that she knew it was he all along. The agony of it is that he still does not know whether she is faithful to him or not. This gay but slight comedy made a great hit in several countries. Nowhere was it more liked than in America, where the noted acting team of Alfred Lunt and Lynn Fontanne treated it to a thoroughly delightful performance.

Among his other plays are: *The Wolf* (played in the United States as *The Phantom Lover*, 1912), which again plays with the idea of a wife's unfaithfulness; *The Swan* (1914), a Graustarkian fantasy in re-verse; and *Fashions for Men*, which deals with a man so simple and generous that nothing can hurt him. *The Red Mill* (1913, acted by Lenore Ulric for David Belasco under the title *Mima*) was a mechani-cal nightmare laid in hell. *The Play in the Castle* (1926), staged in New York under the much more satisfactory title of *The Play's the Thing*, provided Holbrook Blinn with his last acting part. It was a play within a play, with delightful dialogue which depended upon a superlative cast to breathe life into it. None of his more recent pieces has been of more than passing interest. His novel *The Paul Street*

Boys, a touching allegory of war, was filmed as *The Power and the Glory*.

Two of the playwright's wives have been actresses for whom he has written some of his dramas. In fact all of his plays seem to come out of some phase of his love affairs. His second wife was the singer-actress Sári Fedák and his third, Lili Darvas, who attracted as much attention playing in Reinhardt's company as she did in Molnár's plays.

FERENCZ HERCZEG (1863-   ) was the first to raise the standards of Hungarian drama to meet the general European standards of the nineteenth century. His plays were primarily historical but he is also credited with having written a successful farce-comedy *The Three Bodyguards*. He was not content merely to pander to a pleasure-loving public for he wrote a number of plays which were aimed at improving the morals of his audiences. However, it is in his historical dramas that Herczeg stands the best chance of survival. Of these the best known are *Brigadier Ocskay* and *The Orphan King Ladislas*.

SIGMUND MÓRICZ (1879-   ) wrote realistic plays of Hungarian peasant life which really reflected the people and their problems. He was primarily a novelist and frequently reworked sections of his novels, or other fictional material, for the stage. His best known drama is *Justice of the Peace Sári*.

ALEXANDER BRÓDY (real name Alexander Brodski, 1879-   ) introduced naturalism into Hungary in his two principal plays *The Nursemaid* and *The Teacher*; while DESIDER SZOMORY (1873-   ) wrote such historical dramas as *Hapsburg Trilogy* and *Ludwig II*; and ENDRE NAGY (1877-   ) created the literary aspect of the Hungarian theatre-cabaret.

Among the Hungarian dramatists best known outside their country are: Lajos Zilahy (1891-   ) with *The Firebird*; Lajos Bibó (1890-   ) with *The Inheritance*; Ladislas Fodor, who wrote *The Jewel Robbery*, *A Church Mouse* and *I Love an Actress*; Ladislas Bush-Fekete with *The Lady Has a Heart*; Ernö Vajda with the cynical yet touching *Fata Morgana* and *The Crown Prince* which told the story of Crown Prince Rudolph and Maria Vetsera; Menyhért Lengyel with *The Czarina* (with Lajos Biró), *Antonia* and *Angel*; and Baroness Lili Hatvany who wrote the original version of the comedy *Tonight or Never*, adapted by Frederic and Fanny Hatton, 1930.

Budapest is a city of playhouses and once was one of the most prosperous theatrical centers of the world. Those were the days when there were a great many translators and adapters in other countries waiting anxiously to adapt the froth into English, French or German. The Hungarian vogue seems to have passed and many of the theatres are dark.

There have been few Hungarian actors of any lasting ability, though like the second-rate plays they performed, they had a surface charm that was temporarily irresistible. Lili Darvas and Franciska Gaal are the best known modern actresses. The leading directors have been Alexander Hevesi and Jeno Kemendy. Ladislas Czettel was their principal designer though much of his work has been done outside his native land. Hungary's theatre was primarily distinguished for charm, which is indeed an evanescent quality.

YUGOSLAVIA

This post-war country is made up of portions of the former Austro-Hungarian Empire together with Serbia, which freed herself from Moslem-Turkish rule in the nineteenth century. To understand its theatrical history it is necessary to consider the three principal sections which compose the country. Croatia, with its capital at Zagreb, has the oldest culture because it includes Dalmatia and the city of Ragusa (Renaissance Dubrovnik). It was here that performances of pastoral drama as well as local farces and even tragedy took place from the beginning of the sixteenth century. Classical farces, particularly those of Plautus, were admired. As early as 1555 a local dramatist, Drzic, made a Dalmatian version of *Aulularia*. During the eighteenth century this province came under French influence, particularly that of Molière, but not long after the theatre went into a period of decline as Ragusa itself declined in importance.

This was the period when Yugoslavian drama began its rise in Slovenia, the capital of which is Ljubljana. Its first local play was an adaptation of Jean Paul Richter's *Feldmuehle* (*The Windmill in the Field*) which was performed in the capital in 1789. The Slovene theatre was largely under Austrian and German influence, particularly Kotzebue, Iffland and Nestroy. During the Illyrian movement which began in the third decade of the nineteenth century, an intense wave of patriotism blended Croat and Serb literatures into a single language and the folk-ballads of these countries began to develop into crude historical plays. Taking Shakespeare and Schiller as models, the local literary men turned out patriotic dramas of no value whatsoever except that they assisted in a political movement, gave the authors practice in writing, and stimulated the building of regular playhouses for these performances.

Serbia emerged last of the three because it was not until 1814 that she escaped from Turkish rule. Abortive theatrical beginnings in 1834 came to nothing. In Novi Sad, then a part of Hungary, a theatre was built but Belgrade, capital of Serbia, had none until 1864. Once begun however the movement spread over the country through touring troupes. Both Croatia and Slovenia were still under German influence, though local dialect companies were established by 1870 in Zagreb and Ljubljana.

With the formation of Yugoslavia as a nation, following the war, the three separate capitals remained. In 1920 the theatre was nationalized and Central National Theatres were established in Belgrade, Zagreb and Ljubljana. These operate under the Board of Education on a national subsidy; actors are paid by the year and have pension rights. In this perhaps it can be said that the Yugoslav theatre is the most advanced socially in the world. The amazing thing is that a relatively poor nation so felt its responsibility for the encouragement of local culture as to take this step.

The German-Austrian influence on the theatre changed to a Russian one. This was due in part to Pan-Slavism, though the advent of Bolshevism in Russia reduced contacts to a minimum. The widespread influence of the Moscow Art Theatre is probably the reason for this shift in artistic allegiance. The leading directors of the country have all been identified at some time with the Russian theatre and some have been pupils of Stanislavski. Rakitin, Vereshchagin and Mansvyetov work in Belgrade and Ossipovitch and Boris Putyata in Zagreb and Ljubljana. The last named city had even more connection because the native producers, O. Šest and Pavel Golia, when prisoners of war in Russia, studied under Stanislavski. Many of the designers too are of Russian background as for instance Vassili Ulyanichev, though the native Ljubo Babic and Ernst Franz are equally prominent. Actors are primarily Yugoslav and their standards, though uneven, are frequently quite high. The reputations of none extend beyond the borders of the country but at home the best known are Paranos, Gosic, Ginic, Milutinovic, Stojanovic, and Zlatkovic. Now all of the smaller cities and even little towns have theatres (as well as the three capitals, where performances are well patronized) because touring troupes, made up of the best actors, play outside Belgrade, Zagreb and Ljubljana in the summer months.

Yugoslavia has also developed a drama in the present century which should be mentioned. Of the playwrights perhaps the most important is Ivo VOJNOVIC, who is a native of Ragusa and is particularly interested in subject matter from that section of the country. His two best known plays are *Dubrovnik Trilogy* and *The Death of the Jugovici Mother*. Other dramatists include the erotic Milan Begovic, author of the two-character play, *Without a Third Partner*; Pecija Petrovic who wrote the normal, noisy comedies *Storm* and *Knot*; Josip Kosor; Miroslav Krleza; and Josip Kulundzic.

ROUMANIA

The theatre in this country dates back only a little over a century to 1830, when, under the influence of western culture, a group of young people formed the Filarmonic Society and staged Byron's *Marino Falieri*. Not long after the Revolution of 1848, the prominent actor Mihail Pascally acted *Hamlet* for the first time in Roumanian. He repeated and improved his performance in 1866, when he again produced the play on the stage of the National Theatre in Bucharest, which had been built in 1852. In the beginning, naturally all dramatic development centered in the country's capital, but towards the end of the century it began to spread to the other principal cities.

Shakespeare has always been this country's favorite foreign dramatist, thirteen of his plays having been staged, but Ibsen, Shaw and Maugham have also been popular. Ion Luca Caragiale, who was responsible for the much played drama *Scrisoarea pierduta* (*The Lost Letter*), was Roumania's greatest writer.

Cultural development in the theatre has been largely due to the naturalistic Caragiale, the scholarly director Pompiliu Eliade and the playwright-producer Alexandru Davilla. The Dramatic Society, which was laid out along the lines of the *Comédie-Française*, was founded in Bucharest in 1877. It contributed a great deal to the improved staging of foreign classics as well as the work of native playwrights.

Among the earlier Roumanian dramatists are to be found the names of Cathon Theodorian, author of the psychological middle-class drama *Bujoresti;* the comic A. de Herz with *Paiajenul* (*The Spider*); the romantic Victor Eftimiu with the rhetorical *Insirt'te Margarite;* and Mihail Sorbul with *Patima Rosie* (*Red Passion*), a somewhat florid title. Later and contemporary writers include the piercing Liviu Rebreanu with *Plicul* (*The Envelope*); the psychological and socially-minded Camil Petrescu with *Danton* and *Suflete Tari* (*Hardy Souls*); Victor Ion Popà who dealt with the social problems of the *petit bourgeois* and the well-to-do villager, and was responsible for *Muscata din Fereastra* (*The Geranium in the Window*); and the mystical and metaphysical poet Lucian Blaga who composed such emotional historical dramas as *Cruciade Copiilor* (*Children's Crusades*).

The National Theatre in Bucharest under the direction of Soare Z. Soure, follower of Reinhardt, forged ahead in producing standards, particularly in revivals of *King Richard III* and *Hamlet*. When Prince Ion de Ghika was director he employed Shakespearean translations made by his two sons, Princes Scarlat and Dmitri, to impressive effect. Paul Gusty, senior producer, is responsible for fine presentations of *Macbeth, The Comedy of Errors,* and *The Merry Wives of Windsor.* Alexandru Davilla's staging of *Salomé* in his own theatre was noteworthy. Victor Barnowski and Karlheinz Martin have acted as guest directors in the restaging of some of their best foreign productions.

Roumania is fortunate in having reared many acting talents including Griogore Manolescu, whose Hamlet, under the direction of Grigore Cantacuzino, was extremely popular; Aristitza Romanescu, leading Roumanian actress of all time and renowned for her portrayal of Ophelia; C. Nottara; Tony Bulandra; Ion Manelescu; Maria Filotti, who plays high comedy; and Arstid Demetriad. Most of these names are not known abroad but a definite acting technique was established within the country which took what was best from afar and adapted it to native needs.

BULGARIA

The Bulgarian theatre seems literally to have come out of the library. The local reading rooms were used for performances even before the end of Turkish rule in 1878 and in the present time many of the village libraries are constructed so as to permit their theatrical use.

Bulgaria developed a literature early but the drama did not keep pace with the other literary forms so that it was necessary (as in Roumania) to bring in translations of plays, and many foreign directors (as in Yugoslavia). However, a sound acting tradition grew so early that by 1900 such actors as Ognyanov, Kirkov, Kirchev, Sarafov, Budveska and Snezhina had appeared. These men and women were primarily individualists. The newer group, some of whom received their training in the Tsarist theatres of Russia, including the Moscow Art Theatre, were sounder in their technique and truly devoted to the enlargement of their art. Of these perhaps the best known are Irena Tasseva, Zorka Iordanova, Tenev, Khranov, Atanassov and Andreev. The responsibility for their training and development can be ascribed to N. O. Massalitinov, who in 1925 was invited to leave his position as actor for the Moscow Art Company and leader of its Second Studio to assume the direction of the Dramatic School of the Bulgarian National Theatre. The principal playhouse of the country, naturally enough, is the National Theatre in Sofia, built in 1907. In 1923 it was burned and the German architect, Duelfer, designed one of the most modern and best equipped stages in Europe to replace it. Many of the smaller cities have built new municipal theatres for such professional companies as Varna and Russé, and receive some state aid as well as city support. The National Theatre is directly supported by the central government to the extent of 15,000,000 leva a year. Since

1935, all tickets to cinemas have been taxed one-half leva for the support of the legitimate stage, a system of subsidy which might very well be applied successfully in other countries.

Massalitinov was placed in charge of the selection of the repertory for the National Theatre, a highly important post. In addition to that he staged productions and designed the brilliant settings for *The Masters, Albena* and *Golemanov*, all Bulgarian plays, in addition to *Twelfth Night,* Pagnol's *Marius* and *The Cricket on the Hearth.* Chryssan Tsankov, who came under Reinhardt's influence, staged expressively such widely differing plays as *Androcles and the Lion;* Langer's *Periferie;* and *Le Bourgeois Gentilhomme.* Other important directors include I. David and Iuriy Iakovlev who produced Vicki Baum's *Grand Hotel* and Elmer Rice's *Street Scene.*

Bulgarian drama is still young and no great plays have as yet emerged, but there are several thoroughly competent writers such as Ivan Vazov, with *Berislev* and *Toward the Precipice;* Rache Stoianov who wrote *The Masters* (acted in America by the National Theatre Company on tour in 1937); the nationalistic Iovkov with *Albena;* and the urban comedies *The Gold Mine* and *Golemanov* by St. Costov.

CZECHO-SLOVAKIA

The Czech theatre had an honorable beginning, like the western European nations, in the religious drama of the Middle Ages. As in all countries secular interludes crept into these liturgical plays, but their characteristic satirical quality so shocked the religious reformer, John Huss, that he fulminated against them. One fragment called *Mastičkář (The Quack)* still survives, and is enough to give us an inkling as to why the stern Protestant reformers so frowned upon the theatre. A formal Protestant drama for the inculcation of religious truths was combated by the Jesuit School Plays, and the idea of a playhouse as such was anathema. Whenever the thing was even suggested the righteous grew frightened and those who held such dangerous ideas were forced into exile. Austrian and German political domination did not help because a nationalist drama was frowned upon. Italian opera, which had already retarded the development of Austrian drama for a century and a half, together with German plays, were the approved theatrical fare. The combination effectively displaced any glimmerings of a Czech theatre until after the first quarter of the nineteenth century.

Theatre buildings in Prague came into existence before there were native plays to fill them and housed German drama and Italian music. The *Stavovské divadlo* (Estate Theatre) was opened in 1783 with a Lessing drama and the première of Mozart's opera *Don Giovanni* was performed there with rapturous applause. It was not until 1862 that a second playhouse was added, this time for Czech drama, with the building of the *Prozatímní divadlo* (Provisional Theatre). From almost the first it was seen to be inadequate for the expanding drama and no money could be expected from the government of Austria which opposed the rise of Czech nationalism. The people of the nation from the poorest to the richest gave voluntarily to a fund to build a new building. The cornerstone was laid in 1868 but it was not until August 1881 that the *Národní divadlo* (National Theatre) was opened with the acclamation of the whole country. Soon after, it was severely damaged by fire and new funds were necessary to rebuild it. Perhaps it was due to the desire of having a great theatre of their own without help from the Austrians that the money was raised so rapidly the second time, and November 1883 saw the opening of the present massive building. It is handsomely situated on the banks of the Vltava, which bisects the beautiful mediaeval city of Prague.

Then came the handsome *Vinohrady divadlo* (Vineyard Theatre) which was erected in the Vinohrady district in 1907. When this became a part of the city of Prague in 1922, the theatre was renamed the *Městské divadlo* (Municipal Theatre). In 1920 the Estate Theatre was reconstructed and turned over to the National Theatre as a second house for dramatic performances. Opera and ballet were kept in the mother house by the river. The Municipal Theatre secured an experimental studio in 1929, which was subsequently named the *Komorní divadlo* (Chamber Theatre) and is run as an adjunct to the older playhouse, primarily for comedy and lighter drama because its size is suitable for intimate productions.

The *Švandovo divadlo* (Svanda Theatre) was a private playhouse opened in 1871 by Pavel Švanda and was responsible for the introduction of realistic drama at a time when the policy of the National Theatre was much more conservative. During the war it was conducted by his actress-wife. From 1919 to 1925 it was managed by Jan Bor, who produced plays by such Czech playwrights as Jan Bartoš, František Langer and others. After Bor transferred to the Municipal Theatre, Vlasta Burian took over the management for some years. He is not to be confused with E. F. Burian, who conducted a communist and proletarian experimental theatre called *D 36*. Vlasta Burian was a great actor of farce, particularly of the musical variety and has been called the Czech Chaplin. Comedians used to flourish in Prague for *Osvobozené divadlo* (Theatre Unbound) was founded by the two actors, Voskovec and Werich, and was based on the informal theatre society of the same name. Their satirical and highly sophisticated revues appealed to the intellectual and their theatre continued from

1929 to 1935, when they closed it to devote their entire time to the cinema. They have since transferred their allegiance to the United States and have presented English adaptations of two of their shows at the Play House in Cleveland. There were several other theatres in Prague, two of the best known being German language playhouses for the benefit of the German minority in that city, the *Neues Deutsche Theater* (New German Theatre) and *Kleine Buehne* (Small Stage).

During the nineteenth century several Czech dramatists of note appeared, the first being Vaclav Kliment Klicpera (1792-1859) who wrote peasant comedies and parodies of chivalric German drama as well as the historical pieces for which he is best remembered. Those which have survived are *Hadrian z Rímsu* (1821) and *Veselohra na mostě* (*Comedy on the Bridge*, 1828). His pupil Josef Kajetan Tyl (1808-56) was a poor wandering actor but he contributed two plays which were considered important. The first was the musical comedy *Fidlovačka* (1834), which contained the song "Where is My Home," which eventually became the Czech national anthem; the second was *Strakonický dudák* (*The Bagpiper of Strakonice*, 1847), a Bohemian fairy-play. The Francophile Emanuel Bozédch (1841-1889) borrowed his technique from the French, particularly from Scribe, in his most popular comedy *Zkouška státníkova* (*A States-man's Ordeal*, 1874).

A number of playwrights such as Alois Jirásek, Arnošt Dvořák, František Zavřel, the professor and dramatic critic Otokar Fischer, Ladislav Stroupeznický, Jaroslav Vrchlický, Viktor Dyk and Otokar Theer should be mentioned before we discuss the better known moderns. Karel Capek (1890-1939) and Josef Capek (1887-) are known wherever people are interested in modern drama. This is due principally to Karel Capek's expressionist drama *R.U.R.* (1921). The story of Rossum's Universal Robots has gained fresh meaning with the nazification of Karel Capek's Czecho-Slovakia before his death in London. He alone was responsible for *Věc Makropulos* (*The Macropoulos Secret*, 1922) which is a disillusioned drama about longevity. No good comes of living three hundred years and one gets tired of the world long before the end. In this he differs from Shaw, whose *Back to Methuselah* (1921) holds that tremendous advantages may result from living to be ancient. However Capek was not answering Shaw and had indeed conceived the play before he began to write *R.U.R.* With his brother he wrote *Ze zivota hmyzu* (*The Insect Comedy, The Life of Insects, The World We Live In*, depending on the adaptation, 1921). This play depicts mankind as a race of insects and shows only too clearly our distressing habits of living. It was an immense success in Prague.

Adam stvořitel (*Adam the Creator*, 1927) was written by both the Capeks but was a muddled and insufficiently interesting play about human pride. After this piece, neither wrote any more plays until Karel alone wrote *The White Plague, Power and Glory* (1938) and *The Mother* (1939), which are all anti-dictator pieces, though the last named is also pacifist.

FRANTISEK LANGER (1888-   ) has been content for the most part to write pleasant and unimportant comedies which are popular in his own country. Several have been translated, including *Velbloud uchem jehly* (1923, produced successfully by the Theatre Guild as *The Camel Through the Needle's Eye* in 1929). The single exception to this rule is *Periferie* (1925), a sardonic piece of underworld drama in which a man commits a murder for which he does not pay the death penalty and is harassed by his own guilt. He tells everyone and no one will believe him. Finally the woman who loves him commits suicide in his arms and ironically he is executed for the crime he did not commit. Basically this is also the plot of *Payment Deferred*, by Jeffrey Dell, 1931.

We have already mentioned such *entrepreneurs* and *régisseurs* as the Burians, Bor, Voskovec and Werich, but the three most important are yet to be named, Šubert, Kvapil and Hilar. FRANTISEK ADOLF ŠUBERT (1849-1915) was the National Theatre's first director. He was naturally a conservative and his work was sound but far from brilliant as he sought to build up a repertory of classic and patriotic native dramas. The style of acting was romantic and Saxe-Meiningen's innovations did not penetrate the state playhouse for a long time. When the Vinohrady Theatre was built, he assumed its direction and inaugurated a repertory of French plays, notably by Sardou.

JAROSLAV KVAPIL (1868-   ) went to the National Theatre as literary adviser in 1900 and in 1908 was promoted to the directorship, which post he held until 1918. Stanislavski and Reinhardt influenced his course and he introduced Chekhov, Ibsen and Strindberg into national repertory. It was his sensitive handling of Shakespeare which won him his fine reputation, however. In this he was ably assisted by the leading Czech actor of Shakespearean roles, Eduard Vojan. After three years in a political post at the Ministry of Education, he returned to the stage as director of the Municipal Theatre from 1921 to 1927, when he was succeeded by Jan Bor. At the city playhouse he staged *Troilus and Cressida, Cymbeline, King Henry IV, Parts I and II*, Schiller's trilogy *Wallenstein* and introduced such dramatists as Maeterlinck, Verhaeren, Claudel and the native Jirásek and Langer.

KAREL HUGO HILAR (*nom de théâtre* for K. H. Bakule, 1884-1935) began his stage innovations at the Municipal Theatre going to the National Theatre as director in 1921. He began as a disciple of Reinhardt but progressed to the position where he combined the realism of Stanislavski with Gordon Craig's theatrical vision and high imagination. He staged Strindberg and Marlowe, Kleist's *Penthesilea; The Master Builder; Romeo and Juliet; Antony and Cleopatra;* and *Peer Gynt* among a host of exciting productions. The distinguished scene designer, Vlastislav Hofman, collaborated with him just as Josef Wenig and Josef Capek (better known as a designer than as a dramatist) had worked with Kvapil. Hilar had little interest in, nor patience with Shaw's intellectuality nor the metaphysics of Pirandello. These he left to another director, Karel Dostal. The plays of these men were produced at the municipal playhouse which has traditionally had an interest in American and English plays. This custom has been largely fathered by its most recent literary director, Frank Tetauer, who translated many of O'Neill's plays into Czech.

It is impossible to learn just what is the present situation in the Czecho-Slovak theatre since the absorption of the country by Germany. Many of its brilliant creative minds, such as Karel Capek and Antonin Heythum and his wife, fled to more hospitable lands. Some of the men who are spoken of as incumbents of posts may have been removed or may be dead. There is no way of finding out now.

It must not be thought that Prague was the only production center in the country for Bratislava (the former Pressburg), capital of Slovakia, and Brno (Bruenn), capital of Moravia, have had flourishing theatres. What held true for brave and beautiful Prague held true in general for the whole country. Some day perhaps Czecho-Slovakia will take its place again as one of the vital theatrical centers of the world.

XXVI

NATIONALIST ITALY

(1815-1940)

THE unification of Italy was the thought that constantly coursed through the minds of the people as Napoleon's rule drew to a close. They had hoped, when the French first came in the seventeen-nineties, that there was to be an Italian republic, but Napoleon succumbed to imperial temptations. The kingdoms and grand duchies of Italy were useful for the rewarding of brothers, sisters and devoted friends. Still the ordinary run of folk did not give up hope. Even when the Austrian bayonets restored the Italian rulers to their thrones in 1814-15, they hoped without hope. The next forty years constituted a period of constant subterranean struggle on the part of the people behind such leaders as Cavour, Mazzini and Garibaldi, against the machinations of the popes to preserve their temporal rule and the kings, princes and dukes to hold on to their precarious thrones.

There was no man who felt this struggle more keenly or who did more through his poetry and plays to bring it about than that follower of Alfieri, GIOVANNI BATTISTA NICCOLINI (1782-1861). He came of an impoverished Tuscan noble family but managed to secure a good education and received his doctorate from the University of Pisa in 1802. This was fortunate as it was by teaching that he supported himself through life. He would never accept any financial return from his tragedies. He was frugal by nature, so that when an uncle left him a small piece of property on the river Agna between Parto and Pistoia, he was happy. It gave him a place to entertain his friends, where they might talk and plan a united Italy. He never travelled. On one occasion he took a train trip to Pisa but never repeated the experience.

Niccolini was a propagandist and, though this was not apparent in his first play *Polissena* (1813), it became clear in *Nabucco* (1819) even though he was historically accurate and objective. This was a play about Napoleon and was directed at religious and political despotism. In style it lies between classicism and romanticism and its author was claimed by both factions. *Antonio Foscarini* (1827) was acclaimed as a magnificent drama because it came at a moment when any strong play directed against absolutism would have been called a masterpiece. It is definitely romantic in style, though Niccolini was still giving lip service to the unities.

His next play was dangerous because it showed the Italian people revolting against a foreign tyrant. *Giovanni da Procida* (1830) was shaky in its history but its political intentions were clear and it was hailed with enthusiasm. It was intended to promote the cause of unity and independence just as was his better constructed *Lodovico Sforza* (1834). Needless to say public performance was forbidden. He then turned his attentions to *Arnaldo da Brescia* (1843) which struck at even higher opponents, the popes. As publication was not permitted the play was printed abroad and the separate pages were smuggled into Florence in balls of sugar. Had the writer been less well-known and less highly respected, or had he lived in any other part of the country than under the mild rule of Tuscany, Niccolini would undoubtedly have been imprisoned. He lived however to see the unification of Italy, though not long enough to witness the curtailing of the Church's temporal powers.

ALESSANDRO MANZONI (1785-1873) was modest, chaste, and beloved. He was timid and hated crowds. His life was plagued by the early deaths of those he loved, both his wives and one of his sons died before him. He was better known as a novelist and poet than as a playwright; his novel *I Promessi sposi* (*The Betrothed Lovers*) is particularly admired. He did not begin his first drama until 1816 and was four years in the writing of it. *Il Conte di Carmagnola* (1820) was a lyrical historical tragedy, romantic in style and religious in feeling, showing the influence of Schiller's *Wallenstein*. *Adelchi* (1822) lacks unity and force, so Manzoni was probably wise in not again attempting the dramatic form.

PAOLO FERRARI (1822-1889) was the last of the romantic writers. In the beginning he wrote high-sounding romantic plays that are absurd and have not enough literary value to redeem them. It was not until he turned to comedy in imitation of Goldoni that he produced anything worth remembering. He vulgarized everything he touched, particularly *Amore senza Stima* (1868), which he took from Goldoni's *Moglie Saggia*. His best play, *Goldoni e le sue sedici commedie nuove* (1851) was a charming comedy about Goldoni and the company of actors at the Sant' Angelo with the evil Gozzi in the background.

Among the other dramatists who contributed slightly or not at all to the important and all-embracing problem of unifying Italy, were

Giovanni Giraud, Alberto Nota, Martini, Gerardi del Testa, Paolo Giacometti, Cavalotti, Achille Torelli, and Pietro Cossa. Giacometti wrote melodramas, though one play *La Morte civile* (*Civil Death*) contributed something to social reform.

Once Italy had become a nation, with the elimination of the Vatican as a temporal power in 1870, the dramatists sought a new subject for drama and a new interest in life. The growth of realism in France, the country to which Italy has most frequently turned in cultural matters, had its influence in the development of the Verist school, which was the equivalent of German and Scandinavian naturalism. However, the Verists never achieved the extreme realism of Germany and Russia, nor even the less extended social drama of England and France. This was due in part to the firm hold the Church had upon the conscience and intelligence of the nation. The national government had only just been set up so that it was too soon to find flaws in their own handiwork. Problems of social reform such as labor legislation, woman's place in the world, divorce and the liberalizing of marriage laws never interested Italian writers because those problems were outside their habits of thought. Adultery intrigued them in comedy and provided a solemn subject for drama, just as it did in France.

The earliest Verist was LUIGI CAPUANA (1839-1918), whose *Malia* (*Enchantment*, 1894) was outstanding, but the real leaders of the movement were Giacosa and GIOVANNI VERGA (1840-1922) who began as a romanticist of the most emotional type but turned into a thorough realist. He considered it a pleasure and a duty to write about the most unpleasant subjects possible without determining whether it was a social duty or an artistic need, or perhaps neither. He is best known for the familiar *Cavalleria Rusticana* (*Rustic Chivalry*, 1884), his dramatization of his own short story, which Pietro Mascagni turned into an opera; *La Luppa* (*The She Wolf*, 1896) and *La Caccia al lupo* (*The Wolf Hunt*, 1901) are violent and ugly.

GIUSEPPE GIACOSA (1847-1906) established professional dramatic authorship in Italy just as Ostrovski did in Russia. He had a great sense of the theatre without having much dramatic originality. He wrote feelingly of family relationships; drew his characters as honestly as he knew how; and did not stack the cards for or against his heroes. His first drama, the one-act *La Partita a scacchi* (*A Game of Chess*, 1871), is a modern play in spite of its mediaeval background. Its purely Italian quality quickly won Giacosa recognition, for critics and public alike were clamoring for a real national drama. *Il Trionfo d'amore* (*The Triumph of Love*, 1872) was characteristic of his period of comedy of wit, but his best work came after he turned to social drama with *Tristi Amori* (*Sad Loves*, 1888). In this play he honestly drew the believable portrait of a husband too preoccupied to give his wife the attention she needs. The wife drifts unknowingly into a love affair with her husband's best friend and is tortured by the thought that she is being unfaithful to a fine man. The friend and lover refuses to aid the husband, who is in financial difficulty. This refusal opens the husband's eyes to his wife's infidelity but she will not leave her child. Disregarding the physical side of their marriage, they settle down to train their child properly, but there is always the hope that some day their marriage will again be consummated.

Come le foglie (*Like Falling Leaves*, 1900) is perhaps Giacosa's best play. In this he presents a study of a wealthy family which has come upon evil days. Individual characteristics reveal themselves for better or worse as straitened circumstances cause a complete readjustment of lives. In this play Giacosa upholds middle-class virtues and draws life-like and honest characters. *Il Più forte* (*The Stronger*, 1904) is a study of a business man's chicanery and his son's idealism which force them apart.

It is of theatrical interest that he composed a starring vehicle for Sarah Bernhardt, *La Dame de Challant* (*The Lady of Challant*, 1891) a piece of no dramatic merit, and that in collaboration with Luigi Illica he was librettist for the operas *La Bohème* (1896), *La Tosca* (1900) and *Madame Butterfly* (1904), for all of which Puccini composed the music.

GEROLAMO ROVETTA (1853-1910) was primarily a short-story writer and novelist. As a playwright he composed only inconsequential pieces. Variations on the theme of adultery were the best he had to offer, except for a single patriotic drama, *Romanticismo* (*Romanticism*, 1901). This idealistic play was rooted in the mid-nineteenth century effort to rid Italy of Austrian rule. It is an honest and, at moments, masterful drama of the *Risorgimento*.

MARCO PRAGA (1862-1929) began his theatrical career with a one-act drama, *L'Amico* (*The Friend*, 1886), which violated the code that a husband should kill his faithless wife. Instead, he showed her the door. This shocked his Italian audiences but it revealed the bent of his mind. In *Le Vergini* (*The Virgins*, 1889) he drew an interesting picture of a mother and three daughters who are careless about their virtue when there is profit to be made therefrom. One daughter, however, falls genuinely in love with a young man who wants to marry her. Having it on her conscience that she had given herself to a man to help out her family, she confesses to her lover. Her honesty leads him to withdraw his offer of marriage and hint that something less would satisfy him. She refuses and he goes away. In *La Moglie ideale* (*The*

Ideal Wife, 1890) Praga paints the picture of a woman who is successful in having a lover and being a good wife at the same time.

It is easy to see that adultery or other forms of illicit love are the topics which interest this author. Perhaps his best play is *La porta chiusa* (*The Closed Door*, 1913), in which Eleonora Duse acted when she was playing mother parts toward the end of her career. This is primarily a character study, rather than a skilfully plotted drama. It concerns an illicit connection into which a woman enters after her marriage. The play actually begins when the son of the illicit mating has reached maturity bearing falsely the name of his mother's husband. Somehow he learns of his illegitimacy and when he is refused permission to join a colonizing project in East Africa, he tells his mother that he knows the truth. Recognizing her responsibility for the situation, she gives her consent, breaks with her lover and remains alone. It is in drama of this kind that Praga was most successful, but most of his pieces remain undistinguished because his plots dwelt tiresomely on variations of the same subject.

ROBERTO BRACCO (1862-1943) is perhaps the best dramatist of the realistic group and, though he lacks the brilliance and sensationalism of d'Annunzio, Benelli and Pirandello, he was really a sound writer. He did not hesitate to resort to romanticism if it would serve the ends of balanced drama. *Una Donna* (*A Woman*, 1893) and *Maschere* (*Masks*, 1894) show the influence of Dumas *fils*, for the French influence had by this time penetrated as far south as his native city of Naples. His next piece was a realistic comedy that might have come straight from Schnitzler, *L'Infedele* (*The Unfaithful*, 1894). It was produced in America in 1907 under the title *The Countess Coquette* and starred Alla Nazimova.

In 1895 Bracco turned to the low life of Naples for the plots of his plays and it is to this that he owes his reputation. The first was *Don Pietro Caruso*, a realistic picture of a lawyer who stoops to every underhanded method of flattering politicians so that he may make enough money to promote his beloved daughter's well-being, only to discover that one of the politicians has seduced her. Since the seducer is a nobleman he declines to marry her, and the father kills himself because his scheming has been in vain. *Sperduti nel buio* (*Lost in Darkness*, 1901) is the story of a blind violinist's futile, selfless love for a beautiful girl who he thinks is ugly. Though these were not profound dramas, they were simply and honestly written within the limits of Bracco's experience and technique.

In *Il Diritto dell' animo* (*The Right to Live*, 1900), which was influenced by Ibsen, he attempted to treat a social problem in direct fashion, but it merely suggests a pallid copy of Hauptmann's *The*

Weavers. He is at his best in such plays as *La Piccola fonte* (*The Hidden Spring*, 1905), which, like *Lonely Lives*, suggests the unhappiness of the wife of a literary man; and in *Il Piccolo Santo* (*The Little Saint*, 1909). The latter is the simple story of a man who turns to the priesthood after he loses the girl he loves. Withdrawn into a quiet country community, he finds that faith brings peace to his soul. Eventually the daughter of the girl he had loved comes to him for spiritual aid and he is reminded of the love he had borne her mother. The emotion is intensified by the fact that the girl is going to marry his worthless brother whom he despises. His faithful servant, knowing his master's emotions, kills the brother. When the priest accuses his servant of the murder, he tells his motive for the deed. Thus the thought is planted in the gentle ecclesiastic's mind that he has sought to aid others when he has yet to master himself.

GABRIELLE D'ANNUNZIO (1863-1938) was not an admirable character and this fact is certainly evident in his writing. He was brilliant, uneven, sensational, romantic, lyric and colorful; but his "purification by pleasure" thesis, his brutal treatment of Duse and his showy raid on *Fiume* all add up to present an unpleasant picture of the man. This voluptuary began his literary career as a novelist and established something of a reputation for himself in that field before turning to the drama. In the latter form, he amused himself by composing *saynètes* on themes from the New Testament by turning parables into drama. Then he came strongly under the influence of Maeterlinck and wrote a series of dream plays about the seasons, but in no way did he measure up to the standard of the Belgian's writing.

His first full-length play was *La Città morta* (*The Dead City*, 1898), in which the great Duse was to appear for twenty-five years. It is a play of near-incest and superhuman abnegation and in addition to bearing the stamp of Maeterlinck, it was a conscious effort to modernize the Greeks. In the same year he wrote the famous *La Gioconda* which celebrated Duse's beautiful hands. This is d'Annunzio's one play which might be said to contain an idea and is his most restrained piece. It is a study of a sculptor who deserts his wife for his beautiful model because she inspires him to create more beauty. In other words it is Oscar Wilde's thesis, "Art for Art's sake."

Francesca da Rimini (1902) is a flaming reproduction of an episode in Dante's *Inferno*. The lovely Francesca marries the ugly Gianciotto thinking that he and his handsome brother, Paolo, are one and the same. She soon discovers her mistake and eventually yields to her desire for her brother-in-law. A younger brother who is even more repellant than Gianciotto makes advances to her and upon being rebuffed he informs the deceived husband of Francesca's guilt and the lovers are killed. This highly emotional drama should be compared with the more ethical versions of the story as told by George Henry Boker in his play of the same name and by Stephen Phillips in *Paolo and Francesca*.

D'Annunzio's best play is probably *La Figlia di Jorio* (*The Daughter of Jorio*, 1904). It has considerable lustful power and is the best constructed of his dramas. The scene of the play is laid among the Abruzzese peasants who have retained much of their paganism. Mila, the young daughter of a sorcerer, flees from the lust of drunken men to the hut of the shepherd Aligi, who protects her. The shepherd's own father is among the pursuers, but so potent is her spell that the boy takes her up into the hills to live idyllically with him. When the drunken father follows, the son kills him. As a parricide, he is condemned to a frightful death but his mother forgives him and administers a drug that will daze him during the tortures he must undergo. At the last moment, Mila rushes in and takes the blame for the crime, saying that she had bewitched Aligi. She acts so convincingly that her lover himself believes her and curses her as she is taken away to be burnt as a witch. (Irma Gramatica created a sensation as Mila and Ruggiero Ruggeri was excellent as Aligi.)

After this the author turned more and more to such spectacular plays of lust and death as *Fiaccola sotto il moggio* (*Light Under a Bushel*, 1905) and the operatic *La Nave* (*The Ship*, 1908) which was cinematic in scope and was appropriately turned into an opera by Italo Montemezzi. D'Annunzio took the austere *Hippolytus* of Euripides and as *Fedra*, he turned its heroine into a nymphomaniac who is slain by a ray of moonlight.

Displaying his bilingualism, he turned to the French for his next three plays, the first two of which were written for the beautiful Ida Rubinstein. *Le Martyre de Saint Sébastien* (*The Martyrdom of St. Sebastian*, 1911) is a modern mystery play written in archaic French, and was staged with settings designed by Léon Bakst and incidental music by Claude Debussy. *La Pisanella* (*The Pisan Woman*, 1911) was concerned with revenge and sex, two subjects which interested the writer enormously. The final French drama, *La Chèvrefeuille* (*The Honeysuckle*, 1913), is another bloody play of revenge which reverses Hamlet's sex and echoes *Electra* in its macabre lust.

D'Annunzio had a good deal of influence on contemporary dramatists in the decade before the war of 1914-18, but it soon disappeared. Benelli, Morselli and Berrini were his followers, but Benelli is the only one who has any chance of survival. Sensationalism, rank theatricality, lust and revenge run through the work of all these men.

Before continuing with the dramatists, it would perhaps be wise to examine general theatrical conditions in Italy after the defeat of Napoleon. Each important city had one or more theatres devoted to drama and opera. Sometimes both forms of entertainment shared quarters, but usually there were at least two playhouses. The great theatrical architects of the Galli-Bibiena family had built many of the theatres of the eighteenth century so that Verona, Venice, Florence, Turin, Naples and Rome, to name a few, were all handsomely provided with theatrical facilities. These theatres maintained permanent companies but stars moved from place to place. With the coming of the eighteen-hundreds, scenery became heavier and more gloomy in appearance as the graceful lightness of the baroque gave way to the neo-classicism and romanticism so well typified in Germany by Schinkel, Antonio de Pian and Joseph Platzer. In Italy it was Alessandro Sanquirico who established the ponderous style and set the heavy mood which endured to the end of the century and the architectural palaces gave way to verism in scenery as in dramaturgy. The quality of scenic and costume design degenerated after 1815 and it has never reached the same heights since. In the period since the First World War, several interesting scenic talents have developed and will be mentioned later.

There were three great acting personalities who stood above all others in the nineteenth century, Ristori, Salvini and Duse. ADELAIDE RISTORI (1821-1906) was an outstanding tragic actress who played not only in Italy but in France, England and America, where she appeared with Edwin Booth in *Macbeth*. Her mournful beauty and grace of movement coupled with real dramatic power allowed her to play the noblest parts with unusual success. She was Rachel's greatest rival. Her portrayals of Francesca in Pellico's *Francesca da Rimini* and of Mirrha in Alfieri's tragedy of the same name were particularly effective. Other roles in which she excelled were Lady Macbeth, Mary Stuart in Schiller's play, Marie Antoinette in Giacometti's tragedy about the unhappy queen of France, Elizabeth of England in another play by the same author, and her coldly classic Deborah.

The fiery TOMMASO SALVINI (1829-1915) was a native of Milan and pupil of the actor Gustavo Modena. He had tremendous power but it must not be thought that he was merely a ranter. He had an inner fire which not only inspired his audiences but also his fellow actors. No less a technician than Stanislavski said that Salvini was a great inspiration to him and that he went night after night to see him act during his Russian tour. He created his first sensation in Alfieri's *Saul* and his playing of *Wallenstein* was greatly admired. However, it is as *Othello* that he will always be remembered. He is said to have terrified his Desdemonas with the fire of his attack in the smothering scene. His fine figure and musical voice enchanted Londoners when he appeared at Drury Lane in 1875. Clement Scott, who could be very captious, said, ". . . Salvini was not only great in *Othello*. His performance in *The Gladiator* was superb. . . . I have never in my life seen an actor fill the stage as Salvini did . . . He was a torrent, a tornado, a mountain. He was the dominant force that seemed in his righteousness capable of crushing the crowd. This was great acting." *

Salvini's Hamlet was less successful but his Ingomar, his Samson and, surprisingly enough, the comic role of Sullivan in *David Garrick* were others of his best parts. His son, Alessandro, was known for his beauty and romantic attitudinizing rather than for any special acting ability. His Don César de Bazan was his best role, though his Hamlet was attractive to look at if not to hear.

ERNESTO ROSSI (1829-1896) was well known both as an actor and as a playwright, though in the latter capacity he had little merit. He wrote *Adèle* for Ristori and such other plays as *Les Hyènes* (*The Hyenas*), *La Prière d'un soldat* (*The Soldier's Prayer*) and *Consorzio Parentale* (*Parental Partnership*). He appeared many times with Ristori and played with her in Paris in 1855 but he made his greatest success in the tragedies of Alfieri and Shakespeare and was even called the "Italian Talma." The differentiations in his playing of the Ghost scenes in *Hamlet* were much admired.

The artist whom modern critics tend to worship was ELEONORA DUSE (1859-1924) who was literally a daughter of the theatre. Her father Alessandro Duse and her grandfather Luigi Duse were also actors. She was born on a train between Venice and Vigevano while her parents were on tour; she remained with the company and made her debut at the age of four as Cosette in *Les Misérables*. Her next noteworthy performance was at the age of fourteen; when she played Juliet in Verona, home of the Capulets. She is said to have made beautiful use of her hands, an accomplishment she was to exploit greatly throughout her theatrical career. In 1878 she established herself with Augier's *Les Fourchambault* and in 1879 became Rossi's leading lady, just as he had been Ristori's leading man. The great tradition is handed down from one artist to another.

With Rossi, and later with her own company, she acted such tried and true favorites as Sardou's *Théodora*, *Divorçons*, *Fédora*, Goldoni's *La Locandiera*, and Dumas' *La Dame aux Camélias*. In 1885 she toured South America and in 1892 (the year in which many great artists appeared in Vienna at the first international theatre exhibition, out of which grew some of the great theatre collections of the world) she displayed her genius in the Austrian capital. In 1893 she first appeared

* Scott, Clement, *The Drama of Yesterday and Today*, 2 vols. London: Macmillan. 1899.

in New York to the delight of the critics, though there were those who were accustomed to the more florid and theatrical playing of Bernhardt and so were not impressed at the uncorsetted woman who scorned make-up and left her hair untouched by dye. She introduced several of the plays of d'Annunzio, not only to Italy but to the world. Many people were horrified by their themes and were only persuaded to sit through them because she offered them. Their love affair and the dramatist's subsequent cruel treatment of the woman who was but five years his senior alienated many of his admirers. Duse's playing in *La Gioconda*, *Francesca da Rimini* and *La Città Morta* was enthralling; and her performances in *Ghosts* and *The Lady from the Sea*, by Ibsen, were considered finer than those of any other actress.

James Huneker says of her in his *Iconoclasts*, " . . . her face is the mirror of her soul. Across it flit the agonies, the joys, of the modern anaemic, overwrought woman. She excels in the delineation of listless, nervous, hysterical, and half-mad souls . . ." (and in another place, he says) ". . . she is still Eleonora Duse, the woman with the imagination, the glance and the beautiful hands."*

Her poor health and shattered nerves forced her to retire shortly before the First World War, but she was persuaded to reappear for special matinees in London in 1923 and soon after in New York, where eight performances at the Metropolitan Opera House aroused overwhelming enthusiasm. The theatre was too large. She was a slight figure with grey hair and a faded face, but the glance and the hands were still hers. Thousands cheered and every actor in New York crowded in to watch and learn as she played *The Lady from the Sea* and other of her earlier successes. While on tour she was not able to throw off the effects of a severe chill and died in Pittsburgh in April, 1924. Mussolini ordered that her body should be taken back to Italy at public expense and she was buried at Asolo with highest state honors. It has been said that no one could act Ibsen as successfully, wringing as much from the lines as could Duse.

On the literary side the talents of the great Scandinavian were not congenial to Italy. No dramatist of that nation was able to surpass or even to equal him. Such an effort was made by ENRICO ANNIBALE BUTTI (1868-1915). His second drama *L'Utopia* (1894) was an attempt to write a play of ideas. In this case he merely shows the breakdown of liberal theorizing when it is faced with reality. *La Fine d'un Ideale* (*The End of an Ideal*, 1898) was a reactionary study of feminism. Perhaps his best play was *Fiamme nell' Ombra* (*Flames in Darkness*, 1904), an unresentful observation of a man who through no fault of his own is injured by society. A priest has a dissolute sister who by

* *Iconoclasts* by James Huneker, New York, Charles Scribner's Sons, 1907.

her conduct destroys his every chance of advancement within the church, so that he finally gives up his parish and retires with her to a remote village, where, perhaps, he may save at least one soul.

The brothers ANTONA-TRAVERSI, CAMILLO (1857-1934) and GIAN-NINO (1860-   ) were both realistic writers and were the authors of many plays, most of which were of but slight value. Camillo interested himself in extreme naturalism and the macabre and ended up by writing in French for the Grand Guignol in Paris. His best known plays are *Le Rozeno* (*The Rozeno Family*, 1891) and *Parassiti* (*The Parasites*, 1899). Giannino was exceedingly accomplished in his one-act pieces which served as curtain raisers. Some of his witty and mocking satires of the aristocracy and upper middle-classes, of which an early one was *Civetta* (*The Coquette*, 1893), have been most successful. Two of his more recent plays of this type were *Le Sale di Augia* (*The Wit of Augia*, 1931) and *Battistrada* (*The Guide*, 1931).

DARIO NICCODEMI (1877-1934) has been called the Henry Bernstein of Italy. He was an expert craftsman without much dramatic imagination. His plots are trite but his plays are eminently actable and adaptations of several of them have been seen in this country. He wrote both in French and Italian and some of his dramas had their premières in Paris, which was natural as he was Réjane's secretary. *La Refuge* (1909) was performed by John Drew as *The Prodigal Husband; La Ombra* (*The Shadow*, 1905), his most thoughtful play, was acted in New York by Ethel Barrymore; and Gladys Unger prepared three of his plays for Broadway in 1925 under the titles *Stolen Fruit, Seeking* and *The Schoolmistress*. He reached his high point in dramatic ingenuity in his two-character play *L'Alba, il giorno e la notte* (*The Dawn, the Day and the Night*, 1921). In addition to being a playwright Niccodemi was an accomplished stage director and managed his own acting company from 1920 to 1930. The troupe was known for the brilliance of its playing in a catholic repertory of native and foreign plays and had great success in its Spanish and South American tours.

Something must be said of the dialect plays, which occupy something of the same position in Italy as did the earlier pieces of Anzengruber, and the peasant plays of Raimund in Austria and Klipcera in Czecho-Slovakia. These minor dramas have something of the people in them; their speech and habits make them of interest to us; but the plays themselves are certainly not important. AUGUSTO NOVELLI (1867-1927) is a Florentine who has written such gay dialect comedies as *L'Acqua cheta* (*Still Waters*, 1908) and *La Vergine del Lippi* (*Lippi's Virgins*, 1891); and SALVATORE DI GIACOMO (1862-1934), a Neapolitan follower of Giovanni Verga, wrote *Il Voto* (*The Vow*), *Mese Maria* (*Month of Mary*).

However, the real flow of Italian drama descended in the national language of the country. SEM BENELLI (1877-), a Florentine Jew, is a follower of the romantic drama of d'Annunzio. His third play, but his first to be remarked, was *Tignola* (*The Bookworm*, 1904), which the theatre historian and dramatic critic, Silvio d'Amico, considers his best. It is the story of a young woman who thought she could leave her library and take part in the great adventure of living; but she was crushed by life, and returned to her comfortable spot on the sidelines. As this prose drama was comparatively a popular failure, Benelli turned to the florid, poetic drama, imitative of the Poet of Fiume, in *La Maschera di Bruto* (*The Mask of Brutus*, 1905). His best known play was written in the same style, *La Cena delle beffe* (*The Jest*, 1909), and it achieved as much success abroad as in Italy. It is an historical melodrama laid in the Florence of Lorenzo the Magnificent and is concerned with the youngest and weakest of three brothers who has been bullied and tortured by the others, until cunning comes to his aid. The boy's studied revenge is so effective that it causes the insanity of one brother and the death of the other and that is what makes the play so absorbing. It has been successfully staged twice in New York, first with John and Lionel Barrymore and later with Basil Sidney and Mary Ellis. His *L'Amore dei tre re* (*The Love of the Three Kings*, 1910) became the libretto for a successful opera by Italo Montemezzi.

The famous *Teatro Argentina* in Rome brought out Benelli's plays as well as the experimental dramas of ERCOLE LUIGI MORSELLI (1882-1921). His first play, *Orione* (1910), was dedicated to a study of the sexual urge which can have no ending but in the ashes of desire. His plays always have the same bitter ending for their hero. No matter how much he may have achieved in life, he always loses the one thing that he prized above all others, and realizes too late that he might have accomplished his desire had he but scorned the less important things.

GIOVACCHINO FORZANO (1884-) is a popular playwright, whose success with the public is second only to that of Niccodemi. He is chiefly noted for his tetralogy of the Napoleonic period which includes the titles *Il Conte di Brechard* (1923); *I Fiordalisi d'oro* (*The Golden Fleur-de-lis*, 1925); *Danton* (1930); and finally *Campo de Maggio* (*The Hundred Days*, in collaboration with none other than Benito Mussolini, 1931). Of these, the first is the best dramatically, but the last has been most often performed in the capitals of Europe (notably Budapest, Prague, and London) purely for political reasons. Apparently the co-author was not to be cajoled. For some years Forzano has been working on a second cycle of plays dealing with the *Risorgimento*. Of these he has succeeded, to date, with the brilliant *Villafranca* (1931).

Before considering Pirandello, it is necessary to discuss two other post-war writers, Rosso di San Secondo and LUIGI CHIARELLI (1886-). The latter is chiefly known for his comedy *La Maschera e il volto* (*The Mask and the Face*, 1916), which is the revolting study of a cowardly braggart and a faithless wife. Though popular in Italy, where both its style and its subject matter are admired, the play has failed in two adaptations in New York. What Chiarelli did in comedy PIER MARIA ROSSO DI SAN SECONDO (1889-) may be said to have done in grotesque drama. The near-expressionist play *Marionette, che passione!* (*What Passion, Ye Marionettes!* 1918) is stimulating and exciting but lacks the depth of feeling which the title and plot would suggest. *La Bella addormentata* (*The Sleeping Beauty*, 1919) is a well-constructed allegorical drama about woman's awakening of desire for motherhood. Probably his most successful play has been *La Scala* (*The Stairs*, 1925) which shows Pirandello's influence. Since the death of the older man, Rosso di San Secondo is probably the leading dramatist of Italy, having for contemporaries such men as Sabatino Lopez, Luigi Antonelli, Enrico Cavacchioli, Nino Berrini, Fausto Maria Martini, Guglielmo Zorzi, and Cesare Vico Lodovici.

LUIGI PIRANDELLO (1867-1936) was the leading playwright of twentieth century Italy and one of the most outstanding men in her theatrical history. His plays are a curious mixture of chicanery, whimsy, irony, philosophy, dramatically effective scenes, excellent acting parts, and cynically tempting ideas. As a purveyor of his thoughts, however, he is probably no clearer to the *average* play-goer than William Saroyan. Born of a well-to-do Sicilian middle-class family he was brought up in comfortable circumstances and married a woman of his parents' choice.

When his family's circumstances were considerably reduced by a flood which ruined his father's mines, Pirandello became an ill-paid professor in a girls' school in Rome. For seventeen years his life and that of his three children was made intolerable by his wife, whose mind had become unbalanced; domestic happiness was not effected until he had made enough money to have her placed in a private sanitarium.

He first attracted attention by his brilliant novel *Il Fu Mattia Pascal* (*The Late Mattia Pascal*, 1904), which broke the ground for his dramatic perversities some years later. His first play, the long one-act *Lumie di Sicilia* (*Sicilian Limes*, 1910), was an honest drama of the unhappiness of a simple peasant who is confronted with ingratitude in a sophisticated setting. His first important play, *Pensaci, Giacomino!* (*Just Think, Giacomino!* 1914), establishes the typically Pirandellian situation of an elderly teacher who agrees to marry a young woman whom he loves in spite of the fact that she is going to have a baby by a young lover. He agrees to find a job for the man and care for them all; and when the lover protests he threatens him with exposure. The question of the paternity of the child is not important, as is again evidenced by a similar situation in *Tutto per bene* (*All for the Best,* 1920). In this play a man has unknowingly been betrayed by his wife and he mourns for her as a faithful honest woman for twenty years. When he discovers the truth and learns that his friends thought he knew all along and was only playing a comedy, he is enraged and plans revenge; but the more he thinks over his plans the more he realizes that the only thing he can do is to go on pretending he still grieves for his wife.

The question of masks and the impossibility of knowing each other's real selves, and often not even our own, intrigued the dramatist his entire life. He returns to the problem of illusion and belief over and over again. The impossibility of forcing stock situations on anyone is demonstrated in his brilliant and poignant *Sei personaggi in cerca d'autore* (*Six Characters in Search of an Author,* 1921). In this play the impossibility of transmitting thoughts and the ironic tragedy of being unable to communicate with each other, is set in a theatrical background that naturally attracted the dramatist. It was a device he was to resort to several times, notably in *Trovarsi* (1932) and *Questa sera si recita a soggetto* (*Tonight We Improvise,* 1930).

Così è (se vi pare) (*Right You Are! If You Think You Are,* 1918) shows that what we recognize as truth is merely relative. A man's mother-in-law contends that she is the mother of his second wife, while he insists that she is the mother of his first wife who is dead. The mother-in-law in turn declares that the first wife never died and it is she to whom he is still married. The wife is willing to be daughter to the woman and wife to the husband, and at the very end the gossips of the town remain puzzled as to who is telling the truth. It is by such devices as these that the dramatist makes his points.

In *Enrico IV* (*Henry IV,* 1922) a man is thrown from his horse which has been injured by a rival. The fall renders the man insane and he believes himself to be the German emperor, Henry IV. Wealthy relatives hire people to act as retainers and help him preserve his imperial illusion. At some point, however, the man recovers his sanity and merely pretends to be mad, though it is not made clear to the audience when this takes place. Twenty-five years pass and an alienist is summoned again to try to restore his mind. The woman he loved, her daughter, and the lover who had caused the accident come together in an effort to re-enact the past. Henry murders the lover so it is now necessary for him to pretend insanity for the rest of his existence or forfeit his life. He chooses the former course.

It would be impossible to detail all of his plots. Suffice it to say that these are typical, for this is the man who wrote: "Ask the poet what is the saddest sight, and he will reply, 'It is laughter on the face of a man.' Who laughs does not know."

Pirandello's other outstanding dramas include: *Il Piacere dell'onestà* (*The Price of Honesty*, 1914), *Il Berretto a sonagli* (*Cap and Bells*, 1915), *Liola* (1917), *Tutto per bene* (*All for the Best*, 1920), *Vita che ti diedi* (*The Life Which I Gave You*, 1923), *Ciascuno a suo modo* (*Each in His Own Way*, 1924), *Vestire gli ignudi* (*Naked*, 1922) and *Lazzaro* (1929).

In addition to his writing, Pirandello was the manager of a theatrical company in which he had the collaboration of the distinguished actress Marta Abba. She appeared in the chief parts of all of his later dramas and was seen in this country as the star of Robert Sherwood's adaptation of Deval's *Tovarich*. For some time in 1925 he managed the tiny *Teatro Odescalchi* in Rome where Vittorio Podrecca's marionette organization *Teatro dei Piccoli* played from 1913 on. Podrecca's puppets have since toured the world and have been welcomed everywhere for their truly remarkable performances. Pirandello received Mussolini's patronage and imported for the small intellectual class some of the most significant of European dramas. In addition to Marta Abba, Ruggiero Ruggieri was a member of the company which not only acted in Rome but toured France, England and Germany.

Pirandello was honored with the Nobel Prize for Literature in 1934 and continued to write up until the time of his death. Some of his literary views were distasteful to Il Duce and he was in conflict with the official viewpoint for a while, until he cynically defended Mussolini's Ethiopian conquest when he was interviewed in New York in 1935. Then all was forgiven at home. He died one of the most respected dramatists to have practiced in the present century. What the future may hold for his work is another question. William Archer declared it fleeting, but contemporary criticism still rates him near the top.

Italian acting and direction had a distinguished heritage handed down from Ristori, Salvini, Rossi and Duse. Fortunately there were certain men and women who were worthy of it. Ermete Zacconi was one of the principal interpreters of the verist school and remains one of the soundest actors in the country, though he is no longer playing. His best foreign roles were Petruchio, Othello and Lear. Giovanni Grasso played romantic Sicilian characters and was well known all over Europe and in America. Irma Gramatica's acting somewhat resembles that of Duse, and her sister, Emma Gramatica, plays many modern English and American characters and is particularly well known in South America. The older actor who had a reputation as a ranter, Ermete Novelli, could nevertheless really create character. Alexander Moissi, who was bilingual, played again in Italy after Hitler's advent. The farce-comedian Angelo Musco, Ruggiero Ruggieri, the subtle Neapolitan Raffaele Viviani, and that great inheritor of the *commedia dell'arte* tradition, Ettore Petrolini, are the finest Italian actors of the present century.

Before Pirandello organized his troupe and Paolo Milano ran his experimental theatre, and even before the First World War, there was a highly untraditional theatre in Italy. This was run by the poet and dramatist FILIPPO TOMMASO MARINETTI (1876-1944), who founded a movement which he called futurism. The object of this was to destroy the bourgeois theatre and replace it with a "simultaneous," "illogical" and "unreal" playhouse where all wit and gaiety would reside. From 1909 on, despite Marinetti's own plays and vaudeville skits, the Futurist Manifesto (1913, and another in 1915) remained a programme rather than a practical theatre. There were a number of little theatres which experimented with the new artistic and dramatic technique. One of the most successful of these was *Teatro degli Indipendenti*, which endured for eight or nine years after the war. It was designed and built in an underground room in the old Roman baths by the architect and scenic artist, Virgilio Marchi, for the director-producer, Anton Giulio Bragaglia. This studio was literary and synthetic and never really represented Italian feeling, nor did it develop a dramatist or first rate actor.

In Milan, there were several of these experimental groups during the nineteen-twenties. A representative one, the *Sala Azzurra*, was under the brilliant direction of the producer Gualtiero Tumiati whose productions of plays by Tagore, Maeterlinck and Shakespeare were noteworthy. All of these little theatres were fleeting because they did not answer a need in the people themselves. (Italian audiences have never really supported their playhouses as they should.) They did, however, give more of an opportunity for experimentation by scenic artists than did the commercial or state playhouses. Among the best-known Italian theatre designers of the twentieth century are: Giacomo Balla, Enrico Pampalini, Fortunato Despero, Guido Salvini, Nando Tamberlani, Giorgio de Chirico, Bruno Angoletta, Vittorio Grassi, Mario Pompei and Carlo Rende.

In 1930 Mussolini organized a fascist corporation for the theatre. This is known as *La Corporazione dello Spettacolo* and was planned to produce on a broad scale state-approved plays that would really reach the people. In spite of its restrictions, it represented an advance in thinking because it set up a regularly constituted theatre. Only in Russia, Italy and Yugoslavia, to a lesser extent in Germany, and for the few years of our own late lamented Federal Theatre Project were the theatrical energies of a country harnessed for creative effort. (In America, this experiment was tied to work relief, so that we did not have an opportunity for a wholly fair trial.) Many excellent services are provided by this organization. Traveling companies are sent to the most remote districts of the country during the summer; it encourages productions of the old *Maggi* (May Festivals); passion plays are more generally given; open air performances of opera and drama are handsomely staged in Florence, Venice, Syracuse, Taormina; the theatre is really brought to the people, regardless of what we may think of the dramatic fare which they are fed.

XXVII

SPAIN (1800-1940) AND

SPANISH AMERICA (1538-1940)

THE Spanish theatre continued to produce actors and plays all through the eighteenth century. Many of the dramas were in imitation of Calderón while others showed French influence. The drama of these two countries has always been susceptible to the influence of one another but the dominating force has usually emanated from Paris rather than Madrid. With the coming of the nineteenth century and Napoleon's disruption of the political situation in France, there began to emerge a drama that again showed something of national character. The first writer to develop (though his comedies were strongly influenced by Molière) was LEANDRO FERNANDEZ DE MORATIN (1760-1828), son of the lesser dramatist Nicolás Fernández de Moratín (1737-80), whose six-act *Hormesinda* (1770) was a failure. The younger man drew on *L'École des Femmes* for his brilliant *El viejo y la niña* (*The Old Man and the Girl*, 1786). *Le Misanthrope* and *Les Femmes Savantes* were in part the basis for *La Comedia nueva* (1792) which was written as an annoyance to a fellow playwright, Luciano Francisco Comella. In this prose comedy he ridiculed Comella by making him a ludicrous character. His later play *El sí de las niñas* (*The Girls' Acquiescence*, 1805) was also written in prose though the playwright was as noted for his versification as for his amusing dialogue.

Though Spain had a perfectly healthy romantic tradition of her own, in the plays of Lope de Vega and Calderón de la Barca, she sought foreign sources for the so-called romantic movement of the nineteenth century. This was largely due to FRANCISCO MARTINEZ DE LA ROSA (1787-1862), who for political reasons had been forced to take refuge in Paris where he found the French romantic school headed by Victor Hugo in the process of development. The early tragedies *La Viuda de Padilla* (*The Widow of Padilla*, 1814) and *Moraima* (1818) are of slight value. Like Moratín, he displays a predilection for Molière in his comedies. One of these *La niña en casa y la madre en la máscara* (*The Girl at Home and the Mother at the Masked Ball*, 1821) served Theaulon de Lambert as the basis for *La Mère au Bal et la Fille à la Maison* (1826) and its success so flattered Martínez de la Rosa that he tried his hand at writing in French. Because romanticism was fashionable he became a devotee, a fact which was at once apparent in his *Aben Humeya ou la révolte des Maures sous Philippe II* (*Aben Humeya; or, The Revolt of the Moors under Philip II*, 1830). This drama was produced at the *Théâtre Porte-Saint-Martin* without setting Paris afire.

The death of reactionary Fernando VII in 1833 made it possible for liberals to return to Spain, and Martínez de la Rosa took advantage of the amnesty. He composed the first Spanish romantic drama of the nineteenth century, *La Conjuración de Venecia* (*The Conspiracy of Venice*, 1834), which was remarkably successful, though his Castillian translation of his own French piece was a failure in 1836. In the imitation of French comedy he shared honors with MANUEL EDUARDO DE GOROSTIZA (1789-1851), the Mexican playwright, who wrote *Indulgencia para todos* (*Indulgence for All*, 1818). On the romantic side he found a rival in the liberal ANGEL DE SAAVEDRA, DUQUE DE RIVAS (1791-1865). This noble playwright's *Ataulfo* (1814) and *Lanuza* (1822) show the influence of the earlier nationalist dramatists Meléndez Valdés and Quintana. In 1835, however, he espoused the cause of Martínez de la Rosa and offered the fiery and romantic *Don Álvaro ó la fuerza del sino* (*Don Alvaro; or, The Force of Destiny*) which, with its mixture of the comic with the sublime, created an absolute sensation on the Madrid stage. Verdi utilized it as the libretto of his opera *La forza del destino* (1862).

ANTONIO GARCIA GUTIÉRREZ (1813-84) followed in the footsteps of the first two romantic writers which his extraordinarily successful *El Trovador* (*The Troubadour*, 1836), which also served Verdi in the familiar *Il Trovatore* (1853). Neither *Simon Bocanegra* (1843), which the Italian composer also borrowed for his opera of the same name (1857); *Venganza catalana* (*Catalan Vengeance*, 1864); nor *Juan Lorenzo* (1865) were as popular as the author's initial effort.

The last writer of the true romantic movement was JUAN EUGENIO HARTZENBUSCH (1806-1880), a Spanish Jew of genuine scholarship. His best play was *Los Amantes de Teruel* (*The Lovers of Teruel*, 1837), which he weakened by twice rewriting, so anxious was he that it should be meticulously correct; but with each revision he lost some of the fire and excitement. Probably the fact that he was employing a subject already used by Tirso de Molina, among others, made him so excessively zealous in the matter of form. Though they achieved contemporary fame neither *Doña Mencia o la boda en la Inquisición* (*Donna Mencia; or, The Wedding During the Inquisition,* 1838) nor *La Jura en Santa Gadea* (*The Oath of St. Gadea,* 1844) approached the success, or the inherent good qualities, of his first play.

Though a Byronic romanticist and a political revolutionary, JOSÉ DE ESPRONCEDA (1808-42) is primarily considered a lyric poet. His contribution to literature lies largely in that field, but he collaborated on two dramas. The first naturally enough was in verse, *Ni el Tío ni el Sobrino* (*Neither Uncle Nor Nephew,* 1834), written with Antonio Ros de Loano (later Marqués de Guad-el-Jelú). With Eugenio Moreno Lopez he composed the prose play *Amor venga sus agravios* (*Love Takes Vengeance on Its Abusers,* 1838).

The lyric poet JOSÉ ZORRILLA (1817-98) had a great gift for improvisation and was able to turn out countless poems as well as a number of plays. He resembled Lope de Vega in his speed of composition but not in dramatic conception or finish. His first play was *El Zapatero y el Rey* (*The Shoemaker and the King,* 1840) but best known is the fantastic *Don Juan Tenorio* (1844), which he based on works by Mérimée, Dumas, and Zamora. From 1855 to 1866 he lived in Mexico where he was the recipient of many royal favors from the Emperor Maximilian. The last named drama became so popular there that it is presented to this day by nearly every theatre in the land, early each November.

MANUEL BRETÓN DE LOS HERREROS (1796-1873) belonged to the school of the younger Moratín but he must be forgiven for his occasional essays into romanticism. He was one of the most prolific writers of Spain, having composed no less than one hundred and seventy-five pieces between 1817 and 1867. His best play was probably *La Escuela de Matrimonio* (*The School for Matrimony,* 1852) and is still readable. Though he wrote too much and too rapidly he had an amusing and felicitous way of expressing himself, a fact which keeps *Marcela o ¿ cual de los tres?* (*Marcella; or, Which of the Three?* 1831) still on the boards.

The foreign influence marked in Moratín and Bretón de los Herreros is most evident in VENTURA DE LA VEGA (1807-1865), an Argentinian domiciled in Spain. Extreme poverty, coupled with a desire to improve his own dramatic accomplishments, induced him to translate at least sixty French plays for the Spanish stage before he undertook the writing of an original play himself. Gallic comedies and farces were so in demand that he was able to maintain himself in this fashion. Irony which often degenerated into caricature predominates in *El Hombre del Mundo* (*A Man of the World*, 1845), a play of real merit. The fact that he was not at home in tragedy is perfectly evident in *La Muerte de César* (*The Death of Caesar*, 1848).

From Cuba came GERTRUDIS GÓMEZ DE AVELLANEDA (1814-73) who made a real contribution to poetry. Her plays were all poetic dramas; *Alfonso Munio* (1844); *Saul* (1849); and *Baltasar* (1858), which had almost masculine vigor; and constituted a definite advance in feeling in this theatrical genre. ADELARDO LÓPEZ DE AYALA (1829-1879) was another lyric writer who might be called a follower of Calderón. His sincerity and idealism are apparent in such of his early plays as *Un hombre de estado* (*A Man of State*, 1851), *Rioja* (1854), and the later *Consuelo* (1878).

MANUEL TAMAYO Y BAUS (1829-1898), born of an actor family, must have absorbed a great deal of his knowledge of stagecraft as a child. This would explain the actability of his plays. Inspiration for them was found in such widely varying sources as Schiller and Alfieri. In addition to his original pieces he adapted the work of such popular French writers as Augier, Feuillet and even Laya and Féval. In *La Bola de Nieve* (*The Snowball*, 1856) and *Un drama nuevo*, (1867), a play which depicts *Othello* as a play within a play, he argued against jealousy. After producing these he left the theatre and became librarian at the *Biblioteca Nacional* in Madrid.

Almost the diametrical opposite of the theatricality of Tamayo y Baus are the curiously undramatic plays of RAMÓN DE CAMPOAMOR (1819-1901). It has been suggested that such plays as *Guerra a la Guerra* (*From War to War*, 1890) and *Dies Irae* (1873) were intended to be read and not acted, which might explain their lack of adaptability to the stage. MARIANO JOSÉ DE LARRA (1809-1837) did not live long enough to write many plays. But the two written in the brief years before he committed suicide over an unhappy love affair were truly theatrical pieces. He coupled a shrewd observation of life and a knowledge of the technique of Scribe in *No más mostrador* (*No More Counter*, 1831), which was based on *Les Adieux aux Comptoirs;* and in *Macías* (1834). His journalistic powers were shared in part by a Peruvian writer FELIPE PARDO (1806-1868) whose comedy *Una Huérfana en Chorrillos* (*An Orphan in Chorrillos*, 1833) won him a reputation in South and Central America.

Not to be confused with the earlier Mexican dramatist is PEDRO ANTONIO DE ALARCÓN (1833-1891) who is principally remembered for the picaresque novel *El sombrero de tres picos* (1874) but he was also responsible for a single play *El Hijo pródigo* (*The Prodigal Son,* 1857) which was hissed off the stage.

At last we come to the first of the more important Spanish dramatists of the last century and a half. JOSÉ ECHEGARAY (1832-1916) was a versatile man; he had been a teacher, mathematician, politician and engineer, besides other professions, before he wooed the dramatic muse. The combination of political exile in France; the success of the comedies of his younger brother (MIGUEL ECHEGARAY, 1848-1927, who wrote the buoyant *La Viejecita* and *Gigantes y Cabezudos*) and his own reforming spirit, inspired him to attempt the writing of plays.

His first was a one-act drama *El libro talonario* (*The Check Book,* 1874) which was followed in the same year by the romantic *La Esposa del Vengador* (*The Wife of the Avenger*). He did not hesitate to stoop to cheap effects to achieve his results in such melodramas as *En el Puño de la Espada* (*At the Hilt of the Sword,* 1875) and *En el Seno de la Muerte* (*In the Bosom of Death,* 1879).

In the more than sixty plays he poured on to the Madrid stage between 1874 and 1908, there is but one that ranks with the best plays of the last century of world theatre; *El Gran Galeoto* (*The Great Galeoto,* 1881) was written under the influence of Ibsen. Despite all his extravagance and clap-trap, his shoddiness and frequent triviality, Echegaray was a moralist and employed the drama to prove his points. The crusader in Ibsen naturally appealed to him, so it is no mere coincidence that his best play comes closest to the social dramas of the great Norwegian. This is a thesis play with a real social problem, that of the evil effects that befall a family when thoughtless or malicious gossip is spread. A man, his wife and their young ward are living together happily until someone chooses to see a non-existent affair between the young man and the wife. By means of a casually spoken word, a smile, a raised eyebrow, the slander spreads until it brings death to the husband and unhappiness to the wife and their ward.

The problem in *Ghosts* so fascinated Echegaray that he frankly set out to explore it in *El Hijo de Don Juan* (*The Son of Don Juan,* 1892). To him the fault lay not in society but in the impure life of the boy's father. He does not spare the audience the details of this degeneracy which brought unhappiness and death to the son.

His other plays which divide the early romantic pieces already mentioned and his later return to that form, are all frankly thesis plays and derive principally from Dumas *fils* and others of his school in France. We can accept his moral purpose but, with the exceptions noted, we must reject his dramas. As Isaac Goldberg said in *The*

Drama of Transition (1922), "Echegaray, in general, is an inferior dramatist because the plays themselves are vitiated at the source. They do not develop from a core of passion, produced inevitably by the clash of character and circumstance. They are the artificial result of a passion that they do not contain."

The plays of the great novelist BENITO PÉREZ GALDÓS (1845-1920) were the absolute antithesis of Echegaray. Whereas the latter belonged in the theatre of Tamayo y Baus (with whom he had much in common), Pérez Galdós overflowed the stage into the auditorium. He has been accused of having the novelist's lack of restraint, and general inability to accommodate himself to the proscenium arch. For a long time most people thought that he was simply a great novelist (no one questioned that) who had perhaps condescended to employ the playhouse, but such a criticism is a misunderstanding of the man. Nothing could be further from the truth because he did his first work for the theatre which he truly loved. These plays were not produced and were put away, but the thought of the drama was always in the back of his mind. He has been compared with Dickens and Balzac, but the only resemblance lies in the fact that each managed to convey on paper something of the national characteristics of his country.

By 1892, the year in which he first made a play available to the public (*Realidad*, based on two of his novels), he had already composed a large part of that vast canvas called *Episodios nacionales*, a series of forty novels depicting nineteenth century Spanish life. In *La Duquesa de San Quintín* (*The Duchess of St. Quintín*, 1894) he advances his favorite theory which permeated his novels: the artistocracy needed a complete transformation, its blood to come from peasant stock and its brains from intellectual liberals. *El Abuelo* (*The Grandfather*, 1904) has been compared with *King Lear* by Spanish enthusiasts. Pérez Galdós had great power as a writer but his admirers do him a disservice when they seek to compare him with Shakespeare. Such a comparison only serves to point out the Spaniard's deficiencies though he possessed an undoubted talent which approached genius.

Electra (1901), in which he sets forth his anti-clerical views, is one of the most interesting of the plays that he wrote directly for the stage. It depicts the plight of a healthy young girl who is being over-persuaded to enter the church rather than marry the man to whom her parents object. Symbolism is apparent because of Máximo's definite stand in favor of science as opposed to religion. The play created an uproar and was attacked bitterly by the Church. Some religious adherents went so far as to drive a company of actors from a theatre where *Electra* was to be performed. In another place the troupe was denied lodgings and was forced to spend the night in the streets. It was just such a spirit of intolerance that Pérez Galdós attacked.

He was the author of perhaps a dozen additional plays, for Spanish writers are proverbially fecund. The thesis play *Mariucha* (1903), the heroine of which is likened to Nora and Hedda, was particularly successful. *Bárbara* (1905), *Pedro Minio* (1908), *Casandra* (1910), and *Alcestis* (1910) were the best of his later dramas. He continued writing almost up to the time of his death, though he had lost his eyesight and was reduced to poverty.

ÁNGEL GUIMERA (1847-1924), who was born in the Canary Islands, was a protégé of Echegaray who was most generous in aiding him to translate and adapt his Catalan plays for the stage. Guimerá spent most of his life in Barcelona and therefore used Catalan speech in his plays. Due to his repeated reading of Shakespeare and Victor Hugo, his early poetic plays *Gala Placidia* (1879), *Mar y Cel* (*Sea and Sky*, 1884), and *L'Anima Morta* (*The Dead Soul*, 1892) were highly romantic. To his second period belong the peasant tragedies of love and hate among the fishermen and country people of Catalonia, the best known of which are *Maria Rosa* (1895) and *Terra Baixa* (*Marta of the Lowlands*, 1897). Then he came under the influence of the Scandinavians and such German naturalists as Hauptmann and Sudermann and attempted psychological drama in *La Miralta* (1905). The failure of this play led him into his fourth period (a repetition of the first); *Andrónica* (1905) is one of the best of these.

Part of the intellectual movement, whose aim was to separate Catalonia from the rest of Spain, appeared in the dramas of such men as Guimerá, Rusiñol, Soler, Iglesias and Gual. This separationist sentiment continued up to the Civil War of 1936-39 when the urban Barcelonians decided that they preferred the liberalism of an elected Madrid régime to the fascist rebels led by Franco, but the result was an abandonment of their hopes for autonomy. Since Franco's victory no word of their feelings has been allowed to escape from the prison which is present day Spain.

However, in 1864, even before the appearance of Guimerá, a group of men who were consciously Catalonian organized *La Gata* under the leadership of FREDERICH SOLER (1839-1895). The purpose of the organization was to create a dramatic literature for the Catalonian people. The group took form as *Teatre Catalá* and first played at the small, inadequate *Odeón* in Barcelona, and later transferred to the larger but remote *Teatre Romea*. The movement proved so popular that it became necessary to move to the *Novetats* in the central part of the city and eventually to the *Teatre Principal*, the largest playhouse in Catalonia. The director, Soler, wrote one hundred and seven plays for the company under the pen name of Serafí Pitarra. The first were light trifles which he referred to as *gatadas* (squawks) but he contrived many serious plays as well for the people, for this was a popular theatre. The best remembered of these are *Las Joyas de la Rosa* (*Rose's Jewels*, 1866) and *Batalla de Reynas* (*A Queen's Quarrel*, 1887).

Soler's biographer, José FELIU Y CODINA (1845-97) worked for a number of years with the *Teatre Catalá* and produced several plays in verse and prose in which romance was sharpened by realism. The best of them were *Lo Gra de Mesch* (*A Grain of Musk*), *Cofys y Mofys* (*Fools Will Be Fools*) and *La Rambla de les Flors*. Somewhat influenced by Echegaray, who had interested himself in Guimerá and the Catalan movement, he turned to Spanish as his dramatic medium. In that language he wrote the vivid and vigorous *La Dolores* (1892), *Maria del Carmen* (1896), and *La Real Moza* (*The Royal Maid*, 1896) among other character plays.

As might be expected, a movement such as this did not attract actors and dramatists exclusively. The painter and art connoisseur SANTIAGO RUSINOL (1861-1931) became interested, and chose to aid by experimenting with various kinds of plays. Of these the most interesting were the unworldly *El Mistic* (*The Mystic*, 1901), the poetic idyll of the Spanish Levant in *El Patì Blau* (*The Blue Patio*, 1903) and the satiric marionette one-acter for live actors, *El Titella Prodig* (*The Prodigal Doll*, 1911). His study of the Negro problem ¡ *Libertat!* (*Liberty!*) was translated by Benavente into Spanish. In collaboration with Martínez Sierra, Rusiñol himself wrote *Vida y dulzura* (*Sweetness and Life*, 1907) in that language.

The last of the important Catalan dramatists was IGNASI IGLESIAS (1871-1928) who sprang from the working classes and so had considerable sympathy for their problems, as is evidenced by such of his humanitarian plays as *La Mare Eterna* (*The Eternal Mother*, 1902), *El Cor del Poble* (*Heart of the Town*, 1902) and *En Joan dels Miracles* (*John of the Miracles*, 1908). Probably his best plays were the dismal *Els Vells* (*The Aged*, 1903) and the satire of greed in its relation to a national lottery, *Les Garces* (*The Magpies*, 1905). Much of his work is sentimental; a characteristic which appears in the work of all Catalan writers.

ADRIA GUAL (1872-   ) is less important as a writer than as a scene designer and director. Having come under the influence of Antoine and the *Théâtre Libre* he founded the imitative *Teatre Intím* in his native Barcelona and imported many novelties from abroad.

301. ALICE KOONEN AS SALOMÉ. KAMERNY THEATRE.

300. SHAW'S *St. Joan.* KAMERNY THEATRE.

302. *Sakuntala.* THE KAMERNY THEATRE.

303. BRECHT'S *Three-Penny Opera.* KAMERNY THEATRE.

Theatre Collection, N. Y. Public Library

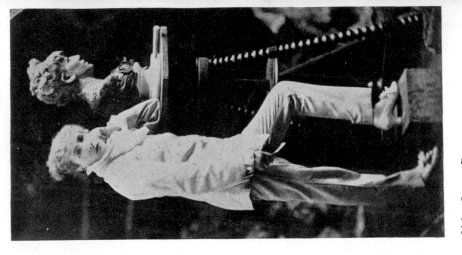

306. SARAH BERNHARDT.

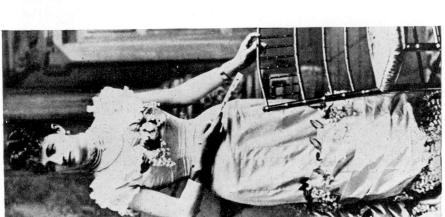

305. HELENA MODJESKA.

Theatre Collection, N. Y. Public Library

304. ELEANORA DUSE.

307. Setting For *The Magic Flute* By Karl Friedrich Schinkel.

Schinkel, "Sammlung von Theater-Dekorationen"

308. Setting For *Nostradamus*, Carlo Ferarrio, 1802.

Ferarrio, "Scenografia"

309. Setting By André Dérain.

310. Setting By Pablo Picasso.

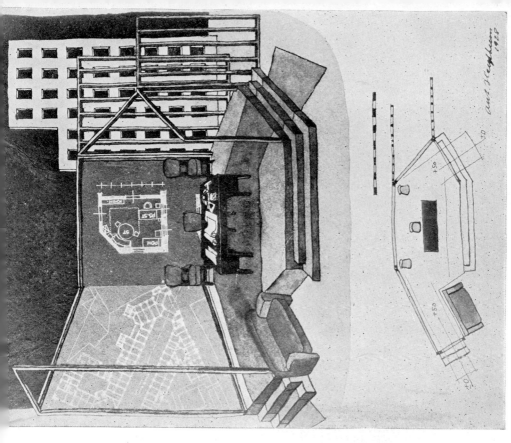

312.   *The Great God Brown.* SETTING BY ANTONIN HEYTHUM.

Museum of Modern Art

311.   *King Lear.* SETTING BY OSCAR STRNAD.

313. SEAN O'CASEY.

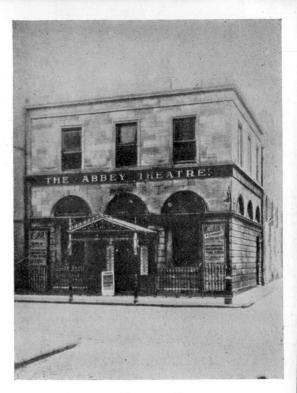

314. THE ABBEY THEATRE, DUBLIN.

316. W. B. YEATS.

317, 318.   ALBERT RUTHERSTON. COSTUMES FOR *A Winter's Tale*.

320. Irving as Mathias, in *The Bells*.

321. Ellen Terry.

323. Oscar Wilde.

322. Sir Arthur Wing Pinero.

325. Mr. Forbes-Robertson to W. Shakespeare: "I've done something for you, William." Shakespeare: "Yes, and don't forget that I have done something for you." Caricature of Forbes-Robertson as Hamlet.

Entr' Acte Annual, 1898

324. Luigi Pirandello.

326. Fermin Gemier and Max Reinhardt.

327. Karel Capek.

328. Ernst Toller.

329. Set For Toller's *Hoppla, Wir Leben*. Production By Erwin Piscator, Berlin.

330. SETTING FOR *The Emperor Jones*. WALTER RENE FUERST.

331. BACK CLOTH FOR *The Tempest*. GEORGE SHERINGHAM.

332. JONEL JORGULESCO. SETTING FOR *The Tempest*.

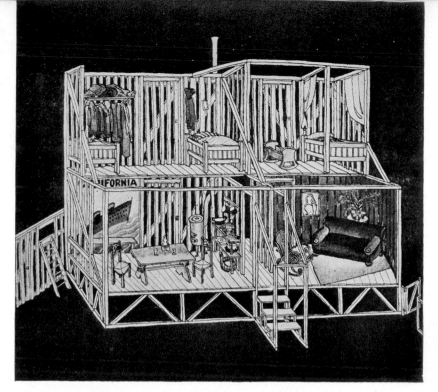

333. Setting For *Desire Under the Elms*, By Heythum.

334. Setting For *R. U. R.*, By Vlastislav Hofman.

335. SETTING BY LUDWIG SIEVERT FOR *The Broad Highway*.   *Museum of Modern Art*

336. SETTING BY V. RINDIN FOR *The Unknown Soldiers*.

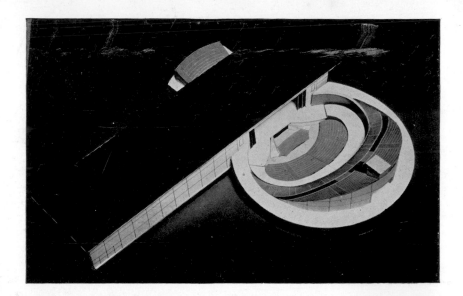

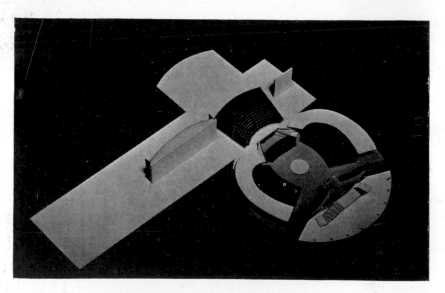

341, 342. THE SPACE STAGE. The "space stage" was invented by Frederick J. Kiesler with a mind for the future. This is a plastic, architectural unit. Plays in general require a proscenium stage, opera and musical revue a peripheral stage, concert requires a focal auditorium, dance a circular stage or arena, circus and sporting events an arena, and conventions need a hall with large seating capacity and good acoustics. Kiesler's building combines all of these features and is shown both open and closed in the model above.

Due to the excessive cost of repertory, handsome and startling scenic experiments were not practical so Gual's staging of Greek tragedies in the open air was a bold step for so conservative a theatre as the Catalonian or Spanish. His only play which attains even second-rate standards is *Misteri de Dolor* (*Mystery of Pain*).

To return to the main current of the Spanish theatre, we find that Echegaray found few followers: LEOPOLDO CANO (1844-1878) wrote *La Mariposa* (1879) and *La Pasionaria* (1883); EUGENIO SELLÉS (1844-1926), who had a better command of versification than Echegaray but little originality, is best known for *El Nudo Gordiano* (*The Gordian Knot*, 1878); the most popular and most inventive of this group was JOAQUIN DICENTA (1863-1917) who wrote such proletarian plays as *Juan José* (1895) and *El Crimen de Ayer* (*A Crime of Yesterday*, 1904), but his principal claim to fame is that he widened the horizon of the Spanish theatre.

After Pérez Galdós and Echegaray the most important modern Spanish dramatist is JACINTO BENAVENTE (1866-   ) whose versatility and originality are prodigious. His work has been sweepingly praised by such authorities on the Spanish drama as John Garrett Underhill who claims that he anticipated Chekhov's *The Cherry Orchard* with *La Comida de las Fieras* (*The Banquet of Wild Beasts*, 1898); wrote *Love Shocks* (1907) two years before Schnitzler created *Countess Mitzi;* Molnár borrowed the color and movement for *The Swan* from *La Escuela de las Princesas* (*The School for Princesses*, 1909). All of these assertions are strongly defended but seem no more warranted than the pronouncements of Pérez de Ayala, distinguished critic and defender of Pérez Galdós, who agrees that Benavente has everything a dramatist could wish for in talent but that "all these gifts together entail particularly vituperable and harmful consequences, for they are pressed into the service of a mistaken conception of dramatic art." It seems fairly obvious that the truth lies between these two extremes. Benavente probably has more varied talents than any living dramatist, but the tremendous output of which Spanish writers are capable makes any estimate of his work difficult. However, he has been writing long enough for us to have perspective on certain of his most important dramas, whether or not we grant him the profundity some of his partisans claim for him.

The Spanish-American War of 1898 had an intense moral effect on Spain. Having lost the last of her colonies she realized that she was no longer an Empire and that it was time to take stock of her resources. The same was true of her theatre. For the most part it had been looking backwards. Echegaray and Pérez Galdós were the only playwrights who had been conscious of the outside world, though the latter drew little from it that showed in his work. Spain had once more become a part of Europe so that Italy, France, Scandinavia and Russia were sources for inspiration which might very well aid even the most nationalistic to build a new Spanish literature. Benavente is the most outstanding of the leaders in this movement and he has attempted almost every technique in playwriting that has been practiced in the western theatre world.

His first play to attract real attention and make people conscious of a new dramatic force in Spain was *Gente Conocida* (*People We Know*, 1896) which is a satire on the decayed aristocracy of the country. He followed this with another realistic satire, *The Banquet of Wild Beasts,* which is a study of a wealthy family who discover the worth of their friends when they lose their money. Contrary to Underhill, this is much more reminiscent of Björnson's *A Bankruptcy* than *The Cherry Orchard.* Following this, are *La Farandula* (1897), *Lo Cursi* (1901), and *La Gobernadora* (*The Governor's Wife*, 1901). This latter is perhaps the best of the group and in plot seems remarkably close to Pinero's *His House in Order* (1906). Both plays are concerned with the problem of remarriage after the death of a beloved spouse. A commemorative statue is planned for the departed. Complications arise from the cropping up of unexpected truths about the dead one, together with family objections to the nudity of the sculptured figures in the memorial.

In *Gregorio Martínez Sierra and the Modern Spanish Drama* (1924) Walter Starkie broke down the plays of Benavente by type in the most lucid manner. The present classification follows his scheme in part. The second group consists of such middle-class plays as *El Hombrecito* (*The Perfect Man*, 1903), and *Rosas de Otoño* (*Autumn Roses,* 1905) which deals with a philandering husband who in the end is regenerated by his patient wife; *Por las Nubes* (*In the Clouds*, 1909) is Chekhovian in its unaccented depiction of the drab family life of a semi-poverty which prevents children from marrying because they must support their elders. *La Losa de los Sueños* (*The Graveyard of Dreams,* 1911) is a study of the impoverished middle-class.

Among his highly imaginative fantastic plays are *Sacrificios* (*Sacrifices,* 1901) which resembles *Autumn Roses* as well as the theme of Maeterlinck's *Aglavaine and Selysette;* and *La Noche del Sábado* (*Saturday Night,* 1903) which is more nearly akin to Andreyev and Evreinov than to the work of any other playwrights. It is a kind of Walpurgis Night in a theatre with Graustarkian princes and noble principles intertwined in a most confusing fashion. *Más Fuerte que el Amor* (*Stronger Than Love*, 1906) deals with woman's protective instinct toward man. The last of this group are *Los Ojos de los Muertos* (*The Eyes of the Dead*, 1907); and *El Dragón de Fuego* (*The Fire Dragon*, 1903) which is an Indian fantasy and may have been influenced by *The Little Clay Cart*.

His romantic comedies include: *La Princesa Bebé* (1904), which describes the love affairs and social problems of Graustarkian nobility on the Riviera; *La Escuela de las Princesas* (1909) which demonstrates that woman's lot is to submit, particularly if she is royal (Benavente's women for the most part do not put passion above sacrifice); and *Los Malhechores del Bien* (*The Evil Doers of Good*, 1905) which is a satiric comedy about women who, in trying to help their protégés, only bungle their love affairs for them.

Two of his peasant dramas are outstanding: *Señora Ama* (1908) is the story of a woman who accepts her husband's philandering on the principle that each return increases her triumph by placing her above his passing conquests, but who demands his reformation when she finds she is with child. *La Malquerida* (*The Passion Flower*, 1913) is a hot-blooded drama of a girl who loves her step-father. He eventually returns her love and kills her mother when she would stop their running away, but the mother dies happy in the knowledge that her husband could never marry the child of one he has murdered. Many authorities declare this to be Benavente's masterpiece, though the author himself reserves that honor for *Señora Ama*. Nance O'Neil made this play memorable in America by her portrayal of the girl.

His plays of morality do not offer a very wide range of interest so that a list of some of their titles is perhaps sufficient: *Campo de Armiño* (*Field of Ermine*, 1916); *El Mal que Nos Hacen* (*The Evil That We Do*, 1917); *La Inmaculada de los Dolores* (*Our Lady of Sorrows*, 1918); and *La Vestal de Occidente* (*The Vestal of the West*, 1919) which is a psychological study of Elizabeth and Essex.

Benavente has been known to write five plays in a single year. Out of all those as yet unmentioned, and they number more than a hundred, including even *zarzuelas* (musical comedies), the most important and probably the best known is *Los Intereses Creados* (*The Bonds of Interest*, 1916). Benavente drew on old Italian comedy for this picaresque play. It is a fantasy of the young mercenary Leander who seeks the hand of an heiress only to be redeemed by her love and to rise above the materialism which first held him in bondage. *The Bonds of Interest* was first performed at the *Teatro Lara*. In America it was produced by the Theatre Guild in 1919, and its translator, John Garrett Underhill, says it "suffered from pernicious anaemia."

In addition to being a playwright, Benavente has managed a circus, acted as theatre director in Madrid, and organized a children's playhouse with the actor Porredón. He has adapted or translated the work of such writers as Shakespeare, Molière, Bulwer-Lytton, Augier, Hervieu, Dumas and the Americans J. H. Benrimo and George Hazelton (their charming fantasy *The Yellow Jacket*). He edited a magazine called *La Vida Literaria* and from 1908 to 1912 wrote weekly critiques for *El Imparcial*. He is the actor-playwright-manager *par excellence* and was awarded the Nobel Prize for Literature in 1922.

Late nineteenth century writers are Vega and GASPAR NUNEZ DE ARCE (1832-1903), the latter having written what is generally accepted to be the best historical drama of his century in *El Haz de Leña* (*The Face of Wood*, 1872), which is poetic in treatment and thought (so much so that he thereafter turned to poetry as his literary medium). RICARDO DE LA VEGA (1839-1910) was, in contrast, primarily a comic writer on themes of lower class life. Over a period of twenty years he wrote many musical pieces, but it is for his merry comedy *La Verbena de la Paloma, o El Boticario y las Chulapas, y Celos mal Reprimidos* (1894) that he is best known.

Among the comic talents which crowded on to the stage was MANUEL LINARES RIVAS (1867-   ), a shrewd observer of morals and manners, who began with unassuming farces and gradually worked up to the comedy of manners in *María Victoria* (1904); *La Garra* (*The Claws*, 1914) which is a justification of divorce; and *El Caballero Lobo* (*The Gentleman Wolf*, 1919). FEDERICO OLIVER (1873-   ) has written more solid drama in *La Nena* (*The Young Girl*); *El Crímen de Todos* (*A Common Crime*, 1916); *Los Cómicos de la Legua* (*Troupers of the Road*, 1925); and *Los Pistoleros* (*The Bandits*, 1931) which deals with class struggle.

The poetic theatre underwent a revival in the present century and as such it has become a lineal descendant of the true romanticism which came out of the Golden Age. The poetic tradition is one of the oldest in Spain and is never entirely absent from its theatre. The pioneer of the present revival, however, is EDUARDO MARQUINA (1879-   ). His first play was perhaps his most popular, *Las Hijas del Cid* (*The Daughters of the Cid*, 1908), and drew on the twelfth century poem for information and inspiration. In blank verse Marquina effected the dramatization of many national legends in such dramas as *Doña María la Brava* (1909), and *En Flandes se ha puesto el Sol* (*The Sun Has Set in Flanders*, 1909), which were written for María Guerrero. Of his more recent plays the best are probably the very original *El Pobrecito Carpintero* (*The Poor Carpenter*, 1924); *Fu-*

ente Escondida (*The Hidden Spring*, 1931); and *Teresa de Jesús* (1932). Other poetic writers include Cristóbal de Castro, Ramón de Godoy, Enrique López Alarcón, Francisco Villaespesa, Luis Fernández Ardavín and the versatile Joaquín Montaner. The brothers MACHADO, MANUEL (1874-   ) and ANTONIO (1875-   ) have perhaps contributed more to this form of Spanish drama than anyone else. Their tragi-comedy *Desdichas de la Fortuna o Julianillo Valcarcel* (*The Blows of Fortune*, 1926) translated Spanish classicism into modern theatre terms. *Don Juan de Mañara* (1927) and the comedy *La Duquesa de Benamejí* (1932) are the best of their other plays.

Sentimentalism, which ran through the Catalan theatre, is just as characteristic of Spain as the poetic strain. Perhaps the high priests of this movement might be said to be the Martínez Sierras and SERAFIN and JOAQUIN ÁLVAREZ QUINTERO, Serafín (1871-1944) and Joaquín (1873-1938) have been the pets of the public since they began their career in the theatre. Their wit has been compared to no less a standard than Lope de Rueda. Each year from 1900 to the beginning of the last decade four or five collaborations have emanated from this source. Perhaps two hundred pieces can be credited to them including their farces (*sainetes*, with and without music) of lower class life. Among their early plays, the comedy *Los Galeotes* (*The Galley Slaves*, 1900) was filled with Andalusian humor and the natural goodness of man (characteristic traits of all their work). *Las Flores* (*The Flowers*, 1901), a sentimental and smiling comedy, is still popular.

Among the best known plays by the Álvarez Quintero brothers are *Malvaloca* (1912); *La Flor de la Vida* (*The Flower of Life*, known in America as *The Fountain of Youth*, 1910); *Los Mosquitos* (1928) which treats jealousy lightly and deftly; *La Consulesa* (*The Lady from Alfáqueque*, 1914); *Papá Juan: Centenario* (1909, popularized in this country as *A Hundred Years Old* by Otis Skinner).

GREGORIO MARTINEZ SIERRA (1881-   ), with the unsigned collaboration of his wife María, has written many sentimental dramas of hope and tenderness. He underwent an apprenticeship to the Catalan Santiago Rusiñol, with whom he collaborated and whose work, together with that of such Frenchmen as Tristan Bernard and Robert de Flers, he translated into Castilian. The play for which Martínez Sierra is best known is *Canción de Cuna* (*Cradle Song*, 1911). Its tenderness and charm are cherished in many countries. The quiet portrait of convent life, with its gentle insight into feminine psychology within its holy precincts, has attracted both critical praise and popular following. There is a romantic, if artificial, charm about *Sueño de una Noche de Agosto* (*The Romantic Young Lady*, 1918). Ecclesiastical life is again treated in *Los Pastores* (*The Shepherds,* 1913), and *El reino de Dios* (*The Kingdom of God,* 1916), with which Ethel Barrymore opened the Ethel Barrymore Theatre in New York in 1928; a magnificent performance of an intensely moving play.

A follower of the poetic tradition who has not been so successful as those mentioned previously in JACINTO GRAU (1877-   ). His work shows the influence of Hebbel on the one hand and d'Annunzio on the other. *El Señor de Pigmalión* (1923), which was produced in Prague before Madrid, is concerned with a group of puppets who turn against their master and demand an existence of their own. It is reminiscent of Pirandello's *Six Characters in Search of an Author.* His only other noteworthy play is *El Conde Alarcos,* written about 1910 but not produced until 1917.

JOSÉ LÓPEZ PINILLOS (1875-1922) had a brutal approach to drama which shows in such comedies as *Las Alas* (*Wings,* 1918), and *Caperucita y el Lobo* (*Little Red Riding Hood and the Wolf,* 1919), as well as in his serious plays *Esclavitud* (*Slavery,* 1918) and *La Red* (*The Net,* 1919). The fact that he worked alone may explain something of his force, for in Spain collaboration is used as a means of speeding up the number of plays turned out and not as an improvement in the quality of the plays. This weakness which occurs in so many plays is one of the many reasons why contemporary Spanish drama has meant so little to the outside world. Both CARLOS ARNICHES (1866-   ), with many plays to his name, the most important being *Es Mi Hombre* (*My Man,* 1921) which has overtones of *He Who Gets Slapped;* and PEDRO MUÑOZ SECA (1881-   ), who composed farces in the manner of the *commedia dell' arte,* have a weakness for collaboration. Muñoz Seca provided plots which permit the introduction of funny stories and incidents, a form which is known as *astrakán.* His *La Venganza de Don Mendo* is a burlesque of poetic drama and is probably his best known piece. Notable among his other works is *¡Usted es Ortiz!* (*Ortiz Himself,* 1927), which considers the possibility of dual souls in one body. He has usually collaborated with Pedro Pérez Fernández or with Enrique García Alvarez, who also worked with Arniches.

There are a large number of other writers who are either of Spanish birth, or who despite their Latin American parentage have long practiced in Spain. Their names can be listed but any mention of their works is out of the question because of the lack of space or for the simple reason that their customary hurried method of composition is too often hostile to proper dramatic development. The fact that some names are not included in this list is no disparagement, for perhaps not enough time has elapsed to properly evaluate their work as yet. The Spanish attitude toward the theatre has always been conservative both from the point of view of writing and staging, which perhaps explains the rapid and careless collaborations. Even foreign plays of an experimental nature rarely flourish on Iberian soil.

Those to be mentioned are: Azorín (José Martínez Ruiz, 1873-); Manuel Azaña (1879-1940); the Peruvian, Felipe Sassone (1884-); Jorge de la Cueva (1884-); Manuel Abril (1884-); Francisco Serrano Anguerita (1887-); José de la Cueva (1887-); Ramón Goy de Silva (1888-); Cipriano Rivas Cherif (1891-); Luis Araquistain (1896-); Angel Lázaro (1900-); Enrique Jardiel Poncela (1901-); the Argentine-born Enrique Suárez de Deza (1906-); José María Penman; Eduardo L. del Palacio; and Luis Martínez Kleiser.

MIGUEL DE UNAMUNO (1864-1936) wrote a tremendous number of plays most of which have neither been acted nor printed. His novels are much better known. Among his play titles perhaps the most important *Fedra* (privately acted in Madrid in 1917, publicly produced in 1924), which takes the *Hippolytus* of Euripides and translates it into modern times, though it has very little meaning to the average reading audience. It is only significant when staged by an imaginative director.

RAMÓN DEL VALLE-INCLAN (1869-1936) was the author of numerous plays which are now termed *comedias bárbaras* and were intended to be read, not acted. Valle-Inclán, like Unamuno, was interested in developing an aesthetic program which would influence stage reform. Though he showed preference for farce, he divided his efforts between satiric verse of a definite lyric quality and prose dramas (*esperpentos*) which combined the present with the historical. The individual titles of his plays are not meaningful in themselves because each was but a piece in the artistic pattern he was fashioning.

The writings of FEDERICO GARCIA LORCA (1899-1936) were all much influenced by music, particularly that of his friend, Manuel de Falla (1876-). *El Maleficio de la Mariposa* (*The Naughty Butterfly*, 1920) should be compared with the Capeks' *Insect Comedy*. *The Naughty Butterfly* was produced by Martínez Sierra at the *Teatro Eslava*. *Mariana Pineda* (1927), *La Zapatera Prodigiosa* (*The Mighty Shoemaker's Wife*, 1930), and *Bodas de Sangre* (*Bitter Oleander*, 1935, produced in New York with Nance O'Neil by the Neighborhood Playhouse) are his other principal plays.

Spanish acting has always borne some resemblance to the Italian in its florid attack upon a part. Naturalistic playing rarely appeals to the Latin mind. The first modern actors to measure up to international standards are MARIA GUERRERO and FERNANDO DIAZ DE MENDOZA.

They followed in the footsteps of such splendid native players as Rafael Calvo, Antonio Vico, Matilde Díez, Teodora Lamadrid, and Antonio García-Gutiérrez, who stemmed from the fine acting tradition of the sixteenth and seventeenth centuries through the veins of such innovators as Isidro Maiquez and Andrés Prieto, who carried the reforms to Mexico. In addition, the Guerrero-Mendoza company benefited from the introduction of what was considered realism, by Emilio Mario, who managed the *Teatro de la Comedia* in Madrid, where María Guerrero (d.1928) made her debut in 1885. Mendoza was twice a grandee of Spain and began his acting career in the private theatre of the Duchess de la Torre where he met her daughter, the Marchioness de Castellón, whom he married. After her death, he renounced his titles and joined the company of María Guerrero, whom he married in 1896. They are credited with having elevated the social position of the acting profession in Spain just as Sir Henry Irving and Sir George Alexander had done in England. From 1896 to 1909 they managed the *Teatro Español*, which has been considered the national theatre of Spain though it has not been subsidized. Then they transferred to the *Teatro de la Princesa,* where they presented their outstanding repertory from 1909 to 1924. This theatre, now named the *Teatro María Guerrero,* is used for the National Conservatory (or was until the Civil War, perhaps the dramatic school has now been resumed). They made twenty-two Latin American tours and Mme. Guerrero appeared in New York in 1926. They also established their own theatre, the *Cervantes,* in Buenos Aires.

There have been few first rate actors on the Spanish stage, though there are many low comedians of considerable ability. The position of star is usually occupied by a woman, who is generally manager and director of the company. The next actress, in point of chronology, to come to the fore was Catalina Bárcena who made her reputation in the wistful roles of Martínez Sierra. The actress who stood for the highest achievement at the time of the Civil War was Margarita Xirgu, whose scope was from Medea and Electra through such popular characters as appear in the pieces of the modern García Lorca. She reorganized the practices at the *Teatro Español* which had become hackneyed, after the Guerrero-Mendoza company had transferred its headquarters. Enrique Borrás can be called Spain's leading actor. The dance has contributed enormously to the Spanish theatre, particularly through such fine artists as Antonia Mercé, known as La Argentina (1888-1936), and Encarnación López (La Argentinita).

In addition to the theatres already mentioned there are several outstanding playhouses, such as the experimental *Teatro Lara* which was established in 1880 by Don Cándido Lara, when Balbina Valverde played leading parts. It was the first to offer such important plays as *The Bonds of Interest* in 1907 and *Cradle Song* in 1911. Besides the permanent playhouses, efforts were made to reach the people by out-of-door performances and by such touring companies as *La Barraca*, which was an amateur organization drawn from the faculty and students of the University of Madrid. This company, with which the dramatist García Lorca was most active, enlisted the help of the other arts in designing its scenery and sent its production around the countryside in trucks. For a time this effort was subsidized but support was finally almost completely withdrawn. Subsequently the Educational Commission sent its company to one hundred and fifteen villages in central Spain. Both of these organizations drew on such dramatists as Lope de Rueda, Juan del Encina, Cervantes and Calderón de la Barca because it was believed that these men spoke a language that country people would understand. This proved to be true.

It is completely impossible to get any accurate picture of the Spanish theatre today. Some of the theatres which kept open throughout the Civil War are still functioning and others have reopened. However, with the purge of liberalism and the fascist triumph, many of the finest talents were dispersed by death, imprisonment or flight. Newspaper reports are meagre and refugees fleeing from France and other beleaguered countries have had little time to observe what is actually happening. It is a broken and hungry country and it will be a long time before we can expect it to assume even the lesser role it formerly played in world theatre.

LATIN AMERICA

The countries in the Western Hemisphere south of the Rio Grande have largely drawn their culture from Spain. Brazil, which fell to Portugal when the Pope divided the New World between Spain and the former country several centuries ago, has been as dependent on Madrid as have the rest. Between 1821 and 1883 the Latin American countries freed themselves from the corrupt political rule of the Spanish, but that does not mean that they had severed cultural ties. These bonds are still strong and the present task of international relations which the United States is undertaking with its ideal of hemisphere defense will demonstrate just how strong they are. Undoubtedly Hollywood, with the enormous number of films which it prepares especially for the Spanish speaking public, has influenced Latin America; whether this has been for good or bad is for others to determine. Certainly until 1936 almost all the theatrical fare which these countries had enjoyed emanated from Spain in one way or another. What held true for the mother country was more or less true for her children. Allowances must be made for crudeness of production, paucity of dramatists and actors, scarcity of theatres, interruptions caused by revolutions, and lack of audiences due to the sheer poverty of the people.

MEXICO

The earliest performance of which we have record, south of the Rio Grande, took place on June 24, 1538, *Corpus Christi* day, at Tlaxcala, Mexico on the occasion of the Emperor Charles V's granting that community the status of a city. The plays were entirely religious, the first *auto* being the Annunciation of the Nativity of St. John the Baptist. The secular theatre was not yet admitted, for the drama was to be used to educate the natives in Christianity. It is highly probable that before the Spanish Conquest there was some sort of aboriginal theatre among the Mexicans for the development of their dances and their religious rituals point in that direction.

As in Europe, the mysteries began within the church buildings and later came out into the plaza. Comic elements were introduced to hold the attention of the natives and, as was the case in all other parts of the world, these secularities separated the theatre, in time, from the church, and the clergy who had used plays as religious propaganda turned against the drama. By the middle of the sixteenth century the Church had ranged herself on the attacking side.

By 1597 there was a theatre in Mexico City called *La Casa de Comedias*. It was near the hospital and its profits were turned over to that institution to insure the free care of patients. Two hundred years later a public playhouse was established in Buenos Aires in similar fashion, thus dissolving public opposition by making the devil do the Lord's work.

The secular drama in Mexico developed side by side with the liturgical, and by the last third of the sixteenth century Fernán González de Eslava, a priest from Andalusia was writing both types of plays. Juan de la Cueva, who at one time lived in Mexico, and the great Alarcón who was native born, have already been mentioned in an earlier chapter on the Spanish theatre. The latter undoubtedly influenced Sor Juana Inés de la Cruz (1651-95) whose contribution of five plays to the Mexican theatre include *El Divino Narciso* (*The Divine Narcissus*, 1690); *Amor es más Laberinto* (*Love is a Labyrinth*, in collaboration with Fr. Juan de Guevara); and *Los Empeños de una Casa* (*The Determinations of a Household*) in which later critics have discerned the influence of Lope de Vega.

By 1673 Mexico City possessed a *coliseo* (playhouse) under the direction of the Hippolitan Brothers, the profits of which were used to maintain the Royal Hospital for Natives. Mondays and Thursdays were free and the performances of cape-and-sword plays, farces, and short musical pieces combined to form a function known as *Guananjos*. These performances continued through the entire eighteenth century and into the early part of the nineteenth.

Due largely to Spanish influence and the prosperous condition of the colony, there was a flowering of the theatre in the last few years of the eighteenth century. Spanish actors and actresses appeared to the delight of the Spanish and upper-class Mexicans. Simple plays called pastorals or colloquies (*los pastores*), which were semi-religious in character and interpolated a good deal of the amusing secular life of the shepherds, were performed for the benefit of the native audiences. The thoughtful novelist and playwright JOSÉ JOAQUIN FERNANDEZ DE LIZARDI (c.1774-1827) did not hesitate to contribute to this native form which derived so largely from the *eclogues* of Juan del Encina. These colloquies continued to be performed in the capital up to the present century and are still seen in the rural districts as well as in the Spanish-settled sections of the southwestern part of the United States.

The years immediately preceding the Mexican War of Independence, which culminated in the freedom of the country in 1821, were bad ones for the theatre because its natural patrons were either fighting or had been driven out. Five years later, however, the distinguished Spanish actor Andrés Prieto, made his first appearance. He is credited with having improved acting standards and assisted in the training of Mexican actors. In 1852 this desire for improvement found expression in the National Conservatory of Declamation, which was under the direction of José Cejudo, another Spanish actor. The playwright Zorrilla spent more than ten years in Mexico and his plays are still presented.

The musical revue has afforded the Mexicans their most potent outlet for theatrical expression. After the Madero revolution and the flight of Díaz, political satire was permitted in the theatre and it became an integral part of the revue.

Among such Mexican actors and actresses as María Teresa Montoya; Fernando Soler; Alfredo Gómez de la Vega; María Luisa Villegas; Dora Vila; and Francisco Cardona; the actress Virginia Fábregas is outstanding. Mme. Montoya organized and directed the government supported *Teatro Municipal* in 1923. In addition various art theatres have cropped up such as the Synthetic Theatre organized in 1923 by Rafael Saavedra, Carlos González and Francisco Domínguez. (That same year the Union of Dramatists [UDAD] was formed.) The Theatre of the Bat, which was under the influence of the *Chauve-Souris*, came into being in 1924 due to Luis Quintanilla, González, and

Domínguez. The *Teatro de Ulises* was formed in 1928 by Celestino Gorostiza for the purpose of informing the Mexican people of what was happening in the theatrical world outside of Spain. In 1932 Mauricio Magdaleno and Juan Bustillo formed the Theatre of Today to present political dramas written by its founders, who are among the best modern Mexican playwrights. This venture failed like all the others. Perhaps the people are no longer theatre-minded or the theatre itself has lost touch with the people. These experiments have been conducted largely with amateur and semi-professional actors; some of them have real talent as in the case of Andrea Palma who has become a star in Mexican films.

SOUTH AMERICA

The South American Indians performed dances and ritual dramas (many of which were concerned with death and immortality) just as their North American brothers and the corresponding natives of the Pacific Islands and the continents of Australia, Asia and Africa had done. A formal drama, however, awaited the coming of the Spanish and Portuguese.

Very little has been written in English about the development of the theatre on this continent and not a great deal of that is authentic. The problems which arose are remarkably similar in all countries and to a certain extent parallel the experience of Mexico. The earliest professional company known to have visited this side of the Atlantic came in 1599, and on June 28th drew up articles of partnership in Callao in wealthy Peru, which was still sending Inca treasure to enrich Spain and make possible her vast European wars. The company was headed by Francisco Pérez de Robles. It is believed that many such companies came out and played in the wealthy provincial capitals of New Spain, but evidence is lacking so far. Thanks to a recently-discovered document in the possession of Dr. A. S. W. Rosenbach, we are granted evidence of this Peruvian tour. Probably in the libraries of monasteries and noble families of Spain there are still more treasures that will become available to theatre scholarship, but war and reconstruction will undoubtedly delay any such discoveries.

Wars of by-gone years, which caused the sinking or capture of Spanish ships by the British, probably kept many acting troupes at home, so it was necessary for the South American people to improvise or do without any theatre. Such performances surely date back into the seventeenth century but no documentary evidence exists. In fact it was not until 1747 that written evidence proved there had been a theatrical performance in Buenos Aires, now one of the leading capitals of the world with a flourishing theatre.

These earliest performances took place on the nights of November 15th and 16th, 1747 in honor of the coronation of Fernando VI of Spain. Calderón's *Las Armas de la Hermosura* and *Efectos de Odio y Amor* were chosen for the occasion. The next performance to be recorded took place in 1775, but the present capital of the Argentine Republic was soon to have a theatre. This was due to the enlightened efforts of the Viceroy, Don Juan José Vertiz who was opposed by the clergy and the bigoted elements in the population. He opened the *coliseo* in 1781, but people pretended they were afraid to go out after dark. He arranged for the streets to be lighted on the way to the theatre and persuaded the nearby residents to illuminate their houses so people could travel safely. The opposition was finally overcome by allotting the profits to the maintenance of the Asylum for Foundlings. The playhouse *Casa de Comedias* was located in the slave quarter (*la Ranchería*) so it was soon referred to as the *Teatro de la Ranchería*.

There is no need to describe this theatre for it was like all other Spanish and European playhouses of the period. There was still no curtain and candles were used for lighting. In 1792 the theatre burned down and a new one, the *Gran Coliseo*, was erected in 1802, but its location was so poor that it failed. In 1803 Don José Olaguer Feliú and his brother petitioned for the right to erect a new theatre at their own expense. The request was granted and in 1804 the *Teatro Provisional de Comedias* was built. After its completion in 1812 it was successively called *Coliseo Chico* and *Coliseo Provisorio* but in 1838 it became the *Teatro Argentino*. This was a much handsomer theatre with many boxes and at the rear of the top gallery was that Spanish survival, the *cazuela*, where the ladies might sit unmolested. This unattractive location was reached by the ladies via a stairway reserved for their use alone.

During the second and third decades of the nineteenth century the gentry ceased going to the theatre and the general populace was a poor substitute. The favorite actress, Trinidad Guevara, left Buenos Aires for the Uruguayan capital of Montevideo. With the reign of terror under the political leadership of Rosas all theatres were closed and intellectuals left the country not to return until after the fall of his régime.

The native theatre declined and its place was taken by the Spanish. In addition to the best known theatre of the period, *El Alcázar*, which was opened in 1856, there were eight or nine other playhouses built between 1845 and 1887. This was one of the most flourishing periods of the Argentine theatre. Plays by Calderón and Alarcón, as well as undistinguished native efforts were presented. Native drama had its

true inception in *El Amor de la Estanciera* (1787), probably written
by a Dr. Maziel, which was the first *criollo* (a play having a ranch
house setting with native types as characters). In 1823 came the next
important piece, *Molina* by Manuel Belgrano, which was also *criollo*.
This was the tradition which fired the greatest native dramatist, Sánchez. Side by side with the native, grew the play of European inspiration, the best known of which is *Rosas* (1860) by Pedro Echagüe,
called the first Argentine national drama.

Just as Mexico found puppets popular among the lower classes from
the eighteenth century on, the Uruguayans developed the *Teatro de
Títeres* in Montevideo. Such playhouses continued to be popular
through the nineteenth century. The most characteristic development, however, came in the rise of the *gaucho* plays, which were in a
sense descendants of the criollo. In 1879-80, the novelist Eduardo
Gutiérrez published *Juan Moreira* which was based on *gaucho* life.
Alfredo Cattaneo, manager of the theatre where the Carlo Brothers'
equestrian troupe was playing, asked Gutiérrez to arrange the novel
as a pantomime. "Pepino 88" was the circus name of the clown, José
J. Podesta who was performing with the *Teatro-Circo Humberto
Primo*. His family was chosen to perform the play. The *gaucho* pantomime was staged in 1884 and played thirteen times before the
company had to leave to fill an engagement in Rio de Janeiro where
they played *Juan Moreira* before the Emperor Dom Pedro II. In 1885
the Podesta family formed its own troupe. In the beginning their
stock play had no written dialogue, but this was soon added to give
continuity to the various episodes. This type of drama celebrated the
conflict between the *gaucho* and city authorities and later turned attention to the resentment felt towards European immigrants; then
the episodes progressed to pictures of ranch life and social and political
conflict among the *gauchos* themselves.

Leguizamon's *Calandria* (1896) had considerable influence on Sánchez and marked the final step in the development of a National Theatre; which was really a joint creation of the Uruguayans and Argen-
tinians, for their capitals are not far apart on the River Platte. This
geographic situation gave the name *Rioplatense* to their dramatic efforts. Its chief artist, Florencio Sanchez (1875-1910), was born in
Montevideo, did most of his writing in the Argentine, and died in
Italy. After the First World War his body was returned to South
America and buried with highest honors.

Sánchez was a hasty writer; he never revised and frequently did not
think out his effects as carefully as he might have. When he attempted
to produce a style, it was a failure. He used to steal blanks from the
local telegraph office and even when he became famous he found that

he wrote most easily on his former stationery. His best known play is *M'hijo el Dotor* (*My Son the Doctor*) which was produced in 1903 and was the high point of his career. This realistic drama presents the conflict of ideas between the new and the old, and employs the medical profession as the most telling channel for demonstrating the change. *La Gringa* (1904) and *Los Muertos* (*The Dead*, 1905) are two other plays of interest. The first shows the conflict between the natives and those coming from abroad; the second is a brutal drama of the dissolution of an urban family by the excessive drinking of the father. *Nuestros Hijos* (*Our Sons*, 1908) is autobiographical and his last important play *Los Derechos de la Salud* (*The Rights of Health*, 1908) is an inherently cruel study of the right of the healthy to love. This portrayal of the harshness of nature and passionate crudity is typical of Sánchez. It has been said that he came under the influence of Roberto Bracco but this seems rather unlikely in spite of the fact that he had been impressed by performances given in 1904 by an Italian company headed by Ermite Zacconi. The gracefulness of Bracco is not to be found in the vivid earthiness of the South American writer.

Unfortunately there have been no dramatists of importance to follow Sánchez either in the Argentine or in the rest of South America. There are several other men of talent who might readily be mentioned. Perhaps out of its experience this great continent will develop a culture comparable to its importance in the modern world. The theatres have been largely strangled by such short-sighted commercial managers as those who formed the Theatrical Syndicate in our own country forty years ago. Certain countries, notably Colombia, have state-supported playhouses where permanent companies are engaged and touring attractions have the opportunity of playing. The *Teatro de Colón* in Bogotá is notable. Opera and the dance speak an international language and so have been more successful than the drama in passing from one country to another.

Brazil's leading playwright is CLAUDIO DE SOUZA, who has developed a following in such principal cities as Rio de Janeiro and São Paulo, both of which were big enough to support three hundred performances of his *Flores de Sombra* (1916); a respectable run in any country. It is a sentimental drama with its thought rooted largely in the past; but it is nationalistic and interprets his native country, as does his later drama *A Jangada* (*The Raft*).

Raul Roulien is the principal actor of Brazil. He usually appears with his company at the small but very modern *Gloria* in the capital, and frequently plays his own comedies. As recently as September 1938, he was still playing in Brazil. Usually several Portuguese or

Brazilian musical revues are to be found each year and Carmen Miranda, singer and diseuse, is Brazil's gift to the New York stage.

In Cuba, Spanish or American companies are certain of welcome. Barring some writers mentioned as Cuban-born in the earlier Spanish part of the chapter, the leading playwright is the Cuban diplomat, JOSÉ ANTONIO RAMOS. Of his play *Libertad* no lesser judge than Benavente wrote, "Your play is a work of art and it is something more." However he advised Ramos against permitting it to be acted by an inferior company and wound up the letter with this cynicism (which is certainly true of many theatres), "But, you know it as well as I; if you wish to be a popular author, don't look for plays in life; thumb over the theatrical archives and be one of the regular gang." * The quality of the writing in *Libertad* (a play about free love) was natural and lucid. His patriotic plays are less effective. Of these *El Hombre Fuerte* (*The Strong Man*, 1915) is the most sincere and the best.

Perhaps out of the new rapprochement between the Americas will come an artistic development to make us all proud of our western heritage and willing to reject all foreign ideologies for the cultivation of our own cultural impulses.

* Goldberg, Isaac, *The Drama of Transition*, Cincinnati, Stewart Kidd, 1922.

XXVIII

THE IRISH NATIONAL THEATRE
(1899-1940)

BRITISH theatre has been immeasurably influenced by Irish dramatists and actors from its very beginnings because of the theatrical spirit in that land of poets, warriors, politicians, bigots, partisans and lovers. Congreve (though not of Irish birth), Farquhar, Oliver Goldsmith, Richard Brinsley Sheridan, Oscar Wilde and George Bernard Shaw have immensely enriched the noble English drama. The first half of the nineteenth century saw the development of a dramatist in Dion Boucicault who later went to England and America. Though he discarded his nationality, many of his plays came out of his native land and were appreciated in Irish playhouses. When the quality of English plays declined after Sheridan, it was on acting alone that the theatre subsisted and thanks to English and Irish talent, there was no lack of that kind of enjoyment for Irish audiences. However, the star system and the touring actor-managers milked the provincial theatres dry and destroyed the resident stock companies.

When Robertson emerged to lead the realistic movement in England and so revived its drooping dramatic laurels, the artistic break with Erin was complete. The Irish did not like Robertsonian plays and no matter how well they were acted, they could not slip them down their gullets.

It was then that Boucicault's plays, which were liked by the Irish-Americans, were performed for the keen pleasure and enjoyment of that most critical of audiences, Dublin. They satisfied the need for national expression, but with his death it became evident that the stage could not subsist forever on revivals of his plays nor even on such super-patriotic dramas as J. W. Whitbread's *The Irishman* and *Shoulder to Shoulder*. Though these were imitative of Boucicault they lacked his skill; at the same time they were popular and continued to be played in small towns as late as 1914.

481

Having taken these matters into consideration and having observed the success of the *Théâtre Libre*, the *Freie Buehne*, the Independent Theatre in London, and having heard of the Moscow Art Theatre, WILLIAM BUTLER YEATS (1865-1939) was determined that Ireland should have a National Theatre. J. T. Grein's venture in London was receiving its greatest support from such Irishmen as Shaw, George Moore and Yeats himself. With these thoughts running through his mind, he sought counsel from Edward Martyn, Moore and that thoroughly remarkable woman, Lady Gregory. As a result of many consultations, the Irish Literary Theatre was founded and a national drama was born.

It was ironic that in the beginning it was necessary to import English actors to interpret their plays but this was unfortunately the case as the Irish Literary Theatre began to function. The first performance of Yeats' *The Countess Cathleen* (written 1892) and Martyn's *The Heather Field* took place on May 8, 1899 at the Ancient Concert Rooms in Great Brunswick Street, Dublin. Yeats' play of self-sacrifice was attacked as being anti-Catholic and anti-Irish; but this was absurd; most of the political and clerical criticism of the whole movement was without foundation. In considering the recent Irish theatre it must never be forgotten that it exists in a Catholic section of the country which has a hostile church. This is all the more amazing when one considers that in other Catholic countries the Roman church soon saw the advantages of inculcating Christian thought through drama and an active theatre. Students in the University College were exhorted to proceed to the Ancient Concert Rooms and demonstrate against this "insult to their faith" and so riotous were they that the police had to be called out. This antagonism has been an integral part of their feeling towards the theatre ever since; both newspaper and clerical criticism has been bigoted, chauvinistic and unbelievably stupid.

The first play of Yeats to be produced was the delightful one-act poetic fantasy, *The Land of Heart's Desire* (1894), (which was staged in London in the spring of 1894 by the Independent Theatre). Yeats was unrepresented in the second bill of the Irish Literary Theatre for which an English company was again brought to Dublin's Gaiety Theatre in 1900 to perform Martyn's *Maeve*, George Moore's *The Bending of the Bough* and *The Last Feast of the Fianna* by Alice Milligan.

Yeats was strongly influenced by Maeterlinck and longed for a poetic theatre; a desire which was always to be denied him after the organization became the Abbey Theatre. Disregarding his personal disappointment, he was loyal to the group even when privately he must have disagreed with many of their methods and many of their ends. His own principles were an integral part of *The Shadowy Waters* (1900), a beautifully poetic play of Irish dreams. Some of this was apparent in the symbolic *Cathleen ni Houlihan* (1902) in which Ireland was portrayed as a haggard, gaunt old woman who is restored to youth and vigor by the sacrifices of a young man. Yeats joined with George Moore to write the naturalistic *Diarmuid and Grania* (1901), unpublished but acted in Dublin and London by Sir F. R. Benson with an English company. Then came the slight farcical play, *The Pot of Broth* (1902), in collaboration with Lady Gregory; after this appeared his most important drama, *The Hour Glass* (1903). Andrew E. Malone calls it "the greatest morality play of the contemporary theatre." * It is a fascinating and moving study of reason and faith in the modern world and its tremendous emotional power is especially moving to an audience, particularly when acted before the magnificent settings of Gordon Craig.

In *The King's Threshold* (1903) he defended the poet's right to take his place in national life, a dogma which was strengthened by his utilization of Ireland's proud legend. In mingled poetry and prose, *On Baile's Strand* tells a story out of Ireland's past, and it was first performed at the opening of the Abbey Theatre, December 21, 1904. He again returned to Ireland's history for *Deirdre* (1906); it is this fact that makes the play so familiar; its author was perhaps never more successful in creating characters and understandable humanity. His other plays need not hold our attention for long; the best are *The Player Queen* (1916) and his theatrically unimpressive translations of Sophocles' *Oedipus Rex and Oedipus Coloneus*. Yeats contributed as much to the promotion of a national theatre in Ireland through his managerial efforts, his tact and inspiring leadership as through his fine, poetic plays.

EDWARD MARTYN (1859-1923) was as devout a Catholic as Lady Gregory was Protestant. (This Irish national dramatic movement managed to combine the two main divisions of Christianity just as it brought in all component people of the country, even the Anglo-Irish.) Martyn was a man of culture, wealth and background; had he been less well-provided with the goods of this world, he might have written more and better. It has been stated that he was unwilling to learn technique where he could (as Lady Gregory and Yeats did) and disdained any helping hand at home and so remained the perfect amateur. His tastes led him towards the naturalistic movement in Europe which influenced his work; yet he was an idealist who believed that he would find fresh and unspoiled audiences in Ireland who were untainted by English commercialism.

* Malone, Andrew E., *The Irish Drama*, New York, Charles Scribner's Sons, 1929.

The Heather Field (1890, acted 1899) is a magnificent combination of searing realism and high poetic imagination. It is a study of man's idealism and unquenchable hope, a striving after the unattainable, and is placed in a domestic Irish setting. Mary Bruin in *The Land of Heart's Desire* resembles *Maeve*, a play of high poetic symbolism. Realism and fairyland are again combined in *An Enchanted Sea* (1902); *Grangecolman* (1912) is almost straight realism; and *The Dream Physician* (1914) is an attempt at comedy. However, Martyn will be remembered for his first two plays rather than for his later efforts.

GEORGE MOORE (1853-1933) was primarily a novelist, as his plays amply illustrate. Having flayed the practicing English playwrights in an essay, *Our Dramatists and Their Literature*, Moore was challenged by George R. Sims to write a play. Sims offered to pay £100 for a seat at the first performance and the Irishman was nothing loath (as always) to accept publicity. He wrote the feeble *The Strike at Arlingford*, which the Independent Theatre produced in 1893; *The Bending of the Bough* (1900) was equally insignificant. Moore's value to the Irish theatre came largely through his position as a novelist and the fact that he was a potential source of advice. He took increasingly less and less interest in Ireland and eventually wrote only in terms of England. None of his other plays, *Esther Waters* (1911), *Elizabeth Cooper* (1913) or *The Coming of Gabrielle* (1924) are of much importance.

AUGUSTA, LADY GREGORY (1859-1932) probably did more to popularize the Irish dramatic movement than any other person. Her plays do not rank so high as those of Synge, nor did she have the poetry of Yeats, nor the great poetic imagination of Martyn, but she did have a wonderful feeling for ordinary people and their problems. Sometimes she deliberately chose a farcical form to portray a serious subject, as in *Spreading the News* (1904) where she treats comedy as farce, and in *The Rising of the Moon* (1907) where she arbitrarily forced a change in the character of the English policeman to give a happy whimsicality to the ending. Both of these comedies have delighted audiences since their first performances, but they definitely demonstrate the author's weakness.

Comedy and even farce were her weapons for propaganda. In the theatre laughter converts more people than preaching, and Lady Gregory was out to convert the widest possible public. *Hyacinth Halvey* (1906) is an entertaining comedy of a young man whose reputation is (despite the false premise on which it is based) so good that nothing he can do will destroy it. Contrived or not, it is typical Irish humor and is as thoroughly enjoyable in the playhouse as most of her other plays; certainly she has proved to be the most enduring popular dramatist of the Abbey Theatre repertory.

The Workhouse Ward (1907) belongs in a higher category than the afore-mentioned plays because the comic situation arises naturally and logically out of the characters themselves. It is the story of two old men who carry a life-long quarrel into the workhouse. When a niece of one of them offers to take her uncle away he refuses to leave his crony because he has grown to be dependent on his antagonistic companionship.

Lady Gregory is at her best in the one-act form; the entertaining central idea in *The Image* (1909) is not strong enough to sustain a three-act play. *The Gaol Gate* (1906) is a distinct contrast to most of her work for it is tragic and in the vein of *Riders to the Sea*. It is the study of the characters of two women who go to visit their son and husband who they think is still alive because he betrayed his friend; they discover that he died out of loyalty instead. It is a deeply sincere and moving play. Her *Grania* (1912) is probably the best of her historical folk-tragedies, but it has not been widely understood nor appreciated outside her native country. There it is admired extravagantly and Malone says "Here she is superior to the Ibsen of *The Vikings at Helgeland*, the Strindberg of *Gustavus Vasa*, or the Hauptmann of *Florian Geyer*. In emotional content and poetic intensity *Grania* can bear the comparison with Synge's *Deirdre* to which it has been subjected." *

Undoubtedly the most important dramatist of the earlier group of Irish playwrights was JOHN MILLINGTON SYNGE (1871-1909). He wrote few plays but all of them are significant both because of his long preparation for writing and his own genius. At the instance of Yeats, he spent several years in the Aran Islands where he studied the language and the rhythms of the Irish peasants' speech. He was as much concerned with their thoughts and the small doings of their lives as with their vocabularies. All these stood him in good stead when in 1903 he produced his first play *In the Shadow of the Glen*. It was called a libel against peasant women and was hostilely treated upon its production by the Irish Literary Theatre. In its expert depiction of native character there are none of the faults of a first play and there is no suggestion of the apprentice; the strokes are sure and telling, and every single line counts towards the creation of an Irish Nora.

Hard on its heels came *Riders to the Sea* (1904) which demonstrates the nobility and resignation of womankind when face to face with the harshness of Nature. There is no desperate striving against

* *Op. cit.*

fate; the end is discounted once the mother realizes that her youngest son is determined to follow the sea as did his four brothers who had been drowned. This too is the work of a master stylist. *The Well of Saints* (1905) was the only one of his plays in which he introduced something of the supernatural; perhaps because of this it has always been the least popular, or it may be that audiences have always felt that his symbolism was aimed at them. It is concerned with two blind beggars whose sight is restored by a miracle. Upon examining their deficiencies and trying to adjust themselves to living, they realize that they do not like what they see and feel and are only too glad to be again blinded by a second miracle.

Synge's greatest play and the one which has stirred up more resentment than any modern play of merit was the comedy *The Playboy of the Western World* (1907). The enemies of the stage howled with rage; it was obscene; it accused the Irish people of admiring murderers; it was calumny upon a fair land. When the Abbey Players announced its inclusion in the repertory for their American tour (under the management of Liebler and Company in 1911-12) the professional Irish-Americans began to attack it in advance and caused a riot on opening night at Maxine Elliott's Theatre in New York. The prompt championing both of the play and the troupe by Theodore Roosevelt (who had been present at the opening) in the magazine, *Outlook*, did much to soften opposition and insure the success of Synge's drama and the company's tour.

This play has attracted wider attention and more favorable reaction from critics than any of his others. Maxim Gorki in the *English Review* for April, 1924, says, "In it the comical side passes quite naturally into the terrible, while the terrible becomes comical just as easily." Its characters prefer a pleasant dream to reality and in their childish search for a hero, Synge has the opportunity to satirize their love for appearances.

Taking advantage of the success of *The Playboy of the Western World*, he published and had produced in 1909 a farcical comedy *The Tinker's Wedding*, which had probably been written about 1902. Its rollicking humor undoubtedly comes out of his observation of peasant customs during his stay in the Aran Islands. At his death he left unfinished his tragedy *Deirdre of the Sorrows*, which was produced at the Abbey on January 13, 1910. The humanity and vitality in this treatment of the old legend stamp this as perhaps the most satisfactory play on the subject. His ability to characterize, his masterly command of language and his economy of writing make it necessary to rank him with the finest writers of the last hundred years.

The men and women who created the roles of Yeats, Martyn,

Gregory and Synge were of high order. Miss A. E. F. Horniman offered to build and maintain the Abbey Theatre and to train a repertory company for Yeats, Martyn, Gregory and Synge. The poet, A. E. (George Russell), was interested in the movement and introduced Frank and William Fay to Yeats, who presented them with *Cathleen ni Houlihan* which was to be produced with A. E.'s *Deirdre* in 1902 as the first productions of the Irish National Dramatic Company. The history of the triumphs and vicissitudes of the Abbey Theatre is partly told in the story of her playwrights. However, it is true that without the wonderful training Miss Horniman gave the talented group of young people, the theatre could never have achieved its eminence.

Among the directors of the Abbey Theatre are to be found the names of Conal O'Riordan (under the *nom de théâtre* of Norreys Connell) who produced three of his own plays, *The Piper* (1908) an unusual piece of political propaganda, *Time* (1909) and *An Imaginary Conversation* (1909); Nugent Monck, who was later to manage the famous Maddermarket Theatre, utilized many of the ideas he had used previously when he ran an acting school and produced a cycle of miracle plays; and the playwright Lennox Robinson became associated with the theatre as manager and producer from 1909 until 1914; in 1919 he returned for four years and later became producer with the assistance of the actor Arthur Shields. During the war years the theatre had four managers, each staying about a year for these were trying times and Ireland was in a state of rebellion or siege from 1916 on. In 1914-15 A. Patrick Wilson staged Lennox Robinson's *The Dreamers* and his own *The Slough*. He was followed by the playwright-critic, St. John Ervine, who had violently attacked the Dublin press for its severe criticism of his *The Magnanimous Lover* (1912) in the satirical burlesque, *The Critics* (1913), so his reception was warm during his encumbancy. Ervine, who had lost most of his Ulster Irish in becoming English, was enamored of the idea of a chain of repertory theatres throughout the British Isles of which the Abbey was to be a member. His most notable achievement was the staging of his finest drama, *John Ferguson* (1915). Ervine's departure brought J. Augustus Keogh to the fore and he in turn was followed by Fred O'Donovan. During the latter's régime, 1916-19, he produced Robinson's *The Lost Leader* (1908). Sara Allgood filled in until Robinson's return, at which time Michael J. Dolan took over the management to relieve Robinson of any onerous duties so that he might devote himself to problems of staging.

In addition to the talented Fay brothers, the early group of actors included the brilliant Arthur Sinclair, Dudley Digges, (who left in

1904 to come to America where he has been a successful actor ever since), J. A. O'Rourke, Sydney Morgan, Fred O'Donovan, and J. M. Kerrigan (long an Irish-American actor). The leading actresses were the tragic Maire NicShuibhlaigh, the excellent comedienne, Maire O'Neill, and her sister Sara Allgood who shines in comedy or tragedy without seeming to have a preference. Miss O'Neill has been a favorite actress in England and Miss Allgood has become domiciled in America, where she is one of the brightest lights of the contemporary stage.

The personnel of the theatre has changed many times as actors leave for the greener pastures of America or England. In the nineteen-twenties such men as Dolan and F. J. MacCormick were added while the painstaking Eric Gorman and the brilliant comedian, Barry Fitzgerald have since become actively allied to the American stage and films. Eileen Crowe, who has taken over many of Sara Allgood's roles, is the best of the younger actresses, while Maureen Delaney, May Craig and Kate Curling are actresses of real talent.

To return to the dramatists who provided the plays after Synge's death, Yeats' excursions into a formless poetic theatre and Lady Gregory's gradual slowing down of writing, there are a number of names which deserve some attention before we consider the latter day O'Casey and Carroll. In the earlier days it was thought that PADRAIC COLUM (1881-   ) would develop into a great dramatist but his preoccupation with children's stories and fairy tales precluded this. His most important plays, which derive both from the folk and the realistic tradition, are the imaginative *The Broken Soil* (1903, revised as *The Fiddler's House,* 1907); the serious comedy, *The Land* (1905); and that study of misery, *Thomas Muskerry* (1910).

WILLIAM BOYLE (1853-1923) had real comic talent but there was not much distinction in his writing. Perhaps his very flatness of structure and language popularized his plays for they have retained a general following throughout the country to this day. His comedies always necessitated the placing of the "House Full" sign on the doors of the Abbey Theatre (the Irish equivalent of the American "Standing Room Only"). The best of these were *The Building Fund* (1905), *The Eloquent Dempsey* (1906), *The Mineral Workers* (1906), *Family Failing* (1912) and *Nic* (1916).

GEORGE FITZMAURICE is a folk dramatist of some power, though his plays have never secured the following that they deserve nor have they attracted a foreign reputation. *The County Dressmaker* (1907) contains some of the best written Irish comedy and an interesting analysis of feminine character. His one-act tragedy, *The Piedish* (1908), has always attracted laughter from its audiences rather than sympathy for the central character who represents the artist's striving for perfection. Perhaps the triviality of his creation has something to do with this. His other plays have received even less response and several have not even been acted.

LORD DUNSANY (Edward John Moreton Drax Plunkett, 1878-   ) wrote fantasy which was at one time highly admired but his reputation has declined sharply in the past decade, probably due to his exotic excursions into never-never-land. His two plays which still merit some attention are the poetic one-act *The Glittering Gate* (1909), and the short thriller, *A Night at an Inn* (1916), which has had tremendous popularity with men's colleges and boys' schools on both sides of the water because of its gruesome qualities and all male cast of characters. The best known of his other plays are *King Argimenes and the Unknown Warrior* (1911), *The Gods of the Mountain* (1911) and the somewhat better *if* (1921).

LENNOX ROBINSON (1886-   ) is as well known for his playwriting as he is for his direction of the Abbey Theatre and his acting. His early plays are of so little present importance that the mere mention of their titles, *The Clancy Name* (1908), *The Cross Roads* (1909) and *Harvest* (1910), is sufficient. *Patriots* (1912) deals sincerely and realistically with a problem which is truly characteristic of his country. This is concerned with the tragic (and at the same time, ironic) plight of an Irish patriot who has gone to prison for his political principles, only to emerge to discover that everything for which he has suffered has become old-fashioned; he can not even attract an audience to listen to his talk because everyone has gone to the movies. Despite the seeming comedy of the gods, this play is at least tragic in its implications.

He followed this with a biographical play that was somewhat similar in theme. *The Dreamers* (1915) purports to describe the career of Robert Emmet, Irish patriot, whose fate was sealed in the general shiftlessness of his followers. Then came the play which up to date of writing best represents him in the theatre, *The Whiteheaded Boy* (1916). This is one of the merriest comedies written by an Irishman; there is a gay feeling of fun about it that has an irresistible appeal for audiences. The author claimed a political connotation for the play which the audiences overlooked in their laughing; but they had no such difficulty with the much less successful *The Lost Leader* (1918). Of his later plays, *Crabbed Youth and Age* (1922) has satirical charm; *The Big House* (1926) mourns the passing of the Anglo-Irish culture while welcoming the New Ireland, which unconsciously echoes the plays of the Russian Civil War which followed that country's revolution. His most recent pieces have little to recommend them.

T. C. MURRAY (1873-   ) is a poignant realist whose plays substantially represent the educated Catholic viewpoint of Eire. Several that stand out above others are: *Birthright* (1910), which transfers the Cain and Abel story from the Bible to an Irish setting and also bears a resemblance to O'Neill's *Beyond the Horizon; Maurice Harte* (1912) which is a study of o'erweaning father love and the too-strong application of parental discipline which destroys a young man; *Spring* (1918) and *Aftermath* (1922) are grim dramas, but they are not so clearly defined and steadfastly developed as *Autumn Fire* (1924) which is probably his best play; *The Blind Wolf* (1928) recalls both Lillo's bourgeois tragedies and the fate dramas of early nineteenth-century Germany.

SEUMAS O'KELLY (1881-1918) was a novelist who contributed several plays to his native stage. His best work was shown in *The Shuiler's Child* (1909), a drama of mother love and self sacrifice in which Maire NicShuibhlaigh triumphed. *The Bribe* (1913) condemns the characteristic vice of nepotism in no uncertain terms. Besides several one-act plays, his only other drama, *The Parnell* (1917), is a study of moral cowardice growing out of Parnell's downfall.

ST. JOHN ERVINE (1883-   ), despite his Belfast birth, might just as well be considered an English dramatist along with Shaw and Wilde if it were not for his various connections with the Abbey Theatre. Though his recent plays have been of little interest except as commercial successes, he has written several plays which bulk large in English dramatic literature.

His first play, *Mixed Marriage* (1911), deals with the controversial subject of marriage between Catholics and Protestants, in this case typified both by the bigotry of an older man pitted against a more tolerant attitude held by the younger people, and the growing realization that no religious differences should divide the working class. Though written earlier, his next produced play, *The Magnanimous Lover* (1912), honestly discusses the problems of seduction and the idea that "an honest woman" must be made of the girl. It recalls *Hindle Wakes,* but probably was written before that play was produced. Neither the critics nor the public cared for it; for intellectual Irishmen feel that social problems of this kind are unwelcome on their native stage.

His next and much better play, *Jane Clegg* (1913), was staged at the Gaiety Theatre in Manchester. This is a character study of a woman who lives under the most adverse circumstances, with poverty, unhappiness and misery about her. The catharsis of the play comes out of her strength which enables her to send her weak and snivelling husband away Though Ervine gave this play to the English rather than the Irish stage, his next and probably best play, *John*

Ferguson (1915), was handed over to the Abbey. It is a play which develops from the staunch protestantism of Ulster; John Ferguson may be a bigot but he is also a stoic. Though Ervine introduces some melodramatic elements which weaken the play as a whole, his characterization and mood hold an audience enthralled. This play saved the life of the struggling Theatre Guild during its early days and many foundering community or little theatres have found it a source of strength. It is that anomaly—a truly fine play which is also a box office attraction. Despite the comparative weakness of his farewell to the Irish stage in the one-act piece, *The Island of Saints, and the Way to Get Out of It* (1920), the memory of *John Ferguson* remains untarnished. Since that time he has written the light comedy *The First Mrs. Fraser*, which that expert comedienne of enormous popularity, Dame Marie Tempest, acted in 1929, *Anthony and Anna* (written and staged in Liverpool, 1926 and subsequently performed for two years in London), and the equally popular problem play *Robert's Wife* (1937). Ervine has become thoroughly English and understands how to gauge London taste.

BRINSLEY MAC NAMARA is better known outside Ireland as a novelist than as a playwright, though he has written several plays of more than passing interest which show real ability. His first play, *The Rebellion in Ballycullen* (1919) is a satire on over-patriotism; and in *The Land for the People* (1920, revised and restaged in 1927) he turned his attention to the land agitators who had been active in Ireland. *The Glorious Uncertainty* (1923) is a brisk racing comedy which is absolutely redolent of the turf. This, naturally enough, was well-received in Dublin and has been happily revived on several occasions. He turned with equal success to local and amorous intrigue for the delightfully characterized comedy, *Look at the Heffernans!* (1926). His best play to date is *The Master* (1928), which in mood goes back to his first piece and contrasts the idealism of Young Ireland with the selfishness and greed of older people.

SEAN O'CASEY (1884-   ) is the greatest dramatist of post-war Ireland, though his individual plays vary in merit. He takes his rank as one of the finest playwrights of the modern world theatre largely through the merit of three plays, *Juno and the Paycock* (1924), *The Plough and the Stars* (1926) and *Within the Gates* (1934). The impact of his first play, *The Shadow of a Gunman* (1923), was so terrific that he was famous over-night, but it was not until *Juno and the Paycock* that we could be sure that this was not merely a flash in the pan. The latter play is a mordant tragedy of the Dublin slums, balanced with comic scenes in the best Irish tradition. This last fact has always made a problem for the producer, for Irish actors have a tendency to go overboard on the comedy and so shift the balance, thereby destroying the unity of the play. O'Casey's study of the background out of which he came makes this perhaps the most poignant of his work. The essential decency of the poor is typified by Juno, the universal mother, and her haplesss daughter, Mary, and the bereaved Mrs. Tancred; unreasoning shiftlessness is personified in Jack Boyle and his cadging friend, Joxer; the son Johnny stands for the hopelessness and fear which poverty breeds.

The Plough and the Stars (1926) is a tragedy of the Easter Rebellion of 1916, which provoked an outbreak amongst the audience on opening night. It would sometimes seem to be indicated that the Irish are an essentially intolerant people. Over and over again they show hostility toward any ideas that do not fit in with their cherished national ideal and their hatred of England. It took poor Yeats, whose dream of a poetic theatre was again shattered, to quiet the mob. In this play of embattled Dublin, O'Casey tries to be scrupulously fair, even to the point of seeming to encourage the shiftless Boyle as well as Fluther Good, and old, heavy drinking Peter. The tragedy of the people involved in this situation, the idealistic Jack Clitheroe who must go out to die for their cause, and his pregnant wife, Nora, who is half-crazed with fear for him, is almost too moving to be endured.

Turning to expressionism, O'Casey wrote the annihilating drama, *The Silver Tassie* (1929), which excoriates the horrors of the aftermath of war. It was too strong meat for the Abbey Theatre and was first performed in London. As might have been expected, the reaction of the English critics was mixed, but Shaw championed it for its brutal realism. Nevertheless, it lacks the trenchant quality of the two preceding plays.

In *Within the Gates* (1934) he retained the expressionistic method and produced a symbolic allegory that meant many things to his audience, but his efforts to explain the meaning of the play were not successful. Nonetheless, it is a moving drama which provides real opportunities for an imaginative producer; these opportunities were not realized in the New York production, except for Lillian Gish's excellent clear-eyed interpretation of The Young Whore. O'Casey's use of music and dance was theatrically stirring and some of his best writing and most pointed outbursts have gone into this play.

Even his champion, George Jean Nathan, was unable to follow him into communism in *The Star Turns Red* (1940), as yet unproduced. His most recent play, *The End of the Beginning*, was staged by the *Théâtre de l'Oeuvre* in May, 1939 in Paris. O'Casey obviously has much more to give to the theatre that will be hard, bitter and brilliant, but only time can tell what form it will take.

After O'Casey's severance with the Abbey, GEORGE SHIELS (1886-
) became their leading playwright. This talented comic writer
began his career with two plays which provoked harmless laughter
without adding to the distinction of national drama, the one-act *Bed-
mates* (1921) and *Insurance Money* (1921). *Paul Twyning* (1922)
has a central character who lifts the play above the calibre of the
others. Others of his plays are, *The Retrievers* (1924), a comedy of
complicated plot; *Professor Tim* (1925), a slapstick comedy that
was well received both in Dublin and London; and *The New Gossoon*
(1933), which is a delightful character-comedy of Irish peasants that
was well received in Ireland and America.

During a period of dissatisfaction with the Abbey Theatre, Micheál
MacLiammóir, Hilton Edwards, D. Bannard Cogley and Gearoid
O-Lochlainn founded the Dublin Gate Theatre in 1927 and the Earl
of Longford and his wife, Christina, became associated with it in
1931. Many experimental productions have been effected by this
group and their effort to present such outstanding general writers as
Sophocles, Ibsen and Shaw has given Dublin an ever-expanding vista.
In addition they developed such playwrights as the Longfords and
DENIS JOHNSTON (1901-   ), who wrote the strictly Irish comedy,
The Old Lady Says "No" (1929), which was staged by the Gate. His
best play, *The Moon in the Yellow River* (1931) was performed by
the Abbey and subsequently in New York, Malvern and London.
This study of the incompetence of idealism facing the modern world
is one of the most satisfactory plays of the post-war period; neither
A Bride for the Unicorn (1922) nor *Storm Song; or, Letters in Lights*
(1934) measures up to it. From 1931 to 1936 he directed for the Gate,
and subsequently staged television performances for the British
Broadcasting Corporation. Besides Johnston, the Gate has had the
native plays of Longford, whose play about Dean Swift, *Yahoo* (1933)
was his best.

TERESA DEEVEY, who is also the author of the moving play *Katie
Roche* (1936), shared honors with PAUL VINCENT CARROLL (1900-
) for the Abbey prize with *Things That Are Caesar's* (1932).
The latter's first play was *The Watched Pot* (1931), but it was not
until *Shadow and Substance* (1934) that he really hit his stride. A
school teacher himself, he thoroughly understood the problem of the
young liberal professor whose duties suffer from priestly interference
and the threat of being supplanted by an incompetent choice of the
canon. The play is heightened, however, by the introduction of the
saintly serving-maid, Brigid, who is in love with the school-master and
reveres and loves his opponent, the Canon Skerritt. She dies to save
the younger man and by her holy death, the implacable opponents

are reconciled. It may not be a perfect play, but Carroll created characters of rich distinction and dialogue that sweeps and flows. *The
White Steed* (1938) did not live up to its expectations in the American production, for the basic revolt of young intellect as exemplified
by the teacher and the librarian, was swamped in the quarrel between
the tolerant old priest and the bigoted young one. The audiences'
sympathies, as inspired by the comic performance of Barry Fitzgerald, were held by the old priest, and the problems of the young
seemed footling. The author's dialogue, however, had grown even
finer. *Kindred* (1939) was a frequently unresolved play of mother
love, as opposed to petty town rivalries, but in this, Carroll, or his
actors as personified by Aline MacMahon, or his director in the person of Robert Edmond Jones, had risen above the low comedy which
marred the effect of his major plays.

Living in the shadow of war, the Irish playhouses are still functioning, though their finest writing talents seem to have gone elsewhere and many of their best actors are in New York or Hollywood.
However, the Dublin stage has risen triumphantly before from a
prostrate and humbled condition.

XXIX

FROM YOUNG GERMANY TO HITLER

(1830-1940)

IN Germany, in the 1830's, a group of writers, feeling the need to extricate themselves from the escapism of the Romantic movement, with its nature poetry and historical dramas, banded together to found *Das junge Deutschland* (*The Young Germany*). Their spokesman was the critic, Ludolf Wienbarg (1802-72) and their ideals were roughly those of the French romanticists and liberals of the Paris Revolution of 1830. They demanded that the theatre be nationalistic and democratic, truly national rather than merely historical, and that it be in opposition to any reactionary tendencies. In other words they wished to take up the cudgels where *Sturm und Drang* had left off half a century before. Their leaders were Gutzkow and Lauber. Heine was regarded as the father of the movement rather than an active participant.

HEINRICH HEINE (1797-1865) had little to contribute to the theatre and that which he did write actually came under the influence of the fate-drama dominated by Werner and Muellner. *William Ratcliff* and *Almansor* (1823) were failures when acted, partly because of prevailing anti-Semitism. Heine's aid to the development of a nationalist theatre came through his beautiful and inspiring poetry and his good advice to his friends who were participating more actively. He contributed no more to the theatre than did KARL IMMERMANN (1796-1840) with his three year experiment with theatre management in Duesseldorf. KARL SEYDELMANN (1795-1843), a noted realistic actor, came to play in *Nathan der Weise* for him and Felix von Mendelssohn staged two operas, but Immermann was unable to obtain a state subsidy and had to close his theatre. He was the author of several classic dramas such as *Petrarca* and *Cardenio und Celinde* (1826), the latter of which celebrated his beautiful and talented lady-love, Elisa von Luetzow, the divorced, noble Danish wife of a German general.

It was not from the mellifluence of Heine nor from the classic qualities of Immermann that Young Germany was to find its typical expression but in younger writers whose experience was not yet defined. Its dramatic leader was KARL GUTZKOW (1811-79) who had little or no sympathy with the puerility of the dramas written during the Napoleonic era. He had real talent and his best play *Uriel Acosta* (1847) reflects the liberal sentiments of the movement, though he seems to have made as much use of historical drama as the earlier writers whom he decried. He managed however to maintain the point of view of Young Germany even when using the literary media of the earlier group. An example of these historical comedies was his *Zopf und Schwert* (*Pigtail and Sword*, 1843) a light-hearted comedy about Friedrich Wilhelm I and his court, written under the influence of Scribe, which held the stage for the rest of the century as did *Der Koenigslieutenant* (1849). This unassuming comedy about Goethe's younger days was written to celebrate the centenary of the great dramatist's birth. Gutzkow's other plays are unimportant, though *Das Urbild des Tartueffe* (*The Prototype of Tartuffe*, 1847) was extremely successful.

But it is the tragedy celebrating free thought, *Uriel Acosta*, for which he is remembered. It was based on a story of his own, called *Der Sadducaeer von Amsterdam*, which he had been inspired to dramatize by the acting he saw in Paris in 1846. The play has been compared with *Nathan der Weise* in its plea for tolerance. It has been acted all over the world and as recently as this present year, when the Artef Players revived it in Yiddish in New York.

GEORG BUECHNER (1813-37) was undoubtedly a genius but his death at twenty-four robbed the theatre of the plays he might have written. What is left to us indicates his dramatic power though it is not proof positive of great work. *Dantons Tod* (*Danton's Death*, 1835) is his only full-length play to survive. He had begun, as Gutzkow's protégé, as a revolutionist, and is considered to have written brilliantly on socialism in the days before Karl Marx. However, by the time he composed his play on the French Revolution, he had become discouraged by the fruits of revolutionary doctrines, which explains why his hero goes to his death, a disillusioned man. Max Reinhardt's masterly staging of this play won it many adherents in both Germany and America, but Orson Welles' highly abbreviated version in 1938 was a deserved failure. Welles reduced it to a series of soliloquies delivered in the manner of arias.

In addition to this drama, Buechner wrote *Pietro Aretino*, which does not survive because the woman he loved did not approve of it;

the brief romantic comedy *Leonce und Lena* (posthumous), the portion of a drama, *Wozzek*, which was turned into an opera not long after the First World War by the composer, Alban Berg. These and an unfinished novel, *Lenz,* are all that are left to us, though the output seems fairly considerable at that, considering his short life.

HEINRICH LAUBE (1806-84) in the beginning came under French influence, which he never entirely threw off even during the short period of his identification with the Young Germany movement. When Gutzkow was imprisoned for irreligion and political offenses and all of the people identified with the group were barred from publication, he turned against the movement. This apostasy is unfortunate but understandable when one realizes that he had just been released from a nine months' imprisonment because he had been too openly sympathetic toward the Revolution of 1830 in France. Chastened by this and a still later imprisonment, he became a moderate, leaning to the right in politics. In 1849 he was offered the post of director of the *Burgtheater* in Vienna which he held until 1866. He improved the acting of the company, raised the standards of training, and enlarged the repertory of the theatre. It was as a director and manager that he contributed most. His own plays *Monaldeschi* (1834), *Struensee* (1844), and *Die Karlsschueler* (1846) are of little importance, though the last, which dealt with the early life of Schiller, achieved a good deal of popularity after its initial suppression by the civil authorities. This was probably because it reflected the period in which the romantic dramatist had difficulties with Duke Karl of Wuerttemberg.

Laube's *Graf Essex* (1856), his last play, was another telling of the Essex-Elizabeth story which has been so popular a subject in drama.

There were a number of followers of Young Germany despite the scandal, three of which deserve brief mention, Brachvogel, Bauernfeld and Freytag. EMIL BRACHVOGEL (1824-78), though the author of many plays, is remembered for only one drama, *Narziss* (1856), which was a great favorite with touring actors because of the starring opportunities it offered. He chose his subjects from eighteenth century France in the days before the Revolution. EDUARD VON BAUERNFELD (1802-90), poet and playwright, like Gutzkow shows the influence of Scribe in his graceful pictures of Viennese society. He was spontaneous and enthusiastic and his comedies are fresh and delightful though artificial. His best play was *Buergerlich und Romantisch* (*Simple and Romantic,* 1835); he was the author of many other plays including *Die Bekenntnisse* (*The Confessions,* 1834), *Grossjaehrig* (*Aged,* 1846) and *Ein deutscher Krieger* (*The German Warrior,* 1847).

GUSTAV FREYTAG (1816-95) was well known as a formulator of dramatic technique as well as for his own playwriting. His first plays, *Die Valentine* (1846) and *Graf Waldemar* (*Count Waldemar*, 1850), were colorful but uneven. His best known play was *Die Journalisten* (*The Journalists*, 1853), a realistic comedy of newspaper life which has been praised for its balance. He is best known outside of Germany for his study of dramatic construction, *Die Technik des Dramas* (*Dramatic Technique*, 1863); this included "Freytag's Pyramid" which was a diagram of the development of action in a play. Revised by Brander Matthews, it is still accepted in some quarters as a workable blueprint for the average drama. His general theory that drama should provide release, "a feeling of security" rather than Aristotle's *katharsis* (purgation); and his rejection of Brunetière's contention that dramatic conflict is the result of man's will pitted against the outside world which would circumscribe it, are no longer considered tenable.

There were innumerable dramatists of small, and in many cases of infinitesimal, talents who were busily writing in these days just before and just after the Revolution of 1848. With the downfall of Napoleon and the enacting of severely repressive measures by the reactionary princes, no professional direction in important theatres was tolerated. The Royal (or National) Theatre in Berlin, on the death of Iffland, was turned over to a court official, Count Karl Moritz von Bruehl, who with the best will in the world managed to destroy all of his predecessor's work. He built up a bureaucratic régime with scores of clerks and so much red tape that a new building was required to house the complicated clerical machinery. It took so much of Bruehl's time that it ended by his becoming completely divorced from the back-stage end of affairs. It was necessary for him to hire a professional director to do the work he might have been expected to do if it had not been beneath the dignity of a nobleman. However the professional director no longer had sufficient authority to make decisions and naturally lost interest in his work. For that reason the state theatres, for a long time, amounted to very little in an artistic way. Their financial losses were borne by the state, or by the king, or by some princeling. Yet all these theatres had to be supplied with plays because they could not repeat their old repertory indefinitely. This afforded an opportunity to many mediocrities, who could and would work under an intellectually stultifying censorship.

Some writers managed to thrive on it. One who was prolific in the Vienna of his time was JOHANN NESTROY (1802-62), whose farces were played all over Germany. He piled absurdity upon absurdity and drew his humor from the most far-fetched impersonations. He parodied the work of others and his writing was pointed, though not sufficiently to be called true satire. One of his plays served as a basis for Thornton Wilder's *The Merchant of Yonkers*, in 1938. Weighted down by cumbersome direction at the hands of Max Reinhardt, the play was an undeserved failure. The most successful of Nestroy's plays was *Lumpacivagabundus*, with its story of two ingenues wearing pants and enjoying adventures as vagabonds in taverns, a typical device of the time.

Another Viennese writer of this period was Franz Joseph Freiherr von Muench-Bellinghausen, who wrote under the pseudonym of FRIEDRICH HALM (1806-71). At this time the principal theatres would present only the kind of drama which was considered "artistic." Folkdrama and plays in dialect were banished from the leading theatres. Of all those who wooed the Hellenic ideal, the most successful in securing productions for his plays (for this group did not have a very firm grip on dramaturgy) was Halm. His first play, *Griseldis* (1834); his most influential drama, *Der Sohn der Wildnis* (*The Son of the Wilderness*, 1842); the hollow and patriotic *Fechter von Ravenna* (*The Swordsman of Ravenna*, 1854); and a play in which the heroine is brought up as a boy without anyone suspecting it, *Wildfeuer* (*Wildfire*, 1863) are his best work. Though his plays were trivial he did have the ability, through the insertion of a lyric passage or by some happy turn of plot, to give the whole thing a fillip which was pleasing to Austro-German audiences. SOLOMON HERMANN RITTER VON MOSENTHAL (1821-77), another of the Viennese group, wrote one of the most popular and successful plays of the nineteenth century in *Deborah* (1848). The title role in this plea for self-mastery and tolerance fascinated many actresses and kept the play alive longer than its slight literary merits could have done.

CHRISTIAN FRIEDRICH HEBBEL (1813-63) was the leading dramatist of the mid-nineteenth century. His was the only considerable talent to arise between Goethe and Hauptmann. His very first play, *Judith* (written in 1839, and acted in Berlin, July 6, 1840), showed few if any marks of immaturity. His study of the Biblical story retains little more than the outline of its original. He was interested in the psychology of a young widow who has heard of the sexual prowess of Holofernes and who persuades herself that she can save her people by giving herself to him. After the experience, she realizes that no noble motive had inspired her action, but her own personal and physical need. In a sense it was the first modern German drama in its psychological approach to a problem of motive. *Genoveva* (1840-41) is still in the somewhat romantic tradition of his first drama but it takes a modern approach toward the problem of the wife unjustly suspected of infidelity. *Der Diamant* (1841) was one of his minor pieces and small preparation for his most important play, *Maria Magdalena* (1844). This is a tragedy of the lower middle-class, which can be more bigoted than any other when its sense of moral values is violated. The betrayed girl, Clara, has yielded to her fiancé and not to a nobleman, so there is no raising of class distinction as was customary in plays of seduction. It was a problem of family pride and a father already broken by his son's false arrest for theft. Knowing that she is going to have a child, abandoned by her lover who wants to avoid any connection with a family with a prison record, and with her dowry gone to aid an old friend of her father's who has had bad luck, Clara drowns herself. This play is the real beginning of naturalism in the German theatre.

Trauerspiel in Sizilien (*Sicilian Tragedy*, 1846) and *Julia* (1846), which was in part a reflection of Clara's tragedy, did little to raise his reputation. The latter play has slight hints of the coming social drama and was intended to portray conditions of the middle-class in Italy before the Revolution of 1848. His *Herodes und Mariamne* (*Herod and Mariamne*, 1847-48) was written because Herod lived at a turning point of history when two great points of view clashed. It was this that interested him in the subject. He saw his opportunity of taking the theme of the jealous husband and the wife whose love means sacrifice of self and so depicting in graphic fashion the contrasts between the old Jewish religion and the new Christianity. This play was acted in several cities outside of New York, in 1938, by Katharine Cornell and Fritz Kortner, but dissatisfaction with translation and production compelled them to abandon the play before it was played in New York.

Then came *Der Rubin* (*The Ruby*, 1849), which masqueraded as an eastern fairy-tale, and *Michel Angelo* (1850), which was concerned with the rights of the individual artist in his struggle with the communal mass. In 1851 came the play which many think was the most beautiful of his tragedies, *Agnes Bernauer*. It is the story of a woman whose great beauty is her crime because it causes the heir of the state to fall in love with her and to put his personal interests before those of the people he must serve as ruler. The reigning Duke, his father, orders her death, though he knows she is innocent of conscious ill-doing, because he realizes that the death of the individual will be for the good of society as a whole. This was the conclusion of the theme which Hebbel had begun in *Michel Angelo*.

Gyges und sein Ring (*Gyges and His Ring*, 1854) was a retelling of the story, in Herodotus' history, of the Queen of Lydia whose husband exposed her beauty unadorned. Then came the trilogy, *Die Nibelungen* (1855-1862), based on the German legends that have attracted many dramatists, including Fouqué, Raupach, and Richard Wagner, who had but recently completed his music dramas. Hebbel undertook this series of plays because he wanted to bring the "great national epic dramatically nearer to the public" without adding anything to it himself. Like Schiller, he was writing a *Demetrius* (1855-63), when he died leaving the drama incomplete. Hebbel made a definite contribution to German national drama and brought it many steps along the path toward the present day conception of playwriting.

OTTO LUDWIG (1813-65) might possibly have attained the rank of Hebbel had it not been for his self-mistrust. He was always working at his technique, trying to improve it, instead of writing plays. That the beautiful could become still more beautiful if only you were to work at it long enough, was his thesis. At the same time, he sought the utmost in realism because he wanted to be faithful to the truth. This he carried out in his first play to be acted, *Der Erbfoerster (The Forester*, written 1845-49, acted 1853). In this case the victim of circumstance is driven to crime not by fate, as in the plays of Werner and Muellner, but through a decision made by himself. In this Ludwig was obviously influenced by *Othello* and by his great admiration for Shakespeare. He chose the story of Leah and Naomi for *Die Makkabaeer. (The Maccabees*, 1854), which was structurally weak and failed to realize its author's intention. These two were his only finished plays, though he left several others on which he had been working for years without ever bringing them to a point at which he was willing to entrust them to the stage or to print. This is but another evidence of that fatal inner indecision which characterized his whole literary life and blocked his writings.

Before embarking on the Saxe-Meiningen venture, which grew in part out of Charles Kean's Shakespearean revivals in London at the Princess Theatre, we must mention a fresh writing talent in the Austrian theatre. LUDWIG ANZENGRUBER (1839-89) revitalized folk and dialect-plays when they were scorned in all of the principal theatres. He realized that there was a value in colloquial speech for the unsophisticated if you could only contrive a language which would be understood in various parts of the country while still retaining the rustic flavor. This he succeeded in doing, though he was nearly at the end of his life before the critics and the best theatres perceived it.

Before depression settled on the world after the First World War, it was impossible to get a play accepted in European repertoire, or to rent a Shaftesbury Avenue or Broadway Playhouse no matter how much money you had, if the theatrical "upper crust" felt your work would endanger the prestige of the theatre. 1930 changed all that, but in the eighteen seventies and eighties, when Anzengruber was doing his principal work, the stage was snobbish. His plays had no great literary merit then or now, but in their day they definitely had something to contribute. We probably shall never know how many talents have been deliberately cold-shouldered by this attitude. Today it is often a fear of "box office trouble," as Broadway so succinctly puts it, the fear that a play may neither make money nor pay for its production.

Der Pfarrer von Kirchfeld (*The Priest of Kirchfield*, 1870), Anzengruber's first play, was written when the Vatican Council of 1870 had promulgated the doctrine of papal infallibility, which stirred controversy in Catholic Austria. The thoughtful priest in this drama won immediate acclaim; and the question of rebellion against the Church attracted the author in his companion piece, *Die Kreuzelschreiber* (*The Cross Signers*, 1872), which was a merry comedy with serious implications. The village radical has persuaded many of the illiterate peasants to make their mark (sign their cross) to a petition which annoyed the priest. Their wives, under the priest's influence, declared a cessation of marital relations until the men made a solemn pilgrimage to Rome to ask forgiveness for their sin. "Sleep in the hayloft or go to Rome" was the alternative in this variation of the *Lysistrata* story. Anzengruber wrote numerous other plays during his nearly twenty years of productivity, once he had given up the idea that he must write the formal drama expected of playwrights contributing to the leading theatres. Perhaps his best works were *Der Doppelselbstmord* (*Double Suicide*, 1875), a variation of the *Romeo and Juliet* story in peasant setting, and *Das vierte Gebot* (*The Fourth Commandment*, 1877), which was a realistic drama and an attack on hypocrisy. The precept "Honor thy father and thy mother" becomes a mockery when the children are sacrificed to the veniality and outrightful sinfulness of the older generation. In this, as in other plays of Viennese life, Anzengruber does not spare the feelings of his audience, which enhances his value as a dramatist, perhaps, but did not make contemporary Austrians comfortable in the playhouse.

Simultaneously with the resurgence of peasant-drama and Anzengruber's excursions into urban drama, there were numerous other writers who wooed their public with middle-class comedies, farces, and the more literary type of play. The names of most of them have perished but a single farce, *Der Bibliothekar* (*The Librarian*, 1878) by GUSTAV VON MOSER (1825-1903) still remains in repertory. Its honest fun won it success, though its literary merits are about on a par with Brandon Thomas' *Charley's Aunt*, that perennial favorite of the English stage. (Popular belief contends that *Charley's Aunt* has been acted continuously since its première in 1893, and now, at the beginning of the season of 1940-41, a new revival is one of the reigning hits on Broadway.

GEORGE II, DUKE OF SAXE-MEININGEN (1826-1914) undertook to free the German stage of the absurdity of solo acting in dead center at the footlights, with mob scenes looking like present day chorus-work at the Metropolitan Opera House. Kean and some of the others may have gotten off on the wrong foot, so to speak, with their overly academic staging, but the conception of staging that went beyond the operatic aria was a revolutionary change. It may be recalled that Schroeder had some conception of ensemble acting, but those slight beginnings were to flower under the innovations of the German duke. He reduced the power of the star, introduced "the collective personality of the group," and established historical accuracy in staging. Costumes and scenery designed by such men as Lieberman and Israel emerged from the rag-bag of stock sets and standardized costume to which they had degenerated from the great days of *décor* in the seventeenth and eighteenth centuries. By that it is not meant that the earlier periods had provided authenticity, or even suitable backgrounds for dramatic action, but they had supplied what was just as important: a beauty which stimulated the imagination of the spectator. The inappropriateness of their costuming was proverbial, but it at least adhered to a high aesthetic standard which the first three-quarters of the nineteenth century reduced to a mockery.

Saxe-Meiningen, in lowering the importance of the individual actor and creating ensemble acting, as we understand the term, brought the stage director to the fore. From that day to this, the power of the director has increased until with Meyerhold, Piscator, and their followers the world over, he has over-reached himself. We are now in a period of establishing a new balance, which re-admits the intelligent actor to participation in the planning of production. This, of course, can be said to have come out of the actors' theatre, the great Moscow Art Theatre. Ten years ago we thought perhaps we had been wrong in allowing the actor so much power, but now we know we were right in the first instance, *if* the actor has the intelligence and artistic ability to equal or surpass the dramatist and *régisseur*.

The Meiningen Players (or Meiningers as they were often called),

between 1874 and 1890, visited nine countries and sowed their seed
in thirty-eight cities. America learned of them mainly by hearsay and
through actors, producers and designers who had been influenced by
their work. At the magnificent theatre exhibition held by the Museum
of Modern Art in New York in 1924 (and subsequently shown in
part to many of the principal cities of the United States), we had an
opportunity to examine at first hand many of the costumes and scene
designs for their epoch-making productions.

Julius Caesar, in May 1874, inaugurated the new régime and
European audiences felt that they had never seen the play before as
its dramatic values emerged in a three-dimensional staging. They had
learned not only from Kean, through the visit of their critic-adviser,
Bodenstedt, to London; but from Wagner's synthesis of the arts, and
from the strong spirit of communism in Russian thought to which
Bodenstedt had also been subjected. To such Shakespearean productions as *Twelfth Night* and *A Winter's Tale*, they added Schiller's
Die Raeuber, *Fiesco*, *Die Jungfrau von Orleans* and above all, *Wallenstein* (one of their most successful productions) to round out their
repertory. Ibsen, Björnson, Tolstoi and Echegaray also contributed to
their success. By 1890, however, they had done their work. Stanislavski
and Nemirovitch-Danchenko, in Moscow, had seen them and Antoine,
who observed them when they played in Brussels, was entranced by
their performances. Their final financial failure and disbanding in
Odessa was an anti-climax but their influence is still at work in the
world.

RICHARD WAGNER (1813-83) was an innovator in more than music.
He was a dramatist, lighting expert, designer and choreographer. He
believed in the universality of art and that only through returning
to the first principles of the theatre as a great synthetic force, as in
the time of the Greeks, could we make full use of its limitless powers.
Stimulation of the imagination is one of the most potent influences in
the world at any time. Those who would separate the theatre into
narrow compartments of drama (how the academicians like to pin
the theatre down to the printed page), staging, designing, incidental
music, or solo acting, destroy one of the greatest social influences for
good which exists. The theatre is a universal language which should
never be forgotten and at no time in the world's history have we had
more need of remembering it than at the moment these words are
being set down on paper.

Wagner understood this. Like the Greeks he also understood the
value of utilizing the mythology and religion of his country from
its most ancient times. For this, perhaps more than anything else,

(though it can lead people into false conclusions as the present government of Germany clearly demonstrates) caused him to be understood and revered in his own country, when the academic mind still thought his music-dramas ugly and harsh. Even a good thing can be carried too far, however, and Wagner has become a cult with many who have no real understanding of the basic principles on which his art was based.

Wagner found an interpreter in ADOLPHE APPIA (1862-1928), born in the French-speaking portion of Switzerland, who twelve years after the composer's death produced *La mise en scène du drame Wagnérien* (1895), with eighteen designs for the great music dramas. Perhaps no one has understood Wagner scenically, even the composer himself, as well as the mystic Appia. He developed his theories further in *Die Musik und die Inscenierung* (1899). His settings seem to dissolve into air as they near the horizon of the cyclorama through his use of light as a constructive part of design. The third dimension and hints of a fourth are defined in his shading off, as well as in his intensification of light. No one in the theatre, perhaps, has recognized more completely the power of light as an element of design. Long overshadowed by his well-publicized follower, Gordon Craig, Appia has received little but praise in the twelve years since his death. This recognition has been led by that fine designer, able writer and coiner of pungent phrases, Lee Simonson, who can carry a torch with the best of them once his highly critical intelligence is convinced. It is interesting that Appia's art, which was a synthesis of music, light, and form, should develop almost simultaneously with naturalism, which was the antithesis of everything for which he stood. Unlike Craig, however, his designs could readily be adapted to the practical theatre.

Immediately before the era of naturalism, had come a chauvinistic resurgence of nationalism, which began with *Sturm und Drang* and revived with Young Germany. The emergence of Prussia as the leader of Germany through the Prusso-Danish War of 1864 and the Austro-Prussian War of 1866 culminated in the establishment of a new German Empire in Paris, after the defeat of Napoleon III in the Franco-Prussian War of 1870. This had produced its effect on the literature of the country and ERNST VON WILDENBRUCH (1845-1909) won the vocal expression of thanks from Kaiser Wilhelm I for his devotion to Prussia's great past and the need for national unity, expressed in his plays.

In May 1881, the Meiningen Players produced his *Die Karolinger* (*The Carolingians*). This won his audience as well as the Emperor because his poetic flights blinded them to the essential weakness of his structure. His plays were numerous and mostly in praise of Hohen-zollern exploits. Though sympathetic German critics deny their servility, they seem uncommonly like flag-waving, particularly *Die Quitzows* (1888), *Der Generalfeldoberst* (*The Commander-in-Chief*, 1889) and *Der neue Herr* (1891). His most interesting drama was *Das neue Gebot* (*The New Commandment*, 1886) in which he made an effort to establish connection with the modern naturalist move-ment. This drama so revolted the average Berlin managers that it had to be performed in a suburban house, where it ran for more than a hundred performances. It dealt with a Roman priest who, with the coming of Christianity, found that by the teachings of the Church his wife, with whom he was very much in love, must be considered his mistress. In *Die Haubenlerche* (*The Crested Lark*, 1891), Wilden-bruch wrote in the Berlin dialect of the city poor, but it was in the old style of historical drama that he was most successful in the popu-lar theatre.

Saxe-Meiningen might undertake reforms in staging and improve the technique of the theatre, but the repertory of the theatres needed modernizing. He had brought in foreign dramatists, who were a part of the naturalist movement, or who were closely allied to it, but the serious encouragement of native dramatists did not come from his playhouse. It remained for the so-called "free stages" to do that, in-spired by the revolutionary work of Antoine and his *Théâtre Libre* in Paris, the great naturalistic novels of Zola, the critical encourage-ment of the Goncourt brothers, and the novels of Flaubert.

The scholarly OTTO BRAHM (1856-1912), with Theodor Wolff and Maximilian Harden, organized the *Freie Buehne* (Free Stage), which was a subscription organization like the *Théâtre Libre*, and so escaped the rigors of German police censorship. The commercial managers were not interested in the new drama because they believed (prob-ably quite rightly) that it would annoy and bore their bourgeois au-diences. The police would permit nothing to be performed which might be taken as a criticism of the status quo and under no circum-stances was anyone to be offended.

This was the situation when the *Freie Buehne* opened its doors on September 29, 1889 with Ibsen's *Ghosts*. The choice of this play was characteristic of Brahm, its first director, who later was to write an informative, critical treatise on Ibsen. He was to become the foremost exponent of naturalism among the theatre managers and directors of Germany. Comparatively his position was that of David Belasco in this country and similar to that of Antoine in France and Stanislavski in Russia. His critical and literary background was excellent and he had even received a Ph.D. degree in 1879, before launching forth as a drama critic and spokesman for the realistic work of Anzengruber, Ibsen, and Björnson. When he became a producer he built up a fine company of naturalistic actors with whom he worked in the greatest harmony. One of the most distinguished acting talents to be brought out by him was that of Albert Bassermann, who went on to triumph after triumph, most recently in American films.

Naturalism sought as violently as had the romantic movement, to break with the formalized theatre which did not permit the representation of life as it really is. Abnormality in human conduct, the lives of the proletariat, crime, and disease became subjects for drama. This was the substance of naturalism and became closely interwoven with the artistic side of this movement, which is reflected in natural speech and integration of character. There will always be division between those who are mostly concerned with the sociological aspects of drama and those who are interested primarily in artistry. Brieux and the thesis play are at the opposite end of the scale from Chekhov and Hauptmann, who combined sociological materials with the achievement of beauty in the theatre.

Because there was no place for naturalism in the commercial theatre, play-producing societies were formed. The *Freie Buehne* performed an important service in producing Hauptmann's *Vor Sonnenaufgang* (*Before Sunrise*, 1889), thus giving to Germany its first great modern dramatist. It must not be thought that the society encountered nothing but hostility from those already established, for Emanuel Reicher emerged as its active champion, as did the fine actress Agnes Sorma. Enthusiasm rose high with the establishment by Julius and Heinrich Hart, Michael Georg Conrad, Karl Bleibtreu, and others, of a new movement called *Juengstdeutschland* (Youngest Germany), named for the earlier movement. This group of writers helped largely in a critical fashion with the creation of literary and dramatic journals to assist the cause. Oskar Blumenthal, director of the *Lessing Theater*, offered the use of his theatre for performances, which was accepted.

That the *Freie Buehne* lasted for less than three seasons was due to the fact that there were few naturalist dramas to perform, but the impetus toward a free theatre had been auspiciously inaugurated. The *Freie Volksbuehne* (*Free People's Stage*) was established by Bruno Wille, in 1890, and continued as a social-democratic theatre (in 1908 it had 12,000 subscribers). Many of these experimental producing organizations were established throughout Germany and Austria. Some of them were amateur societies which either perished or advanced to professionalism, particularly in Berlin, Munich and Vienna. Wille also founded the *Neue Freie Buehne* (New Free Stage) in 1892. Despite attempted police interference it managed to survive until 1933, though it almost ended when it staged *Die Weber.* In 1914 it had 50,000 subscribers. Not long before that it had merged with the *Freie Volksbuehne.* A new *Volksbuehne* now functions which has no labor union or democratic connections.

With the encouragement of the *Freie Buehne* GERHART HAUPT-MANN (1862-1946) was launched on a career which was to distinguish him as one of the world's greatest humanitarian dramatists. (He is reputed to have been the model of the renegade dramatist in S. N. Behrman's *Rain from Heaven,* who deserts the liberal cause in the face of German National Socialism.) He early joined the ranks of the *Freie Buehne,* which was to produce his first play in 1889. Somewhat under the influence of Anzengruber, his naturalism shocked many of the critics and provoked a riot at the première of his first play. He was called both a saviour and an anarchist, types usually not too far removed from each other.

Before Hauptmann had a second play to offer to the group, they had presented Tolstoi's *The Power of Darkness* with great success, following that with Anzengruber's *Das vierte Gebot,* which had not yet been staged in Berlin. The veteran playwright was invited to attend but was too ill and died a few days after the performance.

Then came the play which had an enormous influence on the development of naturalism in Germany, though nothing that its authors, Arno Holz and Johannes Schlaf, did subsequently had any lasting value. *Die Familie Selicke* (*The Happy Family,* 1890) is the pathetic story of a girl, whose father is a drunkard, and whose mother adores her younger sister, a dying child. The older girl is in love with Toni, a young divinity student, whom she hopes to marry. The sick child dies and, in the absence of any moral support from her husband, the mother transfers her affection to the remaining daughter. Realizing that she is the spiritual prop of the household, the girl breaks off her engagement, or rather postpones it to some day in the nebulous future. The play's very simplicity and naturalness, as well as its expert depiction of character, are its most engaging qualities. It had great influence at the time, and even in the present day Gustav Eckstein's *Christmas Eve* (1939) has marked similarities both of plot and mood.

Gerhart Hauptmann's second play *Das Friedensfest* (*The Festival of Peace,* 1890) closed the first season of the *Freie Buehne.* This study of heredity and melancholy bordering closely on insanity suggests Ibsen with whom Hauptmann's name is often associated. The next season the society performed Strindberg's *The Father,* and Anzengruber's *Der Doppelselbstmord* among other plays, as well as Hauptmann's *Einsame Menschen* (*Lonely Lives,* 1891). This was one of his most important plays and is said to be the last to show Ibsen's influence, though there are traces in later dramas. It is a play of religious doubt in which a man seeking the truth is enveloped by a world which destroys him and a love which is maladjusted. Ludwig Lewisohn in his *The Modern Drama* (1915) compares it in detail with Ibsen's *Rosmersholm* which he feels has striking similarities. This German play was one of the early productions of the Moscow Art Theatre.

In 1892 the play, *Die Weber* (*The Weavers,* 1893) was denied performance at the *Deutsches Theater* (with which the *Freie Buehne* was later to merge, in 1894, Brahm becoming director of both until 1905, when Reinhardt succeeded him at the *Deutsches*). The society rallied to Hauptmann's support and offered the play as a special production though they were no longer giving regular performances. The need for them to function constantly had passed as the commercial playhouses became willing to produce modern dramas.

L'Arronge staged *Einsame Menschen* at the *Deutsches Theater* (built about 1884 as a rival to the *Théâtre Français*) not long after its try-out. This producer had inherited his classical and historical productions from the Meiningen Players. The soundness of this inheritance was eventually to pass into the hands of Brahm, and some of it to the neo-romantic Reinhardt in the course of time.

The crowd is the hero in Hauptmann's *Die Weber,* a play of the workers, which is the best known abroad of Hauptmann's dramas, both for production and reading. Its characters are compelling down to the least part, even those without lines being well-defined. It has been called one of the world's great revolutionary plays. In his *Iconoclasts* (1905), James Huneker, the American critic, said, "*The Weavers* was a quivering transcript from life—and such life! Germany took fire from the blaze of the dramatist's generous wrath. Socialism or anarchy, what you will, were swallowed up in the presentment of this veracious document of wretched lives. . . . He paints the picture; his audience finds the indictment. Here is a new German art at last."

In his depiction of poverty and the brutalization of the Silesian peasants in *Die Weber* and *Hannele* or *Hanneles Himmelfahrt* (*The Assumption of Hannele,* 1893), Hauptmann's people are remarkably close to the Georgia crackers of *Tobacco Road,* as Anita Block shrewdly pointed out in her excellent study of social theatre in *The Changing World in Plays and Theatre* (1939). Despite the naturalism of the background of this study of terrified adolescence, *Hannele* was at least a tentative venture from his previous style into romanticism. *Florian Geyer* (1895) was a drama of the Peasants' War, which had little success when first produced. But since the First World War it has been acclaimed, particularly in Reinhardt's massive production at the *Grosse Schauspielhaus* in 1920. *Fuhrmann Henschel* (*Teamster Henschel*, 1898) was a bleak, fatalistic peasant drama of unrelieved naturalism. In contrast to this was the poetic and timeless *Die versunkene Glocke* (*The Sunken Bell*, 1896). In this fairy-tale like drama in verse is the allegory of man's struggle between domesticity and artistic freedom, which may have been a reflection of the author's unhappy first marriage.

Michael Kramer (1900) was the tragedy of a father's failure to understand his son. The boy's repression by his parents drives him out of the house to a cafe where he falls in love with the daughter of the owner and is rebuffed by her and mocked, in her presence, by the loafers. This is the last blow. He kills himself, leaving his father to find comfort in the fact that the worst possible thing has happened to him, but with still no understanding of the boy in his heart.

Rose Berndt (1903) was another tragedy of the peasant class. This time it was the tragedy of a girl with three admirers, a meek one whom her father favors, a married man to whom she is attracted, and a farm laborer who desires her. She yields herself to the married man and is detected in the act by the farmhand, who blackmails her into becoming his mistress as well. Rose strangles her babe in the fields, when it is born, rather than let it grow up to endure, from love, what its mother has suffered. This highly effective drama has moved audiences in many countries. It ranked as one of Arthur Hopkins' best productions when he staged it with Ethel Barrymore in New York, in 1922, though it achieved little more than a *succès d'estime*. Hauptmann repeats the theme on a higher social plane in his *Dorothea Angermann* (1926).

Of the dozen other plays he has written, perhaps the most important is *Gabriel Schillings Flucht* (*The Flight of Gabriel Schilling*, 1912), wherein the artist Gabriel seeks death to avoid the endless claims of his wife and mistress after they have pursued him to the island where he has gone to seek freedom for his work. In recent years Hauptmann has turned more and more to the novel for expression and has achieved, perhaps, as great success in that medium as he has in the drama. Certainly he is the finest German dramatist since Goethe and his plays have weathered the winds of time more satisfactorily than those of any other dramatist of this period.

Unlike Hauptmann, the fame of HERMANN SUDERMANN (1857-1932) has declined with the years. Almost all of his best work was done by 1900 and since then his reputation has diminished in his own country as well as in the rest of the world. There is a tendency to dismiss him as one does Pinero, which is definitely a mistake, for Sudermann's early naturalistic plays contributed a great deal to the development of drama in Germany. Notwithstanding his limitations he had high aims, whereas the English dramatist was a Shaftesbury Avenue writer with all that that implies. Sudermann was a successful publicist for naturalism. His semi-naturalistic plays persuaded the German public of the worth of the whole movement.

His first play *Die Ehre* (*Honor*, 1889) concerned itself with two families, one of the lower and one of the upper middle-class, showing the influence of Ibsen as well as of the apostles of the well-made play, Augier and Dumas *fils*. Its ending however was contrived and far from honest. That was one of Sudermann's greatest weaknesses. If his characters did not develop along the lines of plot which he considered appropriate, he bent them to his way of thinking, ruthlessly disregarding their natural growth. His situations were usually naturalistic but he falsified them to suit his conception of public taste.

Sodoms Ende (*The Destruction of Sodom*, 1890) directed attention to the corruption existing in upper middle-class circles in Berlin. A young artist is destroyed by the lust of a banker's wife, so that he loses all his sense of values and begins to corrupt others. The play ends on the weak note of the natural death (through a hemorrhage) of the young man, Willy. The principal character never convinces us of his charm however, so that his corruption and destruction fail to move us.

His third play is the one for which Sudermann is best remembered because it had an enormous success wherever it was played, though now it is recognized as shoddy stuff. *Die Heimat* (*Magda*, 1893) was blessed with an excellent starring part in the strong-willed Magda, daughter of an army officer, who rejects the proposal of a clergyman whom her father favors. When he insists, she leaves home and goes to Berlin, where she becomes a singer. While there she has a child by a man who deserts her. She is selected as the soloist for a music festival in her home town and enjoys herself thoroughly while she ridicules the local Mrs. Grundies. Her father learns that the man who betrayed her was the local councillor, Keller, and insists on their marriage. When Magda hears that the child may not be allowed to join them, for the protection of Keller's local reputation, she declines the offer. Enraged, her irascible father threatens to kill both her and himself, but has an apoplectic stroke before he can carry out his threat. It was obviously Sudermann's intent to dramatize the struggle between the old and the young, but he chose melodramatic means to do it. The play abounds in what were called "strong situations," and was a favorite starring vehicle for Mrs. Patrick Campbell, Modjeska, Bernhardt and Duse, whom the author admired above all.

Of his other early plays, the most outstanding was *Es Lebe das Leben* (*The Joy of Living*, 1902), which repeated the *Magda* theme in a more distinguished society and with a finer type of woman. Certainly the character of the Countess Beata interested the author most, but he did present a really good picture of the German upper-class *Das Glueck im Winkel* (*The Vale of Content*, also known as *Happiness in a Corner*, 1896) argued the comparative values of altruism and individualism. This play recalls Ibsen's *Lady from the Sea* by the touching way in which a really fine man wins back his wife's love through his tolerance and complete understanding of her motives. The play had its first performance at the *Lessing Theater*, Berlin, in April, 1896.

Sudermann's comedies are not so well remembered, but the broad social humors of *Der Sturmgeselle Sokrates* (*Storm Brother Socrates*, 1903) are extremely amusing. This is a gay satire on the old man who belonged to the Liberal movement, preceding the Revolution of 1848, who forty years later are still meeting in secret and attacking the government which they have brought about, after a fashion.

We have called Sudermann a contact-man for naturalism with the average German public, which is true, but we must not lose sight of the fact that beyond the choice of much of his subject matter, he was influenced more by the well-made play in France than he was by the naturalistic sources in his own country which inspired Hauptmann and Wedekind. Sudermann was primarily a man of the theatre and his plays reflect the fads and fancies in Germany quite as aptly as Pinero in England and de Curel, Lavedan and Bataille in France.

Sudermann had a long list of followers, in Germany, who came into the theatre just as the staging techniques were changing and the names of such new producers as Max Reinhardt and Leopold Jessner were beginning to be known. It was a time of ferment in the theatre when Germany was forging to the front, even into the advance guard, of the new techniques of staging and dramaturgy.

LUDWIG FULDA (1862-1939) wrote both comedies and dramas in a pseudo-naturalistic style. In *Talisman* (1892) he satirized Wilhelm II and his efforts at personal rule; *Kameraden* (*Comrades*, 1894) laughs at the New Woman; *Das verlorene Paradies* (*The Lost Paradise*, 1890) was a naturalistic drama of class conflict; *Herostrat* (1898) was his most ambitious effort, being a verse tragedy of ancient Greece, a highly rhetorical effort and a failure.

KARL HAUPTMANN (1858-1921) was the younger brother of Gerhart and wrote naturalistic dramas in a somewhat similar fashion which dealt with a burning love for the soil and the ownership of land as well as with sexual passion. *Ephraims Breite* (*Ephraim's Heiress*, 1898) celebrates peasant ownership; *Die lange Jule* (*Tall Jule*, 1913) dealt with a similar subject, complicated in this instance with sexual yearnings; *Krieg, ein Tedeum* (*War—A Te Deum*, 1914) was an allegory in which the symbolism seems as remote as in some of the plays of Andreyev and Evreinov.

MAX HALBE (1865-1944) has a real command of dramatic structure which is shown in his many dramas of mental struggle. *Emporkoemmm-ling* (*The Self-Made Man*, 1889) is not unlike the theme of Haupt-mann's *Michael Kramer*. In each the stubborn, unbending father drove his sensitive son to suicide. These unbending fathers, who used to be a stock in trade in Anglo-Saxon drama, have gone out of fashion with their originals, but their barbarism seems to have been retained longer in Germany. *Jugend* (*Youth*, 1893) was a tender and understanding study of adolescence among the Poles and Germans in East Prussia. The natural political antagonisms enter into the lives of the young lovers, who are thus destroyed by heredity. *Mutter Erde* (*Mother Earth*, 1897) is a sympathetic study of the New Woman who gives up her husband to his childhood sweetheart because he has a right to freedom of choice in modern marriage, as she understands it. After yielding to each other in ecstasy, the lovers commit suicide and so presumably return to Mother Earth. *Der Strom* (*The Stream*, 1903) and *Der Eisgang* (*The Ice Drift*, 1892) have much in common. Both of these dramas have to do with ownership of property and its at-tendant problems, resolved in each instance through accidental death by drowning. The endings are not contrived but proceed realistically from the plot premise.

GEORG HIRSCHFELD (1873-   ) was a stout adherent of naturalism, which brought him fame in his own country, though his reputation has not spread much abroad. His one-acter *Zu Hause* (*At Home*, 1896) created a strong impression with his study of a man who is trapped in a hopeless and inescapable environment. *Die Muetter* (*The Mothers*, 1896) is a study of the problems which arise in a family when the prodigal artist son returns bringing his lower-class mistress with him. Faced with the Jewish background from which he has sprung, she realizes that marriage between them is out of the question, and leaves him without telling him that she is bearing his child. The third play for which Hirschfeld is well known (his later comedies are not important) is *Agnes Jordan* (1898). This was a panoramic family drama of the type which Arnold Bennett and Edward Knob-lock popularized in *Milestones* and which Noel Coward broadened into a patriotic spectacle, *Cavalcade*, for the huge Drury Lane.

Education and school life have been favorite subjects in modern German drama and we find the abuses of the system attacked in many plays. There are also those sentimental or romantic plays, with school or university backgrounds, which are supposed to fill their audiences with nostalgia. Among writers of this latter type, the best known is

WILHELM MEYER-FOERSTER (1862-1934) with *Alt Heidelberg* (*Old Heidelberg*, 1901), which Richard Mansfield popularized in America. In its musical version *The Student Prince* (1924), under the aegis of the brothers Shubert, it has been played almost constantly for fifteen years throughout the United States.

Two playwrights of North Germany, MAX DREYER (1862-   ) and OTTO ERNST SCHMIDT (1862-1926) turned out serious plays on the school subject. Dreyer's *Der Probekandidat* (*The Practice Teacher*, 1899) dealt with a young teacher who runs afoul of the anti-Darwin views of his bigoted superiors, and who must conceal his knowledge of biology and his belief in evolution in order to retain his position. This recalls America's famous Scopes' trial in Tennessee, not so many years ago. Ernst Schmidt wrote two plays directed against reactionary principles in education, *Jugend von Heute* (*Youth Today*, 1899) and *Flachsmann als Erzieher* (*Flachsmann as Teacher*, also known as *Master Flachsmann*, 1900).

The problem plays of naturalism fortunately were leavened by several humorous writers including Otto Erich Hartleben (1864-1905), Ludwig Thoma (1867-1921), and CARL STERNHEIM (1881-1943), who was the most important. Hartleben wrote plays which combined seriousness with satire as in *Die Erziehung zur Ehe* (*Education for Marriage*, 1893) and in *The Moral Demand* (1897). His *Angèle* (1891) is entirely frivolous. Ludwig Thoma is probably best known for his satire, *Moral* (1908), which tells the merry tale of the female proprietor of a house of ill fame who is arrested. But her books carry the names of most of the important and respectable citizens of the city, so that the case is hastily dropped and the books destroyed. His *Die Lokalbahn* (*The Local Railway*, 1902) is an ironic comedy of small-town life with a turncoat mayor and a set of stupid burghers.

Carl Sternheim is a caricaturist of bourgeois social customs which aroused his cynicism as to the motives of the middle-class world. Comedy after comedy attested to his distrust and detestation of the artificialities of a society which countenanced hypocrisy, snobbishness, and materialism. He wrote a cycle of satires on this subject, which were known as *Bilder aus dem buergerlichen Heldenleben* (*Pictures of Middle-Class Heroes*, 1908-13). The first of these was *Die Hose* (*The Trousers*), which ridiculed romantic notions in a tale of the loss of a respectable wife's drawers. *Die Kassette* (*The Treasure Chest*) reveals bourgeois avarice, even where family dishonor is involved. *Buerger Schippel* (*Burgher Schippel*) is about a social climber who is a first rate opportunist and succeeds because of his complete lack of scruples. Actually the man came from the proletariat so that it is his middle-class aspirations which Sternheim attacks. *Der Snob* is, as the name implies, the exposure of the ignoble motives and dubious means by which Christian Maske, son of the lady who lost her unmentionables in the earlier play, attains success which, to him, is marriage with an aristocrat. *1913* (1915) is another sequel, depicting the same man, now ennobled, whose daughter marries his socialist secretary immediately after his death. The secretary then discards his leftist views, which is the culmination of the satire. Sternheim wrote a number of other plays including *Oscar Wilde* (1924), which was based on a portion of Frank Harris' biography of the dramatist. He chose some of the same scenes of Wilde's life for dramatization as did Leslie and Sewell Stokes in their *Oscar Wilde* (1937).

Almost simultaneously with this group of North and South German writers, there was growing up in Vienna a school of playwriting headed by ARTHUR SCHNITZLER (1862-1931), who transformed naturalism into realism with the gracefulness of accomplished hands. Trained in the French tradition of the theatre, and like the French being interested in love as a dramatic problem, he wrote highly polished vignettes about casual amours. These cynical pieces are redolent of old Vienna. His other style was that of the artist who writes contemplatively, and in loneliness, of lonely lives. *Anatol* (1893) is entirely characteristic of his first style in his study of love's mutations. Today this cycle of one-act plays still has charm, but it is always the charm of something past, for its humor is faded and its serious notes seem sentimental. Granville-Barker caught its spirit admirably in his translation, or rather adaptation, which he calls *The Affairs of Anatol* (1911).

The serious side of his nature came to the fore in *Liebelei* (*Light o' Love*, 1895). It is the tragedy of the daughter of a humble musician, used for a convenient love affair by the irresponsible Fritz, who is taking refuge for a few weeks from the inconveniences of an intrigue with a fashionable married woman. This brief connection had been advised by a friend because a scandal is threatening in the older affair. Fritz is killed in a duel by the lady's husband. The faithful young Christiane kills herself upon his grave, loving him to the end; unresentful of his defection and the casualness of his feeling towards her.

In *Reigen* (*Hands Around*, 1900) Schnitzler reached as far into naturalism as he was ever to go in his almost clinical treatment of sexual connection. This cycle of ten short two-character plays was not printed, even privately, until 1909, and was aptly termed an "erotic dance of death" by Frank Chandler. It was not staged until 1920 in Vienna and a private performance in New York in 1923 was prevented, though a poor production of it was given in 1926, in Greenwich Village.

Der einsame Weg (*The Lonely Way*, 1901) is the first of the static dramas for which Schnitzler is famous, but which have unfortunately proved of little interest to English and American taste. In this country we are prone to become restless during a slow-moving drama that does not seem to be approaching a definite climax. For that reason many plays fail in this country which deserve thoughtful treatment, and this drama is an example. Perhaps it is our way of living, perhaps it is our national tendency to take mental short cuts, that robs us of much in the theatre, which a little more thoughtfulness might bring to us. *Der einsame Weg* depicts the kind of loneliness which selfishness causes. If you prefer yourself and your own comfort above all else, you can only expect that some day will bring retribution.

Professor Bernhardi (1912) is a far from faultless play about anti-Semitism, which is robbed of much of its force because its author began it with a situation which was insufficient to explain the forces released, and because the conclusion of the play seems ineffectual.

To turn to his one-act plays, Schnitzler is perhaps more satisfactory in this field than in his longer dramas. It is too bad that there is no professional outlet for the short drama in this country, but it is evident that present day audiences do not care for it. Colleges and little theatres are its only outlet and the last ten years have seen a decline even there, except where the study or production of the form is stimulated, as at the University of North Carolina under the inspiring leadership of Frederick H. Koch.

Of course both the *Anatol* and *Reigen* cycles were made up of short dialogues technically called one-act plays. However, Schnitzler wrote many others closer to the type with which we are familiar. *Der gruene Kakadu* (*The Green Cockatoo*, 1899) is a psychological study of the beginnings of the French Revolution on the night of the storming of the Bastille. *Der Schleier der Beatrice* (*Beatrice's Veil*, 1900) is a psychological romance of the Renaissance in five acts.

Lebendige Stunden (*Living Hours*, 1902) is the study of two men who are affected by a woman's death. The older is her former lover, the younger, a poet, is her son. Suffering from a long illness which she realizes is sapping the creative powers of her son, she kills herself so that he may go on writing. The older man tells him about it so that he may measure up to his mother's estimate of him. It is in quiet and contemplative plays of this kind that Schnitzler is at his best. However, many of his one-acters are light comedies such as *Literatur* (1902). Similar in feeling are *Zwischenspiel* (*Intermezzo*, 1905) and *Das Bacchusfest* (*The Festival of Bacchus*, 1915), title play of a series of three one-acters.

Komtesse Mizzi oder der Familientag (*Countess Mitzi*, 1909) deals with a noblewoman who has an illegitimate son by a prince, whom she declines to marry, preferring her freedom in affairs of the heart. However, the sight of the boy at twenty so moves her that she consents to regularize the union and allow the youth his father's name. There are many more of the short pieces for this was perhaps the author's favorite dramatic form.

Schnitzler also wrote many novels, and in the last few years novelettes, which were to fiction what his long one-acters were to drama. His ability to portray character and to establish a mood were two of his strongest characteristics. His medical training and psychiatrical knowledge stood him in good stead, as well as his understanding and appreciation of life. His dramas were mostly static and plot development was evidently not of special interest to him. Though this quality has made some of his best plays unpalatable to the average play-goer in English-speaking countries, it is precisely that quiet nostalgia which attracts the attention and evokes the admiration of his strongest admirers. *Der einsame Weg* establishes a mood and holds its audience enthralled just as surely as *The Cherry Orchard* and other seemingly static plays by Anton Chekhov.

HERMANN BAHR (1863-1934) had wide theatre connections, for in addition to writing eighty plays, he staged productions for the *Freie Buehne;* became director of the *Deutsches Theater* in 1906; founded *Die Zeit*, a Viennese weekly (1892); and wrote dramatic criticism for the *Tageblatt* and the *Volkszeitung* of the Austrian capital.

The single work for which he is known wherever there is a theatre is *Das Konzert* (*The Concert*, 1909). This is a highly entertaining comedy about a great musician who loves his wife and needs her tact and understanding. At the same time he requires love affairs to soothe his vanity. The wife realizes this, and when he pretends that he has a concert at a distant place not on his schedule, she suspects a clandestine meeting with a young woman. Taking the lady's husband with her, she follows them. Then, pretending a love affair of her own, she arouses her husband's jealousy, and happiness is restored to their temperamental household. Contrived, stock stuff you might say, were it not for its genuine wit and the slightly off-color humor of the lines. It has provided a favorite acting part for male stars. In this country, Leo Ditrichstein adapted it and played the lead himself in New York and on the road for several years with great success.

None of Bahr's other plays need concern us save *The Mongrel*, which tells the pathetic story of a roadmender and his mongrel dog. The animal is shot by a forester and the workman goes nearly frantic seeking what he considers justice. His mind becomes affected and he starts to strangle the forester's daughter in an argument over the matter. Coming to himself he is horrified at what he has attempted and flees. He returns and surrenders himself to justice, but the girl declines to bring any charges against him and the judge, deciding, refuses to order punishment. His surprise at this restores balance to the lonely roadman's mind. The play is touching and human. It shows something of the influence of Schnitzler, to whom Bahr was indebted as founder of a school of realism in comedy and drama.

KARL SCHOENHERR (1868-   ), was perhaps chiefly known for *Die Kindertragoedie* (*The Children's Tragedy*, 1919), which tells the story of a woman's affair through the eyes of her three children. This device was subsequently used to fine effect by Leopold Atlas in *Wednesday's Child* and somewhat more stagily by Martin Berkeley and Marie Baumer in *Seen But Not Heard* (1936). It is highly effective when employed with honesty and high purpose.

It is easy to see by this play that Schoenherr was heart and soul a part of the naturalist movement. He has been so inclined from the first when he came from the Tyrol to Vienna to practice medicine. *Sonn-wendtag* (*The Solstice*, 1902) is an anti-clerical drama, and his first play, *Die Bildschnitzer* (*The Carvers*, 1895), a one-act drama, is beautifully written. It deals with a man who deliberately allows himself to die so that his wife and his friend, to whom he owes everything, may be happy. In *Caravan Folk* (1904), a half-starved boy is tempted by a loaf of bread to betray his own father to the police. Remorseful at his act, he kills himself. In *Erde* (*Earth*, 1907), avarice and sardonic humor divide the honors in what has been called Schoenherr's best play. An old peasant, who has dominated his family and kept his fifty-year-old son under his thumb, has his coffin built and keeps it by him (a device also used in Noel Langley's melodrama, *Farm of Three Echoes*) while he pretends he is waiting to die. He watches two girls quarrel over which shall marry his son and get the inheritance. The younger one wins out by getting herself with child. The son is building a cradle but when spring comes, his old father rises out of his bed, smashes the coffin for firewood, and dashes the hopes of his son by his evident intention of living forever.

Of Schoenherr's other plays perhaps the most outstanding is *Der Weibsteufel* (*The She-Devil*, 1914), which involves the sordid situation of an ailing smuggler who persuades his wife to flirt with the customs inspector so as to make things easier for him in his illegal profession. It is not long before she is enjoying the affair and pretense is over. The lover tires first and tries to withdraw from the situation because the husband has grown suspicious and has reported him to the higher officials. The wife is enraged when the inspector is forced to resign. She turns on both men. Plying her lover with drink and dancing wildly with him, she manages to work him up into a rage in which he kills her husband. Thus the woman gets the new house her husband had built from his ill-gotten funds and revenges herself upon both of the men who have humiliated her.

When naturalism passed out of the theatre as a strong dramatic force, the creative energy which had brought it about took several forms. Barely had it been established before Appia, Craig, and others were hard at it trying to remove what they considered abject representationalism. Realism, which had its beginnings in the 1840's in Germany, flowered in the work of such men as Schnitzler and Bahr, to name only those most recently discussed. However, another form taken by the naturalist impetus was the symbolism of Maeterlinck, Andreyev, Meyerhold, Evreinov, and the Austrian HUGO VON HOFMANNSTHAL (1874-1929), who has also been described as a neoromanticist.

Perhaps it would be fairer to say that Hofmannsthal was a follower of Victor Hugo (though D'Annunzio could claim some credit, as could a number of others, for there has scarcely ever been a playwright who clearly showed as many influences as Hofmannsthal). He modelled himself after Sophocles, or so he thought, and for a long time was taken almost at his own estimate of himself. His plays lend themselves to lavish use of color, music and scenic effects, which naturally has delighted designers and *régisseurs* of a certain kind: primarily those who consider a play largely an excuse for a production. Reinhardt has fallen into this error as in the instance of his staging of *Das Spiel von Jedermann* (1912), Hofmannsthal's adaptation of the beautiful English morality play, *Everyman*. Here the short simplicity of the original was more than tripled in length and interlarded with trick theatrical effects. There is no doubt about the great effectiveness of staging the play in front of the cathedral in the baroque little town of Salzburg on the Salzach, most picturesque corner of Austria. When Death calls "Jedermann" from the housetops, from the cathedral towers, from above, from below, the emotional pull made one's scalp prickle. Nevertheless it was this sacrifice of simplicity for theatrical effect that was characteristic of both author and director.

Hofmannsthal was a prolific playwright as well as poet, the latter capacity probably overshadowing the drama in the long run. His work began with a dramatic poem, at seventeen, and he continued to write poems, plays and opera librettos almost until the day of his death. The style of his plays constantly changed and his audiences were hard put to it to keep up with the newest form his work would take. In 1923 he said to Barrett H. Clark, "What my earliest public will never forgive me is my refusing to repeat myself. I am growing and they refuse to grow along with me." These words are recorded in *A Study of the Modern Drama* (1925) and show Hofmannsthal's half-realistic, half-admiring appraisal of himself and of his public. His erotic version of *Electra* (1904), the adaptation of *Venice Preserved*, known as *Das gerettete Venedig* (1905) and *Oedipus und die Sphinx (Oedipus and the Sphinx,* 1906) are among his best known dramas.

The opera librettos, which are sufficiently well written to be plays in their own right (a most unusual accomplishment in which he is to be compared with Metastasio), are variously styled and drawn from contrasting subject matter. *Der Rosenkavalier (The Knight of the Rose,* 1910) is perhaps the best. *Die Frau ohne Schatten (The Woman without a Shadow,* 1919) was given a magnificent production by the *Wiener Staatsoper* (Vienna Opera Company). Richard Strauss composed the music for these operas as well as for *Electra*. Gordon Craig designed the scenery for Otto Brahm's production of Hofmannstahl's adaptation of Otway's *Venice Preserved.*

Now we must turn our attention to another movement which gradually found favor in Germany. The theory of expressionism needs discussion before we can speak of the great directors, actors and designers who collaborated for thirty years to provide their country with a live, vigorous theatre. The first name in this dramatic movement is that of the brilliant and eccentric FRANK WEDEKIND (1864-1918). His work contains much that is abnormal and shocking, both in thought and in expression.

"Expressionism" is a term taken from painting where it signified the revolt against "impressionism" or realism. In both arts it reflects the inner reality of the subject as the eye of the artist or the brain of the dramatist sees it. Its external form, or seeming unreality to the mind of the audience, is of no primary concern to the theatre artist.

Wedekind's background was varied; combining newspaper work, publicity for a circus, vaudeville management, contributions to the famed comic magazine, *Simplicissimus,* and acting for Carl Heine at the *Krystal Palast* in Leipzig and for a Munich theatre. His wide reading in Nietzsche, Max Stirner, Ibsen, and Strindberg influenced him, as did the early naturalism of Gerhart Hauptmann. However, he reflected Ibsen's dramas, in which he thought life had been transformed into a principle. His first play was of no value; his second *Die Junge Welt (The World of Youth,* 1890) revealed conditions of sexual repression in a girls' boarding school and caricatured Hauptmann. *Fruehlings Erwachen, eine Kindertragoedie (The Awakening of Spring,* 1891) burst upon a largely unprepared world. This was the first drama to deal simply and honestly with problems of adolescence (for the first concern of *Romeo and Juliet* was hardly concupiscence in its more clinical forms). The sexual awakening of boys and girls in their middle teens is handled with honesty and candor, though the naturalistic details of the first part of the play turned to symbolism at the end.

Erdgeist (*Earth Spirit*, 1895), and *Die Buechse der Pandora* (*Pandora's Box*, 1904) are both concerned with the lusts of Lulu, who personified Sex the Destroyer, and the final terrible retribution meted out to her. The Parisian pimp who blackmails Lulu in the first drama turns up as a principal character in *Totentanz* (*The Dance of Death*, 1906), where a woman social reformer meets him and is so fascinated by his lust-theories that she begs him to marry her. This he scornfully declines and in desperation she offers herself without marriage. In a complete reversal of all his former ideas, he rejects her offer, condemns lust, warns all the girls of his establishment that he has deceived and perverted them, and kills himself. Even in these few words it is not difficult to detect the similarities between his viewpoint and that of Strindberg, who always wrote of the terrible duel between the sexes. It is not only in these three plays that this idea is maintained by Wedekind. In fact, it is the theme that runs through most of his writing, for his heroes have a real appetite for living dangerously and terribly. He rejected the literary approach to life and literature and believed that the only true survival comes from a return to the life-giving, procreating forces of Nature.

Der Kammersaenger (*The Tenor*, 1899), *Musik* (1907) and *Schloss Wetterstein* (*Castle Wetterstein*, 1910), a trilogy, all celebrated the struggle for supremacy between man and woman, with the man always triumphant. Wedekind departs from the morbid fear of woman which dominated Strindberg. Of his other plays, half-symbolic, half-bitter reflections on his own inability to persuade the world to accept his sexual reforms, the best remembered are *So ist das Leben* (*Such Is Life*, 1902), *Karl Hetmann* (also known as *Hidala*, 1908), *Samson, oder Scham und Eifersucht* (*Samson*, 1914) and *Herakles* (published in 1919 after his death). With his wife Tilly Niemann, whom he married in 1908, he toured Germany in his own plays, in order to impress their social philosophy upon the public. He was scarcely appreciated during his lifetime but Post-War Germany took him and his teachings to heart and made him one of its gods.

Of the dozen or more followers of Wedekind and the school of expressionism, Kaiser, Toller, Werfel and WALTER HASENCLEVER (1890-1940) are the most outstanding and contributed most to the development of the theatre. Hasenclever's first play *Der Juengling* (*The Youth*, 1913) was of little value but his next, *Der Sohn* (*The*

Son, 1914) startled German audiences with his suggestion that sons should murder their parents if they stood in their way. In fact, he implied, all tyranny of family and state should be bathed in blood and so removed. His technique was expressionist; that is, abrupt and extravagant. *The Son* had its first performance in Dresden, in 1916, with Ernst Deutsch giving a brilliant performance in the leading part. Then came the War, into which Hasenclever was inevitably drawn. This, however, did not prevent his writing two anti-war plays, which the government promptly suppressed. These were *The Savior* (1915) and an adaptation of Sophocles' *Antigone* (1917), which he turned into an indictment against war and destruction. In *Mensch* (*Men*, 1918) the protagonist is a corpse who lends his grave to a murderer, takes the sack which contains the head of the killer's victim, and sets out on a night of adventure. The phantasmagoria of the next few hours provides an incoherent and frequently unintelligible drama. Notwithstanding his erratic form, Hasenclever had an ordered intelligence. It is simply his insistence that everything on the stage should be a reflection of the ego of the dramatist, regardless of its seeming irrelevance to the audience, which makes his plays frequently hard to understand without studied attention and reflective interpretation.

Die Entscheidung (*The Decision*, 1919) is an ironic drama of social and political revolution, the futility of which is made clearer by the use of types, rather than characters, in order not to invite irrelevant sympathies. *Jenseits* (*Beyond*, 1920) is a two-character drama in five acts. It is saved from too great monotony by the ghost of the woman's husband. The lovers are literally haunted, in their effort to find happiness, by the comings and goings of the dead man. This play was one of the most interesting productions of the Provincetown Players, in 1925. Of Hasenclever's other plays, including *Gobseck* (1921), *Der Mord* (*Murder*, 1926), the most interesting was his intellectual comedy, *Napoleon greift ein* (*Napoleon Enters on the Scene*, 1930) which was almost prophetic of the dictatorship in Germany which came about three years later.

Reinhard Sorge (1892-1916) won the Kleist Prize with *Der Bettler* (*The Beggar* or *The Mendicant*, 1912). This was a weird drama of death and insanity which interestingly enough called for the "spotted area" style of staging; that is, certain portions of the stage were spotlighted while the rest remained in darkness. This was in advance of the popularization of that technique by Max Reinhardt and others.

Reinhard Goering (1887-1936) wrote two notable pacifist dramas. *Die Seeschlacht* (*Sea Battle*, 1917) was acted in 1918 at the Stadttheater, Dresden and later in Berlin. It was the occasion of the emergence of the great acting talent of Werner Krauss. *Scapa Flow* followed in 1919.

Paul Kornfeld (1889-) wrote a gory drama, *Die Verfuehrung* (*The Seduction,* acted at Frankfort-am-Main in 1916); the eclectic *Himmel und Hoelle* (*Heaven and Hell,* 1919), in which various strange love-relationships are revealed; and the burlesque *Palme oder der Gekraenkte* (*Palme; or, The Hypochondriac,* 1924). The poet Anton Wildgans (1881-1932) wrote plays which usually were on a realistic base even though he decorated them with expressionistic details as in *Liebe* (*Love,* 1916) and *Dies Irae* (1918). The painter-playwright, Oskar Kokoschka (1886-) ran wild in such fantastic plays as *Moerder, Hoffnung der Frauen* (*Murderer, Hope of Women,* 1917) and *Hiob* (1917). Fritz von Unruh (1885-) was another pacifist writer who has to his credit several worthwhile plays, including *Ein Geschlecht* (*One Family,* 1918), *Platz* (*Room,* 1920), though his historical drama *Bonaparte* (1927) is inept. Arnolt Bronnen (1895-) in *Vatermord* (*Parricide,* 1920) celebrated the Oedipus complex which had become a stock in trade of twentieth century dramatists. His mordant *Katalaunische schlacht* (*Underground Battle,* 1924) is almost meaningless, as was the frenzied work of Hans Henny Jahn (1894-), author of a gory *Medea.*

GEORG KAISER (1878-1945) is a dramatist of uneven abilities, half sound and reliable and half opportunist, who seizes upon any trick to attract attention and advance himself and his work in the theatre. *Der Brand im Opernhaus* (*Fire in the Opera House,* 1916), *Gas,* (1918-20) and *Gats* (1928) are examples of one half of his nature. The first is showy and pretentious. It has been produced a good deal because of its splendid opportunities for spectacular staging. This is an incompletely resolved drama of woman's unfaithfulness set against the florid background of a conflagration. The fantastic *Gats* has some of the fine qualities of *Gas,* which remains Kaiser's best work, but its method of presentation and its inchoate dramaturgy handicap an idea which might have made an extremely interesting realistic drama. The fundamental human desire of the race to perpetuate itself, and the fact that the poor will always take advantage of this even if the wealthy and intellectual forego the privilege, would make an excellent subject for the genius of an O'Neill rather than the crude expressionism of a Kaiser.

Kaiser's plays have many excellent qualities and it is this part of his ability which proves interesting to us. His *Von morgen his mitternacht* (*From Morn to Midnight,* 1916) is a moving drama of the futility of modern civilization. A bank clerk impulsively steals a sum of money because he believes that the lady who has been refused the right to cash a bank-draft might grant him love if he offered her the money. Rebuffed, the theft already discovered, he launches on a day which he thinks will prove pleasurable and exciting. He runs the gamut of emotion and ends it by being denounced to the police by the virtuous lady whom he has thought above money, so that she may claim the reward for his capture. This drama proved one of the most exciting productions of the Theatre Guild in New York in 1922.

In spite of the many plays this prolific writer has contributed to the stage, there are but two others that stand out. This is not an attempt to minimize any of his plays which were of real merit, but merely to emphasize the importance of those which might be said to have advanced the theatre.

Die Buerger von Calais (*The Burghers of Calais*, 1914) is an honest effort to write an historical play about a moving episode in Franco-British history. This tells the tragic yet hopeful story of the plight of the citizens of Calais after the victory of the English at Crécy. In order that they might save the city itself and the lives of its citizens, not six, but seven men offer to surrender their lives to save their home. Only six may go and seven have volunteered and not one is willing to withdraw his offer. At the time set for their departure, Eustache de Saint-Pierre, who had suggested the plan, is not there and the fickle citizens denounce him as a coward. Soon after, his dead body is brought in with his father, who is blind, and who explains that his son has killed himself so that he might be the first to die for his natal city. As the six advance, news comes that English Edward III will spare Calais and wishes to worship God there because a royal son has been born. Kaiser violates history in this drama, and it is an interesting point as to which is the more dramatic situation: Kaiser's device, or the true historical situation (there were but six in all and it was the eloquence of Eustache that saved the city). It may be recalled that one of the most celebrated sculptures of the great Rodin is of these self-same citizens.

BERTHOLT BRECHT is perhaps not so important a writer as Kaiser, Toller or Werfel, but he deserves separate mention if only for his collaboration with the composer Kurt Weill in the brilliant rewriting of *The Beggar's Opera* in their *Die Dreigroschenoper* (1928). This protest in satiric form against sinful weakness, staged by Erich Engel, has fine ironic qualities in the writing and gay spitefulness in its music. Some of the anger against cupidity displayed in the light opera was also present in Brecht's *Trommeln in der nacht* (*Drums in the Night* 1922), which won the Kleist Prize that same year. It deals with the unseeing rage of a soldier who returns from war to discover the activities of the profiteers who have been destroying the people during his absence.

Brecht, with the help of Lion Feuchtwanger, turned Marlowe's *Edward II* into an expressionistic play, which scarcely improved it. One of his most successful dramas was his adaptation of Gorki's *Mother*, which was an example of epic drama or *Lehrstuecke* which was to teach people truth (as he, his fellows and followers saw it!) This didactic example of proletarian drama has been widely acted; in New York it was played by the Theatre Union to mixed critical opinion of its merits, though its impact was not denied. Another example of this form, which had a marked similarity to the living newspaper technique developed by the Federal Theatre Project, is *Die Massnahme* (*The Expedient*, 1931). This was given massive and impressive staging at the *Grosse Schauspielhaus* in Berlin. Epic drama was brilliantly satirized in the musical revue *Pins and Needles* (1937) in New York.

ERNST TOLLER (1893-1939) became involved more or less accidentally with communism when he was drawn into active participation in a strike in the munitions industry in Munich in 1918. When the Bavarian Soviet Republic was formed he was made a member of the government, against his will as he said, but his subsequent imprisonment turned him into a full-fledged communist. (He was in prison in 1919 when his first play, *Wandlung* [*Transformation*] was acted in Berlin, with the oratorical Fritz Kortner, at the experimental theatre, *Die Tribuene*, under the direction of Karlheinz Martin.) This conviction lasted at least until he wrote *Masse-Mensch*, which indicated that he was as distrustful of the cruelty of the masses as of the few. Perhaps he always kept his political allegiance but it is probable that it was as an honest liberal unhappy at the turn of world events, that he died by his own hand in New York, May 22, 1939.

Masse-Mensch (*Man and the Masses*, 1921) was a remarkable drama devoted to anti-militarism. A woman works with labor to promote a protest against war, but feeling flames high and despite all her efforts the men swing into revolt against the government, which is but another war. The revolution is suppressed and she is wrongly charged with having been its leader. She refuses to accept even her own possible rescue at the hands of mob violence and is executed. This fine and exciting play was performed for two seasons in Berlin when it was first staged. Its production in New York was greeted with a great deal of critical enthusiasm, in the Theatre Guild's performance, in 1924.

Die Maschinenstuermer (*The Machine Wreckers*, 1922) lost much of its force because of its excessive bitterness and exaggeration. This play dealt with the Luddite riots among English workers early in the nineteenth century when they feared that the machines were going to rob them entirely of their jobs and therefore of their existence. The capitalist villains are too black for belief, despite the fact that history paints them unpleasantly enough, so that much of the audience's sympathy is weakened or lost. It is nonetheless a horrifying and fascinating play.

Hinkemann (1923) was as bitter, though more realistic in form than the earlier expressionist dramas. It dealt with a soldier who is emasculated in the war. Therefore his wife turns to another man for physical pleasures and her husband is rendered miserable. He is so Christian and forgiving that she is overcome with remorse and repents of her act. Interestingly enough this play's première was marred by an anti-Semitic demonstration because its author was a Jew.

Among his other plays *Hoppla wir leben* (*Whoopee, We Live,* staged by Erwin Piscator at the *Piscatorbuehne,* Berlin, 1927) is interesting because of his employment of the cinema as an integral part of the play, though the subjects of the films seem extraneous. *No More Peace* (1937), written after a long period of exile, is a satiric comedy about dictatorship. Toller was a burning force in the drama and his theatre influence was considerable. His last years were spent in aiding the Dramatists' Guild of the Authors' League of America to work out its copyright problems from his own considerable knowledge of the workings of various regulations of this kind in Europe.

FRANZ WERFEL (1890-1945) was born in Prague of German-Jewish parentage. He is a poet of distinction and in the popular mind is perhaps more readily identified as a novelist than as a dramatist. His first important play was the expressionist trilogy *Der Spiegelmensch* (*Mirror Man,* 1920), which depicts the mental struggle of a man between his normal, friendly self and the being which is anti-social. *Schweiger* (1922) is a study of double personality, a psychiatric treatment of schizophrenia. *Bocksgesang* (*Goat Song,* 1921) is one of the most important plays to come out of Europe in the present century. Despite some confusion in thinking and writing, its qualities in the theatre are exciting and occasionally overwhelming. Bestiality in man is symbolized by a monster who leads a revolution of homeless people in the eighteenth century. The revolt is suppressed and the beast slain, but his seed is in the body of a woman so that the spirit of revolution will continue.

Werfel wrote two historical dramas, *Paulus unter den Juden* (*Paul Among the Jews,* 1926) and *Juarez und Maximilian* (1924), which was more successful. *The Eternal Road* was a patriotic, historical pageant about the Jews, which was produced by Max Reinhardt at enormous expense, in New York in 1937. Despite high critical praise of the kindly variety and a run of several months it was a financial failure because of the grandiose ideas of the *régisseur*.

Lesser dramatists who definitely have something to say in the theatre are the left-wing FRIEDRICH WOLF (1888-   ), who is at present living in the U.S.S.R.; and CARL ZUCKMAYER (1896-   ) who is at present in this country after fleeing to England when Hitler came to power. Wolf is responsible for two plays of contemporary interest though their place in the scheme of things dramatic is probably not too high. Examples of *Reportage Drama* (Journalistic Plays) are *Die Matrosen von Cattaro* (*The Sailors of Cattaro*, 1930) and his strong anti-Nazi drama *Professor Mamlock* (1937), which was made into an excellent film by the Russians not long before their alliance with Nazi Germany in 1939. Zuckmayer does not seem to share many of Wolf's sentiments. He early abandoned expressionism in favor of comic folk drama. He attracted favorable attention with his comedy *Der froehliche Weinberg* (*The Happy Vineyard*), which won the Kleist Prize in 1926. His best known and most enduring comedy is *Der Hauptmann von Koepenick* (*Captain von Koepenick*, 1928) which is a satire on German militarism. He turned to a fairy-tale style of play in *Der Schelm von Bergen* (*The Rogue of Bergen*) which was performed in Vienna at the *Burgtheater*.

Zuckmayer was assisted in turning the German stage from expressionism back to realism by ERNST BARLACH (1870-   ), the South-German sculptor-playwright. The two best dramas which he contributed to spiritual realism were *Die echte Sedemunds* (*The Genuine Sedemunds*) and *Der blaue Boll* (*The Blue Boll*, 1936). Because of this quality in his writing and his development of realistic characterization the highly stylized production by Leopold Jessner of the former drama was a failure, with Kortner standing with the author against the superimposed expressionism of the director. It was not until the highly gifted Juergen Fehling staged the play that it was successful, perhaps because he, too, came from South Germany and understood Berlach's people. The collaboration of author and *régisseur* in *Der blaue Boll* in the 1930-31 season, with the assistance of the designer Rochus Gliese, and the actors Heinrich George, Helen Fehdmer and Margarethe Melzer, achieved resounding and deserved success according to Julius Bab, who considers Fehling perhaps the most distinguished stage director of Germany since the First World War.

Since the rise of fascism in Germany there have been no first class writing talents. Hans Johst and Richard Euringer have been the most competent but none of their plays has genuine literary merit.

But besides the dramatists who supplied the substance which justified the maintenance of a professional theatre there are the other artists of the stage, *régisseurs*, managers, designers, and actors. These are the men and women who, by the use of their minds and bodies, create theatre from the words written down by playwrights. In any study of the German stage since the founding of the free stage societies, which were noted earlier in the chapter, the list of these men must begin with Max Reinhardt (1873-1943) who, whatever may be his faults, has contributed enormously to both German and world theatre.

Reinhardt was born in Austria near Vienna, with the theatre of which city he was frequently identified until shortly before the Nazi *anschluss*, at which time he was in the United States. He was first a character actor at Salzburg and was brought by Otto Brahm to Berlin about 1894 where he continued his acting career, later becoming a director. Perhaps that is why his theatre has always been described as an actors' theatre like Stanislavski's, because he has an innate comprehension of the actor's problems and generally has the solution for them. He has taken many actors who are definitely of the second or even the lower rank and made them seem first-rate talents. The moment they left his management much of this slipped away and they were revealed as they really were. This was true of many of the actresses whom Belasco sponsored. This is not to suggest Svengali tactics but to indicate that he could see clearly a player's deficiencies and so know just what had to be filled in by the director to make him give a good performance. The possession of such ability is no inconsiderable talent in itself and a tremendous aid to a *régisseur*.

Reinhardt's faults developed when he was no longer content with the straight, simple, well-grounded performances with which he began at the *Schall und Rauch* cabaret of the *Kleines Theater* in 1902; as well as the *Neues Theater* from 1902 to 1905; the *Deutsches* (1905); and the *Kammerspiele*, somewhat later. When he felt the need to stage great, massive productions, with glaring colors and overwhelming music and mob scenes, he began to decline as a director, despite the fact that his handling of crowds has been proverbially good. He can and does achieve interesting results which have moved critics and audiences in general into extravagant expressions of wonder, but he frequently sacrifices the meaning of the play to achieve his stupendous ends. His four different stagings of *A Midsummer Night's Dream* have excited his audiences, but Shakespeare's fairy drama disappeared in the midst of hundreds of actors and elaborate revolving stages. He repeated this failure in his filming of the play when again he was unable to recognize the possibilities of his medium. His fairies might have made miraculous appearances and dissolved into thin air on the screen instead of remaining heavy realities. This misunderstanding of cinematic technique is cited to illustrate his deficiencies elsewhere as well.

Shortly before the war, he took over the *Zirkus Schumann* and staged Sophocles' *Oedipus Rex*, in what was supposed to be a Greek theatre created by Ernst Stern; as well as his original production of Hofmannsthal's *Jedermann*, and Karl Vollmoeller's pantomime *Das Mirakel* (*The Miracle*, 1912, an expansion of Maeterlinck's *Soeur Béatrice*). Between 1917 and 1920 Reinhardt staged some of the most interesting modern German plays for *Das Junge Deutschland*, an advanced theatrical group named for the earlier organization.

After the war, at the *Grosses Schauspielhaus*, sometimes called the *Theatre of the Five Thousand*, he staged more of his monster spectacles. Hauptman's *Florian Geyer;* Rolland's *Danton; Hamlet;* and *Julius Caesar* were among the productions, but as might be expected, the venture was a financial failure. Angered by this Reinhardt left Berlin for Vienna where he established himself in 1922 in the *Theater in der Josephsstadt*, where he staged some delightful performances. He was also connected with the *Redoutensaal*. This perfect gem of a baroque theatre was in the Hofburg Palace ballroom which had been designed in 1744 as the Empress Maria Theresa's *salle de danse*. Only the slightest and most perfect small plays could be performed in this tiny playhouse where he utilized the acting services of Moissi, Pallenberg and Krauss, with Alfred Roller as scene designer. Later he returned to Berlin, though still maintaining, somewhat indifferently, his Viennese playhouse, to manage the *Deutsches*, the *Kammerspiele* and the newly opened *Komoedie*. There he staged many foreign as well as German plays in the sensuous style in which he excels, until the advent of Hitler, when he withdrew to Austria to work in Vienna and Salzburg. His productions in this country have been mentioned elsewhere. In addition he has installed a theatre school in Hollywood, where he has gathered around him many of his satellites of former days.

LEOPOLD JESSNER (1878-   ) began his career as a director in Hamburg, working especially with trade union groups because he was a socialist. During the First World War he took over the management of the *Neues Schauspielhaus* in his native Koenigsberg in East Prussia. With the collapse of the monarchy, he went to Berlin, where in 1919 he was made director of the *Schauspielhaus*, formerly referred to as the Royal, Court, or National Theatre. During the next six years he created one brilliant and eccentric production after another until the whole nation rang with his exploits and foreign theatre men went especially to Berlin to see his productions. Then his influence crept over the border, notably toward Moscow, where Meyerhold undoubtedly felt it. This does not mean to say that the great Russian director took his famous staircase, which he was so fond of using, from Jessner, but the German's constant re-use of this device naturally interested him. Such men as Robert Edmond Jones and Kenneth Macgowan went to Berlin to see this new master of technique and recorded his brilliance in their informative and reliable *Continental Stagecraft* (1922), which for nearly a generation has been a standby for American students of theatre arts.

Jessnertreppen ("Jessner's steps," first introduced in *Wilhelm Tell*) dominated the settings for his early productions as he felt that they released the mind of the audience in drama, whether naturalistic, realistic or expressionistic. His own technique was developed along the last named line. He was more successful in staging the plays of Wedekind than anyone else in Germany including the author himself. He directed them at twice the tempo, so that individual speeches and lines were delivered like pistol shots. This method suited the plays ideally. (An interesting parallel lies in the staging of O'Neill's *Strange Interlude*, where the thought speeches, if played at full speed, came across to the audience but when the same members of the London company of the play sought to "interpret" the so-called asides, the tempo went to pieces and the whole play suffered so much that its success was destroyed.) Fritz Kortner was one of Jessner's principal actors and *King Richard III; Macbeth; Herodes und Marianne; Othello*; C. D. Grabbe's *Napoleon;* as well as the *Marquis von Keith* and other Wedekind dramas, constituted some of his most important productions.

That really outstanding director, who still carries on his work under the Nazi régime, Juergen Fehling has already been briefly discussed. His staging of *Masse-mensch* against Hans Strohbach's towering and magnificently lighted settings was memorable, and Mary Dietrich's Woman was superb. Other distinguished productions of his were *The Comedy of Errors; King Lear*; Lenz's *Soldaten*, and Hebbel's *Nibelungen*.

Leading *régisseurs* also include such names as Heinz Hilpert, whose approach to his work at the *Deutsches* since 1933 has been unspoiled and charming, particularly in such a comedy as *As You Like It;*

Berthold Viertel; Erich Ziegel; Karlheinz Martin; Friedrich Kayssler; Erich Engel, and particularly ERWIN PISCATOR (1893-), whose activities in communist circles in Germany gave him the reputation of being their greatest director and the outstanding interpreter of their principles. He employed constructivism after he had exhausted expressionism and was more truly the exponent of "epic drama" than Brecht, carrying preachments to the point of becoming lectures (speakers talked from the stage during the intermissions), and bringing theatre as close to political reality as he could with films and projections. He rewrote his authors' work ruthlessly to secure the end he had in mind. His effects were breath-taking and Berlin was swept off its feet by such productions as his dramatization of Dreiser's *An American Tragedy*, Schiller's *Die Raeuber* and his own anti-war play, *Die Abenteuer des braven Soldaten Schweik* (*The Good Soldier Schweik*, 1927). However, his appeal was to the communistic elements and his audiences were largely of the middle class, whom he violently attacked. In time they grew bored or annoyed and did not return to his theatre ventures, three of which failed for that reason. He is like Meyerhold and Orson Welles in his desire to rewrite a play until it pleases him regardless of the dramatist's original idea. With the coming of Hitler, though he is descended from a long line of Protestant pastors, he left Germany, because of his radical and anti-Nazi affiliations. In this country he staged Shaw's *St. Joan* with Luise Rainer in 1940 in Washington, with indifferent results. He is now director of the Dramatic Workshop of the New School for Social Research in New York.

Most of the outstanding actors of this period have been mentioned with the exception of ALEXANDER MOISSI (1880-1935). He was born of Italian-Albanian parentage, in Austria, and when he first acted in Berlin his accent was jeered by the audience. Apparently only in America and the British Empire is there any courtesy at all shown to foreigners who are endeavoring to learn our language but wish to act while they are still learning, for artistic or financial reasons. That does not mean that our audience does not complain of too many German or Russian accents, but they are too considerate to express themselves vocally in the theatre. A good deal has been said about the placidity of American and British audiences, and sometimes their late-coming and early-leaving habits are excoriated as well, but they do treat their actors decently.

Moissi became Reinhardt's leading actor appearing in practically all of his productions. He was a remarkably expressive actor, though at times his background and the florid style of his director betrayed him into overacting. When Reinhardt's company was disbanded and he appeared on his own, this fault became most apparent.

ELISABETH BERGNER (1900-   ) is an actress of charm, but from what she has displayed on the English-speaking stage and screen, her abilities and reputation from Germany seem over-rated. Her whimsical personality suits a few roles, but it is hard to see how it could have been adapted to *St. Joan*, or to Nina in *Strange Interlude*, or Portia in *The Merchant of Venice*. Her Tessa in *The Constant Nymph* and Gemma Jones in *Escape Me Never* are within her scope of playing.

The enormously versatile Werner Krauss; the Thimig family of good stock actors with no top flights of performance; Max Pallenberg (who had a trace of old *Hanswurst* in his acting); Ernst Deutsch; Rudolf Forster; Else Lehmann; Agnes Straub; Gerda Mueller; Rudolf Rittner; Oscar Sauer; the Viennese, Paula Wessely; Emil Jannings of the films; Maria Solveg; Paul Hartmann; and Eugen Kloepfer, are all among the outstanding acting personalities in the German and Austrian theatre. Especially important was the great Austrian actor of the last century, Josef Kainz (1858-1910), whose Hamlet and Romeo were famous; and likewise notable was the distinguished Adalbert Matkowsky (1877-1909), character actor of high standing.

Scenic design reached a very high development in Germany between the 1870's and the present day. Only a brief roll-call need be given of the leaders in this special field. For there are many excellent volumes on scenic design including those of Sheldon Cheney, Lee Simonson, Donald Oenslager, Robert Edmond Jones and Kenneth Macgowan. Saxe-Meiningen's designers, Israel and Liebermann, began the march toward modern design. Then came the Swiss Appia and the lighting expert Adolf Linnebach. Reinhardt's collaborators, Stern and Roller, as well as Oscar Strnad and Benno von Arent, Adolph Mahnke, Hans Poelzig (architect for the *Grosses Schauspielhaus*), Fritz Schumacher, Winkler Tannenberg and the naturalized American Friedrich Kiesler (who was responsible for the development of the "space stage" and who has been for years one of the outstanding architect-designers in America).

With the advent of Hitler and the departure of the non-Aryan stars from Germany, the minor Jewish players were left almost entirely without livelihood. These, numbering several hundred, constituted three per cent of all the theatre folk. Jews were excluded from most of the theatres or found it impossible to attend because of financial or other restrictions. A Jewish Cultural Society was formed in Berlin and soon established branches all over the country with a permanent dramatic and opera company in the capital and at least one touring troupe was formed. Their performances are given in German for German-Jewish audiences.

This ends our survey of the stage history of Germany and Austria since the death of Goethe. One great writer in Hauptmann, and several first-class talents such as Hebbel, Anzengruber, Wedekind, Schnitzler, and Toller have emerged. Structural changes in the theatres were enormous. The drafty barns were cast aside and well-constructed playhouses with revolving stages and the world's first adequate lighting systems came into being. Theatres were equipped with proper dressing-rooms and storage space for scenery. Adequate subsidies were granted by the state. These have been increased (unhealthily, as it happens) since the advent of National Socialism and the practical disappearance of the independent and unsubsidized theatre manager in the German-speaking countries. Such directors as L'Arronge, Brahm, Reinhardt, Jessner have had their influence everywhere and today some of their finest actors are appearing on the various stages of the world. Much of this evolution can be documented through the assembling of records in fine theatre libraries and museums under the aegis of Franz Rapp, Josef Gregor, Heinrich Schnitzler (the stage director, and Gregor's collaborator), Ralf Badenhausen, and the late Winfried Klara.

THE FLUORESCENT RUSSIAN THEATRE

(1898-1940)

IT IS customary to date the modern Russian theatre from the famous eighteen-hour conversation between Constantin Stanislavski and Vladimir Nemirovitch-Danchenko on the twenty-first and twenty-second of June, 1897. Both of the men involved have written about it, as has everyone who has discussed the Russian stage. It has stirred the imagination in a fashion which would seem almost incredible were it not for the enormous influence of the Moscow Art Theatre on the stage of the world.

However, there had been tentative attempts to establish proper rehearsal methods, ensemble acting, and intelligent direction ever since the visit of the Duke of Saxe-Meiningen's Company to St. Petersburg. The hasty and ill-rehearsed productions which had been slapped onto the stage in order to provide a series of novelties for the few who could afford the theatre, were being supplanted. Before this a play had sometimes not been permitted its proper run simply that the nobility might have a new dramatic production to titillate its jaded tastes.

Slavophilism claimed the responsibility for the development of the great theatrical innovations of Saxe-Meiningen. The proponents of that movement told us that the invaluable critical assistance of the German, F. M. Bodenstedt (1819-1892), who had come under their influence, was truly responsible for the Duke's triumphs. Whether you accept this theory or not, Bodenstedt certainly was instrumental in aiding his noble master to establish true ensemble acting which later swept Europe and America. The triumphs of this troupe have been noted in their proper niche in the history of the theatre but their initial Russian success and subsequent debacle must be considered in the light of the development of native *régisseurs* and acting companies.

In 1885, the Saxe-Meiningen Company visited St. Petersburg and Moscow to the accompaniment of almost unanimous critical applause. There were, however, dissenters who contended that all of the individual acting was mediocre and that there were hundreds of native actors who were superior in every way. In every way, that is, but the power to blend themselves into a perfect acting whole. It was this ability that distinguished the German company for they had learned to create atmosphere and background without words, employing pantomime and naturalistic business, which might include natural sounds, and even broken speech, all of which was not included in the drama itself. It was in the trilogy of *Wallenstein* and in *Julius Caesar* that they surpassed themselves. These plays won the intellectual interest of their audiences and stimulated the attempt to recapture these effects with their own actors.

F. A. Korsh in his New Theatre, also referred to as the Moscow Dramatic Theatre, established an acting company in 1882, the first year that private theatres became legal after Ostrovski had won his fight to deprive the Imperial Theatres of the exclusive privilege of play production. This troupe continued in existence even after the Revolution, until 1933, when it was disbanded and the building was handed over to the Moscow Art Theatre for its dramatic school and "Small Stage." Opinions vary concerning Korsh's contribution but he had a number of good actors with him including Ivan Moskvin, the great player of high-comedy, who was to come into his own with the First Art Theatre. Another player was the fine actor Alexander Ivanovitch Youzhin, born Prince Sumbatoff (1857-1927), who was celebrated for his Shakespearean roles. Davidov excelled in his performance in Chekhov's *Ivanov*, which was first staged by Korsh's theatre. The author was inclined to be highly critical of the production, as he was not yet enamoured of the theatre, and all things pertaining to it were somewhat distasteful. Furthermore, Kiselevski, who next to the brilliant Davidov was the best actor, was drunk at the opening. All in all, it cannot have been a happy experience. Korsh's first aesthetic experiments seem to have worn thin and he soon became an obtuse commercial manager and as a figure of importance in the everlasting theatre, he lost caste.

As in New York, restaurants and public night clubs played a large part in the artistic and theatrical development of the city of Moscow. It was at the famous Slavyanski Bazaar that Stanislavski and Nemirovitch-Danchenko met. It was at the Hermitage Restaurant that many of the business affairs of the Moscow Art Theatre were to be transacted. It was there that the great singer-actor, Chaliapin, as well as

Michael Provitch Sadovski, scion of a famous acting family, spent their days, eating, writing, receiving their friends and talking—beyond everything else talking. People came to listen to the brilliance of their conversation. All artistic matters came to be decided in the Hermitage in Moscow.

VLADIMIR IVANOVITCH NEMIROVITCH-DANCHENKO (1858-1943) was born in the Caucasus and was Armenian on his mother's side. That is the reason assigned by some for his astuteness in business matters, which through the long years carried him and his enterprises through financial strain and stress. His talent as a dramatist has long been over-shadowed by his unusual abilities as an entrepreneur. In 1881 he wrote *The Eglantine*, a comedy which was staged at the Mali Theatre on October 5, 1882. Its stage setting of a two-story house, like that of Elmer Rice's *Street Scene*, won acclaim for its novelty. Later the facade was lifted and the interior revealed as in *Desire Under the Elms*. Thus his interest in realistic effect and spectacular settings was early and graphically revealed. Several plays followed with little or no success until 1888 brought *The Last Will*. He received the Vuchina Prize, offered by Odessa University, for the excellence of his *Gold*, staged in 1895 at the Mali in Moscow and the Alexandrinski in St. Petersburg. In this he endeavored to follow the neo-classicism of Racine in compressing his action into a single day in a single spot. In his autobiography, he states that he spoiled the piece, making it monotonous, artificial and overweighted. *The Price of Life* (published in 1896; acted, 1897) won the Griboyedov Prize. His plays, though possessing some qualities, indicate that it was directing and scenic investiture that primarily interested him and it was in the production and managerial side of the theatre that he won his most deserved fame.

He became an instructor in dramatic art at the Moscow Philharmonic School in 1890 and the next year was given full charge of this work. There he propounded the principles of theatrical art which the distinguished critic, S. A. Yurev, outlined in his article published in the periodical, *Russian Thought*, in 1883. *The Significance of the Theatre, its Decay, and the Need for a School for Scenic Art* states definitely that the experiments of the Meiningen Company in ensemble playing are the fundamental first step. Yurev contended that it would be a Russian problem to develop what the Germans had begun because the dramas of Turgenev, Gogol and Ostrovski, in fact all of their native drama, tended to emphasize the importance of the group rather than a single hero. It was the collective personality displayed in drama which required a technique of acting different from that of the western theatre. Nemirovitch-Danchenko read and was impressed by these sentiments, which he proceeded to carry out in his teaching and to employ later with Stanislavski in the Moscow Art Theatre. Some of these principles appear in the so-called Stanislavski system of acting, which is much admired and widely practiced in the non-Russian theatre.

At this point, we must digress to sketch the beginnings of the second half of the famous team, C. S. Alexeyev, better known to us as CONSTANTIN STANISLAVSKI (1863-1938). Born into the well-to-do merchant class, he early distinguished himself as an amateur actor and stage manager of considerable merit. He was deeply drawn to the theatre, perhaps partly due to his French grandmother, Mlle. Varley who married a rich quarry owner, Yakovlev, in Finland. After having two children she divorced her husband. The children remained with him. From the time Stanislavski was two or three, on the authority of his magnificent autobiography, *My Life in Art* (1924), he began to appear in amateur theatricals in the private theatre at their country-place. This continued throughout his youth until he began to teach at the Russian Musical Society and Conservatory in Moscow. It was then that he saw the great Italian actor, Ernesto Rossi, whose finished technique made a great impression on him. From 1877, the Alexeyev family had an amateur circle named for them when they performed at home. In 1888, there was organized a more formal amateur circle called the Society of Art and Literature, where many experimental productions were given, which was to prepare Stanislavski for his collaboration with Nemirovitch-Danchenko.

To the new theatre, which was first called the Moscow Art and Popular Theatre, the latter brought his pupils and the younger male members of his acting circle. This was not until they reassured themselves that their ideal of art was the same, to free the stage from its commercialism and pettiness, to achieve the inner interpretation of the role, the secret understanding that lies within one's self, the inductive approach to acting. To Nemirovitch-Danchenko was assigned the literary and administrative direction and to Stanislavski the artistic and stage direction. It was this ability to trust each other's judgment even in disagreement that brought their company to the high pinnacle of success which it reached. For forty years they labored and the result was very nearly perfection of its own kind.

Their first productions were prepared in the country during the summer of 1898 in anticipation of the first public testing of their theories. On the 14th of October, 1898, they opened the doors of the refurbished Hermitage Theatre with Alexei Tolstoi's *Tsar Fyodor Ivanovitch* which was followed a week later by *The Merchant of Venice*. On December second came *La Locandiera* and *Greta's Joy* and on the seventeenth the play which brought them their greatest fame, *The Sea Gull,* which is now the symbol of the playhouse, appearing on their curtain and on their programs. This production so pleased Chekhov that he wrote, "The *mise en scène* is wonderful. The Mali Theatre has paled, and as to the *mise en scène* and staging, even the Meiningers are far from the new Art Theatre, which so far plays in a miserable building." This was written after he saw a performance acted especially for him in May, 1899.

From then on came a succession of important plays, some highly successful, others but indifferently received. Notable among these productions were *The Death of Ivan the Terrible* and *Uncle Vanya* (1899); *Three Sisters;* and Hauptmann's *Lonely Lives* (1901); and four of Ibsen's dramas, *Hedda Gabler* (1899), *The Enemy of the People* and *When We Dead Awaken* (1900), and *The Wild Duck* (1901). They never quite caught Ibsen's spirit, however, though Nemirovitch-Danchenko knew and admired the great Norwegian. All of these plays were staged in the building which Chekhov disparaged. In the autumn of 1902, they moved to the new Kamergerski Playhouse, with its revolving stage which provided them with new opportunities for innovations and magnificence in staging, which in the beginning they deliberately used to cover up acting deficiencies. In their later years, this was no longer necessary and now their productions are frequently very simple scenically.

To read the list of their repertoire is to find many of the greatest Russian dramas together with many of the most important dramas of western Europe, though it is not the ideal repertory for its professed aims. In comparison with Eva LeGallienne's Civic Repertory Theatre, the play reader did not measure up favorably. Three of its most successful productions were *A Month in the Country* (1909), *Enough Stupidity in Every Wise Man* and *The Brothers Karamazov* (1910).

When you have the trainer of actors *par excellence,* you expect a whole school of great players to develop and the Moscow Art Theatre is naturally the fountain head of all. Ivan Moskvin, who gave a great performance as *Tsar Fyodor,* and whose Luka in *The Lower Depths,* and Yepihodov in *The Cherry Orchard* are unforgettable, has already been mentioned; as has Olga Knipper-Chekhova (whose seventieth birthday has just been celebrated in Moscow with her performance in *Tartuffe*). Vassili Kachalov is perhaps the most versatile actor of the whole company. It was he who played Hamlet, in the production designed by Gordon Craig in 1912. His Baron in *The Lower Depths;* Don Juan in *The Stone Guest;* Ivan Karamazov in The *Brothers Karamazov;* the title role in *Ivanov;* and Ratikin in *A Month in the Country* are among his best known parts. Others in the company were Vladimir Gribunin, Vassili Luzhski, Alexander Vishnevski, Nikolai

Massalitinov and Michael Tarkanov, among the men. In addition to Mme. Chekhova, there have been Maria Petrovna Lilina, wife of Stanislavski; Nadiezhda Butova, Maria Germanova, Maria Zhdanova, Maria Ouspenskaya, and their most recent leading lady, Alla Tarasova (who once acted for the abortive Second Studio).

As is natural over a period of forty years actors have come and gone. Vsevolod Meyerhold spent the first few years with the company and then went his own way, only later to cooperate with Stanislavski in the first attempt to establish a Studio Theatre for experimental productions. The Revolution of 1905 ended this, after both men had decided that the young actors were not ready to display their work publicly. Meyerhold returned for a time to the company as an actor. However the artistic disagreement was too strong to permit a symbolist and a theatre-for-theatre's sake man to remain in the comfortable atmosphere of Nemirovitch-Danchenko's enterprise. It was not until Meyerhold's fall from power shortly before Stanislavski's death that he returned to the older man for what protection he could offer him. Afterwards he was made director of Stanislavski's Opera Theatre, but not long ago he was removed from that post and reports of the imprisonment of the man whom the Soviet régime so much admired for so long have been circulated abroad.

But to return to the Art Theatre, as usual they made a virtue of necessity. With the country disturbed by the revolution and the failure of *The Children of the Sun*, a Berlin season was planned. After receiving an enthusiastic critical acclaim upon their opening in 1906, popular attendance languished until the Emperor Wilhelm II elected to attend due to the interest and enthusiasm of the Empress, and with the characteristic desire of the Germans to do whatever their leader did, they followed suit. The season was a financial as well as an artistic success, to the great relief of the company's impresarios who might have had to disband their troupe. Berlin was followed by a highly successful tour which included Dresden, Leipzig, Prague and Vienna. Their intention was to play in Paris at the *Théâtre Sarah Bernhardt*, but as has been usual in the history of the stage of that city, the indifference of the audience toward foreign artists prevented it. Such exorbitant demands for money to advertise and push the enterprise were made that it was quite out of the question to play there. This was the experience of Duse, who took an enormous loss on her first engagement in order to return with financial success in after years. Other foreign companies reported the same provincial attitude. It was not until their American tour was planned that they decided to risk a French season of a month, and again in 1937, when the Russian government financed the tour, the Art Theatre came to Paris to play at the French International Exposition. The reasons for this appearance were political, not artistic.

The enormous success of the Art Theatre in this country cannot be too highly rated. In 1923 and again in 1924, New York and eleven other large cities were visited by the full company, with all of its scenery and artists. Three hundred and eighty performances of thirteen plays were given in two seasons. Americans, except, of course, those who had seen them play in Europe, got their first view of the great ensemble organization. Oliver Sayler, whose writings on the Russian stage are of real importance, heralded their approach and prepared us for the magnificent art which we saw. It is not too much to say that the whole American theatre was affected by this visit, which left memories, methods and a number of the actors who preferred life in America to the more restricted freedom of their native land.

The temptation is to write in even more detail concerning the exploits of this group and of their many important productions, but though it is the greatest theatre that Russia possesses, it is far from being the only important one. What the Russian stage might have accomplished in the free air of America is incalculable when one considers the results achieved in the atmosphere of censorship and suspicion which has accompanied its development from the very beginning. There were a few years when the sword of Damocles was withdrawn, perhaps between 1930 and 1936, or at least this has been the impression of foreigners. Since 1936, however, the official restraint and political pressure, together with the execution or imprisonment of many of her first talents, has lowered the standards of her magnificent stage.

Nemirovitch-Danchenko and Stanislavski developed not only their own theatre but many off-shoots, either together or separately. The First Studio brought out the talent of Richard Boleslavski and the brilliant Michael Chekhov and developed as the Second Art Theatre (now liquidated).

The Third Studio found its god in Eugene Vakhtangov and grew into the theatre bearing his name. The Moscow Art Musical Studio was the particular protégé of Nemirovitch-Danchenko and he set out to reform the staging of light opera and operetta. Americans saw his magnificent success along these lines during the Studio's New York engagement in 1925. *Carmencita and the Soldier*, *La Perichole* and *Lysistrata* were staged in a fashion which will never be forgotten. Not that it affected that stronghold of conservatism, the Metropolitan Opera, which will probably continue in its stodgy way until a new opera-theatre is formed and the ground cut away beneath its feet, but all musical production was influenced. The American Opera Company was certainly influenced and even the producers of America's most characteristic musical shows learned much.

The off-shoots and ramifications of the great Moscow Art Theatre are too complicated to be followed in a short history of the theatre. Its great contribution has been made. This theatre of the actor, this "theatre of inner feeling" is established as perhaps the First Theatre of the World, as well as of Moscow.

But now we must go back to the year when *The Cherry Orchard* won its first success, 1904, and turn our eyes toward St. Petersburg and the theatre of the greatest Russian actress of the present century. VERA KOMISSARZHEVSKAYA (1864-1910) made an appearance with Stanislavski's semi-amateur Society of Art and Literature in 1896 in Tolstoi's *The Fruits of Enlightenment,* as Betsy. This was natural as she was the daughter of F. P. Komissarzhevski, who was one of Stanislavski's teachers. Having created something of a reputation for herself as an actress, she opened her own theatre in St. Petersburg in 1904. She created the part of the actress in *The Sea Gull,* when it was staged first at the Alexandrinski. Chekhov felt it was a failure, though the financial success throughout the country was considerable. She repeated the Chekhov play successfully as well as several of Ibsen's, including *The Wild Duck,* and the dramas of Naydenov. In 1906 Meyerhold came to her theatre as *régisseur.* Seeking plays with possibilities of symbolic stylization, they chose Maeterlinck's *Sister Beatrice,* Ibsen's *A Doll's House,* and curiously enough S. S. Yushkevich's *In a City,* which did not belong in such distinguished company.

Perhaps it might be well, at this point, to give Meyerhold's definition of stylization, as at that time Komissarzhevskaya subscribed to it and Meyerhold continued to hold views along somewhat the same lines throughout his artistic career. Anna Irene Miller in her excellently conceived volume *The Independent Theatre in Europe* (1931) gives a translation as follows: stylization is "the expression by all expressive means of the internal synthesis of a given epoch or phenomenon, the reproduction of their concealed characteristic features, such as are to be found in a deeply concealed style of any artistic production."

In Sologub's *The Victory of Death* (November, 1907), Meyerhold made use of the famous staircase that was likely to characterize any of his "architecturally" staged productions. The audience was amazed, alarmed and distressed by his experiments. He went too rapidly for them and for the actress-manager. Perplexed herself, she said that, "The thread between the auditorium and us was persistently broken, and every meaning of our work was disappearing." Feeling that his style of production was nullifying the actor and leading along the way to the marionette show, she wrote him that the end had come, "I look the future straight in the face and I say we cannot walk together upon this path."

Taking on her brother Fyodor Komissarzhevski as *régisseur* (his later productions, both at the Shakespeare Memorial Theatre at Stratford and for the Theatre Guild in New York, of *The Tidings Brought to Mary* and *Peer Gynt* are well known and are regarded with mixed emotions), she continued her theatre. Matislav Dobuzhinski was her scenic artist and their production of A. M. Remizov's *The Devil Play* (1907) was a complete failure. The actress decided to make an attempt to recoup her fortunes in America and came with a repertory of Ibsen, Sudermann, Molière, Gorki and Ostrovski to Daly's Theatre in New York. Despite high critical praise, the public was unprepared for drama in a foreign tongue. Opera it accepted because of the music but a play you couldn't understand didn't make sense to the average play-goer of 1908. Her only consistent support came from the Russian speaking population, largely Jewish and on the East Side. She moved to the Thalia Theatre on the Bowery to be nearer her audience but the heavy transportation expenses of her company ruined her. Besides, her *amour propre* was wounded as she took the public neglect as personal to her, when it would have been directed to any artist other than Bernhardt in those days. French and Italian were comprehensible but Russian was not fashionable. Komissarzhevskaya returned to St. Petersburg and opened a season at her theatre with Evreinov as stage director. That collaboration has already been mentioned. She died in 1910 having never recovered from her failure in New York.

It is obviously impossible in a history of this kind to detail the chronological record of such ancient playhouses as the Alexandrinski in St. Petersburg, which celebrated its centenary in 1932 (known since 1937 as the Pushkin State Theatre of Drama); the Bolshoi in Moscow (founded in 1825) which is the great opera house on Theatre Square famous for its restaging of the conventional operas; and the Mali (the oldest theatre in Russia, having been established in 1824). It was in this latter playhouse that many of Ostrovski's plays were produced and it is sometimes called "The House of Ostrovski." A statue of the dramatist was erected in front of the theatre in 1929. Towards the end of the nineteenth century it was the house of French farce but that period has long been over. There were several great actors associated with the Mali, Michael Shchepkin, P. S. Motchalov and the Sadovski family. In 1923 it established a branch in southeastern Moscow to reach the people of that district who found it inconvenient, because of poor transportation, to come all the way to the Theatre Square for performances in the evening. This is called the Safonov Theatre. It was part of a movement to take drama to the people in a fashion they could most enjoy and utilize. It was part and parcel of the touring system of workers' districts and collective farms and the general encouragement of the peasant theatres by displaying the achievements of the best artists of the Moscow and Leningrad playhouses. In 1937, the Mali was awarded the Order of Lenin for its services to Russian drama.

Next to Stanislavski and Nemirovitch-Danchenko the brightest name is that of VSEVOLOD EMILIEVITCH MEYERHOLD (1873-   ). After he left the Moscow Art Theatre in 1902, he formed a Society of the New Drama and he played a number of the Art Theatre's successes on tour in the south. In 1905 he returned to the parent organization as an actor but soon was working on the abortive attempt to establish a Studio, which was to prepare troupes for the provinces and to experiment with new forms. Maeterlinck's *The Death of Tintagiles* was the symbolic drama which attracted Meyerhold as a director. The designers Nikolai Sapunov and Sergei Soudeikine collaborated on this project with him in an effort to throw off the naturalism charged against the older organization, but which has been steadfastly denied as a permanent policy by its founders. This movement away from representationalism began, perhaps, with Adolphe Appia and was continued by Peter Behrens and soon after by Gordon Craig in his *The Art of the Theatre* (1905) and Georg Fuchs later *régisseur* at the *Muenchen Kuenstler Theater*, and author of *The Stage of the Future* (1905). It was along these lines that Meyerhold was working in his dramatic productions at the Alexandrinski and the operas at the Mariinski (home of the famous Russian ballet). His production of *Don Juan* in November, 1910, was epoch-making. Disliking realism as an imitation of life and loving theatre for theatre's sake, he relished the fact that Molière brought the action of the drama down on to the very edge of the stage and made it mingle with the life of the audience. That very fact brought the spectators into active participation, making them a vital and contributing force in the performance, and greatly appealed to Meyerhold's imagination and enthusiasm.

A considerable part of the success of *Don Juan* and the other productions of this great *régisseur* was due to the participation of the scenic artist, Alexander Golovin (1863-1930). The colorful and poetic fancies of his *décor* for the Russian Ballet are as much a part of his artistic palette as the precision and correctness which was the framework upon which he placed the seemingly careless and easy freedom of his designs for Meyerhold's productions.

Among the director's most successful work was the production of Lermontov's *Masquerade,* which opened on the night of the outbreak of the March, 1917 revolution. With the coming of the Bolshevik revolution, he suppressed any disagreement he might have had with A. V. Lunacharski, who had been made Commissar of Education in charge of theatres. Many of the directors and actors resented and fought the Soviet ideology and methods but it was not long before Meyerhold embraced them with open arms. No one yet knows whether this was sincere or mere opportunism. The other theatres eventually had to accept, with whatever grace they could muster, this change in their manner of living and thinking. Meyerhold, however, had the advantage of being in the forefront of the change. Undoubtedly the new and younger group was entirely sincere in its acceptance of the régime, but the older hands added Soviet plays to their repertory with the reluctance that bad playwriting always produces. The new young writers, and the recently converted, wavered between a misunderstanding of dramaturgic rules, in the effort to put across their new and simple ideas, and the awkwardness that essential dislike of an idea brings in its train.

Meyerhold, however, became the white hope of the Russian theatre with his acceptance of the state ideology. Some of his most electrifying productions came after this, including the magnificent staging of *Revizor,* which to most people the world over stands for Meyerhold. Of his later period perhaps Crommelynck's *The Magnificent Cuckold* with its use of constructivism, is the most characteristic of his productions, though it has been said that he creates a new theatre and a new technique for each play. This would seem to bring him in line with Vakhtangov, though no two men could have been further apart. Meyerhold might be said definitely to typify the theatre of the *régisseur* as opposed to the theatre of the actor, Stanislavski's style. Because of this he wrenches a play shamelessly apart to rebuild it with his own lines or parts taken from other plays. In this he approaches the synthetic theatre of Tairov, but he was as far from the principles of the Kamerni Theatre as he was from Stanislavski's and Vakhtangov's. He was an individualist in a collective world, yet in sympathy with that world. However he went too far for the whole; he was the crusader *par excellence,* but there came a time when crusaders were no longer needed and a collective state has small sentimentality about an individual, no matter how important he has been, when his usefulness is deemed over. That is the epitaph of Meyerhold even though he may still be alive.

ALEXANDER TAIROV (1885-   ) came into the theatre in 1912, when he abandoned a legal career to become stage manager of a St. Petersburg cabaret, The Stray Dog. This was followed by his *Théâtre Mobile,* which was a travelling repertory company, and a year as *régisseur* of the newly established Free Theatre, which only lasted out the season of 1913-14. Then with his actress-wife, Alice Koonen, he founded the Kamerni Theatre, which was to be an intimate "chamber" playhouse. He believed in theatre for theatre's sake, just as Meyerhold did, but he translated it into different terms because he saw scenes as a whole, in the large, while Meyerhold always saw with the eye of the individual actor. That, perhaps, is why the latter's small scenes were so good while Tairov's always seemed watery and unresolved. The truth of it was that Tairov became bored when he approached these and his productions always showed it.

Koonen is the connecting link with the Art Theatre for she was the original Mytyl in Stanislavski's tenderly symbolic direction of *The Blue Bird* (1908) as well as Anitra in his staging of *Peer Gynt* (1912). The Kamerni's first production was the Hindu play, *Shakuntala* (1914). *Salomé,* which is no longer in their repertory, is the play with which the theatre has been most closely identified, both inside and outside Russia. Its theatricality and stylized production are characteristic of Tairov's method. He is the most European of all of the *régisseurs.* He has looked beyond the confines of the Soviet State and has staged O'Neill's *All God's Chillun Got Wings, The Hairy Ape* and *Desire Under the Elms;* Shaw; Chesterton; Sophie Treadwell's *Machinal;* and John Dos Passos' *Fortune Heights.* He has apparently had little interest in the propaganda plays of modern Russia but of necessity has had to stage a few to keep his theatre open and to retain his state subsidy. Of these, perhaps his most successful has been Vsevolod Vishnevski's best play, *The Optimistic Tragedy* (1933), which has thrilling moments of surging crowds. It is at this that Tairov is most effective. His handling of the dance of the red sailors on the battleship was not to be forgotten, once seen. The role of the woman commissar was particularly effective in the hands of Alice Koonen.

This chamber theatre has expanded its horizon in its handsome new playhouse. They maintain however their tradition of the integral use of music in all their productions and the ideal of keeping their company pliable by retaining light opera and a curious kind of musical comedy in their repertory. In this last, they seem least effective; it is rather like a third road company of a Broadway musical. In 1937, Okhlopkov, who had been director of the Realistic Theatre since 1932, was made co-director and the Kamerni merged with the Moscow State Realistic Theatre under the new name of *Krasnaya Presna.* This latter playhouse, which undertakes a different approach to every play, including the rearrangement of stage and audience, was begun as the Fourth Studio of the Moscow Art Theatre in 1922. Two of their most noted performances were an adaptation of Gorki's *Mother* and Pogodin's *Aristocrats*. An American reflection of Okhlopkov's method, though not in any way following his treatment of plays, is to be found in the experimental Play Box stage of the Pasadena Community Playhouse under the direction of Gilmor Brown.

One of the most vital theatres of present day Russia is that named for and founded by EUGENE VAKHTANGOV (1883-1922). He was a student of Stanislavski, deemed by many to be the most brilliant and certainly one of the most beloved of all. He was associated with the First Studio for which he acted, among other roles, Tackleton in their colorful performance of *The Cricket on the Hearth*. In 1921, granted funds from the state and securing the large house of Prince Gagarin in Arbat Street, on which thoroughfare the present commodious playhouse is located nearby, he staged Maeterlinck's *The Miracle of St. Anthony* (what a favorite the Belgian symbolist has been with the Russians, who have well understood his mysticism).

Early in 1922, he presented his last and most famous production, *Turandot*. Influenced by the Chinese theatre in the staging of Gozzi's comedy, he brought the full force of his talent to bear. Unfortunately the rigors of bitter Russian winters in ill-heated or unheated buildings, together with the near-starvation under which they all operated for so long, took its toll. He died of tuberculosis at the very point in his career when he might have been expected to contribute most. The actors in his company rallied around to carry out his artistic ideals in his name, hence the Vakhtangov Theatre. Perhaps this enthusiastic support came because it was one of Vakhtangov's precepts that the whole company must concur in the production-plot prepared by the *régisseur* and the dramatist or else they will not understand what they are doing and the final result can only be faulty. Perhaps their most successful presentations have been Leo Slavin's *Intervention* (1933), *Yegor Bulychev and Others* (1932) and Pogodin's *Aristocrats*. Their sovietization of *Hamlet* in 1933, staged and designed by the brilliant *régisseur*, Nikolai Akimov (1901-   ) was in the long run unsuccessful as it departed too far from the real meaning of the play, and has since been dropped from their repertoire.

The foreign language theatres have flourished in Russia. This has been particularly true since the Revolution, when national minority theatres have been encouraged, but certain Yiddish and Hebrew groups existed before that time. Of these the most important and outstanding is the Habimah, to which both Vakhtangov and Stanislavski contributed their time and artistic energies. This group was founded shortly after the revolution of 1905 by N. L. Zemach (brother of Ben-

jamin Zemach, prominently identified with the activities of the Labor
Stage in New York and once a member of the Habimah himself).
They were forced "underground" by the tsarist persecution of the
Jews in 1911. They emerged after the Revolution, and were suppressed
again but such influential friends as Gorki and Stanislavski interceded
successfully on their behalf. Their production of S. Ansky's play, *The
Dybbuk*, was staged by Vakhtangov and Huntley Carter has suggested
that his methods were strongly influenced by the Tibetan mystery
plays. If this is true it is easy to see why those dramas have fixed so
firm a hold on the imaginations of the travellers who have beheld them.
Ansky's play of primitive Jewish emotions caught the imagination of
the world, when this group left Russia and toured Europe and America in 1925 and 1926. In New York they displayed this drama as well
as Henning Berger's *The Deluge*, Penskom's *The Eternal Jew*, and
Richard Beer-Hoffman's *Jacob's Dream*. *The Dybbuk* was eloquently
staged in English at the Neighborhood Playhouse in 1925 under the
management of Alice and Irene Lewisohn. In the season of 1928-29
the Habimah removed to Palestine, the center of the Zionist movement to reorient Jews in their former home. There they merged with
the Stanislavski pupil, Gnessin, and his Hatai Company and built a
handsome new playhouse at Tel-Aviv, where they still play in Hebrew. Also in Tel-Aviv is the Hebrew (and leftist) Ohel troupe.

Before turning to the period of Soviet playwriting, we must speak
of two organizations which came out of Russia, where they no longer
are at home, though once their roots were deep in the land of the tsars.
These are the Russian Ballet and the *Chauve-Souris*. This does not
mean that the dance, either classic ballet, revolutionary ballet, or modern interpretive dance has been neglected in Russia since the Revolution. The Mariinski and the Bolshoi are still hospitable to this art form
and several pieces, more interesting from the point of view of mass
movement and colorful staging than from the point of view of dancers' merits, have been performed. *The Red Poppy* (1927) and *The
Flames of Paris* (1932) are the most notable. Leningrad is the center
of the ballet just as she used to be when she was St. Petersburg, but
the Bolshoi in Moscow has staged many interesting productions.

The ballet was introduced into Russia by the Tsar Alexis in the seventeenth century and was fostered there always. Toward the end of
the nineteenth century it reached a very high peak of technical perfection under the Frenchman Marius Petipa (1822-1910), who
became *maître de ballet* at the Mariinski in 1858. Under the rigors of
his régime such dancers as Pavlova, Mordkin and Nijinski were trained.
In the early years of the present century, under the artistic prompt-
ings of that masterful entrepreneur Serge Diaghilev (1872-1929), the

whole scope of the ballet was widened and fresh talents were introduced. Michael Fokine was beginning to chafe under the restrictions of the old line. In 1907, the great American dancer, Isadora Duncan (1878-1927) went to St. Petersburg. The inspiration of her free dancing was invigorating and through Fokine and Diaghilev the great new tradition was established. In 1909, with the permission of the Mariinski, they took a company to Paris and the whole world became ballet-conscious because of the fame of its dancers, Pavlova, Nijinski, Karsavina, Fokine (also the choreographer); the great designers, Léon Bakst, and Alexander Benois, and the composer, Igor Stravinski. They continued to alternate between their native land and western Europe. In 1916 they paid their only visit to this country. From this group have come the various ballet companies which play all over the world, from London, New York, Buenos Aires to Sydney and Melbourne.

The *Chauve-Souris* (*The Bat*) is almost invariably referred to by its French name, though it originated as a cabaret in Moscow under the leadership of Nikita Baliev (1877-1936), who had been associated in a minor capacity with the Moscow Art Theatre. He had acted in *The Blue Bird* and in Ibsen's *Brand*, but it was not until he emerged as an entertainer and comedian that he came into his own. Beginning as a club for Moscow actors and their friends in 1908, he eventually opened his doors to the general public. His pieces were primarily comic and accompanied with music and song, frequently pantomime. Who will ever forget his *Chauve-Souris Parade of the Wooden Soldiers?* He played short plays of Pushkin and Gogol and occasionally serious short dramas such as Gorki's *Mother*. He had such scenic artists associated with him as Nikolai Remisov and Sergei Soudeikine, whose bold, poster colors caught the imagination of the whole world. His composer was Alexei Arkhangelski. Baliev's greatest actress was that incomparable mistress of make-up and changing moods, Tamara Daykharhanova, who today conducts her own dramatic school in New York, basing her work on the methods of the master Stanislavski under whom she served in her youth. The troupe led a nomadic life, playing in one European capital after another for fifteen years after leaving Moscow. They were disbanded after Baliev's death but members of the troupe are scattered in the various theatres of the world, where their fine creative abilities have long been cherished.

The list of writers who began their careers after the Revolution is long but, as has been stated before, is hardly distinguished. There are a few names which stand out above the others because of more than average ability. Perhaps the finest talent is that of ALEXANDER NIKO-LAYEVITCH AFINOGENOV (1904-   ), whose plays have been performed more widely than any other's after Gorki. His first play was

On the South Side of the Slot (1926), based on Jack London's San Francisco story. In the same year came *At the Turning Point in the Ranks* and the next year he wrote *Keep Your Eyes Open*, a didactic play about a student who disgraced himself by letting his Communist Party membership card be used by counter-revolutionists, and *The Trail of the Wolf*, which concerned sabotage. He ridiculed the hopeless confusion of the bourgeoisie in modern Russia in *Raspberry Jam* (1928). *The Crank* (1929), *The Portrait* (1934), and the anti-fascist *Spain, We Salute Thee* (1936) are other plays by him. His two best dramas are *Fear* (1931), and *Dalekoe* (1935), which painted an interesting picture of unselfishness. The first concerns itself with the irritation of a great scientist who is exposed to suspicion and intolerant attacks because he does not conform to the ideology of "the party line," that bugbear of all intellectuals in Russia. Though he presents the point of view of the professor with sympathy and understanding, he proves him wrong by rather spurious reasoning and ends the play on his conversion. The Moscow Art Theatre gave this play one of its most interesting productions and it remained in its repertory until Afinogenov himself came into conflict with the ever-changing party line in 1938 and 1939. His plays were no longer allowed to be staged anywhere in the U.S.S.R., though he has actually been released from prison according to recent unverified reports.

It is this constantly shifting line of conformity which is demanded of Soviet writers, which has had as much to do with their failure to produce worthwhile drama as anything else. It is never possible to know from day to day what may be considered counter-revolutionary. At any moment a previously praised play or novel may be discovered to contain Trotskyist or other suspect doctrines as political ideologies vary and the author or *régisseur* may find himself imprisoned and his productions banned from Russian theatres. This would seem to point to an inner feeling of insecurity which is not allowed to appear on the surface through rigorous censorship of news dispatches and hesitation to bring official reprisals upon relatives or friends still in that country, if the man himself has escaped to freedom. It is this kind of persecution which has been one of the most powerful methods of the totalitarian nations in suppressing criticism in foreign countries.

MICHAEL BULGAKOV (1891-   ) has had a number of his plays suppressed because of his unwillingness to curb his writing. Two of his dramas are outstanding; *The Last of the Turbins* (produced by Michel St. Denis in London as *The White Guard*) in 1926, and *Dead Souls* (1932), a dramatization of Gogol's great novel for the Moscow Art Theatre. It was there that his sympathetic portrayal of the family of a White Guard during the Civil War was staged. This play has more meat than is customary in this period and the characters have real depth. It was produced in this country experimentally by the undergraduate Yale Dramatic Association with Blanche Yurka as the star. The problems are largely personal and the piece has been compared with *The Cherry Orchard*, not too unfavorably. Bulgakov is responsible for *Molière* (1936) among other lesser plays.

NIKOLAI FEDOROVITCH POGODIN (1900-　　) has written a number of plays about workers and collective farms, the most interesting of which is *Aristocrats* (1935). This macabre comedy about the attempts to rehabilitate civil and political prisoners in a work-camp established for enforced labor on the Baltic-White Sea Canal project shows their eventual regeneration and pride in their accomplishments. *Tempo* (1930); *After the Ball* (1934); *The Man with the Rifle* (1937), concerning the personal inspiration Lenin held for people; and *The Silver Field* (1938) are probably his best plays after *Aristocrats*.

VLADIMIR MICHAELOVITCH KIRSHON (1902-　　) has offered us two plays, out of the common run of unthinking self-praise or political experiment common to most writers of this period. *Red Rust* (1927), in collaboration with A. O. Uspenski, concerns itself with the degeneration of a hero of the Civil War who is entrusted with civil administration and who succumbs to capitalist greed. This play was excitingly staged by Herbert Biberman for the Theatre Guild Studio, forerunner of the present day Group Theatre in New York in 1930. *Bread* (1931) is an arbitrary study of the farm movement with black, black villains and heroes too pure for belief. It is this over-simplification which robs most of these plays of any literary value and of much of their dramatic force.

VALENTIN PETROVITCH KATAYEV (1897-　　) is probably the best writer of comedy on the present day Russian stage. His most successful play, having been staged in many countries, is *Squaring the Circle* (1928), which is a genuinely comic farce about two young men who marry and bring their young wives (one is less regularly attached) home to the one room which they possess. The girls do not care for this arrangement, one being a peasant and the other a party-worker. After an exchange of mates, the farcical situation is happily resolved. In *The Path of Flowers* (also called *The Flowery Way*, 1934), it is a man who is torn between two women, but the comedy is more strained and less spontaneous. This was produced in New York by the Federal Theatre Project. His last two plays, after a series of comedies, *Lonely White Sail* (1937), and *I, Son of the Working People* (1938) are entirely serious.

SERGE MICHAELOVITCH TRETYAKOV (1892-　　) wrote *The Earth Rampant* (1923), an adaptation of Martinet's play, *La Nuit*; and *Gas*

Masks (1924), which had to do with an outbreak on the part of German workers in a poison gas factory, who were denied proper gas masks for their own use. However the play for which he is best known, despite the crudity of its propaganda, was his highly effective *Roar China* (1926). It is concerned with the revolt of Chinese coolies against British imperialism in China in 1926. It was provocatively staged by Herbert Biberman with a memorable permanent setting, by Lee Simonson, of a battleship at anchor in harbor, with the docks stretching out into the auditorium. This play was produced by the Theatre Guild in New York in 1930.

ALEXEI MICHAELOVITCH FAIKO (1893-   ) has written a number of plays including *Lake Lull* (1923), *The Teacher Bubus* (1925), *The Thankless Role* (1932), and *The Concert* (1936). However, his most admired play is *The Man with a Portfolio* (1927), which is highly melodramatic and typical of contrived drama. A scientist hostile to bolshevism, because his father was a general, murders a professional associate for fear his anti-communist views might be exposed, drives his aristocratic wife to suicide, and is finally revealed as a murderer. After a public confession, reminiscent of the malodorous public trials of 1936-37, he kills himself.

ANATOLE GLEBOVITCH GLEBOV (1899-   ) has written plays having to do with factory problems which have been highly popular with an audience made up of factory-workers and other artisans. *Inga* (1928) is probably the best known but it is extremely tedious to an outside public. It is concerned with the difficulties of a woman factory manager who involves herself in a love affair with a married man, and the efforts of the factory committee to extricate her from her unpleasant situation which only get her into worse trouble. It is arranged that she give up her lover (the wife being removed by the committee) and devote herself to industrial problems. This kind of thinking is characteristic also of *Zagmuk* (1925), *Growth* (1926), *Power* (1927); in *Gold and Brains*, the rescue of the inter-planetary ship from the fascists for scientific use is not unlike the comic strip, *Flash Gordon*. In *The Necktie* (1930) Glebov ridicules communists who suspect a man of counter-revolutionary tendencies because he wears a necktie. Perhaps he was right, for a British dramatic critic was once heard saying that he preferred the Moscow Art Theatre because the audience wore neckties and coats, and was humorously shushed for his sentiments by a group of theatre enthusiasts present at a theatre festival in 1934. There is not much difference between Glebov's efforts to be facetious and his efforts to be serious.

YURI KARLOVITCH OLESHA (1899-   ) is responsible for three plays. The first is *The Conspiracy of the Feelings* (1929); the children's play, *The Three Fat Men* (1930), who were Capitalism, Militarism and Clericalism; and his most impressive piece, *The List of Advantages* (1931). This deals with an actress who gets fed up with the Soviet noble experiment, flees to Paris and becomes involved in the intrigues of the Russian *émigrés*, of which she also grows tired and disgusted.

The last of the writers to be considered individually is VSEVOLOD VYACHESLAVITCH IVANOV (1895-   ), who is chiefly noted for the much performed *Armored Train 14-69* (1927). This recounts the capture of an armored train of the White Russian forces by a group of peasants in Siberia. His other plays are *Blockade* (1929), *The Compromise of Naib Khan* (1931), and *Doves of Peace* (1938).

The principal contribution of the Russian theatre since 1917 has been largely on the side of staging and acting, and in the enormous expansion of theatregoing facilities. It has tremendously increased its coverage of the country, for according to the authority on the Soviet theatre, Henry Wadsworth Longfellow Dana, seventy million theatre admissions are used in a single year. The approximately two hundred and fifty theatres inherited from the tsars have been increased to more than a thousand regular playhouses and over five thousand stages controlled by collective farms, factories, workers' clubs as well as informal amateur groups. These statistics hold good as of 1938. Presumably these facilities have been increased since then.

This is a brilliant and highly provocative theatre which is flowering. It is to be hoped that world conditions and internal politics will permit this stage to continue the expansion that the trials of 1936-37 interrupted. It has a great future in which the entire theatre world is interested, regardless of political or economic sympathies.

XXXI

ENGLAND—NAPOLEON TO THE BATTLE

OF BRITAIN

(1815-1940)

The expense of building the new Drury Lane * in 1812 had been heavy and the committee of amateurs, headed by Samuel Whitbread would have proved incompetent to bring back the public to a theatre which fire and disaster had closed for three years. However they were saved by a miracle which was more than providential in the war-torn Napoleonic years. The name of the miracle was Edmund Kean (1787-1833), who in the years before had striven hard for recognition and to whom small parts had occasionally been tossed. But what are bits to a man torn by the terrible anguish of genius? Londoners had crowded in to see the boy wonder, Master Betty, give his totally inadequate performances and passed by, unheedingly, the man who was to carry the fate of the nation's playhouse, Drury Lane, on his narrow shoulders. His lithe figure, his slender face, his dark and burning eyes overtopped by black, curly hair as yet had attracted no notice.

Reputed son of an architect's clerk, Edmund Kean, and an actress, Ann Carey, granddaughter of the playwright, Henry Carey, he made his debut on the stage in his fourth year as Cupid in Noverre's ballet, *Cymon*. After a checkered career, he was taken under the wing of his uncle, Moses Kean, the mimic. At fourteen he ran away and acted with various troupes of strolling players. He learned equestrian tricks in Saunder's circus, something about music from Charles Incledon, dancing from the ballet maestro, James Harvey D'Egville and fencing from the celebrated master, Henry Angelo.

In 1807 he played leading parts with statuesque Mrs. Siddons, who took a dislike to him, calling him "a horrid little man." After watching his work, however, she admitted that Kean "played very, very well" but that unfortunately "there was too little of him to make a great

* Damaged by bombs, November, 1940.

553

actor." The usually far-sighted Sarah lived to see herself proved wrong on that famous night of January 26, 1814 when he electrified his audience and took London almost literally by storm as Shylock, in the great reaches of Drury Lane. Then came Richard III, Hamlet, Othello, Macbeth and Lear and his mastery of the situation was apparent even to the most obtuse of his detractors. He saved the licensees of the theatre from bankruptcy and for several years he triumphed there. The critics and the poets went night after night to watch the fiery wonder of this little man, whose natural approach to the great Shakespearean parts put the recitative method of Kemble to retreat. After Kean all the great actors followed, in a sense.

However he had little control over his personal feelings and the long bitter years of gruelling poverty had ill prepared him for prosperity. He began to drink too much, and ran up debts that only more triumphs and more money could dissolve. As the bad effects of his ill-living crowded upon him, he was less and less able to play, so that the debts grew worse and he drank even more to forget them. He treated his wife badly, raised his son, Charles, extravagantly to be a gentleman, and quarrelled with him when he went on the stage because his father was no longer supporting him. In addition to this the elder Kean involved himself in an affair with a Mrs. Cox, whose husband divorced her and named him responsible. Mrs. Kean left him and matters went from bad to worse until he was only able to act when sustained by brandy. A reconciliation was effected with Charles who was acting with him at Covent Garden, when on March 25, 1833, during *Othello*, he faltered and fell saying "I am dying. Speak to them, Charles." This was his last appearance, Mrs. Kean rallied to him and was with him when he died in his home at Richmond, May 15. Thus died one of England's greatest actors, who was incomparable in Shakespeare, but whose greatest role was probably Sir Giles Overreach in Massinger's *A New Way to Pay Old Debts*.

While Kean was revolutionizing acting, ROBERT WILLIAM ELLISTON (1774-1831), the handsome, the correct, the stage gentleman was performing in an imitation of the Kemble manner. On one occasion, as a *tour de force*, he played Hamlet and Macbeth on the same bill, which showed the variety and scope of his talent. His Romeo was physically attractive rather than fiery. Perhaps his best work as an actor was as Duke Aranza in John Tobin's popular and romantic drama *The Honey Moon* (1805). At various times he served as manager for the Olympic, the Surrey and Drury Lane theatres, having been an actor at the latter from 1804 to its destruction in 1809 and again with the new playhouse from 1812. He became lessee after 1819 and managed Kean, Mme. Vestris and

Macready. He was much admired as an actor by no less than Leigh Hunt and Charles Lamb. He had failed ignominiously when he attempted Falstaff in 1826 and this damaged his reputation. When he was managing the Surrey, all did not go too well for him. However he was saved by the rising talent of DOUGLAS JERROLD (1803-1857), who had tired of the exactions of William Davidge, manager of the Coburg (present day Old Vic). For several years, Jerrold had been turning out dramas and farces for the Coburg with little financial reward. He offered *Black-eyed Susan; or, All in the Downs* (1829) to the drowning Elliston, who produced it with avidity and skill. The fresh, salty flavor of the piece was heightened by T. P. Cooke's breezy acting. The town crowded into the Surrey and Elliston closed his career in a blaze of glory. Jerrold went on to ever-increasing fame with *The Bride of Ludgate* (1831) and play after play until he drew his writing career to a close with *The Heart of Gold* (1854).

While Matthew Gregory Lewis (1775-1818) was chilling the blood of London play-goers with his Gothic drama, *The Castle Spectre* (1798), among other pieces, the hot blood of English romanticism was rising and soon the poets, Coleridge, Keats, Shelley and Byron turned to the theatre. Of these, the man with the most to offer to the stage and with the widest influence throughout Europe was GEORGE GORDON BYRON, 6th Baron Byron (1788-1824). John Keats' *Otho the Great* (written about 1819) was intended for Drury Lane but was never produced, nor does it seem to merit production. The German writers had overinfluenced Samuel Taylor Coleridge in his *Remorse* (1803). Charles Lamb also failed at poetic drama with his *John Woodvill* (1801) and at farce with *Mr. H.* (1805). Shelley's best play was his tragedy, *The Cenci* (1820), which has high poetic and considerable theatrical value. It is perhaps rated higher than it merits because of the almost dead level of dramatic writing surrounding it.

Byron's first drama, *Manfred* (1817), was characteristic of his thinking. His misanthropy and his passionate love of nature appear in this weakest of his poetic dramas. *Marino Falieri* (1820) and *The Two Foscari* (1821) are Venetian tragedies of some merit. Though they do not flow easily, they are truly theatrical for Byron had had ample opportunity to observe rehearsals when he was on the managing committee of the Drury Lane. He endeavored to bring some of the feeling of the Old Testament into *Cain* (1821), which shocked his readers, for this is really closet drama and not intended for the playhouse. *Sardanapolis* (1821) presented an effeminate hero, but the action of the piece was heroic and the leading character managed to rise to the occasion when the situation required it. His *Werner; or, The Inheritance* (1822) was his most effective piece for the theatre; Macready's performance illumined the script and the play had a considerable success for some years. His other two plays were *Heaven and Earth, a Mystery* (1823) and *The Deformed Transformed* (1824). His poetic dramas repay rereading and perhaps *Werner* might stand revival today.

This was a time of great spectacles at Drury Lane, Covent Garden, Sadler's Wells and the other houses. Pantomimes flourished and the great clown Grimaldi was entertaining countless audiences. It was not a period of great drama; most of what was written was mediocre. W. T. Moncrieff, Henry Hart Milman, Gilbert à Beckett, William Dimond, Walter Savage Landor, Sir Thomas Noon Talfourd, Edward Fitzball, J. B. Buckstone; John Oxenford, Henry J. Byron, Charles Reade, and George R. Sims were among the many who contributed to the stage until the dramatic revival at the end of the century. More and more theatres were being built in various parts of London; the stage was flourishing in the provinces. This was due almost entirely to heightened public interest in acting which Mrs. Siddons, Kemble, and Kean had inspired. Comparison of acting techniques and love of elaborate scenic display with unusual mechanical effects drew people to the playhouse.

There are a few names which are enough above the average to mention but their inclusion does not imply unusual merit nor do they warrant more than passing reference. Of these men, one of the best known and the most representative of the early part of the century is JAMES SHERIDAN KNOWLES (1784-1862) with *Leo* (1810), in which Kean was successful; *Brian Boroihme* (1811) created a sensation in Belfast but brought its author little financial return. Then came *Caius Gracchus* (1815), staged in the same city, where he was still teaching school. *Virginius* (1820) was written for Kean and enjoyed wide fame at Covent Garden and elsewhere for the next thirty years. *William Tell* (1825) provided one of Macready's best roles. The last three, with *The Wife, a Tale of Mantua* (1833), constituted his contribution to the poetic tradition in English drama, while *The Love Chase* (1837) was a popular comedy.

JAMES ROBINSON PLANCHÉ (1796-1880) wrote mostly burlesques, musical pieces and pantomimes. Also he designed the costumes for Charles Kemble's production of *King John* at Covent Garden in 1823 (the first time a revival had been costumed with authenticity). He was frequently employed to provide accurate historical costuming. Mme. Vestris desired him to dress his burlesque, *Olympic Revels*, which opened her management of the Olympic in 1831. She had engaged him to write a series of plays for her, which he followed with *Fair One with the Golden Locks* (1843) for Benjamin Nothingham Webster, manager of the Haymarket. When Mme. Vestris took over the Lyceum in 1847, Planché once more became her designer and author; his greatest success was with *The Island of Jewels* (1849).

TOM TAYLOR (1817-1880) stood for the well-constructed play designed for performance in the theatre, with little or no idea of its being read. His pretentious historical pieces in blank verse, such as *Joan of Arc* (1871) and *Anne Boleyn* (1875), were failures. He collaborated with Charles Reade on the popular *Masks and Faces* (1852). He was one of the favorite playwrights of the nineteenth century and was responsible for over a hundred plays. The best known of these are *Our American Cousin* (staged under Buckstone's management at the Haymarket, 1858), which was played for Abraham Lincoln by Laura Keene, at Ford's Theatre, on the night he was shot by John Wilkes Booth; as well as *Still Waters Run Deep* (1855), and *The Ticket of Leave Man* (1863), a hardy perennial.

While the elder Kean was still playing, CHARLES KEMBLE (1775-1854) was acting parts which were enhanced by his handsomeness, such as Charles Surface, Doricourt in *The Belle's Stratagem*, and Ranger in Hoadley's *The Suspicious Husband*. He became manager of Covent Garden where he staged many handsome productions with careful historical preparation, such as *The Tempest* and the aforementioned *King John*. These were so expensive that he began to run into financial difficulties. The fortunate result of this was that his daughter, FRANCES ANNE KEMBLE (1809-93) determined to go on the stage to restore the family fortunes, despite an intense dislike for acting. Her mother, Maria, played Lady Capulet so as to present the debutante as Juliet, as Mrs. Pritchard had done years before. Fanny obviously knew what she was about, for the audience, led by her aunt Mrs. Siddons in a box, cheered her and she played Juliet for twenty-nine performances during the season of 1829-30. Her American career has already been noted. After her return to the stage in 1847 to raise money, and her divorce in 1849, she became a reader like her father, because it permitted her to use her full, rich voice to move her auditors without the vulgarity of acting.

Like Charles Kemble, LUCIA ELIZABETH BARTALOZZI VESTRIS (1797-1856) began as a player and later turned to management and production. She started as a singer and found her pleasing voice a valuable adjunct to her acting. In Paris she appeared as Camille (in *Horace*) opposite Talma, and in London she created a sensation in James Cobb's *The Siege of Belgrade* (1820) at Drury Lane. She was excellent in "breeches parts" because of her enchanting figure, and in light comedies such as Planché's *The Loan of a Lover*, Poole's *Paul Pry*, and Dance's *Naval Engagements*, she bewitched her audiences. In 1831 she took over the Olympic where she made a reputation for her productions of extravaganzas. After an American tour with Charles James Mathews (1803-1878), whom she married in 1838, the two of them undertook the management of Covent Garden. They collaborated with Boucicault as their playwright and brought out his successful *London Assurance*, 1841, and sincerely tried to effect reforms in the drama but there was not enough interest on either side of the footlights for them to succeed. They relinquished the patent house in 1842 and in 1847 took over the reins at the Lyceum, where the public demanded yet more extravaganzas and farces as in the old Olympic days. In addition to Planché, Mme. Vestris secured the services of the fine designer and stage painter, William Beverley. She retired in 1854 and upon her death, two years later, Mathews gave up the Lyceum lease and embarked on another American tour, from which he returned with another wife, and continued to act with brilliant skill for the next twenty years.

Mme. Vestris' predecessor at Covent Garden was WILLIAM CHARLES MACREADY (1793-1873), whose difficulties with Forrest in Edinburgh and later in New York have already been described. He was the son of the provincial theatre manager, William Macready. He made his debut at the age of seventeen as Romeo, at Birmingham. After a quarrel with his father, the younger Macready went to Bath in 1814, where he acted for the next two years. He made a hit as Orestes in Phillips' *The Distrest Mother* in 1816 at Covent Garden. He played mostly romantic parts for some years, notably in Pocock's *Rob Roy* (made from Scott's novel). His Richard III in 1819, his William Tell in 1825, his Werner in 1830, and his Sardanapolis were all successful. In 1837 he took over the management of Covent Garden and his first concern was in building up the puny drama. He encouraged ROBERT BROWNING (1812-1889) to write for the stage and in 1837 produced his *Strafford*, which had able characterization but was static and not readily adaptable to the stage. Then came the poetic *Pippa Passes* (1842), the well characterized and actable *King Victor and King Charles* (1842), the somewhat melodramatic *The Return of the Druses* (1843), and the indifferently received *A Blot in the 'Scutcheon* (1843) which was dramatically effective. Browning was over rhetorical, always, and nowhere did it show more than in *Colombe's Birthday* (1844, acted 1853) and *Luria and a Soul's Tragedy* (1846).

Almost all of the important poetic figures undertook the drama at some time. ALFRED, LORD TENNYSON (1809-1889) was invariably unsuccessful even when well acted. His *Queen Mary* (1875) was staged by Irving in 1876. *The Falcon* (1879) was acted by the Kendals. He also wrote *The Cup* (1881); *The Promise of May* (1882); *Becket* (1884), a hit with Irving after Tennyson's death; *The Foresters* (1892), produced by Augustin Daly; and *Harold* (1876), which was not acted. Because of his strong critical interest in the theatre ALGERNON CHARLES SWINBURNE (1837-1909) tried his hand at writing plays. These were poetic in form, free in expression, glorious in his choice of words, but none of them were really suitable for the stage and are likely to remain "closet dramas". Among these are *The Queen Mother* (1860), *Rosamond* (1860), *Atalanta in Calydon* (1865), *Bothwell* (1874), and *Mary Stuart* (1881.) His Shakespearean criticism was vital and arresting and was published in *Study of Shakespeare* (1880) and *The Age of Shakespeare* (1909).

Macready was also responsible for encouraging EDWARD BULWER-LYTTON, LORD LYTTON (1803-73), the novelist, to attempt the dramatic form. Though his work was marked by sensationalism and sentimentality it did much towards raising dramatic standards. Macready was the sponsor of *The Lady of Lyons* (1838), which became the most popular romantic play of the century. Bulwer-Lytton then followed with *Richelieu; or, The Conspiracy* (1839), which is still revived as an excellent acting vehicle; the summer of 1940 saw a performance at Charles Coburn's Mohawk Drama Festival with Walter Hampden hurling the famous curse of Rome, which caused audiences to shiver all through the nineteenth century. The author's other plays were *Money* (1840), *Not as Bad as We Seem* (1851), and *Walpole; or, Every Man Has His Price* (1869).

Macready followed his management of Covent Garden with that of Drury Lane from 1841 to 1843. There he continued honestly to give the people the best and most up-lifting productions that he could manage but he failed because the old classical repertory no longer interested London audiences and the important new dramatists had yet to make their appearance. In 1851 Macready retired from the stage and spent the balance of his life in quiet and pleasant retirement at the charming spa of Cheltenham.

Another actor who went on to managership was SAMUEL PHELPS

(1804-78). He began, about 1826, as an actor on the York circuit of theatres at eighteen shillings a week but soon progressed to important tragic roles at the theatres in the south of England, where he was well regarded. His first London appearance came as Shylock, at the Haymarket, in August, 1837. Not long after, Macready drew him to the Covent Garden where he remained, playing opposite the actor-manager in the other male leads for six years. Macready acknowledged the power of Phelps' acting when on one occasion he yielded Othello to him, retaining Iago for himself. Being an actor, as well as a manager, he never made that mistake again. Phelps leaned rather to the older style of playing but his admirers were inclined to rank him above Charles Kean and even Fechter, in his heyday, which last may have been mere partisan zeal.

Phelps' principal contribution to the stage was not his acting but the pioneer work he did at Sadler's Wells. That theatre had fallen into disrepute and the reputation of the neighborhood was bad; the most recent tradition of the house was melodramatic. Phelps had expected to give them melodrama mixed in with revivals of the classics, but he found their natural taste drew them to Shakespeare, Massinger, Beaumont and Fletcher, Otway and the others. The only melodramas he offered were better by far than the ordinary. He staged Boucicault's version of Delavigne's *Louis XI* and Tom Taylor's *The Fool's Revenge* (1859). However, during the years between 1844 and 1862 (his business partner, Thomas L. Greenwood retired in 1861), Phelps staged thirty-four of Shakespeare's plays in the most highly satisfactory educational experiment of the nineteenth century. It was undoubtedly his experience which heartened Lilian Baylis to undertake the rehabilitation of the Old Vic, as a place for popular-priced revivals of the classics, with fine actors, for the benefit of the neighborhood. Her success was comparable with that of Phelps and she later included Sadler's Wells in her circuit for it had again fallen into desuetude. However, Miss Baylis's theatre became the favorite stamping ground for actors from the West End who wished to experiment with lung-filling parts. Phelps kept together a more or less permanent company headed by Mary Warner, Isabella Gly, William Hoskins and himself, which gave them the opportunity to run the full range of Shakespeare's characters. Despite this, Phelps' best performance perhaps was the comic Sir Pertinax Macsycophant in Macklin's *The Man of the World*.

While Phelps and Greenwood were running the Sadler's Wells playhouse yet another acting managership was set up by one who had formerly appeared under the sponsorship of others. CHARLES KEAN

343. Eugene O'Neill, America's Most Distinguished Dramatist.

*Brugière Collection,
N. Y. Public Library*

344. The Pasadena Playhouse Production of *Lazarus Laughed*, By Eugene O'Neill.

Courtesy of Gilmor Brown

345. The Members of the Playwrights' Company. Left to right: Robert E. Sherwood, S. N. Behrman, the late Sidney Howard, Maxwell Anderson, and Elmer Rice.

Courtesy of the Playwrights' Company

346. LIONEL BARRYMORE AS MACBETH
Brugière

347. JOHN BARRYMORE, WITH BLANCHE YURKA, IN *Hamlet*. *Brugière*

48. MAUDE ADAMS AS PETER PAN.
N. Y. P. L.

349. HELEN HAYES IN *Victoria Regina*.
Vandamm

350, 351, 352. SETTINGS BY JOSEPH URBAN. Above, two sets for the Ziegfeld Follies. Left, setting for *Don Carlos.*

353. SETTING BY NORMAN BEL GEDDES FOR *The Miracle*, STAGED BY MAX REINHARDT. (1924).

354. SETTING BY NORMAN BEL GEDDES FOR *Dead End*, BY SIDNEY KINGSLEY (1935).

355. Design By Robert Edmond Jones For *Mourning Becomes Electra* (1931).

Courtesy of Eugene O'Neill

356 Setting For *Macbeth*, Robert Edmond Jones (1921).

357. Setting For *The Green Pastures*. Robert Edmond Jones (1930).

WALTER HAMPDEN'S HAMLET — ACT III, SCENE 6: A HALL IN THE CASTLE

358. Setting By Claude Bragdon For *Hamlet* (1925).

359. SETTING BY JO MIELZINER FOR *Two On An Island*, BY ELMER RICE (1940).

360. SETTING BY JO MIELZINER FOR *Winterset*, BY MAXWELL ANDERSON (1935).

361. SETTING BY JO MIELZINER FOR *Journey to Jerusalem*, BY MAXWELL ANDERSON (1940).

362. THE FUNERAL SCENE FROM *Our Town*, BY THORNTON WILDER. Produced without scenery
(1938).   *Vandamm*

363. SETTING BY WATSON BARRATT FOR *The Case of Clyde Griffiths*, BY ERWIN PISCATOR. Group Theatre Production (1935).

364. SETTING BY WATSON BARRATT FOR *Bitter Sweet* (NOEL COWARD). The pylon set with panel designed for the St. Louis Opera Co. to meet the problem of outdoor production. The pylon are also used, without panels, for formalized settings.

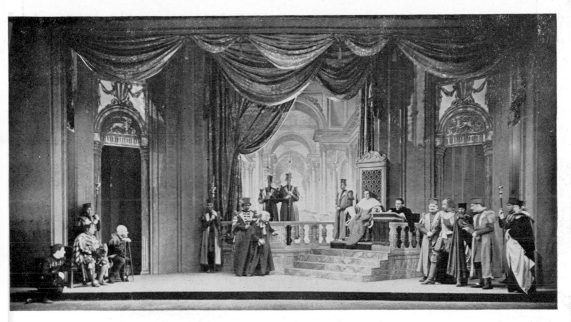

365. Setting By Lee Simonson For *Volpone* (1927).   *Vandamm*

366. Setting By Lee Simonson For *Goat Song*, By Franz Werfel (1926).   *Vandamm*

367. Setting By Lee Simonson For *Amphitryon 38*, With Alfred Lunt and Lynn Fontanne (1938).

368. Alfred Lunt and Lynn Fontanne in *The Taming of the Shrew*. Costumes by Claggett Wilson (1937).

Vandamm

369. SETTING BY HENRY DREYFUS, FOR *Fine and Dandy*. Dreyfuss subsequently left the theatre for the field of industrial design (1930).

370. SETTING BY ALBERT JOHNSON, FOR *The Great Waltz*. This was the most lavish and expensive set ever built for the modern stage (1934).

371. SETTING BY WOODMAN THOMPSON FOR *What Price Glory?* (1924).

372. SETTING BY WOODMAN THOMPSON FOR WINTHROP AMES' PRODUCTION OF THE KAUFMAN-
CONNELLY *Beggar On Horseback* (1924).

373. SETTING BY RAOUL PENE DU BOIS FOR *Panama Hattie* (1940).

374. SETTING BY SERGEI SOUDEIKINE FOR *Porgy and Bess* (1935).

375. SETTING BY BORIS ARONSON FOR THE BALLET, *The Great American Goof* (1940).

376. SETTING BY BORIS ARONSON FOR *The Gentle People*, BY IRWIN SHAW (1939).

(1811-68) made his first appearance as Norval in *Douglas* in 1826 and in October, 1828, he acted in Glasgow with his father, for the first time, in Payne's *Brutus*. The younger Kean was not a fine enough actor to stand the stiff competition of London, so he acted more and more in the provinces. However, his Hamlet at Drury Lane in 1838, was well received, it being considered that his technique had improved. His voice and appearance were against him for great tragedy so he concentrated on acquiring perfection in small details, and in planning magnificent historical productions. In 1842 he married Ellen Tree, with whom he appeared in America from 1845 to 1847 and subsequently at the Haymarket. He joined Robert Keeley in managership of the Princess's Theatre. There he staged a series of notable Shakespearean revivals, which are still spoken of respectfully because of their attention to historical accuracy, though they were accused of lacking the essential fire which marks great performances. It may be recalled that it was these performances, which Friedrich von Bodenstedt saw and reported to the Duke of Saxe-Meiningen before he undertook his epoch-making productions at Mannheim. Clement Scott, English critic, historian and playwright found Kean's staging of *A Midsummer Night's Dream* in 1856 the most delightful. He saw ensemble playing at its highest, up to this point, coupled with imaginative scenery by Lloyds, W. T. Grieve, and George Gordon, music by the accomplished J. L. Hatton, and choreography by Oscar Byrne. He found himself in complete agreement with Kean's biographer, John William Cole, when he said, *"Nothing could exceed the consistent harmony with which all the varied elements of the play were blended together." It was in that province that Kean was pre-eminently successful.

The names of the next actor-manager to be considered, SIR SQUIRE BANCROFT (1841-1926) and his wife, Marie Wilton (d. 1921 at the age of 82), are intertwined with that of THOMAS WILLIAM ROBERT-SON (1829-71). The dramatist was the son of a provincial actor-manager, being the eldest of a large family of which the youngest was the actress, Margaret, later famous as Madge Kendal. His success came late in his career though he had some minor recognition for the farce-comedy *A Night's Adventure* (1851), staged by Henry Farren at the Olympic Theatre under William Farren's management. But the farce, *A Cantab* (1861), at the Strand, brought him so little financial return that he considered leaving the theatre altogether.

He was a wide reader of French drama, from which he may have

* Cole, John William. *The Life and Theatrical Times of Charles Kean.* London: 1859.

acquired the realistic virus, which infected his plays and made them stand out as the beginning of a new school. As far as Robertson was concerned, anything that would improve the shoddiness of English plays would be an improvement. His first success came with *David Garrick* (1864), from a French source, at the Haymarket, under Buckstone, through the good offices of the elder Sothern. So pleased was the author that he wrote *Society* (1865) with the Haymarket company in mind. However, it was the Prince of Wales' Theatre, with Bancroft and that superb comedienne, Marie Wilton, that finally produced it. This began a collaboration which extended until the playwright's death. The talents of the Bancrofts and John Hare, together with the smallness of the theatre, permitted realistic playing which was impossible in the larger houses. Though Robertson has been accused of drabness, and certainly the plays lack most of the romantic characteristics of preceding drama, he made an important contribution. He looked at life and reported it in the theatre, proving that it was possible for the two to mingle. His speeches were characterized by a naturalness which was hitherto unknown to the English playhouse. Native drama did not have to wait for Ibsen for its first naturalistic stirrings.

The Bancrofts produced the concisely titled *Ours* (1866), *Caste* (1867), *Play* (1868), *School* (1869) and *M. P.* (1870), all by Robertson. After his untimely death they continued producing such plays as Bulwer-Lytton's *Money* (1872), Boucicault's *London Assurance* (1877), and Clement Scott's and B. C. Stephenson's *Diplomacy* (1878), adapted from Sardou's *Dora*. The cast for the latter included the Kendals, the Bancrofts, and Arthur Cecil. Their performances were so successful financially that, to the regret of all, they retired from the stage in 1885.

These were Victorian days and Robertson could not speak out too strongly, though Dickens and Thackeray had been vocal in the novel. The stage in England, for a long time, had been in puritanica! leading strings and the loosening came later, though the Lord Cham berlain still exists to be sure that no political or royal feelings are hurt and that the public's general standards of decency are not violated. Men like Jones and Pinero had only the examples of Robertson and Byron, in England, when they began to write and in 1879 Matthew Arnold could say quite honestly and with too much accuracy that "in England we have no drama at all." The poets wrote magnificent verse but their plays were not for the theatre. Sir Edmund Gosse had discovered Ibsen for the British public in an article in the *Fortnightly Review* and William Archer was to be-

gin his life work of translating the Norwegian's plays in 1879, with
A Doll's House, and his adaptation of *Pillars of Society* was played
at the Gaiety Theatre in 1880. The serious drama developed through
Jones and Pinero to Galsworthy and later dramatists of their ilk.

HENRY ARTHUR JONES (1851-1929), by his own confession, came
of puritanical background and never saw a play until he was eighteen, and was not inclined to look too far afield when he did. In 1882
his collaboration with Henry Herman, *The Silver King,* in Wilson
Barrett's production, proved to be one of those melodramas which
catch the public fancy. It brought him affluence and the opportunity
to take stock of English drama, which he was to write about with
mingled hope and despair in *The Renascence of the English Drama*
(1895), *Foundations of a National Drama* (1913), and the *Theatre
of Ideas* (1915), among other critical volumes. He had glanced at
Ibsen and made an adaptation, with Herman, of *A Doll's House* as
a "sympathetic play" under the title *Breaking a Butterfly* (1884).
The perception of the play was superficial.

Jones had real honesty and he did not hesitate to condemn his
earlier melodramas. Despite seeming evidence to the contrary he
did not bend his head to the ruling theatrical ideas but labored long
and hard in his appeal to the hearts of men, in his effort to persuade
them to rebuild the fundamental conception of the theatre and its
place in the contemporary world as a force for social reform. Both
The Middleman (1889) and *Wealth* (1889) were efforts in this
direction. Though well acted by Sir Charles Wyndham and Mary
Moore at the Criterion Theatre, *The Case of Rebellious Susan*
(1894) seems only to skim the surface and to be retrogressive. His
Michael and His Lost Angel (1896) possesses a strange power,
which was too strange for London audiences who stayed away. It
is of the essence of tragedy and Jones regarded it as his best play,
though some of his admirers preferred the problem drama, *Mrs.
Dane's Defence* (1900). Jones' two best comedies were *The Mas-
queraders* (1894), whose characters are well conceived in a background of a decaying society whose standards are gone, and *The
Liars* (1897) which in its completely different approach to the same
fundamental problem should be compared with Clyde Fitch's *The
Truth.* In Jones' play it is the effect of the lie on the group rather
than on a single individual which is interesting.

SIR ARTHUR WING PINERO (1855-1934) was the leading exponent
of the famous well-made play, in this period, which had considerable
influence on all of the writers of the late eighties until well into the
present century. In his more than forty plays, he tried all of the

various forms, from farce to fantasy, sentimental comedy to comic opera. It was, however, the problem play for which he is best remembered and in which he scored his greatest success. *The Magistrate* (1885) is pure comedy of no importance but of considerable popular success, which was repeated with the sentimental Victorian piece reflecting Robertson, *Sweet Lavender* (1888). However in 1893, he sounded what has been called the first note of modern English drama in *The Second Mrs. Tanqueray*, in which that fine emotional actress, Mrs. Patrick Campbell, appeared. Though this play of a woman with a past seems dated now, it had a tremendous awakening effect on the stage for it seemed to its audiences that Pinero had brought life in the raw before their eyes. Despite its creakiness it has served many actresses in revivals, notably Ethel Barrymore in 1924, and Tallulah Bankhead in the summer theatres of 1940.

In 1895 Pinero wrote *The Notorious Mrs. Ebbsmith* for Mrs. Campbell. This gave her a better role despite the false construction of character. Pinero, who had been examining Ibsen, had had a bad case of indigestion for despite a certain advance in conception, the play as a whole is muddled. Mrs. Campbell found a *vis-à-vis* in Sir Johnston Forbes-Robertson, who had played in Pinero's *The Profligate* (1889) and who was to go on to one of the great impersonations of Hamlet.

The Benefit of the Doubt (1895) and *Iris* (1901) show a definite advance in structure, while *Mid-Channel* (1909) represents the culmination of his achievement in the theatre. The theatricality of *The Second Mrs. Tanqueray* had passed into an honest study of neurasthenia. With *The Thunderbolt* (1908), which dealt with provincial family life, *Mid-Channel* represents the ultimate in Pinero's contribution to the theatre. He created a number of interesting characters, and cleared the air in the commercial theatre for popular treatment of serious themes.

Existing along side Pinero was a man who must have understood him very well in his concern for society but who ranks far above him as a man of the theatre, OSCAR WILDE (1856-1900). This brilliant Irishman received both the adulation and ridicule of his London world and the great world outside. He fascinated people with his essays which propounded the theory of "Art for Art's sake". His epigrams convulsed dinner tables and tickled the risibilities of the world. He was one of America's most publicized lecturers, though our newspapers and press agents did him disservice. When he met his audiences face to face, he delivered extremely well conceived lectures, which were far removed from the shocking wit which they expected. His fads and their followers led to much intentional and unintentional silliness.

It was this that the coruscating wit of SIR WILLIAM SCHWENK GILBERT (1836-1911) and the lilting music of SIR ARTHUR SULLIVAN (1842-1900) chose as a subject for their perennially successful *Patience* (1881). In 1871 these men had become acquainted and in 1875 they formed the profitable (for them and for us) association with Rupert D'Oyly Carte, which brought about the famous D'Oyly Carte Company which still exists. Out of the collaboration of the three came their first smash hit, *Trial by Jury* (1875) at the Royalty Theatre. Then at the Opéra Comique Theatre came *The Sorcerer* (1877) with George Grossmith. In 1878 came *H. M. S. Pinafore* (which ran for 700 performances), following which the author and composer went to New York to superintend its production there in 1879. Because of the pirating of their work (and that of others) by completely unscrupulous American producers, they produced *The Pirates of Penzance* (1879) first in New York, with tremendous acclaim and a succession of crowded theatres. *Patience* was transferred from its original London home to the Savoy to inaugurate their successful occupancy there for many years. It was in that playhouse that the witty musical satires appeared: *Iolanthe* (1882), *Princess Ida* (1884), the ever popular *The Mikado* (1885), *Ruddigore* (1887), *The Yeomen of the Guard* (1888), *The Gondoliers* (1889), and after a disagreement between the collaborators, the less successful *Utopia, Limited* (1893) and *The Grand Duke* (1896). Their operettas are perennial and some enthusiasts have made them a cult like the ballet or Wagnerian music-drama.

Once Oscar Wilde's witty comedies began to emerge, the public flocked to hear the lines which may have shocked them but certainly titillated their risibilities. When his plays are taken apart and the window dressing of his epigrammatic lines removed, the plots are like Pineroesque problem plays. After beginning with a Russian melodrama of no importance, *Vera; or, The Nihilists* (1883), and the florid *The Duchess of Padua* (1891), written about 1883 for Mary Anderson who never played it, he shifted to comedy of manners which really displayed his talent. The first of these was *Lady Windermere's Fan* (1892), which was staged by that excellent actor-manager, Sir George Alexander at his St. James's Theatre (now controlled by Gilbert Miller). Alexander excelled in the plays of Wilde and Pinero because their West End point of view was his own. For the first two nights the identity of Mrs. Erlynne (played by Marion Terry of the brilliant

Terry family) was kept from the audience but afterwards the pretense of mystery was dropped. Next to *The Importance of Being Earnest* (1895), this is Wilde's most acted play.

He wrote *Salomé* in French for the great Sarah Bernhardt and when it was refused license by the Lord Chamberlain for its decadence, it was staged successfully in Paris but without Bernhardt. Its Oriental sensuousness, and lines seemingly influenced by Baudelaire and Rimbaud, lent themselves to the operatic form with the music of Richard Strauss.

Though at one time in love with the lovely Lily Langtry, whose acting scarcely measured up to her classic beauty, he never wrote a play for her. *A Woman of No Importance* (1893), despite its sentimentality as to basic theme, is brilliant in its dialogue and was successful in Sir Herbert Beerbohm Tree's production at the Haymarket. The critics and audiences liked Wilde's epigrams, for this was a time of quips by Whistler and Max Beerbohm, of the decadences of the Yellow Book, and Aubrey Beardsley's macabre drawings. It was all very *fin de siècle* and every one was conscious of it.

The handsome actor-manager, Lewis Waller, staged *An Ideal Husband* (1895) at the Haymarket, for all its political intrigue, and Alexander offered that brilliant farce-comedy *The Importance of Being Earnest*, which is frequently called, with some justification, the wittiest since Sheridan. Unhappily this brilliant career was interrupted by Wilde's suit for libel against the Marquis of Queensbury, father of young Lord Alfred Douglas, which led to the pressure of criminal charges for immorality against the dramatist and to his imprisonment. This phase of his life has been told and retold from Frank Harris to Leslie and Sewell Stokes, in their play on the subject, which Robert Morley, whose physical resemblance to Wilde was astonishing, acted brilliantly. Probably Wilde would have written himself out as Pinero did, but his unwritten lines might have brought laughter to countless audiences.

In contrast to Wilde, Jones and Pinero, STEPHEN PHILLIPS (1868-1915) kept to the poetic tradition of the English drama. His aim was to revitalize the Greek method, but he was most successful when, as in his first play, *Paolo and Francesca*, he was closest to the Elizabethan tradition. His poetry attracted so much attention that Sir George Alexander decided to heed the cry of the critics for literary drama and commissioned Phillips to write a play. His first was written in 1900 but was not produced until 1901, after Sir Herbert Beerbohm Tree had already staged *Herod, A Tragedy* (1900) at Her Majesty's Theatre. This began an association with Tree, which lasted for several years. A somewhat flamboyant actor, Tree staged colorful productions of *Hamlet*, and *King Richard II* and other Shakespearean dramas, creating a considerable reputation for himself. His company was good and included Sir Frank Benson, who is always associated with the perennial Shakespeare Memorial Theatre at Stratford-upon-Avon. Benson was a cousin of Phillips and so came into the Tree orbit from that of Irving with whom he had formerly played. Neither *Ulysses* (1902), *The Sin of David* (1904, not played until 1914), nor *Nero* (1906) measured up to his first play, but they attracted a literary public both in book form and in the theatre.

The theatre attracted several other poets, notably Masefield, Drinkwater, and Flecker. JOHN MASEFIELD (1875-   ), poet laureate since 1930, began his stage career with *The Campden Wonder* (1907), a realistic domestic tragedy, in prose, which was produced at the Court Theatre. *The Tragedy of Nan* (1908) is a moving romantic drama which he followed with an adaptation from the Norwegian, *The Witch*. In *Pompey the Great* (1910) he tried to make a modern human being of the leading character just as Shaw tried to do with Caesar in *Caesar and Cleopatra*, and he was less successful. *Philip the King* was a true poetic drama as was that lyric tragedy of Japan, *The Faithful* (1915). He turned to Christ's Passion for the subject of *Good Friday* (1917) and *The Trial of Jesus* (1926) while he borrowed the method of Euripides in his study of Jezebel in *A King's Daughter* (1928). Spiritualism and characters from beyond the grave enter into *Melloney Holtspur* (1923). His other plays include the Cornish story of *Tristan and Isolt* (1927) and an adaptation of a French miracle play in *The Empress of Rome* (1937).

JOHN DRINKWATER (1882-1937) began with a spirited protest against Victorianism in *Rebellion* (1914) and followed it with *Four Poetic Plays* published in 1917. These included *The Storm*, which contrasts the viewpoint of the tourist with that of a shepherd, each of whom sees nature's titanic display with different eyes, and *X=O: A Night of the Trojan War* which borrows from Euripides and preaches pacifism even in wartime. Then came the play for which he is to be respected and remembered, *Abraham Lincoln* (1919), which caught the sincerity and integrity of our great President. He did not do so well with *Oliver Cromwell* (written 1920, published 1921, acted 1922), nor with *Robert E. Lee* (1923), for the lives of neither of these dissimilar crusaders seems suited for the proscenium arch. *Mary Stuart* (1922) was a failure, but some people feel that this study of a woman whose heart is so large that she needs many men to fill it, is subtle and profound and should be compared with Maxwell Anderson's dissimilar poetic drama, *Mary of Scotland* and Schiller's *Maria Stuart*.

JAMES ELROY FLECKER (1884-1915) was known for but one play,

(though his *Don Juan*, written 1911, published 1925, excited some admiration from Shaw), *Hassan* which he never saw published or played. He beat himself against the doors of the theatre which declined to open before his short life was ended. He achieved a good deal in this imaginative Oriental drama, though some of his critics were disinclined to rate it much higher than Edward Knoblock's *Kismet* (1912). It was even referred to as *Chu-Chin-Chow* made more glorious. Those who admire it, however, have been extravagant in their praise of its poetry and color. When it was produced in 1923-24 with Fokine's ballets and Delius' music, it ran through the season.

Probably the most famous acting team of the nineteenth century, when all is said and done, was that of SIR HENRY IRVING (born John Henry Brodribb, 1838-1905) and DAME ELLEN TERRY (1847-1928). Both in Shakespeare and in melodrama their playing excited admiration; Irving's performances were more easily analyzed, but Dame Ellen's were a product of pure magic which no one ever quite fathomed.

Though Irving had been acting for ten years, he attracted little attention until he played Doricourt in *The Belle's Stratagem* in 1866 at the St. James's Theatre. The next year he joined the company at the recently built Queen's Theatre, which included such actors of outstanding ability as Mr. and Mrs. Alfred Wigan, Sir Charles Wyndham, Lionel Brough, J. L. Toole, John Clayton, Nelly Farren and Ellen Terry. In 1870, he made his first smash hit in James Albery's *The Two Roses* at the Vaudeville Theatre. After two hundred and ninety-four performances in that play, H. L. Bateman secured him as leading man for his company at the Lyceum Theatre. There Irving appeared opposite Bateman's daughter Isabel. Affairs had been bad for some time at the Lyceum when a tremendous success revived the drooping fortunes of the Batemans: *The Bells* (1871), which was Leopold Lewis's adaptation of Erckmann-Chatrian's *Le Juif Polonais*. Irving, as Mathias, gave one of his best performances, which he revived from time to time. Then came W. G. Wills' *Charles I* (1872) and *Eugene Aram* (1873). In 1874, Irving acted Hamlet, with brilliance and an unconventionality which became the talk of the town. He had the satisfaction of setting the record of two hundred consecutive performances, which no one has equalled and only John Gielgud, in 1934-35, threatened.

In 1878 he took over the management of the Lyceum himself and chose Ellen Terry for his leading lady, a partnership that continued until his death. She had created a sensation with her Portia, always one of her best parts, in the Bancroft revival of *The Merchant of Venice* at the Prince of Wales's Theatre. This, coupled with her delightful impersonation in *Olivia*, W. G. Wills' dramatic version of Goldsmith's *The Vicar of Wakefield*, in 1878, opposite the brilliant William Terriss at the tiny Court Theatre, led to her engagement by Irving. The costumes by Marcus Stone and the scenery at the Court Theatre were scarcely altered when the play was revived seven years later at the Lyceum.

Irving's Shylock had great dignity, which was characteristic of his work as a whole. His Iago, to Edwin Booth's Othello, and Ellen Terry's Desdemona, in 1881, brought out the elite of London to see three such great actors. These were the great days at the Lyceum when scenery and costumes and music were given intelligent attention. Irving's acting was rarely up to his conception of a part, but his performances were intellectual delights. In 1882 they did *Much Ado About Nothing; Twelfth Night*, in 1884; and subsequently Watts Phillips' *The Dead Heart* (1889), and Herman Merivale's *Ravenswood* (1890), an adaptation of Scott's *Bride of Lammermoor*.

In 1885 they played Goethe's *Faust*, which the English critics did not receive well, though the Germans did. Despite the severe panning received by Irving's Mephistopheles, the play was a great financial success, partly because of Ellen Terry's delightful Marguerite. People had a way of saying they preferred the play with music, meaning the sentimental tunes of Gounod, which had prettied up Goethe's great drama. Terry's Lady Macbeth, in 1888, was probably her greatest contribution to the theatre and is recorded forever by the painting by John Singer Sargent, which hangs in the Tate Gallery in London. Sargent caught all she hoped to portray in the part according to her own testimony. Poor Irving's Macbeth was not well regarded and eventually brought about the decline in financial fortune, which with his wretched health, took the Lyceum away from them, despite several artistically and financially successful American tours. The whole company took part and with them went Sir John Martin-Harvey, who will go down in history for his playing of one role, Sydney Carton in *The Only Way* (1899).

Ellen Terry continued to act after Irving's death, notably in the plays of Ibsen, Shakespeare, Heijermans, and George Bernard Shaw, who was her close friend. Their published correspondence is an invaluable record of the whole period. These were dynamic days, for then a young man who had begun as an actor found himself becoming more interested in *décor* and in broadening the horizons of the theatre than in reciting the lines of others. Ellen Terry's son, EDWARD GORDON CRAIG (1872-) made his stage debut when he was six in *Olivia* at the Court Theatre. From 1885 to 1897, he played steadily with the Lyceum company but grew much interested in engraving and began to think more clearly about the possibilities of the theatre. In 1900 he staged Purcell's *Dido and Aeneas* with his own *décor*, which beautifully suggested the background and thus released the imagination of his audience. He was doing in England what Appia had already begun in Germany. In his famous and electrifying *The Art of the Theatre*, translated into German, Dutch, Russian, and Japanese, he states his thesis that the theatre is a medium with which men * "should be able to show us life in all its beautiful forms. The theatre should not be a place in which to exhibit scenery, in which to read poems, or preach sermons; it should be a place in which the entire beauty of life can be unfolded, and not only the external beauty of the world, but the inner beauty and meaning of life. It should not only be a place to show facts in a material way, but *the* place to show the whole world of fancy, and in a spiritual way."

This miracle Craig set out to perform himself. He never quite achieved it in his own work, because of his disregard of the architectural limitations of theatres. What the audience saw on the stage was not what he had set down in his designs or envisioned in his mind. However, he freed the imagination of others and with Appia is responsible for the great surge of interest in developing the scenic aspects of production; the exquisite collaboration in which the eye of the artist depicts what is perhaps only dreamed of by the author and silently thought by the director. Designers like Robert Edmond Jones, Lee Simonson, Norman Bel Geddes, Donald Oenslager, Jo Mielziner, and Mordecai Gorelik, in America; Paul Shelving, Norman Wilkinson, Albert Rutherston, George Sheringham, and Oliver Messel in England; in Germany, Heinz Daniel, Heinrich Heckroth, and Adolph Mahnke; in Russia, Alexander Golovine, Nikolai Akimov, and Moisei Levine; in France, Pablo Picasso, André Dérain, and Henri Matisse; all of these men created *décor* with superb originality, quite apart from their standing as painters, because of the freedom of imagination which Appia and Craig brought into the theatre.

Among the British dramatists of the modern world, the man who takes unquestioned precedence is the Irishman, GEORGE BERNARD SHAW (1856-   ). He is both an iconoclast and a moralist. He was the Fabian *par excellence* and he believed that his witty comedies would reform the world. That they have not succeeded in doing so is not the fault of their author. He has written and spoken more on the subject of every kind of reform, within or without the theatre, than any man living today.

In 1882 he began a collaboration with William Archer, which was to have taken form in an adaptation of Augier's *La Ceinture Dorée*, as

* Craig, Edward Gordon. *The Art of the Theatre*. London, 1905.

a well-made play. That it was never completed was due to Archer's dismay at the form it took in Shaw's hands. However, in 1891, J. T. Grein established The Independent Theatre to produce important foreign plays for the small group which might be interested in them and to discover any great English plays which native managers were fearful of producing. The scheme was modelled on Antoine's sub-scription playhouse, the *Théâtre Libre,* and its dramatic inspiration came from Ibsen. With Archer as translator, Janet Achurch, Charles Charington and Elizabeth Robins produced several of his plays. Shaw had helped along the movement with his *The Quintessence of Ib-senism* (1891) and *Ghosts* was chosen as Grein's first subscription bill for private performance. The condemnation of the play as filth by the London critics was the answer. The hostility of the press and the public was so great, that for a time it appeared that even private per-formances by this producing society would have to be abandoned. The furor finally died down and after several plays were produced, there still had been no great English drama staged, so Grein tackled Shaw on the subject. Having at first scornfully rejected the idea that he could write a play, he bethought himself of his collaboration with Archer, resurrected it, rewrote the first two acts, gave it a third, and called it *Widower's Houses* (1892). This play about slum-proprietor-ship created a tremendous stir in the London of its day and the lib-erals applauded it while the conservatives condemned. That it is still a vital topic is evidenced by the audience reaction in New York, in 1938, to the Federal Theatre Project's excellent production of Arthur Arent's Living Newspaper, . . . *one-third of a nation.* . . .

Thus one of the most prolific and lively writers of the modern theatre was transferred from dramatic criticism, which profession he decorated, to being the foremost writer of thoughtful drama in Eng-lish. Though his last plays have displayed the inevitable slowing down from age and an increase of one of his most pronounced character-istics, loquacity, half a century later he still has something to offer to modern audiences. His plays have been discussed and rediscussed, analyzed and criticized by almost every historian of the modern drama. Archibald Henderson has done a great service to theatre scholarship with his brilliant studies of this dramatist and most recently the fine Shavian actor, Maurice Colbourne, has contributed what might in truth have been called the quintessence of Shaw in *The Real Bernard Shaw* (1940).

The Philanderer (1893) discussed sexual relations, while *Mrs. War-ren's Profession* (1894) deals with prostitution, which the author points out is not confined to women who sell themselves but is shared with politicians, newspaper men, lawyers, and clergymen, who conceal their real sentiments and act without real conviction, a worse sin, in the eyes of Shaw. This completed what he called his "unpleasant plays." Then came the "pleasant" ones: the anti-romantic *Arms and the Man* (1894); his best comedy, *Candida* (1895), which many actresses have found a completely irresistible role; the bravura *The Man of Destiny* (1895); then followed an attempt to answer the charge that he was uncommercial with *You Never Can Tell* (1896), one of his least characteristic plays. His delightful melodrama, *The Devil's Disciple* (1896) employed a villain as hero; he attempted to rival Shakespeare with *Caesar and Cleopatra* (1897), but was unsuccessful in the attempt. The anti-imperialistic *Captain Brassbound's Conversion* (1898) was written for the pervading charm of Ellen Terry. *The Admirable Bashville* (1900) was an adaptation of his novel, *Cashel Byron's Profession.* At the suggestion of the then dramatic critic of the *Times,* in London, A. B. Walkley, that he write a play about Don Juan, Shaw wrote *Man and Superman* (1901), which Colbourne calls * "a parable of Creative Evolution," and which Shaw himself admits he decorated too lavishly. He even admitted the unplayability of its tremendous length, though that Shavian sympathizer Esme Percy acted all of it on several occasions. In the summer of 1939 an uncut production was staged by Jasper Deeter, at the Hedgerow Theatre, on the occasion of its annual Shaw Festival.

Shaw's attentions were concentrated upon England, and Ireland had disappeared into the back of his mind until William Butler Yeats asked him to write a play for the Abbey Theatre. He complied with *John Bull's Other Island* (1904) which was beyond the slim producing resources of that organization. His characterization, both of the English and Irish, is excellent and is basically sound even with changed political relations between the two countries.

He wrote *How He Lied to Her Husband* (1904), a kind of companion piece for *Candida,* at the request of Arnold Daly, who was acting *The Man of Destiny* and wanted a short play to fill out the evening. *Major Barbara* (1905) considers the evils of poverty in its relation to the uplift of the Salvation Army and the positive evil of private munitions manufacture. Social medicine, which still is revolutionary enough to precipitate endless quarrels in the press and among doctors, is considered in *The Doctor's Dilemma* (1906). The play without an intermission, *Getting Married* (1908), considers the system of English marriage and divorce, while *The Shewing-up of Blanco Posnet* (1909) is really a religious tract. After four "tomfooleries" as he calls them, which are entirely insignificant, he offered his plea for a National Theatre in *The Dark Lady of the Sonnets* (1910). Eu-

* Colbourne, Maurice. *The Real Bernard Shaw.* N. Y.: Dodd, Mead: 1940.

genics and the relations between parents and children are considered in *Misalliance* (another play with no intermission, 1910) and suburbia is urged to awake in *Fanny's First Play* (1911), which is notable chiefly for the thinly hidden identities of contemporary dramatic critics in the prologue and epilogue to this play.

Christianity, in its beginnings, is likened to all so-called "subversive doctrines" in *Androcles and the Lion* (1912). In *Pygmalion* (1912), he wrote a kind of Cinderella story for Mrs. Patrick Campbell who succeeded brilliantly in the role, as did Lynn Fontanne in the Theatre Guild's revival and Wendy Hiller in the film version of 1938, which was both good cinema and good Shaw. *Overruled* (1912) was a farcical comedy of appearances. *The Great Catherine* (1913), which was written for Gertrude Kingston, treats the Russian Empress as an object of fun. Then came the five short plays written during the First World War, when Shaw was perspicacious enough to accept the fact that the public wished to be amused by such trivia as Oscar Asche's *Chu-Chin-Chow* (1916), which ran for four years and holds the record for long runs on the English stage.

However, during this time, Shaw was thinking about the problems involved, in *Heartbreak House* (1919), which he had begun to write in 1914. This play about the break-up of European civilization is still timely and Robert Briffault captured some of Shaw's feeling in the panoramic novel, *Europa* (1935). This concern for the evolution of civilization is continued *ad infinitum* in his pentalogy, *Back to Methusaleh* (1919-21), which received its first production at the hands of the Theatre Guild.

Unquestionably Shaw's finest play is the historical drama, *Saint Joan* (1923), a true interpretation of history and a model for plays of this type. Winifred Lenihan created the part of the protesting Joan, the French nationalist leader; Dame Sybil Thorndyke, a fine English actress, appeared in the part in London; Elisabeth Bergner triumphed in the part in Berlin, as did Mary Newcomb in the Old Vic revival under Shaw's inspiration in 1934; Katharine Cornell in Guthrie McClintic's production in 1936 and Luise Rainer in Piscator's staging of the play in Washington, were also notable.

None of his last plays has risen anywhere near the level of *Saint Joan*. These include *The Apple Cart* (1930), *Too True to Be Good* (1931), *Village Wooing* (1932), *On the Rocks* (1933), *The Simpleton of the Unexpected Isles* (1934), *The Six of Calais* (1934), *The Millionairess* (1936), *Geneva* (1938), and the last (to date) of all, *In Good King Charles's Golden Days* (1939). In these, as in all of his plays, are passages of magnificent writing, actable parts, provocative thinking, and a good deal of garrulousness. Shaw has always declined to allow his plays to be cut for production, which has robbed many of them of the effectiveness in the theatre which they might have had. Taken all in all, however, he is the real giant of British drama of the past century and a half.

One of the most interesting periods of Shaw's long life came at the time of J. E. Vedrenne's management of the Court Theatre, when many of his plays were staged under the masterly direction of Granville-Barker from 1904 to 1907. Then followed the transfer of the Vedrenne-Barker regime to the Savoy. Until 1910, these productions were to be seen in London and on the road.

The man who produced Euripides and Shaw, and introduced Galsworthy and others to such great advantage, is the director-dramatist, HARLEY GRANVILLE-BARKER (1877-   ). He began his career as an actor, at the age of fourteen, in Miss Sarah Thorne's company at Margate, and including a season with Sir Philip Ben Greet's famous Shakespearean touring organization in 1895. He worked successfully with the Elizabethan Stage Society and later with the Incorporated Stage Society, doing productions for several years of significant foreign and English drama.

The period at the Court Theatre was one of the most provocative. It was there that he experimented with simplified productions and the new scenic and lighting principles, which characterized his later work, notably in his famous season at Wallack's, in New York, in 1915-16. He opened the eyes of many American producers to modern methods of staging, which Belasco and MacKaye had already inaugurated.

Granville-Barker is not only a lecturer of renown, but his translations from the Spanish in collaboration with his wife, Helen, are also noteworthy. They have done much to familiarize the English-speaking stage with the best modern work out of Spain. Before that, however, he busied himself writing plays of his own, beginning with *The Marrying of Ann Leete* (1902). His best known plays, however, are *The Voysey Inheritance* (1905) and *The Madras House* (1910), both of which employ what has been called his symphony method. He deals with the English middle class, which he knows and his characters are expertly analyzed and have a forthrightness which is impressive. He is definitely the intelligent man in the theatre, as his expert rephrasing of Schnitzler's *Anatol* into *The Affairs of Anatol* (1911) demonstrates, for it is the perfect example of how a play should be transferred from the stage of one country to that of another.

Granville-Barker was responsible for the introduction into the theatre of the talents of the distinguished novelist, JOHN GALSWORTHY (1867-1933). After a successful career as a novelist, his first play, *The*

Silver Box (1906), was presented at the Court Theatre. This example of realistic drama is characteristic of all his plays for in this he shows his concern for the plight of the poor. He had a real humanitarian interest in his people, both the haves and the have-nots. He was no propagandist in the sense which makes all capitalists villains, for he realized that those at the top are just as much victims of their environment as those who seem to be downtrodden. He was passionately concerned for the wrongs of the little people, but the fine rationalism of his mind prevented him from being one-sided in his judgments. For that reason he has few heroes and no villains and his plays are well-balanced studies of ordinary human beings under favorable or unfavorable circumstances.

He is concerned with the servant class and unemployable unemployed in *The Silver Box.* In *Strife* (1909) he deals with the problem of labor relations in a sane and helpful fashion, which makes a play eminently worth reviving periodically. His *Justice* (1910) brought about some much needed reforms in the English penal system. He pleaded the cause of the artist and the vagabond in a world designed for the Philistine majority in *The Pigeon* (1912). In dealing with the injuries suffered by an individual in wartime, in *The Mob* (1914), he was less successful, as he was likely to be when he personalized his problem too much, as also in *The Fugitive* (1913), and in the sometimes delightful *Escape* (1926). In *The Skin Game* (1920) he is at his best in treating the social struggle between the landed gentry and the pushing manufacturing class. In *Loyalties* (1922), a study of anti-Semitism, he castigates the bigotry of loyalty to one's own class, race, or religion, as compared with a broader decency and honor. These plays are representative of Galsworthy's considerable contribution to the theatre.

Like Galsworthy, another man who had made a reputation as a novelist eventually turned to the stage: the Scotsman, SIR JAMES MATTHEW BARRIE (1860-1937). His first plays do not merit discussion, so concerned were they with the desire to achieve box office success and to follow the current Shaftesbury Avenue fashion without regard to real theatrical distinction. Of his earlier plays, *The Little Minister* (1897) was a dramatization of his sentimental novel, which was hugely popular with the average public in both forms. In 1900 he turned to satire, but as neither the special nor the general public took to *The Wedding Guest,* he returned to the delicately saccharine qualities of his assured successes in *Quality Street* (1902). These plays have undoubted charm and are contrived with skill but the sentimentality which runs through them all has distressed many critics who admire his play structure and deft delineation of character.

He turned to cruel whimsy in his play about a desert island, *The Admirable Crichton* (1903), which may be compared to Ludwig Fulda's *Robinson's Eiland*. If this play represents Barrie's opinion of the English upper classes, it was indeed low for they are represented as liars and cheats. Some of this same feeling crept into *What Every Woman Knows* (1908), where the thesis that every prominent man is a fool and that an intelligent wife must struggle to prevent his learning it, is distinctly depressing. Thanks to a quaint Scotchness and the charming accomplishments of such distinguished actresses as Maude Adams and Helen Hayes neither the audiences of London or New York have discovered the bitterness of the pill they swallowed.

Peter Pan (1904) is a delightful fantasy. It is the best known play for children and for many years it was a popular favorite in America and still is standard diet, at Christmas, for English children.

There is charm, whimsicality, and the inevitable sentimentality which runs through them all, in such of his more important plays as *Alice Sit-by-the-Fire* (1905), *The Legend of Leonora* (1913), *A Kiss for Cinderella* (1916), *The Old Lady Shows Her Medals* (in which Beryl Mercer endeared herself in 1917), *Dear Brutus* (1917, which established Helen Hayes as a Barrie actress in 1918), *Mary Rose* (1920), and *Shall We Join the Ladies?* (1921).

Shaw and Galsworthy, as well as the various play producing societies (many of which functioned privately on Sunday nights to avoid government censorship), were responsible for a tremendous reawakening of interest in writing for the theatre. There were many men in this period, who in a study of British drama would merit special attention. However, in a survey, they tend to merge into each other. Israel Zangwill (1864-1926) is chiefly known for *Children of the Ghetto* (1899) and *The Melting Pot* (1908). St. John Hankin (1860-1909) was introduced by Granville-Barker at the Court Theatre and is best known for his cynical study of English society in *The Cassilis Engagement* (1907). Miss A. E. F. Horniman and her Gaiety Theatre at Manchester first displayed the work of STANLEY HOUGHTON (1881-1913), whose untimely death allowed him time for but one play of importance, *Hindle Wakes* (1912), a realistic drama of Lancashire life which deals honestly with the problem of illegitimacy and forced marriage, at which the girl revolts to the dismay of all concerned. She has carried Nora one step further. Arnold Bennett (1867-1931) collaborated with the American Edward Knoblock (1874-   ) to produce *Milestones* (1912), a drama which pursues its story through three generations of a family and three contrasting periods. Louis N. Parker (1852-1944) is responsible for the star-vehicle for George Arliss, *Disraeli* (1911) and the charming *Pomander Walk*

(1912); while Graham Moffat (1866-   ) provided *Bunty Pulls the Strings* (1911); Harold Brighouse (1882-   ) wrote *Lonesome Like* (1911); Eden Phillpotts (1862-   ) contributed the hugely popular *The Farmer's Wife* (1916); Alfred Sutro (1863-1933), *The Laughing Lady* (1922); and James B. Fagan (1873-1933) charmed audiences with his *And So To Bed* (1926), a play about Samuel Pepys and his wife in which Yvonne Arnaud delighted both London and New York.

Just before the war, in an echo of Miss Horniman at Manchester, SIR BARRY JACKSON (1879-   ) began his Birmingham Repertory Theatre in 1913, which had produced four hundred plays and operas by 1935 and still continued to function up to the present war. His playhouse was never a true repertory company but a more or less permanent stock troupe, which was devoted to producing the best intelligent drama regardless of country, but naturally emphasizing native work when it was possible. *Abraham Lincoln* won him a London reputation and ran for a year at the Lyric Theatre, Hammersmith, establishing Jackson as a manager to be reckoned with, particularly after its production of Shaw's *Back to Methusaleh* and Phillpotts' *The Farmer's Wife* in 1924. The latter ran for nearly three years. His *Hamlet* in modern dress (1925) was responsible for a wave of Shakespeare revivals in contemporary clothes all over the world.

At Malvern, in the summer of 1929, he organized the first English dramatic festival. He also wished to orient it with exhibitions and lectures by such authorities as the playwright-professor Lascelles Abercrombie; Allardyce Nicoll; and Gabrielle Enthoven, whose magnificent theatre collection was presented to the nation and house at the Victoria and Albert Museum under her supervision; and that of the novelist-playwright-curator, James Laver. The South African, H. K. Ayliff, became stage director at Birmingham in 1922 and went over to Malvern where he continued to function through the festival of 1939, as did the designer, Paul Shelving. In recent years the Malvern experiment has dwindled into being a tryout spot for new plays and in 1937 Sir Barry Jackson ceased to take any active part. In the beginning only each new play of Shaw was produced as that playwright had been god-father to the project from the start.

Undoubtedly the most polished dramatist of present day England is WILLIAM SOMERSET MAUGHAM (1874-   ), who descends from the pure English tradition of the comedy of manners of Wycherley, Congreve, Sheridan and Wilde. He has alternated such comedies as *Lady Frederick* (1907), staged by Granville-Barker; the mordant *Our Betters* (1917); the well observed and brilliant *The Circle* (1921); and witty *The Constant Wife* (1927); with the intensely moving and realistic study of the aftermath of modern warfare upon a decent middle class English family in *For Services Rendered* (1932), and the expressionistic *Sheppey* (1933).

In contrast to Maugham is the sentimentalist, A. A. MILNE (1882-), whose principal gift is for the writing of excellent dialogue in such plays as *Mr. Pim Passes By* (1919), *The Truth About Blayds* (1921), and *The Dover Road* (1922). His saccharine qualities are most evident in *The Ivory Door* (1927) and *Michael and Mary* (1929).

NOEL COWARD (1899-) began as an actor of the conversational type and his comedy has been much admired in many of his plays, which are almost always supremely actable. At one time his work was considerably overrated as having serious meaning, which was followed by a period of under-estimating his undeniable talent for discovering what the public wants. *The Vortex* (1924) is a study in neurasthenia and was brilliantly played by the author and that fine actress, Lillian Braithwaite. In *Private Lives* (1930) he painted a coruscating picture of young married people which provided the expert comedienne, Gertrude Lawrence, with an opportunity to appear opposite Coward as she did in his series of one-act plays performed under the collective title of *Tonight at 8:30* (1935). His *Design for Living* of dubious morality was created to permit him to act in triumphant unison with Alfred Lunt and Lynn Fontanne. *Conversation Piece* (1934) showed off his versatility, with Yvonne Printemps, and *Cavalcade* (1931) was created to provide a spectacle for the huge Drury Lane, turned into a patriotic English drama, which had more merit as a film (1933). His contribution to the field of musical revue has been considerable and Beatrice Lillie, a present day clown, won fame in *Charlot's Revue* (1924) and *This Year of Grace* (1928) among others.

There are a number of present day playwrights who are writing literate and occasionally excellent plays, but none of them stands out predominantly. A number of the men and women represented may yet emerge as first rate dramatists but we are too close to their work to tell.

Laurence Housman (1867-) is best known for a series of playlets about the arbiter of English taste in the nineteenth century, which Helen Hayes made famous as *Victoria Regina* (1935). Rudolf Besier (1878-), though he has written a number of plays, is remembered principally for *The Barretts of Wimpole Street* (1930). Gwen Frangcon-Davies created the part of Elizabeth Barrett which Katharine Cornell immortalized in America. Maurice Browne (1881-), with Ellen Van Volkenburg, founded the experimental Little Theatre in Chicago in 1912 and is known particularly for his production of *Jour-*

ney's End (1929). His most important play was written in collaboration with Robert Nichols, *Wings Over Europe* (1928).

Ashley Dukes (1885-   ) is best known as a producer at his tiny Mercury Theatre, which he has conducted since 1933, where he staged *Murder in the Cathedral* (1935). He has adapted numerous plays from the French and German; perhaps his best regarded play is *The Man with a Load of Mischief* (1924). Mordaunt Shairp (1887-1939) will be remembered for his brilliant homosexual drama, *The Green Bay Tree* (1933), in which the leads were created by Frank Vosper, and Hugh Williams, James Dale and Laurence Olivier duplicated the roles in New York.

James Bridie (born Osborne Henry Mavor, 1888-   ) is a prolific Scottish writer, whose works are admired in Great Britain but suffer a sea change when transplanted to the American stage. Perhaps the best known are *Tobias and the Angel* (1930); *The Anatomist* (1931), which Henry Ainsley played and which established that fine tragic actress, Flora Robson, as a star; *A Sleeping Clergyman* (1933), in which Ernest Thesiger appeared to advantage; and *The Black Eye* (1935), with Stephen Haggard in the whimsical part of the young man of the title. Haggard's work will be recalled as Chatterton, opposite Judith Anderson in *Come of Age* (1934) by Clemence Dane (born Winifred Ashton). Dane is most highly regarded for her trenchant play on the Enoch Arden theme, *A Bill of Divorcement* (1921) and for her poetic and finely conceived *Will Shakespeare* (1921).

T. S. Eliot (1888-   ) is an American born poet who has been domiciled in England for many years. He carries on the poetic tradition in the theatre in such plays as the highly choral *Murder in the Cathedral* (1933) and his experiment of transferring a Greek dramatic theme to an English house party in *The Family Reunion* (1939). Sutton-Vane (1888-   ), son of the playwright, Sutton Vane, is associated with a single play, *Outward Bound* (1923), which won its way into the hearts of its audiences, perhaps beyond its merits as a drama. *At Mrs. Beam's* (1923), a comedy of boarding house life, in which Jean Cadell created a sensation as Miss Shoe, will probably be the most enduring play of the Belfast born C. K. Munro (1889-   ). Dorothy L. Sayers (1893-   ) had created a wide public for herself with her detective fiction before she turned to poetic drama. Two of her plays have real merit, *The Zeal of Thy House* (1937) and *The Devil to Pay* (1939).

J. B. PRIESTLEY (1894-   ) probably has the best chance of survival of any of this group of dramatic writers, provided he composes more slowly. His plays have crowded upon the stage almost simultaneously. Of these perhaps the most skilfully constructed are *Dan-*

gerous Corner (1932), which is a theatrical stunt but worth watching on the stage, and the suburban *Laburnum Grove* (1933), in which Edmund Gwenn displayed his fine feeling for comedy. Priestley's most interesting work has been done in his experimentation with time theories in *Time and the Conways, I Have Been Here Before* and *I'm a Stranger Here* (all in 1937). Almost to a man these plays were acclaimed by London critics and damned by their New York confrères. His *Johnson Over Jordan* (1939) is a modern morality play.

R. C. Sherriff (1896-   ) is principally known for his anti-war play *Journey's End* (1928), which has been played around the world after its West End première in London in 1929. In revival in New York, in September 1939, it was overshadowed by the Second World War and seemed to have lost a good deal of its original impact. In 1935 Sherriff collaborated with the South African Jeanne de Casalis in *St. Helena,* in which the role of Napoleon added to Maurice Evans's stature as an actor, when he played it in New York in 1936. Wendy Hiller was similarly served by *Love on the Dole* (1935), which Ronald Gow (1897-   ) wrote with Walter Greenwood. Ronald Mackenzie (1903-1932) was cut off in his prime by an automobile accident so we have no way of knowing whether his Chekhovian *Musical Chairs* (1931) was more than a brilliant flash in the pan. Rodney Ackland (1909-   ) appeared to advantage in this piece as did John Gielgud. Ackland's best play to date is his dramatization of the Hugh Walpole story, *The Old Ladies* (1935).

Ivor Novello (1893-   ) is an actor-playwright whose most important plays are *The Truth Game* (1928), *Fresh Fields* (1933), *Full House* (1935) and *Comedienne* (1938). He was author-composer of *Glamourous Night* (1935), *Careless Rapture* (1936), *Crest of the Wave* (1938) and *The Dancing Years* (1939). Emlyn Williams (1905-   ) is a highly versatile actor who has written several plays of varying merit, the best of which were the thriller, *Night Must Fall* (1935) and the tenderly tragic *The Corn is Green* (1938). John Van Druten (1901-   ) is best known for his comedies *Young Woodley* (1928), *There's Always Juliet* (1931), *The Distaff Side* (1933), *Gertie Maude* (1937). His plays are staged mostly by Auriol Lee with whom he has worked for some years. Keith Winter (1906-   ) has written *The Shining Hour* brilliantly acted by Raymond Massey, Gladys Cooper and Adrianne Allen (1934), *The Rats of Norway* (1933), *Old Music* (1937), which have had wide success. Merton Hodge (1904-   ) wrote the charming sentimental comedy, *The Wind and the Rain* (1933) as well as *Grief Goes Over* (1935) and *The Island* (1939).

W. H. Auden (1907-   ) and Christopher Isherwood have attracted wide attention from intellectuals on both sides of the Atlantic, with two plays, *The Dog Beneath the Skin* (1935) and *The Ascent of F.6* (1936). The former was produced at Anmer Hall's Westminster Theatre in 1936, while Ashley Dukes staged the latter at the Mercury.

Benn W. Levy (1900-   ) achieved a wide success in England and America with *Mrs. Moonlight* (1928), *Springtime for Henry* (1931), *The Devil Passes* (1932) and his adaptation of Gaston Baty's *Mme. Bovary* (1937).

The gossamer touch in recent years has been maintained by Dodie Smith (who formerly wrote under the name of C. L. Anthony) with *Autumn Crocus* (1931) and *Dear Octopus* (1938), which provided Marie Tempest with one of her most rewarding parts. Terence Rattigan (1912-   ) wrote an amusing and popular farce, *French Without Tears* (1936) which recalled the humors of such obvious comediettas as T. J. Williams's *Ici On Parle Français* (1859). Encouraged by Rattigan's easy success, Gerald Savory (1909-   ) replied with an even slighter piece, *George and Margaret*, which ran for two years.

If we leave out such obvious favorites as Dame Marie Tempest, Lillian Braithwaite and Madge Titheradge, probably the two most significant English actresses are Flora Robson and Edith Evans (1888-   ). Miss Evans first attracted attention for her Cressida in *Troilus and Cressida*, when it was revived in 1912 by the Elizabethan Stage Society. She is an extremely versatile actress of beauty, ability and common sense. The range of her capacity is revealed by the calibre of the parts she has played, such as Lady Utterword in *Heartbreak House* (1921), Cleopatra in Dryden's *All for Love* (1922), Mrs. Millimant in *The Way of the World* (1924 and 1927), Helena in *A Midsummer Night's Dream* (1924), a range of Shakespearean comedy roles at the Old Vic (1925-1926), Florence Nightingale in *The Lady With a Lamp* (1929 and 1931), Gwenny in *The Late Christopher Bean* (1933), the Nurse to Katharine Cornell's Juliet in 1934, Sanchia Carson in Ervine's *Robert's Wife* (1937), and Lady Bracknell in Gielgud's revival of *The Importance of Being Earnest* (1939).

Flora Robson (1902-   ) has more compelling power than any actress appearing today on the English speaking stage. She brings intelligence and a knowing prescience to her performances that give a sculptural quality to her work. Her first appearance was as Queen Margaret in *Will Shakespeare* (1921) but it was not until she followed it with Abbie in O'Neill's dark tragedy, *Desire Under the Elms* (1931), Herodias in *Salomé* (1931), and finally Mary Paterson in *The Anatomist*, the same year, that the public realized what a fine artist had appeared upon the scene. Eva in *For Services Rendered* (1932) and then Ella Downey in Andre Van Gyseghem's brilliant staging of *All God's Chillun Got Wings* (1933) at Ronald Adam's experimental

Embassy Theatre heightened the reputations of all concerned. Among other performances in which she has appeared are Varya in *The Cherry Orchard*, Katherine in *King Henry VIII* and Lady Macbeth to Charles Laughton's Macbeth at the Old Vic in the 1933-1934 season. Recently *Anna Christie* (1937) and the play in which she made her American debut, *Ladies in Retirement* (1940), have provided her with the most rewarding roles.

America has the distinct edge on talented actresses but it is from England that actors of talent and genius flow. Maurice Evans will be considered in relation to his New York work, but the leading English actor of today is certainly JOHN GIELGUD (1904-   ). He comes of the talented Terry family which included Ellen, Kate, Marion and Fred. With such a background, he breathed in theatre from the air about him. His first appearance came as the Herald in *King Henry V* at the Old Vic in 1921. He first attracted real attention when he played Romeo in Sir Barry Jackson's revival in 1924. His acting broadened through his playing of Peter Trophimov in *The Cherry Orchard* (1925) and Treplev in *The Sea Gull* (1925). Then came Ferdinand in *The Tempest* (1926) which developed the flowing line which is apparent in his performances. His imagination was stimulated as Oswald in *Ghosts* (1928), but it was not until the 1929-30 season, when he played Hamlet for the first time, that London audiences realized his abilities. From then on each part contributed to his popular and artistic success; his Richard in Gordon Daviot's *Richard of Bordeaux* (1932-33) brought out the faithful followers of the pit, which means that a star of the first magnitude has risen. His Hamlet (for the third time) in 1934-35 reached the longest run of any production of the play since Irving. Then came Noah, in Obey's play (1935). In the 1935-36 season he alternated Mercutio and Romeo with Laurence Olivier to Peggy Ashcroft's Juliet, achieving 186 performances, the longest consecutive run that *Romeo and Juliet* has ever had. His New York triumphs as Hamlet in 1936-37 have been recorded for posterity in Rosamond Gilder's penetrating analysis, *John Gielgud's Hamlet* (1937). The next season he took over the management of the Queen's Theatre (destroyed by German bombs in the autumn of 1940) and assembled a permanent company including Peggy Ashcroft, Michael Redgrave, Harry Andrews, Glen Byam Shaw and Alec Guiness. There he produced *King Richard II, The School for Scandal, Three Sisters* and *The Merchant of Venice*. Subsequently he appeared in other roles including Hamlet (for the fourth time) at Elsinore in Denmark (1939) and most recently (1940) King Lear. But it is as Hamlet that he is likely to be remembered for he is the greatest of our time, and latest in the long line which began with Richard Burbage.

XXXII

AMERICA TAKES ITS PLACE

(1906-1940)

THERE were two main forces that influenced the American theatre early in the present century. One took the form of a developing national drama and the other was a vital standard of play production in all its related aspects. These two were closely intertwined as is always true when both forces are present in any one period. It is only when you have both that a great theatre exists. These two streams of theatrical development will be considered separately as far as the main emphasis is concerned but the close relation between the two must always be borne in mind.

A REAL DRAMA IS BORN

When a country develops as many playwrights of importance and talent as has our country in the past half-century, any study of them in a history of world theatre must be ruthlessly compressed and anything that seems to be even slightly irrelevant must be sheared away so that only those persons and those activities which cleave closely to the main trunk can be considered.

The man who is credited with beginning the American Renaissance is WILLIAM VAUGHN MOODY (1869-1910), a poet who wrote one play of real importance and wide influence. *The Great Divide* (1906) was acted by Margaret Anglin and Henry Miller in a production that toned down the force of the drama, which clearly differentiates between the civilizations of our eastern and western states. The problem of marriage for a sensitive woman who could love the man who had violated her was dynamite. Unfortunately Moody did not sustain this forceful beginning in his later crude psychological drama, *The Faith Healer* (1909). Moody's importance lay in the fact that he honestly made an effort to examine the real psychological basis for drama.

The poetic aspect of his work leads naturally into the writing of JOSEPHINE PRESTON PEABODY (1874-1922), who was a special student of his classes at Radcliffe College. Her most important play was a verse drama, *The Piper* (1907), which was written for Otis Skinner (but not played by him) and which won the Stratford Prize offered for the best play to inaugurate the new Shakespeare Memorial Theatre in Stratford-upon-Avon. Based on the legend of the *Pied Piper of Hamelin* the play was first produced by Sir Frank Benson on July 23, 1910; its American première was given by Winthrop Ames at the New Theatre in January, 1911. Unfortunately a woman was cast for the leading role, though that fine actress Edith Wynne Matthison (for whom Charles Rann Kennedy had provided *The Servant in the House*, 1908) did all she could with the part.

Another associate of Moody's in the poetic drama was PERCY MAC-KAYE (1875-   ) son of the celebrated Steele MacKaye. History and spectacle interested him and appear in almost all of his plays. The tender and simple *Jeanne d'Arc* (1905) was staged by Sothern and Marlowe in 1906. Satire and fantasy are combined in *The Scarecrow* (acted by that sound actor Frank Reicher, 1911). The clever and satirical comedy about those unduly influenced by Ibsen and the Naturalists, *Anti-Matrimony* (acted by Henrietta Crosman, 1910), should be compared with Lennox Robinson's *Drama at Innish* (also known as *Is Life Worth Living?* 1933). MacKaye penetrated into the Kentucky mountain reaches in *This Fine-Pretty World* (staged at the Neighborhood Playhouse, 1923). Of his several masques the most impressive was certainly *Caliban, by the Yellow Sands, a Community Masque of the Art of the Theatre*, which was performed in the stadium of the College of the City of New York, May 25-June 5, 1916, in honor of the Tercentenary of Shakespeare's death. This continued the theme of *The Tempest* and in the vastness of the production drew into it many of the finest talents of the professional and educational theatre.

The realistic phase of Moody's work probably influenced the leading popular playwright, among the many women who have written for the theatre, RACHEL CROTHERS (1878-   ). She began as a critic of life and though her thinking may never have been profound, it has always been felicitously expressed. Among her many plays the most outstanding are *A Man's World* (1909) which dealt with the double standard and has had its complement in the comedy treatment of the same theme in *Let Us Be Gay* (1929); *He and She* (first staged in 1911, produced in New York in 1920) which deals with woman's struggle to maintain both a career and a home; *Nice People* (1920) which considers the immorality of the young but degenerates into an old-fashioned love story; and *As Husbands Go* (1931) which mildly satirizes American husbands as compared with European lovers. Miss Crothers is at her best, perhaps, in *Susan and God* (1937) in which she has fun at the expense of the Oxford Group. Its value was greatly heightened by her casting of Gertrude Lawrence as Susan and by her own gay direction of the piece.

The realistic force which existed in Moody's dramas communicated itself also to EDWARD SHELDON (1886-), who wrote *Salvation Nell* (1908), for Mrs. Fiske, and followed it with two tentative attempts to consider American problems in *The Nigger* (1909) and *The Boss* (1911). He composed the pretty picture, *Romance* (1912), which Doris Keane played successfully for years. His best play is the rather spurious Negro drama written with Charles MacArthur, *Lulu Belle* (1926); he collaborated with Margaret Ayer Barnes to produce the comedy *Jenny* (1929) for Jane Cowl and the melodramatic *Dishonored Lady* (1930) for Katharine Cornell.

While Sheldon was vainly seeking honest, clear-cut realism, there were several older comic writers, who produced many popular plays for the commercial theatre. Langdon Mitchell (1862-1935) wrote two witty comedies, *Becky Sharp* (1899) and *The New York Idea* (1911). Jesse Lynch Williams (1871-1929) is best known as the first winner of the Pulitzer Prize for the best American play, in the season 1917-18, with his satirical study of matrimony, *Why Marry?* (1917). A. E. Thomas (1872-) began brightly with the study of a woman who thinks she is dying, choosing a second wife for the man to whom she is married, in *Her Husband's Wife* (1910). His reputation has sharply dwindled, reviving briefly with his popular farce-comedy, *Come Out of the Kitchen* (1916), a vehicle for Ruth Chatterton. George Ade (1866-1944) went to country Americana for his best known play, *The County Chairman* (1903), which lacks sufficient plot or character invention to carry it through to the weary end. George M. Cohan (1878-1942), genial member of the vaudeville team of the Four Cohans, will undoubtedly be longer remembered as an expert comedian with a whimsical personality than as a playwright. His early plays had considerable popularity but his later work seems to have lost touch with the world today. His titles are better known than his texts. There are few who are not familiar with *Forty-Five Minutes From Broadway* (1906); *Broadway Jones* (1912); *Seven Keys to Baldpate*, from the novel by Earl Derr Biggers (1913); and *The Song and Dance Man* (1923). His ideas are good but his inventiveness as a writer never measures up to them. Besides playing in his own comedies, which are tailored for him, he attracted considerable attention by his sincere study of the father in O'Neill's *Ah, Wilderness!* (1933) and his genial satire of the President, Franklin Delano Roosevelt, in George Kaufman's and Moss Hart's musical comedy, *I'd Rather Be Right* (1937).

James Forbes (1871-1938) is best known for *The Chorus Lady* (1906), expanded from a one-act play, and for *The Famous Mrs. Fair*, his social drama of some brilliance, acted by Blanche Bates and Henry Miller in 1919. Thompson Buchanan (1877-1937) is another one of the earlier writers of social comedy whose plays had some contemporary meaning but who is no longer able to sustain dramatic effort. *A Woman's Way* (1909) and *Civilian Clothes* (1919) represent his best work, though the earlier is the better. Winchell Smith (1871-1933) was an inveterate collaborator whose plays invariably relied on the actor or director to carry them to success. There is but a single one of his pieces worth recording despite the laughter with which audiences have given them. *Lightnin'* (1918), which he wrote in collaboration with the actor, Frank Bacon, ran for 1,291 performances on Broadway. The leading character of *Lightnin'*, Bill Jones, was modelled on Rip Van Winkle both in the writing and Frank Bacon's acting indebtedness to Joseph Jefferson. Frank Craven (1880-   ), who is better known as an actor, particularly as the Stage Manager in *Our Town* (1938), was responsible among other plays for *The First Year* (1920), which with its homely comedy of young married life was hilariously acted despite the shoddiness of the dramatic portraiture. Among the comic writers of a generation ago, none of the men just mentioned was able to reach the sheer delight of the dialogue of Clare Kummer. *Good Gracious Annabelle* (1916); *A Successful Calamity* (1917), which her cousin William Gillette of *Sherlock Holmes* and *Secret Service* fame carried to success; *Be Calm Camilla* (1918); *Rollo's Wild Oat* (1920); and *Her Master's Voice* (1933), with Roland Young and Laura Hope Crews contributing sparkling performances, are her best plays. Regardless of the merit of her work, there is one name that is likely to be long remembered and that is Anne Nichols. She wrote a comic hodge-podge of Irish-Jewish jokes, which had sufficient sentimentality to weave the various racial elements together, and made *Abie's Irish Rose* (1922). Audiences everywhere crowded in to see it, and scores of companies played it simultaneously in this country. It was performed almost everywhere in the world but it stubbornly persists in being a bad play shrewdly written to attract audiences. The English born John Hartley Manners (1870-1928) wrote a much better comedy in *Peg O' My Heart* (1912) for Laurette Taylor and it attracted audiences for two years in New York and for many years on the road. Avery Hopwood (1882-1928) wrote mildly salacious farces which accumulated popularity and wealth for their author. These include *Fair and Warmer* (1915), *The Gold Diggers* (1919), and *Ladies Night* (1920, with Charlton Andrews).

Romance in this country has been served by Edwin Milton Royle (1862-1942) with *The Squaw Man* (1905); Booth Tarkington (1869-) contributed, among others, *Monsieur Beaucaire* (1901) for Richard Mansfield, *The Man from Home* (1907) for William T. Hodge, with the collaboration of Harry Leon Wilson, *Mr. Antonio* (1916) for Otis Skinner, and *Clarence* (1919) as delightfully interpreted by Alfred Lunt, Helen Hayes and Glenn Hunter. Richard Walton Tully (1877-1945), whose romantic *The Rose of the Rancho* (1906) has already been noticed, was also responsible for the scenically beautiful *The Bird of Paradise* (1912), which shows his indebtedness to Belasco. Philip Moeller (1880-), whose name is perhaps better known as a director in recent years, is the author of the delightful travesty, *Helena's Husband* (1915), staged by the Washington Square Players before they became the Theatre Guild. His most important play, however, was the romantic historical drama, *Madame Sand* (1917), which studies some of the love affairs of George Sand and was brilliantly acted by Mrs. Fiske. *Molière* (1919) took warrantable liberties with historical facts; *Sophie* (1918) did little more than provide an acting role for that fine emotional actress, Emily Stevens. Moeller commands the light and comic touch in such plays as his adaptations of Sil-Vara's *Caprice* (1928) and *The Camel Through the Needle's Eye* (1929).

One of the leading practitioners of sophisticated romance in the present century is Zoë Akins (1886-). She provided *Déclassée* (1919) for Ethel Barrymore, *The Varying Shore* (1921) for the beautiful Elsie Ferguson, but her best play, *A Texas Nightingale* (1922) failed because it was miscast. Her characterization was distinctly improved and the play contains her best dialogue. Her most popular pieces have been the wise-cracking *The Greeks Had a Word For It* (1930) and her sentimental adaptation of Edith Wharton's novelette, *The Old Maid* (1935). The fact that so poor a play as this received the Pulitzer Award stimulated so much criticism that the New York Critics' Circle instituted its own award for the best play of the season, feeling that the Pulitzer judges had either lost their critical standards or were too likely to be overruled in their judgments by the Advisory Board.

The next section deals with those dramatists, who have practiced all forms of writing, but much of whose work is of serious nature. Some of the most interesting of these have been composers of one or more plays of contemporary importance and some are obviously yet to let us see their finest writing. Among them, with their best known plays, are Walter Prichard Eaton (*Queen Victoria*, 1923, with David Carb); Austin Strong (*Seventh Heaven*, 1922); John L. Balderston (*Berkeley Square*, 1929, acted by Leslie Howard and Margalo Gillmore); Hatcher Hughes (*Hell-Bent fer Heaven*, 1923); Sophie Treadwell (*Machinal*, 1928); Emmet Lavery (*The First Legion*, 1934); Lula Vollmer (*Sun-Up*, 1923); Mary Kennedy (*Mrs. Partridge Presents*, 1925); Dan Totheroh (*Wild Birds*, 1925, and *Distant Drums*, 1932); Reginald Lawrence (*Men Must Fight*, 1931, with S. K. Lauren); Leopold Atlas (*Wednesday's Child*, 1934); Philo Higley (*Remember the Day*, 1935, with Philip Dunning); John Steinbeck (*Of Mice and Men*, 1937); Robert Ardrey (*Thunder Rock*, 1939); Kenyon Nicholson (*The Barker*, 1927); Robert Turney (*Daughters of Atreus*, 1936); George O'Neil (*American Dream*, 1933); Michael Blankfort (*Battle Hymn*, with Michael Gold); E. P. Conkle (*Prologue to Glory*, 1938); Melvin Levy (*Gold Eagle Guy*, 1934); and Ernest Hemingway (*The Fifth Column*, 1940, with Benjamin Glazer).

Here will be found some of the elder and some of the middle group of playwrights. George Broadhurst (1866-   ), whose name is borne by a New York playhouse, is best known for three farces, *The Wrong Mr. Wright* (1897), *What Happened to Jones* (1897), and *Why Smith Left Home* (1899). He wrote the horse-racing play, *Wildfire* (1908), with George V. Hobart, for Lillian Russell and the melodrama, *Bought and Paid For* (1911), which thrilled audiences when a drunken husband insisting on his marital rights broke down the door to his wife's bedroom to reach her. The fact that he built his play for this second act climax weakened what might have been an interesting piece. Edward Childs Carpenter (1872-   ) turned out contrived comedy dramas of some charm. The best of these are *The Cinderella Man* (1916), *The Pipes of Pan* (1917), *The Bachelor Father* (1928), and *Whistling In the Dark* (with Laurence Gross, 1932).

Zona Gale (1874-1938) was primarily a novelist, who on two notable occasions dramatized her work for the stage. *Miss Lulu Bett* (1920) won the Pulitzer Prize of 1920-21 and Walter Huston's performance of her *Mr. Pitt* (1924) made it memorable. She is definitely allied to some of the playwrights of the American scene, who will be considered later in this chapter. Susan Glaspell (1882-   ) definitely has more to offer the theatre than had Zona Gale. She and her first husband, George Cram Cook, were instrumental in founding the Provincetown Players to whom they contributed the farcical *Suppressed Desires* (1915) and *Tickless Time* (1918). Miss Glaspell's one-act drama, *Trifles* (1916) is perhaps her best play, though *Bernice* (1919) and *The Inheritors* (1921) are serious plays worthy of note. *The Verge* (1921) deals with growing insanity in a powerful manner.

Her *Allison's House* (1930), an oblique study of Emily Dickinson, won the Pulitzer Prize for 1930-31.

Owen Davis (1874-   ) has the reputation of having writiten over a hundred melodramas of no importance and which were never published. His best plays are *The Detour* (1921), and the really moving *Icebound* (1923), with its honest study of New England characters from Davis' native Maine. This play won the Pulitzer Prize for 1922-23 and he was rewarded for his momentary swerving from the popular farces and pleasant little comedies which are more characteristic of his writing.

Gilbert Emery (1875-   ) wrote two plays of considerable merit; *The Hero* (1921), which studies the relationship between two brothers, one quiet, unassuming and honest, the other showy, selfish and a "hero"; and a drama of love, *Tarnish* (1923), which established Ann Harding's first real success as an actress. The honesty of Emery's work contrasts with the pseudo-morality quality in Channing Pollock (1880-   ) in *The Fool* (1922), *The Enemy* (1925), *Mr. Moneypenny* (1928), and *The House Beautiful* (1931). Arthur Richman (1886-   ) has much more penetration and power in his domestic drama, *Ambush* (1921). Martin Flavin (1883-   ) is known primarily for two contrasting plays, *Children of the Moon* (1923), which is a powerful treatment of insanity in a San Francisco family, heightened by the comprehending performances of Henrietta Crosman and Florence Johns; and *The Criminal Code* (1929), which is a study of honor among murderers and the psychology of prison life, to which the acting of Arthur Byron and Russell Hardie contributed.

Lee Wilson Dodd (1879-1933) began as a writer of farces such as *His Majesty Bunker Bean* (1916) (based on Harry Leon Wilson's novel), but it is for his study of marital relations in *The Changelings* (1923) that he is likely to be remembered. John B. Colton is known primarily for his adaptations and collaborations. Born an Englishman he has been domiciled in America for a number of years. His principal achievement was the adaptation of Somerset Maugham's story, *Sadie Thompson*, as *Rain* (1922), in collaboration with Clemence Randolph. To this play that brilliant actress, Jeanne Eagels, contributed the performance of her life, burning herself out in the part. *The Shanghai Gesture* (1925), a study of a Eurasian brothel proprietress, provided Florence Reed with the acting opportunity of her life, making up for the play's numerous demerits.

SIDNEY COE HOWARD (1891-1939) was a dramatist of the American scene despite a long apprenticeship spent in the adaptation of European plays. His *Swords* (1921) was an heroic drama in free blank verse, produced by Brock Pemberton. The Pulitzer prize-winner,

They Knew What They Wanted (1924) proved a much better play, compactly written and clearly characterized. How much he gained from the performances of Pauline Lord, Richard Bennett and Glenn Anders was apparent when the play was revived in 1939. *Lucky Sam McCarver* (1925) was in many ways his most interesting play in its study of the contrasting characters of the highly bred Carlotta (beautifully acted by Claire Eames) and the bootlegger McCarver (played by John Cromwell). It failed largely because of the episodic nature of the play and because, acting in character, McCarver goes off to keep a business appointment and leaves his dead wife alone. This profoundly shocked the audience. In *Ned McCobb's Daughter* (1926), he wrote a New England melodrama which was raised to the level of drama by the satisfactory nature of his character development. This was not true of *The Silver Cord* (1926) for this play of mother-love lacks clearly drawn characters, but was largely redeemed by the extraordinarily fine performance of Laura Hope Crews as the Mother. His adaptation *Marseilles* (1930), based on Pagnol's *Marius*, failed, while his complete reworking of René Fauchois' French piece about art and avarice into a New England setting as *The Late Christopher Bean* (1932) was a huge success. The performances by Walter Connolly, Pauline Lord and Beulah Bondi enhanced the values of the play. Then came *Alien Corn* (1933) for Katharine Cornell and the remarkable adaptation of Sinclair Lewis' novel, *Dodsworth* (1934), which Walter Huston and Fay Bainter made peculiarly their own. In collaboration with Paul de Kruif, Howard wrote *Yellow Jack* (1934), which benefited by Guthrie McClintic's sympathetic production, with such fine young actors as James Stewart, Myron McCormick, Samuel Levene, Millard Mitchell, Eduardo Cianelli, the older John Miltern, Robert Keith and sterling Whitford Kane as the scientist who identifies the carrier of yellow fever. Howard honestly studied the position of an American family at a time of future war in *The Ghost of Yankee Doodle* (1937), an uneven play with many positive virtues. Ethel Barrymore, Eliot Cabot, and Dudley Digges contributed noteworthy performances. His accidental and untimely death in the summer of 1939 robbed our theatre of one of its best realistic dramatists. His last play, *Madam, Will You Walk* (1939) was tried out with George M. Cohan on the road. Cohan was dissatisfied with his performance and withdrew. Because of its content the play is to be withheld from production in the present condition of world affairs.

GEORGE KELLY (1887-   ) began his career as an actor, as is evident in the construction of his plays, which are invariably acting vehicles regardless of their varying dramatic merits. His first success came in that ribbing of the beginnings of our Little Theatre Movement, *The*

Torch-Bearers (1922). This play had as much to do with the general improvement of our amateur standards, with its good-natured laughter, as the quickening of the dramatic pulse throughout the country. *The Show-Off* (1924) is built around one character, Aubrey Piper, whom the title describes. Louis Jean Bartels made him richly unendurable against an accurately painted background of Philadelphia family life. Kelly won the Pulitzer Prize for 1925-26 with his brilliant study of a domineering wife in *Craig's Wife* (1925), which Chrystal Herne played in unrelieved honesty. His approach to *Daisy Mayme* (1926) was broader and less satisfying while in *Behold the Bridegroom* (1928), illuminated by a fine performance by Judith Anderson, he gave us his most purposeful characterization. Then came his exceedingly frank *Maggie, the Magnificent* (1929). Neither *Philip Goes Forth* (1931), nor *Reflected Glory* written for Tallulah Bankhead increased his stature as a dramatist. His own astute direction of his plays has always aided our understanding of them in the theatre.

ELMER RICE (1892-   ) has become one of the foremost directors of his own and other people's plays in our theatre. He has changed direction so frequently, as a dramatist, that it is necessary to take refuge in "versatile" as the only characterizing adjective. He made a sensation with his first play, *On Trial* (1914), which utilized the cinematic technique of the "flash-back" which has become a familiar device in modern drama. He collaborated on *Wake Up Jonathan* (1920), with Hatcher Hughes, for Mrs. Fiske. In *The Adding Machine* (1923) he contributed one of the few expressionistic plays written by an American. This remains one of the most significant productions of the Theatre Guild with Dudley Digges, Helen Westley and Margaret Wycherly. Probably his best play is the realistic drama, *Street Scene* (produced by William A. Brady, 1929), which depicts the movement of life in the streets of New York and behind the façade of the tenement projected on the stage. *The Left Bank* (1931) was an honest appraisal of American expatriates. *Counsellor-at-Law* (1931), a searching portrayal of a Jewish lawyer was acted brilliantly by the versatile actor, Paul Muni (a graduate from the Yiddish speaking stage, whose success in the films, subsequently, has been phenomenal). Rice stacks the cards against the capitalist villains in *We, the People* (1933) and so robs it of much of the force that was inherent in this sympathetic study of the poor. He dramatized the Reichstag fire trial in *Judgment Day* (1934) with its foregone conclusion. *Two on an Island* (1939) was a charming if superficial study of the efforts of two young actors to break into the theatre. They were sympathetically acted by John Craven and Betty Field against the excellent villainy of Luther Adler, in front of some of Jo Mielziner's most exciting settings.

Nevertheless it took all of Rice's direction and the masterly trickery of the theatre to conceal the weakness of its dramatic structure from an audience.

Comedy has been one of the richest resources of our theatre from the beginning and the number of playwrights of passing merit is enormous so that no one playwright in this group can be treated as exhaustively as we might like. Philip Barry, Marc Connelly, George Kaufman with his various collaborators, and S. N. Behrman are discussed as representative of this phase of our drama. This does not mean that there is any merit lacking in such outstanding playwrights as Vincent Lawrence; the inventive Ben Hecht and Charles MacArthur (*The Front Page*, 1928); the facile George Middleton and Guy Bolton (*Adam and Eva*, 1919); the master director George Abbott with such collaborators as Philip Dunning (*Broadway*, 1926); and John Cecil Holm (*Three Men on a Horse*, 1935); Maurine Watkins (*Chicago*, 1926); Don Marquis (*The Old Soak*, 1926); Tom Cushing (*The Devil in the Cheese*, 1926); Preston Sturges (*Strictly Dishonorable*, 1929); Gilda Varesi with Dolly Byrne (*Enter Madame*, 1920); Porter Emerson Browne (*The Bad Man*, 1920); George Haight and Allen Scott (*Goodbye Again*, 1932); Rose Franken (*Another Language*, 1932); Harry Wagstaff Gribble (*March Hares*, 1921); James Hagen (*One Sunday Afternoon*, 1933); the brilliant Spewacks (Bella and Samuel, with their priceless *Boy Meets Girl*, 1935); Samson Raphaelson (*Accent on Youth*, 1934); Arthur Kober (*Having Wonderful Time*, 1937); Paul Osborn (*Morning's at Seven*, 1939); Edwin Justus Mayer (*The Firebrand*, 1924, and *Children of Darkness*, 1930); Lawrence Langner and Armina Marshall (*The Pursuit of Happiness*, 1933); J. P. McEvoy (*The Potters*, 1923, and *Americana*, 1926); and Howard Lindsay with Russel Crouse (*Life with Father*, 1939).

PHILIP BARRY (1896-) was a student at George Pierce Baker's 47 Workshop at Harvard, where he won the Harvard Prize Play contest with *You and I* (1922, staged in 1923). This is a play in which the inherently serious theme of the conflict between love of woman and love of work, as expressed in the terms of art and beauty, is cloaked in the brilliant lines of comedy, which have become a trademark of almost all of Barry's plays. The exceptions to the rule will be dealt with later. *The Youngest* (1924) ridicules social pretension; the remoteness of *In a Garden*, (1925) was illumined by Laurette Taylor's performance. Perhaps his best satirical comedy was *White Wings* (1926), in which the symbolism of the horse completely escaped the understanding of the general public; despite the efforts of the critics to keep this play running, it was a quick failure.

Paris Bound (1927), a comedy which defends the institution of

377. SETTING BY STEWART CHANEY FOR *Twelfth Night*, WITH HELEN HAYES AND MAURICE EVANS (1940).

378, 379. COSTUME DESIGNS BY STEWART CHANEY FOR *Twelfth Night*.

380. SETTING BY ROBERT REDDINGTON SHARPE FOR *Tobacco Road*, Broadway's record-smashing hardy perennial (1933).

381. SETTING BY LAWRENCE GOLDWASSER FOR *A Passenger to Bali*, WITH WALTER HUSTON CAROUSING ON THE UPPER DECK (1940).

382. SETTING BY MORDECAI GORELIK FOR *Processional*, BY JOHN HOWARD LAWSON (1925).

383. SETTING BY MORDECAI GORELIK FOR *Thunder Rock*, BY ROBERT ARDREY (1939).

384. Setting By Donald Oenslager For *Tapestry in Grey* (1935).

385. Setting By Donald Oenslager For *The Flying Dutchman*.

386.   SETTING BY MARCO MONTEDORO FOR *The Twelve Dancing Princesses*. Radio City Music Hall.

387.   SETTING AND COSTUMES BY NAT KARSON FOR *The Hot Mikado*, WITH BILL ROBINSON (1939).

388. *The Shoemakers' Holiday*, PRODUCED BY THE MERCURY THEATRE. Costumes by Millia Davenport (1938).

389. SETTING FOR *Grand Hotel*, DESIGNED BY ALINE BERNSTEIN (1930).

390. SETTING BY
HOWARD BAY
For *Marching
Song* (1937).

391. SETTING BY HOWARD
BAY FOR THE FEDERAL
THEATRE LIVING NEWS-
PAPER . . . *One Third
of A Nation* . . . (1938)

392. PROJECTED SETTING BY
JOHN ROOT FOR *Johnny
Belinda*. NOTE THE
RAKED OVERHANG DE-
SIGNED TO SOLVE THE
"CEILING" PROBLEM IN
AN EXTERIOR SET.

393, 394. Costume Sketches By James Reynolds For *The Greenwich Village Follies.*
Theatre Collection, N. Y. Public Library

395. *The Time of Your Life,* By William Saroyan, With Eddie Dowling and Julie Haydon (1939)

400, 401. SETTINGS BY ROBERT VAN ROSEN FOR THE PROVINCETOWN PLAYHOUSE PRODUCTION OF
Princess Turandot (1926).

403. COSTUME DESIGN BY LUCINDA BALLARD.

402. COSTUME DESIGN FOR *Hold On To Your Hats*, BY RAOUL PENE DU BOIS.

404. COSTUME BY ALINE BERNSTEIN FOR *The Little Clay Cart*

405. CLOWN COSTUME BY SIMON LISSIM FOR *Tsar Saltan*.

406. Costumes By Claude Bragdon For *The Light of Asia.*

407. Costume Design By Robert Edmond Jones For *Much Ado About Nothing.*

409. Cornelia Otis Skinner. Costume designed by Helene Pons.

408. Portrait Costume Sketch By Albertine Randall Wheelan For the Character of Delacroix in *Deburau.*

410. Setting By Tom Adrian Cracraft For *Black Pit* (1935).

412. Katharine Cornell as Lucrece.

411. Alfred Lunt and Richard Whorf in *Amphitryon 38*. Costumes by Valentina.

Vandamm

413. THE THEATRE COLLECTION IN
ACTION AT THE NEW YORK
PUBLIC LIBRARY.

414. GEORGE PIERCE
BAKER, DISTIN-
GUISHED FOUNDER
OF THE 47 WORK-
SHOP AT HARVARD,
LATER AT YALE.

415. THEATRE MUSEUM
AT THE UNIVERSITY
OF NORTH CARO-
LINA. Dr. Fred-
erick Koch stands
beside the seated
students.

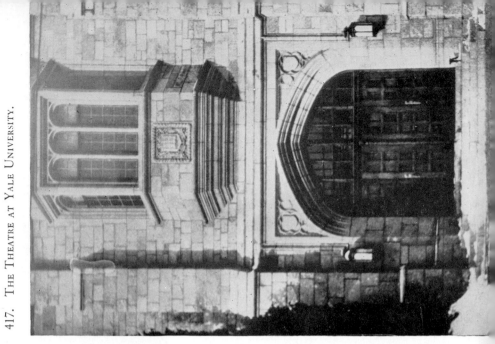

416. THE PLAY HOUSE AT CLEVELAND.

417. THE THEATRE AT YALE UNIVERSITY.

marriage, is one of his wittiest plays. Madge Kennedy starred but Hope Williams, in a minor part, stole the show, so Barry wrote *Holiday* (1928) for her boyish and abrupt style which is eminently suited to his airy lines. *The Animal Kingdom* (1932) is an incompletely motivated comedy of marriage the weakness of which was hidden by the expertness of the cast. *The Philadelphia Story* (1939) is perhaps his best comedy of manners, in which his lines sparkle throughout, with the help of a glowing performance by Katharine Hepburn.

Barry is most interesting when he is writing serious drama but neither the public nor the critics (who profess to misunderstand what, if anything, is overly simple) have cared much for any of them except, perhaps, *Tomorrow and Tomorrow* (1931). In this play the sacredness of marriage and domestic happiness are considered of incalculably greater value than sexual passion and the fierceness of physical love. *Hotel Universe* (1930) dramatizes the truth which is significant for each of us, whether for good or bad. The play and its characters are given the unity of an uninterrupted performance by a technical return to the classic unities of time and space. Each of the characters reveals the truth within him at some moment and so wins through to the end, whether desired or feared. Barry dramatizes religious faith, in its illumination of human impulses and desires, in his quietly moving play, *The Joyous Season* (1934) which critics and public disregarded. *Bright Star* (1935), even more shabbily treated, is an almost unbearable tragedy of two basically fine people. Certainly *Here Come the Clowns* (1938) is Barry's finest play (which uniquely was also given novelistic treatment by him as *War in Heaven*, 1938). This is a study of man's search for the eternal truths and was given an inspired performance by Eddie Dowling. Barry is certainly one of the most significant writers for the stage today. It is singularly unfortunate for him that he must sugar-coat his thoughts for popular consumption. He is an adult writer for an adult theatre.

MARC CONNELLY (1890-   ) has known almost as many collaborators as George S. Kaufman, with whom he has frequently been associated in composition. Their first effort, *Dulcy* (1921) was taken from F. P. A.'s column on the old New York *Tribune*, in which Franklin P. Adams celebrated the worst bromides of the ladies through an imaginary person named Dulcinea. Connelly and Kaufman were shrewd enough to capitalize the dullness of Dulcy (so brilliantly played by Lynn Fontanne as to establish her as a star) and the cleverness of her brother (impersonated by that fine young actor, Gregory Kelly). In *To the Ladies* (1922), they sang the praises of the astute young wife who loves her husband and is intelligent about it. That they succeeded is indicated in the speech which fell to Helen Hayes, as the wife, "Nearly every man that ever got any place . . . has been married, and that couldn't be just coincidence."

It is hard to apportion the praise for the popular success of *Merton of the Movies* (1922) among Connelly and Kaufman, Harry Leon Wilson who wrote the novel, and Glenn Hunter, who so ably portrayed the film-struck hero. *Beggar on Horseback* (1924), was Connelly and Kaufman's most brilliant satire. It has so frequently been called an adaptation of Paul Apel's *Hans Sonnenstoessers Hoellenfahrt*, that it should be made clear that they had not read the play. This is the most imaginative product of their collaboration and certainly the most deserving of praise. It marked the amiable end of their work together.

The Wisdom Tooth (1926) is a fantasy of delightful imagination and tender understanding of shyness and the feeling of inferiority. However, it was in *The Green Pastures* (1930) that Connelly found himself as a dramatist. This is clearly one of the outstanding plays of the century in its honesty, understanding of the Negro, reverence and glorious humor. The play was suggested by Roark Bradford's book, *Ol' Man Adam and His Chillun* (1928) and there were doubts in the minds of some, how much had been the contribution of Connelly and how much of Bradford in this modern morality play. After the production of Bradford's *John Henry* (1940), it was abundantly clear that Connelly was almost solely responsible for the fineness of *The Green Pastures* as a drama. Though Richard B. Harrison was almost perfect as "de Lawd," the play has also been successful with white actors in Stockholm. The perfect collaboration of Negro acting and singing with Connelly's direction and Robert Edmond Jones' *décor* probably made the most memorable play of the decade.

With Frank B. Elser, Connelly wrote *The Farmer Takes a Wife* (1934), a delightful comedy of New York State's canals and the people who plied them, based on Walter D. Edmonds' novel, *Rome Haul*. In this Henry Fonda and June Walker gave their best performances, for Connelly's direction brings out the best in actors. With Arnold Sundgaard's original play as a basis, Connelly and Sundgaard wrote an uneven but frequently fresh and enjoyable drama of the opening of the American frontier in *Everywhere I Roam* (1938). His latest play, *The Land of the Living* has not yet been published nor (because of casting difficulties) produced.

GEORGE S. KAUFMAN (1889-   ) is one of the best directors of comedy and farce in the American theatre and is credited with many of the smart lines and wisecracks in the plays of others, which he has staged. Any play with which he is associated as playwright is likely to be compact in structure and well-developed in its plot. His name has been taken as a synonym for slickness, both in writing and production, so brilliant has been his success in both fields. With Edna Ferber, he has written *Minick* (1924), *The Royal Family* (1927), *Dinner at Eight* (1932) and *Stage Door* (1936). These plays, despite their surface brilliance, possess more humanity, a fact which may be due to Miss Ferber's influence, for her *Show Boat* (with Jules Bledsoe as Joe, and with Jerome Kern's unforgettable music, 1927) made a deep impression on American and English audiences. Kaufman's principal solo effort was *The Butter and Egg Man* (1925), a farce about theatrical types. His principal collaborators include such names as Ring Lardner, Alexander Woollcott, Morrie Ryskind (who collaborated on the book of the Pulitzer Prize-winning musical, *Of Thee I Sing*, 1931), H. J. Mankiewicz, Howard Dietz, and Katherine Dayton.

However, most of his work in the past ten years has been done with Moss Hart (1904-   ), a partnership which began with that extremely funny satire on Hollywood, *Once in a Lifetime* (1930), based on the plight of the author as well as those actors of the silent era who are terrified by sound. Jean Dixon, Hugh O'Connell, Grant Mills and Charles Halton as Mr. Glogauer, the fabulous film executive, gave authenticity to the play, *Merrily We Roll Along* (1934) disguised the obviousness of its plot by having the scenes in reverse order, from futile success to the hopeful beginning. The Pulitzer Prize farce, *You Can't Take It with You* (1936) about a family of zanies has been their most popular play with the public. Capitalizing on the rising feeling of nationalism they composed *The American Way* (1939) for Fredric March and Florence Eldridge as a patriotic spectacle at the large Center Theatre (the smaller of the two Radio City playhouses, the larger being that mecca of tourists, Radio City Music Hall, which combines films with stage presentations).

SAMUEL NATHANIEL BEHRMAN (1893-   ) is the leading American writer of the comedy of manners; his only rival in this form is the English Somerset Maugham. His first play (barring two minor collaborations with Kenyon Nicholson and Owen Davis) was a comedy of the life of a social artist, *The Second Man* (1927), beautifully acted by the Lunts, Margalo Gillmore and Earle Larimore. He dramatized the novel, *Serena Blandish* (1929) into a fabulous comedy for Ruth Gordon, Constance Collier and Henry Daniel. Then came *Meteor* (1929) and *Brief Moment* (1932) which is a comedy about a night club singer who marries into a wealthy family. Then came *Biography* (1932), in which for the first time he introduces his favorite discussion of life and the philosophy of living from various points of view. This continues in varying fashion, with all angles represented, through *Rain from Heaven* (1934), *End of Summer* (1936), *Wine of Choice* (1938) and *No Time for Comedy* (1939).

Four observers of the American scene who are outstanding are Dubose Heyward, Lynn Riggs, Thornton Wilder and Sidney Kingsley. DUBOSE HEYWARD (1885-1940) is known for his keenly observed plays and novels about his native Charleston. With his wife he composed first the novel and then the play, *Porgy* (1927), which gave American audiences their first true portrait of the southern Negro. The people of Catfish Row became real in the cripple Porgy, the prostitute Bess, the bad Negro Crown. Several fine actors appeared in the Theatre Guild production including Frank Wilson, Jack Carter, Georgette Harvey, Leigh Whipper and the fine actress, Rose McClendon, who created leading parts in *In Abraham's Bosom, Deep River* and *Mulatto*. Heyward rewrote the play, for George Gershwin's music, for the folk opera, *Porgy and Bess* (1935). *Mamba's Daughters* (1937, with Mrs. Heyward), which brought that wonderful Negro character, Hagar, to the stage. It was in this role that the musical revue artist, Ethel Waters, was recognized as an actress of the first rank.

The success of *Porgy* and *The Green Pastures* opened the stage to a thrilling spectacle, written by a Negro and played by a Negro cast, *Run, Little Chillun* (1933) by Hall Johnson. Another aspect of the south, the poverty and degradation of the poor white was dramatized in *Tobacco Road* (1933) by Jack Kirkland from Erskine Caldwell's novel of the same name. This play, by its dramatic power, mordant humor, earthiness and frequent obscenity has broken all records for a long run play in a legitimate theatre, not only in New York, but everywhere else in the world. The play is completing its seventh year on Broadway and nearing its three thousandth performance. At first it was believed that it was the superb performance by Henry Hull which attracted audiences after a slow start. Its hold on the imagination of the spectators has not been lessened by such succeeding actors of the Jeeter Lester role as James Barton, James Bell, Eddie Garr, Will Geer (and on the road John Barton and Taylor Holmes).

LYNN RIGGS (1899-　) depicts the west and southwest of our country in his folk comedies and tragedies. The best of his plays are *Green Grow the Lilacs* (1930), which first brought Franchot Tone into prominence, and *Russet Mantle* (1936), which gave free rein to two fine comediennes, Margaret Douglass and Evelyn Varden. THORNTON WILDER (1897-　) is principally known for his sincere and penetrating study of New England *mores* in his tender and moving *Our Town* (1938), which was written to be performed without scenery and so to restore Elizabethan imagination to its audiences. He began his playwriting with *The Trumpet Shall Sound* (1926) and several short plays, notably *The Long Christmas Dinner* (1931). He adapted André Obey's *Lucrece* (1932), *A Doll's House* (1937), and Nestroy's Viennese farce as *The Merchant of Yonkers* (1938).

SIDNEY KINGSLEY (1906-) won the Pulitzer Prize for his first professionally produced play, *Men in White* (1933). He is concerned with urban problems, as in this play of hospital life, and with slums and juvenile delinquency in *Dead End* (1935). After the failure of his play about munitions makers, *Ten Million Ghosts* (1936), he dramatized Millen Brand's tender *The Outward Room*, a novel of a young girl who regains her sanity, as *The World We Make* (1939).

Abuse of privilege by public utilities, communism, labor relations, demonstrations against war, civil liberties, injustice, under-privileged children, slum clearance, and so on, are among the subjects chosen by the playwrights of social protest everywhere and nowhere more strongly than in America. Many of the plays have been weak, so hopelessly weighted on the side being argued as to be dramatically valueless. Many of these were accepted by their audiences at first, because they were delighted at last to have their personal and communal problems spoken of openly in the theatre. The stage as a forum for righting injustice became enormously popular. Such organizations as the Group Theatre with Odets; the Theatre Union with Albert Maltz and George Sklar; the New Theatre League with Irwin Shaw; the Theatre of Action; and Labor Stage came into being.

The Group Theatre still exists because it is primarily a theatre of actors, and the Labor Stage remains prominent because its witty and satirical revue *Pins and Needles* (1937) caught public fancy, and because it exists primarily to provide a social program for the International Ladies Garment Workers Union. The others failed to find sufficiently wide and sustaining audiences to continue. In many instances their sources of plays dried up or their sentiments went so far to the left that they lost the sympathies of their audiences. In many cases the audiences themselves dwindled because of political conditions abroad which made them suspicious of communists and their fellow-travellers. However, while the boom lasted from 1933 to 1939, statements were made upon American stages which would have terrified the D.A.R. or the Union League Club if by chance they had heard them.

However, they had done their work, for all serious dramatists realize the need for inclusion of social vision in their writing today. The most important plays were *Processional* (1925) by John Howard Lawson; *They Shall Not Die* (1934) by John Wexley; *Peace on Earth* (1933) by Albert Maltz and George Sklar; *Stevedore* (1934) by Paul Peters and George Sklar; *1931* (1931) by Clare and Paul

Sifton; *Black Pit* (1935) by Albert Maltz; *Bury the Dead* (1936) by Irwin Shaw; *The Cradle Will Rock* (1937) by Marc Blitzstein; *Marching Song* (1937) by John Howard Lawson; and *Let Freedom Ring* (1935) by Albert Bein from Grace Lumpkin's novel.

LILLIAN HELLMAN (1905-   ) has demonstrated greater dramatic power than any woman now writing for our stage. She began with a brilliant study of the evil that a slander about homosexuality brings upon two women who run a girls' school, in *The Children's Hour* (1934), which ran for two seasons on Broadway. The play suffers from psychological weakness, but its first two acts are notable for dramatic force. Her *Days to Come* (1935) dealt principally with labor relations, but there was a secondary plot about family greed and degeneracy which paved the way for her brilliant study of an avaricious family of southern upstarts in *The Little Foxes* (1939). This play is one of the most satisfactory dramas seen on the New York stage in recent years. Tallulah Bankhead, Frank Conroy, Patricia Collinge, Florence Williams and Abbie Mitchell contributed flawless performances to heighten the general effect.

Unquestionably the greatest American dramatist is EUGENE O'NEILL (1888-   ) son of the distinguished American actor, James O'Neill. He owes much to the invaluable experiences of his early days which were spent backstage and on tour with his father and mother (who was not an actress). His various sea trips took him to the far places of the world as a sailor, not as a passenger. He knew the waterfronts of New York, Buenos Aires, Southampton and the other great ports. It was there that he found the material which he was later to utilize in his sea plays: his sailors, prostitutes, bar-flies and general outcasts. This came to him by a process of assimilation, for he was not seeking "color" or "material" when he traveled. The sea is almost always in the background of his plays even when he seems to be farthest removed from it.

Strindberg is the writer to whom O'Neill seems to be most nearly akin. It has been out of his own experience and his sensitive feeling for life and human relations that his plays have come. He has acknowledged the inspiration and "the courage to believe in his work" which George Pierce Baker gave him. Some also must have come from his many friends and his lovely actress-wife, Carlotta Monterey.

Many of his first plays are unimportant and are not generally available. His earliest seems to have been a vaudeville piece, *A Wife for Life*, which was neither staged nor published. *The Web* (1913) was printed in the same volume which contained the other one-acters, *Thirst* (1914), *Recklessness* (1914), *Warnings* (1914), and *Fog* (1914, acted 1917), which is perhaps the best of these early pieces.

Bound East for Cardiff, was his first mature play and was written in 1914, produced in 1916. This with *In the Zone* (1917), *The Long Voyage Home* (1917), and *The Moon of the Caribbees* (1918) are four sea plays which are frequently performed together (as some of the characters appear in more than one play) as *S.S. Glencairn* and have been filmed in 1940 under the general title of *The Long Voyage Home*. His remarkable study of monotony, *Ile* (1917) came next; his study of avarice in *The Rope* (1918), and in *Where the Cross Is Made* (1918), were utilized in his full-length *Gold* (1921).

The group of friends, professional and amateur, who summered at Provincetown, at the tip of Cape Cod, had begun to function as a producing group in 1915 and in 1916 became the Provincetown Players. This was the agency which gave O'Neill his first hearing and eventually made him known to New York in the MacDougal Street Playhouse from which he progressed to Broadway and the theatre capitals of the world, through the force of his own dramatic power.

Out of *The Dreamy Kid* (1919), he secured practice in working with Negro material which was to emerge in later and more important plays. With *Beyond the Horizon* (1920), his period of apprenticeship was over. In this play he dramatized the longings of a man for the sea, a man who is anchored to a farm, a wife and a child, and a life of which he has made a failure. It is the tragedy of a man who is denied his illusions, and as such moved audiences deeply. In the fall of the year, *The Emperor Jones* (1920) placed the seal of success on O'Neill's career as a playwright and confirmed his position as our leading writer for the theatre. It is a psychological study of fear, in which the great contribution the Negro can make to the theatre was demonstrated by Charles Gilpin and later that great singer and fine actor, Paul Robeson.

Diff'rent (1920) is a naturalistic study of sexual repression and the inevitable explosion, which struck its audience in the face, and nowhere, except in the one-act *Before Breakfast* (1916), is the Strindberg influence so strong. Before the longer play was produced, he had written *Chris Christopherson* (1920) which is a play about the influence of the sea upon character. This, with major changes, remains the theme of *Anna Christie* (1921). The relations between Anna, her father and her lover, both sailors, are poignantly portrayed. Considered realistically the play is not tenable, but symbolically it is not only possible but inevitable. Pauline Lord's playing of Anna, and George Marion's of her father, surely still remain in the memories of those who saw their performances.

The Straw (1921) is a tragedy of love, with mingled hope and helpless struggle against disease, in a tuberculosis sanitarium. It is one of

O'Neill's most actable plays. Otto Kruger and Margalo Gillmore gave their initial love scene almost unbearable poignancy in the first performance at the Provincetown Playhouse. Though written during 1920-21, *The First Man* (1922) was not produced until March 1922 at the Neighborhood Playhouse. The play failed with the public largely because the critics harped upon the minor point of a mother moaning in child-birth, which cast the inference that the play was obscene, which was not true. Though one of his minor plays, it is one of his best portrayals of a family group.

O'Neill's venture into expressionism in *The Hairy Ape* (1922) resulted in one of his most effective plays. The character of the stoker, Yank, at home in his job until the disdainful look given him by the rich girl and his desire for revenge upon her causes a gnawing desire to belong to some group, or someone, proved dramatically effective and emotionally moving. The portrayal of the sailors in the stokehole gave American audiences a new scene in the theatre and broke the ground for later realistic pictures of life in honest crudity. Many of the audiences objected to the profanity but it opened the way for a representation of naturalistic speech which other playwrights were not hesitant to adopt and in some cases to carry to extremes. *Welded* (1924) was produced by the triumvirate of O'Neill, Kenneth Macgowan and Robert Edmond Jones, who formed a producing organization to continue the productions of the Provincetown Players at the Provincetown Playhouse and the Greenwich Village Theatre. This study of the antagonisms between a man and wife in marriage was staged at the Selwyn Theatre in association with the Selwyns. The triumvirate lasted for two seasons and in that time staged Strindberg's *The Spook Sonata* (1924), *Fashion* (1924), *Georges Dandin* (1924), Edmund Wilson's *The Crime in the Whistler Room* (1924), Stark Young's *The Saint* (1924), *Patience* (an excellent revival, 1924), Walter Hasenclever's *Beyond* (1925), Sherwood Anderson's and Raymond O'Neil's *Triumph of the Egg* (1925), Vildrac's *Michel Auclair* (1925), Hatcher Hughes' *Ruint* (1925) and Congreve's *Love for Love* (1925), with Jones' sets and Millia Davenport's costumes; this brilliant combination triumphed again in Jones' revival for The Players in 1940.

These plays, of course, were in addition to revivals of several of O'Neill's plays and premières of three. The first was his dramatic arrangement of Coleridge's poem, *The Ancient Mariner* (1924). This play reflected O'Neill's love and knowledge of the sea. E. J. Ballantine as the mariner was highly effective.

All God's Chillun Got Wings (1924) is a study of miscegenation with the horror of all its implications revealed. Miscegenation is not tne end sought but merely the means to dramatize the aspirations of Jim Harris. It is his personal tragedy that he chose a white woman who did not understand him and was as much below him intellectually as she was above him racially. As interpreted by Paul Robeson and Mary Blair it was a tremendously effective production. The publication of the play in the February 1924 issue of *The American Mercury* had aroused public opinion so there was an effort made on the part of the authorities to interfere with the performance. Despite a fight against the censorship of District Attorney Banton, the opening scene which had children in the cast was not allowed to be played. At the shouted demand of the audience, the lines were read by Kenneth Macgowan and subsequently by Harold McGee.

Then came one of O'Neill's best plays, *Desire Under the Elms* (1924) which provoked even more discussion and public indignation than the previous one. Banton's efforts to interfere were defeated by enlightened public opinion led by the newspapers and such theatrical authorities as Brander Matthews, Percy MacKaye, and Edward Sheldon. The play itself treats of a New England family in which the young wife of an old husband finds her step-son in love with her and reciprocates his passion. She bears his child and murders it and is taken away to be tried. Her old husband still loves her and only mourns that she had not had the child by him in which case he would have stood by her until the end. Walter Huston as the husband, the warm and glowing Mary Morris as the wife, and Charles Ellis as the guilty son, gave extraordinarily fine performances under Jones' sensitive direction. O'Neill, who always takes a strong interest in the scenic background of his plays, indicated just how the house should be represented. Jones caught the spirit in some of his finest designs, which indicated the exterior and four rooms within, which might be used and hidden when the action did not call for them.

The following season the triumvirate were no longer actively associated with the Provincetown and gave their performances at the Greenwich Village Theatre, where on December 10, 1925 they opened O'Neill's poetic drama, *The Fountain*. It was a symbolic romance about Ponce de Leon which Walter Huston played with fine feeling for the beauty of its lines. This play had a short life and on January 23, 1926 the major work, *The Great God Brown*, was produced. Symbolism is the dominant characteristic of this play, in which the author used masks to mark the person as he appeared to others and which he doffed to reveal his real being. It is a passionate cry of the artist in the modern world of commerce. Its mysteriousness, its use of masks did not deter the public and the play with William Harrigan, Anne Shoemaker and Robert Keith attracted a wide public and accustomed its audiences to a higher conception of theatre than they normally held. Almost always, throughout his career, O'Neill has constantly given his auditors new and far reaching goals to achieve.

Lazarus Laughed (1927) was produced by Gilmor Brown at the Pasadena Playhouse, in 1928. It was his and the theatre's greatest contribution to our stage. This symbolic drama of magnificent proportions dramatizes the life of Lazarus after he has risen from the grave. In his rebirth he has lost his fear of death, which is the root of all evil. When he laughs, it is the laughter of joy which comes from his very depths. Perhaps in no other play has O'Neill reached such exaltation, though there is an echo of it in *Days Without End*.

Marco Millions (1928) was a satirical and romantic drama of crass and self-destroying materialism. The almost legendary merchant, Marco Polo, whose journal has long been a source of information concerning the Orient, is his main character. Color and spectacular effects were contributed by Lee Simonson's costumes and settings; swift flow of movement without losing sight of character was aided by Rouben Mamoulian's direction. In this play, O'Neill, the poet, speaks.

Three weeks later with Philip Moeller's interpretive direction and Jo Mielziner's economical use of settings to speed the action, the nine-act drama, *Strange Interlude* (1928) opened. In this play, which reveals the inner life of a neurotic and possessive woman, O'Neill used soliloquies quite arbitrarily and effectively, to reveal the unspoken thoughts of the characters. Nina Leeds is one of the most complex women in modern drama. About her are gathered her father, the man she marries after her fiancé is killed in the war, the doctor who becomes the father of her child, the child who grows to manhood, and the old family friend to whom she turns in the end when all others escape her, either by death or abandonment. The Theatre Guild gave it a superlative production headed by Lynn Fontanne, Glenn Anders, Earle Larimore, Tom Powers and Helen Westley. The performance began at five-thirty in the afternoon and recessed at a quarter to eight, so that both audience and actors might eat, and resumed at nine for slightly more than two hours. The critics accorded the high praise it deserved and it ran for 432 performances in New York, longer than any other play ever produced by the Guild. Judith Anderson and Gale Sondergaard replaced Miss Fontanne in time, and such actresses as Pauline Lord, Elizabeth Risdon and Mary Ellis played it on the road (and the latter in London, which did not popularly begin to accord O'Neill his real position in the theatre until the last few years).

Dynamo (1929) was a failure but contains some of his finest writing. In this the futility of the worship of science is stressed in the study of a sensitive youth, who is in need of some spiritual outlet and who rejects the narrow fundamentalism of his parents' Christianity. Yet he cannot find lasting solace in the cynicism of the engineer father of the girl he loves.

Then came the trilogy, *Mourning Becomes Electra* (1931), which to date represents O'Neill's high point dramatically. In *Homecoming*, *The Hunted* and *The Haunted*, he has transferred the Orestean story to the New England country which he knows so well. This is a modern, psychological drama of tremendous power and into the Mannon family all of his skill of characterization, his great poetic powers, his wonderful ability to create suspense and a sense of impending fate, have been poured. Alice Brady, Alla Nazimova, Lee Baker and Earle Larimore caught his spirit and with Moeller's direction and Jones's setting, the Guild showed that it could match the dramatist's genius.

In *Ah, Wilderness!* (1933) he wrote his nearest approach to a popular drama of laughter. As Arthur Hobson Quinn points out, with his usual prescience, the tender and nostalgic portrait of a small town family surprised only those who had never read or seen the first act of *The First Man*. The role of the father was knowingly played by George M. Cohan and Will Rogers had real success with it on the road.

O'Neill's most recently produced play, *Days without End* (1934), has stirred wide divergence of opinion as to its merits. The majority hold that it is mediocre, while a minority feel that this play of split personality (employing two actors to portray one character) is highly important as it represents O'Neill as finding his own faith again, at the foot of the Cross. New York was lukewarm in its reaction to the play though in Dublin it proved one of the Abbey Theatre's greatest successes.

O'Neill is at present engaged on a cycle of plays representing a long and impressive period in American life. None of the plays is to be published or produced until all are finished. Two other plays, as yet unrevealed, have been completed *outside* the cycle. Whether he has moved into new thought and new techniques or remained in the great tradition of his earlier work is yet to be seen. Regardless of whether he ever writes again, he stands unchallenged as the topmost dramatist of our theatre.

MAXWELL ANDERSON (1888-) is one of the considerable dramatists of our era. Poetic drama with strong realistic validity is his forte though he has written in various styles. His work is of markedly varying quality, but several of his dramas have reached a high standard of near perfection. He began with a tragedy, *White Desert* (1923), which failed, but not before a few had discerned a new imaginative writer.

Then he turned to three collaborations with Laurence Stallings (1894-   ) only one of which was successful. *What Price Glory* (1924) was the first play written by an American to question the sacredness of our mission in the First World War, though John Dos Passos in the novel, *Three Soldiers* (1921), had paved the way. The humorous and profane quarrel till death between Captain Flagg and Sergeant Quirt entertained the audiences and the scene in the cellar-hospital horrified them. Neither *First Flight* (1925) nor *The Buccaneer* (1925) is of any importance; nor was *Outside Looking In* (1925), based on Jim Tully's autobiography, *Beggars of Life*.

Anderson continued in his realistic vein in the much more satisfactory *Saturday's Children* (1927), a restrained and sympathetic comedy of young love and middle-class domesticity. The humor vanished, but the passionate understanding of human frailty continued in *Gods of the Lightning* (1928), with Harold Hickerson, in which they cried out at the injustice of the verdict in the Sacco-Vanzetti case. Anderson was much more effective, when the white heat of his rage had subsided, in *Winterset*.

He continued in the realistic vein in *Gypsy* (1929), a quiet tragedy of a girl who passes from one man to another without finding an anchor, and who resolves her impasse by suicide. Several years before this play, Anderson had begun to experiment with verse in the drama in *Sea Wife* (written about 1926, produced at the University of Minnesota in 1932). He continued his experiments in *Elizabeth the Queen* (1930), a highly moving drama of love and power. He evolved a flexible line, retaining the four stress beat, but breaking the line where the thought was more important than the method of its expression. After passing through the romance of *Night Over Taos* (1932), colorfully staged by the Group Theatre but unsuccessful, and the satiric humors of political corruption in the Pulitzer Prize play *Both Your Houses* (1933), he wrote *Mary of Scotland* (1934). In this he returns to verse with high effect. He sets the scene with Mary, landing friendless, in a country of dark and forbidding enemies. The organized opposition of John Knox, the Scottish nobility, and the scheming Elizabeth, at once win the sympathies of the audience for the hapless queen. Though Anderson introduces a meeting between Elizabeth and Mary which never took place, it is dramatically correct, no matter how far removed from history.

Anderson's sympathy for Washington and his struggle with a dull-witted, pettifogging Congress in *Valley Forge* (1934) is immediately apparent. However, high regard is a poor substitute for drama and the life of Washington, like that of Lee, is a poor subject for playwrights, despite the obviously dramatic episodes in the lives of both.

Both *Hamlet* and the Sacco-Vanzetti case might be said to be responsible for *Winterset* (1935), in many ways his best play. Set beneath the towering Brooklyn Bridge, so magnificently suggested in Jo Mielziner's setting, with Guthrie McClintic's penetrating direction, it caught the mood of all-pervading Fate. The son who is seeking to clear the name of his father from an unjust murder charge; the murderous Trock, of the Underworld, who is really responsible; the frantic judge who has lost his mind from remorse at his biased conduct of the case; all combine to give the play high poetic imagination and power. Burgess Meredith as the boy, Margo as the girl who befriends him, and Richard Bennett as the mad judge gave such moving performances as to identify themselves completely with Anderson's characters.

In *The Wingless Victory* (1936) he chose the same theme which Joseph Hergesheimer employed in his novel *Java Head* (1919), but used it less effectively in this study of a New England sailor who marries an Oriental princess and brings her back to fade away on his native soil in the hostile bosom of his family. Even Katharine Cornell was unable to redeem it. *High Tor* (1936) has much more poetry, real fantasy in its portrayal of a young idealist who declines to yield to materialism, but who finally runs away from civilization when it intrudes upon him. This play contains one of Anderson's comedy scenes, which is as out of place as a vaudeville gag in a Maeterlinck play. The antics of two crooks in a steam shovel are entirely extraneous to the underlying motive of the play.

In *The Masque of Kings* (1936) he explored the story of Crown Prince Rudolph and Maria Vetsera, without either solving the mystery or increasing his stature as a dramatist. The play does, however, contain some isolated, magnificent speeches such as that of Rudolph to his parents before he kills himself.

The quaint New York of Washington Irving's history attracted him because of the opportunity it afforded to draw parallels with modern political events. Blessed with a melodic score by Kurt Weill, *Knickerbocker Holiday* (1938) was launched with a superb characterization of old Peter Stuyvesant, a dictator of the first water, by Walter Huston.

The political theme motivated his turning to the Spanish Civil War for *Key Largo* (1939). Though his feelings on that subject are made quite clear, the story of the play hinges upon a man's cowardice and his efforts to restore his self-respect, which can only come when he has given his life for others. Paul Muni's brooding performance did much to give the play a clarity which it lacked in the writing. His final play, to date, *Journey to Jerusalem* (1940), is an honest effort to portray such aspects of the life of Jesus, at the age of twelve, as may be given modern significance. Though he failed to convince either the critics or his audience that he had written a play for the theatre, many of his speeches are the finest he has composed. Set against Mielziner's exciting, projected scenery, they were cold, yet in reading and re-reading they touch the imagination. Though he understands the playhouse, Anderson has always been a dramatist who requires reading for complete comprehension. His poetry is the finest currently being written in the theatre, though Edna St. Vincent Millay has contributed several one-act plays of charming verse such as *Aria da Capo* (1919) and the more solid opera libretto *The King's Henchman* (1927). Archibald MacLeish (1892-   ) is a poet of distinction who has written several plays for the stage and radio. His highly experimental *Panic* (1935) attracted considerable attention as did his extremely moving radio plays, *The Fall of the City* (1937) and *Air Raid* (1938).

PAUL GREEN (1894-   ) is North Carolina born and a product of the immensely provocative development of folk-drama which came under the direction of Frederick H. Koch (1877-1944). Professor Koch began his work which was to bring plays out of their own local environment, at the University of North Dakota, where he formed the Dakota Playmakers, and in 1918 the University of North Carolina called him to head its department of dramatic art. In the spring of 1940, the twenty-first birthday of the Carolina Playmakers was celebrated with a festival of plays, talks by theatrical experts from all over the country, group discussions and exhibits of pictorial interest. This meeting did more than that. It paid well merited tribute to the man who, with Baker, has been largely responsible for the development of American playwriting. Koch differed from Baker, however, in beginning with the embryo playwright. Green is certainly Koch's greatest student and is the finest writer of folk-drama in our literature. Elizabeth Lay (Mrs. Green) pioneered with her *When the Witches Ride* (1919) but her husband followed with *The Last of the Lowries* (1920), another one-act play. This was based on the story of the infamous band of outlaws, who also figure in his *The Scuffletown Outlaws* (1924). His tragedy of the tenant-farmers, *Fixin's* (1924, with Erma Green) is moving and has been proved a satisfactory introduction to plays of this type by many theatres in the educational field. Then came the story of the vagabond in the charming *The No 'Count Boy* (1925) which is contrasted with another one-acter, *White Dresses* (1926).

Paul Green was more deeply concerned with the fate of the young Negro, Abraham McCranie, than with propaganda for the race, in his tragedy in seven scenes, *In Abraham's Bosom* (1926). As produced by the Provincetown Players with Frank Wilson and Rose McClendon, this play won the Pulitzer Prize for that season. Green turned to religious backwardness and country prejudices of the farmers of eastern North Carolina in *The Field God* (1927, revived in sharply revised and improved form at the Carolina Festival at Chapel Hill, 1940).

The Group Theatre inaugurated its official existence with their production of his almost Chekhovian *The House of Connelly* (1931). This play, which contrasts the virility of tenant farmers with an older family which has run to seed, was weakened by the neurotic performance of an urban-minded cast. The single exception to this was the versatile Mary Morris, whose O'Neill performances had granted her special understanding of the problems involved. Green returned to Negro life in all honesty, leaving out none of the sordid details, in *Potter's Field*, which was published as *Roll, Sweet Chariot* (1934).

He wrote one of the best anti-war plays of the present century in *Johnny Johnson* (1936) which was much better suited to the capabilities of the Group Theatre. Played against Donald Oenslager's imaginative settings with that excellent character actor, Russell Collins (graduate of Frederic McConnell's Cleveland Play House), the play had both satiric power and vitality upon the stage. Laughter, irony and sadness are mingled expertly.

Then, in 1937, he composed the pageant-drama *The Lost Colony* (which might serve as a model to others with a similar problem) to inaugurate the open-air theatre at Manteo, on Roanoke Island. In a perfect setting and in rustic simplicity this playhouse was created to accommodate Green's play of the ill-fated English expedition to establish a colony in the New World. He repeated this feat successfully in *The Highland Call* (1939), at Fayetteville, to mark the exploits of the Scotch-Irish settlers of that section of his state. Many thousands of people have come to see these plays; the first running all summer each year since 1937 and the latter in the late autumn of 1939, also to be repeated annually. In the beginning the Federal Theatre Project assisted Koch and Green on Roanoke Island and each year the young men from the C.C.C. Camp nearby have appeared as extras. Principals have been professionals with assistance from the Carolina Playmakers, but gradually a company of residents is being trained to carry it on in the future.

Green granted to Federal Theatre Project the right to produce two of his later long one-act plays, *Hymn to the Rising Sun* (1936) and *Unto Such Glory* (1936). These were staged brilliantly in 1937 for special matinees. The first, which dealt with the evils of chain-gang labor, was overpowering in the theatre. His many other one-act dramas dealt with various problems of the South from an enlightened point of view, characteristic of North Carolina.

In contrast to Green, ROBERT E. SHERWOOD (1896-   ) has found his experience in the professional theatre. He began as critic and editor for such publications as *Vanity Fair* and *Life* (the former comic weekly) but by 1926 was writing satirical farce comedy of mock-history such as *The Road to Rome* (1926), in which Jane Cowl, Philip Merivale, and Barry Jones gave fine performances, and *The Queen's Husband* (1928) for Roland Young. In *Waterloo Bridge* (1930) he chronicled the minor tragedy of a young soldier and a prostitute in the London of the First World War. In *This Is New York* (1930) he chronicled the New York of the bootleg era and in *Reunion in Vienna* (1931) he wrote a much better play, a romantic drama with satirical emphasis on psychoanalysis. The Lunts made this play delightful both in New York and London, but the production in the Swedish Theatre at Helsingfors was just as brilliant.

The Petrified Forest (1935) was a poor play but Leslie Howard's acting made it both popular and almost credible. In *Idiot's Delight* (1936) he made his first move toward a broader consideration of drama and its social implications, though the preoccupation with the comedy of sex ran through this as it had almost all of his plays before it.

Abe Lincoln in Illinois (1938), while over-praised on its first performance, is nonetheless a sincere and honest chronicle drama of the earlier and still formative years of a great man's career. He picks up at the point where E. P. Conkle left off in *Prologue to Glory*. Raymond Massey brought intelligence and authority to the part of Lincoln and Elmer Rice's staging enhanced the values of the play. The promise of this drama was amply justified by his next (and most recent) play, *There Shall Be No Night* (1940). The tragic events which forced little Finland into a defensive war against the overpowering might of Soviet Russia troubled Sherwood's conscience. He wrote this powerful defense of democracy and took it to the Lunts, already tired by a cross-country tour in their repertory. They felt its timeliness when democracy was fighting for its very existence and produced it in the spring of 1940. It represents the culmination of the theatrical effort of actors, director and playright.

The group of earnest young men and women, many of whom had been working in lesser capacities for the Theatre Guild, brought about the formation of the Theatre Guild Studio, which staged *Red Rust* (1930). Imbued with enthusiasm for the tenets of the Stanislavski system of acting Harold Clurman, Lee Strasberg, and Cheryl Crawford organized the Group Theatre. Having experiments with various playwrights, they eventually found their own dramatist in CLIFFORD ODETS (1906-   ). He was an actor in their organization, playing minor parts and writing plays. *Waiting for Lefty* (1935) an exciting one-act drama, was sponsored by the New Theatre League at the Civic Repertory Theatre. The response of the audience was so instantaneous that the play was hastily rehearsed more fully and shown on Broadway, with his anti-Nazi one-acter, *Till the Day I Die* (1935). His first full-length play, *Awake and Sing* (1935), wholesomely influenced by Chekhov whom he obviously admires but whom he does not imitate, confirmed the belief that a new writer of the first importance had appeared. This study of Bronx family life seemed to have gained in stature when it was revived in 1939. Luther and Stella Adler (brilliant children of the leading Yiddish actor in this country, Jacob Adler) and Jules Garfield, made a great impression in this play. (Garfield's work in *Having Wonderful Time, Golden Boy*, and *Heavenly Express* was also noteworthy.)

Odets' *Paradise Lost* (1935) was less effective, though the work of Morris Carnovsky and Sanford Meisner stood out in a well-integrated cast. *Golden Boy* (1937), despite a forced and melodramatic ending, is his best play so far. His study of a young violinist who is tempted into pugilism to make money to help his family, and in the doing destroys his hands (so that he can no longer play) and eventually his soul, is moving and warmly portrayed. *Rocket to the Moon* (1938) provided Morris Carnovsky and Ruth Nelson with excellent acting opportunities but did not advance Odets as a writer. *Night Music* (1940) was not wholly resolved but it was a much better integrated drama of life in New York for young people trying to establish themselves than Elmer Rice's *Two on an Island*, which had more success with the public. Odets is much more than a propagandist in the theatre; his portrayal of character, his understanding of human behavior, and his sympathy with his own people make him a dramatist to be reckoned with, not only now but in the future.

The Group Theatre, which encouraged Irwin Shaw with its production of his gentle comedy of racketeers and practical idealists, *The Gentle People* (1939), was also responsible for the introduction to the theatre of that paradoxical short-story writer, WILLIAM SAROYAN (1908-   ). He is undoubtedly one of the freshest and most provocative talents to write for the stage since the last war. His long one-act drama, *My Heart's in the Highlands* (1939) is a fantasy of great delight. His unusual use of words, his poetry, humor and imagination won him many admirers, though there were those (some of the same who deny the values of Philip Barry in *Hotel Universe* and *Here Come the Clowns*), who could see nothing in his work, much less understand his meaning. Saroyan followed it with *The Time of Your Life* (1939) a full-length allegory which won both the Critics' Prize as well as the Pulitzer Prize (which Saroyan rejected, though his producers made full use of it in advertising the double award). A company of little people are desperately trying to find happiness in a lowering world and Saroyan's waterfront San Francisco saloon is their haven. The play is filled with humor, pathos, and glorious good sense. Its effect was heightened by the acting of Eddie Dowling, who was the *deus ex machina*. *Love's Old Sweet Song* (1940) deals with a group of "Okies" who descend upon the home of a lovelorn spinster, beautifully played by Jessie Royce Landis, and are fascinated by the efforts of an itinerant pitchman but are finally enticed away by Cupid in the shape of a Western Union messenger. Saroyan's plots rarely make common sense but they add up to something much more exciting in the theatre. Saroyan has written several plays which were performed in the summer theatres during 1940, but none of them has as yet been brought to Broadway or published. It is too early, of course, to place him definitely but he is the newest bright light on Broadway.

THEATRE IN PRODUCTION

Only the pre-Hitler German and the Soviet Russian theatre have truly rivalled the American as a producing force. Many of our greatest designers, directors, producers and technicians have been mentioned in connection with some of their most important productions. A detailed study of their work would be out of place in a volume of this kind which attempts to survey the main channels of theatrical activity and dramatic thought from the beginnings on the Egyptian Nile to fruition on the Hudson.

We have placed particular emphasis on the standards of production in our theatre. Steele MacKaye and David Belasco, Granville-Barker, Robert Edmond Jones, Lee Simonson, Norman Bel Geddes, Jo Mielziner, Donald Oenslager, Arthur Hopkins, Brock Pemberton, Guthrie McClintic among countless others have maintained a high level. One of our first characteristic forms to develop was the lavish revue and musical comedy. Florenz Ziegfeld, George White, and Earl Carroll were responsible for this and later, Dwight Deere Wiman, Sam H. Harris, Vinton Freedley, B. G. DeSylva, Vincente Minelli, Lew Brown, Ray Henderson, George and Ira Gershwin, Irving Berlin, and Rodgers and Hart have created the witty, small musical which holds our attention these days. The list of performers is a long one and includes such personalities as Nora Bayes, W. C. Fields, Will Rogers, Fanny Brice, Victor Moore, Al Jolson, Ed Wynn, Joe Cook, William Gaxton, Jimmy Durante, Beatrice Lillie, Bert Lahr, and Ethel Merman to name but a few to indicate the high point to which the musical comedy stage has been brought in the past quarter of a century.

During the closing days of the fight against the Theatrical Syndicate, three young men from Syracuse came into prominence in the producing field and because of their activities at the time were regarded highly. The Shubert Brothers, Sam (now dead), Lee and Jacob, advanced in power until they now control, directly or indirectly, a large proportion of the theatres still open to so-called legitimate performances throughout the country. Any kind of monopoly, whether recognized or not, hampers the theatre, so the Shuberts frequently find themselves opposed by some of the same men with whom they fought as allies against the Syndicate. Because of their real estate interests, they produce a great many plays, either under their own banner, or, indirectly through the purchase of an interest in the shows of other producers, or through direct financing of managers whose funds are not sufficiently ample to permit their independent financing of productions. Thus they keep their theatres as well filled as a dwindling number of plays permits.

Many of the earlier managers were sharp in their practices and if a play failed, either in New York or on the road, it was always the actor who found himself without payment. Players were stranded in various parts of the country and legal redress was slow and frequently impossible to obtain because of subterfuges practiced by unscrupulous or unfeeling managements.

As a result of this the Actors' Equity Association was formed, in 1912, with a committee which included Albert Bruning, Charles D. Coburn, Frank Gillmore, William Harcourt, Milton Sills, and Grant Stewart. In 1919, the actors resorted to a strike to obtain standard salaries, improved working conditions, and bonds to protect them against giving their services for nothing. The managers, led by that splendid veteran William A. Brady, fought "Equity" tooth and nail. The actors startled Broadway with a parade, constant performances at the Lexington Opera House to raise money, a daily newspaper, and incessant appeals to the public. They probably would not have won their strike had it not been for the united support of the stage hands and other unionized forces of the theatre, who had also banded together for protection against managerial abuses. They, in particular, have gone too far in their restrictions and in their raising of salaries so that the professional theatre has become almost prohibitive in its costs of production. An illuminating survey of this impasse (from all points of view) was published in the May 1940 issue of *Theatre Arts*.

The actors won their strike and have, on the whole, behaved with decency and restraint in the conduct of their affairs with the managers, as represented today by the League of New York Theatres, and with the writers identified with the Dramatists' Guild of the Authors' League of America. The latter organization owed its inception to the Society of American Dramatists and Composers organized by Bronson Howard. (The composers are now taken care of by the powerful American Society of Composers, Authors and Publishers, familiarly known as ASCAP.) One hundred and thirty-one playwrights under the leadership of George Middleton signed a "defensive" agreement saying that they would deal with no manager who would not grant them fair royalties, fifty (now sixty) per cent of film rights, final judgment on casting, and assurance that their lines would not be altered without their consent. Now it is rather the film producers whom they have to guard against as they enter more and more into the financing of plays to insure sufficient dramas for Hollywood's film output. Producing from all points of view has become so expensive, complicated and heartbreaking, that one can easily understand the point of view of those who raise their hands in horror and flee to the educational theatre or the easier (comparatively) form of novel writing or criticism.

Not all of the managers are rank individualists, as Joseph Verner Reed suggests in his satirical and occasionally hysterical *The Curtain Falls* (1935). The brilliant, uneven, usually impractical, ever-changing personnel of the Provincetown Players shows as much in its years between 1915 and 1929. The Neighborhood Playhouse (founded in 1915 in Grand Street by those sincere and high-minded women, Irene and Alice Lewisohn, to bring dramatic culture to the lower East Side of New York) was social in its implications. References to their productions have appeared throughout these pages because their theatre interests were broader than those of any other managers our theatre has yet produced. With them were associated such men and women (outstanding in their fields) as Helen Arthur, Agnes Morgan, Dorothy Sands, Albert Carroll, Aline Bernstein, Aline MacMahon and others.

The Theatre Guild began as the Washington Square Players in 1915 who found their experimental career interrupted by the First World War; afterwards they resumed, in their present capacity, and under their corporate name in 1919. Among the various persons of talent who have been associated with them since their inception the nucleus of six are those with whom we associate the organization, Helen Westley, Philip Moeller, Lawrence Langner, Theresa Helburn, Lee Simonson and Maurice Wertheim. In recent years the talents and energies of the directors have been so largely vitiated by work in Hollywood, and in other outside fields, as to cause a strong deterioration in their artistic standards. They have now become like the regular Broadway managers, differing only in the subscription list which patronizes their plays sight unseen. This list reached the total of thirty thousand, in New York alone, a few years ago. Depression and other factors have decreased their hold in New York but in connection with the Shubert-controlled American Theatre Society, they have a large and healthy subscription list in many eastern and middle-western cities.

From 1926 to 1933, Eva LeGallienne controlled the only professional repertory company New York has had. The Civic Repertory Theatre worked to build an audience in the lower-priced ticket brackets which would come again and again to see Ibsen, Shakespeare and the plays of other standard writers. The depression, plus the exorbitant cost of maintaining repertory in New York, caused the abandonment of this enterprise, to the regret of all.

Walter Hampden for some years maintained his own theatre as an actor-manager to the delight of the college and university audience who could count on the production of plays normally included in their courses of dramatic study. Besides Shakespeare and Ibsen, he included such works as Arthur Goodrich's *Caponsacchi* (1926), dramatized from Browning's *The Ring and the Book*, and *Cyrano de Bergerac* in Brian Hooker's admirable version.

A unique producing organization is the Playwright's Company, which was organized in 1938 by Sidney Howard, S. N. Behrman, Maxwell Anderson, Elmer Rice, and Robert E. Sherwood to produce their own plays and those of any other playwright in whom they might take an interest and whom they might wish to see produced under their own auspices.

Most of the actors have been mentioned throughout the chapter in connection with plays with which they have been associated. Special mention should be made of the actress-playwright, Jane Cowl, whose performances have given so much pleasure. Her plays (with Jane Murfin), *Lilac Time* (1917) and *Smilin' Through* (1919), in which she also appeared, were very popular. Perhaps her finest performance was that of Juliet to Rollo Peters' Romeo, which was given for 157 performances in 1923. Katharine Cornell, Helen Hayes, Ruth Gordon, Lynn Fontanne and Alfred Lunt have been hailed in their various acting triumphs. Maurice Evans, English actor now domiciled in America, has contributed a series of brilliant performances, chiefly remarkable for their popularity and extraordinary elocution. His Romeo to Katharine Cornell's Juliet (1935), Napoleon (in *Saint Helena*, 1936), Richard II, (1937, perhaps his best performance), the full length *Hamlet* (1938), Falstaff (1939) and Malvolio (1940) have owed much to the remarkable powers of the director-actress, Margaret Webster, who has been associated with him since *King Richard II*.

Much influence in the development of the theatre has been wielded not only by the forceful dramatic criticism to be found in the New York and Boston newspapers, but by the various stage periodicals. Just as the *Era* and *Stage*, in England, have influenced critical thought, the *Morning Telegraph*, *New York Dramatic Mirror*, *Theatre Magazine*, *Drama*, *Stage* (in both incarnations), Robinson Locke's splendid *Toledo Blade*, and above all, *Theatre Arts* under the editorship of Sheldon Cheney, Edith J. R. Isaacs, Kenneth Macgowan, John Mason Brown, Carl Carmer, Stark Young and Rosamond Gilder, have raised the standards of writing and production in our theatre.

In 1935, in response to active pressure by stage forces, an effort was made to combat unemployment in the legitimate theatre by the establishment of the Federal Theatre Project. Under the brilliant direction of Hallie Flanagan, this organization sought to combine its primary function as a relief organization with the noteworthy object of becoming a national theatre. With all its inefficiency, governmental red-tape, sabotage from radicals within, it acquitted itself brilliantly. Some of the most interesting productions of recent years were made in its many centers of theatre activity, New York, Philadelphia, Boston, Chicago, New Orleans, San Francisco and Los Angeles.

The technique of the living newspaper was developed though it has found no following on the commercial stage except for Carly Wharton's and Martin Gabel's production of *Medicine Show*, by Oscar Saul and Hammond R. Hays (1940). Some of the outstanding productions were *Murder in the Cathedral*, *Power*, the Negro *Macbeth*, *Doctor Faustus* (these two staged by Orson Welles and John Houseman), . . . *one third of a nation* . . . , and *The Swing Mikado*. The organization carried the seeds of its own destruction within it, which many of its sincerest friends pointed out more than once. Mounting political opposition killed it in the summer of 1939.

The only important producing organization to come out of it was the Mercury Theatre, under the direction of Orson Welles, actor-director-writer and John Houseman. Since leaving the federal fold they have produced a brilliant politically-minded modern dress version of *Julius Caesar* (1937) without scenery, a brisk and amusing revival of *The Shoemakers' Holiday* (1938), *Heartbreak House* (1938), and Buechner's *Danton's Death* (1938).

It has been said over and over again that with the dwindling of the road, the invasion of the films and radio, the theatre will find survival in what Edith Isaacs has so often called "the tributary theatre." Much of the impetus for the educational theatre came out of George Pierce Baker's pioneer work at Harvard, and later at Yale, in his famous 47 Workshop. Certainly Frederick Koch contributed with his folk dramas at Dakota and Carolina. Much has come out of the Drama League of America with such men and women as Walter Prichard Eaton, Walter Hartwig, Mrs. John Alexander, Kate Oglebay, Florence Overton, Barrett H. Clark, to name but a few of the earlier workers whose enthusiasm is carried on by May Newton today.

Out of this has grown a theatre which numbers all of the universities and most of the colleges and secondary schools of America. There is no city and scarcely a town or village which does not have a community or little theatre. There are rural drama movements in many states. Several organizations exist to care for the problems which arise in connection with the multitudinous productions. The foremost is the National Theatre Conference, with headquarters at Cleveland, headed by an executive committee including Gilmor Brown, Allardyce Nicoll, Barclay S. Leathem, Frederic McConnell and C. H. Meredith. There are also the American Association of Community Theatres and the American Educational Theatre Association.

It is difficult to select theatres out of this group for mention because of the growing excellence in this field. Probably the most outstanding are the Pasadena Community Playhouse; the Play House, of Cleveland; the Dock Street Theatre, of Charleston, S. C.; the Hedgerow Theatre, at Moylan-Rose Valley, Pa., the only actual repertory organization in our country; and *Le Petit Théâtre du Vieux Carré* in New Orleans. In addition to these are the theatres of Yale, Dartmouth, the University of Washington, Indiana University, Western Reserve University, Syracuse University, University of Iowa, Carnegie Institute of Technology, the University of California, University of California at Los Angeles, the University of Southern California, and, of course, the Carolina Playmakers of the University of North Carolina.

Though the summer theatre had its inception at Elitch's Gardens in Denver in the last century, followed by the brilliant success of the Lakewood Theatre at Skowhegan, Maine, its real flowering was reserved for the nineteen twenties and thirties. Young actors and graduates of drama schools began the establishment of rural playhouses in barns, schools and churches. So successful were they that the stars and featured players of Broadway followed them into the countryside. In recent years this has become one of the most characteristic facets of our theatre and handsome, well-equipped stages have been built. Some of the most outstanding are those at Stockbridge (Mass.), Dennis on Cape Cod, Ogunquit (Me.), New Hope, (Pa.), and East Hampton, Long Island.

It is a hopeful theatre that helps itself, this American theatre of ours, and one of which we can all be sincerely proud, regardless of our connection with it. It is a theatre of power, dynamics, and above all, song; the song of democracy.

EPILOGUE

THE theatre as our forefathers knew it has expanded beyond our fondest dreams and maddest imagination. What began in the Pyramid Texts and Passion Plays of ancient Egypt has ended in performances in highly sophisticated playhouses, upon the screen with recorded sound, in the air waves and finally in televised portrayals of drama.

From 1889 to 1896 fantastic experiments were going on which made it possible to photograph people and objects so rapidly that they moved upon the screen when the film was projected. Once the producers, men like Edison, Lumière, Kleine and countless others were able to control the medium and began to realize its potentialities, other men followed in their footsteps to commercialize the output so that everyone could see it readily. In 1903 came the feature picture, *The Great Train Robbery* and in a few years men like D. W. Griffith, William Fox, David Selznick, Thomas Ince, Charles Chaplin began to come to the force. The silent film became an art form, which in its high development of pantomime attracted wide audiences.

For many years inventors had been working on the possibilities of introducing sound effects and hoped that synchronized speech would become possible. Warner Brothers were the first to exploit this novelty and they with Al Jolson in *The Jazz Singer* (1927) made a fortune. The talking film did two things for the stage. It destroyed a large part of the road business by offering cheap mechanical competition with the finest actors, writers and directors that money could buy. Besides it led to buying up theatres throughout the country and closing them to touring attractions. This is the purely negative side. The more roseate viewpoint is that it broadened the aspects of the theatre by widening its audience, permitting endless duplication of the same artistic effort, and offered greater employment for all concerned than the legitimate stage had ever done in its palmiest days.

One of the most interesting developments that has appeared in recent years has scarcely been noted by Hollywood, which usually prides itself that it has its ear to the ground to detect trends. This is that the audience, just as the stage audience has always been, is no longer satisfied with seeing films, it wishes to read them. Those libraries such as the New York Public Library, the Dartmouth College Library, the Museum of Modern Art Film Library (under the guidance of John and Iris Abbott) and the Academy of Motion Picture Arts and Sciences Library (headed by Donald and Margaret Gledhill) which have collected scripts for their reading public are meeting a national demand. Perhaps, as this trend is observed, a wider and freer distribution of film scripts to libraries will come in the natural course of events.

Since 1920, a new phase of theatre came into being in Radio, which has drawn its talent not only from stage and screen, but from dying vaudeville, burlesque and the ever present night clubs. Beginning as a news agency, music was added, and not long after, plays were presented over the air. At first little effort was made to adapt them to their new medium. Plays were read and necessary business explained through the microphone to the listeners, but no real use was made of radio potentialities. Eventually men came to write for air production just as they wrote for the screen and for the stage. Maxwell Anderson, Archibald MacLeish and Arch Oboler are some of the men who have been most effective in realizing the possibilities of this new medium.

Television has scarcely been realized in this country except by a few thousand owners of receiving sets and the several hundred people who are experimenting for the National Broadcasting Corporation and the Columbia Broadcasting System. Both England and the Continent had gone further along these lines than had America when the Second World War broke out. Practically all telecasting abroad has been suspended for the duration.

However, neither there nor in this country has there been any real comprehension of the potentialities of this new force for entertainment, education and culture. Plays have been telecast from the stages of theatres or from broadcasting studios. Spot-news reporting of political or sporting events has been the imaginative as well as the practical limit in this new field.

Regardless of the spreading use of these various mechanical devices, there still remains (and probably always will) a public which is unsatisfied unless it experiences that electric spark which only comes through the combination of audiences and actors. It is this excitement that has brought about the vast educational theatre movement with its countless theatres and its unnumbered spectators. It is hard to be thrilled by a shadow or a disembodied voice unless more artistry and intelligence is displayed in these media than the past half century has brought.

When all is said and done, the greatest thrill in life for theatre-lovers is that moment when the house-lights dim, the latecomers scurry to their seats, the ushers' flashlights pierce the gloom like the ghosts of long dead actors, the footlights grow in intensity, the music dims and the curtain rises. Out of the darkness comes Bernardo's voice in Shakespeare's line, "Who's there?"

SELECTED BIBLIOGRAPHY

THE titles are arranged alphabetically by author and numbered in sequence. A cross-index for these numbers by country and special topics follows this list.

1 ADAMS, J. Q. *Shakespearean Playhouses.* Boston: Houghton, Mifflin, 1917.

2 ADAMS, W. DAVENPORT. *A Dictionary of the Drama.* A Guide to the Plays, Playwrights, Players and Playhouses of the United Kingdom and America, from the Earliest Times to the Present. Philadelphia: Lippincott, 1904. Vol. 1 A-G.

3 AGATE, JAMES. *The English Dramatic Critics.* An Anthology, 1660-1932. London: Arthur Barker, 1932.

4 ALLEN, JAMES TURNEY. *Stage Antiquities of the Greeks and Romans and Their Influence.* New York: Longmans, Green and Company, 1927.

5 ANDERSON, JOHN. *The American Theatre.* New York: Dial Press, 1938.

6 ANDERSON, JOHN. *Box Office.* New York: Jonathan Cape and Harrison Smith, 1929.

7 APPIA, ADOLPHE. Fifty-six reproductions printed by the Art Institute, Orell, Fusseli, Zurich, 1929.

8 APPIA, ADOLPHE. *Die Musik und die Inscenerung.* Munich: F. Bruckmann, 1899.

9 ARCHER, WILLIAM. *Introductions* (to individual volumes of Ibsen's plays). New York: Scribner, 1929. 12 vols.

10 ARCHER, WILLIAM. *Play-Making, a Manual of Craftsmanship.* Boston: Small, Maynard, 1923.

11 ARCHER, WILLIAM and GRANVILLE-BARKER, HARLEY. *A National Theatre.* Scheme & Estimates. London: Duckworth, 1907.

12 ARLINGTON, L. C. *The Chinese Drama.* From the Earliest Times until Today. With a *Pien* by Mei Lan-fang. Foreword by H. A. Giles. Shanghai: Kelly & Walsh, 1930.

13 ARRIGTONI, PAOLO and BERTARELLI, ACHILLE. *Ritratti di Musicisti ed Artisti di Teatro conservati nella Raccolta delle Stampe e dei Disegni.* Catalogo Descrittivo. Milan: Comune di Milano, Istituti di Storia e d'Arte. 1934.

14 ARTHUR, SIR GEORGE. *From Phelps to Gielgud.* Reminiscences of the Stage Through Sixty-Five Years. With an introduction by John Gielgud. London: Chapman & Hall, 1936.

15 ARVIN, NEIL COLE. *Eugène Scribe and the French Theatre* 1815-1860. Cambridge: Harvard University Press, 1924.

16 BAIRD, JOHN F. *Make-up.* New York: Samuel French, 1930.

17 BAKER, BLANCH M., compiler. *Dramatic Bibliography.* Introduction by Milton Smith. An Annotated List of Books on the History and Criticism of the Drama and Stage and on the Allied Arts of the Theatre. New York: H. W. Wilson, 1933.

18 BAKER, DAVID ERSKINE, REED, ISAAC and JONES, STEPHEN. *Biographia Dramatica, or, A Companion to the Playhouse.* London: Longman, Hurst, Rees, Orme, and Brown: 1812. Vol. 1, 2 parts.

19 BAKER, GEORGE PIERCE. *The Development of Shakespeare as a Dramatist.* New York: Macmillan, 1917.

20 BAKER, GEORGE PIERCE. *Dramatic Technique.* Boston: Houghton Mifflin, 1919.

21 BAKER, H. BARTON. *History of the London Stage. and Its Famous Players* (1576-1903). London: George Routledge, 1904.

22 BARSHY, ALEXANDER. *The Path of the Modern Russian Stage.* London: C. Palmer & Hayward, 1916.

23 BALL, ROBERT HAMILTON. *The Amazing Career of Sir Giles Overreach.* Princeton: Princeton University Press, 1939.

24 BALMFORTH, RAMSDEN. *The Ethical and Religious Value of the Drama.* London: Allen & Unwin, 1925.

25 BALMFORTH, RAMSDEN. *The Problem-Play, and Its Influence on Modern Thought and Life.* New York: Holt, 1928.

26 BARBER, PHILIP W. *The Scene Technician's Handbook.* New Haven: Whitlock's Book Store, 1928.

27 BARING, MAURICE. *An Outline of Russian Literature.* New York: Holt, n.d.

28 BARRAS, MOSES. *The Stage Controversy in France from Corneille to Rousseau.* New York: Institute of French Studies, Inc., 1933.

29 BARTON, LUCY. *Historic Costume for the Stage.* Foreword by B. Iden Payne. Boston: Baker, 1935.

30 BATES, ALFRED, editor. *The Drama.* London: Smart and Stanley, 1903. (20 vols.)

31 BATES, KATHARINE LEE. *The English Religious Drama.* New York: Macmillan, 1893.

32 BEERBOHM, MAX. *Around the Theaters.* New York: Knopf, 1930. 2 vols.

33 BELASCO, DAVID. *Plays Produced under the Stage Direction of David Belasco.* Privately printed. New York, 1925.

34 BELL, AUBREY F. G. *Portuguese Literature.* Oxford: The Clarendon Press, 1922.

35 BELL, AUBREY F. G. *Contemporary Spanish Literature.* New York: Knopf, 1925.

36 BERNHARDT, SARAH. *The Art of the Theatre.* Translated by H. J. Stenning, Preface by James Agate. London: Geoffrey Bles, 1924.

37 BERNHEIM, ALFRED L. *The Business of the Theatre.* New York: Actors' Equity Association, 1932.

38 BIEBER, MARGARETE. *The History of the Greek and Roman Theatre.* Princeton: Princeton University Press, 1939.

39 BISHOP, G. W. *Barry Jackson and the London Stage.* Foreword by Charles B. Cochran. London: Arthur Barker, 1933.

40 BLAKE, BEN. *The Awakening of the American Theatre.* New York: Tomorrow Publishers, 1935.

41 BLANKNER, FREDERIKA, editor and compiler. *The History of the Scandinavian Literatures.* New York: Dial Press, 1938.

42 BLOCK, ANITA. *The Changing World in Plays and Theatre.* Boston: Little, Brown, 1939.

43 BOLESLAVSKY, RICHARD. *Acting: The First Six Lessons.* New York: Theatre Arts, 1937. Fourth printing.

44 BOSWELL, ELEANORE. *The Restoration Court Stage* (1660-1702). With a particular account of the production of CALSITO. Cambridge, Mass.: Harvard University Press, 1932.

45 BOYD, ERNEST A. *The Contemporary Drama of Ireland.* Boston: Little, Brown, 1928.

46 BRADBROOK, M. C. *Themes and Conventions of Elizabethan Tragedy.* New York: MacMillan (Cambridge), 1935.

47 BRANDES, GEORG. *Main Currents in Nineteenth Century Literature,* 6 Vols. New York: The Macmillan Company, 1904.

50 BRANDES, GEORG. *Wolfgang Goethe.* Authorized Translation From the Danish. By Allen W. Porterfield. New York: Frank-Maurice, Inc., 1925. 2 vols.

51 BRASOL, BORIS. *The Mighty Three—Pushkin, Gogol, Dostoievsky.* New York: William Farquhar Payson, 1934.

52 BREASTED, JAMES HENRY. *Ancient Records.* Chicago: University of Chicago Press, 1906-07. 5 vols.

53 BREASTED, JAMES HENRY. *The Development of Religion and Thought in Ancient Egypt.* New York: Scribner, 1912.

54 BROOKE, C. F. TUCKER. *The Tudor Drama.* Boston: Houghton, Mifflin, 1911.

55 BROWN, IVOR. *First Player.* The Origin of Drama. New York: Wm. Morrow & Co., 1928.

56 BROWN, IVOR. *Parties of the Play.* London: Benn, 1928.

57 BROWN, JOHN MASON. *The Art of Playgoing.* New York: Norton, 1936.

58 BROWN, JOHN MASON. *Letters from Greenroom Ghosts.* New York: Viking, 1934.

59 BROWN, JOHN MASON. *The Modern Theatre in Revolt.* New York: Norton, 1929.

60 BROWN, JOHN MASON. *Upstage.* New York: Norton, 1930.

61 BROWN, T. ALLSTON. *History of the American Stage.* New York: Dick & Fitzgerald, 1870.

62 BROWN, T. ALSTON. *A History of the New York Stage from the First Performance in 1732 to 1901.* New York: Dodd, Mead, 1903. 3 vols.

63 BRUNETIERE, FERDINAND. *The Law of the Drama.* New York, Columbia University Dramatic Museum, 1914.

64 BURRUS-MEYER, HAROLD and COLE, EDWARD C. *Scenery for the Theatre.* Boston: Little, Brown, 1938.

65 BUSS, KATE. *Studies in the Chinese Drama.* Boston: The Four Seas Company, 1922.

66 BUSSE, BRUNO. *Das Drama.* Leipzig: B. C. Teubner, 1922. 4 vols.

67 BUTCHER, S. H. *Aristotle's Theory of Poetry and Fine Art.* London: Macmillan, 1911. 4th edition.

68 BYRNE, DAWSON. *The Story of Ireland's National Theatre.* Dublin: The Talbot Press, 1929.

69 CAMPBELL, LILY B. *Scenes and Machines in the Renaissance.* Cambridge: University Press, 1923.

70 CAPPS, EDWARD. *Vitruvius and the Greek Stage.* Chicago: University of Chicago Press, 1893.

71 CARSON, WILLIAM G. B. *The Theatre on the Frontier.* The Early Years of the St. Louis Stage. Chicago: University of Chicago Press, 1932.

72 CARTER, HUNTLY. *The New Spirit in Drama & Art.* New York: Mitchell Kennerley, 1913.

73 CARTER, HUNTLY. *The New Spirit in the European Theatre,* 1914-1924. London: Benn, 1925.

74 CARTER, HUNTLY. *The New Spirit in the Russian Theatre.* 1917-28. And a sketch of the Russian Kinema and Radio 1919-28, showing the new communal relationship between the three. London: Brentano's, 1929.

75 CARTER, JEAN and OGDEN, JESS. *The Play Book.* New York: Harcourt, Brace 1937.

76 CHAMBERS, SIR E. K. The Elizabethan Stage. Oxford: Clarendon Press, 1923. 4 vols.

77 CHAMBERS, SIR E. K. *The Medieval Stage.* Oxford: Clarendon Press, 1903. 2 vols.

78 CHAMBERS, SIR E. K. *William Shakespeare:* A Study of Facts and Problems. London: Oxford University Press, 1930.

79 CHANDLER, FRANK W. *The Contemporary Drama of France.* Boston: Little, Brown, 1925.

80 CHANDLER, FRANK W. *Modern Continental Playwrights.* New York: Harper & Brothers, 1931.

81 CHATFIELD-TAYLOR, H. C. *Goldoni:* A Biography. New York: Duffield, 1913.

82 CHENEY, SHELDON. *The Art Theatre.* Its character as differentiated from the commercial theater; its ideals and organization; and a record of certain European and American examples. Revised and enlarged edition. New York: Knopf, 1925.

83 CHENEY, SHELDON. *The New Movement in the Theatre.* New York: Mitchell Kennerley, 1914.

84 CHENEY, SHELDON. *The Open-air Theatre.* New York, 1918.

85 CHENEY, SHELDON. *Stage Decoration.* New York: John Day, 1928.

86 CHENEY, SHELDON. *The Theatre:* Three Thousand Years of Drama, Acting and Stagecraft. New York: Longmans, Green, 1929.

87 CHISHOLM, CECIL. *Repertory.* An Outline of the Modern Theatre Movement. London: Peter Davies, 1934.

88 CIBBER, COLLEY. *Apology for the Life of Mr. Colley Cibber.* New edition by R. W. Lowe. London: Nimmo, 1889.

89 CLARK, BARRETT H. *Eugene O'Neill:* The Man and His Plays. New York: McBride, 1927.

90 CLARK, BARRETT H. *European Theories of the Drama.* An Anthology of Dramatic Theory and Criticism from Aristotle to the Present Day, in a Series of Selected Texts, with commentaries, biographies, and bibliographies. New York: D. Appleton, 1925.

91 CLARK, BARRETT H. *Maxwell Anderson:* The Man and his Work. New York: Samuel French, 1933.

92 CLARK, BARRETT H. *A Study of the Modern Drama.* A Handbook for the Study and appreciation of Typical plays, European, English and American of the last Three-quarters of a Century. New York: Appleton-Century, 1938. Revised edition.

93 CLARKE, SIDNEY W. *The Miracle Play in England,* an account of the early Religious Drama. London: W. Andrews, 1897.

94 COAD, ORAL SUMNER and MIMS, EDWIN JR. *The American Stage.* The Pageant of America Series. New Haven: Yale University Press, 1928.

95 COGNIAT, RAYMOND. *Décors de Théâtre.* Paris: Éditions des Chroniques du Jour, 1930.

96 COHEN, GUSTAVE. *Histoire de la mise-en-scène dans le théâtre, religieux français du moyen age.* Paris: Champion, 1926.

97 COLBOURNE, MAURICE. *The Real Bernard Shaw.* New York: Dodd, Mead, 1940.

98 COLEMAN, ARTHUR P. *Humor in the Russian Comedy From Catherine to Gogol.* New York: Columbia University Press, 1925. Columbia University Slavonic Studies. Vol. 2.

99 COLLIER, J. P. *The History of English Dramatic Poetry to the Time of Shakespeare:* and Annals of the Stage to the Restoration. London: C. Bell Sons, 1879. New Edition.

100 COOPER, LANE. *Aristotle on the Art of Poetry.* New York: Ginn & Co., 1913.

101 CORDELL, RICHARD A. *Henry Arthur Jones and the Modern Drama.* New York, 1932.

102 CRAIG, EDWARD GORDON. *On the Art of the Theatre.* New York: Dodd, Mead, 1925.

103 CRAIG, EDWARD GORDON. *Scene.* New York: Oxford University Press, 1923.

104 CRAIG, EDWARD GORDON. *The Theatre Advancing.* Boston: Little, Brown, 1919.

105 CRAIG, EDWARD GORDON. *Towards a New Theatre.* London: Dent, 1913.

106 CRAWFORD, MARY CAROLINE. *The Romance of the American Theatre.* Boston: Little, Brown, 1925.

107 CUNLIFFE, J. W. *Modern English Playwrights.* From 1825 to 1927. New York: Harper, 1927.

108 DAMERON, LOUISE. *Bibliography of Stage Settings.* To which is attached an Index to Illustrations of Stage Settings. Baltimore: Enoch Pratt Free Library, 1936.

109 DANA, HENRY WADSWORTH LONGFELLOW. *Handbook on Soviet Drama.* Lists of Theatres, Plays, Operas, Ballets, Films and Books and Articles About Them. New York: The American Russian Institute, 1938.

110 DEAN, ALEXANDER. *Little Theatre Organization and Management.* Preface by Walter Prichard Eaton. New York: Appleton, 1926.

111 DEUTSCH, HELEN and HANAU, STELLA. *The Provincetown.* New York: Farrar and Rinehart, 1931.

112 DICKINSON, THOMAS H. *The Contemporary Drama of England.* Boston: Little, Brown, 1931. Revised edition.

113 DICKINSON, THOMAS H. *An Outline of Contemporary Drama.* Boston: Houghton, Mifflin, 1927.

114 DICKINSON, THOMAS H. *The Theater in a Changing Europe.* In collaboration with sixteen European and American authorities on the theater of the Continent. New York: Holt. 1937.

115 DISHER, M. WILSON. *Music Hall Parade.* New York: Scribner, 1938.

116 DOBRÉE, BONAMY. *Restoration Comedy,* 1660-1720. New York: Oxford, 1924.

117 DOBRÉE, BONAMY. *Restoration Tragedy,* 1660-1700. New York: Oxford University Press, 1927.

118 DORAN, JOHN. *Annals of the English Stage, from Thomas Betterton to Edmund Kean.* Edited and revised by Robert W. Lowe. London: Nimmo, 1888. 3 vols.

119 *Dramatic Index, The.* Edited by Frederick Withrop Faxon. Boston: Boston Book Co., 1909 to date. From 1936 to date the editor has been Mary E. Bates.

120 DREW, ELIZABETH. *Discovering Drama.* New York: Norton, 1937.

121 DRIOTON, ÉTIENNE. *Le Drame sacré dans l'antique Égypte,* in *Flambeau,* Vol. I, Brussels: January 1, 1928.

122 DRIOTON, ÉTIENNE. *Une scène des Mystères d'Horus* in *Revnue de l'Égypte Ancienne,* Vol. II, Paris: Librairie Ancienne Honoré Champion, 1929.

123 DUBECH, LUCIEN J. DE MONTBRIAL and HELÈNE HORN-MONVAL. *Histoire Genérale illustrée du Théâtre.* Paris: Librairie de France, 1931-1934. 5 vols.

124 DUCHARTRE, PIERRE. *Italian Comedy.* Translated by Randolph T. Weaver. New York: John Day, 1928.

125 EATON, WALTER PRICHARD. *The Drama in English.* New York: Scribner, 1930.

126 EATON, WALTER PRICHARD. *The Theatre Guild,* the First Ten Years. New York: Brentano, 1929.

127 EDWARDS, H. SUTHERLAND. *Idols of the French Stage.* London: Remington, 1889. 2 vols.

128 ELDREDGE, H. J. (Clement Scott, pseud.) *The Drama of Yesterday & Today.* London: Macmillan, 1899. 2 vols.

129 ELDREDGE, H. J. (pseudonym, Clement Scott) *The Stage Cyclopedia.* A bibliography of plays. London: The Stage, 1909.

130 ELLIS-FERMOR, U. M. *The Jacobean Drama.* London: Methuen, 1936.

131 ELOESSER, ARTHUR. *Modern German Literature.* New York: Knopf, 1933.

132 ENCYCLOPAEDIA BRITANNICA: *The Theatre and Motion Pictures.* A selection of articles from the new 14th edition of the E.B., an aid to the fuller appreciation of the theatre, motion pictures, and kindred arts together with descriptions of the technique relating thereto. New York: Encyclopaedia Britannica, Inc., 1933.

133 ENGLAND, SYLVIA L. *An Unrecognized Documen. in the History of French Renaissance Staging.* In: *The Library.* Fourth Series. Vol. XVI., No. 2. September, 1935. Transactions of the Bibliographical Society. London: Oxford University Press, 1935.

134 ERMAN, ADOLF. *Ein Denkmal Memphitischer Theologie.* Berlin: Sitzungsberichte der Koeniglich Preussischen Akademie der Wissenschaften, 1911.

135 ERVINE, ST. JOHN. *The Organised Theatre.* A Plea in Civics. London: Allen & Unwin, 1924.

136 EUSTIS, MORTON. *B'Way, Inc.* New York: Dodd, Mead, 1934.

137 EUSTIS, MORTON. *Players at Work.* New York: Theatre Arts, Inc., 1937.

138 FAY, W. G. and CARSWELL, CATHERINE. *The Fays of the Abbey Theatre:* An Autobiographical Record. New York: Harcourt, Brace, 1935.

139 FILON, AUGUSTIN. *The English Stage.* Being an Account of the Victorian Drama. Translated by Frederic Whyte. Introduction by Henry Arthur Jones. London: Milne and New York: Dodd, Mead, 1897.

140 FILON, AUGUSTIN. *The Modern French Drama.* Seven Essays by Augustin Filon. Translated by Janet E. Hogarth. With an introduction by W. L. Courtney. London: Chapman and Hall, 1898.

141 FILOTTI, MARIA. *English Plays on the Roumanian Stage.* 1938.

142 FIRKINS, INA TEN EYCK, compiler. *Index to Plays,* 1800-1926. New York: H. W. Wilson, 1927. Supplement in 1935.

143 FITZMAURICE-KELLY, JAMES. *Lope de Vega and the Spanish Drama.* London: R. Brimley Johnson, 1902.

144 FITZMAURICE-KELLY, JAMES. *A New History of Spanish Literature.* Oxford University Press, 1926.

145 FLANAGAN, HALLIE. *Shifting Scenes of The Modern European Theatre.* New York: Coward-McCann, 1928.

146 FLEAY, F. G. *A Chronicle History of the London Stage,* 1559-1642. London: Reeves & Turner, 1890.

147 FLEXNER, ELEANOR. *American Playwrights:* 1918-1938. The Theatre Retreats from Reality. Preface by John Gassner. New York: Simon & Schuster, 1938.

148 FLICKINGER, R. S. *The Greek Theater and its Drama.* Chicago: Chicago University Press, 1926.

149 FOSS, KENELM. *Here Lies Richard Brinsley Sheridan.* New York: Dutton, 1940.

150 FOWLER, HAROLD N. *A History of Roman Literature.* New York: Oxford University Press, 1932.

151 FOWLER, W. W. *The Roman Festivals of the Period of the Republic:* an Introduction to the Study of the Religion of the Romans. 1899. (Handbooks of Archaeology and Antiquities.)

152 FRANCKE, KUNO. *A History of German Literature As Determined by Social Forces.* New York: Holt, 1901.

153 FRANKFORT, HENRI. *The Cenotaph of Seti I at Abydos.* Translated by Adriaan DeBuck. 1933. 2 vols.

154 FREYTAG, GUSTAV. *Technique of the Drama.* Tr. by Elias J. MacEwan. Chicago: S. C. Griggs & Co.. 1895.

155 FUCHS, THEODORE. *Stage Lighting.* Boston: Little, Brown, 1929.

156 FULLOP-MILLER, RENÉ and GREGOR, JOSEPH. *The Russian Theatre.* Philadelphia: Lippincott. 1930.

157 FUERST, WALTER RENÉ and HUME, SAMUEL J. *XXth Century Stage Decoration.* Introduction by Adolphe Appia. London: Knopf, 1928. 2 vols.

158 GAMBLE, WILLIAM BURT. *The Development of Scenic Art and Stage Machinery.* A List of References in the New York Public Library.

New York: The New York Public Library, 1928. Revised with additions.

159 GARDINER, ALAN HENDERSON. *Description of a Hieratic Papyrus with a Mythological Story.* Oriental Institute, 1931.

160 GASSNER, JOHN. *Masters of the Drama.* New York. Random House, 1940.

161 GASSNER, JOHN, editor. *Twenty Best Plays of the Modern American Theatre.* New York: Crown, 1939.

162 GENEST, JOHN. *Some Account of the English Stage.* From the Restoration in 1660 to 1830. Bath: H. E. Carrington, 1832. 10 vols.

163 GHERARDI, WILLIAM. *Anton Chekhov:* A Critical Study. London: Duckworth, 1923.

164 GILBERT, DOUGLAS. *American Vaudeville Its Life and Times.* New York: Whittlesey House, 1940.

165 GILDER, ROSAMOND. *Enter the Actress,* The First Women in the Theatre. Boston: Houghton Mifflin, 1931.

166 GILDER, ROSAMOND. *John Gielgud's Hamlet.* New York: Oxford University Press, 1937.

167 GILDER, ROSAMOND and FREEDLEY, GEORGE. *Theatre Collections in Libraries and Museums:* An International Handbook. New York: Theatre Arts, Inc., 1936.

168 GILDER, ROSAMOND. *A Theatre Library.* A Bibliography of One Hundred Books Relating to the Theatre. New York: Theatre Arts, Inc., 1932.

169 GOLDBERG, ISAAC. *The Drama of Transition.* Native and Exotic Playcraft. Cincinnati: Stewart Kidd, 1922.

170 GOLDIE, GRACE WYNDHAM. *The Liverpool Repertory Theatre,* 1911-1934. Liverpool: The University Press, 1935.

171 GRANVILLE-BARKER, HARLEY. *The Study of the Drama.* New York: Macmillan (Cambridge), 1934.

172 GRAPOW, HERMANN. *Die Publikation von Kurt Sethe der "Pyramidentexten,"* in Zeitschrift der Deutschen Morgenlandischen Gesellschaft, Vol. 91, 1937.

173 GRAVES, T. A. *The Court and the London Theatres during the Reign of Elizabeth.* Menasha (Wis.): Collegiate Press, 1913.

174 GREG, WALTER WILSON. *A List of English Plays written before 1643, and printed before 1700.* London: Bibliographical Society, 1900.

175 GREG, WALTER WILSON. *A List of Masques, Pageants, etc.* Supplementary to a list of English Plays. London: Bibliographical Society, 1902.

176 GREGERSEN, HALFDAN. *Ibsen and Spain.* A Study in Comparative Drama. Cambridge: Harvard University Press, 1936.

177 GREGOR, JOSEPH. *Die Masken Der Erde.* Munich: R. Piper, 1936.

178 GREGOR, JOSEPH. *Monumenta Scenica. Denkmaler des Theaters.* Vienna and Munich: National Library and R. Piper, 1925-1930.

179 GREGOR, JOSEPH. *Wiener Scenische Kunst.* Vienna: Wiener Drucker: 1924, 1925. 2 vols.

180 GREGORY, LADY ISABELLA AUGUSTA. *Our Irish Theatre.* New York: Putnam, 1913.

181 HAIGH, A. E. *The Attic Theatre.* A Description of the stage and theatre of the Athenians, and of the dramatic performances at Athens. Third edition revised and in part re-written by A. W. Pickard-Cambridge. Oxford: The Clarendon Press, 1907.

182 HAIGH, A. E. *The Tragic Drama of the Greeks.* Oxford: Clarendon Press, 1925.

183 HALL, LILLIAN ARVILLA. *Catalogue of the Dramatic Portraits in the Theatre Collection of the Harvard College Library.* Cambridge: Harvard University, 1930-32. 4 vols.

184 HAMILTON, CLAYTON. *The Theory of the Theatre,* and other Principles of Dramatic Criticism. Foreword by Burns Mantle. New York: Holt, 1939.

185 HAMILTON, EDITH. *The Greek Way.* New York: Norton, 1930.

186 HAMILTON, EDITH. *The Roman Way.* New York: Norton, 1932.

187 HAPGOOD, NORMAN. *The Stage in America.* 1897-1900. New York: Macmillan, 1901.

188 HARDWICKE, SIR CEDRIC. *The Drama Tomorrow.* Cambridge: University Press, 1936.

189 HARRISON, G. B. *The Story of Elizabethan Drama.* New York: Macmillan (Cambridge), 1924.

190 HARVEY, SIR PAUL. *The Oxford Companion to English Literature.* Oxford: Clarendon Press, 1932.

191 HASTINGS, CHARLES. *The Theatre.* Its development in France and England, and a history of its Greek and Latin origins. With an introductory letter from Monsieur Victorien Sardou. Authorised translation by Frances A. Welby. London: Duckworth and Co., 1901.

192 HAWKINS, FREDERICK. *The French Stage in the Eighteenth Century.* London: Chapman & Hall, 1888. 2 vols.

193 HAWKINS, FREDERICK. *Annals of the French Stage from its Origin to the Death of Racine.* London: Chapman & Hall, 1884.

194 HENDERSON, ARCHIBALD. *European Dramatists.* New York: Appleton, 1926.

195 HENDERSON, ARCHIBALD. *G. Bernard Shaw: His Life and Works.* New York: Appleton, 1932.

196 HERVEY, CHARLES. *The Theatres of Paris.* London: John Mitchell, 1847.

197 HILL, FRANK PIERCE, compiler. *American Plays.* Printed 1714-1830. A Bibliographical Record. Palo Alto, California: Stanford University Press, 1934.

198 HONE, WILLIAM. *Ancient Mysteries Described especially the English Miracle Plays,* founded on Apocryphal New Testament Story, extant among the unpublished manuscripts in the British Museum; including notices of Ecclesiastical Shows. London: William Hone, 1823.

199 HORNBLOW, ARTHUR. *A History of the Theatre in America.* Philadelphia: Lippincott, 1919. 2 vols.

200 HOTSON, LESLIE. *The Commonwealth and Restoration Stage.* Cambridge: Harvard University Press, 1928.

201 HOUGHTON, NORRIS. *Moscow Rehearsals.* An Account of Methods of Production in the Soviet Theatre. New York: Harcourt, Brace and Company, 1936.

202 HOUSSAYE, ARSÈNE. *Behind the Scenes of the Comédie Française.* And Other Recollections. Translated and edited, with notes by Albert D. Vandam, London: Chapman and Hall, 1889.

203 HOUSSAYE, ARSÈNE. *La Comédie Française,* 1680-1880. Paris: L. Bachet, 1880.

204 HUBBELL, JAY B. and BEATY, JOHN O. *An Introduction to Drama.* New York: Macmillan, 1927.

205 HUGHES, GLENN. *The Story of the Theatre.* A short history of theatrical art from its beginnings to the present day. New York: Samuel French, 1928.

206 HUNEKER, JAMES GIBBONS. *Iconoclasts.* A Book of Dramatists. New York: Scribner, 1907.

207 HUTTON, LAURENCE. *Curiosities of the American Stage.* New York: Harper, 1891.

208 ISAACS, EDITH J. R. *Architecture for the New Theatre.* New York: Theatre Arts, Inc., 1935.

209 ISAACS, EDITH J. R., editor. *Theatre.* Essays on the Arts of the Theatre. Introduction by Edith J. R. Isaacs. Boston: Little, Brown, 1927.

210 JAMESON, STORM. *Modern Drama in Europe.* New York: Harcourt, Brace & Howe, 1920.

211 JÉQUIER, GUSTAVE. *Fouilles à Saqqarah; La Pyramide d'Aba.* Cairo: L'Institut français d'archéologie orientale, 1935.

212 JÉQUIER, GUSTAVE. *Fouilles à Saqqarah; les pyramides des reines Neit at Apouit.* Cairo: Institut français d'archéologie orientale, 1933.

213 JONES, INIGO. *Designs by Inigo Jones.* For Masques and Plays at Court. Introduction and

notes by Percy Simpson and E. F. Bell. Cambridge: Oxford University Press, 1924.

214 JONES, ROBERT EDMOND. *Drawings for the Theatre.* New York: Theatre Arts, Inc., 1925.

215 JORGENSEN, THEODORE. *History of Norwegian Literature.* New York: Macmillan, 1933.

216 JOSSIC, YVONNE FRANÇOISE, compiler. *Stage and Stage Settings.* Philadelphia: H. C. Perleberg, 1933.

217 JUSSERAND, JEAN JULES. *Le Théâtre en Angleterre dépuis la Conquête jusqu'aux Prédécesseurs immédiats de Shakespeare.* Paris: E. Leroux, 1881. 2nd edition.

218 JUSSERAND, JEAN JULES. *A Literary History of the English People. From the Origins to the End of the Middle Ages.* New York: G. P. Putnam's Sons, 1926. Third edition.

219 KEITH, A. B. *The Sanskrit Drama in Its Origin, Development, Theory and Practice.* Oxford: Clarendon Press, 1924.

220 KENNARD, JOSEPH SPENCER. *The Italian Theatre.* New York: William Edwin Rudge, 1932. 2 vols.

221 KENNARD, JOSEPH SPENCER. *Masks and Marionettes.* New York: Macmillan, 1935.

222 KINCAID, ZOË. *Kabuki, the Popular Stage of Japan.* New York: Macmillan, 1925.

223 KLENZE, CAMILLE VON. *From Goethe to Hauptmann.* New York: Viking Press, 1926.

224 KOEPFLE, LEO G., editor. *Copyright Protection Throughout the World.* Washington: Department of Commerce, Bureau of Foreign and Domestic Commerce, May, August, September, October, 1936; January, 1937. 7 parts.

225 KOHLER, CARL. *A History of Costume.* Edited and augmented by Emma von Sichart. Translated by Alexander K. Dallas, London: Harrap, 1929.

226 KOHT, HALDAN. *The Life of Ibsen.* New York: Norton, 1931. 2 vols.

227 KOMISARJEVSKY, THEODORE. *The Costume of the Theatre.* London: Geofrey Bles, 1931.

228 KOZLENKO, WILLIAM, editor. *The One-Act Play Today.* A Discussion of the Technique, Scope and History of the Contemporary Short Drama. New York: Harcourt, Brace, 1938.

229 KROWS, ARTHUR EDWIN. *Playwriting for Profit.* New York: Longmans, Green, 1928.

230 KRUTCH, JOSEPH WOOD. *The American Drama since 1918.* New York: Random House, 1939.

231 LANCASTER, H. C. *A History of French Dramatic Literature.* Baltimore: Johns Hopkins Press, 1935.

232 LAWRENCE, W. J. *The Elizabethan Playhouse and Other Studies.* Philadelphia: Lippincott, 1913.

233 LAWRENCE, W. J. *Old Theatre Days and Ways.* London: Harrap, 1935.

234 LAWSON, JOHN HOWARD. *Theory and Technique of Playwriting.* New York: Putnam, 1936.

235 LEA, K. M. *Italian Popular Comedy. A Study in the Commedia Dell'Arte. 1560-1620.* Oxford: Clarendon Press, 1934. 2 vols.

236 LEAVITT, M. B. *Fifty Years in Theatrical Management.* New York: Broadway Publishing Co., 1912.

237 LEE, SIR SIDNEY. *A Life of William Shakespeare.* New York: Macmillan, 1929.

238 LEGOUIS, ÉMILE and CAZMANIAN, LOUIS. *A History of English Literature.* New York; Macmillan, 1930.

239 LEWISOHN, LUDWIG. *The Modern Drama.* An Essay in Interpretation. New York: B. W. Huebsch, Inc., 1921.

240 LITTLEWOOD, S. R. *Dramatic Criticism.* Foreword by Sir Barry Jackson. London: Pitman, 1939.

241 LOGASA, HANNAH and VER NOOY, WINIFRED, compilers. *An Index to One-Act Plays.* Boston: Faxon, 1924, 1932. 2 vols. Supplement published in 1932.

242 LOMBARD, FRANK ALANSON. *An Outline History of the Japanese Drama.* With an introduction

by George Pierce Baker. Boston and New York: Houghton, Mifflin, 1929.

243 LORD, LOUIS E. *Aristophanes, His Plays And His Influence.* Boston: Marshall Jones Company, 1925.

244 LOWE, ROBERT W. *A Bibliographical Account of English Theatrical Literature from the Earliest Times to the Present Day.* London: Nimmo, 1888.

245 LYONNET, HENRY. *Dictionnaire des Comédiens Français. Biographie, Bibliographie, Iconographie.* Genève: Bibliothèque de la Revue Universelle Internationale Illustrée, 1911-1912. 2 vols.

246 MACCLINTOCK, LANDER. *The Contemporary Drama of Italy.* Boston: Little, Brown, 1920.

247 MACGOWAN, KENNETH. *Footlights Across America.* Towards a National Theater. New York: Harcourt, Brace, 1929.

248 MACGOWAN, KENNETH. *The Theatre of Tomorrow.* New York: Boni and Liveright, 1921.

249 MACGOWAN, KENNETH and JONES, ROBERT EDMOND. *Continental Stagecraft.* New York: Harcourt, Brace and Co., 1922.

250 MACKAY, CONSTANCE D'ARCY. *Costume and Scenery for Amateurs.* New York: Holt, 1932.

251 MACMILLAN, DOUGALD, compiler. *Catalogue of the Larpent Plays in the Huntington Library.* San Marino, California: The Huntington Library, 1939.

252 MACMILLAN, DOUGALD, editor. *Drury Lane Calendar 1747-1776.* Compiled from the Playbills. Introduction by Dougald MacMillan. Oxford: The Clarendon Press, 1938.

253 MAHR, AUGUST C. *The Origin of the Greek Tragic Form.* New York: Prentice-Hall, 1938.

254 MALONE, ANDREW E. *The Irish Drama, 1896-1928.* New York: Scribner, 1929.

255 MANTLE, BURNS. *American Playwrights of Today.* New York: Dodd, Mead & Company, 1938.

256 MANTLE, BURNS, ed. *The Best Plays of 1919-20,* 1920-21, 1921-22, 1922-23, 1923-24. And the Year Book of the Drama in America. Boston: Small, Maynard, 1920-24. 5 vols.

257 MANTLE, BURNS, ed. *The Best Plays of 1924-25,* 1925-26, 1926-27, 1927-28, 1928-29, 1929-30, 1930-31, 1931-32, 1932-33, 1933-34, 1934-35, 1935-36, 1936-37, 1937-38, 1938-39, 1939-40. And the Year Book of the Drama in America. Boston: Dodd, Mead, 1925-40. 16 vols.

258 MANTLE, BURNS. *Contemporary American Playwrights.* New York: Dodd, Mead, 1938.

259 MANTLE, BURNS and SHERWOOD, GARRISON P., ed. *The Best Plays of 1909-1919.* And the Year Book of the Drama in America. New York: Dodd, Mead, 1933.

260 MANTZIUS, KARL. *A History of Theatrical Art in Ancient and Modern Times.* 6 volumes. Tr. by Louise von Cossel and C. Archer. New York: Peter Smith, 1937.

261 MARTINOVITCH, NICHOLAS W. *The Turkish Theatre.* New York: Theatre Arts, Inc., 1933.

262 MASON, A. E. W. *Sir George Alexander and the St. James Theatre.* London: Macmillan, 1935.

263 MASPERO, GASTON. *Les inscriptions des pyramides de Saqqarah.* Paris, 1894.

264 MATTHEWS, BRANDER. *A Book About the Theater.* New York, 1916.

265 MATTHEWS, BRANDER. *The Development of the Drama.* New York, 1903.

266 MATTHEWS, BRANDER. *French Dramatists of the Nineteenth Century.* New York: Scribner, 1905.

267 MATTHEWS, BRANDER. *Molière: His Life and His Works.* New York: Scribner, 1910.

268 MATTHEWS, BRANDER. *The Theatres of Paris.* London: Sampson Low, Martson, Searle, and Rivington, 1880.

269 MAYORGA, MARGARET G. *A Short History of the American Drama.* Commentaries on Plays Prior to 1920. New York: Dodd, Mead, 1932.

270 MCCANDLESS, STANLEY R. *A Method of Lighting Stage.* New York: Theatre Arts, Inc., 1932.

271 McCandless, Stanley R. *A Syllabus of Stage Lighting.* New Haven: Whitlock's Book Store, 1931.

272 McCleery, Albert and Glick, Carl. *Curtains Going Up.* Foreword by Gilmor Brown. New York: Pitman, 1939.

273 McGill, V. J. *August Strindberg, the Bedevilled Viking.* New York: Brentano's, 1930.

274 McKechnie, Samuel. *Popular Entertainment Through the Ages.* London: Sampson Low, Marston & Co., Ltd., 1931.

275 Melville, Lewis. *More Stage Favourites of the Eighteenth Century.* London: Hutchinson, 1929.

276 Melville, Lewis. *Stage Favourites of the Eighteenth Century.* London: Hutchinson, 1928.

277 Messel, Oliver. *Stage Designs and Costumes.* Introduction by James Laver; Foreword by Charles B. Cochran. London: John Lane, 1933.

278 Miller, Anna Irene. *The Independent Theatre in Europe 1887 to the Present.* New York: Ray Long & Richard R. Smith, Inc., 1931.

279 Millett, Fred B. and Bentley, Gerald Eades. *The Art of the Drama.* New York: Appleton-Century, 1935.

280 Mirsky, Prince D. S. *A History of Russian Literature.* London: Routledge, 1927.

281 Mirsky, Prince D. S. *Contemporary Russian Literature (1881-1925).* New York: Knopf, 1926.

282 Mitchell, Roy, *Creative Theatre.* New York: John Day, 1929.

283 Monro, Isabel and Cook, Dorothy E., editors. *Costume Index.* A Subject Index to Plates and to Illustrated Text. New York: H. W. Wilson, 1937.

284 Morgan, A. E. *Tendencies of Modern English Drama.* New York: Scribner, 1924.

285 Morley, Malcolm. *The Theatre.* Foreword by George Arliss. London: Pitman, 1935.

286 Moses, Montrose J. *The American Dramatist.* Boston: Little, Brown, 1925.

287 Moses, Montrose J. *Famous Actor-Families in America.* New York: Crowell, 1906.

288 Moses, Montrose J. *Henrik Ibsen. The Man and His Plays.* New York: Kennerley, 1908.

289 Moses, Montrose J. and Brown, John Mason, editors. *The American Theatre as Seen by Its Critics, 1752-1934.* Introduction by John Mason Brown. New York: Norton, 1934.

290 Motherwell, Hiram Kelly. *The Theatre of To-Day.* New York: Dodd, Mead and Co., 1925.

291 Moussinac, Léon. *The New Movement in the Theatre.* Introduction by R. H. Packman; Foreword by Gordon Craig. London: Batsford, 1931.

292 Murray, Gilbert. *Euripides and his Age.* New York: Holt, 1913.

293 Museum of Modern Art, The. *International Exhibition of Theatre Art.* New York: Museum of Modern Art, 1934.

294 Nemirovitch-Dantchenko, Vladimir. *My Life in the Russian Theatre.* Translated from the Russian by John Cournos. Boston: Little, Brown, and Company, 1936.

295 Nettleton, George Henry. *English Drama of the Restoration and Eighteenth Century, 1642-1780.* New York: Macmillan, 1914.

296 Newton, H. Chance. *Crime and the Drama or Dark Deeds Dramatized.* Introduction by Sir John Martin-Harvey. London: Stanley Paul & Co., 1927.

297 Nicoll, Allardyce. *British Drama.* New York: Crowell, 1925.

298 Nicoll, Allardyce. *The Development of the Theatre.* A Study of Theatrical Art from the Beginnings to the Present Day. London: Harrap, 1937. Revised edition.

299 Nicoll, Allardyce. *The English Theatre.* A Short History. London: Thomas Nelson and Sons Ltd., 1936.

300 Nicoll, Allardyce. *A History of the Restoration Drama, 1660-1700; Early Eighteenth Century Drama,* 1700-1750; *Late Eighteenth Century Drama,* 1750-1800; *Early Nineteenth Century Drama,* 1800-1850. 2 vols. Cambridge: Cambridge University Press, 1923-1930. 5 vols.

301 Nicoll, Allardyce. *Masks, Mimes and Miracles.* New York: Harcourt, Brace, 1931.

302 Nicoll, Allardyce. *Stuart Masques and the Renaissance Stage.* New York: Harcourt, Brace, 1938.

303 Nicoll, Allardyce. *The Theory of Drama.* London: Harrap, 1931. Revised edition.

304 Norwood, Gilbert. *Greek Tragedy.* London: Luce, 1920.

305 Noyes, George Rapall. *Masterpieces of the Russian Drama.* Selected and Edited with an Introduction by G. P. Noyes. New York: D. Appleton, 1933.

306 Nungezer, Edwin. *A Dictionary of Actors,* and of Other Persons Associated with the Public Representation of Plays in England before 1642. New Haven: Yale University Press, 1929.

307 Odell, George C. D. *Annals of the New York Stage.* New York: Columbia University Press, 1927 to date. 12 volumes.

308 Odell, George C. D. *Shakespeare from Betterton to Irving.* New York: Scribner, 1920.

309 Ormsbee, Helen, *Backstage With Actors.* From the Time of Shakespeare to the Present Day. New York: Crowell, 1938.

310 Oenslager, Donald. *Scenery Then and Now.* New York: Norton, 1936.

311 Palmer, John. *Molière.* New York: Brewer & Warren, 1930.

312 Palmer, John. *Studies in the Contemporary Theatre.* Boston: Little, Brown, 1927.

313 Parker, John, compiler and editor. *Who's Who in the Theatre.* A Biographical Record of the Contemporary Stage. London: Pitman, 1912-1939. Nine editions. 9 vols.

314 Parsons, Charles S. *A Guide to Theatrical Make-up.* Foreword by Sir Cedric Hardwicke. London: Pitman, 1932.

315 Pawley, Frederic. *Theatre Architecture.* A Brief Bibliography. New York: Theatre Arts, Inc., 1932.

316 Perry, Clarence Arthur. *The Work of the Little Theatres.* New York: Russell Sage Foundation, 1933.

317 Perry, Henry Ten Eyck. *Masters of Dramatic Comedy and Their Social Themes.* Cambridge: Harvard University Press, 1939.

318 Petit de Julleville. *Le Théâtre en France.* Paris: Librairie Armand Colin, 1921.

319 Petrie, Flinders. *Seventy Years in Archaeology.* New York: Henry Holt and Company, 1932.

320 Pollak, Gustav. *Franz Grillparzer and the Austrian Drama.* New York: Dodd, Mead & Company, 1907.

321 Pollard, A. W., editor. *English Miracle Plays, Moralities, and Interludes: Specimens of the Pre-Elizabethan Drama.* Oxford: Clarendon Press, 1927.

322 Pollock, Thomas Clark. *The Philadelphia Theatre in the Eighteenth Century.* Together with the Day Book of the same period. Foreword by Arthur Hobson Quinn. Philadelphia: University of Pennsylvania Press, 1933.

323 Pougin, Arthur. *Acteurs et Actrices d'Autrefois.* Histoire Anecdotique des théâtres à Paris. Dépuis trois cents ans. Illustrated. Paris: F. Juven et Cie, 1896.

324 Quinn, Arthur Hobson. *A History of the American Drama.* From the Civil War to the Present Day. New York: Crofts, 1936.

325 Quinn, Arthur Hobson. *A History of the American Drama, from the Beginning to the Civil War,* vol. 1; From the Civil War to the Present Day, vols. 2-3. New York: Harper, 1923, 1927. 3 vols.

326 RASI, LUIGI. *I Comici Italiana. Biografia, Bibliografia, Iconografia.* Firenze: Fratelli Bocca. Vol. 1, 1897; vol. 2. 1905.

327 REED, JOSEPH VERNER. *The Curtain Falls.* New York: Harcourt, Brace, 1935.

328 REICH, HERMANN. *Der Mimus.* Ein litterar-entwickelungsgechichtlicher Versuch. Berlin: Weidmann, 1903.

329 RENNERT, HUGO ALBERT. *The Spanish Stage in the Time of Lope de Vega.* New York: Hispanic Society, 1909.

330 RENTON, EDWARD. *The Vaudeville Theatre.* Building, Operation, Management. New York: Gotham Press, 1918.

331 RICCI, CORRADO. *La Scenografia Italiana.* Milan: Treves, 1930.

332 RICHARDSON, RUTH. *Florencio Sánchez and the Argentine Theatre.* New York: Instituto de las Españas en Los Estados Unidos, 1933.

333 RIDGEWAY, WILLIAM. *The Dramas and Dramatic Dances of Non-European Races.* Cambridge: University Press, 1915.

334 ROBERTSON, JOHN GEORGE. *Lessing's Dramatic Theory.* Being an introduction to and commentary on his *Hamburgische Dramaturgie.* Cambridge: The University Press, 1939.

335 ROBINSON, LENNOX, editor. *The Irish Theatre.* Lectures delivered during the Abbey Theatre Festival held in Dublin in August 1938. London: Macmillan, 1939.

336 RODWAY, PHYLLIS PHILIP and SLINGSBY, LOIS RODWAY. *Philip Rodway and a Tale of Two Theatres.* Birmingham: Cornish Brothers, 1934.

337 ROLLAND, ROMAIN. *The People's Theater.* Translated from the French by Barrett H. Clark. New York: Holt, 1918.

338 ROSE, ENID. *Gordon Craig and the Theatre.* London: Sampson Low, Marston, 1931.

339 ROSENFELD, SYBIL. *Strolling Players and Drama in the Provinces, 1660-1765.* Cambridge: University Press, 1939.

340 ROSSE, HERMAN. *Designs and Impressions.* Chicago: Ralph Fletcher Seymour, 1920.

341 ROURKE, CONSTANCE. *Troupers of the Gold Coast or the Rise of Lotta Crabtree.* New York: Harcourt, Brace, 1928.

342 RYAN, KATE. *Old Boston Museum Days.* Boston: Little, Brown, 1915.

343 ST. JOHN, CHRISTOPHER, editor. *Ellen Terry and Bernard Shaw.* A Correspondence. Preface by George Bernard Shaw. New York: Putnam, 1931.

344 SAINTSBURY, GEORGE. *A History of Elizabethan Literature.* London: Macmillan. 1887.

345 SAINTSBURY, GEORGE. *A Short History of French Literature.* Oxford: Clarendon Press, 1884.

346 SAYLER, OLIVER M. *Inside the Moscow Art Theatre.* New York: Brentano's, 1925.

347 SAYLER, OLIVER M. *Max Reinhardt and His Theatre.* New York: Brentano's, 1924.

348 SAYLER, OLIVER M. *Our American Theatre.* New York: Brentano's, 1923.

349 SAYLER, OLIVER. *The Russian Theatre.* New York: Brentano's, 1922.

350 SCHAEFER, KURT (HEINRICH). *Die Mysterien des Osiris in Abydos unter Koenig Sesostris III* in Untersuchungen zur Geschichte und Altertumskunde Aegyptus, Vol. IV, No. 2. Leipzig: J. C. Hinrichs, 1904.

351 SCHICK, JOSEPH S. *The Early Theatre in Eastern Iowa.* Cultural Beginnings and the Rise of the Theatre in Davenport and Eastern Iowa, 1836-1863. Chicago: The University of Chicago Press, 1939.

352 SCHLEGEL, AUGUST WILHELM. *Lectures On Dramatic Art and Literature.* Translated by John Black. Second edition, revised by Rev. A. J. W. Morrison. London: George Bell & Sons, 1909.

353 SCOTT, MARIAN. *Chautauqua Caravan.* New York: Appleton-Century, 1939.

354 SEGALL, J. B. *Corneille and the Spanish Drama.* New York: The Columbia University Press, 1902.

355 SETHE, KURT (HEINRICH). *Dramatische Texte zu Altaegyptischen Mysterienspielen.* Leipzig: J. C. Hinrichs, 1928.

356 SETHE, KURT (HEINRICH). *Uebersetzung und Kommentar zu den Altaegyptischen Pyramidentexten.* Glueckstadt und Hamburg: J. J. Augustin, 1934-37. 3 volumes and three pamphlets of Volume 4. Publication interrupted by the Second World War.

357 SEXTON, R. W. *American Theatres of Today.* Vol 2. New York: New York Architectural Book Publishing Co., 1930.

358 SEXTON, R. W. and BETTS. B. F. *American Theatres of Today.* Vol. 1. Foreword by S. L. Rothafel, New York: New York Architectural Book Publishing Co., 1927.

359 SHAND, PHILIP MORTON. *Modern Theatres and Cinemas.* London: Batsford, 1930.

360 SHARP, R. FARQUHARSON. *A Short History of the English Stage.* London and New York: Walter Scott, 1909.

361 SHAW, G. BERNARD. *Dramatic Opinions and Essays.* New York: Brentano's, 1907. 2 vols.

362 SHAY, FRANK, compiler. *A Guide to Longer Plays.* A List of Fifteen Hundred Plays for Little Theatres, Professional and Stock Companies, Art Theatres, Schools, Amateurs and Readers. New York: Appleton, 1925.

363 SHERINGHAM, GEORGE and LAVER, JAMES. *Design in the Theatre.* London: The Studio, 1927.

364 SHERINGHAM, GEORGE and MORRISON, R. BOYD, ed. *Robes of Thespis.* Costume Designs by Modern Artists. Preface by Rupert Mason. London: Benn, 1928.

365 SHOEMAKER, WILLIAM HUTCHINSON. *The Multiple Stage in Spain During the Fifteenth and Sixteenth Centuries.* A dissertation presented to the faculty of Princeton University in candidacy for the degree of Doctor of Philosophy. Princeton: Princeton University Press, 1935.

366 SHORT, ERNEST and COMPTON-RICKETT, ARTHUR. *Ring Up the Curtain.* Being a Pageant of English Entertainment Covering Half a Century. London: Herbert Jenkins, 1938.

367 SIBLEY, GERTRUDE MARIAN. *The Lost Plays and Masques.* 1500-1642. Ithaca, New York: Cornell University Press, 1933.

368 SIMONSON, LEE. *The Stage is Set,* New York: Harcourt, Brace, 1932.

369 SIMONSON, LEE, editor. *Theatre Art.* New York: Norton, 1934.

370 SKINNER, OTIS. *Mad Folk of the Theatre.* Indianapolis: Bobbs-Merrill, 1928.

371 SKINNER, R. DANA. *Our Changing Theatre.* New York: Dial Press, 1931.

372 SMITH, HUGH ALLISON. *Main Currents of Modern French Drama.* New York: Henry Holt and Company, 1925.

373 SMITH, MILTON. *Guide to Play Selection.* A Descriptive Index of Full-Length and Short Plays for Production by Schools, Colleges and Little Theaters. New York: Appleton-Century, 1934.

374 SMITH, SOL. *Theatrical Management,* in the West and South for Thirty Years. New York: Harper, 1868.

375 SMITH, WILLARD. *The Nature of Comedy.* Boston: Badger, 1930.

376 SMITH, WINIFRED. *The Commedia dell' Arte.* New York: Columbia University Press, 1912.

377 SMITH, WINIFRED. *Italian Actors of the Renaissance.* New York: Coward-McCann, 1930.

378 SOBEL, BERNARD, editor. *The Theatre Handbook and Digest of Plays.* Preface by George Freedley. New York: Crown, 1940.

379 SPEAIGHT, ROBERT. *Acting:* Its Idea and Tradition. London: Cassell, 1939.

380 *Spectacles à travers les ages, Les.* Prefaces by Denys Amiel and Henri Fescourt. Paris: Aux Editions du Cygne, 1931-32. 3 vols.

381 SPELEERS, LOUIS. *Traduction index et Vocabulaire des Textes des Pyramides Égyptiennes.* Brussels, 1936.

382 STANISLAVSKY, CONSTANTIN. *An Actor Prepares.* Translated by Elizabeth Reynolds Hapgood. New York: Theatre Arts, Inc., 1936.

383 STANISLAVSKY, CONSTANTIN. *My Life In Art.* Translated from the Russian by J. J. Robbins. Boston: Little, Brown, 1938.

384 STAUFFER, RUTH M. *The Progress of Drama Through the Centuries.* New York: Macmillan, 1928.

385 STEIN, ELIZABETH P. *David Garrick, Dramatist.* New York: Modern Language Association of America, 1938.

386 STEVENS, THOMAS WOOD. *The Theatre from Athens to Broadway.* New York: Appleton, 1932.

387 STOCKWELL, LA TOURETTE. *Dublin Theatres and Theatre Customs (1637-1820).* Kingsport, Tenn.: Kingsport Press, 1938.

388 STRATTON, CLARENCE. *Theatron.* New York: Holt, 1928.

389 STREIT, ANDREAS. *Das Theater: Untersuchungen ueber das Theater—Bauwerk bei den klassischen und modernen Völkern.* Vienna: Lehmann and Wentzel, 1903.

390 STRENKOVSKY, SERGE. *The Art of Make-up.* Edited by Elizabeth S. Taber. New York: Dutton, 1938.

391 STRONG, L. A. G. *Common Sense about Drama.* New York: Alfred A. Knopf, 1937.

392 STUART, DONALD CLIVE. *The Development of Dramatic Art.* New York: D. Appleton-Century Company, 1928.

393 SUMMERS, MONTAGUE. *The Restoration Theatre.* New York: Macmillan, 1934.

394 SYMONDS, JOHN ADDINGTON. *Renaissance in Italy.* New York: Modern Library Giant, 1935. 2 vols.

395 *Theatre Arts.* A quarterly, 1916-1923. A monthly, 1924 to date. An indispensable bibliographical tool and the most comprehensive history of the theatre in English.

396 *Theatre Arts Prints.* Introduction by John Mason Brown. New York: John Day, 1929.

397 *Theatrical Designs.* From the Baroque through Neoclassicism. Introduction by George Freedley. New York: H. Bittner, 1940. 3 vols.

398 THOMAS, CALVIN. *A History of German Literature.* New York: Appleton, 1928.

399 THORNDYKE, ASHLEY H. *English Comedy.* New York: Macmillan, 1929.

400 THORNDYKE, ASHLEY H. *Shakespeare's Theatre.* New York: Macmillan, 1916.

401 THORNDYKE, DAME SYBIL and RUSSELL. *Lilian Baylis.* London: Chapman & Hall, 1938.

402 TICKNOR, GEORGE. *History of Spanish Literature.* London: John Murray: 1849. 3 Vols.

403 URBAN, JOSEPH. *Theatres.* New York: Theatre Arts, Inc., 1930.

404 VITRUVIUS. *The Ten Books on Architecture,* tr. by M. H. Morgan. Cambridge, Mass., 1914.

405 VITTORINI, DOMENICO. *The Drama of Luigi Pirandello,* Foreword by Luigi Pirandello. Philadelphia: University of Pennsylvania Press, 1935.

406 WALEY, ARTHUR. *The Noh Plays of Japan.* New York: Alfred A. Knopf, 1922.

407 WARD, A. W. *A History of English Dramatic Literature to the Death of Queen Anne.* 2nd ed. 3 vols. 1899.

408 WARD, A. W. and WALTER, A. R., editors. *The Cambridge History of English Literature.* Vols. V and VI, The Drama. New York: Putnam, 1910.

409 WATSON, ERNEST BRADLEY. *Sheridan to Robertson.* A study of the Nineteenth-Century London Stage. Cambridge: Harvard University Press, 1926.

410 WAXMAN, S. M. *Antoine and the Théâtre Libre.* Cambridge: Harvard University Press, 1926.

411 WELLS, HENRY W. *Elizabethan and Jacobean Playwrights.* New York: Columbia University Press, 1939.

412 WELSFORD, ENID. *The Court Masque.* New York: Macmillan, 1928.

413 WEYGANDT, CORNELIUS. *Irish Plays and Playwrights.* Boston: Houghton, Mifflin, 1913.

414 WHITMAN, WILLSON. *Bread and Circuses.* New York: Oxford University Press, 1937.

415 WIENER, LEO. *The Contemporary Drama of Russia.* Boston: Little, Brown, 1924.

416 WILLIAMS, H. NOEL. *Later Queens of the French Stage.* New York: Scribner, 1906.

417 WILLIAMS, H. NOEL. *Queens of the French Stage.* London: Harper, 1905.

418 WILLIAMS, RONALD BOAL. *The Staging of Plays in the Spanish Peninsula Prior to 1555.* In UNIVERSITY OF IOWA STUDIES. Spanish Language and Literature. Number 5. Iowa City, Iowa: University of Iowa, 1934.

419 WILLIS, EOLA. *The Charleston Stage in the XVIII Century.* With Social Settings of the Time. Columbia, S. C.: The State Company, 1924.

420 WILSON, A. E. *Christmas Pantomime.* The Story of an English Institution. London: Allen & Unwin, 1934.

421 WILSON, ARTHUR HERMAN. *A History of the Philadelphia Theatre, 1835 to 1855.* Foreword by Arthur Hobson Quinn. Philadelphia: University of Pennsylvania Press, 1935.

422 WILSON, N. SCARLYN. *European Drama.* London: Nicholson and Watson, 1937.

423 WINTER, WILLIAM. *Vagrant Memories.* Being Further Recollections of Other Days. New York: George H. Doran, 1915.

424 WINTER, WILLIAM. *Other Days, Being Chronicles and Memories of the Stage.* New York: Moffat, Yard, 1908.

425 WITKOWSKI, GEORG. *The German Drama of the Nineteenth Century.* Authorized translation from the second German edition by L. E. Horning. New York: Henry Holt and Company, 1909.

426 YAJNIK, R. K. *The Indian Theatre, Its Origins and Its Later Developments under European Influence.* New York: Dutton, 1934.

427 YOUNG, KARL. *The Drama of the Mediaeval Church.* Oxford: Clarendon Press, 1933. 2 vols.

428 YOUNG, STARK. *The Flower in Drama.* New York: Scribner, 1923.

429 YOUNG, STARK. *Theatre Practice.* New York: Scribner, 1926.

430 ZINKEISEN, DORIS. *Designing for the Stage.* London: The Studio, 1938.

431 ZUCKER, A. E. *The Chinese Theater.* Boston: Little, Brown & Co., 1925.

432 ZUCKER, PAUL. *Theater-Dekoration des Barock.* Berlin: R. Kaemmerer, 1925.

433 ZUCKER, PAUL. *Theater-Dekoration des Klassizismus.* Berlin: R. Kaemmerer, 1925.

General Works

2, 11, 13, 17, 18, 30, 42, 55, 59, 60, 66, 72, 82, 86, 92, 113, 114, 119, 122, 124, 129, 132, 135, 145, 160, 165, 167, 168, 169, 171, 183, 184, 188, 191, 194, 198, 204, 205, 206, 208, 209, 210, 224, 234, 239, 241, 248, 249, 260, 264, 274, 278, 285, 290, 298, 312, 313, 328, 333, 352, 362, 368, 369, 373, 375, 378, 380, 384, 386, 388, 389, 391, 392, 395, 396, 422, 427, 428, 429.

Austria

47, 80, 92, 113, 131, 178, 179, 249, 320, 395, 397, 425, 432, 433,

Belgium

92, 113, 114.

Bulgaria

114, 395.

INDEX